THE
RIVERSIDE
GUIDE
TO
Writing

THE RIVERSIDE GUIDE TO *Writing*

DOUGLAS HUNT

University of Missouri

HOUGHTON MIFFLIN COMPANY   BOSTON

Dallas   Geneva, Illinois   Palo Alto   Princeton, New Jersey

Printed in the U.S.A.

Library of Congress Catalog Card Number: 90-83059

ISBN: 0-395-53498-4

ABCDEFGHIJ-D-9876543210

ACKNOWLEDGMENTS

Marbleized designs on cover and inside book designed by Mimi Schleicher.
Calligraphy by Mandy Young.
Line art created by Commonwealth Printing, Hadley, MA.

Photograph of James Weldon Johnson on page 88 by Carl Van Vechten, reproduced by permission of the Van Vechten estate, Joseph Solomon, Executor. Print from Yale University Library.

Portrait of Edward DeVere on page 177 © Minos Publishing Company. Reproduced by permission of David J. Hanson, Susan L. Hanson, and Trustees of the Minos D. Miller Sr. Trust, Jennings, Louisiana.

Acknowledgments are continued on pages 679–682, which constitute an extension of the copyright page.

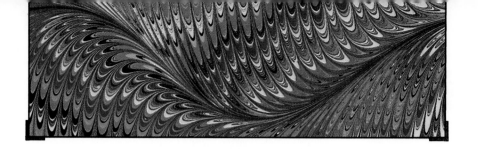

BRIEF CONTENTS

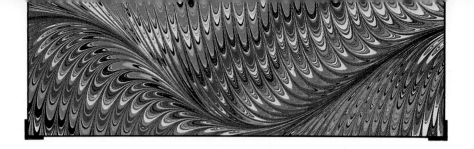

TABLE OF CONTENTS

PART III   *Professional & Academic Applications*   260

CHAPTER 8
PROPOSALS   262

PROFILE
George Orwell, 275

CHAPTER 9

EVALUATIONS   316

◆ *The Range of Evaluations: From Technical to
Interpretive, 317* ◆ *A Technical Evaluation, 318* ◆ *A
Middle Case: Critical Notices, 324* ◆ *The Interpretive
Evaluation: Increased Attention to the Critic's Frame of
Reference, 328*

CHAPTER 10
WRITING ABOUT LITERATURE   358

◆ *A Story for Analysis: "The Blue Eyes" (Isak Dinesen),
359* ◆ *A Poem for Analysis: "Summer Solstice, New
York City" (Sharon Olds), 370*

Section II
Usage and Diction   583

PREFACE

Sixteen years ago, when I taught my first section of composition, I was alarmed to discover that several of my colleagues were using such assignments as "Compare your mother to a 1954 Ford" and "Describe the process of tying a shoe." The prevailing view of the composition class in those days was discouraged and discouraging. Students saw it almost entirely as a course in correctness: "grammar boot camp," they used to say. The graduate students and junior faculty members who did the bulk of the teaching had no coherent view of the course's goals and simply saw it as something else to get done, with good humor if possible. But on every college campus there were a few composition teachers with gleams in their eyes, talking about the relationship between writing, revising, and re-thinking; talking about encouraging students to take a critical attitude toward "facts"; talking about helping them understand the indirect messages conveyed by the choice of this word rather than that, this form of the sentence rather than the other. Talking, in short, as though this course really could become an introduction to college-level thinking, reading, and writing.

The discipline of composition has matured enormously since 1974, both in its guiding theories and in its applied research. We are now in a much better position to construct a course that is grafted to the central purpose of college education: to help students become lucid and flexible thinkers who can present their ideas persuasively to others. *The Riverside Guide to Writing* is designed to serve as the textbook for such a course.

The book divides into four parts. The first part, *Writing and Thinking*, shows that writing involves interpretation (the placing of subjects in frameworks), explains how the writing process improves the mind's ability to create convincing interpretations, and gives students a chance to write interpretations based on memory or direct observation. The second part, *Writing and Argument*, extends the notion of interpretation into argument and persuasion, distinguishing between arguments about facts and arguments about rules and teaching students methods of pursuing each. The third part, *Professional and*

Academic Applications, builds on insights gained in the first two and shows students how to write proposals, evaluations, essays about literature, and research papers. The fourth, *Matters of Form and Style,* discusses organization, introductions and conclusions, and the principles of style. Users of the longer edition will find a fifth part: a handbook of grammar and usage, including exercises.

FEATURES

The principal features of *The Riverside Guide to Writing* are these:

♦ Forty-three assignments prepare students for the kinds of writing they will do throughout their college careers. Modeled on assignments used in courses across the curriculum, the assignments allow students to practice in simplified form the skills in research and analysis that they will use in courses in history, sociology, literature, biology, and other disciplines. The number and variety of assignments should allow instructors to choose their own emphases and to tailor their courses to their students' abilities and interests.

♦ Abundant, engaging essays serve as models. The assignment-centered chapters (3–10) include several professionally written examples short enough to serve as models for student essays. At the ends of chapters are forty-seven longer selections for analysis and discussion. This reading program is enriched by featuring a "panel" of twelve writers whose works and ideas appear in several chapters. These panelists were chosen for their skill and their variety but also because most of them have valuable information to impart about the process of writing, and so they serve students as a sort of coaching staff. Students learn, for example, about the drafting practices of E. B. White, the research methods of Barbara Tuchman, the way that Maya Angelou prepares herself to write, and the way that Charles Darwin used daily journal writing to sharpen his powers of analysis and observation. Other members of the panel are Joan Didion, George Orwell, Annie Dillard, James Weldon Johnson, Mary McCarthy, Mark Twain, Theodore White, and George Will.

♦ Each assignment-based chapter concludes with a compact statement of "Points to Consider" in the process of drafting and revising the type of essay covered, plus a short set of "Questions for Peer Review."

- Exercises scattered through the chapters prepare students for the writing assignments. These exercises can often serve as a focal point for an entire class period. Almost all of them are designed with a dual purpose: not only to help students digest the information in the chapter, but to allow them to practice critical thinking skills they will use in a variety of classes. Instructors committed to collaborative learning will find these exercises particularly engaging.

- A chapter on writing about literature looks at elements of fiction and poetry and provides three poems and four stories for analysis. This chapter should be useful in programs where the composition course serves as a prerequisite to literature courses.

Also available are

- An Instructor's Resource Manual that offers commentary on the chapters and on each full-length reading, plus techniques for teaching and ideas for working through the assignments. In putting this instructor's manual together, Carolyn Perry and I have paid special attention to the needs of programs like our own, where a great many composition courses are taught by inexperienced instructors.

- Forty additional assignments available in printed and computerized form. These supplemental assignments should keep the text from going stale after two or three semesters of use. Their availability on computer disk allows instructors to modify them to suit their own needs.

- A package of sample student papers for class discussion. Written by students who used *The Riverside Guide* in draft form, these papers are not offered as patterns of perfection but as realistic examples of student writing. These are useful in class discussion because they have both strengths to praise and faults to criticize. We have provided instructors with commentary on each paper to help them prepare for class discussion.

The abundance of readings and assignments in *The Riverside Guide* makes it appropriate not only for one-term composition courses but for sequences that stretch over two or three courses with somewhat varied emphases. It would be possible, for example, to use the book for a series of courses that focus on (1) the writing process and personal writing, (2) argumentation, and (3) writing from research.

ACKNOWLEDGMENTS

Like many textbook writers, I am tempted to acknowledge the contribution of every rhetorician, old and new, who ever lived and wrote. Writers of rhetorics today stand on some massive shoulders and hope that this perch allows them to take in a broad horizon.

I will, however, avoid the long list that begins with Aristotle and ends with the most recent issue of *College Composition and Communication*. My more immediate debts are two: first, to Carolyn Perry of the University of Missouri, who is co-author of the Instructor's Resource Manual and who critiqued and class-tested the chapters in their draft form; next, to a remarkable set of reviewers, who were generous with their advice and time and who contributed to some important changes. These reviewers are Julia M. Allen, Sonoma State University (CA); Chris Anderson, Oregon State University; Ray Anschel, Normandale Community College (MN); Linda Bensel-Meyers, University of Tennessee at Knoxville; Annette Briscoe, Ball State University (IN); Patsy Callaghan, Central Washington University; Toni-Lee Capossela, Boston University; James V. Catano, Louisiana State University at Baton Rouge; Ian Cruickshank, St. Louis Community College at Florissant Valley; Beth Rigel Daugherty, Otterbein College (OH); John Dick, University of Texas at El Paso; Sandra A. Engel, Mohawk Valley Community College (NY); Fritz Fleischmann, Babson College (MA); Irene Gale, University of South Florida; G. Dale Gleason, Hutchinson Community College (KS); Barbara S. Gross, Rutgers Newark College of Arts and Sciences; John Hanes, Duquesne University (PA); Patricia Harkin, The University of Akron; Glenda A. Hudson, California State University at Bakersfield; Maurice Hunt, Baylor University (TX); Michael L. Johnson, University of Kansas; Mary A. McCay, Loyola University (LA); Grace H. McNamara, DeKalb College (GA); Elizabeth Metzger, University of South Florida; Margaret Dietz Meyer, Ithaca College (NY); G. Douglas Meyers, University of Texas at El Paso; Michael Miller, Longview Community College (MO); Walter S. Minot, Gannon University (PA); Patrick Parks, Elgin Community College (IL); Joseph Powell, Central Washington University; Susanna Rich, Kean College of New Jersey; Duane H. Roen, University of Arizona; Shirley K. Rose, San Diego State University; Carolyn H. Smith, University of Florida; MaryJean Steenberg, Metropolitan Community College (NE); Martha Tolleson, Collin County Community College District (TX); George Y. Trail, University of Houston; Margaret Urie, University of Nevada at Reno; William Vande Kopple, Calvin College (MI); Linda G. Wadleigh, El Camino College (CA); Steven C. Weisenberger, Uni-

versity of Kentucky; James D. Williams, University of North Carolina at
Chapel Hill; Michael Williamson, Indiana University of Pennsylvania; Ben
Wilson, Greensboro College (NC); and Robert Wiltenburg, Washington Uni-
versity (MO).

Finally, I want to thank my editors at Houghton Mifflin and also the
design and production staff. Their faith in this project from its inception, as
well as their hard work, encouraged me.

DOUG HUNT
University of Missouri

PART I

Writing
AND THINKING

The thinking mind will analyze,
and the creative imagination will link instances,
and time itself will churn out scenes—
scenes unnoticed and lost,
or scenes remembered, written, and saved.

ANNIE DILLARD

WRITING WHEN FACTS DON'T SPEAK FOR THEMSELVES

TEXTBOOKS ABOUT WRITING TEND TO BEGIN WITH SOME SUCH PASSAGE as this: "What is good writing? How can a person improve his or her ability to write effectively? Is good writing always time-consuming and laborious? If you are just beginning a writing course, you are probably asking yourself questions like these." In fact, unless you are a very strange person indeed, you are asking yourself no such things. The world is filled with far more interesting questions. So let's turn our backs on writing for a moment and think a bit about the world in which writing takes place. We will find our way back to writing *per se* within a few paragraphs, and we may be refreshed by the detour.

The detour will take us through some events that were in the news when this chapter was being drafted, during the summer of 1989. The events are not particularly remarkable: you could probably name four comparable ones that have happened in the last few months. But each event illustrates the bedrock assumptions of *The Riverside Guide to Writing:* that we live in a world that needs interpretation, that facts don't speak for themselves, and that those who learn to interpret the mute facts shape the realities with which all of us must live.

THE DETOUR: FOUR EXAMPLES OF INTERPRETED REALITIES

Example 1: Brian De Palma's film *Casualties of War* was getting enthusiastic reviews in some quarters and being roundly condemned in others. In an interview, De Palma said that his film, the story of a squad of American soldiers who raped and murdered a Vietnamese woman and of one man whose conscience rebelled, "epitomizes the Vietnam experience." John Wheeler, the former chairman of the Vietnam Veterans Memorial Fund, denounced the movie as a lie built on "false stereotypes":

> By focusing on a rape, De Palma declines to tell the greater truth, that in Vietnam the overwhelming number of us were decent, built orphanages, roads, hospitals, and schools. It is a lie about what we were really like in Vietnam.

The dispute here is not about facts but about what the facts mean. Wheeler wouldn't deny that the rape and murder took place, and De Palma wouldn't

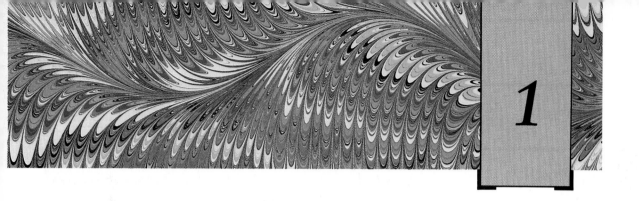

deny that American soldiers built orphanages. What is disputed is the "greater truth." Which action typifies America's role in Vietnam (or in the world)? How should the war make Americans feel about themselves? What will we tell the children and grandchildren of those who fought in it or those who fled to Canada to avoid fighting in it? These are questions that we can never settle to everyone's satisfaction, questions that may make our heads spin. But it is not enough for us to shrug our shoulders and say, "Who knows?" Reaching some sort of understanding with the past is essential for our political health and probably for our mental health as well.

Example 2: At about the same time that *Casualties of War* was released, the United States Supreme Court heard the case of Gregory Johnson, a man who had burned an American flag during the Republican Convention in 1984 to protest policies that he believed increased the chances of a nuclear war. A Texas court had found Johnson guilty of violating a state law forbidding desecration of the American flag and had sentenced him to a year in prison, and a $2,000 fine. Johnson appealed, arguing that the law was unconstitutional. Five of the nine justices of the Supreme Court agreed, saying that Johnson's action was a political protest, protected under the First Amendment to the U.S. Constitution. "It is poignant but fundamental," Justice Anthony Kennedy wrote, "that the flag protects those who hold it in contempt." Four other justices vehemently disagreed, seeing flag burning not as an example of the political speech that the Amendment was designed to protect, but, in Chief Justice William Rehnquist's words, as the equivalent of "an inarticulate grunt or roar . . . indulged in not to express any particular idea, but to antagonize others." Had Rehnquist and the other dissenting justices persuaded one member of the majority to see things their way, Johnson would have gone to jail and the meaning of free speech in the United States would have been narrowed. Cases like this remind laymen of what lawyers and judges know very well: the law—even the constitutional law—is not a fixed set of truths, but a body of opinions argued over, interpreted, and sometimes overturned.

Example 3: Soon after the Supreme Court decision on flag burning, *The Atlantic* ran an article casting doubt on the widely publicized scientific "fact" that lower cholesterol will decrease chances of fatal heart attacks. While such groups as the American Heart Association have persuaded most Americans to join the war on cholesterol, many researchers and physicians have looked at the *same studies* used by the Heart Association and become skeptics and resisters. Some experts argue that changing to a low-cholesterol diet is actually more likely to produce death from cancer than to prevent death from heart disease. It is too early to know whether the link between dietary cholesterol and heart disease will become one of the thousands of scientific "facts" that are relegated to the wastebasket every year, but those who know science know that the wastebasket fills quickly. Professor Craig Nelson of the National Center for Science Education estimates that "the half-life of biological knowledge is about twenty years": half the facts students learn in an introductory course will not be accepted as facts by the next generation of biologists. "The problem," he says, "is that we don't know which half." And the solution, he says, is to learn how scientists work in a world of uncertainty.[1]

Example 4: The same month that *The Atlantic* published the cholesterol article, *Esquire* published an essay in which Joan Didion recalled her brief internship assisting photographers who were preparing features on famous women. If the women wondered what to wear for a sitting, Didion and the other assistants told them to "be themselves," to wear whatever they were comfortable in. "We accepted without question, in other words, the traditional convention of the portrait, which was that somehow, somewhere, in the transaction between artist and subject, the 'truth' about the latter would be revealed. . . ." Didion quickly learned, however, that the woman photographed would eventually become not "herself" but the creature the photographer preferred to portray.

> I recall mainly little tricks, small improvisations, the efforts required to ensure that the photographer was seeing what he wanted. I remember one sitting for which the lens was covered with black chiffon. I remember another during which, after the "anything at all" in which the subject had apparently believed herself comfortable had been seen in the Polaroids and declared not what was wanted, I lent the subject my own dress, and worked the rest of the sitting wrapped in my raincoat. Here, then, was an early lesson: there would be in each such photograph a "subject," the woman in the studio, and there would also be a subject, and the two would not necessarily intersect.

Outside the closed world of mathematical logic, there are very few areas where the revelation of the truth is simply a matter of recording objective reality. Lawyers, teachers, engineers, managers, administrators, physicians—almost all professionals—repeatedly find themselves in situations where reasonable people can disagree about the meaning of data and experience. *To understand means to go beyond the facts, to interpret and to argue.* This much established by our detour, we can return to the campus and to this class.

---

[1] On the role of frameworks in scientific thought, see Thomas Kuhn's *The Structure of Scientific Revolutions* (1962).

INTERPRETATION, COLLEGE EDUCATION, AND THE ROLE OF RHETORIC

In 1852, John Henry Newman argued that the teaching of simple facts is largely the business of primary and secondary schools. The business of the university is to teach students what they can *do* with the facts at their disposal, how they can use them to form the ideas that keep a mind and a culture alive. The university, he said, should "give a man a clear conscious view of his own opinions and judgments, a truth in developing them, an eloquence in expressing them, and a force in urging them."

In our own time Adrienne Rich, addressing the women of Douglass College, has pointed out that the university can never quite "give" these things, students must take them: "Responsibility to yourself means refusing to let others do your thinking, talking, and naming for you; it means learning to respect and use your own brains and instincts. . . ." Most professors agree that students must go beyond the collection and memorization of facts. They want students to understand how "facts" are established, and they want them to construct from data their own structures of thought, their own interpretations.

In this scheme of education, a class in rhetoric or composition can be especially important. Rhetoric has a very long tradition of teaching us how to conduct discussions in areas where the truth is disputable. Twenty-five hundred years ago, the Greek philosopher Aristotle was telling his students that as valuable as pure logic was, they would need other tools to deal with a world full of uncertainties. He saw rhetoric as the discipline that taught people to reason together about questions where the "truth" is at best a matter of probabilities to be weighed and considered. The class for which you are reading this book derives from this long rhetorical tradition. It is intended to improve more than your ability to "compose" in the narrow sense. It aims to improve your ability to handle yourself in a college and a world where facts seldom speak for themselves and where we are therefore forced to interpret them.

SUBJECTS AND FRAMEWORKS

Let's begin with a working definition of the kinds of interpretations you will be writing in this course. Fortunately, John Wheeler and Joan Didion have provided us with clues that make such a definition easier. Wheeler said that he objected to De Palma's film not because it was inaccurate in its particular details but because it didn't tell the "greater truth" about the Vietnam War. Didion said that in every photograph there was the "subject" (a flesh-and-blood woman) and the *subject,* an idea that existed in the mind of the photographer. Both statements imply that an interpretation has two parts.

One part we will call the *subject* or the "smaller truth"; the other we will call the *framework* or "greater truth." This rather vague terminology will acquire more meaning as we apply it to various types of writing in later chapters. For now, we'll conceive of *framework* in a rather simplistic way, by analogy to the frame around a picture. The majority of the justices of the Supreme Court framed the Gregory Johnson case this way:

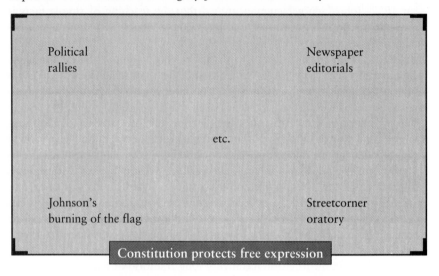

However much they may have been offended by what Johnson did, they felt it had to be seen in the context of the free expression of ideas the First Amendment was written to protect. As Justice Brennan noted in the majority opinion, "Johnson burned an American flag as part—indeed, as the culmination—of a political demonstration. . . . The expressive, overtly political nature of this conduct was both intentional and overwhelmingly apparent."

The dissenting justices framed the subject differently:

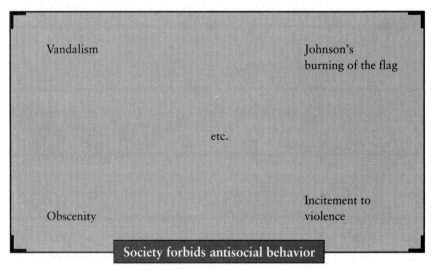

They rejected the idea that burning the flag should be viewed as belonging to the same class of activity as writing a newspaper editorial or delivering a speech on a street corner. In his written dissent Chief Justice Rehnquist argued that "one of the high purposes of a democratic society is to legislate against conduct that is regarded as evil and profoundly offensive to the majority of people—whether it be murder, embezzlement, pollution, or flag burning."[2]

The justices of the Supreme Court have special training, of course, but the workings of their minds are essentially like those of any other serious thinkers who must reach a tough decision in a world of uncertainties. The word *decide* comes to us from Latin, and it is worth remembering that it originally meant "to cut off." The act of interpretation puts a subject into a framework that cuts off other interpretations, at least tentatively and temporarily. Writer A encourages readers to see the subject his or her way, which is not the way Writer B or C would see it. Wise readers, aware that each essay presents a version of the truth, are as alert to the framework as they are to the subject. "What *idea* shapes this essay?" they ask themselves. "What good can this idea do me or the world? What harm?" We may decide that the author's framing creates a lie, a mistake, a reminder of an old truth, or the creation of a new one. For better or worse, forceful writing gives us something more decisive and meaningful than an unframed subject.

FRAMEWORKS: LOGIC AND EMOTION

Some people trained in logic may look at the metaphor of the physical frame and assume that all we will mean by *framework* is a logical category and that what we mean by an interpretation is a fitting of the subject into the right philosophical pigeonhole: "All men are mortal; Socrates is a man; therefore, Socrates is mortal"—that sort of thing. That is, indeed, one aspect of what we mean by framework, but there is much more. As Adrienne Rich says, you must learn to use both your brains and your instincts. In some cases, the framework is created as much by emotional association or life experience as it is by reason. Writing the dissent in the flag-burning case, Chief Justice Rehnquist didn't restrict himself to legal logic-chopping. He quoted parts of Ralph Waldo Emerson's "Concord Hymn," the entire "Star-Spangled Banner" and John Greenleaf Whittier's "Barbara Frietchie." In short, he put Johnson's flag burning in a framework having at least as much to do with feeling and association as with cold reasoning.

---

[2] In the year following the Johnson decision, the flag-desecration debate continued in the courts, the Congress, and the media. An interesting research paper might be written on the way that the national news magazines, especially, created the framework in which readers would view President Bush's repeated calls for a constitutional amendment to protect the flag.

To get a sense of the range of notions we will collect under the term *framework,* consider the following synonyms, some of which stress logic, some emotion:

intellectual context	concept
frame of reference	principle
point of view	rule
perspective	context of experience
model	emotional context
generalization	predisposition
habit of thought	archetype — bluePrinT— original—groundwork
bias	gestalt how you puT things Together
thesis	paradigm model
idea	world view
premise	insight

To this list, compare some synonyms for what we are calling *subject:*

facts	details
data	phenomenon
raw material	event
experience	observations
instances	examples
case	evidence

SUBJECTS AND FRAMEWORKS IN THE EXPOSITORY ESSAY

A key characteristic of the successful writer is the ability to bring subjects and frameworks together effectively, enclosing data with theory, detail with generalization, event with context. As an example, we can look at a passage in which journalist Theodore White discusses John F. Kennedy. Some information about White is worth noting before you begin to read because it will help you see the way that writers can build frameworks from the whole of their experience, from emotion as well as logic. White was a third-generation American, born into a poor family in Boston's Jewish ghetto, which had not long before been a ghetto for Irish immigrants. He rose in the world through scholarship, distinguishing himself at the Boston Latin School, which meant steeping himself not only in the Latin language but in the history and politics of Ancient Rome. When poverty forced him to leave school and sell newspapers on street corners, he sometimes shouted the headlines in Latin or belted out a quotation from a Roman orator. All of this background affects the frameworks in which he puts his fellow Bostonian:

He was the man who ruptured the silent understanding that had governed American politics for two centuries—that this was a country of white Protestant gentry and yeomen who offered newer Americans a choice for leadership only within their clashing rivalries. He made us look at ourselves afresh. Kennedy ended many other myths and fossil assumptions, and with him, an old world of politics and government came to a close.

But how the new world that he ushered in will take shape remains yet to be seen—and thus we cannot finally measure him.

Kennedy was, whether for good or bad, an enormously large figure. Historically, he was a gatekeeper. He unlatched the door, and through the door marched not only Catholics, but blacks, and Jews, and ethnics, women, youth, academics, newspersons and an entirely new breed of young politicians who did not think of themselves as politicians—all demanding their share of the action and the power in what is now called participatory democracy.

Some people are in the habit of distinguishing between expository and "creative" writing, between the "personal essay" and workaday prose. If we look at what is happening here, though, we can see that White's reporting creates a fresh interpretation of Kennedy partly from the stuff of White's own experience. The subject is the same Kennedy about whom millions of words have been written, but the framework comes from White, comes from being an immigrant, being poor, being excluded, and discovering to his enormous excitement that there was a way for him to succeed. How does White's "created" Kennedy compare with the "objective" Kennedy of another reporter? The question is impossible to answer simply because the "objective reporter" is a largely mythological creature. All writers have frameworks to impose.

Just a bit after White's "gatekeeper" passage comes another that we might call the "*gravitas*" passage:

> Liberals, generally, could not see the weight and dignity in Kennedy until well on into the campaign year of 1960; with such outstanding exceptions as Arthur M. Schlesinger, Jr., they considered him a lightweight who had bought his Senate seat with his father's money. Practical politicians saw him more clearly. John Bailey, the "boss" of Connecticut, a veteran of the regular ranks of old politics, once described to me his movement in four years from Stevenson to Kennedy. He had supported Stevenson in both 1952 and 1956, said Bailey, because Stevenson had "heft," and that's what voters wanted in their Presidents. Bailey had probably never heard of the Roman civic phrase *gravitas,* the weightiness that is so becoming to a man of public affairs. But by 1958 Bailey could feel the "heft" he wanted in John F. Kennedy and was mobilizing for him. And by the time he was killed, John Kennedy was accepted fully for his *gravitas* by liberals, just as much as by politicians and common people who had elected him chiefly because he was elegant, gay, witty, young and attractive.

Here is White, at age 63, doing what he had done at age 18: shouting today's headlines in Latin, seeing contemporary America against the backdrop of Roman politics. This, again, is a personal and creative act: it could be argued that White's lifetime project was to show that American "current events" during his lifetime had the "heft" of classical history.

White's description of Kennedy, developed in a great deal more detail than we can show here, is a fairly typical example of expository prose—prose that announces its frameworks as it goes. The naive tend to think of exposition as writing that simply tells the truth, which makes it seem a drab creature compared to fiction or poetry. In fact, since the truth that a writer gives us is created by an interaction between his or her frame of reference and the data, it is dangerous to talk about *the* truth. At most the writer knows some reliable facts from which he or she constructs *a* truth or *some* truths. Exposition creates a version of reality: it is a way of coming to grips with the world.

SUBJECT AND FRAMEWORK IN THE NARRATIVE

Other types of writing—particularly the narrative—create the backdrop more subtly: if we expect to discover the framework neatly expressed in a thesis statement, most narratives will disappoint us. Nonetheless, a story is also an interpretation of reality, and a careful reader will find in it indications of the "larger truths" the writer brings to the subject.

The following passage is from James Weldon Johnson's autobiography, *Along This Way*. As you read it, look for the touches by which the writer establishes frameworks for his story. The choice of words may be important in some cases, the emphasis on a particular detail in others. To better understand the interaction between the writer and the subject, bear in mind that Johnson was a college graduate studying law at the time the incident he describes took place and that by the time he wrote about it, he had served as U.S. Consul in Venezuela and Nicaragua and as executive secretary of the NAACP. Once again, the whole writer—intellect and emotion—is thrown into the creation of the frameworks in which the subject is presented.

"Jim Crow Train"
–JAMES WELDON
JOHNSON

Why does Johnson insert the parenthetical sentence?

In 1896 I was returning from New York to Jacksonville. I went by steamer to Charleston, and from there to Jacksonville by train. When I boarded the train at Charleston I got into the first-class car. (South Carolina had not yet enacted its separate car law; and all my life I have made it a principle never to "Jim Crow" [3] myself voluntarily.) The car was almost full, but I found a seat to myself, arranged my luggage, and settled down comfortably. The conductor took my ticket quietly, and made no reference whatever to the fact that the train carried a special car for me. A while later, however, he came to me and said that I would have to go into the

------

[3] Segregate. As an adjective, *Jim Crow* means "for blacks only."

car forward. His manner was not objectionable; in fact, it was rather apologetic. I asked him why. He replied that we had just crossed the Georgia line, and that it was against the law in Georgia for white and colored people to ride in the same railroad car. I then asked him what he proposed to do if I did not move. We were discussing the question without heat, and he answered in a matter-of-fact manner that he would call the first available officer of the law and have me arrested. I realized that my opposition to the law and all the forces of the state of Georgia would have hardly any other effect than to land me in some small-town jail; but I said to the conductor that I would first take a look at the car designated for me.

Why does he comment on the conductor's manner?

I went forward and looked at the car. It was the usual "Jim Crow" arrangement: one-half of a baggage coach, unkempt, unclean, and ill smelling, with one toilet for both sexes. Two of the seats were taken up by a pile of books and magazines and the baskets of fruit and chewing gum of the "news-butcher." There were a half-dozen or more Negroes in the car and two white men. White men in a "Jim Crow" car were not an unusual sight. It was—and in many parts still is—the custom for white men to go into that car whenever they felt like doing things that would not be allowed in the "white" car. They went there to smoke, to drink, and often to gamble. At times the object was to pick an acquaintance with some likely-looking Negro girl. After my inspection I went back and told the conductor that I couldn't ride in the forward car either. When he asked why, I gave as a reason the fact that there were white passengers in that car, too. He looked at me astonished, and hastily explained that the two men were a deputy sheriff and a dangerously insane man, who was being taken to the asylum. I listened to his explanation, but pointed out that it didn't change the race of either of the men. He pleaded, "But I can't bring that crazy man into the 'white' car." "Maybe you can't," I said, "but if I've got to break this law I prefer breaking it in a first-class car." The conductor was, after all, a reasonable fellow; and he decided to stand squarely by the law, and bring the two white men into the "white" car.

Why does Johnson give a detailed description of the car?

How are you affected by the mention of the behavior of these men?

What ironies do you find in this conversation?

What is the effect of the word *pleaded?*

While this colloquy between the conductor and me was going on the passengers were fully aware of what it was about. There had been no open talk or threats regarding my being in the car. Probably they felt that the matter was in capable hands or it may be that there was no individual among them to take the initiative in stirring up protest or action. However, when I began to get my belongings together, there were smiles and nudges and *sotto voce*[4] comments all through the car. The sheriff and his insane charge were brought in, and I began to move out. The first thing the insane man did after sitting down was to thrust his manacled hands through the glass of the window, cutting himself horribly. Then he not only let out a stream of oaths and ordinary obscenity, but made use of all the unprintable (perhaps no longer so) four-letter words of Anglo-Saxon origin. As I left the car, there were protests from men and women against the change. The maniac continued his ravings; but both I and the conductor stood squarely by the law.

Why does Johnson mention the smiles?

What is the effect of the word *squarely?*

---

[3] Italian: "under the breath."

Different readers will see somewhat different frameworks here, but perhaps we can agree on three. First, Johnson shows the incident as a slice of racial history from the days of American apartheid: notice how carefully he dates the episode and explains the laws and customs of the time. Second, he presents the episode as an example of the foolishness and hypocrisy of laws attempting to separate two races that must inevitably live together. In his autobiography, he introduces this anecdote by saying that it was one of two Jim Crow incidents so "ridiculous" that "all sense of indignity was lost in the absurdity of the situation." Third, its ridiculousness notwithstanding, he presents the episode against the backdrop of one of life's most important and universal struggles, a person's attempt to maintain dignity in difficult circumstances. Notice that he establishes this struggle as a framework almost immediately, by saying that he "made it a principle" not to ride in Jim Crow cars voluntarily. He keeps the idea of personal dignity before us by contrasting the grave and courteous exchanges between himself and the conductor with the description of the indignities of the Jim Crow car. One of the delights of this narrative is the way that its conclusion satisfies our feelings about all of the frameworks. When the insane man disrupts the "white" car, readers (if I can judge from my own reaction) don't merely feel that an individual incident has ended. They feel that racism has taken a slap in the face, the foolishness of the law has been exposed, and human dignity has been vindicated.

THESIS AND DETAILS

The distinction between the framework and the subject helps us make sense of two common pieces of advice given to student writers: "state a definite thesis early in the paper" and "use concrete detail."

The advice that you should state your thesis early makes sense if you consider the importance of showing your reader what your framework is. There must be an emphasis, a sense of what is important. A writer like Theodore White doesn't attempt to pour out the whole content of his notebooks at once, leaving us to assemble the pieces as we will. Instead he creates for each section of his book (indeed, for almost every paragraph, as we will see in Chapter 15) a framework in which selected facts will "make sense." Often the writer will express the controlling idea of an essay or section in an explicit thesis statement, the controlling idea of a paragraph in a topic sentence. Sometimes a single phrase or even a single word stands for the complete framework: *gravitas* or *gatekeeper*. Sometimes the framework is established so indirectly that we cannot associate it with a single word, phrase, or sentence, but it is there, organizing our perception of the subject.

In expository prose, this organization is done by statements of ideas, not by statements that are purely emotional or factual. "I liked John Kennedy" might be a valid observation, but as a framework to shape our perceptions, it hasn't much power. We almost instinctively say "Why?" and look for an idea

JOAN DIDION

"I write entirely to find out what I'm thinking, what I'm looking at, what I see and what it means. What I want and what I fear."

© 1990 Jerry Bauer

Joan Didion's great-great-great grandmother separated from the Donner party just before that group of pioneers was trapped in a snow-blocked pass high in the Sierras in the winter of 1846–47. Those who survived did so by eating the flesh of the dead. "A lot of the stories I was brought up on," Didion once said, "had to do with extreme actions—leaving everything behind, crossing the trackless wastes. . . ." When she was five years old, Didion wrote the first of her own stories: it was about a woman who believed she was freezing in the Arctic until she awoke and discovered she was baking in the desert.

Didion's family history and early writing suggest the kinds of subjects she is attracted to and the kinds of frameworks she imposes on them. With few exceptions, Didion's essays and novels do not reassure: they reflect the author's awareness of a world filled with chaos and contradiction. "Slouching Towards Bethlehem," for instance, the key essay of her early career, describes the "hippie" subculture of San Francisco in 1967. But, as Didion says, the essay is "about something more general than a handful of children wearing mandalas on their foreheads":

> I went to San Francisco because I had not been able to work in some months, had been paralyzed by the conviction that writing was an ir-relevant act, that the world as I had understood it no longer existed. If I was to work again at all, it would be necessary for me to come to terms with disorder.

Most of Didion's work deals with disorder, with situations and places that are out of control: terrorism and political upheaval in Latin America, ethnic friction in Miami, a murder near San Bernardino. Yet if disorder fascinates Didion, it fascinates as a powerful enemy does. Writing allows her to fight back, to impose order on chaos. Remembering a day when she was "scattered, upset, not myself," she described her instinctive reaction: ". . . I went to my office and just sat in front of the typewriter, and it was okay. I got control. I calmed down. I'm only myself in front of the typewriter." ◆

and some supporting data. "Kennedy was only 42 when he began his Presidential campaign," an undisputed fact, makes us ask, "So what?" Or, if you prefer, "In what framework is that fact significant?" If you have had teachers insist that you end your introduction with a thesis statement, please understand this apparently mechanical bit of advice as encouraging you to express an idea that can enclose the details to come.

There must, of course, be something to enclose. Within the framework of a strong idea, the writer arranges details, large and small, that make the idea understandable and believable. A history professor on my campus told me that when the Nazis were rising to power, their secret agents identified potential enemies of the Reich by eavesdropping on conversations. The man or woman who responded to Nazi ideas by insisting that the person who advocated them must "specify" the details on which they were based immediately became a suspect. People who insist that frameworks be linked to details are thinkers, and thinkers are threats to a totalitarian state.

The force of concrete details set in larger frameworks can be seen in a passage from historian Barbara Tuchman's *Bible and Sword*. One of the largest frameworks in this book is Tuchman's thesis that religion shaped Victorian politics to a degree almost unimaginable today. To illustrate that thesis, she introduces the particular case of Lord Shaftesbury. And to illustrate the nature of Lord Shaftesbury, she introduces a number of small details. Schematically, we might represent the situation this way:

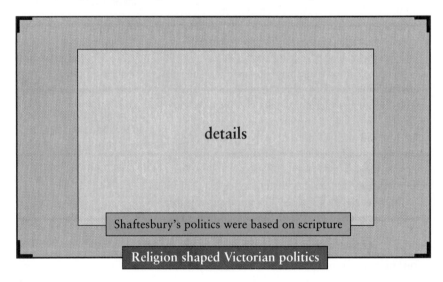

Bear this representation in mind as you read the following passage from *Bible and Sword*. Pay special attention to the way that Tuchman's details not only demonstrate her assertions about Lord Shaftesbury but give clearer meaning to the generalization that the religion and politics of the time were intertwined.

It was said of Lord Shaftesbury that he had "the purest, palest, stateliest exterior of any man in Westminster." His cold and classic face always called forth comparison to a marble bust. Every separate dark lock of hair, said one acquaintance, seemed to curl from a sense of duty. Yet this impeccable peer was in reality a compassionate, deeply religious man who had based his life on literal acceptance of the Bible. The Bible, he said, "is 'God's word written' from the very first syllable down to the very last and from the last back to the first. . . . Nothing but Scripture can interpret Scripture. I should reject it if announced to me by man. I accept it, believe it, bless it, as announced in Holy Writ . . . and like the Israelites, I bow the head and worship."

This was what made him a philanthropist: the Bible enjoined him to be exactly that—to love his fellow man. Born into the ruling aristocracy, related by marriage to the two great Whig prime ministers of his time, sought after by both parties for cabinet office, which he consistently refused in order to remain above party for the sake of his welfare work, Lord Shaftesbury was the personification of *noblesse oblige*.[5] He really believed he *was* his brother's keeper—especially the wretchedest brother's. He really believed that his endowments of rank, ability, and influence obligated him to help the underprivileged. He really believed that the charity and love preached by the gospels was the sum total of all man needed to know or practice, and he practiced them. To say that he was a friend and benefactor of the poor is to use one of those overfamiliar phrases that will pass under the reader's eye unnoticed. Yet Lord Shaftesbury was literally and exactly what the phrase says: a doer-of-good to the poor, to thieves, to lunatics, to cripples; to children, chained at five years to coal carts underground, to wizened "climbing boys" squeezed into soot-filled chimneys, to all humans who existed in the half-starved, ragged, sick, shivering sixteen-hour-a-day squalor that was the life of the laboring class in those happily unregulated days. It was Lord Shaftesbury who forced through Parliament the Ten Hour Bill (the Factory Act), credited with staving off revolution in the industrial counties, as well as the Mines Act, the Lunacy Act, and the Lodging House Act, which Dickens called the finest piece of legislation ever enacted in England up to that time.

"Bible and Sword"
—Barbara Tuchman

How does the "marble bust" comparison suit the framework?

How does Shaftesbury's way of expressing himself suit the framework?

What is the effect of the word *really* here?

Why does Tuchman introduce the chains and coal carts?

Why does Tuchman quote Dickens here?

Readers whom I have asked about this passage praise its style and its emotional force: Tuchman has immersed herself enough in the times to appreciate Shaftesbury's importance and to admire him enormously. But the work of the passage is done by the use of details she uncovered in the process of her research. And, as it turns out, the detail she is proudest of is perhaps the smallest in the passage: "every separate dark lock of hair . . . seemed to curl from a sense of duty." Nine years after writing *Bible and Sword* Tuchman remembered Shaftesbury's dutifully curling hair as "the best corroborative

---

[5] Benevolent and honorable behavior considered to be the responsibility of persons of high birth and rank.

detail I ever found. . . . For conveying both appearance and character of a man and the aura of his times, all in one, that line is unequaled."

One thing that makes most writing duller than it needs to be is that the writer doesn't attempt to do anything with Lord Shaftesbury's hair. That is, most of us don't reach outward from the detail to the large frameworks that detail can illuminate. As a result we write essays that creep along at one level, rather like the monologue the traveler too often treats us to as he shows pictures from a summer vacation. "Here I am standing in front of Salisbury Cathedral. Here's Mary at the Houses of Parliament. Here's Bob with one of the mummies from the British Museum. Here's Mary in the Tower of London." This we might call the problem of having a subject with no meaningful connection to a framework. Occasionally we write bad essays of the opposite sort. Contests with themes like "freedom" or "love" or "duty" tend to produce essays that make the reader long for any concrete detail, even Mary standing in front of the Houses of Parliament. The interpretation of experience, in writing and in our heads, is a dynamic process. Its essence is moving from assertions to observations, from small details to larger meanings. To move this way requires intelligence and energy. It often requires research, and it always requires nerve.

Dull writing is often dull because the writer refuses to be an interpreter, refuses through a failure of nerve to put the subject into a framework, point to X as an example of Y. In "Why I Write" Joan Didion describes the writer's situation this way:

> In many ways, writing is the act of saying *I*, of imposing oneself upon other people, of saying *Listen to me, see it my way, change your mind.* It's an aggressive, even a hostile act. You can disguise its aggressiveness all you want with veils of subordinate clauses and qualifiers and tentative subjunctives, with ellipses and evasions—with the whole manner of intimating rather than claiming, of alluding rather than stating—but there's no getting around the fact that setting words on paper is the tactic of a secret bully, an invasion, an imposition of the writer's sensibility on the reader's most private space.

It is worth noting that a few minutes before Didion delivered this memorable paragraph to an audience that included some of her former professors at the University of California, she was sitting in a restroom, so nervous that she was afraid she would throw up. Interpretation has its terrors. There is always the chance that your audience will think you are wrong.

Good writers take the chance.

ASSIGNMENT 1: **SOW'S EARS**

One of the home truths about writing is that the writer rarely has an absolutely free choice of subjects and that many assigned subjects leave the writer cold. Faced with this unhappy situation, successful writers manage to make a silk purse out of a sow's ear. Finding a framework in which the subject will come to life is the key.

Listed below are four classic sow's ears, subjects that have produced mountains of bad student writing over the decades. Write a short essay (your teacher will specify the length) that redeems one of them by putting it into a context that brings it to life.

1. What I did on my vacation.

2. A memorable book or movie.

3. An event that changed my life.

4. School days.

VARIATION: In the hands of good writers, these sow's ears have produced a number of silk purses. Listed below are essays or passages that redeem one of the subjects above. Read one and write a paragraph explaining how the writer brings it to life by putting it in an unusual or important framework.

1. *What I did on my vacation.*
   E. B. White, "Once More to the Lake" (p. 29)
   Maya Angelou, "My Sojourn in the Lands of My Ancestors" (p. 33)

2. *A memorable book or movie.*
   Sara Maitland, "Spend It All, Shoot It, Play It, Lose It" (p. 354)
   George Will, "Well, I Don't Love You, E.T." (p. 352)

3. *An event that changed my life.*
   Mark Twain, "The Mesmerizer" (p. 104)
   George Orwell, "Shooting an Elephant" (p. 100)

4. *School days.*
   Mary McCarthy, "Names" (p. 113)
   E. B. White, "Education" (p. 139)

EDITORIAL CARTOONS

Like writers, editorial cartoonists interpret their subjects by placing them within a framework. Each cartoon has a thesis, a message. Unfortunately, as time passes, society loses knowledge of the subject and may not recognize the message. Your mission in this assignment is to explicate one of the editorial cartoons reprinted here by writing a note about 500 words long explaining the subject of the cartoon and the framework in which the cartoonist presents it. (The sample paper on page 22 may serve as an example.) Imagine, if you like, that the cartoon and its accompanying note will appear in an album with the title *Events and Comments: What Editorial Cartoons Tell Us About Who We Were.* Assume that you are writing for an audience with the same level of general knowledge your classmates have. In some cases, you will need (for the sake of that audience) to discuss the subject at some length; in some cases you will want to spend most of your space helping your audience understand the cartoonist's attitude and showing that it is (or is not) representative of its period.

Writing this short paper will involve you in some detective work. Look closely at the cartoon and its date for clues. You will find such simple indexes as *The Reader's Guide to Periodical Literature* and *The New York Times Index* useful in locating background material. If you are not acquainted with these indexes, see Chapter 11, pages 428–431. Yearbooks published by such encyclopedias as *Britannica* and *World Book* may also be helpful.

October 30, 1983

October 23, 1962

October 2, 1960

January 27, 1980

As a variation on this assignment, locate a contemporary cartoon whose context you believe will be obscure twenty-five years from now. Assume that the cartoon is to be included in an album of cartoons inserted in a time capsule to be opened in twenty-five years. Write the note needed for the album.

Sample Student Paper

MAULDIN'S REDNECKS

In the summer of 1962 the Student Non-violent Coordinating Committee (SNCC) sponsored a voter-registration drive among the black citizens of Terrell County, Georgia, a county in which 64% of the residents were black and 98% of the registered voters were white. Some whites resisted the drive with intimidation and violence. Sheriff Z. T. Mathews and his deputies "badgered and harassed" SNCC workers and black residents at a rally in July. In August, the Shady Grove Baptist Church, site of SNCC rallies, was destroyed by fire. On August 31, "night riders" fired several bullets into the home of a black family active in the voter-registration campaign, and on September 5, three shotgun blasts were fired into another Negro home, injuring three college-age activists—two white men and one black woman. Before dawn on September 9, Mount Olive Baptist Church and Mount Mary Baptist Church, both of which had been used by SNCC as rallying points, were burned to the ground. Sheriff Mathews told reporters that he found no

"See you in church."

By Bill Mauldin. Reprinted by permission of North American Syndicate, Inc.

September 16, 1962

evidence of arson and that he did not believe that the burnings were associated with the registration drive. If arson was involved, he said, the cause was probably not the registration drive itself, but the outrage Terrell County residents felt when they saw white SNCC workers living in the same houses with blacks: "It's unusual for white folks to go down there living with niggers—pretty unusual. . . . The niggers are upset about it, too—the better niggers."

These ugly events are the subject of Bill Mauldin's September 16 cartoon captioned "See you in church." In the cartoon Mauldin, drawing for the *Chicago Sun-Times,* expressed attitudes that were probably typical of the northern white liberals of the time. President Kennedy had called the burning of the churches "cowardly as well as outrageous," and Mauldin's cartoon seems to second this judgment and to add *benighted* and *hypocritical* to the list of adjectives. The crescent moon at the upper right reminds us that the church-bombers did their dirty work under cover of darkness. The portrayal of the two men passes a judgment on their state of civilization. Notice the clothing of the man on the left: the untied boots, the ill-fitting, beltless pants with a half-buttoned fly, the gapping undershirt, the battered hat. Only a person this backward, Mauldin seems to be saying, would be capable of such an act. That the men who are on their way to burn a church are themselves church-goers makes them hypocrites, or perhaps even something lower. A hypocrite is someone who consciously professes one set of values and acts on another, but the men Mauldin draws may not have self-consciousness enough to be hypocrites: they may not see the contradiction between Christianity and violent repression.

Mauldin presents the episode in the framework of Southern backwardness and unconscious hypocrisy. His rural white Southerners are stereotyped to the point of being almost ape-like. Thirty years later, we can look at this cartoon and see the Northern stereotyping of white Southerners as unfair, almost as troubling as white stereotyping of blacks. But in the heat of the times, the advocates of civil rights needed an image of the enemy, and the stereotypical Southern redneck was an ideal target.

Sources: *New York Times,* September 1, 1962, p. 20; September 6, 1962, p. 1; September 10, 1962, pp. 1, 21; September 14, 1962, p. 1.

ASSIGNMENT 3: *POEMS, HISTORICAL SUBJECTS, AND FRAMEWORKS*

Like the political cartoons in Assignment 2, some poems are interpretations of historical subjects. The reader of such a poem needs therefore to recognize both the subject and the framework the author imposes on it. Write a brief essay (about 500 words) in which you first explain the historical subject of a poem, then explain the poet's interpretation of it. You may conclude with a brief "framework" comment of your own, evaluating the poet's interpretation. Your paper will follow the same pattern as the one described in Assignment 2.

Gwendolyn Brooks's "The Chicago Defender Sends a Man to Little Rock" (page 384) would be an appropriate poem to write about, as would Robert Browning's "My Last Duchess" (page 381). The subject in Brooks's poem is an episode in American history that you should be able to identify precisely. The episode described in Browning's poem is fictional, but it is grounded in the realities of a historical period. You will not be able to identify the particular Duke, but you should be able to identify and discuss the period in a way pertinent to the poem.

ASSIGNMENT 4: *SUMMARIES IN FRAMEWORKS*

A standard assignment in many college classes is a short essay responding to class readings. There are innumerable ways to handle such assignments, but three of the most common are also three of the most useful in helping you assimilate what you have read. Your assignment will be to write a summary based on one of the patterns that follow. You may be asked to do all three types for the same essay.

OPTION 1: *A DETAIL/FRAMEWORK SUMMARY*. Writers, as we can see from James Weldon Johnson's story about the Jim Crow train and Barbara Tuchman's description of Lord Shaftesbury, do their work largely by finding a relationship between small details of a subject and the larger framework into which the subject fits. One way to summarize a chapter or essay is to write a paragraph that begins with a small detail from the passage you are summarizing, moves quickly to the largest generalization in the essay, and then moves back to other details. The aim in such a summary is not to alter the author's interpretation but to compress it. This encapsulated summary should give an undistorted view of the essay to someone who has not read it or should serve you as a reliable reminder after the essay itself has faded in your memory. The following distillation of Joan Didion's "Marrying Absurd" (page 27) is a fairly typical detail/framework summary.

> In "Marrying Absurd" Joan Didion quotes James A. Brennan, Justice of the Peace in Las Vegas, who says that when he performed sixty-seven weddings in three hours, "I got it down from five to three minutes. . . . I could've married them *en masse,* but they're people, not cattle. People expect more when they get married." The quotation is typical of the essay, which discusses Las Vegas weddings as extreme examples of both the American "devotion to instant gratification" and the American desire for "niceness." The essay concentrates on the speed and impersonality of the weddings, carried out in a city so devoted to gambling and pleasure that events there seem to have "no connection with 'real' life." "Services" (including the providing of rings and witnesses) that ought to make a wedding seem solid and traditional can be rented or purchased on the spot, at any time of the day or night,

"presumably on the assumption that marriage, like craps, is a game to be played when the table seems hot." Didion points out, however, that for many who are married in Las Vegas, speed and convenience are not the only issues. Las Vegas wedding chapels sell " 'niceness,' the facsimile of proper ritual, to children who do not know how else to find it."

OPTION 2: *A SUMMARY IN THE FRAMEWORK OF THE AUTHOR'S LIFE AND WORK.* More difficult than the detail/framework summary, but often more enlightening, is a summary that begins by identifying a dominant theme in the writer's life and work and then shows how the particular essay (down to its particular details) is a part of his or her larger "project" as a writer. Such a summary requires a trip to the library but not necessarily a prolonged one. If the author is well known, you should be able to find adequate information in a good encyclopedia, in *Current Biography,* or in *Contemporary Authors,* which is the source primarily relied on in the following example.

A summary of this sort is necessarily a riskier proposition than the detail/framework summary. You are now making your own interpretation, and if it says anything significant it is certain to conflict with the interpretation of some other readers (including, perhaps, your teacher). Since you will not have time to do in-depth reading, you may develop an interpretation that further research would force you to abandon. For now, however, your job is to be bold: you are not trying to state definitively *the* truth about the relationship between the author and this particular work. Instead, you are creating a clearly expressed tentative interpretation, as the following example does.

A critic once said of Joan Didion (1934–) that "ghastliness and pointlessness" are her "invariable themes." Born into a stable family with conventional values, Didion seems to favor tradition, conservatism, and control. Until she lost interest in political labels, she called herself a Republican, and she has written essays criticizing the women's liberation movement and praising John Wayne's adherence, onscreen and off, to "the Code" of old-fashioned morality. Confronted by the social chaos of the 1960s, Didion became curious and alarmed. In fact, she began *Slouching Towards Bethlehem,* her 1969 collection of essays, by quoting W. B. Yeats's poem "The Second Coming": "Things fall apart; the center cannot hold;/Mere anarchy is loosed upon the world."

"Marrying Absurd" (1966), one of the essays in that collection, shows traditional marriage reduced to an almost pointless parody in the wedding chapels of Las Vegas. Didion emphasizes the extreme impersonality of what should be a most personal ceremony. One justice of the peace, she points out, married sixty-seven couples in three hours, getting the "ceremony" down from five minutes to three. The chapels advertise their services with the sort of garishness that the casinos do, and they offer them around the clock "presumably on the premise that marriage, like craps, is a game to be played when the table is hot." In Las Vegas, Didion sees a typical sight, a drunken bride "in an orange mini-dress and flame-colored hair." More depressing still is the sight of a pregnant bride sitting in a Strip restaurant after her hurried wedding: " 'It was just as nice,' she sobbed, 'as I hoped and dreamed it would be.' " The Las Vegas version of "niceness," "the facsimile of proper ritual," is for Didion another sign that things are falling apart.

OPTION 3:   *A SUMMARY IN A FRAMEWORK THE READER PROVIDES.* A reader who is also a thinker and writer will sometimes want to pluck the subject of an essay or chapter out of the author's framework and place it in a context that comes from his or her own mind. The following example shows how someone skeptical about the economic specialization in twentieth-century life (not a major concern of Didion's) brings Didion's subject into his framework. Notice that the summary characterizes the essay accurately, though from an angle Didion might think slightly odd.

Nearly a century and a half ago, Henry David Thoreau said that our tendency to turn aspects of our lives over to specialists could get us into trouble. "Where is this division of labor to end? and what object does it finally serve? No doubt another may also think for me, but it is not therefore desirable that he should do so to the exclusion of my thinking for myself." In her essay "Marrying Absurd" Joan Didion gives us an example of specialization producing results that are sad and disturbing. The essay describes Las Vegas, "the most extreme and allegorical of American settlements," a place that stands in the middle of the desert and has no traditional industry. The town supports itself by offering entertainment (notably gambling) or weddings, two products that in the nineteenth century were essentially homemade, with very little specialized assistance. Though Didion touches on entertainment, her primary subject is the weddings performed in the city's nineteen "wedding chapels." These weddings are produced with great efficiency: one justice of the peace, faced with high demand for his eight-dollar ceremony, squeezed it down to three minutes. The services the chapels offer are remarkably complete. For a price, they can provide rings, witnesses, transportation, music—all the things that once had to be produced laboriously by those who cared about the bride and groom and wanted to see their marriage properly launched. A ceremony that once belonged to the community and family has been turned over to strangers. It isn't, as Didion points out, merely a matter of convenience. It is also that many rootless people have lost the old knowledge of how to make a wedding. Las Vegas is merchandising " 'niceness,' the facsimile of proper ritual, to children who do not know how else to find it, how to make the arrangements, how to do it 'right.' "

MARRYING ABSURD

Joan Didion

From 1967 to 1969 Joan Didion and her husband, the novelist and screenwriter John Gregory Dunne, alternately wrote a column ("Points West") for The Saturday Evening Post. *The subjects for Didion's columns were often places, seen in the framework of the cultural upheaval of the 1960s. "Marrying Absurd" appeared in the* Post *on December 16, 1967, and was collected in her book* Slouching Towards Bethlehem *in 1968.*

1   TO BE MARRIED IN LAS VEGAS, CLARK COUNTY, Nevada, a bride must swear that she is eighteen or has parental permission and a bridegroom that he is twenty-one or has parental permission. Someone must put up five dollars for the license. (On Sundays and holidays, fifteen dollars. The Clark County Courthouse issues marriage licenses at any time of the day or night except between noon and one in the afternoon, between eight and nine in the evening, and between four and five in the morning.) Nothing else is required. The State of Nevada, alone among these United States, demands neither a premarital blood test nor a waiting period before or after the issuance of a marriage license. Driving in across the Mojave from Los Angeles, one sees the signs way out on the desert, looming up from that moonscape of rattlesnakes and mesquite, even before the Las Vegas lights appear like a mirage on the horizon: "GETTING MARRIED? Free License Information First Strip Exit." Perhaps the Las Vegas wedding industry achieved its peak operational efficiency between 9:00 p.m. and midnight of August 26, 1965, an otherwise unremarkable Thursday which happened to be, by Presidential order, the last day on which anyone could improve his draft status merely by getting married. One hundred and seventy-one couples were pronounced man and wife in the name of Clark County and the State of Nevada that night, sixty-seven of them by a single justice of the peace,

Mr. James A. Brennan. Mr. Brennan did one wedding at the Dunes and the other sixty-six in his office, and charged each couple eight dollars. One bride lent her veil to six others. "I got it down from five to three minutes," Mr. Brennan said later of his feat. "I could've married them *en masse,* but they're people, not cattle. People expect more when they get married."

2   What people who get married in Las Vegas actually do expect—what, in the largest sense, their "expectations" are—strikes one as a curious and self-contradictory business. Las Vegas is the most extreme and allegorical of American settlements, bizarre and beautiful in its venality and in its devotion to immediate gratification, a place the tone of which is set by mobsters and call girls and ladies' room attendants with amyl nitrite poppers in their uniform pockets. Almost everyone notes that there is no "time" in Las Vegas, no night and no day and no past and no future (no Las Vegas casino, however, has taken the obliteration of the ordinary time sense quite so far as Harold's Club in Reno, which for a while issued, at odd intervals in the day and night, mimeographed "bulletins" carrying news from the world outside); neither is there any logical sense of where one is. One is standing on a highway in the middle of a vast hostile desert looking at an eighty-foot sign which blinks "STARDUST" or "CAESAR'S PALACE." Yes, but what

does that explain? This geographical implausibility reinforces the sense that what happens there has no connection with "real" life; Nevada cities like Reno and Carson are ranch towns, Western towns, places behind which there is some historical imperative. But Las Vegas seems to exist only in the eye of the beholder. All of which makes it an extraordinarily stimulating and interesting place, but an odd one in which to want to wear a candlelight satin Priscilla of Boston wedding dress with Chantilly lace insets, tapered sleeves and a detachable modified train.

3   And yet the Las Vegas wedding business seems to appeal to precisely that impulse. "Sincere and Dignified Since 1954," one wedding chapel advertises. There are nineteen such wedding chapels in Las Vegas, intensely competitive, each offering better, faster, and, by implication, more sincere services than the next: Our Photos Best Anywhere, Your Wedding on A Phonograph Record, Candlelight with Your Ceremony, Honeymoon Accommodations, Free Transportation from Your Motel to Courthouse to Chapel and Return to Motel, Religious or Civil Ceremonies, Dressing Rooms, Flowers, Rings, Announcements, Witnesses Available, and Ample Parking. All of these services, like most others in Las Vegas (sauna baths, payroll-check cashing, chinchilla coats for sale or rent), are offered twenty-four hours a day, seven days a week, presumably on the premise that marriage, like craps, is a game to be played when the table seems hot.

4   But what strikes one most about the Strip chapels, with their wishing wells and stained-glass paper windows and their artificial bouvardia, is that so much of their business is by no means a matter of simple convenience, of late-night liaisons between show girls and baby Crosbys.[1] Of course there is some of that. (One night about eleven o'clock in Las Vegas I watched a bride in an orange minidress and masses of flame-colored hair stumble from a Strip chapel on the arm of her bridegroom, who looked the part of the expendable nephew in movies like *Miami*

---

[1] baby Crosbys: Male singers; the name alludes to crooner Bing Crosby (1904–77).

Syndicate. "I gotta get the kids," the bride whimpered. "I gotta pick up the sitter, I gotta get to the midnight show." "What you gotta get," the bridegroom said, opening the door of a Cadillac Coupe de Ville and watching her crumple on the seat, "is sober.") But Las Vegas seems to offer something other than "convenience"; it is merchandising "niceness," the facsimile of proper ritual, to children who do not know how else to find it, how to make the arrangements, how to do it "right." All day and evening long on the Strip, one sees actual wedding parties, waiting under the harsh lights at a crosswalk, standing uneasily in the parking lot of the Frontier while the photographer hired by The Little Church of the West ("Wedding Place of the Stars") certifies the occasion, takes the picture: the bride in a veil and white satin pumps, the bridegroom usually in a white dinner jacket, and even an attendant or two, a sister or a best friend in hot-pink *peau de soie,* a flirtation veil, a carnation nosegay. "When I Fall in Love It Will Be Forever," the organist plays, and then a few bars of *Lohengrin.* The mother cries; the stepfather, awkward in his role, invites the chapel hostess to join them for a drink at the Sands. The hostess declines with a professional smile; she has already transferred her interest to the group waiting outside. One bride out, another in, and again the sign goes up on the chapel door: "One moment please—Wedding."

5   I sat next to one such wedding party in a Strip restaurant the last time I was in Las Vegas. The marriage had just taken place; the bride still wore her dress, the mother her corsage. A bored waiter poured out a few swallows of pink champagne ("on the house") for everyone but the bride, who was too young to be served. "You'll need something with more kick than that," the bride's father said with heavy jocularity to his new son-in-law; the ritual jokes about the wedding night had a certain Panglossian character, since the bride was clearly several months pregnant. Another round of pink champagne, this time not on the house, and the bride began to cry. "It was just as nice," she sobbed, "as I hoped and dreamed it would be." ◆

ONCE MORE TO THE LAKE

E. B. White

In the summer of 1936, not long after the death of his parents, E. B. White (1899–1985) visited Belgrade Lakes, Maine, the site of memorable family vacations when he was a boy. Soon after the visit, White described it in a long letter to his brother Stanley, a letter that repeatedly used the reassuring phrase "things haven't changed much." Five years later, White vacationed at Belgrade with his son and described the vacation for Harper's Magazine *(August 1941). "Once More to the Lake" was later collected in* One Man's Meat *(1942) and has become one of his best-known essays. Its subject is the most overworked in the world: every year thousands of eighth graders write essays with the title "What I Did on My Summer Vacation." White's experiences and emotions, however, help to put his subject into a significant framework.*

1 ONE SUMMER, ALONG ABOUT 1904, MY father rented a camp on a lake in Maine and took us all there for the month of August. We all got ringworm from some kittens and had to rub Pond's Extract on our arms and legs night and morning, and my father rolled over in a canoe with all his clothes on; but outside of that the vacation was a success and from then on none of us ever thought there was any place in the world like that lake in Maine. We returned summer after summer—always on August 1st for one month. I have since become a salt-water man, but sometimes in summer there are days when the restlessness of the tides and the fearful cold of the sea water and the incessant wind which blows across the afternoon and into the evening make me wish for the placidity of a lake in the woods. A few weeks ago this feeling got so strong I bought myself a couple of bass hooks and a spinner and returned to the lake where we used to go, for a week's fishing and to revisit old haunts.

2 I took along my son, who had never had any fresh water up his nose and who had seen lily pads only from train windows. On the journey over to the lake I began to wonder what it would be like. I wondered how time would have marred this unique, this holy spot—the coves and streams, the hills that the sun set behind, the camps and the paths behind the camps. I was sure the tarred road would have found it out and I wondered in what other ways it would be desolated. It is strange how much you can remember about places like that once you allow your mind to return into the grooves which lead back. You remember one thing, and that suddenly reminds you of another thing. I guess I remembered clearest of all the early mornings, when the lake was cool and motionless, remembered how the bedroom smelled of the lumber it was made of and of the wet woods whose scent entered through the screen. The partitions in the camp were thin and did not extend clear to the top of the rooms, and as I was always the first up I would dress softly so as not to wake the others, and sneak out into the sweet outdoors and start out in the canoe, keeping close along the shore in the long shadows of the pines. I remembered being very careful never to rub my paddle against the gunwale for fear of disturbing the stillness of the cathedral.

3 The lake had never been what you would call a wild lake. There were cottages sprinkled around the shores, and it was in farming country although the shores of the lake were quite heavily wooded. Some of the cottages were owned by nearby farmers, and you would live at the shore and eat your meals at the

farmhouse. That's what our family did. But although it wasn't wild, it was a fairly large and undisturbed lake and there were places in it which, to a child at least, seemed infinitely remote and primeval.

I was right about the tar: it led to within half a mile of the shore. But when I got back there, with my boy, and we settled into a camp near a farmhouse and into the kind of summertime I had known, I could tell it was going to be pretty much the same as it had been before—I knew it, lying in bed the first morning, smelling the bedroom, and hearing the boy sneak quietly out and go off along the shore in a boat. I began to sustain the illusion that he was I, and therefore, by simple transposition, that I was my father. This sensation persisted, kept cropping up all the time we were there. It was not an entirely new feeling, but in this setting it grew much stronger. I seemed to be living a dual existence. I would be in the middle of some simple act, I would be picking up a bait box or laying down a table fork, or I would be saying something, and suddenly it would be not I but my father who was saying the words or making the gesture. It gave me a creepy sensation.

5   We went fishing the first morning. I felt the same damp moss covering the worms in the bait can, and saw the dragonfly alight on the tip of my rod as it hovered a few inches from the surface of the water. It was the arrival of this fly that convinced me beyond any doubt that everything was as it always had been, that the years were a mirage and there had been no years. The small waves were the same, chucking the rowboat under the chin as we fished at anchor, and the boat was the same boat, the same color green and the ribs broken in the same places, and under the floor-boards the same fresh-water leavings and débris—the dead helgramite,[1] the wisps of moss, the rusty discarded fishhook, the dried blood from yesterday's catch. We stared silently at the tips of our rods, at the dragonflies that came and went. I lowered the tip of mine into the water, tentatively, pensively dislodging the fly, which darted two feet away, poised,

------

[1] helgramite: an insect larva used for bait.

darted two feet back, and came to rest again a little farther up the rod. There had been no years between the ducking of this dragonfly and the other one—the one that was part of memory. I looked at the boy, who was silently watching his fly, and it was my hands that held his rod, my eyes watching. I felt dizzy and didn't know which rod I was at the end of.

6   We caught two bass, hauling them in briskly as though they were mackerel, pulling them over the side of the boat in a businesslike manner without any landing net, and stunning them with a blow on the back of the head. When we got back for a swim before lunch, the lake was exactly where we had left it, the same number of inches from the dock, and there was only the merest suggestion of a breeze. This seemed an utterly enchanted sea, this lake you could leave to its own devices for a few hours and come back to, and find that it had not stirred, this constant and trustworthy body of water. In the shallows, the dark, water-soaked sticks and twigs, smooth and old, were undulating in clusters on the bottom against the clean ribbed sand, and the track of the mussel was plain. A school of minnows swam by, each minnow with its small individual shadow, doubling the attendance, so clear and sharp in the sunlight. Some of the other campers were in swimming, along the shore, one of them with a cake of soap, and the water felt thin and clear and unsubstantial. Over the years there had been this person with the cake of soap, this cultist, and here he was. There had been no years.

7   Up to the farmhouse to dinner through the teeming, dusty field, the road under our sneakers was only a two-track road. The middle track was missing, the one with the marks of the hooves and the splotches of dried, flaky manure. There had always been three tracks to choose from in choosing which track to walk in; now the choice was narrowed down to two. For a moment I missed terribly the middle alternative. But the way led past the tennis court, and something about the way it lay there in the sun reassured me; the tape had loosened along the backline, the alleys were green with plantains and other weeds, and the net (installed in June and removed in September) sagged in the dry noon, and the whole place

steamed with midday heat and hunger and emptiness. There was a choice of pie for dessert, and one was blueberry and one was apple, and the waitresses were the same country girls, there having been no passage of time, only the illusion of it as in a dropped curtain—the waitresses were still fifteen; their hair had been washed, that was the only difference—they had been to the movies and seen the pretty girls with the clean hair.

8   Summertime, oh summertime, pattern of life indelible, the fadeproof lake, the woods unshatterable, the pasture with the sweetfern and the juniper forever and ever, summer without end; this was the background, and the life along the shore was the design, the cottages with their innocent and tranquil design, their tiny docks with the flagpole and the American flag floating against the white clouds in the blue sky, the little paths over the roots of the trees leading from camp to camp and the paths leading back to the outhouses and the can of lime for sprinkling, and at the souvenir counters at the store the miniature birch-bark canoes and the post cards that showed things looking a little better than they looked. This was the American family at play, escaping the city heat, wondering whether the newcomers in the camp at the head of the cove were "common" or "nice," wondering whether it was true that the people who drove up for Sunday dinner at the farmhouse were turned away because there wasn't enough chicken.

9   It seemed to me, as I kept remembering all this, that those times and those summers had been infinitely precious and worth saving. There had been jollity and peace and goodness. The arriving (at the beginning of August) had been so big a business in itself, at the railway station the farm wagon drawn up, the first smell of the pine-laden air, the first glimpse of the smiling farmer, and the great importance of the trunks and your father's enormous authority in such matters, and the feel of the wagon under you for the long ten-mile haul, and at the top of the last long hill catching the first view of the lake after eleven months of not seeing this cherished body of water. The shouts and cries of the other campers when they saw you, and the trunks to be unpacked, to give up their rich burden. (Arriving was less exciting nowadays, when you sneaked up in your car and parked it under a tree near the camp and took out the bags and in five minutes it was all over, no fuss, no loud wonderful fuss about trunks.)

    Peace and goodness and jollity. The only thing that was wrong now, really, was the sound of the place, an unfamiliar nervous sound of the outboard motors. This was the note that jarred, the one thing that would sometimes break the illusion and set the years moving. In those other summertimes all motors were inboard; and when they were at a little distance, the noise they made was a sedative, an ingredient of summer sleep. They were one-cylinder and two-cylinder engines, and some were make-and-break and some were jump-spark, but they all made a sleepy sound across the lake. The one-lungers throbbed and fluttered, and the twin-cylinder ones purred and purred, and that was a quiet sound too. But now the campers all had outboards. In the daytime, in the hot mornings, these motors made a petulant, irritable sound; at night, in the still evening when the afterglow lit the water, they whined about one's ears like mosquitoes. My boy loved our rented outboard, and his great desire was to achieve singlehanded mastery over it, and authority, and he soon learned the trick of choking it a little (but not too much), and the adjustment of the needle valve. Watching him I would remember the things you could do with the old one-cylinder engine with the heavy flywheel, how you could have it eating out of your hand if you got really close to it spiritually. Motor boats in those days didn't have clutches, and you would make a landing by shutting off the motor at the proper time and coasting in with a dead rudder. But there was a way of reversing them, if you learned the trick, by cutting the switch and putting it on again exactly on the final dying revolution of the flywheel, so that it would kick back against compression and begin reversing. Approaching a dock in a strong following breeze, it was difficult to slow up sufficiently by the ordinary coasting method, and if a boy felt he had complete mastery over his motor, he was tempted to keep it running beyond its time and then reverse it a few feet from the dock. It took a cool nerve, because if you threw the switch a twentieth of a second too soon you would catch the flywheel when it still had speed enough to go up past center, and the boat would leap ahead, charging bull-fashion at the dock.

We had a good week at the camp. The bass were biting well and the sun shone endlessly, day after day. We would be tired at night and lie down in the accumulated heat of the little bedrooms after the long hot day and the breeze would stir almost impercep-tibly outside and the smell of the swamp drift in through the rusty screens. Sleep would come easily and in the morning the red squirrel would be on the roof, tapping out his gay routine. I kept remembering everything, lying in bed in the mornings—the small steamboat that had a long rounded stern like the lip of a Ubangi, and how quietly she ran on the moon-light sails, when the older boys played their mandolins and the girls sang and we ate doughnuts dipped in sugar, and how sweet the music was on the water in the shining night, and what it had felt like to think about girls then. After breakfast we would go up to the store and the things were in the same place—the minnows in a bottle, the plugs and spinners disar-ranged and pawed over by the youngsters from the boys' camp, the fig newtons and the Beeman's gum. Outside, the road was tarred and cars stood in front of the store. Inside, all was just as it had always been, except there was more Coca-Cola and not so much Moxie and root beer and birch beer and sarsaparilla. We would walk out with a bottle of pop apiece and sometimes the pop would backfire up our noses and hurt. We explored the streams, quietly, where the tur-tles slid off the sunny logs and dug their way into the soft bottom; and we lay on the town wharf and fed worms to the tame bass. Everywhere we went I had trouble making out which was I, the one walking at my side, the one walking in my pants.

One afternoon while we were there at that lake a thunderstorm came up. It was like the revival of an old melodrama that I had seen long ago with childish awe. The second-act climax of the drama of the elec-trical disturbance over a lake in America had not

changed in any important respect. This was the big scene, still the big scene. The whole thing was so familiar, the first feeling of oppression and heat and a general air around camp of not wanting to go very far away. In midafternoon (it was all the same) a curious darkening of the sky, and a lull in everything that had made life tick; and then the way the boats suddenly swung the other way at their moorings with the com-ing of a breeze out of the new quarter, and the pre-monitory rumble. Then the kettle drum, then the snare, then the bass drum and cymbals, then crack-ling light against the dark, and the gods grinning and licking their chops in the hills. Afterward the calm, the rain steadily rustling in the calm lake, the return of light and hope and spirits, and the campers running out in joy and relief to go swimming in the rain, their bright cries perpetuating the deathless joke about how they were getting simply drenched, and the children screaming with delight at the new sensation of bathing in the rain, and the joke about getting drenched link-ing the generations in a strong indestructible chain. And the comedian who waded in carrying an um-brella.

When the others went swimming my son said he was going in too. He pulled his dripping trunks from the line where they had hung all through the shower, and wrung them out. Languidly, and with no thought of going in, I watched him, his hard little body, skinny and bare, saw him wince slightly as he pulled up around his vitals the small, soggy, icy gar-ment. As he buckled the swollen belt suddenly my groin felt the chill of death. ◆

MY SOJOURN IN THE LANDS OF MY ANCESTORS

Maya Angelou

Like E. B. White's "Once More to the Lake," Maya Angelou's essay places a vacation—in this case a "long weekend"—in a much larger framework. The body of "My Sojourn in the Lands of My Ancestors" is an excerpt from Angelou's 1986 book, All God's Children Need Traveling Shoes. Angelou added the italicized introduction when Ms. magazine published the excerpt in August 1986. As you read, consider how the introduction affects your understanding of the body of the essay.

1 *DURING THE EARLY SIXTIES IN NEW YORK City, I met, fell in love with, and married a South African Freedom Fighter who was petitioning the United Nations over the issue of apartheid. A year later, my 15-year-old son, Guy, and I followed my new husband to North Africa.*

2 *I worked as a journalist in Cairo and managed a home that was a haven to Freedom Fighters still trying to rid their countries of colonialism. I was a moderately good mother to a growingly distant teenager and a faithful, if not loving, wife. I watched my romance wane and my marriage end in the shadows of the Great Pyramid.*

3 *In 1962, my son and I left Egypt for Ghana, where he was to enter the university and I was to continue to a promised job in Liberia. An automobile accident left Guy with a broken neck and me with the responsibility of securing work and a place for him to recover. Within months I did have a job, a house, and a circle of black American friends who had come to Africa before me. With them I, too, became a hunter for that elusive and much longed-for place the heart could call home.*

4 *Despite our sincerity and eagerness, we were often rebuffed. The pain of rejection in Africa caused*

the spiritual that black slaves sang about their oppressors to come to my mind:

> *I'm going to tell God*
> *How you treat me*
> *when I get home.*

5 *On the delicious and rare occasions when we were accepted, our ecstasy was boundless, and we could have said with our foreparents in the words of another spiritual:*

> *My soul got happy*
> *When I came out of the wilderness*
> *Came out of the wilderness*
> *Came out of the wilderness.*
> *My soul got happy*
> *When I came out of the wilderness*
> *And up to the welcome table.*

6 I had a long weekend, money in my purse, and working command of Fanti. After a year in Accra, I needed country quiet, so I decided to travel into the bush. I bought roasted plantain stuffed with boiled peanuts, a quart of Club beer, and headed my little car west. The stretch was a highway from Accra

to Cape Coast, filled with trucks and private cars passing from lane to lane with abandon. People hung out of windows of the crowded mammie lorries, and I could hear singing and shouting when the drivers careened those antique vehicles up and down hills as if each was a little train out to prove it could.

I stopped in Cape Coast only for gas. Although many black Americans had headed for the town as soon as they touched ground in Ghana, I successfully avoided it for a year. Cape Coast Castle and the nearby Elmina Castle had been holding forts for captured slaves. The captives had been imprisoned in dungeons beneath the massive buildings, and friends of mine who had felt called upon to make the trek reported that they felt the thick stone walls still echoed with old cries.

8   The palm-tree-lined streets and fine white-stone buildings did not tempt me to remain any longer than necessary. Once out of the town and again onto the tarred roads, I knew I had not made a clean escape. Despite my hurry, history had invaded my little car. Pangs of self-pity and a sorrow for my unknown relatives suffused me. Tears made the highway waver and were salty on my tongue.

9   What did they think and feel, my grandfathers, caught on those green savannas, under the baobab trees? How long did their families search for them? Did the dungeon wall feel chilly and its slickness strange to my grandmothers, who were used to the rush of air against bamboo huts and the sound of birds rattling their green roofs?

10   I had to pull off the road. Just passing near Cape Coast Castle had plunged me back into the eternal melodrama.

11   There would be no purging, I knew, unless I asked all the questions. Only then would the spirits understand that I was feeding them. It was a crumb, but it was all I had.

12   I allowed the shapes to come to my imagination; children passed, tied together by ropes and chains, tears abashed, stumbling in a dull exhaustion, then women, hair uncombed, bodies gritted with sand, and sagging in defeat. Men, muscles without memory, minds dimmed, plodding, leaving bloodied footprints

in the dirt. The quiet was awful. None of them cried, or yelled, or bellowed. No moans came from them. They lived in a mute territory, dead to feeling and protest. These were the legions, sold by sisters, stolen by brothers, bought by strangers, enslaved by the greedy, and betrayed by history.

13   For a long time I sat as in an open-air auditorium watching a troupe of tragic players enter and exit the stage.

14   The visions faded as my tears ceased. Light returned and I started the car, turned off the main road, and headed for the interior. Using rutted track roads, and lanes a little larger than footpaths, I found the River Pra. The black water moving quietly, ringed with the tall trees, seemed enchanted. A fear of snakes kept me in the car, but I parked and watched the bright sun turn the water surface into a rippling cloth of lamé. I passed through villages that were little more than collections of thatch huts, with goats and small children wandering in the lanes. The noise of my car brought smiling adults out to wave at me.

15   In the late afternoon I reached the thriving town that was my destination. A student whom I had met at Legon (where the University of Ghana is located) had spoken to me often of the gold-mining area, of Dunkwa, his birthplace. His reports had so glowed with the town's virtues, I had chosen that spot for my first journey.

16   My skin color, features, and the Ghana cloth I wore would make me look like any young Ghanaian woman. I could pass if I didn't talk too much.

17   As usual, in the towns of Ghana, the streets were filled with vendors selling their wares of tinned pat milk, hot spicy Killi Willis (fried, ripe plantain chips), Pond's cold cream, and antimosquito incense rings. Farmers were returning home, children returning from school. Young boys grinned at mincing girls, and always there were the market women, huge and impervious. I searched for a hotel sign in vain and as the day lengthened, I started to worry. I didn't have enough gas to get to Koforidua, a large town east of Dunkwa, where there would certainly be hotels, and I didn't have the address of my student's family. I parked the car a little out of the town center and

stopped a woman carrying a bucket of water on her head and a baby on her back.

18   "Good day." I spoke in Fanti and she responded. I continued, "I beg you, I am a stranger looking for a place to stay."

19   She repeated, "Stranger?" and laughed. "You are a stranger? No. No."

20   To many Africans, only whites could be strangers. All Africans belonged somewhere, to some clan. All Akan[1]-speaking people belong to one of eight blood lines (Abosua) and one of eight spirit lines (Ntoro).

21   I said, "I am not from here."

22   For a second, fear darted in her eyes. There was the possibility that I was a witch or some unhappy ghost from the country of the dead. I quickly said, "I am from Accra." She gave me a good smile. "Oh, one Accra. Without a home," she laughed. The Fanti word *Nkran,* for which the capital was named, means the large ant that builds 10-foot-high domes of red clay and lives with millions of other ants.

23   "Come with me." She turned quickly, steadying the bucket on her head, and led me between two corrugated tin shacks. The baby bounced and slept on her back, secured by the large piece of cloth wrapped around her body. We passed a compound where women were pounding the dinner *foo foo*[2] in wooden bowls.

24   The woman shouted, "Look what I have found. One Nkran which has no place to sleep tonight." The women laughed and asked, "One Nkran? I don't believe it."

25   "Are you taking it to the old man?"

26   "Of course."

27   "Sleep well, alone, Nkran, if you can." My guide stopped before a small house. She put the water on the ground and told me to wait while she entered the house. She returned immediately, followed by a man who rubbed his eyes as if he had just been awakened.

He walked close and peered hard at my face. "This is the Nkran?" The woman was adjusting the bucket on her head.

"Yes, Uncle. I have brought her." She looked at me, "Good-bye, Nkran. Sleep in peace. Uncle, I am going." The man said, "Go and come, child," and resumed studying my face. "You are not Ga.[3]" He was reading my features.

30   A few small children had collected around his knees. They could barely hold back their giggles as he interrogated me.

31   "Aflao?"

32   I said, "No."

33   "Brong-ahafo?"

34   I said, "No. I am . . ." I meant to tell him the truth, but he said, "Don't tell me. I will soon know." He continued staring at me. "Speak more. I will know from your Fanti."

35   "Well, I have come from Accra and I need to rent a room for the night. I told that woman that I was a stranger . . ."

36   He laughed. "And you are. Now, I know. You are Bambara from Liberia. It is clear you are Bambara." He laughed again. "I always can tell. I am not easily fooled." He shook my hand. "Yes, we will find you a place for the night. Come." He touched a boy at his right. "Find Patience Aduah and bring her to me."

37   The children laughed, and all ran away as the man led me into the house. He pointed me to a seat in the neat little parlor and shouted, "Foriwa, we have a guest. Bring beer." A small black woman with an imperial air entered the room. Her knowing face told me that she had witnessed the scene in her front yard.

38   She spoke to her husband. "And, Kobina, did you find who the stranger was?" She walked to me. I stood and shook her hand. "Welcome, stranger." We both laughed. "Now don't tell me, Kobina, I have ears, also. Sit down, sister, beer is coming. Let me hear you speak."

---

[1]Akan: The Akan languages include Fanti, Ashanti, and five or six others principally spoken in Ghana.
[2]*foo foo* (fufu): a bread made of pounded plantain and cassava.

[3]Ga: The Ga, Alflao, Brong-ahafo, and Bambara are West African ethnic groups.

We sat facing each other while her husband stood over us smiling. "You, Foriwa, you will never get it."

I told her my story, adding a few more words I had recently learned. She laughed grandly. "She is Bambara. I could have told you when Abaa first brought her. See how tall she is? See her head? See her color? Men, huh. They only look at a woman's shape."

41   Two children brought beer and glasses to the man, who poured and handed the glasses around. "Sister, I am Kobina Artey; this is my wife, Foriwa, and some of my children."

42   I introduced myself, but because they had taken such relish in detecting my tribal origin I couldn't tell them that they were wrong. Or, less admirably, at that moment I didn't want to remember that I was an American. For the first time since my arrival, I was very nearly home. Not a Ghanaian, but at least accepted as an African. The sensation was worth a lie.

43   Voices came to the house from the yard.

44   "Brother Kobina," "Uncle," "Auntie."

45   Foriwa opened the door to a group of people, who entered, speaking fast and looking at me.

46   "So this is the Bambara woman? The stranger?" They looked me over and talked with my hosts. I understood some of their conversation. They said that I was nice-looking and old enough to have a little wisdom. They announced that my car was parked a few blocks away. Kobina told them that I would spend the night with the newlyweds, Patience and Kwame Duodu. Yes, they could see clearly that I was a Bambara.

47   "Give us the keys to your car, sister; someone will bring your bag."

48   I gave up the keys and all resistance. I was either at home with friends or I would die wishing that to be so.

49   Later, Patience, her husband, Kwame, and I sat out in the yard around a cooking fire near to their thatched house, which was much smaller than the Artey bungalow. They explained that Kobina Artey was not a chief, but a member of the village council, and all small matters in that area of Dunkwa were taken to him. As Patience stirred the stew in the pot that was balanced over the fire, children and women appeared sporadically out of the darkness carrying covered plates. Each time Patience thanked the bearers and directed them to the house, I felt the distance narrow between my past and present.

50   In the United States, during segregation, black American travelers, unable to stay in hotels restricted to white patrons, stopped at churches and told the black ministers or deacons of their predicaments. Church officials would select a home and then inform the unexpecting hosts of the decision. There was never a protest, but the new hosts relied on the generosity of their neighbors to help feed and even entertain their guests. After the travelers were settled, surreptitious knocks would sound on the back door.

51   In Stamps, Arkansas, I heard so often, "Sister Henderson, I know you've got guests. Here's a pan of biscuits."

52   "Sister Henderson, Mama sent a half a cake for your visitors."

53   "Sister Henderson, I made a lot of macaroni and cheese. Maybe this will help with your visitors."

54   My grandmother would whisper her thanks and finally when the family and guests sat down at the table, the offerings were so different and plentiful, it appeared that days had been spent preparing the meal.

55   Patience invited me inside, and when I saw the table I was confirmed in my earlier impression. Groundnut stew, garden egg stew, hot pepper soup, *kenke, kotomre,* fried plantain, *dukuno,*[4] shrimp, fish cakes, and more, all crowded together on variously patterned plates.

56   In Arkansas, the guests would never suggest, although they knew better, that the host had not prepared every scrap of food, especially for them.

57   I said to Patience, "Oh, sister, you went to such trouble."

58   She laughed, "It is nothing, sister. We don't want our Bambara relative to think herself a stranger anymore. Come let us wash and eat."

---

[4] *kenke, kotomre . . . dukuno: kenke,* corn dough, a staple food of the Fanti people is called *dukuno* in Ashanti; *kotomre (kantamire)* is a green vegetable.

59 After dinner, I followed Patience to the outdoor toilet; then they gave me a cot in a very small room.

60 In the morning, I wrapped my cloth under my arms, sarong fashion, and walked with Patience to the bathhouse. We joined about 20 women in a walled enclosure which had no ceiling. The greetings were loud and cheerful as we soaped ourselves and poured buckets of water over our shoulders.

61 Patience introduced me. "This is our Bambara sister."

62 "She's a tall one, all right. Welcome, sister."

63 "I like her color."

64 "How many children, sister?" The woman was looking at my breasts.

65 I apologized, "I only have one."

66 "One?"

67 "One?"

68 "One!" Shouts reverberated over the splashing water. I said, "One, but I'm trying."

They laughed. "Try hard, sister. Keep trying."

We ate leftovers from the last night feast, and I said a sad good-bye to my hosts. The children walked me back to my car, with the oldest boy carrying my bag. I couldn't offer money to my hosts, Arkansas had taught me that, but I gave change to the children. They bobbed and jumped and grinned.

71 "Good-bye, Bambara Auntie."

72 "Go and come, Auntie."

73 "Go and come."

74 I drove into Cape Coast before I thought of the gruesome castle and out of its environs before the ghosts of slavery caught me. Perhaps their attempts had been halfhearted. After all, in Dunkwa, although I let a lie speak for me, I had proved that one of their descendants, at least one, could just briefly return to Africa, and that despite cruel betrayals, bitter ocean voyages, and hurtful centuries, we were still recognizable. ◆

CHIVALRY

Barbara Tuchman

Barbara Tuchman's A Distant Mirror: The Calamitous 14th Century *(1978) explores the culture of medieval Europe by focusing on a single figure, Eguerrand de Coucy, "the most experienced and successful of all the knights of France." The following excerpt from the book does not discuss Eguerrand directly, but does discuss the "moral system" of chivalry and courtly love that prevailed during his lifetime. Like much of Tuchman's writing, the passage is so detailed that the reader may temporarily lose track of the framework. If you read closely, however, you'll find that she has structured her presentation so as to reinforce her thesis.*

1 OF CHIVALRY, THE CULTURE THAT NURtured him, much is known. More than a code of manners in war and love, chivalry was a moral system, governing the whole of noble life. That it was about four parts in five illusion made it no less governing for all that. It developed at the same time as the great crusades of the 12th century as a code intended to fuse the religious and martial spirits and somehow bring the fighting man into accord with Christian theory. Since a knight's usual activities were as much at odds with Christian theory as a merchant's, a moral gloss was needed that would allow the Church to

tolerate the warriors in good conscience and the warriors to pursue their own values in spiritual comfort. With the help of Benedictine thinkers,[1] a code evolved that put the knight's sword arm in the service, theoretically, of justice, right, piety, the Church, the widow, the orphan, and the oppressed. Knighthood was received in the name of the Trinity after a ceremony of purification, confession, communion. A saint's relic was usually embedded in the hilt of the knight's sword so that upon clasping it as he took his oath, he caused the vow to be registered in Heaven. Chivalry's famous celebrator Ramon Lull, a contemporary of St. Louis,[2] could now state as his thesis that "God and chivalry are in concord."

2   But, like business enterprise, chivalry could not be contained by the Church, and bursting through the pious veils, it developed its own principles. Prowess, that combination of courage, strength, and skill that made a chevalier *preux*,[3] was the prime essential. Honor and loyalty, together with courtesy—meaning the kind of behavior that has since come to be called "chivalrous"—were the ideals, and so-called courtly love the presiding genius. Designed to make the knight more polite and to lift the tone of society, courtly love required its disciple to be in a chronically amorous condition, on the theory that he would thus be rendered more courteous, gay, and gallant, and society in consequence more joyous. Largesse was the necessary accompaniment. An open-handed generosity in gifts and hospitality was the mark of a gentleman and had its practical value in attracting other knights to fight under the banner and bounty of the *grand seigneur*.[4] Over-celebrated by troubadours and chroniclers who depended on its flow, largesse led to reckless extravagance and careless bankruptcies.

3   Prowess was not mere talk, for the function of physical violence required real stamina. To fight on horseback or foot wearing 55 pounds of plate armor,

to crash in collision with an opponent at full gallop while holding horizontal an eighteen-foot lance half the length of an average telephone pole, to give and receive blows with sword or battle-ax that could cleave a skull or slice off a limb at a stroke, to spend half of life in the saddle through all weathers and for days at a time, was not a weakling's work. Hardship and fear were part of it. "Knights who are at the wars . . . are forever swallowing their fear," wrote the companion and biographer of Don Pero Niño, the "Unconquered Knight" of the late 14th century. "They expose themselves to every peril; they give up their bodies to the adventure of life in death. Moldy bread or biscuit, meat cooked or uncooked; today enough to eat and tomorrow nothing, little or no wine, water from a pond or a butt, bad quarters, the shelter of a tent or branches, a bad bed, poor sleep with their armor still on their backs, burdened with iron, the enemy an arrow-shot off. 'Ware! Who goes there? To arms! To arms!' With the first drowsiness, an alarm; at dawn, the trumpet. 'To horse! To horse! Muster! Muster!' As lookouts, as sentinels, keeping watch by day and by night, fighting without cover, as foragers, as scouts, guard after guard, duty after duty. 'Here they come! Here! They are so many—No, not as many as that—This way—that—Come this side—Press them there—News! News! They come back hurt, they have prisoners—no, they bring none back. Let us go! Let us go! Give no ground! On!' Such is their calling."

4   Horrid wounds were part of the calling. In one combat Don Pero Niño was struck by an arrow that "knit together his gorget and his neck," but he fought on against the enemy on the bridge. "Several lance stumps were still in his shield and it was that which hindered him most." A bolt from a crossbow "pierced his nostrils most painfully whereat he was dazed, but his daze lasted but a little time." He pressed forward, receiving many sword blows on head and shoulders which "sometimes hit the bolt embedded in his nose making him suffer great pain." When weariness on both sides brought the battle to an end, Pero Niño's shield "was tattered and all in pieces; his sword blade was toothed like a saw and dyed with blood . . . his

---

[1]Benedictine thinkers: Monks of the Benedictine order were among the most influential teachers of the Middle Ages.
[2]St. Louis: King of France from 1226 to 1270.
[3]*preux*: "valiant."
[4]*grand seigneur*: "great lord"; powerful nobleman.

armor was broken in several places by lance-heads of which some had entered the flesh and drawn blood, although the coat was of great strength." Prowess was not easily bought.

5   Loyalty, meaning the pledged word, was chivalry's fulcrum. The extreme emphasis given to it derived from the time when a pledge between lord and vassal was the only form of government. A knight who broke his oath was charged with "treason" for betraying the order of knighthood. The concept of loyalty did not preclude treachery or the most egregious trickery as long as no knightly oath was broken. When a party of armed knights gained entrance to a walled town by declaring themselves allies and then proceeded to slaughter the defenders, chivalry was evidently not violated, no oath having been made to the burghers.

6   Chivalry was regarded as a universal order of all Christian knights, a trans-national class moved by a single ideal, much as Marxism later regarded all workers of the world. It was a military guild in which all knights were theoretically brothers, although Froissart[5] excepted the Germans and Spaniards, who, he said, were too uncultivated to understand chivalry.

7   In the performance of his function, the knight must be prepared, as John of Salisbury wrote, "to shed your blood for your brethren"—he meant brethren in the universal sense—"and, if needs must, to lay down your life." Many were thus prepared, though perhaps more from sheer love of battle than concern for a cause. Blind King John of Bohemia met death in that way. He loved fighting for its own sake, not caring whether the conflict was important. He missed hardly a quarrel in Europe and entered tournaments in between, allegedly receiving in one of them the wound that blinded him. His subjects, on the other hand, said the cause was Divine punishment—not because he dug up the old synagogue of Prague, which he did, but because, on finding money concealed beneath the pavement, he was moved by greed and the advice of German knights to dig up the tomb of St.

Adelbert in the Prague cathedral and was stricken blind by the desecrated saint.

8   As an ally of Philip VI, at the head of 500 knights, the sightless King fought the English through Picardy, always rash and in the avant-garde. At Crécy[6] he asked his knights to lead him deeper into the battle so that he might strike further blows with his sword. Twelve of them tied their horses' reins together and, with the King at their head, advanced into the thick of the fight, "so far as never to return." His body was found next day among his knights, all slain with their horses still tied together.

9   Fighting filled the noble's need of something to do, a way to exert himself. It was his substitute for work. His leisure time was spent chiefly in hunting, otherwise in games of chess, backgammon and dice, in songs, dances, pageants, and other entertainments. Long winter evenings were occupied listening to the recital of interminable verse epics. The sword offered the workless noble an activity with a purpose, one that could bring him honor, status, and, if he was lucky, gain. If no real conflict was at hand, he sought tournaments, the most exciting, expensive, ruinous, and delightful activity of the noble class, and paradoxically the most harmful to his true military function. Fighting in tournaments concentrated his skills and absorbed his interest in an increasingly formalized clash, leaving little thought for the tactics and strategy of real battle.

10   Originating in France and referred to by others as "French combat" (conflictus Gallicus), tournaments started without rules or lists as an agreed-upon clash of opposing units. Though justified as training exercises, the impulse was the love of fighting. Becoming more regulated and mannered, they took two forms: jousts by individuals, and melees by groups of up to forty on a side, either à plaisance[7] with blunted weapons or à outrance[8] with no restraints, in which case participants might be severely wounded and not

---

[5] Froissart: French historian Jean Froissart (1333?–1400).

[6] Crécy: The battle of Crécy (1346) was one of the great English victories of the Hundred Years' War.
[7] à plaisance: "for pleasure."
[8] à outrance: "to the death."

infrequently killed. Tournaments proliferated as the noble's primary occupation dwindled. Under the extended rule of monarchy, he had less need to protect his own fief, while a class of professional ministers was gradually taking his place around the crown. The less he had to do, the more energy he spent in tournaments artificially re-enacting his role.

11   A tournament might last as long as a week and on great occasions two. Opening day was spent matching and seeding the players, followed by days set apart for jousts, for melees, for a rest day before the final tourney, all interspersed with feasting and parties. These occasions were the great sporting events of the time, attracting crowds of bourgeois spectators from rich merchants to common artisans, mountebanks, food vendors, prostitutes, and pickpockets. About a hundred knights usually participated, each accompanied by two mounted squires, an armorer, and six servants in livery. The knight had of course to equip himself with painted and gilded armor and crested helmet costing from 25 to 50 livres, with a war-horse costing from 25 to 100 livres in addition to his traveling palfrey, and with banners and trappings and fine clothes. Though the expense could easily bankrupt him, he might also come away richer, for the loser in combat had to pay a ransom and the winner was awarded his opponent's horse and armor, which he could sell back to him or to anyone. Gain was not recognized by chivalry, but it was present at tournaments.

12   Because of their extravagance, violence, and vainglory, tournaments were continually being denounced by popes and kings, from whom they drained money. In vain. When the Dominicans denounced them as a pagan circus, no one listened. When the formidable St. Bernard[9] thundered that anyone killed in a tournament would go to Hell, he spoke for once to deaf ears. Death in a tournament was officially considered the sin of suicide by the Church, besides jeopardizing family and tenantry without cause, but even threats of excommunication

had no effect. Although St. Louis condemned tournaments and Philip the Fair prohibited them during his wars, nothing could stop them permanently or dim the enthusiasm for them.

13   With brilliantly dressed spectators in the stands, flags and ribbons fluttering, the music of trumpets, the parade of combatants making their draped horses prance and champ on golden bridles, the glitter of harness and shields, the throwing of ladies' scarves and sleeves to their favorites, the bow of the heralds to the presiding prince who proclaimed the rules, the cry of poursuivants announcing their champions, the tournament was the peak of nobility's pride and delight in its own valor and beauty.

14   If tournaments were an acting-out of chivalry, courtly love was its dreamland. Courtly love was understood by its contemporaries to be love for its own sake, romantic love, true love, physical love, unassociated with property or family, and consequently focused on another man's wife, since only such an illicit liaison could have no other aim but love alone. (Love of a maiden was virtually ruled out since this would have raised dangerous problems, and besides, maidens of noble estate usually jumped from childhood to marriage with hardly an interval for romance.) The fact that courtly love idealized guilty love added one more complication to the maze through which medieval people threaded their lives. As formulated by chivalry, romance was pictured as extramarital because love was considered irrelevant to marriage, was indeed discouraged in order not to get in the way of dynastic arrangements.

15   As its justification, courtly love was considered to ennoble a man, to improve him in every way. It would make him concerned to show an example of goodness, to do his utmost to preserve honor, never letting dishonor touch himself or the lady he loved. On a lower scale, it would lead him to keep his teeth and nails clean, his clothes rich and well groomed, his conversation witty and amusing, his manners courteous to all, curbing arrogance and coarseness, never brawling in a lady's presence. Above all, it would

---

[9] St. Bernard: Bernard of Clairvaux, monastic reformer and promoter of the Second Crusade.

make him more valiant, more *preux*; that was the basic premise. He would be inspired to greater prowess, would win more victories in tournaments, rise above himself in courage and daring, become, as Froissart said, "worth two men." Guided by this theory, woman's status improved, less for her own sake than as the inspirer of male glory, a higher function than being merely a sexual object, a breeder of children, or a conveyor of property.

16   The chivalric love affair moved from worship through declaration of passionate devotion, virtuous rejection by the lady, renewed wooing with oaths of eternal fealty, moans of approaching death from unsatisfied desire, heroic deeds of valor which won the lady's heart by prowess, consummation of the secret love, followed by endless adventures and subterfuges to a tragic denouement. The most widely known of all such romances and the last of its kind was the *Châtelain de Coucy,* written about the time of Enguerrand VII's birth when the *chanson de geste* was dying out. Its hero was not a Seigneur de Coucy but a *châtelain* of the castle named Renault, modeled on a real individual and poet of the 12th century.

17   In the legend he falls madly in love with the Dame de Fayel and through an enormous series of maneuvers occupying 8,266 lines of verse is decoyed into the Third Crusade by the jealous husband, covers himself with glory, and when fatally wounded by a poisoned arrow, composes a last song and farewell letter to be dispatched after his death in a box with his embalmed heart and a lock of the lady's hair. Carried by a faithful servant, the box is intercepted by the husband, who has the heart cooked and served to his wife. On being informed what she has eaten, she swears that after such a noble food she will never eat again and dies, while the husband exiles himself in a lifelong pilgrimage to obtain pardon for his deed.

18   "Melancholy, amorous and barbaric,"[10] these tales exalted adulterous love as the only true kind, while in the real life of the same society adultery was a crime, not to mention a sin. If found out, it dishon-

ored the lady and shamed the husband, a fellow knight. It was understood that he had the right to kill both unfaithful wife and lover.

Nothing fits in this canon. The gay, the elevating, the ennobling pursuit is founded upon sin and invites the dishonor it is supposed to avert. Courtly love was a greater tangle of irreconcilables even than usury. It remained artificial, a literary convention, a fantasy (like modern pornography) more for purposes of discussion than for everyday practice.

20   The realities were more normal. As described by La Tour Landry,[11] his amorous fellow knights were not overly concerned with loyalty and *courtoisie.* He tells how, when he used to ride abroad with his friends as a young man, they would beg ladies for their love and if this one did not accept they would try another, deceiving the ladies with fair words of blandishment and swearing false oaths, "for in every place they would have their sport if they could." Many a gentlewoman was taken in by the "foul and great false oaths that false men use to swear to women." He tells how three ladies who were exchanging opinions of their lovers discovered that the senior Jean le Maingre, Sire de Boucicaut, was the favorite of each, he having made love to all, telling each he loved her best. When they taxed him with his falsity, he was in no way abashed, saying, "For at that time I spake with each of you, I loved her best that I spake with and thought truly the same."

21   La Tour Landry himself, a seigneur of substance who fought in many campaigns, emerges as a domestic gentleman who liked to sit in his garden and enjoy the song of the thrush in April, and loved his books. Contrary to chivalry, he had also loved his wife, "the bell and flower of all that was fair and good," and "I delighted me so much in her that I made for her love songs, ballads, roundels, verelays and divers new things in the best wise that I could." He does not think much of chivalry's favorite theme, that courtly love inspires knights to greater prowess, for though they say they do it for the ladies, "in faith they do it

---

[10]barbaric: Tuchman's notes indicate that she is quoting Gaston Paris (1839–1903), an eminent French scholar.

[11]La Tour Landry: Geoffrey La Tour Landry (1330?–1405?), author of a book of cautionary tales for girls.

for themselves to win praise and honor." Nor does he approve of love for its own sake, *par amours,* either before or after marriage, for it can cause all kinds of crime, of which he cites the *Châtelain de Coucy* as an example.

As suggested by a spectacular scandal of the time, Edward III's[12] rape of the Countess of Salisbury, courtly love was the ideal of chivalry least realized in everyday behavior. Froissart, who believed in chivalry as St. Louis believed in the Trinity, expurgated the story, supposedly after careful inquiries, but more probably out of respect for his beloved first patron, Philippa of Hainault, Edward's Queen. He reports only that the King, on visiting Salisbury Castle after a battle in Scotland in 1342, was "stricken to the heart with a sparkle of fine love" for the beautiful Countess. After she repulsed his advances, Edward is reported (with some historic license) debating with himself about pursuing his guilty passion in words that are a supreme statement of the chivalric theory of love's role: "And if he should be more amorous it would be entirely good for him, for his realm and for all his knights and squires for he would be more content, more gay and more martial; he would hold more jousts, more tourneys, more feasts and more revels than he had before; and he would be more able and more vigorous in his wars, more amiable and more trusting toward his friends and harsher toward his foes."

[23] According to another contemporary, Jean le Bel, who had himself been a knight with few illusions before he took orders as a canon and became a chronicler, matters went rather differently. After sending the Earl of Salisbury to Brittany like Uriah,[13] the King revisited the Countess and, on being again rejected, he villainously raped her, "stopping her mouth with such force that she could only cry two or three cries . . . and left her lying in a swoon bleeding from the nose and mouth and other parts." Edward returned to London greatly disturbed at what he had done, and the good lady "had no more joy or happiness again, so heavy was her heart." Upon her husband's return she would not lie with him and, being asked why, she told him what had happened, "sitting on the bed next to him crying." The Earl, reflecting on the great friendship and honor between him and the King, now so dishonored, told his wife he could live in England no more. He went to court and before his peers divested himself of his lands in such a manner that his wife should have her dowry for life, and then went before the King, saying to his face, "You have villainously dishonored me and thrown me in the dung," and afterward left the country, to the sorrow and wonder of the nobility, and the "King was blamed by all."

If the fiction of chivalry molded outward behavior to some extent, it did not, any more than other models that man has made for himself, transform human nature. Joinville's[14] account of the crusaders at Damietta[15] in 1249 shows the knights under St. Louis plunged in brutality, blasphemy, and debauchery. Teutonic knights in their annual forays against the unconverted natives of Lithuania conducted manhunts of the peasants for sport. Yet, if the code was but a veneer over violence, greed, and sensuality, it was nevertheless an ideal, as Christianity was an ideal, toward which man's reach, as usual, exceeded his grasp. ◆ [24]

---

[12] Edward III: King of England from 1327 to 1377.
[13] Uriah: The husband of Bathsheba, whom David sent to the front lines so that he would be killed in battle (2 Samuel 11).

[14] Joinville's: Jean de Joinville (1224?–1317) was a chronicler of French history.
[15] Damietta: A city in northeast Egypt.

SINGING WITH THE FUNDAMENTALISTS

Annie Dillard

First published in the Yale Review *in January 1985, "Singing with the Fundamentalists" attempts the difficult task of changing the reader's view on a subject about which opinions tend to be rigidly fixed. Dillard knows that many non-fundamentalists, including (one assumes) some readers of* Yale Review, *"dislike and fear Christian fundamentalists." Her essay demands that such readers think again. It creates a fresh interpretation of fundamentalism by altering the framework in which fundamentalists are seen. As in many of her essays, Dillard combines minute observations with curiosity about large questions.*

1   IT IS EARLY SPRING. I HAVE A TEMPORARY OF-fice at a state university on the West Coast. The office is on the third floor. It looks down on the Square, the enormous open courtyard at the center of campus. From my desk I see hundreds of people moving between classes. There is a large circular fountain in the Square's center.

2   Early one morning, on the first day of spring quarter, I hear singing. A pack of students has gathered at the fountain. They are singing something which, at this distance, and through the heavy window, sounds good.

3   I know who these singing students are: they are the Fundamentalists. This campus has a lot of them. Mornings they sing on the Square; it is their only perceptible activity. What are they singing? Whatever it is, I want to join them, for I like to sing; whatever it is, I want to take my stand with them, for I am drawn to their very absurdity, their innocent indifference to what people think. My colleagues and students here, and my friends everywhere, dislike and fear Christian fundamentalists. You may never have met such people, but you've heard what they do: they pile up money, vote in blocs, and elect right-wing crazies; they censor books; they carry handguns; they

fight fluoride in the drinking water and evolution in the schools; probably they would lynch people if they could get away with it. I'm not sure my friends are correct. I close my pen and join the singers on the Square.

4   There is a clapping song in progress. I have to concentrate to follow it:

> Come on, rejoice,
> And let your heart sing,
> Come on, rejoice,
> Give praise to the king.
> Singing alleluia—
> He is the king of kings;
> Singing alleluia—
> He is the king of kings.

Two song leaders are standing on the broad rim of the fountain; the water is splashing just behind them. The boy is short, hard-faced, with a moustache. He bangs his guitar with the backs of his fingers. The blonde girl, who leads the clapping, is bouncy; she wears a bit of make-up. Both are wearing blue jeans.

5   The students beside me are wearing blue jeans too—and athletic jerseys, parkas, football jackets, turtlenecks, and hiking shoes or jogging shoes. They

all have canvas or nylon book bags. They look like any random batch of seventy or eighty students at this university. They are grubby or scrubbed, mostly scrubbed; they are tall, fair, or red-headed in large proportions. Their parents are white-collar workers, blue-collar workers, farmers, loggers, orchardists, merchants, fishermen; their names are, I'll bet, Olsen, Jensen, Seversen, Hansen, Klokker, Sigurdsen.

6   Despite the vigor of the clapping song, no one seems to be giving it much effort. And no one looks at anyone else; there are no sentimental glances and smiles, no glances even of recognition. These kids don't seem to know each other. We stand at the fountain's side, out on the broad, bricked Square in front of the science building, and sing the clapping song through three times.

7   It is quarter to nine in the morning. Hundreds of people are crossing the Square. These passersby—faculty, staff, students—pay very little attention to us; this morning singing has gone on for years. Most of them look at us directly, then ignore us, for there is nothing to see: no animal sacrifices, no lynchings, no collection plate for Jesse Helms,[1] no seizures, snake handling, healing, or glossolalia. There is barely anything to hear. I suspect the people glance at us to learn if we are really singing: how could so many people make so little sound? My fellow singers, who ignore each other, certainly ignore passersby as well. Within a week, most of them will have their eyes closed anyway.

8   We move directly to another song, a slower one.

> *He is my peace,*
> *Who has broken down every wall;*
> *He is my peace,*
> *He is my peace.*
>
> *Cast all your cares on him,*
> *For he careth for you—oo—oo*
> *He is my peace,*
> *He is my peace.*

---

[1] Jesse Helms: (1921–   ), an ultraconservative U.S. Senator from North Carolina.

9   I am paying strict attention to the song leaders, for I am singing at the top of my lungs and I've never heard any of these songs before. They are not the old American low-church Protestant hymns; they are not the old European high-church Protestant hymns. These hymns seem to have been written just yesterday, apparently by the same people who put out lyrical Christian greeting cards and bookmarks.

10   "Where do these songs come from?" I ask a girl standing next to me. She seems appalled to be addressed at all, and startled by the question. "They're from the praise albums!" she explains, and moves away.

11   The songs' melodies run dominant, subdominant, dominant, tonic, dominant. The pace is slow, about the pace of "Tell Laura I Love Her," and with that song's quavering, long notes. The lyrics are simple and repetitive; there are very few of them to which a devout Jew or Mohammedan could not give whole-hearted assent. These songs are similar to the things Catholics sing in church these days. I don't know if any studies have been done to correlate the introduction of contemporary songs into Catholic churches with those churches' decline in membership, or with the phenomenon of Catholic converts' applying to enter cloistered monasteries directly, without passing through parish churches.

> *I'm set free to worship,*
> *I'm set free to praise him,*
> *I'm set free to dance before the Lord . . .*

12   At nine o'clock sharp we quit and scatter. I hear a few quiet "see you"s. Mostly the students leave quickly, as if they didn't want to be seen. The Square empties.

The next day we show up again, at twenty to nine. The same two leaders stand on the fountain's rim; the fountain is pouring down behind them.

14   After the first song, the boy with the moustache hollers, "Move on up! Some of you guys aren't paying attention back there! You're talking to each other. I want you to concentrate!" The students laugh, embar-

rassed for him. He sounds like a teacher. No one moves. The girl breaks into the next song, which we join at once:

> In my life, Lord,
> Be glorified, be glorified, be glorified;
> In my life, Lord,
> Be glorified, be glorified, today.

At the end of this singularly monotonous verse, which is straining my tolerance for singing virtually anything, the boy with the moustache startles me by shouting, "Classes!"

15   At once, without skipping a beat, we sing, "In my classes, Lord, be glorified, be glorified . . ." I give fleet thought to the class I'm teaching this afternoon. We're reading a little "Talk of the Town"[2] piece called "Eggbag," about a cat in a magic store on Eighth Avenue. "Relationships!" the boy calls. The students seem to sing "In my relationships, Lord," more easily than they sang "classes." They seemed embarrassed by "classes." In fact, to my fascination, they seem embarrassed by almost everything. Why are they here? I will sing with the Fundamentalists every weekday morning all spring; I will decide, tentatively, that they come pretty much for the same reasons I do: each has a private relationship with "the Lord" and will put up with a lot of junk for it.

16   I have taught some Fundamentalist students here, and know a bit of what they think. They are college students above all, worried about their love lives, their grades, and finding jobs. Some support moderate Democrats; some support moderate Republicans. Like their classmates, most support nuclear freeze, ERA, and an end to the draft. I believe they are divided on abortion and busing. They are not particularly political. They read *Christianity Today* and *Campus Life* and *Eternity*—moderate, sensible magazines, I think; they read a lot of C. S. Lewis. (One

---

2"The Talk of the Town": a regular feature of *The New Yorker*, consisting of short, unsigned essays.

such student, who seemed perfectly tolerant of me and my shoddy Christianity, introduced me to C. S. Lewis's critical book on Charles Williams.) They read the Bible. I think they all "believe in" organic evolution. The main thing about them is this: there isn't any "them." Their views vary. They don't know each other.

Their common Christianity puts them, if anywhere, to the left of their classmates. I believe they also tend to be more able than their classmates to think well in the abstract, and also to recognize the complexity of moral issues. But I may be wrong.   17

In 1980, the media were certainly wrong   18 about television evangelists. Printed estimates of Jerry Falwell's television audience ranged from 18 million to 30 million people. In fact, according to Arbitron's actual counts, fewer than 1.5 million people were watching Falwell. And, according to an Emory University study, those who did watch television evangelists didn't necessarily vote with them. Emory University sociologist G. Melton Mobley reports, "When that message turns political, they cut it off." Analysis of the 1982 off-year election turned up no Fundamentalist bloc voting. The media were wrong, but no one printed retractions.

The media were wrong, too, in a tendency to   19 identify all fundamentalist Christians with Falwell and his ilk, and to attribute to them, across the board, conservative views.

Someone has sent me two recent issues of *Eter-*   20 *nity: The Evangelical Monthly*. One lead article criticizes a television preacher for saying that the United States had never used military might to take land from another nation. The same article censures Newspeak, saying that government rhetoric would have us believe in a "clean bomb," would have us believe that we "defend" America by invading foreign soil, and would have us believe that the dictatorships we support are "democracies." "When the President of the United States says that one reason to support defense spending is because it creates jobs," this lead article says, "a little bit of *1984* begins to surface."

Another article criticizes a "heavy-handed" opinion of Jerry Falwell Ministries—in this case a broadside attack on artificial insemination, surrogate motherhood, and lesbian motherhood. Browsing through *Eternity*, I find a double crostic.[3] I find an intelligent, analytical, and enthusiastic review of the new London Philharmonic recording of Mahler's second symphony—a review which stresses the "glorious truth" of the Jewish composer's magnificent work, and cites its recent performance in Jerusalem to celebrate the recapture of the Western Wall following the Six Day War. Surely, the evangelical Christians who read this magazine are not book-burners. If by chance they vote with the magazine's editors, then it looks to me as if they vote with the American Civil Liberties Union and Americans for Democratic Action.

21   Every few years some bold and sincere Christian student at this university disagrees with a professor in class—usually about the professor's out-of-hand dismissal of Christianity. Members of the faculty, outraged, repeat the stories of these rare and uneven encounters for years on end, as if to prove that the crazies are everywhere, and gaining ground. The notion is, apparently, that these kids can't think for themselves. Or they wouldn't disagree.

22   Now again the moustached leader asks us to move up. There is no harangue, so we move up. (This will be a theme all spring. The leaders want us closer together. Our instinct is to stand alone.) From behind the tall fountain comes a wind; on several gusts we get sprayed. No one seems to notice.

23   We have time for one more song. The leader, perhaps sensing that no one likes him, blunders on. "I want you to pray this one through," he says. "We have a lot of people here from a lot of different fellowships, but we're all one body. Amen?" They don't like it. He gets a few polite Amens. We sing:

---
[3] double crostic: a difficult word puzzle that requires the solver to re-create a long quotation.

Bind us together, Lord,
With a bond that can't be broken;
Bind us together, Lord,
With love.

Everyone seems to be in a remarkably foul mood today. We don't like this song. There is no one here under seventeen, and, I think, no one here who believes that love is a bond that can't be broken. We sing the song through three times; then it is time to go.

24   The leader calls after our retreating backs, "Hey, have a good day! Praise Him all day!" The kids around me roll up their eyes privately. Some groan; all flee.

25   The next morning is very cold. I am here early. Two girls are talking on the fountain's rim; one is part Indian. She says, "I've got all the Old Testament, but I can't get the New. I screw up the New." She takes a breath and rattles off a long list, ending with "Jonah, Micah, Nahum, Habakkuk, Zephaniah, Haggai, Zechariah, Malachi." The other girl produces a slow, sarcastic applause. I ask one of the girls to help me with the words to a song. She is agreeable, but says, "I'm sorry, I can't. I just became a Christian this year, so I don't know all the words yet."

26   The others are coming; we stand and separate. The boy with the moustache is gone, replaced by a big, serious fellow in a green down jacket. The bouncy girl is back with her guitar; she's wearing a skirt and wool knee socks. We begin, without any preamble, by singing a song that has so few words that we actually stretch one syllable over eleven separate notes. Then we sing a song in which the men sing one phrase and the women echo it. Everyone seems to know just what to do. In the context of our vapid songs, the lyrics of this one are extraordinary:

I was nothing before you found me.
Heartache! Broken people! Ruined lives
Is why you died on Calvary.

The last line rises in a regular series of half-notes. Now at last some people are actually singing; they throw some breath into the business. There is a seriousness and urgency to it: "Heartache! Broken people! Ruined lives . . . I was nothing."

27   We don't look like nothing. We look like a bunch of students of every stripe, ill-shaven or well-shaven, dressed up or down, but dressed warmly against the cold: jeans and parkas, jeans and heavy sweaters, jeans and scarves and blow-dried hair. We look ordinary. But I think, quite on my own, that we are here because we know this business of nothingness, brokenness, and ruination. We sing this song over and over.

28   Something catches my eye. Behind us, up in the science building, professors are standing alone at opened windows.

29   The long brick science building has three upper floors of faculty offices, thirty-two windows. At one window stands a bearded man, about forty; his opening his window is what caught my eye. He stands full in the open window, his hands on his hips, his head cocked down toward the fountain. He is drawn to look, as I was drawn to come. Up on the building's top floor, at the far right window, there is another: an Asian-American professor, wearing a white shirt, is sitting with one hip on his desk, looking out and down. In the middle of the row of windows, another one, an old professor in a checked shirt, stands sideways to the opened window, stands stock-still, his long, old ear to the air. Now another window cranks open, another professor—or maybe a graduate student—leans out, his hands on the sill.

30   We are all singing, and I am watching these five still men, my colleagues, whose office doors are surely shut—for that is the custom here: five of them alone in their offices in the science building who have opened their windows on this very cold morning, who motionless hear the Fundamentalists sing, utterly unknown to each other.

31   We sing another four songs, including the clapping song, and one which repeats, "This is the day which the Lord hath made; rejoice and be glad in it." All the professors but one stay by their opened windows, figures in a frieze. When after ten minutes we break off and scatter, each cranks his window shut. Maybe they have nine o'clock classes too.

I miss a few sessions. One morning of the following week, I rejoin the Fundamentalists on the Square. The wind is blowing from the north; it is sunny and cold. There are several new developments.

Someone has blown up rubber gloves and floated them in the fountain. I saw them yesterday afternoon from my high office window, and couldn't quite make them out: I seemed to see hands in the fountain waving from side to side, like those hands wagging on springs which people stick in the back windows of their cars. I saw these many years ago in Quito and Guayaquil, where they were a great fad long before they showed up here. The cardboard hands said, on their palms, HOLA GENTE, hello people. Some of them just said HOLA, hello, with a little wave to the universe at large, in case anybody happened to be looking. It is like our sending radio signals to planets in other galaxies: HOLA, if anyone is listening. Jolly folk, these Ecuadorians, I thought.

34   Now, waiting by the fountain for the singing, I see that these particular hands are long surgical gloves, yellow and white, ten of them, tied off at the cuff. They float upright and they wave, *hola, hola, hola;* they mill around like a crowd, bobbing under the fountain's spray and back again to the pool's rim, *hola.* It is a good prank. It is far too cold for the university's maintenance crew to retrieve them without turning off the fountain and putting on rubber boots.

35   From all around the Square, people are gathering for the singing. There is no way I can guess which kids, from among the masses crossing the Square, will veer off to the fountain. When they get here, I never recognize anybody except the leaders.

36   The singing begins without ado as usual, but there is something different about it. The students are growing prayerful, and they show it this morning with a peculiar gesture. I'm glad they weren't like this when I first joined them, or I never would have stayed.

37   Last night there was an educational television special, part of "Middletown."[4] It was a segment

<hr>

[4]"Middletown": A 1983 PBS series that updated a book published in 1929, *Middletown: A Study in Contemporary American Culture,* by Robert and Helen Merrell Lynd.

called "Community of Praise," and I watched it because it was about Fundamentalists. It showed a Jesus-loving family in the Midwest; the treatment was good and complex. This family attended the prayer meetings, healing sessions, and church services of an unnamed sect—a very low-church sect, whose doctrine and culture were much more low-church than those of the kids I sing with. When the members of this sect prayed, they held their arms over their heads and raised their palms, as if to feel or receive a blessing or energy from above.

38 Now today on the Square there is a new serious mood. The leaders are singing with their eyes shut. I am impressed that they can bang their guitars, keep their balance, and not fall into the pool. It is the same bouncy girl and earnest boy. Their eyeballs are rolled back a bit. I look around and see that almost everyone in this crowd of eighty or so has his eyes shut and is apparently praying the words of this song or praying some other prayer.

39 Now as the chorus rises, as it gets louder and higher and simpler in melody—

> I exalt thee,
> I exalt thee,
> I exalt thee,
> Thou art the Lord—

then, at this moment, hands start rising. All around me, hands are going up—that tall girl, that blond boy with his head back, the redheaded boy up front, the girl with the McDonald's jacket. Their arms rise as if pulled on strings. Some few of them have raised their arms very high over their heads and are tilting back their palms. Many, many more of them, as inconspicuously as possible, have raised their hands to the level of their chins.

40 What is going on? Why are these students today raising their palms in this gesture, when nobody did it last week? Is it because the leaders have set a prayerful tone this morning? Is it because this gesture always accompanies this song, just as clapping accompanies other songs? Or is it, as I suspect, that these kids watched the widely publicized documentary last night

just as I did, and are adopting, or trying out, the gesture?

41 It is a sunny morning, and the sun is rising behind the leaders and the fountain, so those students have their heads tilted, eyes closed, and palms upraised toward the sun. I glance up at the science building and think my own prayer: thank God no one is watching this.

42 The leaders cannot move around much on the fountain's rim. The girl has her eyes shut; the boy opens his eyes from time to time, glances at the neck of his guitar, and closes his eyes again.

43 When the song is over, the hands go down, and there is some desultory chatting in the crowd, as usual: can I borrow your library card? And, as usual, nobody looks at anybody.

44 All our songs today are serious. There is a feudal theme to them, or a feudal analogue:

> I will eat from abundance of your household.
> I will dream beside your streams of righteousness.

> You are my king.

> Enter his gates
> with thanksgiving in your heart;
> come before his courts with praise.

> He is the king of kings.

> Thou art the Lord.

45 All around me, eyes are closed and hands are raised. There is no social pressure to do this, or anything else. I've never known any group to be less cohesive, imposing fewer controls. Since no one looks at anyone, and since passersby no longer look, everyone out here is inconspicuous and free. Perhaps the palm-raising has begun because the kids realize by now that they are not on display; they're praying in their closets, right out here on the Square. Over the course of the next weeks, I will learn that the palm-raising is here to stay.

46 The sun is rising higher. We are singing our last song. We are praying. We are alone together.

> He is my peace
> Who has broken down every wall . . .

47   When the song is over, the hands go down. The heads lower, the eyes open and blink. We stay still a second before we break up. We have been standing in a broad current; now we have stepped aside. We have dismantled the radar cups; we have closed the telescope's vault. Students gather their book bags and go. The two leaders step down from the fountain's rim and pack away their guitars. Everyone scatters. I am in no hurry, so I stay after everyone is gone. It is after nine o'clock, and the Square is deserted. The fountain is playing to an empty house. In the pool the cheerful hands are waving over the water, bobbing under the fountain's veil and out again in the current, *hola.* ◆

Writing as a Process of Understanding

VERY WRITER, SOONER OR LATER, REALIZES THAT WRITING IS AN UN-natural act. The body was not designed to sit essentially motionless for hours on end. The mind, designed to dart in many directions, rebels when we command it to produce orderly sentences and paragraphs. We may be communicative creatures by nature, but the communication we crave is talk rather than writing, which usually requires us to isolate ourselves from our friends. Many people, probably most people, even in a generally literate country like the United States, are so uncomfortable with the process of writing that they avoid it whenever possible, to the delight of shareholders in telephone companies.

This chapter concerns itself with what happens to the person who decides to (or is forced to) write rather than call. It divides into two parts, the first concerning the writer working in solitude, the second concerning the writer's connection with audiences. In both parts the point is the same: when we address any but the most trivial subjects, the process of writing has one enormous advantage over unplanned talk. Not only does it transfer thought, it improves it.

FOGGINESS: THE WRITER WORKING IN SOLITUDE

Our starting point in understanding this improvement will be disorder—the near chaos that overtakes us all when we attempt to pursue a train of thought. One of the clearest descriptions of this disorder comes from the mouth of Gabrielle Dain, a character in Dashiell Hammett's *The Dain Curse*. Gabrielle, convinced that she has inherited a family curse that produces madness, describes her symptoms to Hammett's hard-boiled detective:

I've not ever been able to think clearly, as other people do, even the simplest thoughts. Everything is always so confused in my mind. No matter what I try to think about, there's a fog that gets between me and it, and other thoughts get between us, so I barely catch a glimpse of the thought I want before I lose it again, and have to hunt through the fog, and at last find it, only to have the same thing happen again and again and again. Can you understand how horrible that can become: going through life like that—year after year—knowing you will always be like that—or worse?

To which the detective replies:

> I can't. It sounds normal as hell to me. Nobody thinks clearly, no matter what they pretend. Thinking's a dizzy business, a matter of catching as many of those foggy glimpses as you can and fitting them together the best you can. That's why people hang on so tight to their beliefs and opinions; because, compared to the haphazard way in which they're arrived at, even the goofiest opinion seems wonderfully clear, sane, and self-evident. And if you let it get away from you, then you've got to dive back into that foggy muddle to wangle yourself out another to take its place.

One way of describing the Dain Curse, a curse shared by almost all of us, is to say that the mind's capacity for focused attention is very small. Our skulls may contain a great deal of information, but we can be conscious of only a small portion of it at a time. A person trying to think coherently, trying to match various memories, facts, and perceptions to an interpretive framework, is like a person with a small flashlight trying to reorganize a dark warehouse.

WHAT COGNITIVE PSYCHOLOGY
TELLS US ABOUT FOGGINESS

Cognitive psychologists have given us a rough idea of how dim the flashlight is. George Miller's research on the size of the "short-term" memory indicates that ordinary people are capable of retaining in the forefront of their consciousness only five to nine separate items at a time, whether those items are digits, letters, words, or short sentences. Suppose that we meet a woman who has memorized an entire book of limericks—150 poems, each identified by a short title. We ask her to recite a dozen of the poems in an arbitrary order: "Parrot," "Irish Priest," "Socks," "Jumbo," "Raincoat," for example. Clearly this woman has a good long-term memory, but unless we allow her to write down our list of requests, she will forget some or most of them. Old information (the 150 limericks) may be safely stored in our minds, but new information and fresh ideas evaporate quickly, like ether from an open bottle.

Miller and other researchers have pointed out, furthermore, that any shift in the focus of our attention will speed the evaporation. "Give a person three consonants—CHS, or MXB, for instance—and then immediately have him count backward by threes until you are ready to test his recall. The counting breaks up his normal processes of transfer from temporary to more permanent memory, so that twenty seconds later the string of consonants, which would ordinarily be perfectly recalled, is forgotten more than 90 per cent of the time." Experiments of this sort have led cognitive psychologists to conceive of "working memory," the pot we keep on the brain's front burner, as a tiny container. Attempts to process information can crowd out the very information we are trying to process.

The implications for anyone who is trying to think clearly and originally about a subject are alarming. If we use only our minds, consulting no one else and putting nothing on paper, we quickly find ourselves in trouble. We begin with a framework and a few details, and we believe we can connect them to create an interpretation. But while we are busy working out the connection between two of the details, we begin to lose our grip on the framework. If we turn back to recover our understanding of the framework, we forget something about the connection we were making between the details. After a few frustrating minutes of rushing back and forth trying to keep our mental plates spinning, our stomach begins to growl, and we give it up. Fresh interpretations are so hard to work out, and the old ones, we tell ourselves, are "wonderfully clear, sane, and self-evident."

THE STABILIZING INFLUENCE OF WRITING

To understand how writing helps us overcome the limitations of our minds, let's return to an image introduced a few paragraphs ago: the metaphor of the flashlight and the warehouse. Suppose you were actually given a flashlight and told to rearrange a darkened warehouse. You would find yourself facing difficulties on at least three levels. At the lowest level, there is the problem of identifying individual objects: what are these flat metal plates with the hole in the center? At the highest level, there is the problem of defining your goal: exactly what a sensible arrangement of the whole warehouse would be. In between, there is the problem of sorting: do the widgets belong in the same bay as the blodgetts, or would it make more sense to put them in the bin next to the thingamajigs? These three levels of difficulty, unfortunately, intertwine. Until you know what sort of objects you are dealing with, you can't come up with a sensible arrangement of the whole. Until you know what the arrangement of the whole is, you can't make rational decisions about how to group widgets and blodgetts. But if you wander around the warehouse trying to examine and identify all the objects one at a time in your flashlight's beam, you will get nothing done. Every attempt to think about organizing the objects will cloud your memory of what the objects are.

But suppose you are carrying a notebook and pencil. Now you can make lists of objects, write yourself notes about various plans for organization, draw maps of the various bins and bays. It will still be a hard task, but time is on your side. You can still only see a few inches in front of your face, and your capacity for concentration is no better than it was before, but the ability to record information and ideas securely keeps them from evaporating and allows you to think about one thing at a time, confident that progress is inevitable.

◆ *A Test of Working Memory.* To test the effect of writing on thinking, work with a partner on the following project. One of you will be allowed to write, the other will not. Each of you should think of eight types of fasteners, arrange the eight fasteners in an alphabetical list, and think of an unconventional use each fastener could be put to. Do not list the same unconventional use for two different fasteners. One item on your list could be the zipper, which could be used to light a match. The first person finished should immediately dictate his or her list to the other, who should then dictate his or her incomplete list back.

EXERCISE 1

WRITING AND THINKING IN STAGES

The notebook that is useful in helping us organize the physical world is even more useful in the more elusive task of helping us organize our mental worlds. It allows us to overcome some of the limitations of our minds and memories. Some scholars go so far as to say that writing makes our mental engines more powerful, but this claim is disputable. It is enough to say that writing creates a kind of mechanical advantage, a leverage, that allows us to do more work with the same mental engine. We can see this leverage at work by looking at a piece of writing passing through several drafts. Consider, for example, the passage on page 51 in which the flashlight metaphor was first introduced:

> One way of describing the Dain Curse, a curse shared by almost all of us, is to say that the mind's capacity for focused attention is very small. Our skulls may contain a great deal of information, but we can be conscious of only a small portion of it at a time. A person trying to think coherently, trying to match various memories, facts, and perceptions to an interpretive framework, is like a person with a small flashlight trying to reorganize a dark warehouse.

These three sentences evolved through three stages which I can reproduce and date accurately, since each was saved on a computer disk. The story of my struggles with them is a fair illustration of the way that writing and revision can help us think.

Version 1. 4:35 P.M., December 31.   The original version of this passage, though it contained only two sentences, was the result of a good deal of thought:

> One way of describing the Dain Curse, which is a curse shared by almost all of us, is to say that the mind's capacity for focused attention is very small. When we try to concentrate on a complex question or situation, we seem to be bailing with a leaky bucket.

When I wrote this, I was nervous about equating the Dain Curse with the mind's limited "capacity for focused attention"; Dashiell Hammett and psychologists like George Miller (to whom I wanted to build a bridge) speak very different languages. It took me some weeks to decide that he and they are discussing the same phenomenon, and I hesitated before committing myself on paper to this connection. The metaphor about "bailing with a leaky bucket" was the one that made the connection clear to me, so I put it in.

Version 2. 6:31 P.M., December 31.   As I wrote further into the chapter, however, I became unhappy with that leaky bucket. It was certainly a clear image for memory loss, the focus of Miller's research, but I didn't find it particularly helpful when I wanted to discuss the relation of writing to thinking. In Version 2, I doubled back to reconsider the metaphor, producing the following draft.

> One way of describing the Dain Curse, which is a curse shared by almost all of us, is to say that the mind's capacity for focused attention is very small. Our minds may contain a greal deal of information, but we can be conscious of only a small portion of it at a time. A person trying to think coherently, trying to create a match between various facts and the framework that will interpret them, is like a person exploring a vast dark building with a penlight they can illuminate only a few inches at a time.

Though the writer's difficulty might actually stem from memory problems, it *feels* like a problem of limited vision, so I came up with the idea of a flashlight in a large building. I liked this image because the beam of the flashlight seems to correspond to the beam of our "focused attention." After some hesitation, I chose the penlight rather than the flashlight because I liked the idea of the tiniest possible flashlight mismatched with a vast building. It also occurred to me that I could help my readers make the connection to college-level thinking and writing by referring to the idea of interpretation via framework from Chapter 1, so I added this reference in the third sentence. Then, it being New Year's Eve and my mental flashlight dimming, I quit.

You'll notice, by the way, that the typographical error in the last sentence of Version 2 (*they* for *that*) escaped my attention. Obviously, I am too pea-brained to be constantly aware of what is going on at every level of even a short passage. So, probably, are you.

Version 3.   7:50 A.M., January 2.   Back at work on January 2, I printed out a draft of the chapter and penciled changes into the margin. In the passage we are considering, I began to realize the flashlight-and-building metaphor wasn't quite specific enough: it didn't suggest that the person with the flashlight, like the thinker or writer, has a job to do. So I changed the building to a warehouse to be rearranged—a change that has obviously affected the rest of the chapter.

> One way of describing the Dain Curse, a curse shared by almost all of us, is to say that the mind's capacity for focused attention is very small. Our skulls may contain a great deal of information, but we can be conscious of only a small portion of it at a time. A person trying to think coherently, trying to match various memories, facts, and perceptions to an interpretive framework, is like a person with a small flashlight trying to reorganize a dark warehouse.

Nervous that not every reader would know what a penlight is, I had checked the word in my dictionary and hadn't found it. Perhaps it is a brand name? At any rate, I decided that "small flashlight," though it pleased me less, might communicate better. Then I turned my attention to issues of style and correctness. I dropped the *which is* from the first sentence to make it move somewhat faster, and considered dropping the *almost.* I changed *minds* to *skulls* in the second sentence because *mind* seems too dull and abstract a word to repeat in back-to-back sentences. Some philosophers, I realized, would object to locating the mind so securely in the skull, but I decided in this case to choose the more graphic word rather than to be mincingly correct. In the third sentence, I hit on a problem that was more than stylistic. I didn't want to suggest that it is only facts that lie around in the warehouse of our mind and can be misplaced. Memories that aggregate hundreds of separate facts may be temporarily lost and so—especially—may the little flashes of insight that have not quite formed themselves into fixed ideas. So may whole ideas, whole systems of thought. As a compromise between oversimplifying and overelaborating, I simply added *memories* and *perceptions.* The third sentence was now becoming cumbersome, so I found a way to shorten it: "interpretive framework" for "framework that will interpret them." Finally, I eliminated the adjective *vast,* a word that seemed rather snooty in this context and was probably unnecessary since warehouses are rarely small.

THE ADVANTAGE OF REVISION:
MENTAL REPROCESSING

It won't have escaped your attention that I have now written more than thirty sentences explaining the evolution of three sentences. Even this ten-to-one ratio is deceptively low since I have left much out of the account to avoid boring you more than was necessary. It won't have escaped your attention, either, that there is a rough correspondence between the levels at which I was forced to think and the levels mentioned in the warehouse problem. At the highest level, I was struggling with what I ought to say, what I could understand, about how the mind works. At the lowest level, I was checking for typographical errors and wondering whether *penlight* was a word my audience would recognize. In between were such decisions as whether to talk about a *vast dark building* or a *dark warehouse*. By writing as I thought my way through the passage rather than trying to compose it in my head, I was able to bring the penlight of my attention to bear on one problem at a time.

It is the recursiveness of writing, the ability it gives us to return to our earlier thoughts and hone them, that makes the unnatural act of writing valuable not only to the reader but to the writer. Writing and revising bring our diffuse thoughts together in a compact form. The process allows us to think about certain sorts of problems more efficiently than we would otherwise be able to do. Certainly the end product is "smarter" than the products of the early steps. The linguist Martin Joos compares this mental reprocessing to careful packing of a suitcase:

> The rewriter is as one who packs his thought for a long journey. Having packed the garment, he does not merely straighten out the folds and close the paragraph. Instead, he unpacks completely and repacks again. And again; and again and again. Each time, he tucks one more thought into this or that pocket. When he quits, there are more of them than of words. So many labors of love on a single sentence, that many rewards for the rereader. On the surface, one teasing half-reward; others at successively greater and greater depths, so that each reading finds one more.

The person who learns to unpack and repack a paragraph has found a medication that relieves the symptoms of the Dain Curse.

WRITER'S BLOCK

The benefits of drafting and redrafting come to us only when we can get something on the page to begin with. Most of us, however, have sat for long periods in front of a blank page or a blank computer screen, a situation so unpleasant that it has made a name for itself: writer's block. Names can be dangerous things: since we have a *name* for writer's block, we tend to invoke it. People will sometimes spend an hour or more suffering at their desks, diagnose themselves as having writer's block, and decide that they may as well knock off for the day. They believe that it is as impossible to write when one is afflicted with writer's block as it is to run a marathon when one is suffering from heart disease.

Professional writers can't afford long unproductive periods. Most work steadily, acting as though there were no such thing as writer's block. A difficult passage may send them out for a brief walk or for a talk with a sympathetic friend, but they return and produce. Maya Angelou goes every morning at 6:30 to her workroom and stays until afternoon, always producing something. Every evening she edits what she has written in the morning. Theodore White followed much the same routine, writing steadily for a few hours early in the day, revising in the afternoon, and falling asleep reading through the material he planned to write about the next morning: "You see, the best writing is always done at night when you're asleep." In interviews, professional writers seem to talk far less than amateurs about writing as an activity that requires inspiration and far more about it as a workaday activity. Even E. B. White, a less methodical worker than Maya Angelou or Theodore White, rejected the notion that the writer should wait for inspiration: "I think that writing is mainly work. Like a mechanic's job. A mechanic might as well say he was waiting for inspiration before he greased your car because if he didn't feel just right he'd miss a lot of the grease points. . . ."

How do these professional writers produce very high quality work with such regularity when so many of us have trouble filling a page? Obviously, this is not a question with a single, simple answer. One part of an answer, though, is that professionals have a realistic view of the writing process. The inexperienced writer may labor for hours on an opening paragraph, writing the first sentence, erasing it, rewriting it. When the clock finally forces her to get something done, right or wrong, she writes her paragraph at one burst, looks it over, and pronounces it dead on arrival: "No. You can't say that. You'll bore them to death."[1] Experienced writers may find getting started just as unpleasant but, knowing that the process of writing and revising will gradually produce an acceptable product, they start. Rather than trying to compose a whole paragraph in their minds before putting pen to paper, they start with a somewhat fuzzy idea and clarify it as they write. Rather than be blocked by their inability to imagine a first paragraph that will grab the reader's attention, they start at some other point in the essay, knowing that as the essay takes physical form in front of them, they will be better equipped to write the introduction.

In effect, writers, like other experienced mental workers, must learn to work more efficiently with their limited equipment. They know that they are working with a small flashlight, so they use their not-for-publication drafts to make their thoughts visible, stable, and accessible to reconsideration. The experienced writer may find herself, as Joan Didion sometimes does, "in a room literally papered with false starts." But the false starts are *there*, and she knows that she can eventually find the most promising one, tinker with it, and be on her way.

---

[1] This account of the behavior of a blocked writer is based on a case study described in Mike Rose's "Rigid Rules, Inflexible Plans, and the Stifling of Language: A Cognitivist Analysis of Writer's Block," *College Composition and Communication*, December 1980.

The best advice a friend can offer a blocked writer is probably that she should lower her standards as much as necessary to get *something* on the page. She needs to remember that she can't get to the top of the stairs at a single leap.

EXERCISE 2

◆ *Rules for Writers.* One problem that may create writer's block among inexperienced writers is a too hasty and too rigid adherence to "rules" of good writing. A writer may block on an opening paragraph, for example, if she has constantly in her mind the "rule" that an opening paragraph should grab the reader's attention. Trying to invent a "grabber" at the same time you are trying to project the general shape of your essay is an impossibly large task. Sometimes you may have to ignore for a draft or two the rule about grabbing attention. The preoccupation with rules is particularly damaging if the rules aren't important ones.

As a step toward evaluating the rules of "good writing" that you follow, list at least six. Don't list rules of punctuation or spelling. Share your list with your classmates and your instructor to get their reactions: How important do they feel these rules are? How early in the writing process should they be observed?

THE WRITER'S CONCERN WITH AUDIENCES

In addition to having a rule on her mind, the blocked writer we have been discussing was composing as if her page were in full view of her audience. Awareness of an audience is one of the psychological conditions that creates logical, coherent prose, but it can also be one of the obstacles to writing. A person preoccupied with the audience may have no attention left for the hard thinking necessary to bring a subject and framework together.

DELAYING CONSIDERATION: FRONT AREAS AND BACK AREAS

Sociologists have provided us with a useful way of talking about this problem. They point out that in most occupations that involve an audience workers must have "back areas" as well as front areas. Onstage, actors are in a classic front area, where everything they do will be scrutinized. But backstage is the green room, where they can shed cumbersome costumes, rehearse lines, complain about the audience, take tranquilizers, or do whatever is necessary to get them through the performance. And "back of" the performance were early read-throughs and rehearsals where the actors could temporarily forget about the audience and concentrate on the difficult business of making sense of characters and situations. A friend of mine once visited a powerful executive whose "front" office was as uncluttered and composed as a room in a museum. But a small door at the rear led to the "back" office, where the

E. B. WHITE

"I have moments when I wish that I could either take a sheet of paper or leave it alone, and sometimes, in despair and vengeance, I just fold them into airplanes and sail them out of high windows, only to have an updraft (or a change of temper) bring them back in again."

© Jim Kalett

I n 1960, when E. B. White won one of his many literary awards, *Newsweek* sent a reporter to interview him. The interviewer found White disappointing; he "hemmed and hawed" and said very little. "I have strong opinions about a lot of things," he explained, "but I can't express them unless I run them through a typewriter." The next day, the reporter received an apology and two pages of witty answers to his questions—neatly typed.

One of America's finest writers, White was never quick with words. His early attempts at newspaper reporting convinced him that he could never be "any good at gathering straight news under great difficulties and with the clock always running out." But when he and *The New Yorker* got together in the 1920s, White found his vocation, and the magazine found its true voice—simultaneously lighthearted and thoughtful. Perhaps his most remarkable essays for *The New Yorker* were his gem-like one-paragraph "comments" in the magazine's opening section. As James Thurber, another great *New Yorker* writer, said, "the art of paragraphing is to make something that was ground out sound as if it were dashed off." (See pages 72–79.)

Success at *The New Yorker* and collaboration with Thurber on a best-seller (*Is Sex Necessary?*) eventually allowed White to buy a farm in Maine, now famous as the setting of *Charlotte's Web*. He gave up his short weekly paragraphs in favor of tending the hen house and producing longer essays, many of them expressing a love of the natural world and a fear about "Man's gradual, creeping contamination of the planet."

When White died, William Shawn of *The New Yorker* issued a memorable tribute: "His literary style was as pure as any in our language. It was singular, colloquial, clear, unforced, thoroughly American and utterly beautiful. Because of his gentle influence, several generations of this country's writers will write better than they might have. He never wrote a mean or careless sentence." ◆

executive worked amid stacks of papers and open books. People seem to need a space, physical or psychological, where they concentrate on their work without worrying about appearances.

Some writers create back areas by free-writing (see Assignment 1, p. 67). Others, like Theodore White and Joan Didion, keep journals: Didion says that hers is filled with "bits of the mind's string too short to use, an indiscriminate and erratic assemblage with meaning only for its maker." Others begin a project by writing their thoughts in a letter to a friend. Personal letters, as Garrison Keillor points out, don't feel like performances: "when you have a True True Friend to write to, a *compadre,* a soul sibling, then it's like driving a car down a country road, you get behind the keyboard and press on the gas." E. B. White's much-praised essay "Once More to the Lake" began as a letter to his older brother, drafted soon after the death of their parents. The public essay is more reserved than the original letter, but the emotion is much the same, and it may be that White could not have written with such feeling if he had not begun with an intimate audience.

Even when writers do not free-write, keep a private journal, or begin with a letter, they may pass through stages of writing essentially for themselves or for a friendly audience before they attend closely to the needs of a more public audience. When I drafted difficult sections of this book, I seemed to pass through a stage of writing primarily to clarify issues in my own mind, then through a stage of imagining how the section would sound to my friends who teach writing classes, and finally through stages of considering it with the ultimate audience in mind. I don't say that the ultimate audience wasn't in some ways on my mind from the beginning, shaping what I undertook. But I do say that if this audience were constantly at the forefront of my attention, it would fog my thinking.

INTERMEDIATE AND ULTIMATE AUDIENCES

Eventually, of course, you must move a draft from the shelter of a back area and put it before an audience. When there is time for multiple drafts, this may happen gradually. As you become increasingly confident about the soundness of your thought, you can pay more attention to presenting it in a way that will satisfy an audience.

But which audience? The question is more difficult than it first appears because many of the things we write pass through several audiences. A lawyer writing an important brief will normally show it to other lawyers in the firm before sending it to the court. An engineer's proposal ordinarily passes over several desks before it is mailed to a potential client. This chapter passed through five audiences before it went to the printer: (1) a friend, (2) a project editor, (3) twenty-five peer-reviewers, (4) the project editor again, and (5) a manuscript editor. Since none of these audiences was the ultimate audience for the book, I did not write primarily to please them, nor did they read primarily to see whether they *personally* were pleased. They read, so far as they were able, through the eyes of the students and teachers who would ultimately use the book in class. In effect, each intermediate reader assumed the roles of a silver-haired professor, a young instructor, a middle-aged student taking night courses to advance her career, a brilliant freshman and his dull roommate, all at once.

With regard to audience, your situation as a student writer is parallel to mine as a textbook writer, and your instructor's situation is parallel to that of my editors and reviewers. Instructors must evaluate writing as representatives of an ultimate audience whose tastes and backgrounds are not necessarily their own. If an assignment requires you to write a letter to the members of a small-town school board, for example, your instructor may say of a given passage, "I find this very amusing, but I doubt that the board members would." The difference between your situation and mine, of course, is that your instructor assigns grades and my editor only gives advice. In order to avoid low grades and unpleasantness, therefore, you should insure at the outset of every essay that you are writing for the same "ultimate" audience that the instructor is reading for.

College professors sometimes say that when no particular audience is specified, students should write to the "general educated reader." This mythological creature might be described as a person with some college education (but no particular major) and a very strange life. The general reader is both male and female, both old and young, both rich and poor, simultaneously left, right, and centrist in politics, and by turns a member of every conceivable ethnic and racial minority. He or she is, in short, both everyone and no one. I always have trouble conceiving of the general reader in the singular and so am inclined to visualize a crowd. The key in dealing with this crowd-creature is not to confuse it with either yourself or your instructor. An instructor who is himself a borderline sexist may quite properly take you to task for writing a sentence that might be offensive to liberated women. An economics professor may criticize you for writing as though the reader already understood the principle of decreasing marginal utility. That *you* understood it and knew that *she* understood it is no defense because the general reader would *not* understand it.

Whether your ultimate audience is a very specific person or the general reader, the attempt to present your material to it will add new complications to the process of writing and thinking. In the early stages of the writing process, as we have seen, you may want to avoid these complications by putting the readers out of your mind, but you will need to return to them before you hand in your final draft.

◆ *Visualizing an Audience.* Consider a paper you will write for this class. Assuming that the instructor will read the paper as a representative of some larger audience, describe the group he or she will represent. Attempt to

EXERCISE 3

visualize the group in some detail, imagining the age, sex, race, socioeconomic class, and educational level of a half-dozen of its typical members. Work to make your typical members represent the broadest possible cross section of the audience. Compare your visualization of the audience with your instructor's.

CONSIDERING THE AUDIENCE:
EXPECTATIONS, KNOWLEDGE, AND OPINIONS

The nearer the essay comes to its final form, the more your audience should be on your mind. In some respects, as we have seen, having an audience on your mind is a nuisance, hampering the movement of your thought. But in the long run, considering the audience is not only a practical necessity but an intellectual stimulant. When we begin to look at our writing from the perspectives of strangers, we learn new things about both our prose and our ideas. Teachers often comment that they learn a subject best when they are "working it up" for a class lecture. All writers are in this respect teachers and every audience a class. Writers enrich their understanding by considering their audience's expectations, knowledge, and attitudes.

Expectations.   Two expectations are shared by virtually all readers: writers should say something significant, and they should write in a way that makes that something clear. Saying something, as we noted in the first chapter, ordinarily means putting a subject into a framework. It is the hard intellectual work that writers do in their back areas. Writing clearly demands not only that the prose be free from distracting errors in spelling, grammar, and punctuation but that it not be too cluttered and ornate. Audiences will differ somewhat in which styles they consider ornate, but few readers enjoy words or phrases that seem to be written to draw attention to themselves rather than to say something about the subject and framework. If you have ambitions as a stylist, a good rule of thumb is that it is better to have the reader admire your prose on a *second* reading. On the first, you ordinarily hope he or she will be paying too much attention to what you say to notice the style.

Beyond substance and clarity, the expectations of audiences are quite variable and depend partly on what sort of writing you are doing. If you are writing a technical evaluation of a new product, for example, your audience ordinarily expects straightforward, clear, highly organized, and rather impersonal prose. If you write an autobiographical sketch like James Weldon Johnson's memoir of his train ride, however, readers will expect writing of an entirely different kind: something that reveals thoughts and feelings as well as facts and conclusions.

What will happen should you fail to meet your readers' expectations? In some circumstances, they may be delighted. If a technical report manages to do its business and inject some mild humor (as some *Consumer Reports* articles do), many readers will be pleased. But this is not so much a failure to meet readers' expectations as a success in exceeding them. Failure to meet readers' expectations of substance and clarity is likely to please no one.

One expectation you can never afford to disappoint is your readers' expectation that they will be treated as reasonable, intelligent people of good judgment. Nothing will lose an audience quicker than the indirect insult of assuming they will believe something that you would never believe yourself.

Knowledge.   Knowing something that your readers don't is a great advantage since it allows you to say things that may surprise and interest them. Few of us had thought for two minutes about the behavior of white men in Jim Crow cars until we read about it in Johnson's narrative or about the connection between Biblical teaching and Victorian social legislation until we read Tuchman's discussion of Lord Shaftesbury.

But an edge in knowledge has disadvantages as well, since there is always the danger that you will fail to explain something essential to the reader's understanding. If you look at James Weldon Johnson's narrative, published in 1933, you'll notice that he expected his reader to know what a Jim Crow car was. Today, *Jim Crow* would send some readers to the dictionary or encyclopedia and others into confusion. The writer who constantly sends readers to a dictionary should not be surprised if many don't return. Worse yet is the writer whose prose is studded with references and allusions that are unknown both to the reader and the dictionary maker. If you write that on the day President Reagan was shot, you hardly noticed because you were so grieved about Bertie's death, the reader will hardly know how to react—not realizing that Bertie was your goldfish and that you were eight years old.

Opinions.   What we are dealing with here is not so much knowledge as "mindset." If the subject is political and your framework is one generally associated with the political right, then you will want to consider how the leftists in your audience will react and how you can persuade them to listen to your view. If you are a Hispanic writer discussing race in America, you will want to look at your essay from the perspective of blacks, whites, Orientals, native Americans, and others who will read what you write.

One way of dealing with potentially conflicting mindsets is to seek common ground—a framework that your audience can easily share with you. Thus when Martin Luther King, Jr., addresses white clergymen who have opposed his call for civil disobedience in Birmingham,[2] he does not begin reminding them that they are white and he is black. Instead, he puts the subject into a religious framework that they and he share: ". . . I am in Birmingham because injustice is here. Just as the prophets of the eighth century B.C. left their villages and carried their 'thus saith the Lord' far beyond the

---

[2] "Letter from Birmingham Jail," page 301.

boundaries of their home towns, and just as the Apostle Paul left the village of Tarsus and carried the gospel of Jesus Christ to the far corners of the Greco-Roman world, so am I compelled to carry the gospel of freedom beyond my own home town."

Sometimes, of course, there is no middle ground, no shared framework, and the writer must persuade readers to substitute his or her view for theirs. King attempts this later in his essay, where he presents his white readers with the perspective of "those who have suffered unduly from the disease of segregation." To persuade the reader to adopt a new framework is, however, an enormously difficult task. As Hammett's detective says, all of us prefer to cling to "even the goofiest opinion" rather than "dive back into that foggy muddle" where our opinions are formed.

A Cautious Overview of the Writing Process

The textbooks of earlier generations sometimes featured lists that told the student writer what to do step-by-step, as though writing an essay were no more mysterious than assembling a bookcase. Research conducted in the last twenty years has shown that these lists bore almost no relation to the writing processes of successful writers, which are so various and complex that no list can describe them. Nonetheless, we can hazard a few generalizations about how experienced writers work in the early, middle, and late stages of the writing process.

Early on, writers struggle to define their goals and their procedures. They consider who their ultimate audience is, what that audience needs or wants to know, how they hope it will react. They define their subject and their framework as clearly as they can at this point, and they may produce a preliminary outline. In some cases, they delay the drafting to do necessary research or direct their thinking along unfamiliar paths. Even professional writers report that they are tempted to protract their planning and research, delaying too long the business of drafting.

Drafting, however, is the essential business. Sometimes, for some writers, drafting is a tidy process neatly following the preliminary plan. For most writers it is not. They begin drafting well before their research and planning are complete, trusting that the process of writing will uncover gaps in research and suggest new lines of thought. Although luck or extraordinary foresight will sometimes allow a writer to use in the finished copy almost every word of the first draft, the typical "survival rate" is lower: some professionals throw away five or ten pages for every page they keep. Early in the drafting process, particularly if the subject matter is difficult, writers close their eyes to the ultimate audience, writing primarily for themselves. In later drafts, the audience will be strongly on writers' minds, and in the process of seeing the essay from the audience's perspective, they may make fresh discoveries about their subject or framework.

After two or three (or more) drafts, the writer will often produce one suitable for reading by friends or colleagues. This semipublic reading can be an exciting stage in the paper's development, comparable to the first dress rehearsal of a play, but the writer's work is not completed. The writer has to consider readers' comments, positive and negative, and read the draft again, ready—if necessary—to go back to square one.

PEER REVIEW: A CHECKLIST

Students in composition classes often act as "peer editors" or "peer reviewers" of each other's papers, just as engineers, lawyers, managers, and other professionals often act as peer reviewers of each other's work. Learning to master the give-and-take of peer review is one of the more practical goals of a composition class. To get the maximum benefit from peer review, you and your reviewers need to act on three assumptions. First, your reviewers need to know that the draft you offer is the result of serious work, serious thinking. You waste your reviewers' time and talent by presenting them with material you have not attempted to organize and present clearly. The appropriate draft for peer review is rarely the first one; it should be a draft ready for a "semi-public" reading, one that you would not be embarrassed by having a stranger read. Second, your reviewers should agree to be as frank as common courtesy will allow in reporting on the essay's strengths and weaknesses. Third, you and your reviewers should acknowledge that even the most painstaking and intelligent peer review leaves responsibility for the draft in *your* hands. Peer reviewers sometimes make brilliant suggestions, but they sometimes contradict each other and sometimes make suggestions that would do more harm than good. The process is valuable because it leaves the writer with reactions to weigh and consider, but the reviewers' judgment can never be substituted for the writer's.

To get the fullest and frankest criticism, you should be certain that your reviewers understand exactly what the assignment is and exactly who your ultimate audience is. You may give them such instructions as the following:

1. State in your own words (avoiding mine) your impression of what the essay's central point is.

2. Underline with a straight line particularly valuable sentences or phrases in the essay. I will interpret these underlines as advice not to substantially rewrite these passages or delete them in a subsequent draft.

3. Underline with a jagged underline (〰〰〰) particularly ineffective or unclear sentences or phrases. I will interpret these jagged underlines as advice to rewrite these passages or delete them.

4. Insert a thunderbolt ($\frac{1}{7}$) between two sentences if you cannot see the logical connection between them.

5. Circle any plain errors of spelling, punctuation, or grammar that you see. These circles will help me proofread.

6. Write a brief marginal note on any passage that you think might offend, confuse, or bore my intended audience.

7. Tell me orally or in writing what you believe are the two or three greatest strengths of the essay.

8. Tell me what you believe are the two or three greatest weaknesses of the essay.

9. Tell me what you would do next if this were your essay.

You'll find additional procedures and questions for peer review at the end of several of the following chapters.

Having friends give you objective feedback of this sort is obviously a great advantage. If you cannot find someone to serve as a reviewer, you may have to follow the advice of the ancient Roman poet Horace: leave the essay in a desk drawer for a few days, then draw it out and try to read it with the cold eyes of a stranger. Actually, Horace recommended nine years. He was not at that time an undergraduate.

ASSIGNMENT 1: *FREE-WRITING AND LOOPING*

A technique some writers use to create a psychological "back area" is free-writing. As its name implies, free-writing is an exercise in unruliness. In fact, its only rule is one intended to prevent rules and an inhibiting awareness of audience from intruding. In free-writing, you write headlong about your topic for a fixed period of time (perhaps ten minutes); the rule is that you must keep your pencil moving forward constantly. You mustn't *pause* to take stock or to consider whether what you are saying makes sense or would bore a reader. If grammar, spelling, and punctuation are off, so be it. You mustn't go back to correct. You may, of course, *write* that you don't think you are making sense or that you think what you are saying is boring. You may find yourself writing for some seconds, "I can't think what to say, I can't think what to say." Eventually, though, you will say something: free-writing tends to turn up nuggets of thought that can later be developed in a more thoughtful way.

In fact, many writing teachers now recommend a technique called "looping" that systematically exploits this tendency of free-writing to produce nuggets. In looping, the writer first free-writes, then stops to read through the result, looking for a nugget about a sentence long that expresses the best observation the writing has turned up. Transferring that sentence to the top of a new page, he or she then launches into another free-writing. In all probability, this second free-writing will produce better material than the first because the writer's head is now clearer, the attention better focused. Obviously, the process can be repeated any number of times: the second free-writing can produce a nugget for the third, the third produce a nugget for the fourth, and so on. Eventually, the writer will weary of looping because he or she is ready to develop the essay more systematically.

Try a twenty-minute looping exercise on a topic you are considering for an upcoming paper. Use five minutes on the first free-writing, then one minute reading the result, choosing the nugget, and writing the nugget at the top of another page; use five minutes for the second free-writing; then one minute reading, choosing, and writing the nugget at the top of another page; use five minutes for a third free-writing, then three minutes to consider the whole exercise and decide whether looping seems to be a technique useful to you.

Like free-writing, listing can be a useful "back area" activity. Unlike the systematic outliner, the list-maker refuses to think too early about coherence or selectivity. He or she merely makes a list—at first in no particular order—of ideas or details that *might* find their way into the paper. If you are writing a memoir in a historical framework (an assignment in Chapter 3), you might begin with a list of times when, as a child, you became aware that you were connected to history. One of the items ("the day Reagan was shot") on this list might lead you to make another list of events that happened to you that

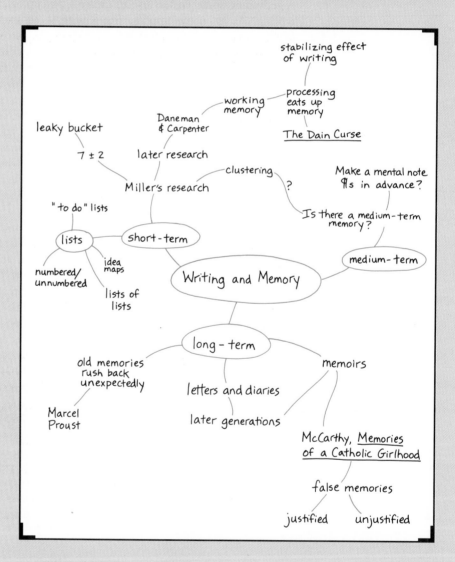

day and perhaps a third of historic events that the shooting brought to mind. List builds on list in much the same way that "loop" builds on "loop."

What form these lists take varies from writer to writer. Some of us automatically number lists, some leave them unnumbered, some prefer lists that line up neatly, others prefer the sort of free-form list that is often called an "idea map" (see the sample idea map on the opposite page). If you are using lists to get a writing project started or to restart it when it stalls, the key is to avoid rigidity. At first you needn't concern yourself about whether a given item is good or bad and whether it belongs on this list or that. The list is merely an aid to memory. It allows the writer to capture a thought before it can disappear into the darkness.

Take ten minutes to list as rapidly as possible ideas and details that might be useful to you in an upcoming paper. Then take two minutes to write yourself a note about the most interesting items on the list.

ASSIGNMENT 3: *ANALYSIS OF YOUR OWN REVISION PROCESS*

Search through drafts of your old papers until you find a short passage that changed fairly dramatically from first draft to last. Write an analysis of the changes comparable to the one on pages 54–55. If you do not have drafts of earlier papers, begin to collect ones for the next paper you write so that you can return to this assignment later.

ERASE YOUR TRACKS

Annie Dillard

Annie Dillard's 1989 book, The Writing Life, *gives a very personal and somewhat controversial view of the subjective experience of being a writer. (Three reviews of the book can be found on page 354.) In the passages below she talks about one of the issues raised in Chapter 2 of* The Riverside Guide to Writing: *the sometimes painful process of revision.*

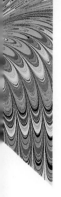

1   WHEN YOU WRITE, YOU LAY OUT A LINE of words. The line of words is a miner's pick, a woodcarver's gouge, a surgeon's probe. You wield it, and it digs a path you follow. Soon you find yourself deep in new territory. Is it a dead end, or have you located the real subject? You will know tomorrow, or this time next year.

2   You make the path boldly and follow it fearfully. You go where the path leads. At the end of the path, you find a box canyon. You hammer out reports, dispatch bulletins.

3   The writing has changed, in your hands, and in a twinkling, from an expression of your notions to an epistemological tool. The new place interests you because it is not clear. You attend. In your humility, you lay down the words carefully, watching all the angles. Now the earlier writing looks soft and careless. Process is nothing; erase your tracks. The path is not the work. I hope your tracks have grown over; I hope birds ate the crumbs; I hope you will toss it all and not look back.

4   The line of words is a hammer. You hammer against the walls of your house. You tap the walls, lightly, everywhere. After giving many years' attention to these things, you know what to listen for. Some of the walls are bearing walls; they have to stay, or everything will fall down. Other walls can go with im-

punity; you can hear the difference. Unfortunately, it is often a bearing wall that has to go. It cannot be helped. There is only one solution, which appalls you, but there it is. Knock it out. Duck.

5   Courage utterly opposes the bold hope that this is such fine stuff the work needs it, or the world. Courage, exhausted, stands on bare reality: this writing weakens the work. You must demolish the work and start over. You can save some of the sentences, like bricks. It will be a miracle if you can save some of the paragraphs, no matter how excellent in themselves or hard-won. You can waste a year worrying about it, or you can get it over with now. (Are you a woman, or a mouse?)

6   The part you must jettison is not only the best-written part; it is also, oddly, that part which was to have been the very point. It is the original key passage, the passage on which the rest was to hang, and from which you yourself drew the courage to begin. Henry James knew it well, and said it best. In his preface to *The Spoils of Poynton,* he pities the writer, in a comical pair of sentences that rises to a howl: "Which is the work in which he hasn't surrendered, under dire difficulty, the best thing he meant to have kept? In which indeed, before the dreadful *done,* doesn't he ask himself what has become of the thing all for the sweet sake of which it was to proceed to

that extremity?"

7   So it is that a writer writes many books. In each book, he intended several urgent and vivid points, many of which he sacrificed as the book's form hardened. "The youth gets together his materials to build a bridge to the moon," Thoreau noted mournfully, "or perchance a palace or temple on the earth, and at length the middle-aged man concludes to build a wood-shed with them." The writer returns to these materials, these passionate subjects, as to unfinished business, for they are his life's work.

8   It is the beginning of a work that the writer throws away.

9   A painting covers its tracks. Painters work from the ground up. The latest version of a painting overlays earlier versions, and obliterates them. Writers, on the other hand, work from left to right. The discardable chapters are on the left. The latest version of a literary work begins somewhere in the work's middle, and hardens toward the end. The earlier version remains lumpishly on the left; the work's beginning greets the reader with the wrong hand. In those early pages and chapters anyone may find bold leaps to nowhere, read the brave beginnings of dropped themes, hear a tone since abandoned, discover blind alleys, track red herrings, and laboriously learn a setting now false.

10   Several delusions weaken the writer's resolve to throw away work. If he has read his pages too often, those pages will have a necessary quality, the ring of the inevitable, like poetry known by heart; they will perfectly answer their own familiar rhythms. He will retain them. He may retain those pages if they possess some virtues, such as power in themselves, though they lack the cardinal virtue, which is pertinence to, and unity with, the book's thrust. Sometimes the writer leaves his early chapters in place from gratitude; he cannot contemplate them or read them without feeling again the blessed relief that exalted him when the words first appeared—relief that he was writing anything at all. That beginning served to get him where he was going, after all; surely the reader needs it, too, as groundwork. But no.

Every year the aspiring photographer brought a stack of his best prints to an old, honored photographer, seeking his judgment. Every year the old man studied the prints and painstakingly ordered them into two piles, bad and good. Every year the old man moved a certain landscape print into the bad stack. At length he turned to the young man: "You submit this same landscape every year, and every year I put it on the bad stack. Why do you like it so much?" The young photographer said, "Because I had to climb a mountain to get it."

12   A cabdriver sang his songs to me, in New York. Some we sang together. He had turned the meter off; he drove around midtown, singing. One long song he sang twice; it was the only dull one. I said, You already sang that one; let's sing something else. And he said, "You don't know how long it took me to get that one together."

13   How many books do we read from which the writer lacked courage to tie off the umbilical cord? How many gifts do we open from which the writer neglected to remove the price tag? Is it pertinent, is it courteous, for us to learn what it cost the writer personally? . . .

14   It takes years to write a book—between two and ten years. Less is so rare as to be statistically insignificant. One American writer has written a dozen major books over six decades. He wrote one of those books, a perfect novel, in three months. He speaks of it, still, with awe, almost whispering. Who wants to offend the spirit that hands out such books?

15   Faulkner wrote *As I Lay Dying* in six weeks; he claimed he knocked it off in his spare time from a twelve-hour-a-day job performing manual labor. There are other examples from other continents and centuries, just as albinos, assassins, saints, big people, and little people show up from time to time in large populations. Out of a human population on earth of four and a half billion, perhaps twenty people can write a book in a year. Some people lift cars, too. Some people enter week-long sled-dog races, go over Niagara Falls in barrels, fly planes through the Arc de Triomphe. Some people feel no pain in childbirth.

Some people eat cars. There is no call to take human extremes as norms.

Writing a book, full time, takes between two and ten years. The long poem, John Berryman said, takes between five and ten years. Thomas Mann was a prodigy of production. Working full time, he wrote a page a day. That is 365 pages a year, for he did write every day—a good-sized book a year. At a page a day, he was one of the most prolific writers who ever lived. Flaubert wrote steadily, with only the usual, appalling strains. For twenty-five years he finished a big book every five to seven years. My guess is that full-time writers average a book every five years; seventy-three usable pages a year, or a usable fifth of a page a day. The years that biographers and other nonfiction writers spend amassing and mastering materials are well matched by the years novelists and short-story writers spend fabricating solid worlds that answer to immaterial truths. On plenty of days the writer can write three or four pages, and on plenty of other days he concludes he must throw them away.

Octavio Paz cites the example of "Saint-Pol-Roux, who used to hang the inscription 'The poet is working' from his door while he slept." [17]

The notion that one can write better during one season of the year than another Samuel Johnson labeled, "Imagination operating upon luxury." Another luxury for an idle imagination is the writer's own feeling about the work. There is neither a proportional relationship, nor an inverse one, between a writer's estimation of a work in progress and its actual quality. The feeling that the work is magnificent, and the feeling that it is abominable, are both mosquitoes to be repelled, ignored, or killed, but not indulged. ◆ [18]

MOON-WALK

E. B. White

In his biography of E. B. White, Professor Scott Elledge of Cornell University has given us a useful tool for examining the process by which a good writer works through a series of drafts, improving both style and thought. In the collection of White's papers at Cornell, Elledge found six drafts of a one-paragraph comment White wrote for The New Yorker *after the July 20, 1969, moon-walk by astronauts Neil Armstrong and Edwin Aldrin, Jr. The six drafts are reproduced on the following pages.*

Elledge notes that White watched the moon-walk on television in his Maine home until about 1:00 A.M. on Monday, July 21, and that he wrote "under some pressure," since his paragraph had to be ready for typesetting in New York at noon the same day. When White completed the third draft, he believed he had done the job and telegraphed the result to The New Yorker. *He soon decided that he didn't like what he had sent, however, and took the piece through three more drafts before sending William Shawn, editor of* The New Yorker, *the following telegram: "My comment no good as is. I have written a shorter one on the same theme but different in tone. If you want to hear it, I'll read it to you." Shawn phoned White back, listened to the new version, and agreed that it was better. White then dictated it to Shawn, who rushed it to the printer.*

*astronaut would never have
reached their goal. But they
sent along something that might
better have been left behind—*

white

comment

Planning a trip to the moon, ~~isxessantiallyxas~~

~~differ~~ differs in no ~~esstial~~ respect from planning a trip

to the beach. You have to decide what to take_{along,} what to leave

behind. Should the thermos jug go? The child's rubber horse?
The dill pickles?
These are sometimes fateful decisions, on which the success or
failure
~~thexhappinexs~~ of the whole ~~expedition~~ outing turns. Something goes

along that spoils everything because it is always in the way.

Something gets left behind that spoils everything because it is
~~were saddled with the~~
desperately needed for comfort or_{for} safety. The men who had to

decide what to take along to the moon must have pondered long and
send *pretty*
hard, drawn up many a list. ~~We're not sure~~ they planned well,
Should the vacuum cleaner go? The peanut butter?
when they included the
~~forxinxyxelextentoviakexalong~~ the little telescoped flagpole and
artificially stiffened
the ~~stiffened~~ American flag, ~~artifimallyxxstiffmed~~ so that it
would fly to the breeze that didn't blow.
~~flew to the breeze that didn't blow.~~ The Stars and Stripes on

the moon undoubtedly gave untold satisfaction to millions of
But
~~who~~ As we watched the Stars and Stripes planted on the surface of

the moon, we experienced the same sensations of pride ~~and~~ that

must have filled the hearts of millions of Americans. But it

the emotion soon turned to *stone in my stomach*
to do something new, and unparalleled in all history.
Here a
~~This was our~~ great chance, and we muffed it. The ~~meen~~ men who
were
stepped out onto the surface of the moon are in a class by
the image of the *of men & women everywhere*
themselves---pioneers of what is universal. They saw the
dark sky *followed*
earth whole---hust as it is, a round ball in a   But they
instruction &
colored the moon red, white, and blue0---~~good colors all---but~~
the moon that is out of the garden of nationality by its very position.
~~out of place in that setting.~~ The moon still ~~influences~~ the
still
tides, and the tides lap on every shore, right around the globe.

still holds the key to madness

Kiss in every land

The moon stil belongs to lovers, and lovers are everywhere--not

just in America. What a pity we couldn't have planted some

          precisely   this unique, this incredible

emblem that ~~exactly~~ expressed the occasion, even if it were

nothing more than a white banner, with the legend: ~~Xhxxkxxxxxxxxxx~~-y."

that simply said:

"At last!"

handkerchief, symbol of the common ...
which, like the moon, belongs to all.
mankind

white

comment

Planning a trip to the moon differs in no essential
respect from planning a trip to the beach. You have to decide
what to take along, what to leave behind. Should the thermos jug
go? The child's rubber horse? The dill pickles? These are sometimes fateful decisions on which the success or failure of the
whole outing turns. Something goes along that spoils everything because it is always in the way. Something gets left
behind that is desperately needed for comfort or for safety. The
men who drew up the moon list for the astronauts, planned long
and hard and well. (Should the vacuum cleaner go?) Among the
to suck up moondust and save
the world?)
items they sent along, of course, was the little jointed flagpole
and the flag that could be stiffened to the breeze that didn't
blow. (It is traditional among explorers to plant the flag.) Yet
the two men who stepped out on the surface of the moon were in a
class by themselves: they were of the new race of men, those
who hadseen the earth whole. When, following instructions, they
colored the moon red, white, and blue, they were stepping out of
character---or so it seemed to us who watched, trembling with awe
and admiration and pride. This was the last scene in the long
book of nationalism, and they followed the book. But the moon
still holds the key to madness, which is universal, still controls
the tides, that lap on every shore everywhere, and still blesses
lovers that kiss in every land, under no particular banner. What
a pity we couldn't have played the scene as it should been played,
planting, perhaps, a simple white handkerchief, symbol of the
common cold, that belongs to mankind impartially and inows no
borders

is   *and trembles*

white

comment

        Planning a trip to the moon differs in no essential respect from planning a trip to the beach. You have to decide what to take along, what to leave behind. Should the thermos jug go? The child's rubber horse? The dill pickles? These are sometimes fateful decisions on which the success or failure of the whole outing turns. Something goes along that spoils everything because it is always in the way; something gets left behind that is desperately needed for comfort or for safety. The men who drew up the moon list for the astronauts planned long and hard and well. (Should the vacuum cleaner go, to suck up moondust?) Among the *inevitable* items they sent along, of course, was the little jointed flagpole and the flag that could be stiffened to the breeze that did not blow. (It is traditional among explorers to plant the flag.) Yet the two men who stepped out on the surface of the moon were in a class by themselves and should have been equipped accordingly: they were of the new breed of men, those who had seen the earth whole. When, following instructions, they colored the moon red, white, and blue, they were fumbling with the past---or so it seemed to us, who watched, trembling with awe and admiration and pride. This moon plant was the last *chapter* scene in the long book of nationalism, one that could well have been omitted. The moon still holds the key to madness, which is universal, still controls the tides that lap on shores everywhere, still guards lovers that kiss in every land under no banner but the sky. What a pity we couldn't have forsworn our little Iwo Jima scene and planted instead a banner acceptable to all---a simple white handkerchief, perhaps, symbol of the common cold, which, like the moon, affects us all.

that

it tusn out;

The moon is a great place for men, a)d when
ad they mocking little
Armstrong and Aldrin danced from sheer exuberance, it was
                                            a poor place for
a sight to see. But the moon is ~~no place for banners~~ flags.
a flag   for the breeze doesn't blow   a flag is out
~~They~~ cannot float on the breeze, and t~~heyxxdonnt~~ belong there
of place on the moon anyway.
anyway. Like every great river, every great sea, the moon
                    none
belongs to ~~no one~~ and belongs to all. What a pity we

couldn't have forsworn our little Iwo Jima flag-lanting

scene and planted instead a universal banner acceptable

to all---a limp white handkerchief, perhaps, symbol of the

common cold, which, like the moon, affects us all.

Of course, it is traditional t hat explorers plant the flag,

and it was inevitable that our astronauts should follow thw
            as we watched
custom. But the act was the last chapter in the long book

of nationalism, one that could well have been omitted---or

~~so it seemed to us.~~ The moon still holds the key to madness,

still controls the tides that lap on shores everywhere, still

guards the lovers that kiss in every land under no banner but th

the sky. What a pity ~~waxxeexidntt~~ that, in our triumph, we
                                                        instead
couldn't have forsworn the little Iwo Jima scene and planted
                                    limp
a banner acceptable to all---a ~~simple~~ white handkerchief,

perhaps, symbo l of the common cold,whcih, like the moon, affects
us all.

white

comment

like two happy children

       The moon, it turns out, is a great place for
men. One-sixth gravity must be a lot of fun, and when Armstrong and Aldrin went into their little dance, bouncy it was a
moment not only of triumph but of gaiety. The moon, on the
other hand, is a poor place for flags. Ours looked stiff
and ~~dopey~~, trying to float on the breeze that ~~did~~ does not blow.
(There must be a lesson here somewhere.) It is traditional,
of course, for explorers to plant the flag, but it struck
us, as we watched with awe and admiration and pride, that our
two ~~unix~~ men were universal men, not national men, and should
have been equipped accordingly. The moon ~~still holds the key~~
~~to madness, looks~~, like every great river, every great sea,
belongs to none and belongs to all; ~~it might be better both to~~
~~itself than to being colored red-white and blue~~ It still holds
the key to madness, still controls the tides that lap on
~~every shores~~ shores on everywhere, still guards the lovers
that kiss in every land under no banner but the sky. What a
pity that, in our moment of triumph, we ~~didn't bless the moon~~
~~because the blue than seem~~ couldn't have forsworn the ~~little~~ old outworn
Iwo Jima scene and planted instead a device acceptable to all:
a limp white handkerchief, perhaps, symbol of the common cold,
which, like the moon, affects us all, unites us all.

white

comment

        The moon, it turns out, is a great place for
men. One-sixth gravity must be a lot of fun, and when Armstrong and Aldrin went into their bouncy little dance, like
two happy children, it was a moment not only of triumph but of
gaiety. The moon, on the other hand, is a poor place for flags.
Ours looked stiff and awkward, trying to float on the breeze
that does not blow. (There must be a lesson here somewhere.)
It is traditional, of course, for explorers to plant the flag,
but it struck us, as we watched with awe and admiration and
pride, that our two fellows were universal men, not national
men, and should have been equipped accordingly. Like every
great river and every great sea, the moon belongs to none and
belongs to all. It still holds the key to madness, still controls the tides that lap on shores everywhere, still guards the
lovers that kiss in every land under no banner but the sky.
What a pity that in our moment of triumph we did not forswear
the familiar Iwo Jima scene and plant instead a device acceptable
to all: a limp white handkerchief, perhaps, symbol of the
common cold, which, like the moon, affects us all, unites us
all!

WRITING AUTOBIOGRAPHICALLY

IN CHAPTER ONE, WE DREW A DISTINCTION BETWEEN THE SUBJECT OF A piece of writing and the framework in which the writer presents the subject. In this chapter, we will examine the use of various frameworks that can reveal meaning in one loosely defined subject: an episode from the writer's past. Most of the examples we will look at are self-contained narratives. They begin, that is, by showing a protagonist (the author) caught in a troublesome situation, and they end when the trouble ends, happily or unhappily. This narrative structure, so familiar to anyone who reads short stories or watches television, is useful in many situations, and becoming a better narrator may be one of the by-products of working with this chapter. Our primary concern, however, is not storytelling for its own sake. We want, once more, to watch the way meaning emerges from the interaction between the subject and the framework.

THE AUTHOR AS CHARACTER
AND THE AUTHOR AS INTERPRETER

As you will see, the memoir is a form of writing that makes the inter-action between subject and framework particularly visible because it divides the author into two personalities. There is the author presented in the story: the "author as character." The experience of this person, what it was like to be *there, then,* is the *subject* of a memoir. But beside the "author as character" is the "author as interpreter." This somewhat older and wiser person establishes the interpretive *framework*.

Textbook authors don't ordinarily turn to their great-aunts' memoirs to illustrate a point, but in this case I can't resist. Consider the following passage from my great-aunt Alberta Carr's handwritten memoir of growing up on a farm just south of the Texas-Oklahoma border. The year was 1897. Oklahoma was not then a state but a U.S. territory made up almost entirely of Indian reservations. The Carr family had hopes of moving into the territory as soon as it was opened for settlement by whites.

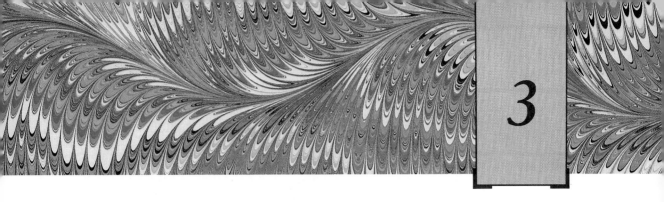

3

"Outlaws"
—ALBERTA CARR

Dad bought a small farm where they resided for 5 yrs before moving into the Okla. Territory. It was a well settled community but—just north of the river only Indians, outlaws & thieves. They preyed on farmers stealing their live stock, food, in fact anything they wanted then crossing the river where the citizens had no recourse. As a result an Anti Horse Thief Society was formed and did much to protect their interests. Dad belonged of course and was active altho we always had a sense of uneasiness. They would come in groups into Nacona on wk.ends and make much trouble for law enforcement officials.

My Dad could plant the straightest rows I ever saw in a field. They were beautiful and every one noticed and admired them. Late one Sat. 5 or 6 of the river bunch came riding by and noticed the beautiful field of young cotton. The house set up about a block from the road there was a fence and a front gate. They whirled their horses and came galloping up in a cloud of dust, shouting with much profanity. They wanted to see the man who could run such straight rows. We were all petrified. Mom was begging Dad not to go out but you don't know my Dad. He kept a revolver (a British Bulldog) laying on top of the cupboard (loaded). He reached up got it and put it in his hip pocket and walked out to the front gate as tho it was nothing out of the ordinary. The leader pulled out a bottle and said By God, I want to drink with the man who ran those rows. Dad said I don't drink fellows whereupon they whirled and galloped away. I was hiding under Mom's apron, but I saw it all and you can bet it made a profound impression on me.

This brief passage, unedited, shows the memoirist's dual perspective at work. Aunt Bert is present "as character," hiding behind her mother's apron and telling us what she sees and what she knows. Part of the pleasure of reading the story is that it takes us back almost a hundred years and shows us what the world then looked like to a six-year-old girl. On the other hand, we feel the presence of the other Aunt Bert, the seventy-three-year-old woman who looks back on the event and sees meaning in it that a six-year-old could not. The "author as interpreter" knows that this confrontation is between two types of men—each presented through carefully chosen details—the outlaw and the solid citizen. She knows that such a confrontation belongs to the history of the period and, in fact, epitomizes the period.

As you read through the examples in this chapter and as you write your own memoir, be aware of the two authors who are present—one as the subject, one as the discoverer or inventor of the framework that will give the subject meaning.

THE IMPORTANCE OF FINDING FRAMEWORKS
FOR THE MEMOIR

The writer of a memoir has one edge most other writers must envy but also faces a peculiar difficulty. The advantage—an enormous one—is that he or she knows the subject intimately. A historian or biographer laboring for decades couldn't possibly amass the amount of information about your life that you are capable of recalling at will. On this subject, you are the world's greatest expert.

The difficulty is that none of this knowledge is likely to be *in itself* interesting to an audience of strangers. As Annie Dillard says, "You have to take pains in a memoir not to hang on the reader's arm, like a drunk, and say 'And then I did this and it was so interesting.' " To some degree, you may be able to create interest by the charm or energy of your writing style, but style alone is rarely enough. The most successful memoirs are generally those in which the author presents private events in frameworks that give them more than personal interest. A memoirist like Maya Angelou, writing about an event from her girlhood in Stamps, Arkansas, can evoke the framework of America's troubled race relations. A memoirist like Mary McCarthy, writing about her girlhood in Seattle, can evoke every child's struggle to discover what her "self" is like. The *subject* of the memoir comes from the world of individual experience—the world of *I*; the *framework* comes from the world of shared experience—the world of *we*.

The world of shared experience is so large that it provides an inexhaustible supply of frameworks. In the following pages, we will look at some examples of memoirs that present the author's personal experience in three broadly defined kinds of frameworks: the historical, the social, and the psychological.

THE HISTORICAL FRAMEWORK

One of the universal experiences of growing up is the discovery (and periodic rediscovery) of the fact that we are a part of history, that the events of our private lives are connected with the events that form the headlines today and will appear in the history books in years to come. All of us at some point literally touch history. As a boy growing up in the 1870s, James Weldon Johnson made a collection of brass buttons and rusty bayonets that he dug up in the yards and fields of Jacksonville, Florida. In 1877, when Ulysses

S. Grant came to the city to deliver a speech, Johnson found a way to shake his hand. At the time both the collection and the handshake were merely exciting, but the mature Johnson, looking back on them from the perspective of a man involved in the later struggles for racial equality, could feel the force of these physical connections with the Civil War and the Reconstruction era.

Annie Dillard, looking back on her childhood in Pittsburgh, realized that the city "like Rome, or Jericho" was "a sliding pile of cities built ever nearer the sky."

> City workers continually paved the streets: they poured asphalt over the streetcar tracks, streetcar tracks their fathers had wormed between the old riverworn cobblestones, cobblestones laid smack into the notorious nineteenth-century mud. Long stretches of that mud were the same pioneer roads that General John Forbes's troops had hacked over the mountains from Carlisle, or General Braddock's troops had hacked for the Chesapeake and the Susquehanna, widening with their axes the woodland paths the Indians had worn on deer trails.

This passage shows in miniature what the discovery of the historical framework of memoir is about—the sense that our lives are interlayered with the lives of those who have gone before us and those who will come after.

An example of such layering can be found in Theodore White's autobiography, *In Search of History*. Early in the book, he describes his experiences with his sixth-grade history teacher, Miss Fuller. White (as you may recall from our first chapter) was born into a family of Jewish immigrants, and his house on Erie Street was in the heart of Boston's Jewish ghetto. This situation created a problem for Miss Fuller, who was, White says, "probably the first Protestant I ever met."

"History Lessons"
–THEODORE WHITE

> She decided we would have a play the day before Thanksgiving, a free-form play in the classroom, in which we would all together explore the meeting of Puritans and Indians, and the meaning of Thanksgiving. She divided the class, entirely Jewish, into those children who were American-born and spoke true English, and those who were recent arrivals and spoke only broken English or Yiddish. I was Elder William Bradford because I spoke English well. "Itchie" Rachlin, whose father was an unemployed trumpet player recently arrived from Russia, and who spoke vivid Yiddish, was Squanto, our Indian friend. Miss Fuller hoped that those who could not speak English would squawk strange Indian sounds while I, translating their sounds to the rest of the Puritans, all of us in black cardboard cone hats, would offer good will and brotherhood. "Itchie" and the other recently arrived immigrant children played the game of being "Indian" for a few minutes, then fell into Yiddish, pretending it was Indian talk. Miss Fuller could not, of course, understand them, but I tried to clean up their Yiddish vulgarities in my translation to the other little Puritans, who could not help but giggle. ("*Vos is dos vor traef?*" said Itchie, meaning: "You want us to eat pig food?" and I would translate in English: "What kind of strange food is this before us?") Miss Fuller became furious as we laughed

How is the "meaning" of Thanksgiving different for this group of students than it might be for another group?

Does White present the play as a success or a failure? Does White as interpreter see it as White the character does?

our way through the play; and when I tried to explain, she was hurt and upset. Thanksgiving was sacred to her.

But she was a marvelous teacher. Once we had learned the names and dates from 1630[1] to the Civil War, she let us talk and speculate, driving home the point that history connected to "now," to "us." America for her was all about freedom, and all the famous phrases from "Give me liberty or give me death" to the Gettysburg Address had to be memorized by her classes—and understood.

What is the connection between Miss Fuller's interpretation of American history and her own situation? What is the connection between her version of history and White's situation or "Itchie" Rachlin's?

She was also a very earnest, upward-striving teacher. I realize now that she must have been working for an advanced degree, for she went to night school at Boston University to take education courses. This, too, reached from outside to me. One day she told my mother about a project her night-school seminar was conducting in how much independent research a youngster of ten or eleven could do on his own— one of those projects now so commonplace in progressive schools. Would my mother mind, she asked, if I was given such an assignment, and then reported on it to her seminar? My mother said yes after Miss Fuller promised to bring me home herself afterward.

My assignment was to study immigration, and then to speak to the seminar about whether immigrants were good or bad for America. Her seminar mates would question me to find out how well I had mastered the subject. The Immigration Act of 1924—the "Closing of the Gates"—had just been passed; there was much to read in both papers and magazines about the controversy, but my guide was my father. He put it both ways: the country had been built by immigrants, so immigrants were not bad. He had been an immigrant himself. On the other hand, as a strong labor man, he followed the A.F. of L. line of those days. The National Association of Manufacturers (the capitalists) wanted to continue unrestricted immigration so they could sweat cheap labor. But the American Federation of Labor wanted immigration restricted to keep the wages of American workingmen from being undercut by foreigners. This was a conundrum for my father: he was against the capitalists and for the A.F. of L.; but he was an immigrant himself, as were all our friends and neighbors. He helped me get all the facts, and I made a speech on the platform of a classroom at Boston University Teachers College at nine one night, explaining both sides of the story and taking no position. I enjoyed it all, especially when the teachers began asking me questions; I had all the dates and facts, and an attentive audience, but no answers then just as I have none now. I must have done well, for Miss Fuller kissed me and bought me candy to eat on the streetcar. It became clear to me, as we talked on our way home, that immigrants were history, too. History was happening now, all about us, and the gossip of Erie Street and the problem of whether someone's cousin could get a visa back in the old country and come here were really connected to the past, and to Abraham Lincoln, Henry Clay, Sam Adams, Patrick Henry and the Elder William Bradford.

What is the connection between the "meaning" of Thanksgiving and the Immigration Act of 1924?

What is the significance of this list? Why is the list in this order?

---

[1] The date the first settlers arrived in Boston.

SEARCHING FOR HISTORICAL FRAMEWORKS FOR YOUR OWN MEMOIR

A prerequisite for writing an effective memoir with a historical framework is to think of your life as belonging to the history of your times. White knew that he was a product of one of the great periods of immigration to the United States; he also knew that when the Great Depression forced him to leave school and sell newspapers, he was sharing in the fate of his generation. James Weldon Johnson learned fairly early in his life that he was living at a pivotal point in America's racial history. The following exercises are intended to help you think about the historical frameworks into which your own life fits and to help you find a topic for a historical memoir.

Identifying a Key Historical Event. Name an event that occurred during your childhood or adolescence that was so obviously historic that you remember the moment you first heard about it. Think, if you can, of some ways that the event affected the course of your life thereafter.

EXERCISE 1

Identifying a Process of Historical Change. Think about at least two groups (ethnic, sexual, economic, social, political, or other) to which you belong. How has the status of each of these groups changed from the day that you were born to the present? Are there widely known events associated with this change? Have you witnessed any events associated with this change?

EXERCISE 2

Identifying Historical Themes from Late Childhood. To a surprising degree, childhood memoirs seem to focus on events that happened to the writer when he or she was ten to fourteen years old. Consider this period in your own life. List at least three major "themes" in the public history of those years. Were any of those themes echoed in your own life?

EXERCISE 3

Remembering Lessons in History. Try to recall a specific occasion when an adult attempted to show you, as Miss Fuller showed Theodore White, that history is connected to "us." What was your reaction to the lesson then? What is it now?

EXERCISE 4

THE SOCIAL FRAMEWORK

No bright line separates the social framework from the historical. Most of us, however, as we look back over our earlier lives will remember some of the shocks of learning that the world included attitudes, values, and social forces unknown in our immediate family or among our close friends. We learn that not all people are like "us" and that what drives "us" may not drive "them." This experience of the peculiarity and importance of others is at the heart of what we will call the social framework. In the passages that follow, one memoir writer recalls her encounters with "whitefolks," and another recalls his first encounter with charismatic Christians. In each case, the writer is faced with the child's constant questions: "Are 'they' like me? Could I, should I, be like them?"

As prologue to the passages, you should know a bit about the books from which they come. The first is from Maya Angelou's *I Know Why the Caged Bird Sings* (1969), a book largely about growing up in "the musty little town" of Stamps, Arkansas. Like any long piece of autobiographical writing, the book places its episodes in a number of frameworks, none more important than the extraordinary racial segregation of the United States before World War II. The second passage is from James Weldon Johnson's autobiography *Along This Way* (1933), which in its early chapters traces the author's struggle to extricate himself from the confining life that would be the fate of most black children born in the Southern United States only a few years after the Emancipation Proclamation. The selection we will look at, however, has to do with another of the book's themes, Johnson's "swing almost from the one extreme almost to the other" on his way to a conception of religion that would strike "an emotional and intellectual balance."

As you read the passages, note techniques that may be useful to you in your own memoir writing. The questions in the margin will give you some clues.

"Whitefolks"
—MAYA ANGELOU

Are these the opinions of Angelou the character or Angelou the interpreter?

In Stamps the segregation was so complete that most Black children didn't really, absolutely know what whites looked like. Other than that they were different, to be dreaded, and in that dread was included the hostility of the powerless against the powerful, the poor against the rich, the worker against the worked for and the ragged against the well dressed.

I remember never believing that whites were really real.

Many women who worked in their kitchens traded at our Store, and when they carried their finished laundry back to town they often set the big baskets down on our front porch to pull a singular piece from the starched collection and show either how graceful was their ironing hand or how rich and opulent was the property of their employers.

I looked at the items that weren't on display. I knew, for instance, that white men wore shorts, as Uncle Willie did, and that they had an opening for taking out their "things" and peeing, and that white women's breasts weren't built into their dresses, as some people said, because I saw their brassieres in the baskets. But I couldn't force myself to think of them as people. People were Mrs. LaGrone, Mrs. Hendricks, Momma, Reverend Sneed, Lillie B, and Louise and Rex. White folks couldn't be people because their feet were too small, their skin too white and see-throughy, and they didn't walk on the balls of their feet the way people did—they walked on their heels like horses.

Do these sound like the observations of a child or an adult?

People were those who lived on my side of town. I didn't like them all, or, in fact, any of them very much, but they were people. These others, the strange pale creatures that lived in their alien unlife, weren't considered folks. They were whitefolks.

"Revival Meeting"
—JAMES WELDON
JOHNSON

After John Barton[2] died I spent a good deal of time at my grandmother's house to keep her company. I made myself handy, especially in the shop, where I served a part of each day as clerk. I often slept at her house. On those evenings, after the shop was closed, she usually read to me for an hour or so. She read from the Bible and from a thick, illustrated book in green cloth called *Home Life in the Bible*. She also read me stories from books that she drew from the library of Ebenezer Church Sunday School. These stories were better written and slightly less juvenile than those in the "library" my father had given me, but they were of the same genre. My grandmother had had very little schooling, and could not read as my mother did; that, however, did not daunt her, she read a great deal, and more and more as she grew older. When she read Bible stories aloud to me she came across many names difficult to pronounce, especially in the stories from the Old Testament, but I never knew her to be stumped by a single one; she'd call it something and pass right on. In this way she coined, I am sure, a number of wonderful words.

It was during this period that she disclosed her consuming ambition, her ambition for me to become a preacher. She lived until I was thirty years old, and I believe she never felt that I had done other than choose the lesser part. She took me to Sunday school each week and to some of the church services. I was practically living at my grandmother's when there came a revivalist to Ebenezer. She attended the meetings every night, taking me along with her, always walking the distance of about a mile each way. Sometimes that homeward mile for my short legs seemed without end. In these revival meetings the decorum of the regular Sunday service gave way to something primitive. It was hard to realize that this was the same congregation which on Sunday mornings sat quietly listening to the preacher's exegesis of his text and joining in singing conventional hymns and anthems led by a choir. Now the scene is changed. The revivalist rants and roars, he exhorts and implores, he warns and threatens. The air is charged. Overlaid emotions come to surface. A woman gives a piercing scream and begins to "shout"; then another, and another. The more hysterical ones must be held to be kept from "shouting" out of their clothes. Sinners crowd to the mourners' bench. Prayers and songs go up for the redemption of their souls. Strapping men break down in agonizing sobs, and emotionally strained women fall out in a rigid trance. A mourner "comes through" and his testimony of conversion brings a tumult of rejoicing.

I was only about nine years old but younger souls had been consecrated to God; and I was led to the mourners' bench. I knelt down at the altar. I was so wedged in that I could hardly breathe. I tried to pray. I tried to feel a conviction of sin. I,

What is the tone of Johnson's description of his grandmother?

What purposes are served by giving this subjective impression of the distance?

---

[2]The second husband of Johnson's grandmother.

JAMES WELDON JOHNSON

"Since I have reached the point in life where the glance is more and more frequently backward, I look searching to discover the Key. I try to isolate and trace to their origins the forces that have determined the direction I have followed."

© Carl Van Vechten estate

The life James Weldon Johnson looked back on when he wrote his autobiography is charged with racial tension and with great accomplishments. He was born in Jacksonville, Florida, only eight years after the signing of the Emancipation Proclamation. Though neither of his parents had been slaves and his home was prosperous and cultured, there was no high school for blacks in his hometown, so Johnson went to Atlanta University for his secondary as well as his college education. After he graduated, he returned to Jacksonville to establish a black high school and become its principal. At the same time, he studied law; he was the first black admitted to the Florida bar after Reconstruction ended.

In 1902 he moved to New York City, joining his brother Rosamond and entertainer Bob Cole to form a highly successful trio of singer-songwriters. While in New York, Johnson also studied theater history at Columbia University and became active in Republican politics. In 1906 President Theodore Roosevelt appointed him a U.S. consul, posted first in Venezuela and later in Nicaragua. During his years as consul he played a role in suppressing a revolution, produced his remarkable novel *Autobiography of an ExColored Man,* and wrote some of his best poems.

In 1912 Johnson returned to New York, where he edited the city's leading black newspaper. Four years later he became national field secretary for the NAACP, and in this role organized the historic silent march against lynching (July 20, 1917). From 1920 to 1930 he was executive secretary of the NAACP but still found time to edit *The Book of American Negro Poetry* and to write both *God's Trombones: Seven Negro Sermons in Verse* (considered his masterpiece) and *Black Manhattan* (a cultural history).

After retiring from his NAACP post, he taught at Fisk University, wrote his autobiography *Along This Way,* and continued to exert a powerful political and literary influence until the day he died in a traffic accident. Among the two thousand mourners at his funeral were several of America's great black writers and leaders, including Langston Hughes and W.E.B. DuBois. ◆

finally, fell asleep. . . . The meeting was about to close; somebody shook me by the shoulder. . . . I woke up but did not open my eyes or stir. . . . Whence sprang the whim, as cunning as could have occurred to one of the devil's own imps? The shaking continued, but I neither opened my eyes nor stirred. They gathered round me. I heard, "Glory to God, the child's gone off!" But I did not open my eyes or stir. My grandmother got a big, strong fellow who took me on his back and toted me that long mile home. Several people going our way accompanied us, and the conversation reverted to me, with some rather far-fetched allusions to the conversion of Saul of Tarsus. The situation stirred my sense of humor, and a chuckle ran round and round inside of me, because I did not dare to let it get out. The sensation was a delicious one, but it was suddenly chilled by the appalling thought that I could not postpone my awakening indefinitely. Each step homeward, I knew, brought the moment of reckoning nearer. I needed to think and think fast; and I did. I evolved a plan that I thought was good; when I reached home and "awoke" I recounted a vision. The vision was based on a remembered illustration in *Home Life in the Bible* that purported to be the artist's conception of a scene in heaven. To that conception I added some original embellishments. Apparently my plan worked out to the satisfaction of everybody concerned. Indeed, for me, it worked out almost too satisfactorily, for I was called upon to repeat the vision many times thereafter—to my inward shame.

What does *gone off* mean? Why does Johnson quote this sentence?

How does the final sentence affect the tone of the whole passage?

SEARCHING FOR SOCIAL FRAMEWORKS FOR YOUR OWN MEMOIR

A key to writing a memoir in a social framework is learning to think of yourself as a creature shaped by the society around you. This shaping may take the form of instructions from family members about the ways that "we" are different from "them": Angelou's grandmother, for instance, very deliberately taught her how to distinguish proper behavior from the behavior of "trashy" families, white or black. It may come directly from an institution that attempts to "socialize" the young: the school, the church or synagogue, the athletic team, the Girl Scouts or Boy Scouts, and so forth. In some cases, it may come less from deliberate instruction than from the example of an adult who lives according to such definite values that we feel an unspoken pressure to adopt those values as our own. Think of yourself as a malleable substance and identify the forces that have shaped you—or attempted to.

The following exercises may help you find social frameworks and subjects for a memoir.

◆ *Recalling Negative Stereotypes.* Adults—especially parents—sometimes try to shape the characters of children by holding up a group as a negative example, an example of what not to be. Do you remember having a group presented to you as a negative stereotype?

EXERCISE 5

EXERCISE 6 ◆ *Recalling Rejected Social Lessons.* Social lessons that you refuse to learn are sometimes more memorable than those you accept. Do you remember instances from your childhood when you recognized a lesson and resisted it?

EXERCISE 7 ◆ *Recalling Lessons About Sex Roles.* Among the most universal (often indirect) "lessons" of childhood is the teaching of feminine and masculine roles. Can you recall the ways that you received clues about how men's behavior should differ from women's (or vice versa)?

EXERCISE 8 ◆ *Recalling an Outsider's Influence.* One common crisis in growing up is falling under the influence of a person outside the family whose values and style of life directly conflicts with much of what the family has attempted to inculcate in us. Do you remember such a crisis in your own life?

THE PSYCHOLOGICAL FRAMEWORK

Just as the historical and social frameworks of our childhoods overlap, the psychological framework overlaps with both. Nonetheless, we can productively think of it as a somewhat different backdrop for the events of our lives. Eventually, most of us find an element in our character that can't be entirely accounted for by the times we live in or by the attempts of society to mold us. We discover that (for better or worse) we have a nature, a personality.

One of the richest themes in memoir writing is the author's discovery of his or her psychological nature. Often writers will recall an event from early life that captures the essence of their personality, not only as it was at that moment but as it will continue to be until the day they die. In the passages that follow, Mark Twain and Mary McCarthy describe such incidents. The "Cadet of Temperance" passage is from Twain's *Autobiography* (published after his death in 1910). "First Communion" is from *Memories of a Catholic Girlhood* (1957). As you read Twain, notice that he sees his personality as typical: though he was fascinated by the differences between people, he believed that down deep there was a universal human nature. McCarthy, on the other hand, feels that she is a fundamentally different type of person than most of those around her.

Whether there is a universal human nature is a question we can leave for now to the psychologists and philosophers. The individual's discovery of his or her nature is certainly a universal experience and one that interests readers of memoirs.

"Cadet of Temperance"
—MARK TWAIN

In Hannibal when I was about fifteen I was for a short time a Cadet of Temperance, an organization which probably covered the whole United States during as much as a year—possibly even longer. It consisted in a pledge to refrain, during membership, from the use of tobacco; I mean it consisted partly in that pledge and partly in a red merino sash, but the red merino sash was the main part. The boys joined in order to be privileged to wear it—the pledge part of the matter was of no consequence. It was so small in importance that, contrasted with the sash, it was in effect nonexistent. The organization was weak and impermanent because there were not enough holidays to support it. We could turn out and march and show the red sashes on May Day with the Sunday schools and on the Fourth of July with the Sunday schools, the independent fire company and the militia company. But you can't keep a juvenile moral institution alive on two displays of its sash per year. As a private I could not have held out beyond one procession but I was Illustrious Grand Worthy Secretary and Royal Inside Sentinel and had the privilege of inventing the passwords and of wearing a rosette on my sash. Under these conditions I was enabled to remain steadfast until I had gathered the glory of two displays—May Day and the Fourth of July. Then I resigned straightway and straightway left the lodge.

What attitude toward humanity does the passage display? Is it the attitude of a child or an adult?

I had not smoked for three full months and no words can adequately describe the smoke appetite that was consuming me. I had been a smoker from my ninth year—a private one during the first two years and a public one after that—that is to say, after my father's death. I was smoking and entirely happy before I was thirty steps from the lodge door. I do not know what the brand of the cigar was. It was probably not choice, or the previous smoker would not have thrown it away so soon. But I realized that it was the best cigar that was ever made. The previous smoker would have thought the same if he had been without a smoke for three months. I smoked that stub without shame. I could not do it now without shame, because now I am more refined than I was then. But I would smoke it just the same. I know myself and I know the human race well enough to know that.

What is the connection between Twain's humor and his view of humanity?

"First Communion"
—MARY MCCARTHY

. . . in St. Stephen's School, I was not devout just to show off; I felt my religion very intensely and longed to serve God better than anyone else. This, I thought, was what He asked of me. I lived in fear of making a poor confession or of not getting my tongue flat enough to receive the Host reverently. One of the great moral crises of my life occurred on the morning of my first Communion. I took a drink of water. Unthinkingly, of course, for had it not been drilled into me that the Host must be received fasting, on the penalty of mortal sin? It was only a sip, but that made no difference, I knew. A sip was as bad as a gallon; I *could not* take Communion. And yet I had to. My Communion dress and veil and prayer book were laid out for me, and I was supposed to lead the girls' procession; John Klosick, in a white suit, would be leading the boys'. It seemed to me that I would be failing the school and my class, if, after all the rehearsals, I had to confess what I had done and drop out. The sisters would be angry; my guardians would be angry, having paid for the dress and veil. I thought of the procession without me in it, and I could not bear it. To make my first Communion later, in ordinary clothes, would not be the same. On the other hand, if I took my first Communion in a state of mortal sin, God would never forgive me; it would be a fatal beginning. I went through a ferocious struggle with

How serious is this conflict from a child's perspective? From an adult's?

my conscience, and all the while, I think, I knew the devil was going to prevail; I was going to take Communion, and only God and I would know the real facts. So it came about: I received my first Communion in a state of outward holiness and inward horror, believing I was damned, for I could not imagine that I could make a true repentance—the time to repent was now, before committing the sacrilege; afterward, I could not be really sorry for I would have achieved what I had wanted.

What is the difference in perspective between the first and second paragraphs?

I suppose I must have confessed this at my next confession, scarcely daring to breathe it, and the priest must have treated it lightly: my sins, as I slowly discovered, weighed heavier on me than they did on my confessors. Actually, it is quite common for children making their first Communion to have just such a mishap as mine: they are so excited on that long-awaited morning that they hardly know what they are doing, or possibly the very taboo on food and water and the importance of the occasion drive them into an unconscious resistance. I heard a story almost identical with mine from Ignazio Silone. Yet the despair I felt that summer morning (I think it was Corpus Christi Day) was in a certain sense fully justified: I *knew myself,* how I was and would be forever; such dry self-knowledge is terrible. Every subsequent moral crisis of my life, moreover, has had precisely the pattern of this struggle over the first Communion; I have battled, usually without avail, against a temptation to do something which only I knew was bad, being swept on by a need to preserve outward appearances and to live up to other people's expectations of me. The heroine of one of my novels, who finds herself pregnant, possibly as the result of an infidelity, and is tempted to have the baby and say nothing to her husband, is in the same fix, morally, as I was at eight years old, with that drink of water inside me that only I knew was there. When I supposed I was damned, I was right—damned, that is, to a repetition or endless re-enactment of that conflict between excited scruples and inertia of will.

Is this in fact "the same fix"?

SEARCHING FOR PSYCHOLOGICAL FRAMEWORKS FOR YOUR OWN MEMOIR

Of the three frameworks we are discussing, the psychological is probably the most difficult to manage well because it requires a clear view of ourselves. It is not easy to pluck out of childhood experience an incident that epitomizes our personalities, to say "I know myself and I know the human race well enough to know that" or "I *knew myself,* how I was and would be forever," as Twain and McCarthy do above. It is probably best to start by recollecting who we are at present before we search our earlier lives. The following exercises may help you with that recollection.

EXERCISE 9

◆ *The Battle of the Virtues and Vices.* In a long poem called the *Psychomachia,* Aurelius Clemens Prudentius (A.D. 348–404) presented the personality as a battleground on which seven sins fought seven virtues. The idea was a catchy one, and became one of the standard ways of thinking about personality during the Middle Ages. On the chart below (and with slight modifications) Prudentius's vices are arranged on the left, his virtues on the right. If you can imagine a hand-to-hand battle between each vice and its corresponding virtue in your own personality, where on the following scale would you say the battle now stands?

Sin Winning	Combat Even	Virtue Winning
Paganism		Religion
Lust		Modesty
Anger		Patience
Pride		Humility
Avarice		Charity
Discord		Harmony
Despair		Fortitude

This exercise may help you think of incidents from your childhood that showed the battle turning in favor of one of your besetting "sins" (which you may not now think of as sinful at all) or one of your redeeming "virtues" (which you may not think of as entirely good things).

◆ *Personality Description from Astrology.* Astrologers, like psychologists, often construct tables of personality traits that acknowledge that a given characteristic can be both a vice and a virtue. The chart on the next page links signs of the zodiac with character traits. Ignoring for now the sign you were born under, decide which set of traits matches your personality best and which matches your personality worst.

    You may find that the cluster of adjectives associated with one of the signs of the zodiac describes you well and provides the right framework for a memoir. Perhaps you will find it useful instead to produce a comparable cluster that doesn't pretend to be written in the stars.

EXERCISE 10

Aries ♈	+ Assertive, energetic, courageous, ardent − Aggressive, angry, egotistical, impulsive
Taurus ♉	+ Conservative, reliable, steadfast, patient, deliberate − Greedy, stodgy, possessive, obstinate
Gemini ♊	+ Intellectual, versatile, communicative, alert − Nervous, undependable, impatient, unable to concentrate
Cancer ♋	+ Protective, domestic, emotional, patriotic − Oversensitive, oblique, crabby, moody, acquisitive
Leo ♌	+ Creative, vital, commanding, expansive, regal − Pleasure seeking, conceited, domineering, lazy
Virgo ♍	+ Practical, modest, analytical, unassuming − Reticent, overdiscriminating, aloof, overcritical
Libra ♎	+ Harmonious, affable, diplomatic, balanced, thoughtful − Indecisive, vapid, discontented
Scorpio ♏	+ Intense, passionate, penetrating, genuine − Blunt, cruel, lustful, vindictive
Sagittarius ♐	+ Expansive, free, enthusiastic, profound − Reckless, outspoken, excessive, boisterous
Capricorn ♑	+ Cautious, ambitious, serious, stable, orderly − Cold, limited, miserly, fearful
Aquarius ♒	+ Instructive, inventive, aspiring, changeable, unconventional − Revolutionary, detached, cool, rebellious
Pisces ♓	+ Intuitive, inspired, sensitive, intangible − Vague, oversentimental, confused, self-pitying

WRITING A MEMOIR: POINTS TO CONSIDER

Successful memoirists tend to start with a story to tell. *Story* implies a struggle with a definite beginning and a definite end, so your first task may be to remember a time when you found yourself in conflict with other people (as in "Whitefolks"), with a social institution, or perhaps with your own nature (as in "Knights of Temperance"). You may find it useful to try out your story by telling it to a friend.

As the story begins to take shape, you need to stretch yourself in two directions. First, you need to think hard about the story's significance. In what framework does it gain importance, not only for you but for your readers? How is it related to history, society, or psychology? James Weldon Johnson might have told himself that his story is significant because it illustrates the contrast between religion imposed on a child from outside and religion that grows from the inside. Theodore White might have told himself that his story was significant because it shows the way that each life is tangled in history. Both writers may have thought the stories were *good* because they were funny, but the stories would have been significant even without the humor. Your finished essay may or may not contain a thesis statement that shows your readers precisely what the significant framework is, but the significance needs to be clear to you and to them.

Second, you need to stretch your memory, searching for precise details. It might be worthwhile to make a list of unexpected items that come to mind, items like the baskets of laundry that Angelou remembers seeing on the porch of her grandmother's store, the "illustrated book in green cloth" that Johnson remembers reading in his grandmother's house, and the merino sash that Twain remembers wearing in parades. Memory is itself a sort of writer or editor. The images it retains often have a strong emotional and intellectual charge that can lead us to new insights about our past.

QUESTIONS FOR PEER REVIEW

When you have composed a draft in what you hope is essentially its final form, you should ask a friend to read it. Ask the friend to give you both general advice (see the checklist on pages 65–66) and responses to three particular questions.

a. Have I shown you anything about how my earlier life connects with history? (or "with the structure of society?" or "with my present personality?").

b. Are there details or incidents vivid enough that you will remember them a week from now? What are they?

c. Are there details or events that are unnecessary or dull? What are they?

Your friend's responses should help prepare you to write the final draft.

GROWING UP IN AMERICA: 10 LIVES

While some memoirs of childhood and youth are intended only for friends and relatives, others are widely read and help shape a nation's image of itself. The ten examples below could serve as a short course on what it means, and has meant, to grow up in America.

1. Fredrick Douglass (1813–95) *Narrative of the Life of Fredrick Douglass: An American Slave* (1845). The first of three volumes of Douglass's autobiography, this book combines eloquence and historical importance. It traces Douglass's life from early childhood to his escape North in 1837.

2. Helen Keller (1880–1968) *The Story of My Life* (1903). Written in Keller's sophomore year at Radcliffe, this autobiography tells the story of her struggle, despite blindness and deafness, to become an educated woman. The book is also a tribute to her teacher, Anne Sullivan.

3. Richard Wright (1908–60) *Black Boy* (1945). The story of Wright's coming of age amid racial repression and violence is a milestone in both social history and literature. Like Douglass's autobiography, Wright's ends with an escape North.

4. Mary McCarthy (1912–89) *Memories of a Catholic Girlhood* (1957). McCarthy's memoirs of living as an orphan among unsympathetic relatives in Minneapolis, then as an uneasy boarder in Catholic schools in Washington state, is sometimes hilarious and sometimes grim.

5. Theodore White (1915–86), *In Search of History: A Personal Adventure* (1979). The first section of White's autobiography is a story of pluck and luck—White's childhood in an immigrant family, his struggles during the Depression, and his success at Harvard.

6. Russell Baker (1925–), *Growing Up* (1982). Baker's autobiography covers the first twenty-four years of his life, including his childhood in a proud Virginia family suffering the hardships of the Depression. The book includes memorable portraits of people who influenced Baker, notably his mother who had "a passion for improving the male of the species."

7. Maya Angelou (1928–), *I Know Why the Caged Bird Sings* (1970). The first of Angelou's several memoirs, this book includes remarkable pictures of life in the highly segregated town of Stamps, Arkansas. It ends in Angelou's sixteenth year, with her graduation from high school and the birth of her son.

8. Richard Rodriguez (1944–), *Hunger of Memory* (1982). Controversial because of Rodriguez's opposition to bilingual education, this autobiography focuses on the tension between the life of the author's Mexican-American family and his new life as a "scholarship boy" increasingly separated from the family's traditions and language.

9. Annie Dillard (1945–), *An American Childhood* (1987). Dillard's memoir recreates a child's life in Pittsburgh in the 1950s and includes fine portraits of her eccentric family, but its chief interest lies in the way it traces the awakening of her own mind and spirit.

10. Patricia Hampl (1946–), *A Romantic Education* (1981). Hampl is a poet, and her memoir—full of arresting images and metaphors—is a meditation on the forces that have shaped her own (and her generation's) sense of identity, history, and beauty. It begins in St. Paul, Minnesota, and ends in Prague, Czechoslovakia, in 1975. ◆

ASSIGNMENT 1:   *ANALYSIS OF A MEMOIR*

Because memoirs are often many-faceted, they give us an excellent opportunity to practice one of the most common assignments in college classes, the analysis of a reading passage. An analysis is different from any of the three types of summaries discussed in Chapter 1 (pp. 24–26) because it requires you to break down your subject (the passage) by viewing it in *several* frameworks. In a sociology or psychology class, for example, you might study five forces that affect self-esteem and then be asked to analyze Maya Angelou's *I Know Why the Caged Bird Sings* to show these forces at work. The terms of analysis become frameworks for your examination of the text.

Such assignments are not easy. You will sometimes feel that you have been handed a block of wood and told to put it into a glove in such a way that all five fingers are filled. Angelou did not, after all, write her book as an illustration of the five forces that affect self-esteem, and you will have to do considerable mental rearrangement of her material to make the analysis work. Remember that this difficult rearrangement is precisely the purpose of such assignments. The professor who assigns the paper hopes that you will discover how his or her discipline can alter your view of a subject. To analyze a text successfully, you will have to see it in a somewhat different way than the author saw it and perhaps in a way that would not entirely please the author. In a sense you might have to read the text against the grain. You are intellectually and ethically obliged to treat the text *fairly*, however, not altering the essence of what it says and not misrepresenting any details.

In this chapter we have a simple set of terms of analysis: the three frameworks for memoir (historical, social, and psychological). The following example uses all three terms in its analysis of White's "History Lessons."

Theodore White's "History Lessons" presents a pair of sixth-grade memories: one of participating in a "free-form" play about the first Thanksgiving, one of delivering a paper to a group of teachers in a night-school education class at Boston University. These memories connect his life to the larger context of immigration in American history. The play was, of course, about an immigrant group (the Puritans) meeting with native-born Americans, and it was presented by a mixed cast of American-born students and newly arrived immigrant children. Thus it gave White a double exposure to the American traditions of cooperation and misunderstanding among various immigrant groups. The paper White later delivered to his teacher's night-school class discussed the Immigration Act of 1924, clearly a part of the same 300-year-old story.

Though this historical framework dominates the memoir, we can also see young White getting an early exposure to serious conflicts between groups with different values and ideologies. This social lesson comes from his conversations with his father, who, because he was an immigrant himself, had reason to oppose "The Closing of the Gates" by the Immigration Act. White's father did not express opposition, however. Being a socialist and a union man, he saw that the importation of cheap labor served the interests of the capitalists by keeping the wages of American workers low. This discussion with his father about the conflict between the trade unions and the capitalists must have been one of White's earliest exposures to politics outside the family and the neighborhood.

On the psychological level, White was learning what he was good at, what he enjoyed, and what abilities would allow him to make his way in the world. In the play, it is his ability to bridge the cultural gap between his American teacher and his immigrant classmates that puts him in a position of responsibility. In the night-school class he learned that he enjoyed explaining contemporary history, enjoyed having "all the dates and facts" and an "attentive audience." The play and speech might be seen as the beginnings of White's career as a writer about American politics.

Almost all extended memoirs and many short ones lend themselves to this three-part analysis. Your assignment is to analyze one of the following selections using *at least two* of our frameworks (historical, social, and psychological) as the terms of analysis:

> George Orwell, "Shooting an Elephant," p. 100
> Mark Twain, "The Mesmerizer," p. 104
> Maya Angelou, "Powhitetrash," p. 110
> Mary McCarthy, "Names," p. 113

ASSIGNMENT 2: *ANALYSIS OF AN INITIATION STORY*

The transition from childhood or adolescence into the adult world is so common a theme in literature that the "initiation story" is sometimes thought of as a special literary genre. Like the memoirs we have read, the initiation story shows a protagonist gaining self-understanding and knowledge of the world. Analyze the protagonist's learning in one of the following stories:

> Joyce Carol Oates, "Where Are You Going, Where Have You Been?" p. 384
> Toni Cade Bambara, "The Hammer Man," p. 394
> Alice Munro, "The Day of the Butterfly," p. 398
> Ethan Canin, "Star Food," p. 403

You may elect to use one or more of this chapter's categories—historical, social, and psychological—in your analysis. You may find other terms more suitable.

ASSIGNMENT 3: **A MEMOIR**

Write a memoir that puts an experience from your past into at least one of the three general frameworks mentioned in the chapter: historical, social, and psychological.

SHOOTING AN ELEPHANT

George Orwell

"Shooting an Elephant" (1936) is the only memoir collected in this group that treats an episode from the writer's adult life. Like the other memoirs, however, it looks backward on an earlier self: the Orwell who writes the essay is clearly a different man from the Orwell who served as a policeman in Burma. As you read the essay, think especially about its historical setting and what that implies about the younger Orwell's predicament and the older Orwell's perspective.

1 IN MOULMEIN, IN LOWER BURMA, I WAS hated by large numbers of people—the only time in my life that I have been important enough for this to happen to me. I was sub-divisional police officer of the town, and in an aimless, petty kind of way anti-European feeling was very bitter. No one had the guts to raise a riot, but if a European woman went through the bazaars alone somebody would probably spit betel juice over her dress. As a police officer I was an obvious target and was baited whenever it seemed safe to do so. When a nimble Burman tripped me up on the football field and the referee (another Burman) looked the other way, the crowd yelled with hideous laughter. This happened more than once. In the end the sneering yellow faces of young men that met me everywhere, the insults hooted after me when I was at a safe distance, got badly on my nerves. The young Buddhist priests were the worst of all. There were several thousands of them in the town and none of them seemed to have anything to do except stand on street corners and jeer at Europeans.

2 All this was perplexing and upsetting. For at that time I had already made up my mind that imperialism was an evil thing and the sooner I chucked up my job and got out of it the better. Theoretically—and secretly, of course—I was all for the Burmese and

all against their oppressors, the British. As for the job I was doing, I hated it more bitterly than I can perhaps make clear. In a job like that you see the dirty work of Empire at close quarters. The wretched prisoners huddling in the stinking cages of the lock-ups, the grey, cowed faces of the long-term convicts, the scarred buttocks of the men who had been flogged with bamboos—all these oppressed me with an intolerable sense of guilt. But I could get nothing into perspective. I was young and ill-educated and I had to think out my problems in the utter silence that is imposed on every Englishman in the East. I did not even know that the British Empire is dying, still less did I know that it is a great deal better than the younger empires that are going to supplant it. All I knew was that I was stuck between my hatred of the empire I served and my rage against the evil-spirited little beasts who tried to make my job impossible. With one part of my mind I thought of the British Raj as an unbreakable tyranny, as something clamped down, in *saecula saeculorum*,[1] upon the will of prostrate peoples; with another part I thought that the greatest joy in the world would be to drive a bayonet into a

---

[1] *saecula saeculorum:* "For ages of ages"; until the end of time.

Buddhist priest's guts. Feelings like these are the normal by-products of imperialism; ask any Anglo-Indian official, if you can catch him off duty.

3   One day something happened which in a roundabout way was enlightening. It was a tiny incident in itself, but it gave me a better glimpse than I had had before of the real nature of imperialism—the real motives for which despotic governments act. Early one morning the sub-inspector at a police station the other end of the town rang me up on the 'phone and said that an elephant was ravaging the bazaar. Would I please come and do something about it? I did not know what I could do, but I wanted to see what was happening and I got on to a pony and started out. I took my rifle, an old .44 Winchester and much too small to kill an elephant, but I thought the noise might be useful *in terrorem*. Various Burmans stopped me on the way and told me about the elephant's doings. It was not, of course, a wild elephant, but a tame one which had gone "must." It had been chained up, as tame elephants always are when their attack of "must" is due, but on the previous night it had broken its chain and escaped. Its mahout, the only person who could manage it when it was in that state, had set out in pursuit, but had taken the wrong direction and was now twelve hours' journey away, and in the morning the elephant had suddenly reappeared in the town. The Burmese population had no weapons and were quite helpless against it. It had already destroyed somebody's bamboo hut, killed a cow and raided some fruit-stalls and devoured the stock; also it had met the municipal rubbish van and, when the driver jumped out and took to his heels, had turned the van over and inflicted violences upon it.

4   The Burmese sub-inspector and some Indian constables were waiting for me in the quarter where the elephant had been seen. It was a very poor quarter, a labyrinth of squalid bamboo huts, thatched with palm-leaf, winding all over a steep hillside. I remember that it was a cloudy, stuffy morning at the beginning of the rains. We began questioning the people as to where the elephant had gone and, as usual, failed to get any definite information. That is invariably the case in the East; a story always sounds clear enough at a distance, but the nearer you get to the scene of events the vaguer it becomes. Some of the people said that the elephant had gone in one direction, some said that he had gone in another, some professed not even to have heard of any elephant. I had almost made up my mind that the whole story was a pack of lies, when we heard yells a little distance away. There was a loud scandalized cry of "Go away, child! Go away this instant!" and an old woman with a switch in her hand came round the corner of a hut, violently shooing away a crowd of naked children. Some more women followed, clicking their tongues and exclaiming; evidently there was something that the children ought not to have seen. I rounded the hut and saw a man's dead body sprawling in the mud. He was an Indian, a black Dravidian coolie, almost naked, and he could not have been dead many minutes. The people said that the elephant had come suddenly upon him round the corner of the hut, caught him with its trunk, put its foot on his back and ground him into the earth. This was the rainy season and the ground was soft, and his face had scored a trench a foot deep and a couple of yards long. He was lying on his belly with arms crucified and head sharply twisted to one side. His face was coated with mud, the eyes wide open, the teeth bared and grinning with an expression of unendurable agony. (Never tell me, by the way, that the dead look peaceful. Most of the corpses I have seen look devilish.) The friction of the great beast's foot had stripped the skin from his back as neatly as one skins a rabbit. As soon as I saw the dead man I sent an orderly to a friend's house nearby to borrow an elephant rifle. I had already sent back the pony, not wanting it to go mad with fright and throw me if it smelt the elephant.

5   The orderly came back in a few minutes with a rifle and five cartridges, and meanwhile some Burmans had arrived and told us that the elephant was in the paddy fields below, only a few hundred yards away. As I started forward practically the whole population of the quarter flocked out of the houses and followed me. They had seen the rifle and were all shouting excitedly that I was going to shoot the elephant. They had not shown much interest in the elephant when he

was merely ravaging their homes, but it was different now that he was going to be shot. It was a bit of fun to them, as it would be to an English crowd; besides they wanted the meat. It made me vaguely uneasy. I had no intention of shooting the elephant—I had merely sent for the rifle to defend myself if necessary—and it is always unnerving to have a crowd following you. I marched down the hill, looking and feeling a fool, with the rifle over my shoulder and an ever-growing army of people jostling at my heels. At the bottom, when you got away from the huts, there was a metalled road and beyond that a miry waste of paddy fields a thousand yards across, not yet ploughed but soggy from the first rains and dotted with coarse grass. The elephant was standing eight yards from the road, his left side towards us. He took not the slightest notice of the crowd's approach. He was tearing up bunches of grass, beating them against his knees to clean them and stuffing them into his mouth.

6   I had halted on the road. As soon as I saw the elephant I knew with perfect certainty that I ought not to shoot him. It is a serious matter to shoot a working elephant—it is comparable to destroying a huge and costly piece of machinery—and obviously one ought not to do it if it can possibly be avoided. And at that distance, peacefully eating, the elephant looked no more dangerous than a cow. I thought then and I think now that his attack of "must" was already passing off; in which case he would merely wander harmlessly about until the mahout came back and caught him. Moreoever, I did not in the least want to shoot him. I decided that I would watch him for a little while to make sure that he did not turn savage again, and then go home.

7   But at that moment I glanced round at the crowd that had followed me. It was an immense crowd, two thousand at the least and growing every minute. It blocked the road for a long distance on either side. I looked at the sea of yellow faces above the garish clothes—faces all happy and excited over this bit of fun, all certain that the elephant was going to be shot. They were watching me as they would watch a conjurer about to perform a trick. They did

not like me, but with the magical rifle in my hands I was momentarily worth watching. And suddenly I realized that I should have to shoot the elephant after all. The people expected it of me and I had got to do it; I could feel their two thousand wills pressing me forward, irresistibly. And it was at this moment, as I stood there with the rifle in my hands, that I first grasped the hollowness, the futility of the white man's dominion in the East. Here was I, the white man with his gun, standing in front of the unarmed native crowd—seemingly the leading actor of the piece; but in reality I was only an absurd puppet pushed to and fro by the will of those yellow faces behind. I perceived in this moment that when the white man turns tyrant it is his own freedom that he destroys. He becomes a sort of hollow, posing dummy, the conventionalized figure of a sahib. For it is the condition of his rule that he shall spend his life in trying to impress the "natives," and so in every crisis he has got to do what the "natives" expect of him. He wears a mask, and his face grows to fit it. I had got to shoot the elephant. I had committed myself to doing it when I sent for the rifle. A sahib has got to act like a sahib; he has got to appear resolute, to know his own mind and do definite things. To come all that way, rifle in hand, with two thousand people marching at my heels, and then to trail feebly away, having done nothing—no, that was impossible. The crowd would laugh at me. And my whole life, every white man's life in the East, was one long struggle not to be laughed at.

8   But I did not want to shoot the elephant. I watched him beating his bunch of grass against his knees, with that preoccupied grandmotherly air that elephants have. It seemed to me that it would be murder to shoot him. At that age I was not squeamish about killing animals, but I had never shot an elephant and never wanted to. (Somehow it always seems worse to kill a *large* animal.) Besides, there was the beast's owner to be considered. Alive, the elephant was worth at least a hundred pounds; dead, he would only be worth the value of his tusks, five pounds, possibly. But I had got to act quickly. I turned to some experienced-looking Burmans who had been there when we arrived, and asked them how the elephant

had been behaving. They all said the same thing; he took no notice of you if you left him alone, but he might charge if you went too close to him.

9   It was perfectly clear to me what I ought to do. I ought to walk up to within, say, twenty-five yards of the elephant and test his behavior. If he charged, I could shoot; if he took no notice of me, it would be safe to leave him until the mahout came back. But also I knew that I was going to do no such thing. I was a poor shot with a rifle and the ground was soft mud into which one would sink at every step. If the elephant charged and I missed him, I should have about as much chance as a toad under a steamroller. But even then I was not thinking particularly of my own skin, only of the watchful yellow faces behind. For at that moment, with the crowd watching me, I was not afraid in the ordinary sense, as I would have been if I had been alone. A white man mustn't be frightened in front of "natives"; and so, in general, he isn't frightened. The sole thought in my mind was that if anything went wrong those two thousand Burmans would see me pursued, caught, trampled on and reduced to a grinning corpse like that Indian up the hill. And if that happened it was quite probable that some of them would laugh. That would never do. There was only one alternative. I shoved the cartridges into the magazine and lay down on the road to get a better aim.

10   The crowd grew very still, and a deep, low, happy sigh, as of people who see the theatre curtain go up at last, breathed from innumerable throats. They were going to have their bit of fun after all. The rifle was a beautiful German thing with cross-hair sights. I did not then know that in shooting an elephant one would shoot to cut an imaginary bar running from ear-hole to ear-hole. I ought, therefore, as the elephant was sideways on, to have aimed straight at his ear-hole; actually I aimed several inches in front of this, thinking the brain would be further forward.

11   When I pulled the trigger I did not hear the bang or feel the kick—one never does when a shot goes home—but I heard the devilish roar of glee that went up from the crowd. In that instant, in too short a time, one would have thought, even for the bullet to get there, a mysterious, terrible change had come over the elephant. He neither stirred nor fell, but every line of his body had altered. He looked suddenly stricken, shrunken, immensely old, as though the frightful impact of the bullet had paralysed him without knocking him down. At last, after what seemed a long time—it might have been five seconds, I dare say—he sagged flabbily to his knees. His mouth slobbered. An enormous senility seemed to have settled upon him. One could have imagined him thousands of years old. I fired again into the same spot. At the second shot he did not collapse but climbed with desperate slowness to his feet and stood weakly upright, with legs sagging and head drooping. I fired a third time. That was the shot that did for him. You could see the agony of it jolt his whole body and knock the last remnant of strength from his legs. But in falling he seemed for a moment to rise, for as his hind legs collapsed beneath him he seemed to tower upward like a huge rock toppling, his trunk reaching skywards like a tree. He trumpeted, for the first and only time. And then down he came, his belly towards me, with a crash that seemed to shake the ground even where I lay.

12   I got up. The Burmans were already racing past me across the mud. It was obvious that the elephant would never rise again, but he was not dead. He was breathing very rhythmically with long rattling gasps, his great mound of a side painfully rising and falling. His mouth was wide open—I could see far down into caverns of pale pink throat. I waited a long time for him to die, but his breathing did not weaken. Finally I fired my two remaining shots into the spot where I thought his heart must be. The thick blood welled out of him like red velvet, but still he did not die. His body did not even jerk when the shots hit him, the tortured breathing continued without a pause. He was dying, very slowly and in great agony, but in some world remote from me where not even a bullet could damage him further. I felt that I had got to put an end to that dreadful noise. It seemed dreadful to see the great beast lying there, powerless to move and yet powerless to die, and not even to be able to finish him. I sent back for my small rifle and poured shot

after shot into his heart and down his throat. They seemed to make no impression. The tortured gasps continued as steadily as the ticking of a clock.

In the end I could not stand it any longer and went away. I heard later that it took him half an hour to die. Burmans were bringing dahs and baskets even before I left, and I was told they had stripped his body almost to the bones by the afternoon.

Afterwards, of course, there were endless discussions about the shooting of the elephant. The owner was furious, but he was only an Indian and could do nothing. Besides, legally I had done the right thing, for a mad elephant has to be killed, like a mad dog, if its owner fails to control it. Among the Europeans opinion was divided. The older men said I was right, the younger men said it was a damn shame to shoot an elephant for killing a coolie, because an elephant was worth more than any damn Coringhee coolie. And afterwards I was very glad that the coolie had been killed; it put me legally in the right and it gave me a sufficient pretext for shooting the elephant. I often wondered whether any of the others grasped that I had done it solely to avoid looking a fool. ◆

THE MESMERIZER

Mark Twain

When Mark Twain died, he left behind hundreds of pages of autobiographical writing. Portions of this autobiography have appeared in various forms; the most complete version is The Autobiography of Mark Twain *(1959, edited by Charles Neider). In the excerpt below, Twain recalls the introduction of mesmerism to his home town, Hannibal, Missouri. Mesmerism, based on a theory of "animal magnetism," had been denounced as a hoax as early as 1784. Only in the middle of the nineteenth century did investigators begin to understand the true nature of hypnotism.*

1   AN EXCITING EVENT IN OUR VILLAGE WAS the arrival of the mesmerizer. I think the year was 1850. As to that I am not sure but I know the month—it was May; that detail has survived the wear of fifty years. A pair of connected little incidents of that month have served to keep the memory of it green for me all this time; incidents of no consequence and not worth embalming, yet my memory has preserved them carefully and flung away things of real value to give them space and make them comfortable. The truth is, a person's memory has no more sense than his conscience and no appreciation whatever of values and proportions. However, never mind those trifling incidents; my subject is the mesmerizer now.

He advertised his show and promised marvels. 2 Admission as usual: 25 cents, children and negroes half price. The village had heard of mesmerism in a general way but had not encountered it yet. Not many people attended the first night but next day they had so many wonders to tell that everybody's curiosity was fired and after that for a fortnight the magician had prosperous times. I was fourteen or fifteen years old, the age at which a boy is willing to endure all things, suffer all things short of death by fire, if thereby he may be conspicuous and show off before the public; and so, when I saw the "subjects" perform their foolish antics on the platform and make the people laugh and shout and admire I had a burning desire to be a subject myself.

3 Every night for three nights I sat in the row of candidates on the platform and held the magic disk in the palm of my hand and gazed at it and tried to get sleepy, but it was a failure; I remained wide awake and had to retire defeated, like the majority. Also, I had to sit there and be gnawed with envy of Hicks, our journeyman; I had to sit there and see him scamper and jump when Simmons the enchanter exclaimed, "See the snake! See the snake!" and hear him say, "My, how beautiful!" in reponse to the suggestion that he was observing a splendid sunset; and so on—the whole insane business. I couldn't laugh, I couldn't applaud; it filled me with bitterness to have others do it and to have people make a hero of Hicks and crowd around him when the show was over and ask him for more and more particulars of the wonders he had seen in his visions and manifest in many ways that they were proud to be acquainted with him. Hicks—the idea! I couldn't stand it; I was getting boiled to death in my own bile.

4 On the fourth night temptation came and I was not strong enough to resist. When I had gazed at the disk a while I pretended to be sleepy and began to nod. Straightway came the professor and made passes over my head and down my body and legs and arms, finishing each pass with a snap of his fingers in the air to discharge the surplus electricity; then he began to "draw" me with the disk, holding it in his fingers and telling me I could not take my eyes off it, try as I might; so I rose slowly, bent and gazing, and followed that disk all over the place, just as I had seen the others do. Then I was put through the other paces. Upon suggestion I fled from snakes, passed buckets at a fire, became excited over hot steamboat-races, made love to imaginary girls and kissed them, fished from the platform and landed mud cats that outweighed me—and so on, all the customary marvels. But not in the customary way. I was cautious at first and watchful, being afraid the professor would discover that I was an imposter and drive me from the platform in disgrace; but as soon as I realized that I was not in danger, I set myself the task of terminating Hicks's usefulness as a subject and of usurping his place.

5 It was a sufficiently easy task. Hicks was born honest, I without that incumbrance—so some people said. Hicks saw what he saw and reported accordingly, I saw more than was visible and added to it such details as could help. Hicks had no imagination; I had a double supply. He was born calm, I was born excited. No vision could start a rapture in him and he was constipated as to language, anyway; but if I saw a vision I emptied the dictionary onto it and lost the remnant of my mind into the bargain.

6 At the end of my first half-hour Hicks was a thing of the past, a fallen hero, a broken idol, and I knew it and was glad and said in my heart, "Success to crime!" Hicks could never have been mesmerized to the point where he could kiss an imaginary girl in public or a real one either, but I was competent. Whatever Hicks had failed in, I made it a point to succeed in, let the cost be what it might, physically or morally. He had shown several bad defects and I had made a note of them. For instance, if the magician asked, "What do you see?" and left him to invent a vision for himself, Hicks was dumb and blind, he couldn't see a thing nor say a word, whereas the magician soon found out that when it came to seeing visions of a stunning and marketable sort I could get along better without his help than with it.

7 Then there was another thing: Hicks wasn't worth a tallow dip on mute mental suggestion. Whenever Simmons stood behind him and gazed at the back of his skull and tried to drive a mental suggestion into it, Hicks sat with vacant face and never suspected. If he had been noticing he could have seen by the rapt faces of the audience that something was going on behind his back that required a response. Inasmuch as I was an imposter I dreaded to have this test put upon me, for I knew the professor would be "willing" me to do something, and as I couldn't know what it was, I should be exposed and denounced.

However, when my time came, I took my chance. I perceived by the tense and expectant faces of the people that Simmons was behind me willing me with all his might. I tried my best to imagine what he wanted but nothing suggested itself. I felt ashamed and miserable then. I believed that the hour of my disgrace was come and that in another moment I should go out of that place disgraced. I ought to be ashamed to confess it but my next thought was not how I could win the compassion of kindly hearts by going out humbly and in sorrow for my misdoings, but how I could go out most sensationally and spectacularly.

8   There was a rusty and empty old revolver lying on the table among the "properties" employed in the performances. On May Day two or three weeks before there had been a celebration by the schools and I had had a quarrel with a big boy who was the school bully and I had not come out of it with credit. That boy was now seated in the middle of the house, halfway down the main aisle. I crept stealthily and impressively toward the table, with a dark and murderous scowl on my face, copied from a popular romance, seized the revolver suddenly, flourished it, shouted the bully's name, jumped off the platform and made a rush for him and chased him out of the house before the paralyzed people could interfere to save him. There was a storm of applause, and the magician, addressing the house, said, most impressively—

9   "That you may know how really remarkable this is and how wonderfully developed a subject we have in this boy, I assure you that without a single spoken word to guide him he has carried out what I mentally commanded him to do, to the minutest detail. I could have stopped him at a moment in his vengeful career by a mere exertion of my will, therefore the poor fellow who has escaped was at no time in danger."

10   So I was not in disgrace. I returned to the platform a hero and happier than I have ever been in this world since. As regards mental suggestion, my fears of it were gone. I judged that in case I failed to guess what the professor might be willing me to do, I could count on putting up something that would answer just as well. I was right, and exhibitions of unspoken sug-

gestion became a favorite with the public. Whenever I perceived that I was being willed to do something I got up and did something—anything that occurred to me—and the magician, not being a fool, always ratified it. When people asked me, "How *can* you tell what he is willing you to do?" I said, "It's just as easy," and they always said admiringly, "Well, it beats *me* how you can do it."

    Hicks was weak in another detail. When the   11
professor made passes over him and said "his whole body is without sensation now—come forward and test him, ladies and gentlemen," the ladies and gentlemen always complied eagerly and stuck pins into Hicks, and if they went deep Hicks was sure to wince, then that poor professor would have to explain that Hicks "wasn't sufficiently under the influence." But I didn't wince; I only suffered and shed tears on the inside. The miseries that a conceited boy will endure to keep up his "reputation"! And so will a conceited man; I know it in my own person and have seen it in a hundred thousand others. That professor ought to have protected me and I often hoped he would, when the tests were unusually severe, but he didn't. It may be that he was deceived as well as the others, though I did not believe it nor think it possible. Those were dear good people but they must have carried simplicity and credulity to the limit. They would stick a pin in my arm and bear on it until they drove it a third of its length in, and then be lost in wonder that by a mere exercise of will power the professor could turn my arm to iron and make it insensible to pain. Whereas it was not insensible at all; I was suffering agonies of pain.

    After that fourth night, that proud night, that   12
triumphant night, I was the only subject. Simmons invited no more candidates to the platform. I performed alone every night the rest of the fortnight. Up to that time a dozen wise old heads, the intellectual aristocracy of the town, had held out as implacable unbelievers. I was as hurt by this as if I were engaged in some honest occupation. There is nothing surprising about this. Human beings feel dishonor the most, sometimes, when they most deserve it. That handful of overwise old gentlemen kept on shaking their heads all the first

week and saying they had seen no marvels there that could not have been produced by collusion; and they were pretty vain of their unbelief too and liked to show it and air it and be superior to the ignorant and the gullible. Particularly old Dr. Peake, who was the ringleader of the irreconcilables and very formidable; for he was an F.F.V.,[1] he was learned, white-haired and venerable, nobly and richly clad in the fashions of an earlier and a courtlier day, he was large and stately, and he not only seemed wise but was what he seemed in that regard. He had great influence and his opinion upon any matter was worth much more than that of any other person in the community. When I conquered him at last, I knew I was undisputed master of the field; and now after more than fifty years I acknowledge with a few dry old tears that I rejoiced without shame.

13   In 1847 we were living in a large white house on the corner of Hill and Main Streets—a house that still stands but isn't large now although it hasn't lost a plank; I saw it a year ago and noticed that shrinkage.[2] My father died in it in March of the year mentioned but our family did not move out of it until some months afterward. Ours was not the only family in the house; there was another, Dr. Grant's. One day Dr. Grant and Dr. Reyburn argued a matter on the street with sword canes and Grant was brought home multifariously punctured. Old Dr. Peake calked the leaks and came every day for a while to look after him.

14   The Grants were Virginians, like Peake, and one day when Grant was getting well enough to be on his feet and sit around in the parlor and talk, the conversation fell upon Virginia and old times. I was present but the group were probably unconscious of me, I being only a lad and a negligible quantity. Two of the group—Dr. Peake and Mrs. Crawford, Mrs. Grant's mother—had been of the audience when the Richmond theater burned down thirty-six years before, and

they talked over the frightful details of that memorable tragedy. These were eyewitnesses, and with their eyes I saw it all with an intolerable vividness: I saw the black smoke rolling and tumbling toward the sky, I saw the flames burst through it and turn red, I heard the shrieks of the despairing, I glimpsed their faces at the windows, caught fitfully through the veiling smoke, I saw them jump to their death or to mutilation worse than death. The picture is before me yet and can never fade.

15   In due course they talked of the colonial mansion of the Peakes, with its stately columns and its spacious grounds, and by odds and ends I picked up a clearly defined idea of the place. I was strongly interested, for I had not before heard of such palatial things from the lips of people who had seen them with their own eyes. One detail, casually dropped, hit my imagination hard. In the wall by the great front door there was a round hole as big as a saucer—a British cannon ball had made it in the war of the Revolution. It was breathtaking; it made history real; history had never been real to me before.

16   Very well, three or four years later, as already mentioned, I was king bee and sole "subject" in the mesmeric show; it was the beginning of the second week; the performance was half over; just then the majestic Dr. Peake with his ruffled bosom and wristbands and his gold-headed cane entered, and a deferential citizen vacated his seat beside the Grants and made the great chief take it. This happened while I was trying to invent something fresh in the way of vision, in response to the professor's remark—

17   "Concentrate your powers. Look—look attentively. There—don't you see something? Concentrate—concentrate! Now then—describe it."

18   Without suspecting it, Dr. Peake, by entering the place, had reminded me of the talk of three years before. He had also furnished me capital and was become my confederate, an accomplice in my frauds. I began on a vision, a vague and dim one (that was part of the game at the beginning of a vision; it isn't best to see it too clearly at first, it might look as if you had come loaded with it). The vision developed by degrees and gathered swing, momentum, energy. It

---

[1] F.F.V.: First Families of Virginia, an elite social organization.
[2] Written in 1903. [author's note]

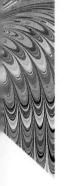

was the Richmond fire. Dr. Peake was cold at first and his fine face had a trace of polite scorn in it; but when he began to recognize that fire, that expression changed and his eyes began to light up. As soon as I saw that, I threw the valves wide open and turned on all the steam and gave those people a supper of fire and horrors that was calculated to last them one while! They couldn't gasp when I got through—they were petrified. Dr. Peake had risen and was standing—and breathing hard. He said, in a great voice:

19   "My doubts are ended. No collusion could produce that miracle. It was totally impossible for him to know those details, yet he has described them with the clarity of an eyewitness—and with what unassailable truthfulness God knows I know!"

20   I saved the colonial mansion for the last night and solidified and perpetuated Dr. Peake's conversion with the cannon-ball hole. He explained to the house that I could never have heard of that small detail, which differentiated this mansion from all other Virginian mansions and perfectly identified it, therefore the fact stood proven that I had *seen* it in my vision. Lawks!

21   It is curious. When the magician's engagement closed there was but one person in the village who did not believe in mesmerism and I was the one. All the others were converted but I was to remain an implacable and unpersuadable disbeliever in mesmerism and hypnotism for close upon fifty years. This was because I never would examine them, in after life. I couldn't. The subject revolted me. Perhaps it brought back to me a passage in my life which for pride's sake I wished to forget; though I thought, or persuaded myself I thought, I should never come across a "proof" which wasn't thin and cheap and probably had a fraud like me behind it.

22   The truth is I did not have to wait long to get tired of my triumphs. Not thirty days, I think. The glory which is built upon a lie soon becomes a most unpleasant incumbrance. No doubt for a while I enjoyed having my exploits told and retold and told again in my presence and wondered over and exclaimed about, but I quite distinctly remember that there presently came a time when the subject was wearisome and odious to me and I could not endure the disgusting discomfort of it. I am well aware that the world-glorified doer of a deed of great and real splendor has just my experience; I know that he deliciously enjoys hearing about it for three or four weeks and that pretty soon after that he begins to dread the mention of it and by and by wishes he had been with the damned before he ever thought of doing that deed. I remember how General Sherman used to rage and swear over "While we were marching through Georgia," which was played at him and sung at him everywhere he went; still, I think I suffered a shade more than the legitimate hero does, he being privileged to soften his misery with the reflection that his glory was at any rate golden and reproachless in its origin, whereas I had no such privilege, there being no possible way to make mine respectable.

23   How easy it is to make people believe a lie and how hard it is to undo that work again! Thirty-five years after those evil exploits of mine I visited my old mother, whom I had not seen for ten years; and being moved by what seemed to me a rather noble and perhaps heroic impulse, I thought I would humble myself and confess my ancient fault. It cost me a great effort to make up my mind; I dreaded the sorrow that would rise in her face and the shame that would look out of her eyes; but after long and troubled reflection, the sacrifice seemed due and right and I gathered my resolution together and made the confession.

24   To my astonishment there were no sentimentalities, no dramatics, no George Washington effects; she was not moved in the least degree; she simply did not believe me and said so! I was not merely disappointed, I was nettled to have my costly truthfulness flung out of the market in this placid and confident way when I was expecting to get a profit out of it. I asserted and reasserted, with rising heat, my statement that every single thing I had done on those long-vanished nights was a lie and a swindle; and when she shook her head tranquilly and said she knew better, I put up my hand and *swore* to it—adding a triumphant, "*Now* what do you say?"

25   It did not affect her at all; it did not budge her the fraction of an inch from her position. If this was hard for me to endure, it did not begin with the blister she put upon the raw when she began to put my sworn oath out of court with *arguments* to prove that I was under a delusion and did not know what I was talking about. Arguments! Arguments to show that a person on a man's outside can know better what is on his inside than he does himself. I had cherished some contempt for arguments before, I have not enlarged my respect for them since. She refused to believe that I had invented my visions myself; she said it was folly: that I was only a child at the time and could not have done it. She cited the Richmond fire and the colonial mansion and said they were quite beyond my capacities. Then I saw my chance! I said she was right—I didn't invent those, I got them from Dr. Peake. Even this great shot did not damage. She said Dr. Peake's evidence was better than mine, and he had said in plain words that it was impossible for me to have heard about those things. Dear, dear, what a grotesque and unthinkable situation: a confessed swindler convicted of honesty and condemned to acquittal by circumstantial evidence furnished by the swindled!

26   I realized with shame and with impotent vexation that I was defeated all along the line. I had but one card left but it was a formidable one. I played it and stood from under. It seemed ignoble to demolish her fortress after she had defended it so valiantly but the defeated know not mercy. I played that master card. It was the pin-sticking. I said solemnly—

27   "I give you my honor, a pin was never stuck into me without causing me cruel pain."

28   She only said—

29   "It is thirty-five years. I believe you do think that now but I was there and I know better. You never winced."

30   She was so calm! and I was so far from it, so nearly frantic.

31   "Oh, my goodness!" I said, "let me *show* you that I am speaking the truth. Here is my arm; drive a pin into it—drive it to the head—I shall not wince."

She only shook her gray head and said with simplicity and conviction—

"You are a man now and could dissemble the hurt; but you were only a child then and could not have done it."

And so the lie which I played upon her in my youth remained with her as an unchallengeable truth to the day of her death. Carlyle[3] said "a lie cannot live." It shows that he did not know how to tell them. If I had taken out a life policy on this one the premiums would have bankrupted me ages ago. ◆

---

[3] Carlyle: Thomas Carlyle (1795–1881), the Victorian prose writer.

POWHITETRASH

Maya Angelou

When Maya Angelou's parents were divorced in 1931, she was sent to Stamps, Arkansas, to be raised by her grandmother, Annie Henderson, whom she soon began to call "Momma." In the rigidly segregated town, Annie Henderson was a pillar of the black community. She owned a store and considerable property, some of it rented to whites. In the following chapter from Angelou's autobiography I Know Why the Caged Bird Sings *(1969), we see an encounter between this formidable grandmother and some of the town's least distinguished white citizens.*

1 "THOU SHALL NOT BE DIRTY" AND "Thou shall not be impudent" were the two commandments of Grandmother Henderson upon which hung our total salvation.

2 Each night in the bitterest winter we were forced to wash faces, arms, necks, legs and feet before going to bed. She used to add, with a smirk that unprofane people can't control when venturing into profanity, "and wash as far as possible, then wash possible."

3 We would go to the well and wash in the ice-cold, clear water, grease our legs with the equally cold stiff Vaseline, then tiptoe into the house. We wiped the dust from our toes and settled down for schoolwork, cornbread, clabbered milk, prayers and bed, always in that order. Momma was famous for pulling the quilts off after we had fallen asleep to examine our feet. If they weren't clean enough for her, she took the switch (she kept one behind the bedroom door for emergencies) and woke up the offender with a few aptly placed burning reminders.

4 The area around the well at night was dark and slick, and boys told about how snakes love water, so that anyone who had to draw water at night and then stand there alone and wash knew that moccasins and rattlers, puff adders and boa constrictors were winding their way to the well and would arrive just as the person washing got soap in her eyes. But Momma convinced us that not only was cleanliness next to Godliness, dirtiness was the inventor of misery.

5 The impudent child was detested by God and a shame to its parents and could bring destruction to its house and line. All adults had to be addressed as Mister, Missus, Miss, Auntie, Cousin, Unk, Uncle, Buhbah, Sister, Brother, and a thousand other appellations indicating familial relationship and the lowliness of the addressor.

6 Everyone I knew respected these customary laws, except for the powhitetrash children.

7 Some families of powhitetrash lived on Momma's farm land behind the school. Sometimes a gaggle of them came to the Store, filling the whole room, chasing out the air and even changing the well-known scents. The children crawled over the shelves and into the potato and onion bins, twanging all the time in their sharp voices like cigar-box guitars. They took liberties in my Store that I would never dare. Since Momma told us that the less you say to white-folks (or even powhitetrash) the better, Bailey and I would stand, solemn, quiet, in the displaced air. But if one of the playful apparitions got close to us, I pinched it. Partly out of angry frustration and partly because I didn't believe in its flesh reality.

8 They called my uncle by his first name and ordered him around the Store. He, to my crying shame, obeyed them in his limping dip-straight-dip fashion.

9 My grandmother, too, followed their orders, except that she didn't seem to be servile because she anticipated their needs.

10 "Here's sugar, Miz Potter, and here's baking powder. You didn't buy soda last month, you'll probably be needing some."

11 Momma always directed her statement to the adults, but sometimes, Oh painful sometimes, the grimy, snotty-nosed girls would answer her.

12 "Naw, Annie . . ."—to Momma? Who owned the land they lived on? Who forgot more than they would ever learn? If there was any justice in the world, God should strike them dumb at once!—"Just give us some extry sody crackers, and some more mackerel."

13 At least they never looked in her face, or I never caught them doing so. Nobody with a smidgen of training, not even the worst roustabout, would look right in a grown person's face. It meant the person was trying to take the words out before they were formed. The dirty little children didn't do that, but they threw their orders around the Store like lashes from a cat-o'-nine-tails.

14 When I was around ten years old, those scruffy children caused me the most painful and confusing experience I had ever had with my grandmother.

15 One summer morning, after I had swept the dirt yard of leaves, spearmint-gum wrappers and Vienna-sausage labels, I raked the yellow-red dirt, and made half-moons carefully, so that the design stood out clearly and mask-like. I put the rake behind the Store and came through the back of the house to find Grandmother on the front porch in her big, wide white apron. The apron was so stiff by virtue of the starch that it could have stood alone. Momma was admiring the yard, so I joined her. It truly looked like a flat redhead that had been raked with a big-toothed comb. Momma didn't say anything but I knew she liked it. She looked over toward the school principal's house and to the right at Mr. McElroy's. She was hoping one of those community pillars would see the design before the day's business wiped it out. Then she looked upward to the school. My head had swung with hers, so at just about the same time we saw a

troop of the powhitetrash kids marching over the hill and down by the side of the school.

I looked to Momma for direction. She did an excellent job of sagging from her waist down, but from the waist up she seemed to be pulling for the top of the oak tree across the road. Then she began to moan a hymn. Maybe not to moan, but the tune was so slow and the meter so strange that she could have been moaning. She didn't look at me again. When the children reached halfway down the hill, halfway to the Store, she said without turning, "Sister, go on inside."

17 I wanted to beg her, "Momma, don't wait for them. Come on inside with me. If they come in the Store, you go to the bedroom and let me wait on them. They only frighten me if you're around. Alone I know how to handle them." But of course I couldn't say anything, so I went in and stood behind the screen door.

18 Before the girls got to the porch I heard their laughter crackling and popping like pine logs in a cooking stove. I suppose my lifelong paranoia was born in those cold, molasses-slow minutes. They came finally to stand on the ground in front of Momma. At first they pretended seriousness. Then one of them wrapped her right arm in the crook of her left, pushed out her mouth and started to hum. I realized that she was aping my grandmother. Another said, "Naw, Helen, you ain't standing like her. This here's it." Then she lifted her chest, folded her arms and mocked that strange carriage that was Annie Henderson. Another laughed, "Naw, you can't do it. Your mouth ain't pooched out enough. It's like this."

19 I thought about the rifle behind the door, but I knew I'd never be able to hold it straight, and the .410, our sawed-off shotgun, which stayed loaded and was fired every New Year's night, was locked in the trunk and Uncle Willie had the key on his chain. Through the fly-specked screen-door, I could see that the arms of Momma's apron jiggled from the vibrations of her humming. But her knees seemed to have locked as if they would never bend again.

20 She sang on. No louder than before, but no softer either. No slower or faster.

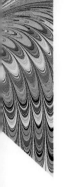

The dirt of the girls' cotton dresses continued on their legs, feet, arms and faces to make them all of a piece. Their greasy uncolored hair hung down, uncombed, with a grim finality. I knelt to see them better, to remember them for all time. The tears that had slipped down my dress left unsurprising dark spots, and made the front yard blurry and even more unreal. The world had taken a deep breath and was having doubts about continuing to revolve.

22 The girls had tired of mocking Momma and turned to other means of agitation. One crossed her eyes, stuck her thumbs in both sides of her mouth and said, "Look here, Annie." Grandmother hummed on and the apron strings trembled. I wanted to throw a handful of black pepper in their faces, to throw lye on them, to scream that they were dirty, scummy peckerwoods, but I knew I was as clearly imprisoned behind the scene as the actors outside were confined to their roles.

23 One of the smaller girls did a kind of puppet dance while her fellow clowns laughed at her. But the tall one, who was almost a woman, said something very quietly, which I couldn't hear. They all moved backward from the porch, still watching Momma. For an awful second I thought they were going to throw a rock at Momma, who seemed (except for the apron strings) to have turned into stone herself. But the big girl turned her back, bent down and put her hands flat on the ground—she didn't pick up anything. She simply shifted her weight and did a hand stand.

24 Her dirty bare feet and long legs went straight for the sky. Her dress fell down around her shoulders, and she had on no drawers. The slick pubic hair made a brown triangle where her legs came together. She hung in the vacuum of that lifeless morning for only a few seconds, then wavered and tumbled. The other girls clapped her on the back and slapped their hands.

25 Momma changed her song to "Bread of Heaven, bread of Heaven, feed me till I want no more."

26 I found that I was praying too. How long could Momma hold out? What new indignity would they think of to subject her to? Would I be able to stay out of it? What would Momma really like me to do?

27 Then they were moving out of the yard, on their way to town. They bobbed their heads and shook their slack behinds and turned, one at a time:

28 "'Bye, Annie."

29 "'Bye, Annie."

30 "'Bye, Annie."

31 Momma never turned her head or unfolded her arms, but she stopped singing and said, "'Bye, Miz Helen, 'bye, Miz Ruth, 'bye, Miz Eloise."

32 I burst. A firecracker July-the-Fourth burst. How could Momma call them Miz? The mean nasty things. Why couldn't she have come inside the sweet, cool store when we saw them breasting the hill? What did she prove? And then if they were dirty, mean and impudent, why did Momma have to call them Miz?

33 She stood another whole song through and then opened the screen door to look down on me crying in rage. She looked until I looked up. Her face was a brown moon that shone on me. She was beautiful. Something had happened out there, which I couldn't completely understand, but I could see that she was happy. Then she bent down and touched me as mothers of the church "lay hands on the sick and afflicted" and I quieted.

34 "Go wash your face, Sister." And she went behind the candy counter and hummed, "Glory, glory, hallelujah, when I lay my burden down."

35 I threw the well water on my face and used the weekday handkerchief to blow my nose. Whatever the contest had been out front, I knew Momma had won.

36 I took the rake back to the front yard. The smudged footprints were easy to erase. I worked for a long time on my new design and laid the rake behind the wash pot. When I came back in the Store, I took Momma's hand and we both walked outside to look at the pattern.

37 It was a large heart with lots of hearts growing smaller inside, and piercing from the outside rim to the smallest heart was an arrow. Momma said, "Sister, that's right pretty." Then she turned back to the Store and resumed, "Glory, glory, hallelujah, when I lay my burden down." ◆

NAMES

Mary McCarthy

"Names" was first published as "C.Y.E." in Mademoiselle *in 1944. Apparently Mary McCarthy enjoyed writing this memoir, for she wrote seven others during the next thirteen years, and collected the lot in* Memories of a Catholic Girlhood *(1957). Written more than two decades after the events it describes, "Names" recreates the world of an eighth-grader with remarkable clarity.*

1 ANNA LYONS, MARY LOUISE LYONS, MARY von Phul, Emilie von Phul, Eugenia McLellan, Marjorie McPhail, Marie-Louise L'Abbé, Mary Danz, Julia Dodge, Mary Fordyce Blake, Janet Preston—these were the names (I can still tell them over like a rosary) of some of the older girls in the convent: the Virtues and Graces. The virtuous ones wore wide blue or green moire good-conduct ribbons, bandoleer-style, across their blue serge uniforms; the beautiful ones wore rouge and powder or at least were reputed to do so. Our class, the eighth grade, wore pink ribbons (I never got one myself) and had names like Patricia ("Pat") Sullivan, Eileen Donohoe, and Joan Kane. We were inelegant even in this respect; the best name we could show, among us, was Phyllis ("Phil") Chatham, who boasted that her father's name, Ralph, was pronounced "Rafe" as in England.

2 Names had a great importance for us in the convent, and foreign names, French, German, or plain English (which, to us, were foreign, because of their Protestant sound), bloomed like prize roses among a collection of spuds. Irish names were too common in the school to have any prestige either as surnames (Gallagher, Sheehan, Finn, Sullivan, McCarthy) or as Christian names (Kathleen, Eileen). Anything exotic had value: an "olive" complexion, for example. The pet girl of the convent was a fragile Jewish girl named Susie Lowenstein, who had pale red-gold hair and an exquisite retroussé nose, which, if we had had it, might have been called "pug." We liked her name too and the name of a child in the primary grades: Abbie

Stuart Baillargeon. My favorite name, on the whole, though, was Emilie von Phul (pronounced "Pool"); her oldest sister, recently graduated, was called Celeste. Another name that appealed to me was Genevieve Albers, Saint Genevieve being the patron saint of Paris who turned back Attila from the gates of the city.

3 All these names reflected the still-pioneer character of the Pacific Northwest. I had never heard their like in the parochial school in Minneapolis, where "foreign" extraction, in any case, was something to be ashamed of, the whole drive being toward Americanization of first name and surname alike. The exceptions to this were the Irish, who could vaunt such names as Catherine O'Dea and the name of my second cousin, Mary Catherine Anne Rose Violet McCarthy, while an unfortunate German boy named Manfred was made to suffer for his. But that was Minneapolis. In Seattle, and especially in the convent of the Ladies of the Sacred Heart, foreign names suggested not immigration but emigration—distinguished exile. Minneapolis was a granary; Seattle was a port, which had attracted a veritable Foreign Legion of adventurers—soldiers of fortune, younger sons, gamblers, traders, drawn by the fortunes to be made in virgin timber and shipping and by the Alaska gold rush. Wars and revolutions had sent the defeated out to Puget Sound, to start a new life; the latest had been the Russian Revolution, which had shipped us, via Harbin, a Russian colony, complete with restaurant, on Queen Anne Hill. The English names in the con-

vent, when they did not testify to direct English origin, as in the case of "Rafe" Chatham, had come to us from the South and represented a kind of internal exile; such girls as Mary Fordyce Blake and Mary McQueen Street (a class ahead of me; her sister was named Francesca) bore their double-barreled first names like titles of aristocracy from the ante-bellum South. Not all our girls, by any means, were Catholic; some of the very prettiest ones—Julia Dodge and Janet Preston, if I remember rightly—were Protestants. The nuns had taught us to behave with special courtesy to these strangers in our midst, and the whole effect was of some superior hostel for refugees of all the lost causes of the past hundred years. Money could not count for much in such an atmosphere; the fathers and grandfathers of many of our "best" girls were ruined men.

4   Names, often, were freakish in the Pacific Northwest, particularly girls' names. In the Episcopal boarding school I went to later, in Tacoma, there was a girl called De Vere Utter, and there was a girl called Rocena and another called Hermoine. Was Rocena a mistake for Rowena and Hermoine for Hermione? And was Vere, as we called her, Lady Clara Vere de Vere? Probably. You do not hear names like those often, in any case, east of the Cascade Mountains; they belong to the frontier, where books and libraries were few and memory seems to have been oral, as in the time of Homer.

5   Names have more significance for Catholics than they do for other people; Christian names are chosen for the spiritual qualities of the saints they are taken from; Protestants used to name their children out of the Old Testament and now they name them out of novels and plays, whose heroes and heroines are perhaps the new patron saints of a secular age. But with Catholics it is different. The saint a child is named for is supposed to serve, literally, as a model or pattern to imitate; your name is your fortune and it tells you what you are or must be. Catholic children ponder their names for a mystic meaning, like birthstones; my own, I learned, besides belonging to the Virgin and Saint Mary of Egypt, originally meant "bitter" or "star of the sea." My second name,

Therese, could dedicate me either to Saint Theresa or to the saint called the Little Flower, Soeur Thérèse of Lisieux, on whom God was supposed to have descended in the form of a shower of roses. At Confirmation, I had added a third name (for Catholics then rename themselves, as most nuns do, yet another time, when they take orders); on the advice of a nun, I had taken "Clementina," after Saint Clement, an early pope—a step I soon regretted on account of "My Darling Clementine" and her number nine shoes. By the time I was in the convent, I would no longer tell anyone what my Confirmation name was. The name I had nearly picked was "Agnes," after a little Roman virgin martyr, always shown with a lamb, because of her purity. But Agnes would have been just as bad, I recognized in Forest Ridge Convent—not only because of the possibility of "Aggie," but because it was subtly, indefinably *wrong,* in itself. Agnes would have made me look like an ass.

The fear of appearing ridiculous first entered my   6 life, as a governing motive, during my second year in the convent. Up to then, a desire for prominence had decided many of my actions and, in fact, still persisted. But in the eighth grade, I became aware of mockery and perceived that I could not seek prominence without attracting laughter. Other people could, but I couldn't. This laughter was proceeding, not from my classmates, but from the girls of the class just above me, in particular from two boon companions, Elinor Heffernan and Mary Harty, a clownish pair— oddly assorted in size and shape, as teams of clowns generally are, one short, plump, and baby-faced, the other tall, lean, and owlish—who entertained the high-school department by calling attention to the oddities of the younger girls. Nearly every school has such a pair of satirists, whose marks are generally low and who are tolerated just because of their laziness and non-conformity; one of them (in this case, Mary Harty, the plump one) usually appears to be half asleep. Because of their low standing, their indifference to appearances, the sad state of their uniforms, their clowning is taken to be harmless, which, on the whole, it is, their object being not to wound but to divert; such girls are bored in school. We in the eighth grade sat directly in front of the two wits in study hall, so that they had us under close observation; yet at first I was not afraid of them, wanting, if anything, to identify myself with their laughter, to be initiated into the joke. One of their specialties was giving people nicknames, and it was considered an honor to be the first in the eighth grade to be let in by Elinor and Mary on their latest invention. This often happened to me; they would tell me, on the playground, and I would tell the others. As their intermediary, I felt myself almost their friend and it did not occur to me that I might be next on their list.

7   I had achieved prominence not long before by publicly losing my faith and regaining it at the end of a retreat. I believe Elinor and Mary questioned me about this on the playground, during recess, and listened with serious, respectful faces while I told them about my conversations with the Jesuits. Those serious faces ought to have been an omen, but if the two girls used what I had revealed to make fun of me, it must have been behind my back. I never heard any more of it, and yet just at this time I began to feel something, like a cold breath on the nape of my neck, that made me wonder whether the new position I had won for myself in the convent was as secure as I imagined. I would turn around in study hall and find the two girls looking at me with speculation in their eyes.

8   It was just at this time, too, that I found myself in a perfectly absurd situation, a very private one, which made me live, from month to month, in horror of discovery. I had waked up one morning, in my convent room, to find a few small spots of blood on my sheet; I had somehow scratched a trifling cut on one of my legs and opened it during the night. I wondered what to do about this, for the nuns were fussy about bedmaking, as they were about our white collars and cuffs, and if we had an inspection those spots might count against me. It was best, I decided, to ask the nun on dormitory duty, tall, stout Mother Slattery, for a clean bottom sheet, even though she might scold me for having scratched my leg in my sleep and order me to cut my toenails. You never know what you might be blamed for. But Mother Slattery, when she bustled in to look at the sheet, did not scold me

at all; indeed, she hardly seemed to be listening as I explained to her about the cut. She told me to sit down: she would be back in a minute. "You can be excused from athletics today," she added, closing the door. As I waited, I considered this remark, which seemed to me strangely munificent, in view of the unimportance of the cut. In a moment, she returned, but without the sheet. Instead, she produced out of her big pocket a sort of cloth girdle and a peculiar flannel object which I first took to be a bandage, and I began to protest that I did not need or want a bandage; all I needed was a bottom sheet. "The sheet can wait," said Mother Slattery, succinctly, handing me two large safety pins. It was the pins that abruptly enlightened me; I saw Mother Slattery's mistake, even as she was instructing me as to how this flannel article, which I now understood to be a sanitary napkin, was to be put on.

9   "Oh, no, Mother," I said, feeling somewhat embarrassed. "You don't understand. It's just a little cut, on my leg." But Mother, again, was not listening; she appeared to have grown deaf, as the nuns had a habit of doing when what you were saying did not fit in with their ideas. And now that I knew what was in her mind, I was conscious of a funny constraint; I did not feel it proper to name a natural process, in so many words, to a nun. It was like trying not to think of their going to the bathroom or trying not to see the straggling iron-grey hair coming out of their coifs (the common notion that they shaved their heads was false). On the whole, it seemed better just to show her my cut. But when I offered to do so and unfastened my black stocking, she only glanced at my leg, cursorily. "That's only a scratch, dear," she said. "Now hurry up and put this on or you'll be late for chapel. Have you any pain?" "No, no, Mother!" I cried, "You don't understand!" "Yes, yes, I understand," she replied soothingly, "and you will too, a little later. Mother Superior will tell you about it some time during the morning. There's nothing to be afraid of. You have become a woman."

10   "I know all about that," I persisted. "Mother, please listen. I just cut my leg. On the athletic field. Yesterday afternoon." But the more excited I grew,

the more soothing, and yet firm, Mother Slattery became. There seemed to be nothing for it but to give up and do as I was bid. I was in the grip of a higher authority, which almost had the power to persuade me that it was right and I was wrong. But of course I was not wrong; that would have been too good to be true. While Mother Slattery waited, just outside my door, I miserably donned the equipment she had given me, for there was no place to hide it, on account of drawer inspection. She led me down the hall to where there was a chute and explained how I was to dispose of the flannel thing, by dropping it down the chute into the laundry. (The convent arrangements were very old-fashioned, dating back, no doubt, to the days of Louis Philippe.)

11   The Mother Superior, Madame MacIllvra, was a sensible woman, and all through my early morning classes, I was on pins and needles, chafing for the promised interview with her which I trusted would clear things up. "*Ma Mère*," I would begin, "Mother Slattery thinks . . ." Then I would tell her about the cut and the athletic field. But precisely the same impasse confronted me when I was summoned to her office at recess-time. *I* talked about my cut, and *she* talked about becoming a woman. It was rather like a round, in which she was singing "Scotland's burning, Scotland's burning," and I was singing "Pour on water, pour on water." Neither of us could hear the other, or, rather, I could hear her, but she could not hear me. Owing to our different positions in the convent, she was free to interrupt me, whereas I was expected to remain silent until she had finished speaking. When I kept breaking in, she hushed me, gently, and took me on her lap. Exactly like Mother Slattery, she attributed all my references to the cut to a blind fear of this new, unexpected reality that had supposedly entered my life. Many young girls, she reassured me, were frightened if they had not been prepared. "And you, Mary, have lost your dear mother, who could have made this easier for you." Rocked on Madame MacIllvra's lap, I felt paralysis overtake me and I lay, mutely listening, against her bosom, my face being tickled by her white, starched, fluted wimple, while

she explained to me how babies were born, all of which I had heard before.

12   There was no use fighting the convent. I had to pretend to have become a woman, just as, not long before, I had had to pretend to get my faith back— for the sake of peace. This pretense was decidedly awkward. For fear of being found out by the lay sisters downstairs in the laundry (no doubt an imaginary contingency, but the convent was so very thorough), I reopened the cut on my leg, so as to draw a little blood to stain the napkins, which were issued me regularly, not only on this occasion, but every twenty-eight days thereafter. Eventually, I abandoned this bloodletting, for fear of lockjaw, and trusted to fate. Yet I was in awful dread of detection; my only hope, as I saw it, was either to be released from the convent or to become a woman in reality, which might take a year, at least, since I was only twelve. Getting out of athletics once a month was not sufficient compensation for the farce I was going through. It was not my fault; they had forced me into it; nevertheless, it was I who would look silly—worse than silly; half mad—if the truth ever came to light.

13   I was burdened with this guilt and shame when the nickname finally found me out. "Found me out," in a general sense, for no one ever did learn the particular secret I bore about with me, pinned to the linen band. "We've got a name for you," Elinor and Mary called out to me, one day on the playground. "What is it?" I asked, half hoping, half fearing, since not all their sobriquets were unfavorable. "Cye," they answered, looking at each other and laughing. " 'Si'?" I repeated, supposing that it was based on Simple Simon. Did they regard me as a hick? "C.Y.E.," they elucidated, spelling it out in chorus. "The letters stand for something. Can you guess?" I could not and I cannot now. The closest I could come to it in the convent was "Clean Your Ears." Perhaps that was it, though in later life I have wondered whether it did not stand, simply, for "Clever Young Egg" or "Champion Young Eccentric." But in the convent I was certain that it stood for something horrible, something even worse than dirty ears (as far as I knew, my ears

were clean), something I could never guess because it represented some aspect of myself that the world could see and I couldn't, like a sign pinned on my back. Everyone in the convent must have known what the letters stood for, but no one would tell me. Elinor and Mary had made them promise. It was like halitosis; not even my best friend, my deskmate, Louise, would tell me, no matter how much I pleaded. Yet everyone assured me that it was "very good," that is, very apt. And it made everyone laugh.

14   This name reduced all my pretensions and solidified my sense of *wrongness*. Just as I felt I was beginning to belong to the convent, it turned me into an outsider, since I was the only pupil who was not in the know. I liked the convent, but it did not like me, as people say of certain foods that disagree with them. By this, I do not mean that I was actively unpopular, either with the pupils or with the nuns. The Mother Superior cried when I left and predicted that I would be a novelist, which surprised me. And I had finally made friends; even Emilie von Phul smiled upon me softly out of her bright blue eyes from the far end of the study hall. It was just that I did not fit into the convent pattern; the simplest thing I did, like asking for a clean sheet, entrapped me in consequences that I never could have predicted. I was not bad; I did not consciously break the rules; and yet I could never, not even for a week, get a pink ribbon, and this was something I could not understand, because I was trying as hard as I could. It was the same case as with the hated name; the nuns, evidently, saw something about me that was invisible to me.

15   The oddest part was all that pretending. There I was, a walking mass of lies, pretending to be a Catholic and going to confession while really I had lost my faith, and pretending to have monthly periods by cutting myself with nail scissors; yet all this had come about without my volition and even contrary to it. But the basest pretense I was driven to was the acceptance of the nickname. Yet what else could I do? In the convent, I could not live it down. To all those girls, I had become "Cye McCarthy." That was who I was. That was how I had to identify myself when telephoning my friends during vacations to ask them to the movies: "Hello, this is Cye." I loathed myself when I said it, and yet I succumbed to the name totally, making myself over into a sort of hearty to go with it—the kind of girl I hated. "Cye" was my new patron saint. This false personality stuck to me, like the name, when I entered public high school, the next fall, as a freshman, having finally persuaded my grandparents to take me out of the convent, although they could never get to the bottom of my reasons, since, as I admitted, the nuns were kind, and I had made many nice new friends. What I wanted was a fresh start, a chance to begin life over again, but the first thing I heard in the corridors of the public high school was that name called out to me, like the warmest of welcomes: "Hi, there, Si!" That was the way they thought it was spelled. But this time I was resolute. After the first weeks, I dropped the hearties who called me "Si" and I never heard it again. I got my own name back and sloughed off Clementina and even Therese—the names that did not seem to me any more to be mine but to have been imposed on me by others. And I preferred to think that Mary meant "bitter" rather than "star of the sea." ◆

WRITING REPORTS AND OBSERVATIONS

THIS IS A CHAPTER ABOUT THE WORK OF REPORTERS—NOT NECESSARILY about journalists, but about people whose task is to observe and to write about what they see. In this sense, the engineer in the field must often be a reporter and so must the diplomat posting dispatches from a foreign capital. In letters home, travelers become for a few paragraphs reporters on life in New Guinea, or New York, or at Aunt Sarah's house.

Though these and many other reports involve journeys, the reporter is not necessarily a traveler: you could present observations made inside the four walls of your home, even observations that come to you by way of television or radio. The essential thing is not traveling but watching and listening for yourself and commenting on what you learn. For the purpose of this chapter, we will not consider strictly autobiographical essays—ones in which writers talk about themselves—to be reports: autobiographical essays are the subject of Chapter 3. Nor will we consider essays based on the observations of others to be reports: such essays will be discussed in Chapter 14.

A passage in John Henry Newman's *The Idea of a University* (1873) suggests one quality that allows a writer to convert raw experience into a meaningful report. Newman complains that "seafaring men" with much material to report on often have nothing to say about it:

> They sleep, and they rise up, and they find themselves, now in Europe, now in Asia; they see visions of great cities and wild regions; they are in the marts of commerce, or amid the islands of the South; they gaze on Pompey's pillar,[1] or on the Andes; and nothing which meets them carries them forward or backward, to any idea beyond itself. Nothing has drift or relation; nothing has a history or a promise. Everything stands by itself, and comes and goes in its turn, like the shifting scenes of a show, which leave the spectator where he was.

Here we come back to a point made in Chapter 1, that writing worth reading involves interpretation. The reporter who gives readers nothing but random comments in which "everything stands by itself" has not done her job. In a

---

[1] A gigantic column (88 feet high) in Alexandria, Egypt, raised circa A.D. 300 in honor of the emperor Diocletian.

successful report, the details observed will have "drift and relation . . . a history and a promise." Each will connect to an "idea beyond itself." To phrase the point differently, the reporter has a framework as well as a subject.

REPORTS ON PLACES

Imagine what would happen if you took a notebook to a restaurant for an hour and attempted to record everything you saw, heard, smelled, tasted, or touched in the place, attempting to be as literal and as detailed as possible. That man sitting over in the corner, for example. It would not be enough to describe his face, with its spots of acne and its drooping mustache. You would also have to describe his clothes minutely, down to the smudge of mud on the instep of his right shoe. And, of course, you would have to describe his actions: the way he held his fork, what he did when his napkin fell off his lap, what vegetables he ate in what order. And then there would be the other two people at the table, and the other ten tables in the room, and the room itself, and your own meal. The task would be simply impossible. And if it could be completed, the result would be useless and dull—probably to yourself and certainly to anyone else.

THE LITERAL PLACE AND THE
IDEA OF A PLACE

Good reporting on places comes from an interaction between the place itself and an idea of the place, constructed in the writer's mind and conveyed to the reader largely by a judicious selection of details. The selection both compresses the subject and reveals the "drift." In this respect, every report tells us not only about the subject but about the writer's view of the world. We can see this interaction of subject and view clearly in the reports George Orwell wrote from various places. His concern with the plight of the poor and down-trodden doesn't change with the latitude; it travels with him. Consider, for example, his description of the ghetto in Marrakech, Morocco (1939).

What is the effect of saying "you go" instead of "I went" in the first sentence?

What effect do Orwell's similes have on you?

Why does Orwell mention the grandson and his age?

When you go through the Jewish quarters you gather some idea of what the medieval ghettoes were probably like. Under their Moorish rulers the Jews were only allowed to own land in certain restricted areas, and after centuries of this kind of treatment they have ceased to bother about overcrowding. Many of the streets are a good deal less than six feet wide, the houses are completely windowless, and sore-eyed children cluster everywhere in unbelievable numbers, like clouds of flies. Down the centre of the street there is generally running a little river of urine.

In the bazaar huge families of Jews, all dressed in the long black robe and little black skull-cap, are working in dark fly-infested booths that look like caves. A carpenter sits cross-legged at a prehistoric lathe, turning chair-legs at lightning speed. He works the lathe with a bow in his right hand and guides the chisel with his left foot, and thanks to a lifetime of sitting in this position his left leg is warped out of shape. At his side his grandson, aged six, is already starting on the simpler parts of the job.

I was just passing the coppersmiths' booths when somebody noticed that I was lighting a cigarette. Instantly, from the dark holes all round, there was a frenzied rush of Jews, many of them old grandfathers with flowing grey beards, all clamouring for a cigarette. Even a blind man somewhere at the back of one of the booths heard a rumour of cigarettes and came crawling out, groping in the air with his hand. In about a minute I had used up the whole packet. None of these people, I suppose, works less than twelve hours a day, and every one of them looks on a cigarette as a more or less impossible luxury.

Who doubts that the details Orwell reports here are presented accurately? And yet someone who has read Orwell's other essays would immediately see that this is a report in the Orwell style, strongly emphasizing the poverty and misery of oppressed people. Perhaps even the blind man crawling across his booth would have described the bazaar in more cheerful terms than Orwell. It is the unrelieved gloom that makes the passage typical of its author and also memorable. No flat description of Marrakech, this is Marrakech as an example of the state in which the world's poor are forced to live.

Recall Newman's complaint that sailors' reports on places often lack "drift and relation . . . a history and a promise." Here the drift is unmistakable, and there is also a history and a promise. Without scanting his description of the present place, Orwell connects it to the past—to the medieval ghettos of Europe. He also, disturbingly, suggests the "promise" of the future: the grandson, aged six, will soon have a warped leg to match his grandfather's.

EXERCISE 1

◆ *Objective and Subjective Language.* Orwell's characterization of the Marrakech ghetto includes several words and phrases that seem to be both accurate ("objective") and emotionally charged ("subjective"). Locate six examples of such words and phrases and explain how they serve both a subjective and an objective function.

A PLACE CHARACTERIZED BY
THE BEHAVIOR OF ITS INHABITANTS

In this chapter, place, event, and personality are treated as separate categories, but they obviously overlap. In many cases the impression of a place is largely an impression of its inhabitants. When young Charles Darwin visited the cattle-ranching region of Banda Oriental (southern Uruguay) in 1832, the people seem to have impressed him more strongly than the flat, featureless countryside. He devotes a long paragraph in *The Voyage of the Beagle* to reporting on their character.

On the first night we slept at a retired little country-house; and there I soon found out that I possessed two or three articles, especially a pocket compass, which created unbounded astonishment. In every house I was asked to show the compass, and by its aid, together with a map, to point out the direction of various places. It excited the liveliest admiration that I, a perfect stranger, should know the road (for direction and road are synonymous in this open country) to places where I had never been. At one house a young woman, who was ill in bed, sent to entreat me to come and show her the compass. If their surprise was great, mine was greater, to find such ignorance among people who possessed their thousands of cattle, and "estancias" [2] of great extent. It can only be accounted for by the circumstance that this retired part of the country is seldom visited by foreigners. I was asked whether the earth or sun moved; whether it was hotter or colder in the north; where Spain was, and many other such questions. The greater number of the inhabitants had an indistinct idea that England, London, and North America were different names for the same place; but the better informed well know that London and North America were separate countries close together, and that England was a large town in London! I carried with me some promethean [3] matches, which I ignited by biting; it was thought so wonderful that a man should strike fire with his teeth, that it was usual to collect the whole family to see it: I was once offered a dollar for a single one. Washing my face in the morning caused much speculation at the village of Las Minas; a superior tradesman closely cross-questioned me about so singular a practice; and likewise why on board we wore our beards; for he had heard from my guide that we did so. He eyed me with suspicion; perhaps he had heard of ablutions in the Mahomadan religion, and knowing me to be a heretick, [4] probably he came to the conclusion that all hereticks were Turks. It is the general custom in this country to ask for a night's lodging at the first convenient house. The astonishment at the compass, and my other feats of jugglery, was to a certain degree advantageous, as with that, and the long stories my guides told of my breaking stones, knowing venomous from harmless snakes, collecting insects &c, I repaid them for their

"Banda Oriental"
—CHARLES DARWIN

Why do you think Darwin mentions the young woman?

How would you describe the tone of Darwin's comments on the ignorance of the villagers?

Does Darwin's own view of the world seem limited by his cultural perspective?

[2] Latin American Spanish for *ranch*.
[3] The promethean match, ignited by breaking a small glass bead wrapped in paper, was first manufactured in London in 1828.
[4] From the perspective of Banda Oriental, Darwin would have been a "heretic" because he was from a non-Catholic country.

hospitality. I am writing as if I had been among the inhabitants of central Africa: Banda Oriental would not be flattered by the comparison; but such were my feelings at the time.

Once again, there can be no mistaking the "drift" of this passage. While there must have been other things to report about the life of the villagers Darwin met, he chose to emphasize their ignorance. It was, from his point of view, a remarkable feature of the region they inhabited. Notice that unlike Orwell, Darwin does not attempt to present his report as a single scene, observed in an hour or day. Instead, he collects incidents that occurred over the course of several days, and he selects them because they have—to use Newman's term—connection. The passage includes some details that are interesting in their own right: the picture of Charles Darwin striking matches with his teeth to amaze cattle ranchers delights me. But no detail "stands by itself": each contributes to the "idea" of the place as Darwin sees it.

EXERCISE 2

◆ *Action as an Element of Description.* Some writers tend, when they describe a place, to stop all action. People and things are described as if they were part of still photographs, and the result can be tedious. Darwin, however, includes a good deal of action in his description of Banda Oriental. Examine his paragraph closely and identify at least ten separate acts reported in it.

FINDING SUBJECTS AND FRAMEWORKS FOR A REPORT ON A PLACE

The passages from Orwell and Darwin touch on an important and fascinating theme: the effect of place on character. If you are searching for a subject, one strategy is to begin by considering the same theme. Recalling your travels, whether to other continents or other neighborhoods, think about how the people there differ from the people in your own community. Then consider ways that the cultural and natural environment may account for this difference. Darwin attributes the ignorance of the villagers of Banda Oriental to isolation from foreign influences. Orwell attributes the poverty and misery of the Jews of Marrakech to laws that denied them ownership of land and forced them into crowded ghettos. What comparable factors (positive or negative) did you find at work in places you have visited? By thinking about the effect of this factor, you may develop a framework for your report.

If you choose to report on a place in or near your own community, you might consider another strategy. Assume the role of a guide, informing people about places they might consider visiting. Imagining your classmates as an audience can be useful here since it is likely that some of them are relative strangers to the city in which your college is located. Can you think of places that they ought to visit or ought to avoid? The reasons you would give for visiting or avoiding the place may become frameworks for an essay.

REPORTS ON OCCASIONS

The passages we have just examined report on the relatively unchanging qualities of a place. That is, though Orwell describes Marrakech as it appeared to him at a particular time, his aim is not to record a passing hour in that city's history. Presumably a traveler who came to the city a week, a month, or a year later would find matters essentially unchanged. Darwin, likewise, reports not on a given occasion in Banda Oriental but on conditions that had existed before his visit and would persist for some time after. Often, however, the writer's job is to report on an event that passes quickly, to capture the essential flavor of a particular day or hour.

A UNIFIED IMPRESSION OF A SINGLE OCCASION

In *Singin' and swingin' and gettin' merry like Christmas*, Maya Angelou describes a party in the apartment of a wealthy San Franciscan in the 1950s. Her description of the party has much in common with Darwin's report, but it is clearly less about a place than about an event.

"Jorie's Party"
—MAYA ANGELOU

One evening I was invited to a wine party at Jorie's apartment after closing time. The house sat on a hilly street. A stranger opened the door and took no more notice of me, so I entered and sat on a floor pillow and watched the guests spin around each other in minuet patterns. There were glamorous young men with dyed hair who rustled like old cellophane. Older men had airs of sophistication and cold grace, giving the impression that if they were not so terribly tired they would go places (known only to a select few) where the conversation was more scintillating and the congregation more interesting.

How does the mention of a minuet help establish the passage's "idea" or "framework"?

There were young women who had the exotic sheen of recently fed forest animals. Although they moved their fine heads languorously this way and that, nothing in the room excited their appetites. Unfashionable red lips cut across their white faces, and the crimson fingernails, as pointed as surgical instruments, heightened the predatory effect. Older, sadder women were more interesting to me. Voluminous skirts and imported shawls did not hide their heavy bodies, nor was their unattractiveness shielded by the clanks of chains and ribbons of beads, or by pale pink lips and heavily drawn doe eyes. Their presence among the pretty people enchanted me. It was like seeing frogs buzzed by iridescent dragonflies. The young men, whose names were Alfie, Reggie and Roddy and Fran, hovered around these fat women, teasing them, tickling them, offering to share a portion of their svelte beauty. None of the company spoke to me. That I was one of the three Negroes in the room, the only Negro woman and a stranger as well, was not a sufficiently exotic reason to attract attention.

How many mentions of color does this passage contain?

How many words in the passage suggest iridescence?

Notice that Angelou's description emphasizes movement, often a key to successful reporting on an occasion. Notice, too, her evocation of our senses. Angelou's emphasis is primarily visual, often concerned with color. But she notes sounds as well: the rustle of clothing, the clank of chains, the buzz of conversation. There are also suggestions of textures and weights that we might feel: the sharp nails of the young women, the cumbersome chains and skirts and shawls of the older ones, the suggestion that the "pretty people" are nearly weightless compared to the heavy older women.

Like Darwin's and Orwell's reports, Angelou's is no mere collection of details: the occasion is made to represent "an idea beyond itself." Different readers might name the idea somewhat differently. Some might say that Angelou presents the party as "exotic," some might say "decadent," some might say "sophisticated," though not in a positive sense. No one, surely, would say that Angelou presents the party as "plain," or "warm," or "friendly," or "joyous," though it is quite possible that another of the party-goers (perhaps one of the "predatory" women) might have chosen such a word.

EXERCISE 3

◆ *Figurative Language in Descriptive Writing.* Angelou's passage contains many similes and metaphors. Locate six and assess their effect. Are they primarily used to help the reader visualize the subject or to express Angelou's impression of the subject?

AN IMPRESSION OF
A SERIES OF OCCASIONS

Writers sometimes need to report on a series of occasions in a single description. A clinical psychologist writing a case study, for example, may report on a patient's behavior under stress by compressing notes from several separate observation periods into one general description. Journalists covering a story that extends over a period of days or weeks frequently compress their stories this way, as Theodore White does in the following description of the crowds that greeted John F. Kennedy in the last days of the 1960 presidential campaign.

"Kennedy Crowds"
—THEODORE WHITE

How is the form of White's first sentence related to its content?

How does White's use of adjectives shape our perceptions?

One remembers being in a Kennedy crowd and suddenly sensing far off on the edge of it a ripple of pressure beginning, and the ripple, which always started at the back, would grow like a wave, surging forward as it gathered strength, until it would squeeze the front rank of the crowd against the wooden barricade, and the barricade would begin to splinter; then the police would rush to reinforce the barricade, shove back, start a counterripple, and thousands of bodies would, helplessly but ecstatically, be locked in the rhythmic back-and-forth rocking. One remembers the groans and the moans; and a frowzy woman muttering hoarsely as if to herself, "Oh, Jack, I love yuh, Jack, I love yuh, Jack—Jack, Jack, I love yuh"; or the harsh-faced woman peering over one's shoulder glowering, "You a newspaperman?—You better write nice things about him, or you watch out" (and she meant it). One remembers the crude signs—hand-lettered, crayoned by school children, chalked on tarpaulin by workmen constructing new buildings, carried on staves by families (in the Bronx: "The home of the *knishes* thinks Jack is delicious" and "The home of the *bagel* thinks Big Jack is Able"). And the noise, and the clamor.

One remembers the motorcades and the people along the road—confetti pouring down at some stops until, when the convertible's door would open to release the candidate, the confetti would pour out like water from a tank. One remembers groups along the road waving, the women unbinding kerchiefs from their heads to wave; the grizzled workingmen and union men, too embarrassed to show emotion publicly, toughness written all over their hard faces, suddenly holding out their hands and waving at him after he had gone by—and the hand stretched out as in a Roman salute of farewell for full seconds *after* the candidate had passed, and then slowly dropping, of itself. One remembers the grabbers, bursting through police lines, trying to touch him or reach him, and the squeezers who grasped his hand and, to prove their affection, squeezed extra hard until, one day in Pennsylvania, even the candidate's callused hand burst with blood.

Every sentence in this paragraph begins with the same words. How does this repetition affect you?

Maya Angelou, who writes from memory about essentially private experience, *attempts* to present details accurately. As a working reporter, White was obliged to go further, to *insure* accuracy. Those who saw him at work remember that he filled one notepad after another with the observations that would allow him to write factual descriptions this detailed. But White's report on the Kennedy crowds is not a coldly objective one. The emotional fervor, bordering on adulation, that White describes is something he later admitted to having felt himself.

In a sense, the passage is about a type of crowd, just as Orwell's description of Marrakech is about a type of city. With a few changes in detail, White could have been describing any crowd responding to a charismatic leader: Roman crowds responding to the presence of Julius Caesar or German crowds responding to Adolf Hitler. In order to give us a sense of the fervor that he found so remarkable, White must have suppressed some details of what he saw, either before they reached his notepad or after. In a crowd of many thousands, wouldn't *some* have been irritated because they couldn't see over the people in front of them? Wouldn't some have been vocal Nixon supporters coming to see the Democratic candidate out of curiosity? Were no hecklers present? Was no one angry about being jostled? White clearly decided that such details would distract readers from what he believed to be the essential truth about the Kennedy crowd. Another reporter, working from equally detailed notes, would have produced a different interpretation of the event.

◆ *Verbs in Descriptive Writing.* Many inexperienced writers associate descriptive writing with the use of colorful adjectives. White's description of a crowd, however, demonstrates the descriptive power of verbs and verb forms (participles, gerunds, and infinitives). To gauge the effect of these verbs and verb forms, find ten that are especially effective in conveying the

EXERCISE 4

energy of the crowd. Replace these with ten less energetic verbs and assess the result.

FINDING SUBJECTS AND FRAMEWORKS FOR A REPORT ON AN OCCASION

Though Maya Angelou's description of the party at Jorie's apartment is drawn from private life, you'll notice that it is not a story with Angelou as the protagonist.[5] The best "occasion" to use as a writing topic for this chapter (as opposed to Chapter 3) is not one that is essentially part of your own life story, the story of your growth and development. You may have a very personal reaction to the event you witness, and this reaction should shape the framework of your essay, but the subject should come from "out there," from the world that other people inhabit and control.

The ordinary course of your life may produce promising subjects of this kind. You may, for example, attend a political rally, a concert, or a sporting event that merits comment. Better subjects may, however, lie somewhat farther afield. Paying attention to the events announced in your local or campus newspaper is a good way to find potential topics.

EXERCISE 5

◆ *A Brainstorming Session on Reportable Events.* Typically, reporters for local newspapers gather for daily or weekly editorial conferences where they either receive assignments for stories from an autocratic editor or discuss assignments democratically. Following the more democratic pattern, meet for a few minutes with a group of your classmates and make a list of at least six upcoming events that could be subjects of interesting reports. For each event, try to think of at least two "angles" or "frameworks" the reporter might use.

REPORTS ON PERSONALITIES

Reports on places and occasions, as we have seen, create an impression of the thing reported on. This impression corresponds to the "framework" we discussed in Chapter 1. It helps us make sense of what could otherwise be a shapeless collection of details, and so it is essential to clear writing. The framework that shapes our understanding, however, also has the potential to warp it. As readers, we may appreciate Darwin's providing us with a perspective on the villagers of Banda Oriental. At the same time, we may remain slightly skeptical of his view, wondering whether their ignorance is exaggerated in the telling.

---

[5]The description is a *part* of such a story, but in these paragraphs Angelou is essentially an observer, outside the action.

I mention this possibility of distortion because it is particularly strong in the case of reports on personalities. When we discuss people, we almost automatically use language like "You know the type" or "What kind of man is he?" We create pigeonholes into which a new acquaintance or a public figure can be put. At its worst, this way of thinking produces crude and unrealistic stereotypes, sterotyping so offensive and destructive that we might wish we could forget about types altogether and deal with each individual as an individual. As an ethical position, this refusal to deal in types has merit. The difficulty is that we confront such a bewildering number of people that our minds are overwhelmed if we don't form some generalizations. Eventually, most of us will conclude—if only for convenience—that some people are flatterers, some are perfectionists, some are bigots, some are liberals, and so forth. Recognizing the type helps us know how to act, even how to feel, when we confront the individual.

THE THEOPHRASTAN CHARACTER: THE CHARACTER TYPE AS FRAMEWORK

To get a clearer picture of how such "types" work in reports on persons, let's begin by examining a short essay that presents a "pure" type—one that doesn't pretend to represent an individual. The author is Theophrastus, an ancient Greek philosopher.

Faultfinding is being unreasonably critical of your portion in life. For example, a friend sends over a serving of the main dinner course with his compliments: the faultfinder is the kind who says to the messenger, "You can go tell your master I said that he didn't want me to have a taste of his soup and his third-rate wine— that's why he wouldn't give me a dinner invitation." And even while his mistress is kissing him he will complain, "I wonder if you really love me the way you say you do." He gets angry with the weather, too, not because it rained but because it didn't rain soon enough.

If he comes on a wallet in the street, his comment is "Always this—never a real find!" Let him get a slave at bargain prices, moreover, after begging and pleading, and what does he say but "I really wonder if the fellow can be in sound shape, seeing that he was so cheap." Or supposing somebody announces, "You've got a baby boy!" He meets this good news with: "You might as well have told me half my estate's down the drain—that's what it really means." What's more, he can win a case with every single ballot in his favor; he will still claim that his lawyer passed over a lot of sound arguments. And when friends have raised a loan to help him out and one of them asks him, "Aren't you pleased?" his answer is "How can I be, when I have to pay everybody back and then act grateful besides?"

"The Faultfinder"
—THEOPHRASTUS

Theophrastus wrote thirty such characters, memorable because of the author's eye and ear for particular details. His Flatterer, for instance, dispenses compliments while "he is pulling a loose thread from your coat or picking a piece of chaff the wind has blown onto your hair." When it is the Pinch-penny's turn to have neighbors over for a meal, he has the meat cut into tiny slices. On shipboard the Coward is the one "who mistakes a rocky headland for a pirate brig, and who asks if there are unbelievers on board when a big wave hits the side."

The formula for a Theophrastan character is very simple. It begins with a sentence defining the character type and then presents a series of details, as precise as possible and with as little commentary as possible. Though they are sometimes humorous, Theophrastus's characters were written for the purpose of moral instruction. By presenting his students with clear pictures of various character faults, he was giving them, indirectly, a series of lessons in morality and psychology. The composition of the characters was an essentially scientific project. Like Aristotle, Theophrastus was a great botanist who delighted in collecting specimens of plants and categorizing them by species, genus, and family according to their similarities. The writing of the characters was, so to speak, human botanizing—an attempt to identify the different species of men who could be found in Athens.

EXERCISE 6

◆ *A List of Character Types.* Theophrastus left us thirty characters, suggesting that he had observed thirty distinct species of Athenians. Consider the community around you. Name at least half a dozen character types that you think are common in the population. Keep this list as a basis for Assignment 2 at this chapter's end.

EXERCISE 7

◆ *A Rewrite of "The Faultfinder."* Theophrastus illustrates "The Fault-finder" with examples drawn from daily life in ancient Athens. Retaining his first sentence, rewrite the character using examples drawn from the daily life of your own community.

THE INDIVIDUAL PERSONALITY IN THE FRAMEWORK OF THE GENERAL CHARACTER

Since it is about a type rather than an individual, the "Theophrastan character" keeps writers out of some kinds of trouble. They may gather details from the study of actual people, but since no one is mentioned by name in the sketch itself, no one would dare to complain. Who would have threatened to sue Theophrastus by claiming to be the model for "The Faultfinder" or "The Pinch-Penny"? Only someone who wanted to appear, unnamed, in "The Dunce."

But readers are usually eager to learn about "real people" rather than about types. Or, rather, they are eager to learn about real people *as* types. When we analyze the profiles of public personalities that appear very frequently in books, newspapers, and magazines, we quickly discover that the individual is being portrayed against the backdrop of a well-known character type. In effect, the framework for a personality profile is something like a

Theophrastan character, and the writer sets out to prove that the subject is an example of the species (perhaps with some variations from the normal type). When such a profile is well done, readers learn on two levels at once. Barbara Tuchman's description of Lord Shaftesbury helps us understand a particular person by associating him with a type we have encountered before, the Man of Duty. At the same time, her description enriches our understanding of the type by giving us a concrete example.

The writer may choose to present a subject as a positive type or a negative one. The important thing is to be clear, to leave in the reader's mind a strong impression of the ways that the individual fits the type. Consider, for example, the following profile of C. Everett Koop by journalist Ellen Goodman. As you may remember, Koop was a controversial figure. Appointed by President Reagan because he seemed to fit the type of the religious conservative, he behaved in office in a way that pleased liberals like Goodman. In her attempt to explain this enigmatic figure, Goodman presents him as an example of another type altogether.

"C. Everett Koop"
—ELLEN GOODMAN

When C. Everett Koop was nominated for the post of Surgeon General in 1981, I was among those who let out a collective and public groan.

Koop? The author of the pro-life tract, "The Slide to Auschwitz"? *That* Koop? The star of a documentary in which he waded through waters surrounded by floating doll-fetuses? The man who delivered an address containing a sci-fi parable about a time when "secular humanism" was the state anti-religion and a gay organization created "100,000 homosexual and lesbian test-tube babies to give the gay movement more political clout"?

It was an ominous resume. And the photo attached—of a stern and patriarchal man—wasn't reassuring. *The New York Times,* not noted for its wit, called him "Dr. Unqualified" and cartoonists caricatured "Chick" Koop as one of the Reagan foxes put in charge of the federal "chicken coops."

Notice that Goodman begins with a view of Koop as someone belonging to a type she dislikes.

But by the time Koop left office last summer, grim predictions had turned into rave reviews. Jeffrey Lewis, executive director of the National Gay & Lesbian Task Force, spoke for many when he said, "The bottom line on Koop is that it shows you never should give up on anyone, whether it's your parents or the surgeon general."

Why does Goodman cite this source?

The brass-buttoned uniform Koop wore was as transforming as a superhero's cape. It took him up, up and away from the narrow perspective of a pediatric surgeon to the viewing post of chief of the nation's health. He rose above both religious and political constituencies.

Within a matter of years, Koop became the nation's family doctor: patriarchal, deadly serious and wholly credible. The man who had made housecalls to his patients became the surgeon general who entered every American living room with messages for our own good.

Chick Koop gradually became a celebrity of the Reagan Era: the surgeon general who didn't mince words. He called a spade a spade, a condom a condom, and the tobacco companies "sleazy." And he did it through a series of surprises that disarmed his old foes and dismayed his political friends.

Can you see any reason
for presenting the sur-
prises in the order
Goodman does?

Why would Goodman
choose this particular
quotation from all
Koop's statements and
publications?

How must Koop *as an
individual* have felt
about this report?

Why is the word *imper-
sonal* important here?

Is an "independent citi-
zen" the same thing as a
"private individual"?

Why does Goodman re-
fer repeatedly to the
uniform?

Surprise One: smoking. Koop went further than any surgeon general in his opposition to tobacco. Using the bully pulpit, he helped toughen the warnings on cigarette packages, argued against exporting the evil weed to Third World countries, and supported smoking restrictions in federal buildings and on airplanes. To the dismay of the Reagan administration, he even talked about smoking as an addiction and testified against tobacco ads.

Surprise Two: AIDS. While many on the Right saw AIDS as a punishment for sexual activity and especially for "sexual deviance," Koop said, "I am the Surgeon General of the heterosexuals and the homosexuals . . . so I can tell you how to keep yourself alive no matter what you are. That's my job." He proceeded to do so in a frank report on AIDS, followed by an equally frank brochure that won him the title of "condom king" among the disappointed Right.

In the name of AIDS he debated setting up needle exchanges for addicts and sex education for children and then videotaped a lecture for soldiers that included this line: "The rectum was not designed for sexual intercourse."

Surprise Three: Abortion. The Reagan-ites asked this ardent pro-lifer to report on the effects of abortion on women. The goal was to portray women as miserable victims of abortionists. He reported back that some women had regrets and others had relief. No report.

As the Phyllis Schlaflys began to rescind their support and their dinner invitations, he said, in a classic Koop understatement: "I am not looked upon as a controllable individual."

And that was the key to Koop.

At some point, when much was being made of the changes in Koop's perspective, he demurred. "I haven't changed one iota during my tenure as Surgeon General." In some respects that was true. Koop was always a man of integrity.

As a doctor, Koop learned that his first obligation is to the patient, and that view didn't waver when he found the entire nation in his waiting room. As a surgeon he was part of a caste of doctors proud of doing their work with a cool, even impersonal emphasis on skill. Koop brought that bias to the work at hand.

Others in Washington may originally have seen the job as a modest political post, with a more modest budget. Who is this person, after all, who reported to a mere undersecretary of HHS? In his uniform Koop sometimes looked like a humorless Dutch ship captain. But this serious man took his job seriously. He didn't behave like a political appointee but like an independent citizen.

"What bothered the very conservative people," he said during the flap over AIDS, "was that I wasn't willing to abandon those who didn't take the message of abstinence and monogamy. Well, I'm their Surgeon General as well." He had a national caseload, not a political message. He put medicine above ideology.

The man in the uniform was no scientific stalwart. To this day, he refutes the key principles of evolution. But he acted out of a sense of duty that won him and his office respect. When presented with evidence on AIDS or abortion or addiction, good medicine was his highest morality.

And of such stuff is heroism made in the '80s. In an era when policy is often set by poll-takers, Koop asked for the evidence, not the numbers. In an era when so-called leaders assess where the majority is on an issue and follow them, Koop tried to assess what was best for our health and he stood firm there. In an era when high-ranking officials try to make issues as uncontroversial as possible, Koop went at them in his own inimitable, straight-ahead fashion.

It may be a commentary on the times that in modern America you can become a hero for everyday honesty. But maybe there's a lesson in the tale of Chick Koop. Today, at the close of the '80s, Americans look at politicians with intense cynicism. But one independent, uncompromising public servant left office with his epaulets unruffled and his brass buttons still shining.

Goodman's sketch of Koop grew out of an assignment: the magazine *Savvy Woman* had set her and nine other writers the task of profiling some of the most significant figures of the 1980s. Under these circumstances the reader's interest naturally starts with the individual, and the question that drives the writing is "What sort of man is X?" In other circumstances, the reader will be interested in the individual only as a representative of a group, and the question that drives the writing may be "What is a Moslem fundamentalist (or a Ku Klux Klanner or an oral surgeon) *really* like?" To answer such a question by presenting a single case is obviously a risky procedure, but the result can be fascinating even to those who reserve judgment on its accuracy.

◆ *A Counter-Characterization.* Obviously, Goodman's characterization of Koop would not be accepted by some of Koop's critics. Using the information Goodman has given you and your own knowledge, construct a brief (100-word) counter-characterization that challenges Goodman's view.

EXERCISE 8

◆ *Preparing to Report on the "Type" Associated with a Group.* Name a well-defined group that interests you and that has members in your community or on your campus—Baptist ministers, for example, or pool sharks. Write a few sentences describing the type of person generally thought to belong to the group. You now have a pattern of expectation that can serve as a basis for research. Imagine that you have an opportunity to interview a member of the group in order to confirm or overturn this pattern of expectation. Develop ten questions that you believe would be particularly useful in the interview.

EXERCISE 9

RESEARCHING AND WRITING A REPORT BASED ON OBSERVATION: POINTS TO CONSIDER

Charles Darwin used to say that no one could be a good observer unless he was an active theorizer. Details become interesting and memorable only when you see them in a framework. Therefore, it is best to begin your observa-

MAYA ANGELOU

© 1990 Jill Krementz

"I have too often hated words, despised their elusive nature. Loathed them for skittering around evading their responsibility to convey meaning. Conversely, they have frequently infuriated me by being inert, heavy, ponderous. Lying like stones on a page, unwilling to skip, impervious to my prodding."

Maya Angelou has been a traumatized child in a racist town, an unwed teenage mother, a streetcar conductor, a Creole cook, a madam, a cocktail waitress, a dancer in nightclubs and on great stages, an actress, a singer and songwriter, a civil rights organizer, a newspaper editor, and a film director. She has lived and worked in various cities in America, Europe, and Africa.

By the time she was forty, she had lived in poverty and wealth, made famous friends and unknown ones, participated in the American civil rights movement, and witnessed the liberation movement in Africa. A group of friends, listening to her stories one night at dinner, convinced her to write her autobiography, and she has thrown herself into the project with gusto.

Reporting on people, places, and events from memory presents some difficulties—details are lost, and even if recovered, they may not revive the spirit of the times. Angelou tries to "get back" by a strict, though somewhat quirky, discipline. "I keep a hotel room in which I do my work—a tiny, mean room with just a bed, and sometimes, if I can find it, a face basin. I keep a dictionary, a Bible, a deck of cards, and a bottle of sherry in the room." She stays in the room at least six hours a day—sometimes for much longer—concentrating so hard on her past life that she temporarily forgets the present: during one intense period of work, she stopped eating for days, until a worried friend appeared silently at the hotel with a casserole in hand.

The discipline has been rewarded. Her first book, *I Know Why the Caged Bird Sings* (1970), was an immediate success and has been followed by four other volumes of autobiography and three of poetry. Today Angelou has a large, diverse, and enthusiastic following. "I speak to the black experience," Angelou once said, "but I am always talking about the human condition—about what we can endure, dream, fail at, and still survive." ◆

tion and note-taking with one or more hypotheses in mind. Reporting on a local athletic star, you might begin with the hypothesis that she is a compulsive worker, someone who constantly drives herself to succeed. If you begin your research with this hypothesis in mind, you may notice that when you interview her, she is compulsively tidying her desk, and you may recognize this as a detail pertinent to the framework of your report. Even hypotheses that are overthrown by research are valuable because they focus our attention.

When you begin your research, gather more details than you think you can possibly use. Only a fraction of these may appear in the final essay, but in the process of drafting, you may change your mind about which details are most important. Begin with an oversupply, and you will be able to pick and choose.

The more you learn about your subject, the more uncomfortable you may be with simplifying it by presenting a single view of it. If your subject is a person, for instance, you may feel that it would be truer to present her as twelve things rather than one: she is a mother, a doctor, a gardener, a faultfinder, a sports fan, a political conservative, an agnostic, an audiophile, the product of a broken home, an overachiever, a liar on petty issues, and an example of someone who got one good break and ran with it. As a practical matter, though, writers always have limited space and readers have limited attention spans. You will be forced to choose some view of your multifaceted subject and make it dominant. As Theodore White once said, "A writer must invent the outline of the man he fitfully glimpses."

Sometimes the writer has space and time to present a somewhat more complex report on a subject; see, for example, White's report on President Carter (page 148). Even in this situation, your reader is likely to be happier and less confused if you limit yourself to a very few aspects of the subject's character. White identifies five for Carter, but concentrates on two.

QUESTIONS FOR PEER REVIEW

If you have an opportunity for peer review, ask your reviewer for both general comments (see the checklist on pages 65–66) and for answers to three particular questions:

1. Do all of my examples contribute to one impression, or do they point in somewhat different directions and so blur the impression? Which examples seem most to the point? Which seems farthest from the point?

2. Are my examples graphic? That is, do they engage the senses and do they show specific actions and objects? Which examples are most lively? Which are least lively?

3. Have I stereotyped my subject in a way that is offensive or clearly false?

Having benefited from this review, revise until you are prepared to stand behind the validity of your characterization, the quality of each supporting detail, and the effectiveness of each sentence. If you are like most writers, you will find plenty to regret even in the most careful "final" draft, but the first draft that goes to your teacher should be one that you were satisfied with, at least temporarily.

ASSIGNMENT 1: ### *A Report on a Place*

For this assignment you will act as a journalist whose job is to characterize a place you presume your readers have not seen. Since you are probably not able to travel far while classes are in session, you may have to rely on memory for your report. The memory of a recent journey may serve you best since success will depend largely on recalling precise details.

Don't overlook the possibility of traveling locally and reporting on a place unfamiliar to many of your classmates. You might produce an interesting report on a club or restaurant, a neighborhood, a museum, or other public building. A visit to the city jail may provide you with more to write about than a vacation to Paris.

ASSIGNMENT 2: ### *A Report on an Occasion*

In this case your assignment is a very common one for reporters on local papers: attend an event and write a report that gives those who did not attend it a sense of what they missed. Angelou's description of a party reminds us, however, that an event needn't be newsworthy to be interesting. The key is that it should arouse curiosity, that people should wonder what such an occasion is like. A concert by a well-known artist might, therefore, be a good subject, but an amateur barbershop quartet contest might be more interesting still. Those who have never been present at a livestock auction, a political protest rally, or a beauty contest may be interested in a report that gives them a strong impression of what such events are like.

ASSIGNMENT 3: ### *A Theophrastan Character*

Following as precisely as possible the formula used by Theophrastus himself, write a "character" that exemplifies a vice or a virtue. Your sketch, though it deals with a general type, should be filled with particular details and actions.

ASSIGNMENT 4: ### *A Report on an Acquaintance*

Write a report on someone you know well and whose personality you believe your classmates will find interesting. The challenge here will be twofold, to show that your acquaintance embodies a "type" worth discussing and to illustrate your characterization with graphic details: actions, words, appearances, contrasts, and so forth.

ASSIGNMENT 5: *AN INTERVIEW-BASED REPORT ON A "PUBLIC FIGURE"*

For this assignment, your mission is to characterize a person who by vocation, avocation, or name is likely to arouse the sort of interest that might result in a story in a local newspaper. Your primary sources of information should *not* be other published reports but direct observation and interviews with the subject and perhaps with others who know the subject. You will want to choose a subject likely to grant you an interview, of course. You might interview a musician, artist, actor or actress (amateur or professional), an especially popular teacher, the writer of a book, a dedicated athlete, a politician in the community or a student politician, or someone committed to a controversial cause. Write for an audience curious to know what makes such a person tick.

ASSIGNMENT 6: *A REPORT ON A CHARACTER IN A SHORT STORY OR POEM*

The people we encounter in literature often approach the complexity of those we meet in life, and they are often presented with very little commentary by the author. To practice the close reading of a literary work and demonstrate your ability to write a focused report, write a 250-word description of one of the following characters.

1. The Duke or the Duchess in "My Last Duchess" (p. 381)
2. Connie in "Where Are You Going, Where Have You Been?" (p. 384)
3. Manny or the narrator in "The Hammer Man" (p. 394)
4. Myra or Helen in "The Day of the Butterfly" (p. 398)
5. Dade or his father in "Star Food" (p. 403)

COPPER MINING IN NORTHERN CHILE

Charles Darwin

Darwin's Journal of Researches into the Natural History and Geology of the countries visited during the Voyage of H.M.S. Beagle Round the World *(usually called* The Voyage of the Beagle) *is one of the great travel books of all time. Like many travel books, Darwin's is organized chronologically: the writer simply takes up the various sights in the order that he encountered them. Such books rarely have a general thesis, but they often have smaller intellectual frameworks—points made in a paragraph or a passage. As you read the following account, notice Darwin's sharp eye, but also notice that he is always dealing in ideas and theories.*

1   FINDING THE COAST-ROAD DEVOID OF INTER-est of any kind, we turned inland towards the mining district and valley of Illapel. This valley, like every other in Chile, is level, broad, and very fertile: It is bordered on each side, either by cliffs of stratified shingle, or by bare rocky mountains. Above the straight line of the uppermost irrigating ditch, all is brown as on a high road; while all below is of as bright a green as verdigris, from the beds of alfarfa, a kind of clover. We proceeded to Los Hornos, another mining district, where the principal hill was drilled with holes, like a great ants'-nest. The Chilian miners are a peculiar race of men in their habits. Living for weeks together in the most desolate spots, when they descend to the villages on feast-days, there is no ex-cess or extravagance into which they do not run. They sometimes gain a considerable sum, and then, like sailors with prize-money, they try how soon they can contrive to squander it. They drink excessively, buy quantities of clothes, and in a few days return pen-niless to their miserable abodes, there to work harder than beasts of burden. This thoughtlessness, as with sailors, is evidently the result of a similar manner of life. Their daily food is found them, and they acquire no habits of carefulness; moreover, temptation and the means of yielding to it are placed in their power at the same time. On the other hand, in Cornwall, and some other parts of England, where the system of sell-ing part of the vein is followed, the miners, from be-ing obliged to act and think for themselves, are a sin-gularly intelligent and well-conducted set of men.

2   The dress of the Chilian miner is peculiar and rather picturesque. He wears a very long shirt of some dark-coloured baize, with a leathern apron; the whole being fastened round his waist by a bright-coloured sash. His trowsers are very broad, and his small cap of scarlet cloth is made to fit the head closely. We met a party of these miners in full costume, carrying the body of one of their companions to be buried. They marched at a very quick trot, four men supporting the corpse. One set having run as hard as they could for about two hundred yards, were relieved by four

others, who had previously dashed on ahead on horseback. Thus they proceeded, encouraging each other by wild cries: altogether the scene formed a most strange funeral.

We continued travelling northward, in a zigzag line; sometimes stopping a day to geologise. The country was so thinly inhabited, and the track so obscure, that we often had difficulty in finding our way. On the 12th I stayed at some mines. The ore in this case was not considered particularly good, but from being abundant it was supposed the mine would sell for about thirty or forty thousand dollars (that is, 6000 or 8000 pounds sterling); yet it had been bought by one of the English Associations for an ounce of gold (3*l*. 8*s*.). The ore is yellow pyrites, which, as I have already remarked, before the arrival of the English, was not supposed to contain a particle of copper. On a scale of profits nearly as great as in the above instance, piles of cinders, abounding with minute globules of metallic copper, were purchased; yet with these advantages, the mining associations, as is well known, contrived to lose immense sums of money. The folly of the greater number of the commissioners and shareholders amounted to infatuation;—a thousand pounds per annum given in some cases to entertain the Chilian authorities; libraries of well-bound geological books; miners brought out for particular metals, as tin, which are not found in Chile; contracts to supply the miners with milk, in parts where there are no cows; machinery, where it could not possibly be used; and a hundred similar arrangements, bore witness to our absurdity, and to this day afford amusement to the natives. Yet there can be no doubt, that the same capital well employed in these mines would have yielded an immense return: a confidential man of business, a practical miner and assayer, would have been all that was required.

4   Captain Head has described the wonderful load which the "Apires,"[1] truly beasts of burden, carry up from the deepest mines. I confess I thought the account exaggerated; so that I was glad to take an op-

portunity of weighing one of the loads, which I picked out by hazard. It required considerable exertion on my part, when standing directly over it, to lift it from the ground. The load was considered under weight when found to be 197 pounds. The apire had carried this up eighty perpendicular yards,—part of the way by a steep passage, but the greater part up notched poles, placed in a zigzag line up the shaft. According to the general regulation, the apire is not allowed to halt for breath, except the mine is six hundred feet deep. The average load is considered as rather more than 200 pounds, and I have been assured that one of 300 pounds (twenty-two stone and a half) by way of a trial has been brought up from the deepest mine! At this time the apires were bringing up the usual load twelve times in the day; that is, 2400 pounds from eighty yards deep; and they were employed in the intervals in breaking and picking ore.

These men, excepting from accidents, are   5 healthy, and appear cheerful. Their bodies are not very muscular. They rarely eat meat once a week, and never oftener, and then only the hard dry charqui. Although with a knowledge that the labour was voluntary, it was nevertheless quite revolting to see the state in which they reached the mouth of the mine; their bodies bent forward, leaning with their arms on the steps, their legs bowed, their muscles quivering, the perspiration streaming from their faces over their breasts, their nostrils distended, the corners of their mouth forcibly drawn back, and the expulsion of their breath most laborious. Each time they draw their breath, they utter an articulate cry of "ay-ay," which ends in a sound rising from deep in the chest, but shrill like the note of a fife. After staggering to the pile of ore, they emptied the "carpacho;" in two or three seconds recovering their breath, they wiped the sweat from their brows, and apparently quite fresh descended the mine again at a quick pace. This appears to me a wonderful instance of the amount of labour which habit, for it can be nothing else, will enable a man to endure. ◆

---

[1]"Apires": mine workers.

EDUCATION

E. B. White

In the fall of 1938 E. B. White, who had for some time been living part-time on a forty-acre farm in Maine, left New York City to live on it permanently. The move created dramatic changes in his life and the life of his family and also produced a much admired series of monthly essays for Harper's *magazine, giving citified readers a fresh view of life in the country. The following passage was first published in* Harper's *in March 1939 and later collected in* One Man's Meat *(1942).*

1   *I* HAVE AN INCREASING ADMIRATION FOR THE teacher in the country school where we have a third-grade scholar in attendance. She not only undertakes to instruct her charges in all the subjects of the first three grades, but she manages to function quietly and effectively as a guardian of their health, their clothes, their habits, their mothers, and their snowball engagements. She has been doing this sort of Augean task for twenty years, and is both kind and wise. She cooks for the children on the stove that heats the room, and she can cool their passions or warm their soup with equal competence. She conceives their costumes, cleans up their messes, and shares their confidences. My boy already regards his teacher as his great friend, and I think tells her a great deal more than he tells us.

2   The shift from city school to country school was something we worried about quietly all last summer. I have always rather favored public school over private school, if only because in public school you meet a greater variety of children. This bias of mine, I suspect, is partly an attempt to justify my own past (I never knew anything but public schools) and partly an involuntary defense against getting kicked in the shins by a young ceramist on his way to the kiln. My wife was unacquainted with public schools, never having been exposed (in her early life) to anything more public than the washroom of Miss Winsor's. Regardless of our backgrounds, we both knew that the change in schools was something that concerned not us but the scholar himself. We hoped it would work out all right. In New York our son went to a medium-priced private institution with semi-progressive ideas of education, and modern plumbing. He learned fast, kept well, and we were satisfied. It was an electric, colorful, regimented existence with moments of pleasurable pause and giddy incident. The day the Christmas angel fainted and had to be carried out by one of the Wise Men was educational in the highest sense of the term. Our scholar gave imitations of it around the house for weeks afterwards, and I doubt if it ever goes completely out of his mind.

3   His days were rich in formal experience. Wearing overalls and an old sweater (the accepted uniform of the private seminary), he sallied forth at morn accompanied by a nurse or a parent and walked (or was pulled) two blocks to a corner where the school bus made a flag stop. This flashy vehicle was as punctual as death: seeing us waiting at the cold curb, it would sweep to a halt, open its mouth, suck the boy in, and spring away with an angry growl. It was a good deal like a train picking up a bag of mail. At school the scholar was worked on for six or seven hours by half a dozen teachers and a nurse, and was revived on orange juice in mid-morning. In a cinder court he played games supervised by an athletic instructor, and in a cafeteria he ate lunch worked out by a dietitian. He soon learned to read with gratifying facility and discernment and to make Indian weapons of a semi-deadly nature. Whenever one of his classmates fell low

of a fever the news was put on the wires and there were breathless phone calls to physicians, discussing periods of incubation and allied magic.

In the country all one can say is that the situation is different and somehow more casual. Dressed in corduroys, sweatshirt, and short rubber boots, and carrying a tin dinner-pail, our scholar departs at crack of dawn for the village school, two and a half miles down the road, next to the cemetery. When the road is open and the car will start, he makes the journey by motor, courtesy of his old man. When the snow is deep or the motor is dead or both, he makes it on the hoof. In the afternoons he walks or hitches all or part of the way home in fair weather, gets transported in foul. The schoolhouse is a two-room frame building, bungalow type, shingles stained a burnt brown with weather-resistant stain. It has a chemical toilet in the basement and two teachers above stairs. One takes the first three grades, the other the fourth, fifth, and sixth. They have little or no time for individual instruction, and no time at all for the esoteric. They teach what they know themselves, just as fast and as hard as they can manage. The pupils sit still at their desks in class, and do their milling around outdoors during recess.

5   There is no supervised play. They play cops and robbers (only they call it "Jail") and throw things at one another—snowballs in winter, rose hips in fall. It seems to satisfy them. They also construct darts, pinwheels, and "pick-up sticks" (jackstraws), and the school itself does a brisk trade in penny candy, which is for sale right in the classroom and which contains "surprises." The most highly prized surprise is a fake cigarette, made of cardboard, fiendishly lifelike.

The memory of how apprehensive we were at   6 the beginning is still strong. The boy was nervous about the change too. The tension, on that first fair morning in September when we drove him to school, almost blew the windows out of the sedan. And when later we picked him up on the road, wandering along with his little blue lunch-pail, and got his laconic report "All right" in answer to our inquiry about how the day had gone, our relief was vast. Now, after almost a year of it, the only difference we can discover in the two school experiences is that in the country he sleeps better at night—and *that* probably is more the air than the education. When grilled on the subject of school-in-country *vs.* school-in-city, he replied that the chief difference is that the day seems to go so much quicker in the country. "Just like lightning," he reported. . . . ◆

SALT LAKE CITY

James Weldon Johnson

Before he achieved political prominence, James Weldon Johnson was a singer and songwriter, collaborating with his brother John Rosamond Johnson and Bob Cole, a more seasoned performer. For a time the trio performed on Broadway and on the "Orpheum Circuit" through the western United States. Travels on the circuit gave Johnson a view of a variety of American cities early in this century. The following report on his experiences in Salt Lake City is from Along This Way *(1933).*

1 JUST BEFORE SPRING IN 1905, BOB AND ROSA-
mond started again over the Orpheum Circuit; I made
the trip with them. Some other performers who were
playing the same circuit and who left Denver for San
Francisco on the same train with us had planned to
stop off for a day at Salt Lake City to visit the Mor-
mon Tabernacle and see the town. They persuaded us
to do likewise. We had our tickets adjusted for a stop-
over until the next day and got off the train at Salt
Lake City. We took a carriage, and directed the
driver, a jovial Irishman, to take us to a good hotel.
He took us to the best. Porters carried our luggage
into the lobby, and I went to the desk, turned the register round and registered for the three. The clerk was
busy at the key-rack. He glanced at us furtively, but
kept himself occupied. It grew obvious that he was
protracting the time. Finally, he could delay no longer
and came to the desk. As he came his expression revealed the lie he was to speak. He turned the register
round, examined our names, and while his face
flushed a bit said, "I'm sorry, but we haven't got a
vacant room." This statement, which I knew almost
absolutely to be false, set a number of emotions in action: humiliation, chagrin, indignation, resentment, anger; but in the midst of them all I could detect a sense
of pity for the man who had to make it, for he was,
to all appearances, an honest, decent person. It was
then about eleven o'clock, and I sought the eyes of the
clerk and asked if he expected any rooms to be
vacated at noon. He stammered that he did not. I
then said to him that we would check our bags and
take the first room available by night. Pressure from
me seemed to stiffen him, and he told us that we
could not; that we had better try some other hotel.
Our bags were taken out and a cab called, and we
found ourselves in the same vehicle that had brought
us to the hotel. Our driver voluntarily assumed a part
of our mortification, and he attempted to console us
by relating how ten or twelve years before he had
taken Peter Jackson (the famous Negro pugilist) to
that same hotel and how royally he had been entertained there. We tried two other hotels, where our ex-

periences were similar but briefer. We did not dismiss
our cabman, for we were being fast driven to the conclusion that he was probably the only compassionate
soul we should meet in the whole city of the Latter-
Day Saints.

2 We had become very hungry; we felt that it was
necessary for us to eat in order to maintain both our
morale and our endurance. Our cabman took us to a
restaurant. When we entered it was rather crowded,
but we managed to find a table and sat down. There
followed that hiatus, of which every Negro in the
United States knows the meaning. At length, a man in
charge came over and told us without any pretense of
palliation that we could not be served. We were
forced to come out under the stare of a crowd that
was conscious of what had taken place. Our cabman
was now actually touched by our plight; and he gave
vent to his feelings in explosive oaths. He suggested
another restaurant to try, where we might have "better luck"; but we were no longer up to the possible
facing of another such experience. We asked the
cabby if he knew of a colored family in town who
might furnish us with a meal; he did not, but he had
an idea; he drove along and stopped in front of a sa-
loon and chophouse; he darted inside, leaving us in
the carriage; after a few moments he emerged beaming good news. We went in and were seated at a
wholly inconspicuous table, but were served with food
and drink that quickly renewed our strength and revived our spirits.

3 However, we were almost immediately confronted with the necessity of getting a place to sleep.
Our cabby had another idea; he drove us to a woman
he knew who kept a lodging house for laborers. It
was a pretty shabby place; nevertheless, the woman
demurred for quite a while. Finally, she agreed to let
us stay, if we got out before her regular lodgers got
up. In the foul room to which she showed us, we
hesitated until the extreme moment of weariness before we could bring ourselves to bear the touch of the
soiled bedclothes. We smoked and talked over the
situation we were in, the situation of being outcasts

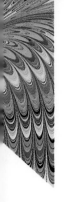

and pariahs in a city of our own and native land. Our talk went beyond our individual situation and took in the common lot of Negroes in well-nigh every part of the country, a lot which lays on high and low the constant struggle to renerve their hearts and wills against the unremitting pressure of unfairness, injustice, wrong, cruelty, contempt, and hate. If what we felt had been epitomized and expressed in but six words, they would have been: A hell of a "my country."

4   We welcomed daybreak. For numerous reasons we were glad to get out of the beds of our unwilling hostess. We boarded our train with feelings of unbounded relief; I with a vow never to set foot again in Salt Lake City. Twenty-three years later, I passed through Salt Lake City, as one of a large delegation on the way to a conference of the National Association for the Advancement of Colored People held in Los Angeles. Our train had a wait of a couple of hours, and the delegation went out to see the town, the Tabernacle, and the lake. I spent the time alone at the railroad station.

5   Concerning this particular lapse from democracy in America, I have heard many people declare that the remedy for the situation is for Negroes to have places of their own. Aside from any principle of common rights, the suggestion is absurd. At the time of which I have been speaking, Negroes in Salt Lake City constituted an infinitesimal element in the community, and Negroes who visited there, a still smaller element; therefore it is evident that no hotel nor even a modest boarding house for "Negroes only" could have been operated on a commercial basis. Such an institution would have demanded a subsidy. Negroes in many localities where their numbers are large have, from necessity, and as often from choice, provided certain places of public accommodation for themselves; but to say that they should duplicate the commercial and social machinery of the nation is to utter an inanity. It takes all New York and its hundreds of thousands of visitors to support one grand opera company. If I want to hear grand opera in New York I must go to the Metropolitan Opera House. To tell Negroes that they ought to get their own opera house

in Harlem if they want to hear grand opera would not be less unreasonable than to tell them to get their own railroads if they want to ride in Pullman cars, and just about as reasonable as telling them to have hotels in all cities and towns in which a Negro traveler might, perchance, stop over.

6   I was delighted with San Francisco. Here was a civilized center, metropolitan and urbane. With respect to the Negro race, I found it a freer city than New York. I encountered no bar against me in hotels, restaurants, theaters, or other places of public accommodation and entertainment. We hired a furnished apartment in the business area, and took our meals wherever it was most convenient. I moved about with a sense of confidence and security, and entirely from under that cloud of doubt and apprehension that constantly hangs over an intelligent Negro in every Southern city and in a great many cities of the North. ◆

REFLECTIONS ON GANDHI

George Orwell

Book reviews often extend beyond an evaluation of the book and become discussions of the book's subject, particularly when the writer is as strong-minded as George Orwell. The following review of Mohandas Gandhi's autobiography clearly became an evaluation of the life of the man whose techniques of nonviolent resistance hastened the British withdrawal from India. The review first appeared in The Partisan Review *in January 1949, about a year after Gandhi's assassination and before the majority of Westerners had decided what view to take of his life and career. It was reprinted in* Shooting an Elephant *(1950).*

1   SAINTS SHOULD ALWAYS BE JUDGED GUILTY until they are proved innocent, but the tests that have to be applied to them are not, of course, the same in all cases. In Gandhi's case the questions one feels inclined to ask are: to what extent was Gandhi moved by vanity—by the consciousness of himself as a humble, naked old man, sitting on a praying mat and shaking empires by sheer spiritual power—and to what extent did he compromise his own principles by entering politics, which of their nature are inseparable from coercion and fraud? To give a definite answer one would have to study Gandhi's acts and writings in immense detail, for his whole life was a sort of pilgrimage in which every act was significant. But this partial autobiography,[1] which ends in the nineteen-twenties, is strong evidence in his favor, all the more because it covers what he would have called the unregenerate part of his life and reminds one that inside the saint, or near-saint, there was a very shrewd, able person who could, if he had chosen, have been a brilliant success as a lawyer, an administrator, or perhaps even a businessman.

---

[1] *The Story of my Experiments with Truth.* By M. K. Gandhi. Translated from the Gujarati by Mahadex Desai. Public Affairs Press. [author's note]

2   At about the time when the autobiography first appeared I remember reading its opening chapters in the ill-printed pages of some Indian newspaper. They made a good impression on me, which Gandhi himself at that time, did not. The things that one associated with him—home-spun cloth, "soul forces," and vegetarianism—were unappealing, and his medievalist program was obviously not viable in a backward, starving, overpopulated country. It was also apparent that the British were making use of him, or thought they were making use of him. Strictly speaking, as a Nationalist, he was an enemy, but since in every crisis he would exert himself to prevent violence—which, from the British point of view, meant preventing any effective action whatever—he could be regarded as "our man." In private this was sometimes cynically admitted. The attitude of the Indian millionaires was similar. Gandhi called upon them to repent, and naturally they preferred him to the Socialists and Communists who, given the chance, would actually have taken their money away. How reliable such calculations are in the long run is doubtful; as Gandhi himself says, "in the end deceivers deceive only themselves"; but at any rate the gentleness with which he was nearly always handled was due partly to the feeling that he was useful. The British Conservatives only became really angry with him when, as in 1942, he

was in effect turning his non-violence against a different conqueror.

But I could see even then that the British officials who spoke of him with a mixture of amusement and disapproval also genuinely liked and admired him, after a fashion. Nobody ever suggested that he was corrupt, or ambitious in any vulgar way, or that anything he did was actuated by fear or malice. In judging a man like Gandhi one seems instinctively to apply high standards, so that some of his virtues have passed almost unnoticed. For instance, it is clear even from the autobiography that his natural physical courage was quite outstanding: the manner of his death was a later illustration of this, for a public man who attached any value to his own skin would have been more adequately guarded. Again, he seems to have been quite free from that maniacal suspiciousness which, as E. M. Forster rightly says in *A Passage to India*, is the besetting Indian vice, as hypocrisy is the British vice. Although no doubt he was shrewd enough in detecting dishonesty, he seems whenever possible to have believed that other people were acting in good faith and had a better nature through which they could be approached. And though he came of a poor middle-class family, started life rather unfavorably, and was probably of unimpressive physical appearance, he was not afflicted by envy or by the feeling of inferiority. Color feeling when he first met it in its worst form in South Africa, seems rather to have astonished him. Even when he was fighting what was in effect a color war, he did not think of people in terms of race or status. The governor of a province, a cotton millionaire, a half-starved Dravidian coolie, a British private soldier were all equally human beings, to be approached in much the same way. It is noticeable that even in the worst possible circumstances, as in South Africa when he was making himself unpopular as the champion of the Indian community, he did not lack European friends.

Written in short lengths for newspaper serialization, the autobiography is not a literary masterpiece, but it is the more impressive because of the commonplaceness of much of its material. It is well to be reminded that Gandhi started out with the normal ambitions of a young Indian student and only adopted his extremist opinions by degrees and, in some cases, rather unwillingly. There was a time, it is interesting to learn, when he wore a top hat, took dancing lessons, studied French and Latin, went up the Eiffel Tower, and even tried to learn the violin—all this was the idea of assimilating European civilization as thoroughly as possible. He was not one of those saints who are marked out by their phenomenal piety from childhood onward, nor one of the other kind who forsake the world after sensational debaucheries. He makes full confession of the misdeeds of his youth, but in fact there is not much to confess. As a frontispiece to the book there is a photograph of Gandhi's possessions at the time of his death. The whole outfit could be purchased for about £5, and Gandhi's sins, at least his fleshly sins, would make the same sort of appearance if placed all in one heap. A few cigarettes, a few mouthfuls of meat, a few annas pilfered in childhood from the maidservant, two visits to a brothel (on each occasion he got away without "doing anything"), one narrowly escaped lapse with his landlady in Plymouth, one outburst of temper—that is about the whole collection. Almost from childhood onward he had a deep earnestness, an attitude ethical rather than religious, but, until he was about thirty, no very definite sense of direction. His first entry into anything describable as public life was made by way of vegetarianism. Underneath his less ordinary qualities one feels all the time the solid middle-class businessmen who were his ancestors. One feels that even after he had abandoned personal ambition he must have been a resourceful, energetic lawyer and a hardheaded political organizer, careful in keeping down expenses, an adroit handler of committees and an indefatigable chaser of subscriptions. His character was an extraordinarily mixed one, but there was almost nothing in it that you can put your finger on and call bad, and I believe that even Gandhi's worst enemies would admit that he was an interesting and unusual man who enriched the world simply by being alive. Whether he was also a lovable man, and whether his teachings can have much value for those who do not accept the religious beliefs on which they are founded,

I have never felt fully certain.

5   Of late years it has been the fashion to talk about Gandhi as though he were not only sympathetic to the Western left-wing movement, but were integrally part of it. Anarchists and pacifists, in particular, have claimed him for their own, noticing only that he was opposed to centralism and State violence and ignoring the other-worldly, anti-humanist tendency of his doctrines. But one should, I think, realize that Gandhi's teachings cannot be squared with the belief that Man is the measure of all things and that our job is to make life worth living on this earth, which is the only earth we have. They make sense only on the assumption that God exists and that the world of solid objects is an illusion to be escaped from. It is worth considering the disciplines which Gandhi imposed on himself and which—though he might not insist on every one of his followers observing every detail—he considered indispensable if one wanted to serve either God or humanity. First of all, no meat-eating, and if possible no animal food in any form. (Gandhi himself, for the sake of his health, had to compromise on milk, but seems to have felt this to be a backsliding.) No alcohol or tobacco, and no spices or condiments even of a vegetable kind, since food should be taken not for its own sake but solely in order to preserve one's strength. Secondly, if possible, no sexual intercourse. If sexual intercourse must happen, then it should be for the sole purpose of begetting children and presumably at long intervals. Gandhi himself, in his middle thirties, took the vow of *brahmacharya,* which means not only complete chastity but the elimination of sexual desire. This condition, it seems, is difficult to attain without a special diet and frequent fasting. One of the dangers of milk-drinking is that it is apt to arouse sexual desire. And finally—this is the cardinal point—for the seeker after goodness there must be no close friendships and no exclusive loves whatever.

6   Close friendships, Gandhi says, are dangerous, because "friends react on one another" and through loyalty to a friend one can be led into wrong-doing. This is unquestionably true. Moreover, if one is to love God, or to love humanity as a whole, one cannot give one's preference to any individual person. This again is true, and it marks the point at which the humanistic and the religious attitude cease to be reconcilable. To an ordinary human being, love means nothing if it does not mean loving some people more than others. The autobiography leaves it uncertain whether Gandhi behaved in an inconsiderate way to his wife and children, but at any rate it makes clear that on three occasions he was willing to let his wife or a child die rather than administer the animal food prescribed by the doctor. It is true that the threatened death never actually occurred, and also that Gandhi—with, one gathers, a good deal of moral pressure in the opposite direction—always gave the patient the choice of staying alive at the price of committing a sin: still, if the decision had been solely his own, he would have forbidden the animal food, whatever the risks might be. There must, he says, be some limit to what we will do in order to remain alive, and the limit is well on this side of chicken broth. This attitude is perhaps a noble one, but, in the sense which—I think—most people would give to the word, it is inhuman. The essence of being human is that one does not seek perfection, that one *is* sometimes willing to commit sins for the sake of loyalty, that one does not push asceticism to the point where it makes friendly intercourse impossible, and that one is prepared in the end to be defeated and broken up by life, which is the inevitable price of fastening one's love upon other human individuals. No doubt alcohol, tobacco, and so forth, are things that a saint must avoid, but sainthood is also a thing that human beings must avoid. There is an obvious retort to this, but one should be wary about making it. In this yogi-ridden age, it is too readily assumed that "non-attachment" is not only better than a full acceptance of earthly life, but that the ordinary man only rejects it because it is too difficult: in other words, that the average human being is a failed saint. It is doubtful whether this is true. Many people genuinely do not wish to be saints, and it is probable that some who achieve or aspire to sainthood have never felt much temptation to be human beings. If one could follow it to its psychological roots, one would, I believe, find that the main motive

for "non-attachment" is a desire to escape from the pain of living, and above all from love, which, sexual or non-sexual, is hard work. But it is not necessary here to argue whether the other-worldly or the humanistic ideal is "higher." The point is that they are incompatible. One must choose between God and Man, and all "radicals" and "progressives," from the mildest liberal to the most extreme anarchist, have in effect chosen Man.

7   However, Gandhi's pacifism can be separated to some extent from his other teachings. Its motive was religious, but he claimed also for it that it was a definite technique, a method, capable of producing desired political results. Gandhi's attitude was not that of most Western pacifists. *Satyagraha,* first evolved in South Africa, was a sort of non-violent warfare, a way of defeating the enemy without hurting him and without feeling or arousing hatred. It entailed such things as civil disobedience, strikes, lying down in front of railway trains, enduring police charges without running away and without hitting back, and the like. Gandhi objected to "passive resistance" as a translation of *Satyagraha:* in Gujarati, it seems, the word means "firmness in the truth." In his early days Gandhi served as a stretcher-bearer on the British side in the Boer War, and he was prepared to do the same again in the war of 1914–18. Even after he had completely abjured violence he was honest enough to see that in war it is usually necessary to take sides. He did not—indeed, since his whole political life centered round a struggle for national independence, he could not—take the sterile and dishonest line of pretending that in every war both sides are exactly the same and it makes no difference who wins. Nor did he, like most Western pacifists, specialize in avoiding awkward questions. In relation to the late war, one question that every pacifist had a clear obligation to answer was: "What about the Jews? Are you prepared to see them exterminated? If not, how do you propose to save them without resorting to war?" I must say that I have never heard, from any Western pacifist, an honest answer to this question, though I have heard plenty of evasions, usually of the "you're another" type. But it so happens that Gandhi was asked a somewhat similar question in 1938 and that his answer is on record in Mr. Louis Fischer's *Gandhi and Stalin.* According to Mr. Fischer, Gandhi's view was that the German Jews ought to commit collective suicide, which "would have aroused the world and the people of Germany to Hitler's violence." After the war he justified himself: the Jews had been killed anyway, and might as well have died significantly. One has the impression that this attitude staggered even so warm an admirer as Mr. Fischer, but Gandhi was merely being honest. If you are not prepared to take life, you must often be prepared for lives to be lost in some other way. When, in 1942, he urged non-violent resistance against a Japanese invasion, he was ready to admit that it might cost several million deaths.

8   At the same time there is reason to think that Gandhi, who after all was born in 1869, did not understand the nature of totalitarianism and saw everything in terms of his own struggle against the British government. The important point here is not so much that the British treated him forbearingly as that he was always able to command publicity. As can be seen from the phrase quoted above, he believed in "arousing the world," which is only possible if the world gets a chance to hear what you are doing. It is difficult to see how Gandhi's methods could be applied in a country where opponents of the régime disappear in the middle of the night and are never heard of again. Without a free press and the right of assembly, it is impossible not merely to appeal to outside opinion, but to bring a mass movement into being, or even to make your intentions known to your adversary. Is there a Gandhi in Russia at this moment? And if there is, what is he accomplishing? The Russian masses could only practice civil disobedience if the same idea happened to occur to all of them simultaneously, and even then, to judge by the history of the Ukraine famine,[2] it would make no difference. But let it be granted that non-violent resistance can be effective against one's own government, or against an

---

[2] Ukraine famine: When peasants resisted Stalin's plan for collectivization in the early 1930s, the Soviet leader refused to send disaster relief; nearly five million people starved.

occupying power: even so, how does one put it into practice internationally? Gandhi's various conflicting statements on the late war seem to show that he felt the difficulty of this. Applied to foreign politics, pacifism either stops being pacifist or becomes appeasement. Moreover the assumption, which served Gandhi so well in dealing with individuals, that all human beings are more or less approachable and will respond to a generous gesture, needs to be seriously questioned. It is not necessarily true, for example, when you are dealing with lunatics. Then the question becomes: Who is sane? Was Hitler sane? And is it not possible for one whole culture to be insane by the standards of another? And, so far as one can gauge the feelings of whole nations, is there any apparent connection between a generous deed and a friendly response? Is gratitude a factor in international politics?

9   These and kindred questions need discussion, and need it urgently, in the few years left to us before somebody presses the button and the rockets begin to fly. It seems doubtful whether civilization can stand another major war, and it is at least thinkable that the way out lies through non-violence. It is Gandhi's virtue that he would have been ready to give honest consideration to the kind of question that I have raised above; and, indeed, he probably did discuss most of these questions somewhere or other in his innumerable newspaper articles. One feels of him that there was much that he did not understand, but not that there was anything that he was frightened of saying or thinking. I have never been able to feel much liking for Gandhi, but I do not feel sure that as a political thinker he was wrong in the main, nor do I believe that his life was a failure. It is curious that when he was assassinated, many of his warmest admirers exclaimed sorrowfully that he had lived just long enough to see his life work in ruins, because India was engaged in a civil war which had always been foreseen as one of the by-products of the transfer of power. But it was not in trying to smooth down Hindu-Moslem rivalry that Gandhi had spent his life. His main political objective, the peaceful ending of British rule, had after all been attained. As usual the relevant facts cut across one another. On the one hand, the British did get out of India without fighting, an event which very few observers indeed would have predicted until about a year before it happened. On the other hand, this was done by a Labor government, and it is certain that a Conservative government, especially a government headed by Churchill, would have acted differently. But if, by 1945, there had grown up in Britain a large body of opinion sympathetic to Indian independence, how far was this due to Gandhi's personal influence? And if, as may happen, India and Britain finally settle down into a decent and friendly relationship, will this be partly because Gandhi, by keeping up his struggle obstinately and without hatred, disinfected the political air? That one even thinks of asking such questions indicates his stature. One may feel, as I do, a sort of aesthetic distaste for Gandhi, one may reject the claims of sainthood made on his behalf (he never made any such claim himself, by the way), one may also reject sainthood as an ideal and therefore feel that Gandhi's basic aims were anti-human and reactionary: but regarded simply as a politician, and compared with the other leading political figures of our time, how clean a smell he has managed to leave behind! ◆

JIMMY CARTER

Theodore White

By the time Theodore White published the following passage in America in Search of Itself: The Making of the President 1956–1980 *(1982), he had reported on the careers of Presidents Eisenhower, Kennedy, Johnson, Nixon, and Ford. He had seen and evaluated, therefore, a diverse set of presidential personalities. Reading his report on Jimmy Carter, however, one feels that he is struggling to understand a nature very different from his own. His struggle produces a report that puts Carter's personality into several conflicting frameworks.*

1   JIMMY CARTER WAS ALWAYS A MYSTERY, THIS man with the straw-colored hair and clear blue eyes, whose enemies came to despise him while those who would be friends could not understand him. Carter fit no mold nor any of those familiar journalistic diagrams by which political writers try to explore the nature of a presidency through the personality of the President. He could not describe himself, as Roosevelt so jauntily did, as having passed from being "Dr. New Deal" to "Dr. Win the War." Nor could he be described, as was Richard Nixon by so many of us, in the twenty years of Nixon's eminence, as being the "Old Nixon" or the "New Nixon," with new Nixons succeeding one another every two or three years in the public print.

2   The personality of Jimmy Carter was the same from the day he decided to run for the presidency until he lost it. And that personality, rather than changing from an "old" to a "new" Carter, had to be examined as a set of layers of faith, of action, even of unpleasantnesses. What made it most difficult was that the most important layer of the personality was a Christianity so devout and concerned that political writers found it awkward to write about.

3   That layer—of true belief—was uppermost and undermost. I encountered it initially before he became President, when I had my first long talk with Carter in Plains, Georgia, in his pleasant middle-class home, surrounded by oak trees—a home comfortable by any standards but by no means the style of mansion so many presidential candidates had acquired. At that time, in 1976, I was pursuing the candidates with a single-track question that might possibly be useful if I was to write a book on that year's campaign. "Where did modern American history really begin?" I would ask, and all had different answers. Jimmy Carter began with civil rights, "the most profound sociological change that's taken place in the country." It was the law as well as Martin Luther King that brought the change in the South, he said. So long as civil rights had been something administered by HEW, and while local and state laws contradicted federal laws, there was this question: "Whose laws do you obey?" But once the federal courts took over, everything changed. The South *wanted* to change, and the federal courts forced it along. Carter rambled on in answering my question and then got to family life. "When I grew up, the family was my community," he said. "I always knew where my mother and father were, they always knew where I was. I never had a problem where there was any doubt or fear except . . . disappointing my family . . . and there was a greater centering of the life in the community, for which our schools and church were the center." He has since been called a "dispassionate President," but when he talked quietly, he could be passionate. And on black rights he was most passionate of all. Sumter County is one of the most segregationist counties of the Old

South; but he had led the fight there for integration, had refused flatly, publicly, to join the White Citizens Council or the "segs." To give the blacks their open and equal opportunity was a matter of faith—of Christianity. Somewhere Carter had crossed a line in his past; blacks as well as whites were the children of God.

4   Much could be said about the archaic fundamentalist underpinning of his Christianity. But it was real. He believed. No other candidate could write, as did Carter, an open letter to a newspaper declaring his belief in creationism.[1] He taught Sunday school in Plains, held prayer breakfasts in the White House, began lunch, even with such amused big-city politicians as Ed Koch, mayor of New York, by asking permission to say grace. "Why not?" Koch, who had come to plead for aid for his city, is reported to have replied. "We can all use a little extra help."

5   It was impossible to ignore that motivation of love and mercy which Christianity brought to the administration of Jimmy Carter. He tried to make real all the promises that a generation of liberal programs had substituted for old faith. He ticked off to me the record of previous Presidents, their shortcomings, their lack of faith. Of Kennedy, he said, he "lacked boldness."

6   Then there was a second layer of the Carter personality—Jimmy Carter the engineer. He had answered my first question by talking of civil rights. Then he gave me an alternative beginning for his reflection on where modern American history began: Sputnik.[2] "Sputnik shook people," he said, "the first dawning of the belief that the Soviets were actually able to challenge us in a world that we thought was uniquely ours from a scientific and technological [view]."

No journalist ever gets to know a President, unless he has known him years before on his way up. Presidents are too busy to spend time on any but those who are useful to them. So a writer must invent the outline of the man he fitfully glimpses. And it seemed to me that one could invent a Jimmy Carter on the model of Sir Isaac Newton. Newton was also a man of science and of God; Newton thought the universe was a clockwork mechanism fashioned by God with some ultimate unfathomed design, and that by exploring the mechanics of things he could bare the larger design.

8   These two layers of Jimmy Carter's personality intersected. A pilot named Peterson had flown me down to Plains for my first visit. I sat beside him and we talked of Carter. Peterson was devoted to him. He had flown Carter from Atlanta to Plains several times. On their flights Carter would sit beside him, ask him how the plane worked, had learned to understand and operate the instruments in the cockpit. Then Peterson added a catching observation. He and Carter attended the same Baptist church in Plains and Carter would say occasionally, "Saw you in church on Sunday." But Mrs. Peterson did not go to services. Peterson recalled Carter asking whether he could call on her someday to talk about it. But he could not have been more surprised when Carter did indeed call (this in the midst of a presidential campaign), to talk with Mrs. Peterson about church, prayer, God, and the importance of Sunday services.

9   The engineer Carter was quite distinct from the Carter of faith. He would rise at five-thirty every morning at the White House and be at his desk before any of his staff. And he worked hard. He seemed to believe that if he could grasp all the facts and figures of a problem, he would understand its dynamics. A prominent New York Democrat, one of the major contributors to the party, visited Carter in midterm and was asked into the private study adjacent to the Oval Office. There sat Carter at his desk, with a pile of papers knee-high beside him. "Do you know what that is?" he asked the visitor. "That's the Air Force budget," said Carter. "I've read every page of it." The astonished executive talked briefly with the President,

---

[1] "The article in Monday's *Atlanta Constitution* incorrectly states," he wrote in the summer of 1976, "that I do not 'believe in such biblical accounts as Eve being created from Adam's rib and other such miracles.' I have never made any such statement and have no reason to disbelieve Genesis 2:21, 22 or other biblical miracles. . . ." [author's note]
[2] Sputnik: the first artificial earth satellite, launched by the USSR on October 4, 1957.

then made his exit through the office of Hamilton Jordan, who acted as chief of staff. There he sat down to enjoy a good conversation on politics and policy. It was as if, said the businessman later, Carter was the chief researcher, Jordan the chief policymaker. This appetite for swallowing detail went with Carter always. At his summit conference with Brezhnev[3] in Vienna, both were invited to a performance of Mozart's *The Abduction from the Seraglio*. Brezhnev, in his box, tired and restless, would doze, nod, occasionally chat and joke with his attendants. But Carter in his box had brought with him the full libretto of the opera and, turning the pages, followed the score act by act, scene by scene, even making notes in the margins. "Carter," said one of those with the President, "is not exactly a bundle of laughs."

10   There were also all the other layers of Carter. Carter the yeoman, for example. He knew the name of every tree he saw, and loved them all. I mentioned to him, on my first visit, that I had seen a stand of Southern cypress a few miles south of his home, near the town of Americus. The observation caught him. "That's a climatological line," he said. "North of that stand of cypress you won't find any more . . . all the way to the North Pole." He pulled the last phrase out with characteristic melancholy of tone, for he loved his Southern homeland. Then there was Carter of the primaries of 1976, a first-class mechanic of politics, aware of every county, city, voting bloc he must deal with, enjoying the adventure. Yet however much the public Carter on the stump, at the town meeting, in a student dormitory, seemed warm and outgoing, there was the other, prickly, private man—shy, soft-spoken, occasionally vindictive, withdrawn, unable to entertain give-and-take except with his Georgians, his wife, and Pat Caddell. This was a wary, small-town Carter, peering at the world and the barons of Washington with the skepticism of a country visitor, fearful of being taken in by them as much as they, on his arrival, feared him.

---

[3] Brezhnev: Leonid Brezhnev (1906–82), a Communist party official considered the leader of the Soviet Union for eighteen years.

11   "You have to understand," said one of Carter's White House guard, "that Carter simply did not *like* politicians. He had set his mind on being governor of Georgia, and he got to be governor by politics; he set his mind on being President, and he got that job done using politicians. But he didn't *like* them. He asked Russell Long over to the White House once to ask for his help on a tax bill, gave Long half an hour, and when the half hour was over, he simply got up and said, 'Thank you.' He wasn't offering friendship. We tried to get him to see the older Democrats, the wise men, people like Clifford and Harriman. He tried that twice and then just stopped. We told him he had to make friends in Congress. Of course, he didn't drink, but he played tennis. So we made a list of congressmen and senators to be invited over for a game. He went through the names, played once with each of them, checked them off the list. And that was that." . . . ◆

AMADO VAZQUEZ

Joan Didion

Originally published as "The Man in a Greenhouse of Orchids" (Esquire, June 1976), Didion's report on Amado Vazquez illustrates the hidden interest that may lie in people and places we encounter every day. She shows us in her second and third paragraphs that her first encounters with her "subject" occurred before she knew he was a subject at all. One of the pleasures of reading the essay is retracing Didion's enlarging awareness of Vazquez's significance. Didion republished the portrait in The White Album *(1979), as a section of the essay "Quiet Days in Malibu."*

1 AMADO VAZQUEZ IS A MEXICAN NATIONAL who has lived in Los Angeles County as a resident alien since 1947. Like many Mexicans who have lived for a long time around Los Angeles he speaks of Mexico as "over there," remains more comfortable in Spanish than in English, and transmits, in his every movement, a kind of "different" propriety, a correctness, a cultural reserve. He is in no sense a Chicano. He is rather what California-born Mexicans sometimes call "Mexican-from-Mexico," pronounced as one word and used to suggest precisely that difference, that rectitude, that personal conservatism. He was born in Ahualulco, Jalisco. He was trained as a barber at the age of ten. Since the age of twenty-seven, when he came north to visit his brother and find new work for himself, he has married, fathered two children, and become, to the limited number of people who know and understand the rather special work he found for himself in California, a kind of legend. Amado Vazquez was, at the time I first met him, head grower at Arthur Freed Orchids, a commercial nursery in Malibu founded by the late motion-picture producer Arthur Freed,[1] and he is one of a handful of truly great orchid breeders in the world.

---

[1] Freed: Arthur Freed (1894–1973) produced *An American in Paris, Show Boat,* and *Singing in the Rain,* among other well-known motion pictures.

2 In the beginning I met Amado Vazquez not because I knew about orchids but because I liked greenhouses. All I knew about orchids was that back in a canyon near my house someone was growing them *in greenhouses.* All I knew about Amado Vazquez was that he was the man who would let me spend time alone in these greenhouses. To understand how extraordinary this seemed to me you would need to have craved the particular light and silence of greenhouses as I did: all my life I had been trying to spend time in one greenhouse or another, and all my life the person in charge of one greenhouse or another had been trying to hustle me out. When I was nine I would deliberately miss the school bus in order to walk home, because by walking I could pass a greenhouse. I recall being told at that particular greenhouse that the purchase of a nickel pansy did not entitle me to "spend the day," and at another that my breathing was "using up the air."

3 And yet back in this canyon near my house twenty-five years later were what seemed to me the most beautiful greenhouses in the world—the most aqueous filtered light, the softest tropical air, the most silent clouds of flowers—and the person in charge, Amado Vazquez, seemed willing to take only the most benign notice of my presence. He seemed to assume that I had my own reasons for being there. He would speak only to offer a nut he had just cracked,

or a flower cut from a plant he was pruning. Occasionally Arthur Freed's brother Hugo, who was then running the business, would come into the greenhouse with real customers, serious men in dark suits who appeared to have just flown in from Taipei or Durban and who spoke in hushed voices, as if they had come to inspect medieval enamels, or uncut diamonds.

4   But then the buyers from Taipei or Durban would go into the office to make their deal and the silence in the greenhouse would again be total. The temperature was always 72 degrees. The humidity was always 60 per cent. Great arcs of white phalaenopsis trembled overhead. I learned the names of the crosses by studying labels there in the greenhouse, the exotic names whose value I did not then understand. *Amabilis* × *Rimestadiana* = *Elisabethae*. *Aphrodite* × *Rimestadiana* = *Gilles Gratiot*. *Amabilis* × *Gilles Gratiot* = *Katherine Siegwart* and *Katherine Siegwart* × *Elisabethae* = *Doris*. *Doris* after Doris Duke.[2] *Doris* which first flowered at Duke Farms in 1940. At least once each visit I would remember the nickel pansy and find Amado Vazquez and show him a plant I wanted to buy, but he would only smile and shake his head. "For breeding," he would say, or "not for sale today." And then he would lift the spray of flowers and show me some point I would not have noticed, some marginal difference in the substance of the petal or the shape of the blossom. "Very beautiful," he would say. "Very nice you like it." What he would not say was that these plants he was letting me handle, these plants "for breeding" or "not for sale today," were stud plants, and that the value of such a plant at Arthur Freed could range from ten thousand to more than three-quarters of a million dollars.

5   I suppose the day I realized this was the day I stopped using the Arthur Freed greenhouses as a place to eat my lunch, but I made a point of going up one day in 1976 to see Amado Vazquez and to talk to Marvin Saltzman, who took over the business in 1973 and is married to Arthur Freed's daughter Barbara.

---

[2] Duke: Doris Duke (1912–   ), a journalist and fashion editor, inherited $70 million from her father, the owner of the Duke Tobacco Farms and founder of Duke University.

(As in *Phal. Barbara Freed Saltzman* "Jean McPherson," *Phal. Barbara Freed Saltzman* "Zuma Canyon," and *Phal. Barbara Freed Saltzman* "Malibu Queen," three plants "not for sale today" at Arthur Freed.) It was peculiar talking to Marvin Saltzman because I had never before been in the office at Arthur Freed, never seen the walls lined with dulled silver awards, never seen the genealogical charts on the famous Freed hybrids, never known anything at all about the actual business of orchids.

6   "Frankly it's an expensive business to get into," Marvin Saltzman said. He was turning the pages of *Sander's List,* the standard orchid studbook, published every several years and showing the parentage of every hybrid registered with the Royal Horticultural Society, and he seemed oblivious to the primeval silence of the greenhouse beyond the office window. He had shown me how Amado Vazquez places the pollen from one plant into the ovary of a flower on another. He had explained that the best times to do this are at full moon and high tide, because phalaenopsis plants are more fertile then. He had explained that a phalaenopsis is more fertile at full moon because in nature it must be pollinated by a night-flying moth, and over sixty-five million years of evolution its period of highest fertility began to coincide with its period of highest visibility. He had explained that a phalaenopsis is more fertile at high tide because the moisture content of every plant responds to tidal movement. It was all an old story to Marvin Saltzman. I could not take my eyes from the window.

7   "You bring back five-thousand seedlings from the jungle and you wait three years for them to flower," Marvin Saltzman said. "You find two you like and you throw out the other four-thousand-nine-hundred-ninety-eight and you try to breed the two. Maybe the pollenization takes, eighty-five per cent of the time it doesn't. Say you're lucky, it takes, you'll still wait another four years before you see a flower. Meanwhile you've got a big capital investment. An Arthur Freed could take $400,000 a year from M.G.M. and put $100,000 of it into getting this place started, but not many people could. You see a lot of what we call backyard nurseries—people who have

fifty or a hundred plants, maybe they have two they think are exceptional, they decide to breed them—but you talk about major nurseries, there are maybe only ten in the United States, another ten in Europe, That's about it. Twenty."

8   Twenty is also about how many head growers there are, which is part of what lends Amado Vazquez his legendary aspect, and after a while I left the office and went out to see him in the greenhouse. There in the greenhouse everything was operating as usual to approximate that particular level of a Malaysian rain forest—not on the ground but perhaps a hundred feet up—where epiphytic orchids grow wild. In the rain forest these orchids get broken by wind and rain. They get pollinated randomly and rarely by insects. Their seedlings are crushed by screaming monkeys and tree boas and the orchids live unseen and die young. There in the greenhouse nothing would break the orchids and they would be pollinated at full moon and high tide by Amado Vazquez, and their seedlings would be tended in a sterile box with sterile gloves and sterile tools by Amado Vazquez's wife, Maria, and the orchids would not seem to die at all. "We don't know how long they'll live," Marvin Saltzman told me. "They haven't been bred under protected conditions that long. The botanists estimate a hundred and fifty, two hundred years, but we don't know. All we know is that a plant a hundred years old will show no signs of senility."

9   It was very peaceful there in the greenhouse with Amado Vazquez and the plants that would outlive us both. "We grew in osmunda then," he said suddenly. Osmunda is a potting medium. Amado Vazquez talks exclusively in terms of how the orchids grow. He had been talking about the years when he first came to this country and got a job with his brother tending a private orchid collection in San Marino, and he had fallen silent. "I didn't know orchids then, now they're like my children. You wait for the first bloom like you wait for a baby to come. Sometimes you wait four years and it opens and it isn't what you expected, maybe your heart wants to break, but you love it. You never say, 'that one

was prettier.' You just love them. My whole life is orchids."

And in fact it was. Amado Vazquez's wife, Maria (as in *Phal. Maria Vasquez* "Malibu," the spelling of Vazquez being mysteriously altered by everyone at Arthur Freed except the Vazquezes themselves), worked in the laboratory at Arthur Freed. His son, George (as in *Phal. George Vasquez* "Malibu"), was the sales manager at Arthur Freed. His daughter, Linda (as in *Phal. Linda Mia* "Innocence"), worked at Arthur Freed before her marriage. Amado Vazquez will often get up in the night to check a heater, adjust a light, hold a seed pod in his hand and try to sense if morning will be time enough to sow the seeds in the sterile flask. When Amado and Maria Vazquez go to Central or South America, they go to look for orchids. When Amado and Maria Vazquez went for the first time to Europe a few years ago, they looked for orchids. "I asked all over Madrid for orchids," Amado Vazquez recalled. "Finally they tell me about this one place. I go there, I knock. The woman finally lets me in. She agrees to let me see the orchids. She takes me into a house and . . ."

11   Amado Vazquez broke off, laughing.

12   "She has three orchids," he finally managed to say. "Three. One of them dead. All three from Oregon."

13   We were standing in a sea of orchids, an extravagance of orchids, and he had given me an armful of blossoms from his own cattleyas to take to my child, more blossoms maybe than in all of Madrid. It seemed to me that day that I had never talked to anyone so direct and unembarrassed about the things he loved. He had told me earlier that he had never become a United States citizen because he had an image in his mind which he knew to be false but could not shake: the image was that of standing before a judge and stamping on the flag of Mexico. "And I love my country," he had said. Amado Vazquez loved his country. Amado Vazquez loved his family. Amado Vazquez loved orchids. "You want to know how I feel about the plants," he said as I was leaving. "I'll tell you. I will die in orchids." ◆

PART II

Writing

AND ARGUMENT

*In many ways
writing is the act of saying <u>I</u>,
of imposing oneself upon other people,
of saying listen to me,
<u>see it my way, change your mind</u>.*

JOAN DIDION

PREPARING TO ARGUE

Y *ARGUMENT,* PEOPLE OFTEN MEAN A COMPLETE DISAGREEMENT ABOUT facts, the sort of thing one often hears between two children and sometimes hears between two nations. From the back seat of the family car it is, "Johnny kicked me!"—"Did not!"—"Did, too!" Or over the airwaves and in the newspapers it is nation X's allegation that nation Y's soldiers have crossed the border and nation Y's denial. Where there is an utter disagreement of facts, argument as we will define it is useless. Battle or investigation may resolve the dispute, but reasoning and persuasion cannot. In Chapter 6 we will discuss a more reasonable approach to disputes about facts.

A related and common meaning of *argument* is a quarrel between people who have things to get off their chests and who translate their anger into what sounds like statements of high principle and time-honored rules. Russell Baker's memoir *Growing Up* (1982) contains a good example of this sort of argument. Baker remembers an encounter between his paternal grandmother (Ida Rebecca), who had just given him a bread-and-jelly snack, and his mother, who came into Ida Rebecca's kitchen in time to protest this violation of the household rules.

> My mother spoke to Ida Rebecca. "You know I don't want him to eat between meals." Her voice was terrible with anger.
>
> So was Ida Rebecca's. "Are you going to tell *me* how to raise a boy?"
>
> "I'm telling you I don't want him eating jelly bread between meals. He's my child, and he'll do as I tell him."
>
> "Don't you come in here telling me how to raise children. I raised a dozen children, and not one of them ever dared to raise their voice to me like you do."
>
> I cowered between them while the shouting rose, but they had forgotten me now as the accumulated bitterness spewed out of them.

Disputes about rights and rules *can,* of course, be true arguments: we will study some examples in Chapter 7. But the arguers in Baker's memoir aren't primarily concerned about reaching a conclusion. They have pet peeves to vent, personal points to score. Even if they believed that curbing their tempers would lead them closer to the argument's end, they would probably refuse to curb them. Arguments of this sort may serve a valuable recreational or therapeutic purpose, but we will leave them to one side.

CATEGORICAL ARGUMENT

We will also leave to one side the purely "categorical" or "syllogistic" argument taught in logic classes. You may recognize the most familiar example of a categorical syllogism:

All men are mortal	[major premise]
Socrates is a man	[minor premise]
Therefore Socrates is mortal	[conclusion]

The ancient Greek philosopher Aristotle, who was a master of the syllogism and thought it was a very powerful logical tool, nonetheless recognized that it is not very useful to the lawyer or other arguer about human affairs. To be valid, a strict categorical syllogism requires a major premise that is *always* and *indisputably* true about a *whole category* of objects (for example, "All men"). This insistence on universal and undoubted truth means that the strict syllogism is of limited use in a world of uncertainty and disputes. In effect, the syllogism can only be used to prove what no reasonable person who understood the definition of its terms would doubt. No one who knows that Socrates was a man ever really doubted that he was mortal.

The syllogism does reveal a useful truth about the nature of arguments, though. Like the other forms of writing we have examined, arguments have both a "subject" component and a "framework" component. The "fact" or "situation" or "minor premise" corresponds with what we have elsewhere called the subject. It must be connected with a "statement of probability" or "statement of principle," a "major premise" or "framework," before the argument can reach a conclusion. However, most arguments define subjects and frameworks far more flexibly than the syllogism allows, as we will see in Chapters 6 and 7.

OUR DEFINITION OF ARGUMENT

Having said that we will use neither the quarrel nor the syllogism as our definition of argument, we need another definition. *By argument, we will mean a writer's attempt, on a question where people can reasonably disagree, to move intelligent readers toward his or her own position.* The acknowledgment that people can reasonably disagree indicates that neither pure logic nor the revelation of "the facts" is likely to decide the issue one way or another. True arguments occur in areas of uncertainty. The notion of moving readers *toward* the writer's position reminds us that total victory need not be the arguer's goal. Often a good argument merely persuades the audience to consider the writer's position more seriously than it had before.

In some cases a "win" may be important—lawyers naturally want their clients to prevail and the writer of a proposal hopes that it will be adopted. But even in these cases, victory is not won by bluster. In fact, the most effective arguers are generally the ones who understand, anticipate, and even sympathize with the arguments of their opponents.

Inexperienced arguers tend to enter the arena like gladiators ready for combat. Experienced advocates are usually cautious, courteous, and reasonable. The inexperienced often allow their commitment to one side of an argument to blind them to the virtues of the other. They argue so aggressively that the audience dismisses them as cranks. Effective advocates argue more temperately, and the best of them seem to argue from a deep understanding of everyone's perspective on the issue, including their opponent's perspective. They give the impression of being reasonable people whose judgment can be trusted.

BLOCKED BY OPENNESS

To argue well you must be capable of understanding how the world looks from a perspective opposed to your own. This ability to enter into the minds of others and to understand their frameworks, their assumptions and experiences, does not come naturally to many of us. Most of us, having developed *one* framework, are ready to rest from our labors.

Think back to Chapter 2, where we discussed the Dain Curse, the mind's very limited capacity for focused attention. One of the results of this curse, as Dashiell Hammett's detective points out, is that people develop opinions hastily and, once they have formed them, cling to them irrationally:

> Thinking's a dizzy business, a matter of catching as many of those foggy glimpses as you can and fitting them together the best you can. That's why people hang on so tight to beliefs and opinions; because, compared to the haphazard way in which they're arrived at, even the goofiest opinion seems wonderfully clear and self-evident. And if you let it get away from you, then you've got to dive back into that foggy muddle and wangle yourself out another to take its place.

This tendency to cling to hasty opinions creates a paradox that British writer Edward de Bono calls being "blocked by openness." Familiarity with one line of thought makes it seem so natural to us that we fail to consider other lines of thought. We are like the motorist who drives down the same streets every day, eventually becoming so channelized that he looks neither right nor left, loses curiosity about the side streets, and finally stops noticing that there *are* other streets that could be used.

As a metaphor for this channelization, de Bono urges us to see the mind as something like the earth's surface and thought as something like water. The first drop of water that hits the surface begins to carve a channel toward the sea. Each subsequent drop in the same area, following the line of least resistance, will naturally run along the channel created by that drop, and eventually the surface will have such clearly marked streams and rivers that wherever a drop falls, its course to the sea is not only predetermined but smoothed and hastened. In the case of the earth, there is a danger that the channelization will become too complete, that too much water will rush to the sea without sinking into the soil, resulting in erosion and deserts.

In the case of the mind, there is a comparable danger: our thoughts may rush so quickly along familiar paths that we fail to examine important alternatives. By staying on what de Bono calls a "cliché route"—the route of ideas we have often considered and "truths" that "everyone knows"—we avoid being confused by new thoughts, but we may pay the price of clinging to old errors. If we were well-educated citizens of the fourteenth century, for example, we would be so used to thinking that the world is flat that we would ignore or simply fail to notice things inconsistent with its flatness: that ships seem to *sink* below the horizon, for instance. In effect, the paths of thought that would lead us to see the world as round would have been *blocked* by the *openness* of the paths created by the conventional "flat-earth" view.

Arguments are particularly inclined to run into familiar channels. When we write about specific people, places, things, and events (the focus of Chapters 3 and 4 of this book), our attention to particulars serves as a brake, keeping us from running along clichéd paths of thought. But when we turn to opinions, proposals, and evaluations, we are more easily pulled along worn paths of thought where "even the goofiest opinion seems wonderfully clear, sane, and self-evident." Listen to the way most people argue about abortion, for example—taking "pro-life" or "pro-choice" stances even though no one is arguing on "anti-life" or "anti-choice" principles. This is not argument, but sloganizing, an extreme case of rushing down an open channel. In describing political speeches, George Orwell gives an alarming example of what the result may be:

> When one watches some tired hack on the platform mechanically repeating the familiar phrases—*bestial atrocities, iron heel, bloodstained tyranny, free peoples of the world, stand shoulder to shoulder*—one often has a curious feeling that one is not watching a live human being but some kind of dummy: a feeling which suddenly becomes stronger at moments when the light catches the speaker's spectacles

and turns them into blank discs which seem to have no eyes behind them. And this is not altogether fanciful. A speaker who uses that kind of phraseology has gone some distance towards turning himself into a machine. The appropriate noises are coming out of his larynx, but his brain is not involved as it would be if he were choosing his words for himself.

MOVING YOUR THOUGHTS OUTSIDE THE FAMILIAR CHANNELS

The danger of channelized thought has been apparent to philosophers and writers since ancient times and has produced a number of methods the thinker can use to dam the predictable channel at least long enough to allow the possibility of fresh thought. One that Edward de Bono repeatedly recommends is to identify the "dominant idea" on the subject at hand and then to think about the problem for a while in a way that avoids the dominant idea or denies its validity. If "everyone knows," for example, that increasing drug use is the cause of an increase in violent crime, de Bono would have us stop for a time to consider the possibility that there is *another* cause. Eventually, we may decide that the "dominant idea" is better than any alternative we can develop, but at least we will have recognized that there *are* alternatives.

A second method that can be applied to any number of problems is what Peter Elbow, one of our best contemporary writing teachers, calls "the believing and doubting game." This method has the writer study a proposition by first assembling as many reasons as possible for believing it to be true, then by assembling as many reasons as possible to doubt its truth. A third method is to consider why it is difficult to prove any answer correct. A fourth is to examine the short-term and long-term consequences of believing or disbelieving a proposition. With slight modifications, these four can be combined into a five-part procedure that can help stave off the danger of automatic thinking:

1. Explain what it is in your past thinking or experience that makes one answer "naturally" appealing to you.

2. List reasons to doubt this answer.

3. List reasons to believe this answer.

4. Explain why this is not an open-and-shut question.

5. Explain the consequences, long-term and short-term, of persuading an audience to accept one answer or another.

Let's examine this five-part procedure at work by seeing how a student[1] used it to freshen her thought before she wrote a proposal on the following question:

Should the college adopt the following "affirmative action" policy: Until our faculty is 50 percent female, we will always hire a qualified woman rather than a man with roughly equal qualifications to fill vacant faculty positions.

1. *Explain what it is in your past thinking or experience that makes one answer "naturally" appealing to you.*
   Because I am a woman who will soon be looking for a job herself, I'm naturally inclined to favor this policy. Also, I grew up in a fairly liberal family. My parents taught me that affirmative action for blacks, Hispanics, and other minorities was good. I also *like* so many of my female teachers. Naturally, these are the teachers that come to mind when I think about the question, and I want to say "hire more of them."

2. *List reasons to doubt this answer.*
   a. From the point of view of a man with "roughly equal qualifications," this could seem terribly unfair. He loses every close call.

   b. Think what would happen when the college tried to enforce this policy. How do they prove that a female candidate has "roughly equal qualifications"? Suppose a man and woman are equal on paper, but when a department talks to the woman, she doesn't seem smart or doesn't seem like she would be a good teacher. Will the college take these subjective considerations into account? If they don't, the policy is bad. If they do, it is unenforceable.

   c. Suppose I got a job at a college that had a policy like this one. Suppose I were to get into an overwhelmingly male department, hired in competition with a man most of the department thought was better but that the college decided had "roughly equal qualifications." Where would that leave me?

   d. Or suppose the department hired me because they thought I was the greatest thing they had ever seen. Wouldn't other people, knowing that I was a woman hired under this new policy, *assume* that I was just so-so and that I only got the job because I was a woman?

   e. Where does the 50 percent come from? Is the idea that 50 percent of the pool of professors is female? But what if it really is true that most really good professors (say 70 percent) are male?

---

[1] This example combines writing from two students and has been retouched in places for clarity's sake. The original versions—brainstormings for an essay—were private documents, filled with peculiar abbreviations and "shorthand" phrases.

f. Aren't there other ways to go about this? College professors and administrators are rational, well-meaning people (I think). Perhaps the best plan would be just to remind them that there are qualified female applicants who deserve consideration.

3. *List reasons to accept this answer.*

a. This is not a men's college. Over half the students are women. One problem with being a woman is that when all the authority figures around you are male, your self-confidence is undermined. I *know* this from my own experience. For the sake of the women students there should be more women faculty members.

b. If you want more women to become college professors, you have to assure them that there will be jobs for them. Supply and demand. I *think* (don't know for sure) that there was a time when women with Ph.D.'s had trouble breaking into the "old boys' network."

c. Letting departments hire on "subjective factors" rather than the objective quality of someone's qualifications *is* the "old boys' network." People hire people who "fit in," their friends' friends. If a department has twelve male professors in it, all of whose best friends are male professors, it's not likely that a female candidate will "fit in."

d. It is true that a woman hired under this new policy would be put in a hard situation. She would have to prove that she *deserved* the job. I just don't think that this would be so hard to do. My mother is an executive in an insurance firm. She says that at first she felt she was on trial as a woman, but pretty soon no one paid attention to this.

e. I'll just bet that if I do some digging in the library, I can defend that 50 percent figure. Perhaps I could find out what percentage of Ph.D.'s graduated in the last ten years are women or what percentage of women are on faculties of other colleges.

4. *Explain why this is not an open-and-shut question.*

One reason it is hard to decide is that the situation looks different to men and women. It is hard to deny that men lose jobs under this plan and women gain them. Not everyone is better off. Another reason it is hard to decide is that I don't know what "roughly equal qualifications" are or should be. Are subjective impressions "qualifications"? Should they be? You have to answer these questions before you can get to the real question.

MARK TWAIN

"It is by the goodness of God that in our country we have those three unspeakably precious things: freedom of speech, freedom of conscience, and the prudence never to practice either of them."

© 1938 FPG International

Samuel Langhorn Clemens, known everywhere as Mark Twain, has become part of American mythology, associated with small towns, innocent childhoods, Mississippi steamboats, and rugged individualism. The image of the elderly Twain, smoking cigars and making droll observations on human nature, is kept alive by actors who imitate his public speeches and by advertisers who want to associate his name with various "family attractions."

It is ironic that the public now reveres Twain as a sort of Midwestern saint, because Twain's writing was consistently irreverent. As a young man he detected silliness and hypocrisy in the ideas of his respectable neighbors, and his resistance to the received wisdom grew stronger as he aged. His first book, *The Innocents Abroad* (1869), reported on a tour of American "pilgrims" to Europe and the Holy Land. Most of his shipmates accepted the idea that Europe's culture was essentially superior to America's. Twain did not. Of one European city he wrote, "It is well that the alleys are not wider, because they hold as much smell now as a person can stand, and of course if they were wider, they would hold more, and the people would die."

In *Huckleberry Finn* (1884), set in slavery days, Twain's protagonist must choose between goodness or evil as defined by his society. "Goodness" tells him to send his black friend Jim back to his owner; "evil" says set him free. Huck pauses:

> Well, I tried the best I could to kinder soften it up somehow for myself by saying I was brung up wicked, and so I warn't so much to blame; but something inside of me kept saying, "There was the Sunday school, you could 'a' gone to it; and if you'd 'a' gone to it they'd 'a' learnt you there that people that acts as I'd been acting about that nigger goes to everlasting fire."

This is one of hundreds of passages in Twain's works where the individual heart and mind are set against settled public opinion. Huck's defiant conclusion to help Jim might almost be Twain's epitaph: "All right, then, I'll *go* to hell." ◆

5. Consider the consequences, long-term and short-term, of persuading an audience to accept one answer or another.

> The best audience is the faculty and administration of the college since they could adopt the policy. In the short run, I think we might be better off if they *didn't,* as it is going to create a lot of friction about hiring and it is likely to make the position of women professors we have even less comfortable. In the long run, I think the rule will make the college into a place with many more women on the faculty, and so it will be a place where both female and male students get used to the idea of women in positions of authority. If a larger audience were convinced—all college administrators and faculties—I think it would encourage a lot of women to get Ph.D.'s because they would know that there are jobs available to them. On the other hand, men might start to be discouraged because they felt their job market was closing. More women would go into college teaching and fewer men, maybe. Would this drive pay down because college teaching would become "women's work," like being a secretary or a nurse? Maybe in the longest run this is a bad policy, after all. *But* the policy would be switched off when the college (or all colleges) reached a 50/50 balance, and the bad effects would be switched off, too.

As you can see from this example, answering a set of questions that slows our judgment somewhat can force our minds to explore channels that would otherwise be untouched. Even though we may arrive at the same conclusion we would have without the delay, we arrive there better informed, and we tend to reason and write more intelligently. We are prepared to argue rather than to chant the familiar slogans, bully, and offend.

EXERCISE 1

◆ *A Prewriting Exercise for Argument.* With your instructor's guidance, identify a question that might be the subject of an argumentative paper you will write this term. To prepare yourself to write the paper, follow the steps below, writing responses that are as comprehensive as possible:

1. Explain what it is in your past thinking or experience that makes one answer "naturally" appealing to you.

2. List reasons to doubt this answer.

3. List reasons to believe this answer.

4. Explain why this is not an open-and-shut question.

5. Explain the consequences, long-term and short-term, of persuading an audience to accept one answer or another.

CORN-PONE OPINIONS

Mark Twain

Mark Twain's skepticism about the ability of humans to think clearly and independently may have begun in childhood (see "The Mesmerizer," p. 104). It grew stronger as he grew older, and in some of his late writings, like "Corn-Pone Opinions" (1900), he seems to challenge the idea that any of us are capable of the sort of critical thinking that lays a foundation for rational argument. The essay was published posthumously in Europe and Elsewhere (1923).

1 FIFTY YEARS AGO, WHEN I WAS A BOY OF fifteen and helping to inhabit a Missourian village on the banks of the Mississippi, I had a friend whose society was very dear to me because I was forbidden by my mother to partake of it. He was a gay and impudent and satirical and delightful young black man—a slave—who daily preached sermons from the top of his master's woodpile, with me for sole audience. He imitated the pulpit style of the several clergymen of the village, and did it well, and with fine passion and energy. To me he was a wonder. I believed he was the greatest orator in the United States and would some day be heard from. But it did not happen; in the distribution of rewards he was overlooked. It is the way, in this world.

2 He interrupted his preaching, now and then, to saw a stick of wood; but the sawing was a pretense— he did it with his mouth; exactly imitating the sound the bucksaw makes in shrieking its way through the wood. But it served its purpose; it kept his master from coming out to see how the work was getting along. I listened to the sermons from the open window of a lumber room at the back of the house. One of his texts was this:

3 "You tell me whar a man gits his corn pone, en I'll tell you what his 'pinions is."

4 I can never forget it. It was deeply impressed upon me. By my mother. Not upon my memory, but elsewhere. She had slipped in upon me while I was absorbed and not watching. The black philosopher's idea was that a man is not independent, and cannot afford views which might interfere with his bread and butter. If he would prosper, he must train with the majority; in matters of large moment, like politics and religion, he must think and feel with the bulk of his neighbors, or suffer damage in his social standing and in his business prosperities. He must restrict himself to corn-pone opinions—at least on the surface. He must get his opinions from other people; he must reason out none for himself; he must have no first-hand views.

5 I think Jerry was right, in the main, but I think he did not go far enough.

6 1. It was his idea that a man conforms to the majority view of his locality by calculation and intention. This happens, but I think it is not the rule.

7 2. It was his idea that there is such a thing as a first-hand opinion; an original opinion; an opinion which is coldly reasoned out in a man's head, by a searching analysis of the facts involved, with the heart unconsulted, and the jury room closed

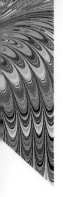

against outside influences. It may be that such an opinion has been born somewhere, at some time or other, but I suppose it got away before they could catch it and stuff it and put it in the museum.

I am persuaded that a coldly-thought-out and independent verdict upon a fashion in clothes, or manners, or literature, or politics, or religion, or any other matter that is projected into the field of our notice and interest, is a most rare thing—if it has indeed ever existed.

9 A new thing in costume appears—the flaring hoop skirt, for example—and the passers-by are shocked, and the irreverent laugh. Six months later everybody is reconciled; the fashion has established itself; it is admired, now, and no one laughs. Public opinion resented it before, public opinion accepts it now, and is happy in it. Why? Was the resentment reasoned out? Was the acceptance reasoned out? No. The instinct that moves to conformity did the work. It is our nature to conform; it is a force which not many can successfully resist. What is its seat? The inborn requirement of self-approval. We all have to bow to that; there are no exceptions. Even the woman who refuses from first to last to wear the hoop skirt comes under the law and is its slave; she could not wear the skirt and have her own approval; and that she *must* have, she cannot help herself. But as a rule our self-approval has its source in but one place and not elsewhere—the approval of other people. A person of vast consequences can introduce any kind of novelty in dress and the general world will presently adopt it—moved to do it, in the first place, by the natural instinct to passively yield to that vague something recognized as authority, and in the second place by the human instinct to train with the multitude and have its approval. An empress introduced the hoop skirt, and we know the result. A nobody introduced the bloomer, and we know the result. If Eve should come again, in her ripe renown, and reintroduce her quaint styles—well, we know what would happen. And we should be cruelly embarrassed, along at first.

10 The hoop skirt runs its course and disappears. Nobody reasons about it. One woman abandons the fashion; her neighbor notices this and follows her lead; this influences the next woman; and so on and so on, and presently the skirt has vanished out of the world, no one knows how nor why; or cares for that matter. It will come again, by and by, and in due course will go again.

11 Twenty-five years ago, in England, six or eight wine glasses stood grouped by each person's plate at a dinner party, and they were used, not left idle and empty; today there are but three or four in the group, and the average guest sparingly uses about two of them. We have not adopted this new fashion yet, but we shall do it presently. We shall not think it out; we shall merely conform, and let it go at that. We get our notions and habits and opinions from outside influences; we do not have to study them out.

12 Our table manners, and company manners, and street manners change from time to time, but the changes are not reasoned out; we merely notice and conform. We are creatures of outside influences, as a rule we do not think, we only imitate. We can not invent standards that will stick; what we mistake for standards are only fashions, and perishable. We may continue to admire them, but we drop the use of them. We notice this in literature. Shakespeare is a standard, and fifty years ago we used to write tragedies which we couldn't tell from—from somebody else's; but we don't do it any more, now. Our prose standard, three-quarters of a century ago, was ornate and diffuse; some authority or other changed it in the direction of compactness and simplicity, and conformity followed, without argument. The historical novel starts up suddenly, and sweeps the land. Everybody writes one, and the nation is glad. We had historical novels before; but nobody read them, and the rest of us conformed—without reasoning it out. We are conforming in the other way, now, because it is another case of everybody.

13 The outside influences are always pouring in upon us, and we are always obeying their orders and accepting their verdicts. The Smiths like the new play; the Joneses go to see it, and they copy the Smith verdict. Morals, religions, politics, get their following from surrounding influences and atmospheres, almost

entirely; not from study, not from thinking. A man must and will have his own approval first of all, in each and every moment and circumstance of his life—even if he must repent of a self-approved act the moment after its commission, in order to get his self-approval *again:* but, speaking in general terms, a man's self-approval in the large concerns of life has its source in the approval of the peoples about him, and not in a searching personal examination of the matter. Mohammedans are Mohammedans because they are born and reared among that sect, not because they have thought it out and can furnish sound reasons for being Mohammedans; we know why Catholics are Catholics; why Presbyterians are Presbyterians; why Baptists are Baptists; why Mormons are Mormons; why thieves are thieves; why monarchists are monarchists; why Republicans are Republicans and Democrats, Democrats. We know it is a matter of association and sympathy, not reasoning and examination; that hardly a man in the world has an opinion upon morals, politics, or religion which he got otherwise than through his associations and sympathies. Broadly speaking, there are none but corn-pone opinions. And broadly speaking, corn-pone stands for self-approval. Self-approval is acquired mainly from the approval of other people. The result is conformity. Sometimes conformity has a sordid business interest—the bread-and-butter interest—but not in most cases, I think. I think that in the majority of cases it is unconscious and not calculated; that it is born of the human being's natural yearning to stand well with his fellows and have their inspiring approval and praise—a yearning which is commonly so strong and so insistent that it cannot be effectually resisted, and must have its way.

14   A political emergency brings out the corn-pone opinion in fine force in its two chief varieties—the pocketbook variety, which has its origin in self-interest, and the bigger variety, the sentimental variety—the one which can't bear to be outside the pale; can't bear to be in disfavor; can't endure the averted face and the cold shoulder; wants to stand well with his friends, wants to be smiled upon, wants to be welcome, wants to hear the precious words, *"He's on the right track!"* Uttered, perhaps by an ass, but still an

ass of high degree, an ass whose approval is gold and diamonds to a smaller ass, and confers glory and honor and happiness, and membership in the herd. For these gauds many a man will dump his life-long principles into the street, and his conscience along with them. We have seen it happen. In some millions of instances.

15   Men think they think upon great political questions, and they do; but they think with their party, not independently; they read its literature, but not that of the other side; they arrive at convictions, but they are drawn from a partial view of the matter in hand and are of no particular value. They swarm with their party, they feel with their party, they are happy in their party's approval; and where the party leads they will follow, whether for right and honor, or through blood and dirt and a mush of mutilated morals.

16   In our late canvass half of the nation passionately believed that in silver lay salvation, the other half as passionately believed that that way lay destruction. Do you believe that a tenth part of the people, on either side, had any rational excuse for having an opinion about the matter at all? I studied that mighty question to the bottom—came out empty. Half of our people passionately believe in high tariff, the other half believe otherwise. Does this mean study and examination, or only feeling? The latter, I think. I have deeply studied that question, too—and didn't arrive. We all do no end of feeling, and we mistake it for thinking. And out of it we get an aggregation which we consider a boon. Its name is public opinion. It is held in reverence. It settles everything. Some think it the voice of God. ◆

ARGUING WHEN FACTS ARE DISPUTED

N CHAPTER 1 WE SAW THAT UNCERTAINTY WAS PART OF THE WRITER'S situation, as it is of everyone else's. In this chapter and the next we will deal with questions that stem naturally from this condition of uncertainty: How can you present an opinion persuasively when both you and your reader know it *is* an opinion rather than an undeniable truth? How can you advocate a position that you cannot be absolutely certain is correct?

The traditional answer, stated in various ways by rhetoricians since Aristotle's day, comes in three parts. Because you believe that facts few people would seriously dispute favor your position, you can point to them. Because you think that there is a line of reasoning that leads from these facts to your conclusion, you can present your argument logically. And because you know that neither facts nor logic can remove the reader's uncertainty, you can present your position in a way that reveals you as a trustworthy person with sound judgment. In the abstract, this combination of factual, logical, and psychological appeal sounds simple. In practice, it is notoriously difficult. There may be fewer master arguers in the world than there are sword swallowers or countertenors.

Though mastering it is difficult, argument can be a source of great pleasure and interest. Like the investigation of a major crime, a large, energetic dispute will draw investigators into curious areas of knowledge and speculation. The long-standing dispute about who wrote the plays and poems attributed to William Shakespeare, for example, has involved not only English professors, but lawyers, historians, X-ray technicians, handwriting experts, statisticians, cryptographers, linguists, and a number of detectives, professional and amateur. The arguments on the subject are so varied that they will be used as illustrations throughout this chapter. In exercises, you will be asked to take part in the Shakespeare controversy, evaluating the effectiveness of arguments for and against the thesis that the man named Shakespeare actually wrote the works attributed to him. In the process of completing and discussing these exercises, you will hone your skills at building and evaluating arguments about disputed facts.

6

A CASE: MARK TWAIN DISPUTES THE AUTHORSHIP OF SHAKESPEARE'S WORKS

Most people assume that Shakespeare wrote *Hamlet, King Lear, Venus and Adonis,* and 154 sonnets simply because everyone says so: his name always appears on the title page. In fact, his name did not appear on any existing title page until the publication of the first folio, seven years after his death, and many people believe that the man named William Shakespeare could not have written the plays attributed to him.

Mark Twain, one of the early doubters, laid out his arguments at great length in a book called *Is Shakespeare Dead?* (1909). After preliminary remarks on the gullibility of the public, he begins his argument proper with a three-page list of "those details of Shakespeare's history which are facts— verified facts, established facts, undisputed facts." Among the key facts are these:

1. He was born in 1564 in the small village of Stratford-on-Avon, England, "of good farmer-class parents who could not read, could not write, could not sign their names" (Shakespeare's father signed documents with an X or cross).

2. In 1587 he moved to London, where he became an actor and a theater manager.

3. While he was in London, his name was "associated with a number of great plays and poems," some of which "were pirated, but he made no protest."

4. In 1597, he bought a good house in Stratford, and in about 1610 moved there permanently, becoming a real estate speculator and moneylender.

5. In 1616 he made his will "a thoroughgoing business man's will" that apparently "named in minute detail every item of property he owned in the

world" but "mentioned *not a single book . . . not a play, not a poem, not an unfinished literary work, not a scrap of manuscript of any kind.*" He died in 1616.

6. His signature appears three times on the will and two times on other documents, but *"there are no other specimens of his penmanship in existence."*

7. "When Shakespeare died in Stratford, *it was not an event.* It made no more stir in England than the death of any other forgotten theater-actor would have made. Nobody came down from London, there were no lamenting poems, no eulogies, no national tears—there was merely silence, and nothing more. A striking contrast with what happened when Ben Jonson, and Francis Bacon, and Spenser, and Raleigh, and all the other distinguished literary folk of Shakespeare's time passed from life! No praiseful voice was lifted for the lost Bard of Avon; even Ben Jonson waited seven years before he raised his."

Twain thought it improbable that the man whose life these facts describe could be the author of Shakespeare's works, and he insisted that the reader consider some obvious questions. Is it likely that a man from an illiterate family in a farming village would have acquired the extensive knowledge of books, geography, history, human affairs, and law that the works display? Is it likely that he would acquire such knowledge without also owning, apparently, a single book? Is it likely that the death of an author whose poems and plays "had been before the London world and in high favor for twenty-five years" would go unnoticed and that no contemporary biographer would have journeyed to Stratford to learn the details of his life? Twain believed all this to be highly unlikely; he accused scholars of perpetuating the "Bard of Avon" myth by "surmising" crucial details of Shakespeare's life. Biographers surmise, for instance, that Shakespeare learned law by serving as a clerk of Stratford court, although there is no record of his having done so. And they surmise that after he moved to London he "amused himself" by studying law, although no one in Shakespeare's lifetime mentioned this studying. Twain compares this surmising to the process by which an archaeologist creates a model brontosaurus from nine bones, a great many assumptions, and tons of plaster of Paris.

Like many people in the nineteenth century, Twain thought the likely author of the poems and plays was Francis Bacon, a writer of demonstrable talent with an extensive knowledge of law, politics, and classical literature. The theory of the "Baconians" was that Bacon had political reasons for not wanting a reputation as a playwright and that he persuaded Shakespeare to serve as a foster father for the plays. In the twentieth century, Bacon has had fewer champions, but there has been a good deal of support for two other candidates: Edward de Vere, a nobleman with literary talent, and Christopher Marlowe, a playwright whose production stopped when Shakespeare's began.

Twain's objections to the surmisings of Shakespeare's biographers reveals something about the nature and difficulty of arguments about disputed facts. "Surmising" is an inevitable part of the process. Indeed, the basic movement of such an argument is from "established facts" (ones generally agreed on), through a statement of probability, to a "surmised" fact. Thus, arguers who disagree may begin with the same facts:

1. The man named Shakespeare had not formally studied law.

2. Some of the plays attributed to Shakespeare show a considerable knowledge of law.

To these facts, the arguers may apply different statements of probability and arrive at different conclusions. Arguer 1 may say that it is highly improbable that informal study of law could give someone the knowledge necessary to write the plays. He will conclude that Shakespeare was probably not the author. Arguer 2 may say that informal study probably could provide the necessary knowledge. If she is inclined to believe that Shakespeare was the author, she will conclude that he very likely studied law informally.

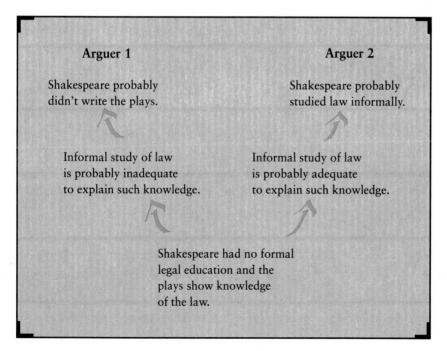

Arguer 1

Shakespeare probably
didn't write the plays.

Informal study of law
is probably inadequate
to explain such knowledge.

Arguer 2

Shakespeare probably
studied law informally.

Informal study of law
is probably adequate
to explain such knowledge.

Shakespeare had no formal
legal education and the
plays show knowledge
of the law.

Arguments about facts involve us inevitably in the process of estimating probabilities and drawing inferences on the basis of probabilities. In the following exercise, you will have an opportunity to practice this process of probabilistic reasoning.

EXERCISE 1 ◆ *Weighing Facts.* To complete the following exercise, you will need to write several short notes about probabilities and inferences, so have a pencil and paper ready.

Imagine a scale numbered from 0 to 100, with each point on the scale representing a level of conviction. For this exercise the zero position will indicate absolute certainty that Shakespeare did not write the works attributed to him. The 100 position will indicate absolute conviction that he did. Begin by estimating your *present* position on the scale (before reading any of the facts below); write a brief note explaining the reasoning behind your position. Then recalibrate your position in light of each of the facts, making notes on your reasoning as you go. To benefit most from this exercise, you must recalibrate and rereason after *each* fact. Treat the facts as cumulative: that is, take Fact 1 into consideration as you think about Fact 2, Facts 1 and 2 into consideration as you think about Fact 3, and so forth.

FACTS

1. One of England's most eminent nineteenth-century lawyers, a man who rose to the office of Lord Chief Justice in 1850 and subsequently became Lord Chancellor, wrote that Shakespeare's plays had to be the work of a man with "a deep technical knowledge of the law" and a thorough acquaintance with "some of the most abstruse proceedings in English jurisprudence." "While novelists and dramatists are constantly making mistakes as to the laws of marriage, of wills, and inheritance, to Shakespeare's law, lavishly as he expounds it, there can be neither demurrer, nor bill of exceptions, nor writ of error."

2. Scholars have located references to Shakespeare's plays in letters, diaries, and other works written by Shakespeare's contemporaries. These documents indicate no doubt that the author's name was actually Shakespeare.

3. During the years when Shakespeare was growing up in Stratford, thirteen of the nineteen men who played important roles in the town government signed documents with a mark, often a cross.

4. Ben Jonson, Shakespeare's contemporary and a well-known playwright, published an introductory poem in the 1623 edition of the plays; the poem praises Shakespeare by name. Jonson also talked about his friendship with

Shakespeare and commented on the virtues and faults of Shakespeare's style in *Timber: or, Discoveries; Made Upon Men and Matter* (1641).

5. The monument to Shakespeare in the parish church at Stratford includes a half-height bust of a man with a pen and paper in his hands and inscriptions both in English and Latin indicating that the man whose life and death are commemorated was a great writer. Most experts who have examined the monument say that it was erected before 1623.

6. Some experts think the monument was erected several years later.

7. An informal survey of twenty citizens in Columbia, Missouri, in 1990 revealed that no one doubted Shakespeare's authorship of the plays and poems attributed to him.

8. An informal survey of the English department faculty at the University of Missouri, Columbia, in 1990 revealed that not a single professor "seriously doubted" Shakespeare's authorship.

A TEMPERATE TREATMENT OF THE SHAKESPEARE QUESTION

Mark Twain argues his case against Shakespeare with combative energy and spices it with a good deal of humor:

> Did Francis Bacon write Shakespeare's Works?
> Nobody *knows.*
>
> We cannot say we know a thing when the thing has not been proved. *Know* is too strong a word to use when the evidence is not final and absolutely conclusive. We can infer, if we want to, like those slaves . . . No I will not write that word, it is not kind, it is not courteous. The upholders of the Stratford-Shakespeare superstition call us the hardest names they can think of, and they keep doing it all the time; very well, if they like to descend to that level, let them do it, but I will not so undignify myself as to follow them. I cannot call them harsh names; the most I can do is to indicate them by terms reflecting my disapproval; and this without malice, without venom.
>
> To resume. What I was about to say was, those thugs have built their entire superstition on inferences, not upon known and established facts.

This confrontational tone may work in the hands of a humorist who is willing to parody himself as well as his opponents. It is a risky business for most writers of arguments, however. Generally, the temperate arguer is more credible, the one who carefully weighs one probability against another. Such a balanced, judicious treatment is particularly valued in the academic community, where even the most ferocious advocates of a position are obliged by the unwritten rules of scholarship to deal fairly with the evidence for the other side. The ethical obligation creates a delicate problem for academic writers, since they must find a middle ground between a cold neutrality and a heated argument. The passage below is the *Encyclopaedia Britannica*'s discussion of the Shakespeare controversy, written by Professor J. R. Brown of the University of Sussex and Professor T. J. B. Spencer of the University of Birmingham. As you read, notice that the professors attempt simultaneously to inform us about views they do not accept and persuade us to accept their views.

"Questions of authorship"
–J. R. BROWN &
T. J. B. SPENCER

Does this seem to be a fair summary of the case against Shakespeare's authorship?

How is the treatment of the case for Bacon different from the treatment given other candidates?

Questions of authorship. The idea that Shakespeare's plays and poems were not actually written by William Shakespeare of Stratford has been the subject of many books and is widely regarded as at least an interesting possibility. The source of all doubts about the authorship of the plays lies in the disparity between the greatness of Shakespeare's literary achievement and his comparatively humble origin, the supposed inadequacy of his education, and the obscurity of his life. In Shakespeare's writings, people have claimed to discover a familiarity with languages and literature, with such subjects as law, history, politics, and geography, and with the manners and speech of courts, which they regard as inconceivable in a common player, the son of a provincial tradesman. This range of knowledge, it is said, is to be expected at that period only in a man of extensive education, one who was familiar with such royal and noble personages as figure largely in Shakespeare's plays. And the dearth of contemporary records has been regarded as incompatible with Shakespeare's eminence and as therefore suggestive of mystery. That none of his manuscripts has survived has been taken as evidence that they were destroyed to conceal the identity of their author.

The claims put forward for Bacon. The first suggestion that the author of Shakespeare's plays might be Francis Bacon, Viscount St. Albans, seems to have been made in the middle of the 19th century, inquiry at first centering on textual comparison between Bacon's known writings and the plays. A discovery was made that references to the Bible, the law, and the classics were given similar treatment in both canons. In the later 19th century a search was made for ciphered messages embedded in the dramatic texts. In *Love's Labour's Lost,* for example, it was found that the Latin word "honorificabilitudinitatibus" is an anagram of *Hi ludi F. Baconis nati tuiti orbi* ("These plays, the offspring of F. Bacon, are preserved for the world."). Professional cryptographers of the 20th century, however, examining all the Baconian ciphers, have rejected them as invalid, and interest in the Shakespeare-Bacon controversy has diminished.

Other candidates. A theory that the author of the plays was Edward de Vere, 17th earl of Oxford, receives some circumstantial support from the coincidence that Oxford's known poems apparently ceased just before Shakespeare's work began to appear. It is argued that Oxford assumed a pseudonym in order to protect his family from the social stigma then attached to the stage and also because extravagance had brought him into disrepute at court. Another candidate is William Stanley, 6th earl of Derby, who was keenly interested in the theatre and was patron of his own company of actors. Several poems, written in the 1580s and exhibiting signs of an immature Shakespearean style, cannot well have been written by Shakespeare himself. One of these is in Derby's handwriting, and three of them are signed "W.S." These initials are thought by some to have been a concealment for Derby's identity (for some such motives as were attributed to Oxford) and to have been later expanded into "William Shakespeare."

Shakespeare has also been identified with Christopher Marlowe, one theory even going so far as to assert that Marlowe was not killed in a tavern brawl in 1593 (the corpse of another being represented as his own) but was smuggled to France and thence to Italy where he continued to write in exile—his plays being fathered on Shakespeare, who was paid to keep silent.

The case for Shakespeare. In spite of recorded allusions to Shakespeare as the author of many plays in the canon, made by about 50 men during his lifetime, it is arguable that his greatness was not as clearly recognized in his own day as one might expect. But, on the other hand, the difficulties are not so great as many disbelievers have held, and their proposals have all too often raised larger problems than they have resolved. Shakespeare's contemporaries, after all, wrote of him unequivocally as the author of the plays. Ben Jonson, who knew him well, contributed verses to the First Folio of 1623, where (as elsewhere) he criticizes and praises Shakespeare as the author. John Heminge and Henry Condell, fellow actors and theatre owners with Shakespeare, signed the dedication and a foreword to the First Folio and described their methods as editors. In his own day, therefore, he was accepted as the author of the plays. Throughout his lifetime, and for long after, no person is known to have questioned his authorship. In an age that loved gossip and mystery as much as any, it seems hardly conceivable that Jonson and Shakespeare's theatrical associates shared the secret of a gigantic literary hoax without a single leak or that they could have been imposed upon without suspicion. Unsupported assertions that the author of the plays was a man of great learning and that Shakespeare of Stratford was an illiterate rustic no longer carry weight, and only when a believer in Bacon or Oxford or Marlowe produces sound evidence will scholars pay close attention to it and to him.

What portions of the authors' case for Shakespeare do you find most persuasive?

⬧ *Weighing Additional Facts.* Once again, imagine our 0 to 100 scale, with 0 representing an absolute conviction that Shakespeare did not write the works attributed to him and 100 representing an absolute conviction that he did. Begin by placing yourself (as you stand after having read Brown and Spencer, but before considering the facts that follow); note your reasoning. Recalibrate your position on the scale after you consider each of the following facts and note why the fact affected your judgment as it did.

EXERCISE 2

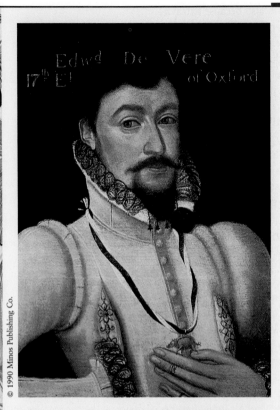

Edward De Vere, 17th earl of Oxford (1550–1604; portrait attributed to Marcus Gheeraedts), was a quarrelsome and extravagant nobleman. He fell into disfavor with Elizabeth I through repeated acts of disobedience, and he waged a fierce quarrel with the poet Sidney, whom he publicly called a "puppy." Though he was described as a fine writer of comedy, none of Oxford's plays have survived; in fact, only some fifteen poems can definitely be attributed to him. He was first proposed as the author of Shakespeare's plays in 1920 by J. T. Looney. Looney devised a psychological profile of "Shakespeare"; then, through intense reading of Elizabethan history, he avowed that De Vere's personality and actions provided an almost perfect fit.

1. Calvin Hoffman, whose book *The Murder of the Man Who Was Shakespeare* (1955) is the cornerstone of the argument for Marlowe, was not a Shakespearean scholar but a Broadway press agent.

2. In January, 1940, a man named Charles Wisner Barrell published in *Scientific American* the results of his scrutiny of three portraits of William Shakespeare. Barrell's analysis using X-ray and infrared photography revealed that all three were originally portraits of Edward de Vere, the 17th earl of Oxford, modified later to disguise the true identity of the subject.

3. In a 1940 article from *Harper's Magazine*, Oscar James Campbell, a Shakespeare scholar and editor, wrote: "Today a man who makes a cross instead of signing his name gives manifest proof of his illiteracy. But in the sixteenth century, this was not so. When we first find a cross serving as a signature on legal documents it was used because of its significance as a religious symbol. As a representation of the Holy Cross it afforded proof that the man who made it was giving religious sanctity to the ceremony of affixing his name. It was regarded as the written equivalent of an oath."

4. In a 1948 letter to the editor of *The Saturday Review of Literature*, Gelett Burgess, a draftsman and designer best known for his suspense fiction and comic poetry, pointed out that Edward de Vere owned copies of several books that are used as sources for the Shakespeare plays.

5. In a 1955 article for *The New York Times Book Review* Alfred Harbage, a leading Shakespeare scholar, wrote that "the identity of playwrights then, like that of screen, radio, and television writers now, was a matter of public indifference. . . . The most popular single piece,

'The Spanish Tragedy,' went through eleven editions without mention of the author, and only a late casual allusion lets us assign it to a scrivener's son named Thomas Kyd."

6. Among those who have doubted Shakespeare's authorship of "his" plays are poets Samuel Taylor Coleridge, Ralph Waldo Emerson, John Greenleaf Whittier, the eminent nineteenth-century Shakespeare scholar W. H. Furness, and the novelist Henry James.

THE LEVEL OF THE AUTHOR'S CONVICTION AND THE AUDIENCE'S

L et's consider for a moment the importance of the writer's position relative to the audience on our 100-point scale of conviction. There are, of course, four general possibilities. The writer may address an audience more skeptical about Shakespeare's being the actual author than she is (let's say author = 90, audience ranging from 10 to 80), in which case she will presumably try to move them up the scale of conviction. She may address an audience less skeptical than she (author = 50, audience = 95 to 100), in which case her purpose will be to shake their confidence. She may address a very mixed audience, including some more skeptical than she and some more convinced, in which case she may only want to show the unreasonableness of either extreme position. Or she may address an audience that stands precisely where she stands on the question, in which case she is not attempting to persuade at all, merely to reassure.

Too often when we think of persuasion or argumentation, we conceive of a situation in which the writer stands at one extreme on a question and tries to win over an audience that stands at the other extreme. This analysis is far too simple. Persuasion more often implies an attempt to adjust an audience's level of conviction about an issue than it does an attempt to win an outright victory, a movement from 0 to 100 or 100 to 0.

Of the few existing contemporary likenesses of Shakespeare, this portrait, painted in 1610 by Cornelius Janssen, is perhaps the most elegant. However, some scholars doubt both that it represents Shakespeare and that Janssen painted it. Three of the five existing Shakespeare signatures are shown below.

Francis Bacon (1561–1626; portrait by Van Somer) was a prominent lawyer, philosopher, and essayist. In 1601 he successfully prosecuted the Earl of Essex, his one-time patron and friend, on charges of conspiring to kill Elizabeth I, and he served briefly as Lord Chancellor in James I's reign but retired in 1621 after being convicted of bribery. Those who claim Bacon was the real Shakespeare cite similarities of vocabulary and knowledge and sometimes point to cryptograms that Bacon is supposed to have written into the plays. These ciphers, when decoded, ostensibly proclaimed him to be the author, but scholars have found instances of certain of the cryptograms as early as 1460, a century before Bacon's birth.

If the author's purpose is to sway the audience rather than overcome it, what tone should she adopt? Tone in writing is usually defined as the author's attitude toward the subject and the audience. In the case of persuasive writing, we might define it as the level of certainty that the writer chooses to express.

One might ask, as a moral question, whether the author has the right to imply any level of certainty other than the one she feels. Doesn't honesty demand that a writer 99 percent convinced that a proposition is true express her near certainty by the way she writes? Perhaps so, but another sort of honesty tells us that our convictions cannot be so neatly pinpointed. On the Shakespeare authorship question, I am capable of fluctuating, on a given day, from about 85 on our scale to about 99.9. If I were writing an essay on the subject, I would choose to write as an 88 rather than a 99 for at least two reasons. One reason is the framework in which I view all such controversies: since I believe that all of us erroneously tend toward extreme and simple answers, I prefer to risk my error on the side of open-mindedness. A second reason is strategic: when the author sounds open-minded, the reader tends to respond open-mindedly. If some of my readers were strong advocates of the Earl of Oxford as the true author, I would arouse their resistance and perhaps their anger by treating the case for Shakespeare as an open-and-shut one. I might force some readers who began as 10's to retreat defensively a notch or two *down* the scale of conviction. If my tone were more moderate, I might persuade them to move a notch or two up toward my position. Working at the moderate end of your own range of conviction shows respect and courtesy, at least, toward those who might disagree with you.

One suspects that Brown and Spencer deliberately work at the moderate end of their range of conviction. In private, they might sometimes refer to the advocates of Francis Bacon or Edward de Vere as *crack-pots* or *hare-brains*. In this very public statement, they are more open-minded and conciliatory. They concede that the anti-Shakespearean hypothesis is "at least an interesting possibility" and they admit that there are "difficulties" in reconciling the known facts of Shakespeare's life with the magnitude of his literary achievement. At the same time, they are far from neutral on the issue. Look carefully at the first paragraph and the last. The first is filled with expressions like *supposed, claimed, they regard, it is said, has been regarded,* and *has been taken:* Brown and Spencer carefully let us know that they endorse none of these views. The last paragraph, on the other hand, after its conciliatory first sentence, states the authors' views strongly, using expressions that show a high level of confidence: *after all, unequivocally, he was accepted* (not *he seemed to be accepted*), *it seems hardly conceivable, no longer carry weight.* We might say that Brown and Spencer start at the moderate end of their range of conviction and end somewhere nearer its middle or even high end. In most cases, this is both an honest approach and a wise strategy.

Twain's strategy is quite different, and is somewhat harder to reconcile with simple honesty. At one point in *Is Shakespeare Dead?,* he says that he is neither a "Stratfordian" (an advocate of Shakespeare) nor a "Baconian," but a "Brontosaurian"—a person who thinks that the Shakespeare biography is, like a model brontosaurus, made up largely of questionable assumptions and plaster of Paris. I take this to mean that his true position is nearer the middle of the scale of conviction than one might guess from reading isolated passages of the book. The tone of absolute conviction he assumes is a pose. To shock the audience out of its complacent assumption that, of course, Shakespeare *must* have written Shakespeare's plays, he deliberately exaggerates his conviction that Shakespeare *could not* have done so. This strategy is occasionally successful in moving people toward a more moderate position, and it provides the writer with an opportunity to exercise his or her gaudier rhetorical skills, but it is prone to backfire. Readers who feel bullied may dig in their heels and resist all persuasion.

Corpus Christi College, England

*Christopher Marlowe (1564–1593) is shown here in an unattributed portrait in Corpus Christi College, Cambridge (where he was educated). He has sometimes been called the first great Elizabethan dramatist. He was a masterful poet: Ben Jonson, himself a great dramatist, cited Marlowe's "mighty line." Of all the candidates for the "true" authorship of Shakespeare's plays, Marlowe produced in four short years a body of work most like Shakespeare's: tragedies—*Tamburlaine the Great, Doctor Faustus, The Jew of Malta, *and* Edward II*—and lyric poetry. Born in the same year as Shakespeare, Marlowe was killed in a tavern brawl in 1593, years before Shakespeare's major plays were performed. His adherents claim, however, that the death was faked and that Marlowe went on to write the plays under the name of Shakespeare.*

THE NECESSARY LEVEL OF CERTAINTY

Our scale of conviction serves us well when we think about another problem every writer and thinker faces constantly. How certain must we be of supposed facts before we can treat them, in Twain's words, as "verified facts, established facts, undisputed facts"? There is no single answer here, but there are useful ways to think about the difficulty.

To begin with, the writer may be content to leave some "facts" in a state of uncertainty. No biographer of Shakespeare *needs* absolutely to resolve the question of whether the poet's father could read and write. If the biographer wants to leave the fact of John Shakespeare's supposed illiteracy in limbo, he or she can simply move on to other things, being careful to make no argument based on this questionable "fact."

Some facts may be moved to a relatively high level of certainty and left there with little comment. A writer 95 percent certain that Shakespeare wrote *Hamlet* and *Coriolanus* and confident that her audience is also nearly certain can usually let the matter rest. That is, she can write, "Shakespeare's imagery in *Coriolanus* is simpler than that in *Hamlet*" without stopping to discuss the possibility that Shakespeare is really Bacon. In a discussion of imagery, biography isn't a matter of great importance. On the other hand, there are occasions where even a 95 percent level of certainty is not high enough for us to let the matter rest. If investigators report that they are only 95 percent sure that Soft Drink X is not highly carcinogenic, then we expect the Food and Drug Administration to take it off the shelves. A 5 percent risk of error in this case would be unacceptable.

The level of conviction the writer aims to bring the audience to depends, therefore, on the situation. A fair rule of thumb is that the more serious the consequences of accepting or rejecting a fact, the higher the level of conviction writers must inspire in their audiences.

THE BURDEN OF PROOF

The case of the Food and Drug Administration brings to mind another important aspect of persuasion, one that is usually named the "burden of proof." The best-known example of an assigned burden of proof comes from the Anglo-American legal system, which tells prosecutors in criminal cases that they must "prove beyond reasonable doubt" that the accused is guilty. Think what this means in terms of our scale of conviction. Use zero to mean that the accused is assuredly innocent and 100 to mean that he or she is assuredly guilty. Under our legal system jurors are instructed to consider the accused "innocent until proven guilty," that is, they *must* start at the zero point. And if the prosecution is to succeed, the prosecutor must bring them very near the 100 point. Unless the prosecution has very strong evidence, this movement will be impossible, *even if the defense says nothing*. The "burden of proof" is on the prosecution.

Rarely does a writer take on so severe a burden of proof as the prosecutor does. But every writer of a persuasive essay needs to think what the audience will or should assume in the absence of any compelling evidence. In the Shakespeare case, most audiences would assume that the man named Shakespeare wrote the works. Someone who wants to prove otherwise therefore faces a heavy burden. "Stratfordians" face a lighter burden: if they refute the arguments of someone like Twain the audience will probably return to its prior assumption that Shakespeare was the author. Logically, audiences should distribute the burden of proof equally in a case like this, but psychologically they may not.

If you look closely at Twain's argument and that of Professors Brown and Spencer, you'll see that arguers sometimes try to shift the burden of proof to their opponents. Twain relentlessly accuses the Stratfordians of "surmising" and "assuming" with "no evidence." Brown and Spencer do the same on the other side: "only when a believer in Bacon or Oxford or Marlowe produces sound evidence will scholars pay close attention to it and to him." Such reminders of points where the other side has failed to shoulder its burden are legitimate, but rarely can the burden be shifted entirely to the other side. The audience will ordinarily adopt the motto of Twain's home state: "I'm from Missouri; you'll have to show me."

SOME LOGICAL FALLACIES THAT CAN (AND SHOULD) HINDER PERSUASION

As every advertiser knows, persuasion is hardly an exact science, and audiences can sometimes be swayed by entirely irrational appeals. Most audiences, however, include reasonable people who will question a logically flawed argument and view with suspicion the position it is supposed to support. Philosophy textbooks present more logical fallacies than we can possibly discuss here, but we can deal with nine of the most common.

1. Circular Argument. Also known as "begging the question," this fallacy occurs when someone "reaches" a conclusion by a logical route that assumes the conclusion to be true: "We can trust the recommendations of the F.D.A. because the F.D.A.'s recommendations are good ones." A circular argument seems to chase its own tail endlessly, and we may be surprised at first that any writer would fall into one or that any audience would fall for one. But circularity is actually very common. In the Shakespeare debate, Twain justly accuses some of Shakespeare's biographers of circular argument. Shakespeare's plays, one argument goes, show a knowledge of the law, and we know that Shakespeare wrote the plays, and therefore we can assume that Shakespeare studied law informally; and since he studied law informally, there is no disparity between Shakespeare's formal education and the level of education shown in the plays, and since there is no disparity, we can continue to assume that Shakespeare wrote the plays. C. S. Lewis mentions a bit of circular reasoning practiced by a friend of his who saw a ghost. She wouldn't deny that she saw the ghost, but she knew that ghosts don't exist, and since ghosts don't exist, this one must have been a hallucination, and since this one was a hallucination, it didn't damage the conclusion that ghosts don't exist.

2. *Either/Or Argument.* Also called "false dilemma" or the "black/white" fallacy, this fault in argument oversimplifies a question by saying that there are only two possible and neatly opposed answers: "Either you love me, or you don't," "Shakespeare was either a university graduate or an uneducated farm boy." In many cases, there is a vast gray area between the extremes where we might look for the truth. Once again, this fallacy is embarrassingly common. Indeed, most participants in the Shakespeare controversy fall into the either/or fallacy by insisting that Shakespeare either wrote the works attributed to him or he didn't. It is at least possible that Shakespeare wrote some of the works and that other authors wrote the rest, in which case some of the difficulties raised by Shakespeare's wide range of knowledge vanish. It is also possible that many of the individual plays were collaborative efforts. Scholars know that some of "Shakespeare's" plays take plots, characters, settings, and even dialogue from books by other authors. They also suspect that some of the members of Shakespeare's theatrical company, better educated and more widely traveled, may have helped him revise drafts of his plays. To say that either Shakespeare wrote *Hamlet* or he didn't is, therefore, to oversimplify the question somewhat. He may have written much of it, borrowed parts from books, and relied on his collaborators for still other parts.

3. *The Bandwagon Fallacy.* This fallacy consists of assuming that the popular position is almost necessarily the correct position. If you are inclined to believe that Shakespeare wrote the works attributed him just because "everyone knows" that this is true (or twenty of the twenty people polled "knew"), then you have fallen victim to the bandwagon fallacy. Remember that everyone used to "know" that the world is flat and that the best treatment for a heart problem is to cut one of the patient's veins periodically to remove excess blood. The bandwagon fallacy has probably gained strength in recent years because the media now bombard us with the results of public opinion polls, and "expert" commentators present the results as if the opinion of the general public was the most expert opinion of all. The general opinion may or may not be correct; by definition it is not expert opinion.

4. *Ad Hominem Argument.* Also known as "poisoning the well," the *ad hominem* (Latin, "to the person") fallacy consists of attacking the character of those who advocate an opposing view in a way that is not logically pertinent to the argument. Someone who argued that Mark Twain's opinion on the

Shakespeare question could not be trusted because he was an atheist or an American would clearly be making an *ad hominem* argument. Rarely, outside the realm of politics, are *ad hominem* arguments so obvious. When one of the defenders of Shakespeare's claim characterized Calvin Hoffman (see Exercise 2, Fact 1) as "a Broadway press agent," however, he was using a more subtle smear tactic. On the one hand, it is fair to consider the credentials of someone who offers an "expert" opinion, and Hoffman was distinctly not a Harvard professor specializing in Shakespeare. On the other hand, he was a graduate of Columbia University and the author of several books of literary criticism and poetry, and his book is the result of nineteen years of research. To label him as "a Broadway press agent" is clearly an attempt to poison the well by suggesting that Hoffman is a shallow sensationalist whose opinions are not worth considering.

5. The Straw Man.   Closely related to the *ad hominem* argument is the setting up of what is called a "straw man," an opponent whose ideas are so clearly wrongheaded that they can easily be refuted. Sometimes the straw man is created by ignoring the strong points of an opponent's position, sometimes by combining the weak points of several opponents who may even disagree among themselves. Mark Twain creates a straw man when he lumps together several unnamed "Stratfordian" biographers and attributes to all of them the silliest speculations made by any of them. Like the *ad hominem* argument, the straw man fallacy is so common in politics that we almost expect to hear Republicans oversimplify and distort "the Democrat position" and Democrats do the same to "the Republican position." Of course, politicians are not generally regarded as trustworthy in such matters.

6. Hasty Generalization.   This fallacy consists of drawing a broad conclusion from a few unrepresentative examples. It is particularly dangerous when the writer then uses the conclusion as a "fact" in the next stage of an argument. Oscar James Campbell (see Exercise 2, Fact 3) offers the generalization that literate men of Shakespeare's time *often* chose to "sign" documents with a cross rather than their signatures. He uses this "fact" to refute the argument that John Shakespeare, William's father, who did sign documents with a cross, was an illiterate man. How legitimate Campbell's argument is depends largely on how many examples of sixteenth-century literate cross-signers his generalization is based on. He gives only *one* example, thus making the cautious reader wonder whether his generalization is a hasty one.

7. False Analogy.   Closely related to hasty generalization is false analogy, a fault in reasoning that comes from comparing things that are not truly comparable and so arriving at questionable conclusions. *Is Shakespeare Dead?* contains a magnificent false analogy in which Twain attempts to show how unlikely it is that a famous author's biography could be as mysterious as

Shakespeare's is by comparing Shakespeare's case to his own. On the face of it, the analogy seems logical. Like Shakespeare, Twain was born in a small village far from any great cultural center, and, like Shakespeare, he rose from obscurity to a high literary reputation. Building on the parallelism Twain points out that *his* biography is fairly easy to substantiate and has been largely substantiated by reporters who have interviewed his Hannibal schoolmates and dozens of other people who knew him well. "If Shakespeare had really been celebrated, like me, Stratford could have told things about him; and if my experience goes for anything, they'd have done it."

But *do* Twain's experiences go for anything here? Twain lived in a country and a period where writers had a high reputation and tended to become celebrities. Apparently writers of Shakespeare's time, particularly playwrights, were not held in high regard; many plays were performed and published without any mention of the author's name. Twain lived in an era when daily and weekly newspapers were eager to fill their columns with stories about celebrities. Shakespeare lived before there were newspapers. Encouraged by his publishers, Twain went on lecture tours that helped spread his fame throughout the country. So far as we know, writers in Shakespeare's time made no such efforts to draw attention to themselves.

8. Post Hoc Fallacy. This fallacy draws its name from the Latin phrase *post hoc, ergo propter hoc:* "after this, therefore because of this." It is a pattern of thinking that confuses sequence with causation. A child may discover that every time she watches her favorite football team on television, its players make some dreadful error. She may conclude that because the error followed her sitting down in front of the television, it was her observation of the game that caused the error. I distinctly remember drawing such a conclusion when I was a child, and I remember congratulating myself on one or two Oklahoma University victories that I caused by staying out of the living room.

Of course, it is sometimes true that the thing that comes before causes the thing that comes after, but the writer needs to give the reader strong reason to believe that this cause-and-effect connection is probable. When the advocates of the Earl of Oxford point out that Oxford's poems ceased just when "Shakespeare's" work began to appear, they imply that there is a causal link between the cessation of Oxford and the commencement of Shakespeare. And they are eager to provide the causal link—that Oxford assumed the pen name Shakespeare. But, as Professors Brown and Spencer point out, the timing of these events may be entirely coincidental. When a writer asserts a causal connection between events, he or she takes on a heavy burden of proof. Showing that one event followed another is simply not enough.

9. Tenuous Chain of Causation. This fallacy is essentially a variation of the *post hoc* fallacy. Perhaps the most delightful example comes from a story most of us learned in childhood:

For want of a nail the shoe was lost,
For want of a shoe the horse was lost,
For want of a horse the rider was lost,
For want of a rider the battle was lost,
For want of a battle the kingdom was lost,
And all for the want of a horseshoe nail.

Since the story is fictional, it is hard to challenge its truth, and yet we may be uneasy with the result. Imagine, for example, that a mob enraged at the loss of the kingdom decided to lynch the blacksmith who failed to hammer the nail securely. Surely this would be unjust. To use distinctions familiar to philosophers, the blacksmith's negligence (if it was negligence) may have been a "contributing cause" of the loss. But it was probably not a "sufficient cause" or a "necessary cause." That is, the kingdom could hardly have been lost *solely* because of the missing nail, and losing the nail would not *necessarily* lead to losing the kingdom.

Outside of the scientific laboratory, where events can be carefully controlled, almost every event has many causes, and almost every cause has many effects. To identify "the" cause of a great event like the loss of a kingdom is impossible. After all, there may have been other blacksmiths who also failed to hammer in nails properly. Perhaps the absence of *their* riders from the battle was as important as the absence of the rider who chose our unfortunate blacksmith. Perhaps some of the knights had eaten too heavy a supper or the general used an unwise strategy. The failure of our rider to show up may have been, as we say, the last straw, but it is unfair to call it *the* cause. Ordinarily, when a writer sets out to convince us that X was the cause of Y, we will insist that he show that this was the most significant cause, not merely a last straw. Sometimes we will insist that the writer show that his proposed cause is the *last* significant cause in a sequence of events. If, for example, in the final hour of the battle that lost the kingdom, the commander for the losing side directed his knights to charge into an ambush, we surely won't want to lynch the unfortunate blacksmith. It may be true that one more rider could have salvaged the situation, but the charge into the ambush contributed more heavily to the loss and contributed nearer to the fatal moment.

◆ *Identifying Flaws in Arguments.* The following statements are taken from published arguments. Removing a statement from its context makes it hard to evaluate, of course, but do your best: decide in each case whether you believe the statement contains a clear logical fallacy, is logically sound, or is in the gray area between. Be prepared to explain your reasoning. If you believe the statement is fallacious, try to identify the fallacy. If it doesn't precisely fit into the categories listed above, explain what is illogical about it in your own words.

EXERCISE 3

1. In 1976, John D. Rockefeller III published a *Newsweek* essay favoring abortion rights. The essay includes the following statement: ". . . those who support legalized abortion—and the opinion polls demonstrate them to be a majority—have been comparatively quiet. After all, they won their case in the Supreme Court decision. Legalized abortion is the law of the land. It is also in the mainstream of world opinion. The number of countries where abortion has been broadly legalized has increased steadily, today covering 60 percent of the world population. In this situation, there is a natural tendency to relax, to assume that the matter is settled and that the anti-abortion clamor will eventually die down. But it is conceivable that the United States could become the first democratic nation to turn back the clock by yielding to the pressure and reversing the Supreme Court decision."

2. In his 1963 essay "Letter from Birmingham Jail," Martin Luther King, Jr., justifies his violation of segregationist laws in the following statement: "One may well ask: 'How can you advocate breaking some laws and obeying others?' The answer lies in the fact that there are two types of laws: just and unjust. I would be the first to advocate obeying just laws. One has not only a legal but a moral responsibility to obey just laws. Conversely, one has a moral responsibility to disobey unjust laws."

3. In her 1977 book *The Plug-in Drug: Television, Children, and the Family*, Marie Winn makes the following statement: "The decreased opportunities for simple conversation between parents and children may help explain an observation made by an emergency room nurse at a Boston hospital. She reports that parents just seem to sit there these days when they come in with a sick or seriously injured child, although talking to the child would distract and comfort him. 'They don't seem to know *how* to talk to their own children at any length,' the nurse observes."

4. In a 1970 anti-abortion speech before the British House of Commons, Jill Knight made the following statement: "As any doctor knows, depression and rejection of the child is quite a normal phenomenon of early pregnancy. Perhaps the mother-to-be feels sick, perhaps she regrets spoiled holiday plans, perhaps she did not intend to start a baby just then. However, before the Abortion Act it would never have entered her head to go along to her G.P. and ask to have the pregnancy ended. Within a few weeks she would not only accept her condition, but usually begin to look forward with pleasure to her baby. Now, with the knowledge that the highest authority in the land has sanctioned it, and the fact that her temporary period of rejection corresponds with the 'best' time to have an abortion, medically speaking, off she goes."

5. In a 1988 essay advocating strict warning labels on alcoholic beverages, Patricia Taylor makes this statement about manufacturers of beer, wine, and liquor: "Some companies do sponsor occasional ads to remind us to drink 'moderately.' Unfortunately, those ads are designed more to undercut prevention-oriented legislative initiatives than to educate drinkers about health risks. The fact is, the $70 billion-a-year booze industry simply can't afford moderate drinking. Its best customers are heavy drinkers, who account for half of all sales. If those drinkers drank less, sales—and profits—would plummet."

EVALUATING FLAWED ARGUMENTS

There are purists who say that they will reject any argument that contains one of the logical fallacies noted above. If they make good on this statement, they must find themselves in an odd position—all alone on the logical mountaintop with no argument to keep them company. In the real world, where writers have limited time, space, and information, and readers have limited attention spans, almost all arguments of any complexity are flawed. It is possible that Oscar James Campbell's research had uncovered hundreds of authenticated examples of literate sixteenth-century individuals who signed their names with a cross. Who would want to read twenty pages laboriously explaining these cases? Sometimes it is better to risk the appearance of hasty generalization than to belabor a point. And sometimes the writer of a short essay is forced to present a complex situation in either/or terms even though he knows this is an oversimplification.

Most readers who learn to recognize logical fallacies also learn to evaluate their importance in the context of the whole argument. If the oversimplifying fallacy deals with a minor point or one on which there is little controversy, the reader may simply notice it and move on. If it deals with the center of a controversy, the reader will be more disturbed. If the author seems in general to be a reliable, honest person of good judgment, the reader will be inclined to assume that the oversimplification is innocent and that the writer is merely streamlining the presentation of a thoroughly considered line of thought. If the writer seems to be a bully or a person irrationally committed to a viewpoint, the reader will be more suspicious.

WEIGHING THE EVIDENCE

As we have seen, persuasive essays are ordinarily based on a body of what Mark Twain called "verified facts, established facts, undisputed facts." We should think briefly about what allows the writer and reader to treat a fact as "established."

There are, of course, philosophers who are willing to doubt everything including their own existence, but let's leave such extreme skepticism aside. Almost everyone will accept the factuality of things that they have encountered with their own senses, particularly if there are other witnesses present who experienced the same thing. If the day comes when I see a flying saucer with my own eyes, turn to my wife and say "Did you just see a flying saucer?" and hear her say "Yes," then I will accept as almost certain the fact that at least one flying saucer exists. Direct observation is the strongest sort of evidence, and it ordinarily overrides any of the weaker sorts we will now examine.

When we can't observe something with our own eyes, we will almost certainly be impressed by the testimony of several impartial eyewitnesses we view as reliable, particularly if their testimony is accompanied by documents or photographs dating from or near the moment of observation. If on July 5, 1994, Joan Didion, Maya Angelou, George Will, Annie Dillard, and George Bush issue independent statements that they saw a flying saucer hovering over the Washington Monument the day before, I will reluctantly accept the existence of this saucer as a fact, especially if I have also seen a photograph of it in the newspaper. As the number and the reliability of the eyewitnesses goes down, the certainty of a fact is diminished. If just one of these people reported the sighting and if there were no photograph, I would be more skeptical. If there were only the photograph, I would be very skeptical.

When the number of eyewitnesses from whom we hear directly is very small, we weigh the credibility of the witnesses carefully. If the only eyewitness to a saucer landing is a convicted perjurer who stands to gain thousands of dollars by selling his story, then most of us will not accept the landing as an established fact.

PHYSICAL EVIDENCE AND RELIANCE
ON AUTHORITIES

Very often, neither the reader nor the writer has direct access to eyewitnesses or their testimony. Now we are dependent on physical evidence, "filtered" testimony, or a combination of the two. Shakespeare's will is physical evidence. Not even Twain would dispute its existence or the existence of three signatures on it, and any argument that does not fit with this physical evidence is unlikely to be convincing.

On the other hand, there is a story that Shakespeare's father was a butcher and that "when he was a boy he exercised his father's Trade, but when he kill'd a Calfe, he would doe it in a *high style*, & make a speech." This story was reported by John Aubrey in 1681 and is, he says, based on an interview with a Mr. Beeston of Stratford. There is physical evidence that Aubrey recorded the story, since we have it in his handwriting, but how reliable is Aubrey? How good is his judgment of Beeston's reliability? From whom did Beeston get the story?

We have now reached a point where we must rely on layers of authority. If experts on Aubrey report that he is a fine judge of a witness's reliability, then we *might* elevate this rumor about the speech-making to the level of fact. If the experts who praise Aubrey are themselves unreliable, however, the situation is different: it is possible that Aubrey was a gullible gossip-monger, that Beeston was a liar, and that Shakespeare never slaughtered a calf. Every expert is a sort of filter through which evidence passes on its way to us. In effect, experts do some of our thinking for us and give us the result of their deliberation. When the evidence is very complex, this filtering process is essential to our knowing anything, but turning our thinking over to someone else is inherently dangerous.

Careful readers and writers use several tactics to protect themselves from being misinformed by the authorities they rely on. First, they inquire into the credentials of supposed experts. What sort of experience do these experts have, what sort of education? Second, they check for bias. Is there reason to think that the expert stands to benefit from the opinion she gives? Third, they consult several authorities, preferably authorities with offsetting biases. If both the Stratfordian experts and the Baconian experts accept the calf-slaughtering story as true, we will be more likely to believe it ourselves. Fourth, and most important, careful readers and writers attempt to examine for themselves at least some of the evidence on which the expert judgment is based. Evidence that has been filtered through several levels of expertise may be interpreted beyond recognition. Before you accept at second or third hand Charles Wisner Barrell's assertion that three Shakespeare portraits are really retouched portraits of Edward de Vere, go to the library shelf, find the January 1940 copy of *Scientific American,* and examine the photographs with your own eyes. You may be shocked to discover that the crucial details are mere blurs and that in some cases Barrell has retouched a photograph to make us see what he imagines himself to have seen.

WRITING A PERSUASIVE ESSAY ABOUT DISPUTED FACTS: POINTS TO CONSIDER

To write persuasively about disputes of fact, you need to have a clear sense of where you stand and good judgment about how firm the ground underfoot really is. If the topic is a familiar one, you may have investigated it thoroughly. You may already have given due consideration to opposing viewpoints and have arrived at a position in which you are reasonably confident without being closed-minded. If, however, there is the least chance that your opinion on the subject needs to be ripened by further consideration, I urge you to use the five-part "dechanneling" procedure described in Chapter 5 (page 160). Often, exploring the question in this way will show you that you need to do more research and thinking before you commit yourself to a position.

Before you become too deeply involved in your argument, gauge your own level of conviction and the level of conviction you aim to inspire in your audience. Must you convince them that some "fact" is virtually certain, or is it enough to convince them that it is more probable than not? Is your aim to raise your readers' confidence in a view they are already inclined to accept, or is it to challenge their view? How heavy a burden of proof are you assuming?

To be sure that you haven't been blinded by your own prejudices, have a draft critiqued by someone who disagrees with your view of the subject. Have your reviewer state her own position before and after reading your essay. Did you get the movement you hoped for? Why or why not?

QUESTIONS FOR PEER REVIEW

You might ask your reviewer to respond to the general peer-review questions from Chapter 2 (pages 65–66), and you may want to add three others:

1. Is my essay entirely free of logical fallacies?

2. Is my evidence, including my use of authorities, unchallengeable?

3. Do I present myself as a reasonable person whose judgment can be trusted in an area of uncertainty?

If your reviewer answers yes to all these questions, you should probably ask for a second opinion before undertaking the final draft. Few arguments are completely untainted by fallacious reasoning, and almost all evidence is challengeable. The best help your reviewer can offer is locating the weakest links in the chain of your argument.

ASSIGNMENT 1: *A TEMPERATE STATEMENT OF YOUR POSITION ON A PUBLICLY DISPUTED FACT*

Each of the following facts (or "facts") has been disputed in the national or international press. In an essay comparable in length and tone to Professors Brown and Spencer's discussion of the Shakespeare question, inform your readers about the nature of the controversy and indicate your own position. Your essay should be written with a tone, content, and style appropriate for publication in an encyclopedia.

1. *The United States landed a man on the moon in 1969.* A poll taken in the early 1970s indicated that fewer than half the people in the world believed this to be true, and a January 1990 article in *The Wall Street Journal* indicates that in many parts of the world skepticism continues to run high. The following sources could serve as starting points for research:

   a. Schadewald, Robert J. "Earth Orbits? Moon Landings? A Fraud! Says This Prophet." *Science Digest* July 1980: 58–63.
   b. Ledeen, Michael. "Those Fun-Loving Pranksters at NASA." *Wall Street Journal* 23 Jan. 1990: A18.
   c. Jensen, Oliver. "They're Keeping It Hushed Up." *Harper's* Dec. 1984: 48.
   d. *Omni* July 1989. [Special Commemorative Issue: Twentieth Anniversary of the First Moon Landing.]

2. *Because of television, Americans today are better informed about international affairs than Americans were in the pretelevision era.* The following sources could serve as starting points:

   a. Mander, Jerry. *Four Arguments for the Elimination of Television.* 1978. [See chapters entitled "Information Loss" and "Expropriation of Knowledge."]
   b. Weisman, John. "Are We Better Informed Now—or Worse?" *Impact of Mass Media.* Ed. Ray Hiebert. 2nd ed., 1988.
   c. "China and the Power of the Tube." *Broadcasting* 26 June 1989: 34.

d. Karp, W. "Where the Media Critics Went Wrong." *American Heritage* March 1988: 76–79.

3. *The United States invaded Grenada in 1983 because the lives of American medical students in Grenada were in danger.* Some people have questioned this fact. The following sources could serve as starting points:

   a. "1,900 U.S. Troops, with Caribbean Allies, Invade Grenada" and "School's Chancellor Says Invasion Was Not Necessary to Save Lives." *New York Times* 26 Oct. 1983: A1, A20.
   b. Buckley, William. "Missing the Point of Grenada." *National Review* 25 Nov. 1983: 1504–45.
   c. Brands, H. W. "Decisions on American Armed Intervention." *Political Science Quarterly* Winter 1987: 607–24.

4. *Reducing serum cholesterol levels will significantly improve the health of Americans.* Some researchers and physicians disagree. The following sources could serve as starting points:

   a. Moore, Thomas J. "The Cholesterol Myth." *The Atlantic* September 1989: 37–70.
   b. "Letters to the Editor." *The Atlantic* Jan. 1990: 8–18.
   c. Gannes, Stewart. "Behind the Battle over Cholesterol." *Fortune* 18 Dec. 1989: 101–116.
   d. Raeburn, Paul. "The Great Cholesterol Debate: Is It a Myth—or a Killer?" *American Health* Jan.–Feb. 1990: 79–85. [Panel discussion.]

5. *Widespread burning of fossil fuel and deforestation are causing a global warming trend.* Some scientists and politicians dispute this fact and do not think that protective measures are warranted. The following sources could serve as starting points:

   a. White, Robert M. "The Great Climate Debate." *Scientific American* July 1990: 36–43.
   b. Brookes, Warren T. "The Global Warming Panic: A Classic Case in Overreaction." *Forbes* 25 Dec. 1989: 96–102.
   c. "Split Forecast: Dissent on Global Warming—A Special Report," *New York Times* 13 Dec. 1989: A1.
   d. "Curing the Greenhouse Effect Could Run into the Trillions," *New York Times* 19 Nov. 1989: 1.

You can probably think of other disputed facts that could be added to this list and serve as good topics for an essay.

ASSIGNMENT 2: *A Strong Advocacy of an Unpopular Opinion*

Write a "minority report" on a subject like those suggested for Assignment 1. To do this assignment properly, you need to identify a "fact" that most people believe to be true and then argue that there is reason to doubt it. You need not, for this assignment, maintain a scholarly decorum. You may, like Twain, adopt a more aggressive tone than would be appropriate for the *Encyclopaedia Britannica*. You might imagine your essay appearing on the opinion/editorial page of a newspaper with a wide circulation.

ASSIGNMENT 3: *A Balanced Treatment of a Factual Dispute Closer to Home*

It is not only questions of national and international interest that produce disputes about facts. Every parent has had to sort through the conflicting stories of children. Every community produces gossip and countergossip about its members. A college or university newspaper will often include conflicting claims about what a person said or did or about what the actual cause of a campus crisis was. Find one of these more local disputes of fact and write an essay in which you explain it clearly and show the reasoning that leads you to accept one version of the truth over another. Strive for the sort of moderate tone that Professors Brown and Spencer adopt in their discussion of the Shakespeare question.

ASSIGNMENT 4: *An Analysis of a Persuasive Essay*

To get a clearer picture of how the principles discussed in this chapter apply to published persuasive essays, subject one to a three-part analysis. First, comment on the author's tone, level of conviction, and purpose: Is this a cocksure writer attempting to win the reader over completely to one side of the issue? A cautious writer attempting to suggest that the reader also be cautious? Something else? Second, examine the logic of the essay: Has the author assumed the burden of truth? Does he or she commit or come close to committing any logical fallacies? If the reasoning is sometimes fallacious, how much damage does this do to the argument's credibility? Third, examine the evidence the author bases his or her reasoning on: does the author refer you to your own experience, write from personal experience, or quote eyewitnesses directly? Does he or she point to physical evidence that you could conceivably examine yourself? Does he or she rely on authorities, and if so, how credible are they? When experts' opinions are cited, does the author describe any of the evidence on which these opinions are based? End your paper by estimating how the essay will affect the opinions of the audience. Consider the different effects the essay will have on readers who are relatively skeptical about the opinion the author advances and on readers who are relatively sympathetic to his or her position. Be sure that your analysis is itself persuasive: cite your evidence and explain your reasoning.

THE TRUTH ABOUT ROY MCCARTHY

Mary McCarthy

In Memories of a Catholic Girlhood, *Mary McCarthy tells the story of her family's disastrous 1918 railroad journey from Seattle to Minneapolis, during which both her father and her mother developed fatal cases of Spanish influenza. Orphaned at 6, McCarthy entered adult life with only fragmented memories of her mother and father. She remembered, for instance, her father's "coming home one night with his arms full of red roses for my mother, and my mother's crying out, 'Oh, Roy!' reproachfully because there was no food for dinner." This poverty contrasted sharply with the wealth of her father's parents, who occasionally sent their son small sums of money and who eventually insisted that he move from Seattle to Minneapolis so that they could "keep an eye on what was happening and try to curb my father's expenditures." In the preface to* Memories, *McCarthy sorts through conflicting stories about her father's character.*

1   AT THIS POINT, I MUST MENTION A THING that was told me, only a few years ago, by my uncle Harry, my father's younger brother. My father, he confided, was a periodical drunkard who had been a family problem from the time of his late teens. Before his marriage, while he was still in Minnesota, a series of trained nurses had been hired to watch over him and keep him off the bottle. But, like all drunkards, he was extremely cunning and persuasive. He eluded his nurses or took them with him (he had a weakness for women, too) on a series of wild bouts that would end, days or weeks later, in some strange Middle Western city where he was hiding. A trail of bad checks would lead the family to recapture him. Or a telegram for money would eventually reveal his whereabouts, though if any money was sent him, he was likely to bolt away again. The nurses having

proved ineffective, Uncle Harry was summoned home from Yale to look after him, but my father evaded him also. In the end, the family could no longer handle him, and he was sent out West as a bad job. That was how he came to meet my mother.

2   I have no idea whether this story is true or not. Nor will I ever know. To me, it seems improbable, for I am as certain as one can be that my father did not drink when I was a little girl. Children are sensitive to such things; their sense of smell, first of all, seems sharper than other people's, and they do not like the smell of alcohol. They are also quick to notice when anything is wrong in a household. I do recall my father's trying to make some homemade wine (this must have been just before Prohibition was enacted) out of some grayish-purple bricks that had been sold him as essence of grape. The experiment was a failure,

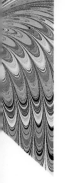

and he and my mother and their friends did a good deal of laughing about "Roy's wine." But if my father had been a dangerous drinker, my mother would not have laughed. Moreover, if he was a drinker, my mother's family seem not to have known it. I asked my mother's brother whether Uncle Harry's story could possibly be true. His answer was that it was news to him. It is just possible, of course, that my father reformed after his marriage, which would explain why my mother's family did not know of his habits, though as Uncle Harry pointed out, rather belligerently: "You would think they could have looked up their future son-in-law's history." Periodical drunkards, however, almost never reform, and if they do, they cannot touch wine. It remains a mystery, an eerie and troubling one. Could my father have been drinking heavily when he came home with those red roses, for my mother, in his arms? It is a drunkard's appeasing gesture, certainly, lordly and off-balance. Was that why my mother said, "Oh, Roy!"?

If my father was a sort of remittance man, sent out West by his family, it would justify the McCarthys, which was, of course, Uncle Harry's motive in telling me. He felt I had defamed his mother, and he wanted me to understand that, from where she sat, my father's imprudent marriage was the last straw. Indeed, from the McCarthy point of view, as given by Uncle Harry, my father's marriage was just another drunkard's dodge for extracting money from his father, all other means having failed. My mother, "your lovely mother," as Uncle Harry always calls her, was the innocent lure on the hook. Perhaps so. But I refuse to believe it. Uncle Harry's derelict brother, Roy, is not the same person as my father. I simply do not recognize him. ◆

3

WHAT WAS THE ACHEULEAN HAND AX?

Eileen M. O'Brien

Begun as an undergraduate research project, Eileen O'Brien's investigation of the possible uses of a prehistoric stone "ax" was so fruitful that it was published in Current Anthropology *(February 1981). The article there caught the attention of the editors of* Natural History, *who asked her to revise it for a more general readership. The resulting essay, published in* Natural History *in July 1984, shows a scientist's careful use of evidence in an argument, but also reveals the amount of speculation and debate that may lie behind a modest statement like "this prehistoric stone tool was thrown as a weapon."*

1   *A*BOUT ONE AND ONE-HALF MILLION YEARS ago, a new type of large, symmetrically shaped stone implement entered the prehistoric tool kit, signaling both an advance in early craftsmanship and the advent of *Homo erectus,* a small-brained but otherwise fairly recognizable form of human being. The tool was the hand ax, which these ancestral humans faithfully made for well over one million years. Named for archaeological finds at Saint Acheul, France, examples of the Acheulean hand ax are found from the Vaal River of South Africa to the lakes, bogs, and rivers of Europe, from the shores of the Mediterranean to India and Indonesia. Such continuity over time and space speaks to us of use, success, and reuse—a design integral to some task, a task appropriate or essential to diverse environments. *Homo erectus* needed tools: tools to cut, slice, and chop; to dig, pound, and grind; tools to defend against predators and competitors, to procure and process food or other materials, even tools to make tools. But which task (or tasks) the hand ax performed is still being debated.

2   The average hand ax looks like a giant stone almond, although some are more ovate and others more triangular. Crafted from a stone core or flake, it can range in size from only a few inches to a foot or more, but more are six or seven inches long. Whether roughly finished or as refined as a work of art, the hand ax always has an eccentric center of gravity and a sharp edge around all or most of its perimeter. Thus in cross section lengthwise, it resembles a stretched-out teardrop.

3   Some have speculated that the hand ax's design was not functional but purely aesthetic or that it was a byproduct of the manufacture of the sharp flakes used in butchering. Most anthropologists, however, assume it was a practical implement. Initially, prehistorians thought it was a hafted, multipurpose tool and weapon like the stone hatchet, or ax, of the aboriginal Americans and Australians. But there is no evidence that it was hafted until much later in time, not until after the evolution of *Homo sapiens.* Another proposal, advanced to explain why excavators find some

hand axes standing on edge, *in situ,*[1] is that the hand ax acted as a stationary tool, one edge embedded in the earth while the exposed edge cut or scraped an object passed over it. But the common and traditional interpretation is that it was a hand-held tool for butchering, cutting, scraping, digging, or as its name implies, chopping.

4   Experiments show that these important tasks can be accomplished with a hand ax. But *Homo erectus* possessed other tools suitable for these purposes— tools that precede and continue alongside the hand ax in the archaeological record. Compared with these, the hand ax was costly to produce in terms of time, labor, and skill, and required larger blocks of fine-grained, faultless stone such as flint or basalt. The hand ax also presented a hazard. Since a heavy object requires effort to wield and carry, we may assume the mass of the hand ax was important to its function. Force in the form of increased momentum would be useful for chopping, for example, as compared with a task like scraping, where the user exerts all the energy in the form of pressure. But without a safe handhold, the sharp edge of the hand ax, when used with force, was (and is) capable of inflicting as much damage on the user as on the material being worked.

5   Whatever its function, the hand ax represented to its users not only an investment of energy but also a source of raw material. They would have saved and reused a hand ax for as long as possible and retouched it when necessary. With time and repeated repair, it would have become smaller; once irreparably damaged, what remained could then have served as a core in the production of still smaller stone tools. Accordingly, except for those hand axes that were misplaced or lost, the hand ax should not be in the archaeological record. Excavators, however, recover hand axes in abundance, mostly at sites that are within or alongside what were once (and may still be) watercourses or wetland environments. For example, at the Acheulean site of Olorgesailie (one of the East

---

[1] *in situ:* in its natural location.

African sites southwest of Nairobi, Kenya, in the Eastern Rift Valley), hundreds of large hand axes were deposited about four hundred thousand years ago in what appears to have been a shallow stream bed. Elsewhere across the landscape, hand axes are rare, although they are occasionally found in some numbers in prehistoric cave sites. This suggests that during some activity that took place near water, hand axes were used and lost with astonishing frequency.

6   If we let the evidence speak for itself, the appropriate question is: What task would require force, call for a tool with a sharp edge around all (or most) of its perimeter but without a safe handhold, occur in or near water, and often result in the loss of a potentially reusable and valuable artifact? The possibility that occurred to me is that the hand ax was a projectile weapon. The idea, I have since discovered, has been thought of before, but not pursued. Use of the hand ax as a weapon has been suggested since at least the sixteenth century, and small hand axes have been proposed as projectiles since the nineteenth century, most enjoyably by H. G. Wells[2] in his *Tales of Time and Space* (1899). More recently, M. D. W. Jeffreys, a South African anthropologist, wrote that the small- to medium-sized Vaal River hand axes would make good bird-hunting weapons if thrown overhand, like a knife ("The Handbolt." *Man*, 1965). But the idea that hand axes were in general used as projectiles has not taken hold, probably because it is not obvious how the larger hand axes could have been thrown.

7   By analogy with modern forms, we understand how prehistoric stone arrowheads and spearpoints were propelled and used as weapons or how a stone ball ("spheroid," to archaeologists) could be thrown or used in a bola (a weighted thong or cord thrown to entangle prey). But what about the hand ax? One way might be overhand, as Jeffreys suggested. Other methods of throwing a small- to medium-sized hand ax might be the side/overhand throw used in baseball and perhaps the backhand throw used in both knife and frisbee throwing. To throw a large, heavy hand ax, however, a sidearm or underhand throw might be

---

[2]H. G. Wells: novelist and science-fiction writer (1866–1946).

preferable. A few years ago, I decided that a practical experiment was what was needed. From my limited knowledge of track and field, I thought that for sidearm throwing, an analogy might be made between a hand ax and the Olympic discus.

8   Like a hand ax, the early discus of the ancient Greeks was unhafted, edged all around, and made of stone. It also varied in size from about half a foot to more than one foot in diameter, and in weight from about two and one-quarter pounds to more than fourteen and one-half pounds. (Actually, the word *discus* means "a thing for throwing" or "a thing thrown"; the discus thrown by Odysseus in Homer's *Odyssey*, for example, is thought by some scholars to refer to a beach cobble.) Unlike a hand ax, the classic Greek discus was perfectly round. (The modern regulation discus, which weighs 2 kilograms, or 4.4 pounds, is made of wood and weighted with metal around the edge to accelerate its spinning motion. The longer and faster it spins, the more stable the flight pattern and the longer the flight, all else being equal.)

9   The hand ax I chose for the throwing experiment was the largest I could find in the Olorgesailie collection at the National Museums of Kenya, Nairobi (I was in Africa at the time doing fieldwork unrelated to this topic). Because the original could not be used—and raw material for making a "real" hand ax of such size was difficult to obtain—a fiberglass replica was made. The original hand ax is a little more than a foot long, ovate shaped, and edged all around. It is made of basalt and weighs about four pounds, three ounces. J. D. Ambrosse Esa (then head of the museum's casting department) supervised the casting and the accurate weighting of the facsimile to within one and one-half ounces of the original.

10   The experiment took place in 1978, in the discus practice area at the University of Massachusetts, where I was then a student. Two student athletes participated: Karl Nyholm, a discus thrower, and George Peredy, a javelin thrower. One day in late April, and again two weeks later, both threw the hand ax discus-style. Peredy also threw it overhand. To maximize potential accuracy in the discus throw, the thrower did not whirl.

11   The first to throw the hand ax discus-style was Karl Nyholm. He took the unfamiliar object in his right hand, grasping it every which way before settling on the butt. He tossed it up and down for balance and "feel," then crouched and practiced his swing. Ready, he paced off from the release line. With his back to the field, he spread his legs apart, bent at the knees, and twisted his right arm far behind him. Then he began the throw: his outstretched left hand grasping at air, weight shifting from right foot to left, he rotated to face the field. The burdened right hand swung wide and low and then raced upward. With a great exhalation of breath, he hurled himself out straight and let go. Silently, gracefully spinning, the hand ax soared.

12   Like a discus, the hand ax spun horizontally as it rose, but changed its orientation in midair. On reaching its maximum altitude, it rolled onto its edge and descended in a perpendicular position, its spinning motion appearing to decline. Then, with a thud, it landed point first, slicing deeply into the thawing earth. In both throwing bouts, regardless of thrower, the hand ax repeated this flight pattern when thrown discus-style. It landed on edge forty-two out of forty-five throws, thirty-one of which were point first. The average throw was about one-third the length of a football field (almost 102 feet), and usually accurate to within two yards right or left of the line of trajectory.

13   The propensity of the hand ax to pivot onto its edge in mid-flight was unexpected and curious. But, as suggested to me by several track coaches, it may be related to the same factors that can produce the "peel-off" pattern in a thrown discus, some function of the manner of release and the thrower's expertise. A full explanation of the physical principles involved must await an interpretation by someone with the relevant expertise. What is important is that it does happen. By so doing, it makes on-edge impact of a thrown hand ax predictable. The further tendency of the hand ax to

© Eileen M. O'Brien

land point first does not appear accidental and adds to the implement's potential to inflict damage. If the hand ax can also be thrown so that it behaves exactly like the discus in both ascent and descent (more recent demonstrations support this possibility), then by simply changing the angle and manner of release it should be possible to strike a target with either a horizontally or vertically directed edge.

14   Modern discus throwing is not known for its accuracy. But in terms of how far a hand ax might ideally be thrown, it is worth noting that the 1980 Olympic record in discus was 218.8 feet. Since the experimental hand ax weighs only two and a half ounces less than the modern Olympic discus, this suggests that as the thrower's skill and/or strength increase, the potential flight distance of the hand ax increases.

15   When grasped and thrown overhand, like a knife, the experimental hand ax performed like one, rotating symmetrically on edge in both ascent and descent. The average throw was just short of discus-style, but more accurate, about half a yard right or left of the line of trajectory. It always landed on edge, but less often point first. Unfortunately, these results are the product of only six throws; owing to its

weight and the ovate, broad point, the experimental hand ax was difficult to grasp and throw overhand. George Peredy, who was the thrower, also appeared to tire more quickly using this method and probably could not have used it at all if he had not had large hands, in proportion to his six-foot six-inch frame. This overhand style would probably be more suitable for lighter, more triangular hand axes. In contrast, weight and shape were of no real concern when throwing the hand ax discus-style. Even a significant increase in weight might not have impeded the throwing motion, although it would have affected the distance of the throw.

16   Further testing is needed (and is currently under way), but these first trials showed that a hand ax could perform appropriately as a projectile. The hand ax demonstrated a propensity to land on edge when thrown overhand or discus-style, a tendency to land point first, and a potential for distant and accurate impact. Its overall shape minimizes the effects of resistance while in flight, as well as at impact. This is not true of an unshaped stone or a spheroid, for example. And despite its sharp edge, the hand ax could be launched without a safe handhold. The only apparent limitations to the hand ax's use as a projectile weapon are the strength, coordination, and skill of the thrower.

17   *Homo erectus* was bipedal, probably dexterous enough to manipulate a hand ax in either of the tested throwing styles, and very much stronger than most modern humans. With their technique perfected over years of practice and use, our ancestors probably surpassed the accuracy shown in the experimental throws. I suspect the hand ax simply reflects a refinement in missile design, one that allowed for successful long-distance offense and defense against larger animals. This is consistent with evidence that big-game hunting appears for the first time in the archaeological record along with *Homo erectus*.

18   Perfected through trial and error, the hand ax would not necessarily have replaced preexisting projectile or handheld weapons, because weapons and strategies probably varied with the predator being deterred or the game being hunted. Hand axes would

have been especially effective in a collective strategy, such as a group of hunters bombarding a herd. To overcome any difficulty in transporting hand axes, *Homo erectus* could have used carrying slings made from hide, stockpiled hand axes near hunting areas, or cached them (in caves, for example) prior to seasonal migrations.

        Hunting near water, where game is relatively   19 predictable and often concentrated, offers a simple explanation of why hand axes are recovered there in abundance—as well as the phenomenon of hand axes embedded on edge *in situ*. Hand axes that missed their mark, landing in water or dense vegetation on the banks of a river, might have been difficult or impossible to retrieve. Over time, with continued exploitation of an area, projectiles would accumulate like golf balls in a water trap. Elsewhere across the landscape, retrieval is more likely and the hand ax should be rare. This distribution pattern, as noted by English archaeologist L. H. Keeley, resembles that of the Indian projectile points across the American Southwest. (Keeley, however, does not believe that the hand ax was a projectile.)

        Homo erectus, like later *Homo sapiens,* was   20 physically defenseless compared with the rest of the animal kingdom. Relatively slow, without canines, claws, tusks, or other natural means of defense, these early humans were easy prey when out of a tree. With handheld weapons they could defend themselves, once attacked. With projectile weapons they could wound, maim, or kill without making physical contact, avoiding assault or retaliation. Modern humans are notoriously expert at killing from a distance. The hand ax may be proof that this behavioral strategy was refined long ago, at a time when truly "giants strode the earth"—when by dint of size the megamammals of the Pleistocene asserted their dominance, when migrating game might pass in a continuous parade for days without a break in their ranks, and humankind struggled to survive, both consumer and consumed. At the other end of time, at the dawn of history, is it possible that the ancient Greeks preserved as a sport a tradition handed down from that distant yesterday? ◆

WHITE LIES

Sissela Bok

Sissela Bok is an expert on professional ethics and has been a lecturer on medical ethics in the Harvard-M.I.T. Division of Health Sciences and Technology. In this selection from Lying: Moral Choice in Public and Private Life *(1978), she argues against the apparently self-evident proposition that white lies harm no one. Arguments on moral questions often involve statements of value rather than statements of fact, but Bok's argument here is practical. She attempts to make her case by demonstrating the effects of supposedly benign deception.*

NEVER HAVE I LIED IN MY OWN INTEREST; BUT *often I have lied through shame in order to draw my- self from embarrassment in indifferent matters [. . .] when, having to sustain discussion, the slowness of my ideas and the dryness of my conversation forced me to have recourse to fictions in order to say something.*

—JEAN-JACQUES ROUSSEAU, Reveries of
a Solitary Walker

When a man declares that he "has great pleasure in accepting" a vexatious invitation or is the "obedient servant" of one whom he regards as an inferior, he uses phrases which were probably once deceptive. If they are so no longer, Common Sense condemns as over-scrupulous the refusal to use them where it is customary to do so. But Common Sense seems doubt- ful and perplexed where the process of degradation is incomplete and there are still persons who may be de- ceived: as in the use of the reply that one is "not at home" to an inconvenient visitor from the country.

—HENRY SIDGWICK, Methods of Ethics

HARMLESS LYING

1 White lies are at the other end of the spectrum of de- ception from lies in a serious crisis. They are the most common and the most trivial forms that duplicity can take. The fact that they are so common provides their protective coloring. And their very triviality, when compared to more threatening lies, makes it seem un- necessary or even absurd to condemn them. Some consider *all* well-intentioned lies, however momentous, to be white; in this book, I shall adhere to the nar- rower usage: a white lie, in this sense, is a falsehood not meant to injure anyone, and of little moral im- port. I want to ask whether there *are* such lies; and if there are, whether their cumulative consequences are still without harm; and, finally, whether many lies are not defended as "white" which are in fact harmful in their own right.

2 Many small subterfuges may not even be in- tended to mislead. They are only "white lies" in the most marginal sense. Take, for example, the many so- cial exchanges: "How nice to see you!" or "Cordially Yours." These and a thousand other polite expressions are so much taken for granted that if someone de- cided, in the name of total honesty, not to employ them, he might well give the impression of an indiffer- ence he did not possess. The justification for continu- ing to use such accepted formulations is that they de- ceive no one, except possibly those unfamiliar with the language.

3 A social practice more clearly deceptive is that of giving a false excuse so as not to hurt the feelings of someone making an invitation or request: to say one "can't" do what in reality one may not *want* to do. Once again, the false excuse may prevent unwar- ranted inferences of greater hostility to the undertak- ing than one may well feel. Merely to say that one can't do something, moreover, is not deceptive in the sense that an elaborately concocted story can be.

Still other white lies are told in an effort to flatter, to throw a cheerful interpretation on depressing circumstances, or to show gratitude for unwanted gifts. In the eyes of many, such white lies do no harm, provide needed support and cheer, and help dispel gloom and boredom. They preserve the equilibrium and often the humaneness of social relationships, and are usually accepted as excusable so long as they do not become excessive. Many argue, moreover, that such deception is so helpful and at times so necessary that it must be tolerated as an exception to a general policy against lying. Thus Bacon[1] observed:

5   Doth any man doubt, that if there were taken out of men's minds vain opinions, flattering hopes, false valuations, imaginations as one would, and the like, but it would leave the minds of a number of men poor shrunken things, full of melancholy and indisposition, and unpleasing to themselves?

6   Another kind of lie may actually be advocated as bringing a more substantial benefit, or avoiding a real harm, while seeming quite innocuous to those who tell the lies. Such are the placebos given for innumerable common ailments, and the pervasive use of inflated grades and recommendations for employment and promotion.

7   A large number of lies without such redeeming features are nevertheless often regarded as so trivial that they should be grouped with white lies. They are the lies told on the spur of the moment, for want of reflection, or to get out of a scrape, or even simply to pass the time. Such are the lies told to boast or exaggerate, or on the contrary to deprecate and understate;[2] the many lies told or repeated in gossip; Rousseau's[3] lies told simply "in order to say something"; the embroidering on facts that seem too tedious in

their own right; and the substitution of a quick lie for the lengthy explanations one might otherwise have to provide for something not worth spending time on.

8   Utilitarians often cite white lies as the *kind* of deception where their theory shows the benefits of common sense and clear thinking. A white lie, they hold, is trivial; it is either completely harmless, or so marginally harmful that the cost of detecting and evaluating the harm is much greater than the minute harm itself. In addition, the white lie can often actually be beneficial, thus further tipping the scales of utility. In a world with so many difficult problems, utilitarians might ask: Why take the time to weigh the minute pros and cons in telling someone that his tie is attractive when it is an abomination, or of saying to a guest that a broken vase was worthless? Why bother even to define such insignificant distortions or make mountains out of molehills by seeking to justify them?

9   Triviality surely does set limits to when moral inquiry is reasonable. But when we look more closely at practices such as placebo-giving, it becomes clear that all lies defended as "white" cannot be so easily dismissed. In the first place, the harmlessness of lies is notoriously disputable. What the liar perceives as harmless or even beneficial may not be so in the eyes of the deceived. Second, the failure to look at an entire practice rather than at their own isolated case often blinds liars to cumulative harm and expanding deceptive activities. Those who begin with white lies can come to resort to more frequent and more serious ones. Where some tell a few white lies, others may tell more. Because lines are so hard to draw, the indiscriminate use of such lies can lead to other deceptive practices. The aggregate harm from a large number of marginally harmful instances may, therefore, be highly undesirable in the end—for liars, those deceived, and honesty and trust more generally.

10   Just as the life-threatening cases showed the Kantian analysis[4] to be too rigid, so the cases of white lies show the casual utilitarian calculation to be inade-

---

[1]Bacon: Francis Bacon (1561–1626), British essayist, philosopher, and statesman.
[2]Aristotle, in *Nicomachean Ethics*, contrasts these as "boasting" and "irony." He sees them as extremes between which the preferable mean of truthfulness is located. [author's note]
[3]Rousseau: Jean Jacques Rousseau (1712–78), French philosopher, author, and political theorist, known as the father of French romanticism.

---

[4]Kantian analysis: based on the belief of Immanuel Kant (1724–1804) that certain rules are essential to our moral consciousness and should under no circumstances be violated.

quate. Such a criticism of utilitarianism does not attack its foundations, because it does not disprove the importance of weighing consequences. It merely shows that utilitarians most often do not weigh enough factors in their quick assumption that white lies are harmless. They often fail to look at *practices* of deception and the ways in which these multiply and reinforce one another. They tend to focus, rather, on the individual case, seen from the point of view of the individual liar.

11   In the post-Watergate period, no one need regard a concern with the combined and long-term effects of deception as far-fetched. But even apart from political life, with its peculiar and engrossing temptations, lies tend to spread. Disagreeable facts come to be sugar-coated, and sad news softened or denied altogether. Many lie to children and to those who are ill about matters no longer peripheral but quite central, such as birth, adoption, divorce, and death. Deceptive propaganda and misleading advertising abound. All these lies are often dismissed on the same grounds of harmlessness and triviality used for white lies in general.

12   It is worth taking a closer look at practices where lies believed trivial are common. Triviality in an isolated lie can then be more clearly seen to differ markedly from the costs of an entire practice—both to individuals and to communities. One such practice is that of giving placebos.

PLACEBOS

13   The common practice of prescribing placebos to unwitting patients illustrates the two miscalculations so common to minor forms of deceit: ignoring possible harm and failing to see how gestures assumed to be trivial build up into collectively undesirable practices.[5] Placebos have been used since the beginning of

---

[5]This discussion draws on my two articles, "Paternalistic Deception in Medicine and Rational Choice: The Use of Placebos," in Max Black, ed., *Problems of Choice and Decision* (Ithaca, N.Y.: Cornell University Program on Science, Technology and Society, 1975), pp. 73–107; and "The Ethics of Giving Placebos," *Scientific American* 231 (1974):17–23. [author's note]

medicine. They can be sugar pills, salt-water injections—in fact, any medical procedure which has no specific effect on a patient's condition, but which can have powerful psychological effects leading to relief from symptoms such as pain or depression.

Placebos are prescribed with great frequency. Exactly how often cannot be known, the less so as physicians do not ordinarily talk publicly about using them. At times, self-deception enters in on the part of physicians, so that they have unwarranted faith in the powers of what can work only as a placebo. As with salesmanship, medication often involves unjustified belief in the excellence of what is suggested to others. In the past, most remedies were of a kind that, unknown to the medical profession and their patients, could have only placebic benefits, if any.

15   The derivation of "placebo," from the Latin for "I shall please," gives the word a benevolent ring, somehow placing placebos beyond moral criticism and conjuring up images of hypochondriacs whose vague ailments are dispelled through adroit prescriptions of beneficent sugar pills. Physicians often give a humorous tinge to instructions for prescribing these substances, which helps to remove them from serious ethical concern. One authority wrote in a pharmacological journal that the placebo should be given a name previously unknown to the patient and preferably Latin and polysyllabic, and added:

16   [I]t is wise if it be prescribed with some assurance and emphasis for psychotherapeutic effect. The older physicians each had his favorite placebic prescriptions—one chose tincture of Condurango, another the Fluidextract of *Cimicifuga nigra*.[6]

17   After all, health professionals argue, are not placebos far less dangerous than some genuine drugs? And more likely to produce a cure than if nothing at all is prescribed? Such a view was expressed in a letter to the *Lancet:*

18   Whenever pain can be relieved with a ml of saline, why should we inject an opiate? Do anxieties or

---

[6]O. H. Pepper, "A Note on the Placebo," *American Journal of Pharmacy* 117 (1945):409–12. [author's note]

discomforts that are allayed with starch capsules require administration of a barbiturate, diazepam, or propoxyphene?[7]

Such a simplistic view conceals the real costs of placebos, both to individuals and to the practice of medicine. First, the resort to placebos may actually prevent the treatment of an underlying, undiagnosed problem. And even if the placebo "works," the effect is often short-lived; the symptoms may recur, or crop up in other forms. Very often, the symptoms of which the patient complains are bound to go away by themselves, sometimes even from the mere contact with a health professional. In those cases, the placebo itself is unnecessary; having recourse to it merely reinforces a tendency to depend upon pills or treatments where none is needed.

20   In the aggregate, the costs of placebos are immense. Many millions of dollars are expended on drugs, diagnostic tests, and psychotherapies of a placebic nature. Even operations can be of this nature—a hysterectomy may thus be performed, not because the condition of the patient requires such surgery, but because she goes from one doctor to another seeking to have the surgery performed, or because she is judged to have a great fear of cancer which might be alleviated by the very fact of the operation.

21   Even apart from financial and emotional costs and the squandering of resources, the practice of giving placebos is wasteful of a very precious good: the trust on which so much in the medical relationship depends. The trust of those patients who find out they have been duped is lost, sometimes irretrievably. They may then lose confidence in physicians and even in bona fide medication which they may need in the future. They may obtain for themselves more harmful drugs or attach their hopes to debilitating fad cures.

22   The following description of a case[8] where a placebo was prescribed reflects a common approach:

23   A seventeen-year-old girl visited her pediatrician, who had been taking care of her since infancy. She went to his office without her parents, although her mother had made the appointment for her over the telephone. She told the pediatrician that she was very healthy, but that she thought she had some emotional problems. She stated that she was having trouble sleeping at night, that she was very nervous most of the day. She was a senior in high school and claimed she was doing quite poorly in most of her subjects. She was worried about what she was going to do next year. She was somewhat overweight. This, she felt, was part of her problem. She claimed she was not very attractive to the opposite sex and could not seem to "get boys interested in me." She had a few close friends of the same sex.

24   Her life at home was quite chaotic and stressful. There were frequent battles with her younger brother, who was fourteen, and with her parents. She claimed her parents were always "on my back." She described her mother as extremely rigid and her father as a disciplinarian, who was quite old-fashioned in his values.

25   In all, she spent about twenty minutes talking with her pediatrician. She told him that what she thought she really needed was tranquilizers, and that that was the reason she came. She felt that this was an extremely difficult year for her, and if she could have something to calm her nerves until she got over her current crises, everything would go better.

26   The pediatrician told her that he did not really believe in giving tranquilizers to a girl of her age. He said he thought it would be a bad precedent for her to establish. She was very insistent, how-

---

[7]J. Sice, "Letter to the Editor," *The Lancet* 2 (1972):651. [author's note]

[8]I am grateful to Dr. Melvin Levine for the permission to reproduce this case, used in the Ethics Rounds at the Children's Hospital in Boston. [author's note]

ever, and claimed that if he did not give her tranquilizers, she would "get them somehow." Finally, he agreed to call her pharmacy and order medication for her nerves. She accepted graciously. He suggested that she call him in a few days to let him know how things were going. He also called her parents to say that he had a talk with her and he was giving her some medicine that might help her nerves.

27   Five days later, the girl called the pediatrician back to say that the pills were really working well. She claimed that she had calmed down a great deal, and that she was working things out better with her parents, and had a new outlook on life. He suggested that she keep taking them twice a day for the rest of the school year. She agreed.

28   A month later, the girl ran out of pills and called her pediatrician for a refill. She found that he was away on vacation. She was quite distraught at not having any medication left, so she called her uncle who was a surgeon in the next town. He called the pharmacy to renew her pills and, in speaking to the druggist, found out that they were only vitamins. He told the girl that the pills were only vitamins and that she could get them over the counter and didn't really need him to refill them. The girl became very distraught, feeling that she had been deceived and betrayed by her pediatrician. Her parents, when they heard, commented that they thought the pediatrician was "very clever."

29   The patients who do *not* discover the deception and are left believing that a placebic remedy has worked may continue to rely on it under the wrong circumstances. This is especially true with drugs such as antibiotics, which are sometimes used as placebos and sometimes for their specific action. Many parents, for example, come to believe that they must ask for the prescription of antibiotics every time their child has a fever or a cold. The fact that so many doctors accede to such requests perpetuates the dependence of these families on medical care they do not need and weakens their ability to cope with health problems. Worst of all, those children who cannot tolerate antibiotics may have severe reactions, sometimes fatal, to such unnecessary medication.[9]

30   Such deceptive practices, by their very nature, tend to escape the normal restraints of accountability and can therefore spread more easily than others. There are many instances in which an innocuous-seeming practice has grown to become a large-scale and more dangerous one. Although warnings against the "entering wedge" are often rhetorical devices, they can at times express justifiable caution; especially when there are great pressures to move along the undesirable path and when the safeguards are insufficient.

31   In this perspective, there is much reason for concern about placebos. The safeguards against this practice are few or nonexistent—both because it is secretive in nature and because it is condoned but rarely carefully discussed in the medical literature.[10] And the pressures are very great, and growing stronger, from drug companies, patients eager for cures, and busy physicians, for more medication, whether it is needed or not. Given this lack of safeguards and these strong pressures, the use of placebos can spread in a number of ways.

32   The clearest danger lies in the gradual shift from pharmacologically inert placebos to more active ones. It is not always easy to distinguish completely inert substances from somewhat active ones and these in turn from more active ones. It may be hard to distinguish between a quantity of an active substance so

---

[9]C. M. Kunin, T. Tupasi, and W. Craig, "Use of Antibiotics," *Annals of Internal Medicine* 79 (October 1973):555–60. [author's note]

[10]In a sample of nineteen recent, commonly used textbooks, in medicine, pediatrics, surgery, anesthesia, obstetrics, and gynecology, only three even mention placebos, and none detail either medical or ethical dilemmas they pose. Four out of six textbooks on pharmacology mention them; only one mentions such problems. Only four out of eight textbooks on psychiatry even mention placebos; none takes up ethical problems. For references, see Bok, "Paternalistic Deception in Medicine and Rational Choice." [author's note]

low that it has little or no effect and quantities that have some effect. It is not always clear to doctors whether patients require an inert placebo or possibly a more active one, and there can be the temptation to resort to an active one just in case it might also have a specific effect. It is also much easier to deceive a patient with a medication that is known to be "real" and to have power. One recent textbook in medicine goes so far as to advocate the use of small doses of effective compounds as placebos rather than inert substances—because it is important for both the doctor and the patient to believe in the treatment! This shift is made easier because the dangers and side effects of active agents are not always known or considered important by the physician.

33   Meanwhile, the number of patients receiving placebos increases as more and more people seek and receive medical care and as their desire for instant, push-button alleviation of symptoms is stimulated by drug advertising and by rising expectations of what science can do. The use of placebos for children grows as well, and the temptations to manipulate the truth are less easily resisted once such great inroads have already been made.

34   Deception by placebo can also spread from therapy and diagnosis to experimentation. Much experimentation with placebos is honest and consented to by the experimental subjects, especially since the advent of strict rules governing such experimentation. But grievous abuses have taken place where placebos were given to unsuspecting subjects who believed they had received another substance. In 1971, for example, a number of Mexican-American women applied to a family-planning clinic for contraceptives. Some of them were given oral contraceptives and others were given placebos, or dummy pills that looked like the real thing. Without fully informed consent, the women were being used in an experiment to explore the side effects of various contraceptive pills. Some of those who were given placebos experienced a predictable side effect—they became pregnant. The investigators neither assumed financial responsibility for the babies nor indicated any concern about having bypassed the "informed consent" that is required in ethical experi-

ments with human beings. One contented himself with the observation that if only the law had permitted it, he could have aborted the pregnant women!

35   The failure to think about the ethical problems in such a case stems at least in part from the innocent-seeming white lies so often told in giving placebos. The spread from therapy to experimentation and from harmlessness to its opposite often goes unnoticed in part *because* of the triviality believed to be connected with placebos as white lies. This lack of foresight and concern is most frequent when the subjects in the experiment are least likely to object or defend themselves; as with the poor, the institutionalized, and the very young.

36   In view of all these ways in which placebo usage can spread, it is not enough to look at each incident of manipulation in isolation, no matter how benevolent it may be. When the costs and benefits are weighed, not only the individual consequences must be considered, but also the cumulative ones. Reports of deceptive practices inevitably leak out, and the resulting suspicion is heightened by the anxiety which threats to health always create. And so even the health professionals who do not mislead their patients are injured by those who do; the entire institution of medicine is threatened by practices lacking in candor, however harmless the results may appear in some individual cases.

37   This is not to say that all placebos must be ruled out; merely that they cannot be excused as innocuous. They should be prescribed but rarely, and only after a careful diagnosis and consideration of non-deceptive alternatives; they should be used in experimentation only after subjects have consented to their use.

LETTERS OF RECOMMENDATION

38   Another deceptive practice where not much may seem to be at stake yet which has high accumulated costs is that of the inflated recommendation. It seems a harmless enough practice, and often an act of loyalty, to give extra praise to a friend, a colleague, a student, a relative. In the harsh competition for employment and

advancement, such a gesture is natural. It helps someone, while injuring no one in particular, and balances out similar gestures on the part of many others. Yet the practice obviously injures those who do not benefit from this kind of assistance; and it injures them in a haphazard and inequitable way. Two applicants for work, who are equally capable, may be quite differently rated through no fault of their own.

39   The existing practices also pose many problems for the individuals caught up in them. Take, for instance, a system where all recommendations given to students are customarily exaggerated—where, say, 60 percent of all graduates are classified as belonging to the top 10 percent. If a professor were to make the honest statement to an employer that a student is merely among the top 60 percent, he might severely injure that student's ability to find work, since the statement would not be taken at face value but would be wrongly interpreted to mean that his real standing was very near the bottom.

40   Or consider officer evaluation reports in the U.S. Army. Those who rate officers are asked to give them scores of "outstanding," "superior," "excellent," "effective," "marginal," and "inadequate." Raters know, however, that those who are ranked anything less than "outstanding" (say, "superior" or "excellent") are then at a great disadvantage,[11] and become likely candidates for discharge. Here, superficial verbal harmlessness combines with the harsh realities of the competition for advancement and job retention to produce an inflated set of standards to which most feel bound to conform.

41   In such cases, honesty might victimize innocent persons. At the same time, using the evaluations in the accepted manner is still burdensome or irritating to many. And the blurring of the meaning of words in these circumstances can make it seem easier, perhaps even necessary, not to be straightforward in others.

42   It is difficult for raters to know what to do in such cases. Some feel forced to say what they do not

mean. Others adhere to a high standard of accuracy and thereby perhaps injure those who must have their recommendations.

    To make choices on the basis of such inflated recommendations is equally difficult. This is especially true in large organizations, or at great distances, where those who receive the ratings never know who the raters are or by what standards they work.

44   The entire practice, then, is unjust for those rated and bewildering for those who give and make use of ratings. It also robs recommendations of whatever benefits they are intended to bring. No one can know what is meant by a particular rating. Such a practice is fraught with difficulties; the costs to deceivers and deceived alike are great.

45   For this reason, those who give ratings should make every effort to reduce the injustice and to come closer to the standard of accuracy which they would accept were it not for the inflated practice. But if one goes against such a practice, one does have the responsibility of indicating that one is doing so, in order to minimize the effect on those rated. To do so requires time, power, and consistency. A counselor at a school for highly sought-after students, for example, can make it clear to college recruiters that he means every word he uses in his recommendations of students. So can colleagues who know each other well, when they discuss job applicants. But many are caught up in practices where they are nearly anonymous, perhaps transient, and where they have no contact with those who ask them to make out ratings for students or staff members or military personnel. They are then quite powerless: while it may be demeaning to participate in the inflated practices, it is hard to resist them singlehandedly. In verbal inflation as with monetary inflation, more general measures are often necessary. It must, therefore, be more excusable for those individuals to cooperate with the general norm, who cannot establish a different verbal "currency" for what they say.

46   Institutions, on the other hand, do have more leverage. Some can seek to minimize the reliance on such reports altogether. Others can try to work at the verbal inflation itself. But it is very difficult to do so,

---

[11] Form DA 67-7, 1 January 1973, U.S. Army Officer Evaluation Report. [author's note]

especially for large organizations. The U.S. Army tried to scale down evaluations by publishing the evaluation report I have cited. It suggested mean scores for the different ranks, but few felt free to follow these means in individual cases, for fear of hurting the persons being rated. As a result, the suggested mean scores once again lost all value.

TRUTHFULNESS AT WHAT PRICE?

47   These examples show that one cannot dismiss lies merely by claiming that they don't matter. More often than not, they do matter, even where looked at in simple terms of harm and benefit. Any awareness of how lies spread must generate a real sensitivity to the fact that most lies believed to be "white" are unnecessary if not downright undesirable. Many are not as harmless as liars take them to be. And even those lies which would generally be accepted as harmless are not needed whenever their goals can be achieved through completely honest means. Why tell a flattering lie about someone's hat rather than a flattering truth about their flowers? Why tell a general white lie about a gift, a kind act, a newborn baby, rather than a more specific truthful statement? If the purpose is understood by both speaker and listener to be one of civility and support, the *full* truth in such cases is not called for.[12]

48   I would not wish to argue that all white lies should be ruled out. Individuals caught up in the practices of making inflated recommendations, for example, may have no other recourse. In a few cases, placebos may be the only reasonable alternative. And certain marginally deceptive social excuses and conventions are unavoidable if feelings are not to be needlessly injured.

49   But these are very few. And it is fallacious to argue that all white lies are right because a few are. As a result, those who undertake to tell white lies

should look hard for alternatives. They should see even these lies as links in much wider practices and should know the ways in which these practices can spread. If they do, white lies, where truly harmless and a last resort—told, for instance, to avoid hurting someone's feelings—can be accepted as policy, but *only* under such limited circumstances.

50   Most of us doubtless come into more frequent contact with white lies than with any other form of deception. To the extent that we train ourselves to see their ramifications and succeed in eliminating them from our speech, the need to resort to them will diminish. If we can then make it clear to others that we stand in no need of white lies from *them,* many needless complications will have been avoided.

51   A word of caution is needed here. To say that white lies should be kept at a minimum is *not* to endorse the telling of truths to all comers. Silence and discretion, respect for the privacy and for the feelings of others must naturally govern what is spoken. The gossip one conveys and the malicious reports one spreads may be true without therefore being excusable. And the truth told in such a way as to wound may be unforgivably cruel, as when a physician answers a young man asking if he has cancer with a curt Yes as he leaves the room. He may not have lied, but he has failed in every professional duty of respect and concern for his patient.

52   Once it has been established that lies should not be told, it still remains to be seen whether anything should be conveyed, and, if so, how this can best be done. The self-appointed removers of false beliefs from those for whom these beliefs may be all that sustains them can be as harmful as the most callous liars. ◆

---

[12] If, on the other hand, one is asked for one's honest opinion, such partial answers no longer suffice. A flattering truth that conceals one's opinion is then as deceitful as a flattering lie. To avoid deception, one must then choose either to refuse to answer or to answer honestly. [author's note]

LOTTERIES CHEAT, CORRUPT THE PEOPLE

George F. Will

Like Sissela Bok's argument against white lies, George Will's argument against state-run lotteries flies in the face of the majority opinion. Most people in the United States seem to believe that state lotteries are a harmless diversion and a relatively painless way to raise revenue. Will argues that the actual effects of "state-sanctioned gambling" make it unacceptable. His argument was originally published in the Hartford *[Connecticut]* Journal, *October 15, 1978.*

1   ON THE OUTSKIRTS OF THIS CITY OF INSURANCE companies, there is another, less useful, business based on an understanding of probabilities. It is a jai alai fronton, a cavernous court where athletes play a fast game for the entertainment of gamblers and the benefit of, among others, the state treasury.

2   Half the states have legal betting in casinos, at horse or dog tracks, off-track betting parlors, jai alai frontons, or in state-run lotteries. Only Connecticut has four (the last four) kinds of gambling, and there is talk of promoting the other two.

3   Not coincidentally, Connecticut is one of just seven states still fiercely determined not to have an income tax. Gambling taxes yielded $76.4 million last year, which is not a large slice of Connecticut's $2.1 billion budget, but it would be missed, and is growing.

4   Last year Americans legally wagered $15 billion, up 8 percent over 1976. Lotteries took in 24 percent more. Stiffening resistance to taxes is encouraging states to seek revenues from gambling, and thus to encourage gambling. There are three rationalizations for this:

5   State-run gambling controls illegal gambling.

6   Gambling is a painless way to raise revenues.

7   Gambling is a "victimless" recreation, and thus is a matter of moral indifference.

8   Actually, there is evidence that legal gambling increases the respectability of gambling, and increases public interest in gambling. This creates new gamblers, some of whom move on to illegal gambling, which generally offers better odds. And as a revenue-raising device, gambling is severely regressive.

9   Gamblers are drawn disproportionately from minority and poor populations that can ill afford to gamble, that are especially susceptible to the lure of gambling, and that especially need a government that will not collaborate with gambling entrepreneurs, as in jai alai, and that will not become a gambling entrepreneur through a state lottery.

10   A depressing number of gamblers have no margin for economic losses and little understanding of the probability of losses. Between 1975 and 1977 there was a 140 percent increase in spending to advertise lotteries—lotteries in which more than 99.9 percent of all players are losers. Such advertising is apt to be especially effective, and cruel, among people whose tribulations make them susceptible to dreams of sudden relief.

11   Grocery money is risked for such relief. Some grocers in Hartford's poorer neighborhoods report that receipts decline during jai alai season. Aside from the injury gamblers do to their dependents, there is a more subtle but more comprehensive injury done by

gambling. It is the injury done to society's sense of elemental equities. Gambling blurs the distinction between well-earned and "ill-gotten" gains.

Gambling is debased speculation, a lust for sudden wealth that is not connected with the process of making society more productive of goods and services. Government support of gambling gives a legitimating imprimatur to the pursuit of wealth without work.

13 "It is," said Jefferson, "the manners and spirit of a people which preserves a republic in vigor." Jefferson believed in the virtue-instilling effects of agricultural labor. Andrew Jackson denounced the Bank of the United States as a "monster" because increased credit creation meant increased speculation. Martin Van Buren warned against "a craving desire . . . for sudden wealth." The early nineteenth century belief was that citizens could be distinguished by the moral worth of the way they acquired wealth; and physical labor was considered the most ennobling labor.

14 It is perhaps a bit late to worry about all this: the United States is a developed capitalist society of a sort Jefferson would have feared if he had been able to imagine it. But those who cherish capitalism should note that the moral weakness of capitalism derives, in part, from the belief that too much wealth is allocated in "speculative" ways, capriciously, to people who earn their bread neither by the sweat of their brows nor by wrinkling their brows for socially useful purposes.

15 Of course, any economy produces windfalls. As a town grows, some land values soar. And some investors (like many non-investors) regard stock trading as a form of roulette.

16 But state-sanctioned gambling institutionalizes windfalls, whets the public appetite for them, and encourages the delusion that they are more frequent than they really are. Thus do states simultaneously cheat and corrupt their citizens. ◆

UNCONSCIOUS SELECTION AND NATURAL SELECTION

Charles Darwin

Charles Darwin's The Origin of Species by Means of Natural Selection or the Preservation of Favoured Races in the Struggle for Life *(1859) must be counted as one of the most successful arguments of all times. Directly or indirectly it has convinced most modern thinkers to believe what their ancestors would not have believed: that it is possible over the course of time for species to change to such an extent that they become quite new species, and that such a process of gradual evolution could have produced today's diverse plants and animals from a single common ancestor.*

The principal obstacle to such a view of evolution until Darwin's time was that no one had proposed an adequate cause for the change. What pressure could force a species to undergo over centuries a series of small changes that seemed directed to produce a new species? Darwin's argument was that small changes occur spontaneously and that in the "struggle for existence" nature would select changes that made creatures better suited to their environment and eliminate changes that were disadvantageous. The passages below give some sense of how Darwin developed this argument. In the first section, he demonstrates that humans alter animal species by selective breeding, even when they do not intend to create a change. In the second section, he builds on this observation, arguing that what man unconsciously does, nature may do without guidance.

1   AT THE PRESENT TIME, EMINENT BREEDERS try by methodical selection, with a distinct object in view, to make a new strain or sub-breed, superior to anything of the kind in the country. But, for our purpose, a form of Selection, which may be called Unconscious, and which results from every one trying to possess and breed from the best individual animals, is more important. Thus, a man who intends keeping pointers naturally tries to get as good dogs as he can, and afterwards breeds from his own best dogs, but he has no wish or expectation of permanently altering the breed. Nevertheless we may infer that this process, continued during centuries, would improve and modify any breed, in the same way as Bakewell, Collins, &c.,[1] by this very same process, only carried on more methodically, did greatly modify, even during their lifetimes, the forms and qualities of their cattle. Slow and insensible changes of this kind can never be recognised unless actual measurements or careful drawings of the breeds in question have been made long ago, which may serve for comparison. In some cases, however, unchanged, or but little changed individuals of the same breed exist in less civilised districts, where the breed has been less improved. There is reason to believe that King Charles's[2] spaniel has been unconsciously modified to a large extent since the time of that monarch. Some highly competent authorities are convinced that the setter is directly derived from the

spaniel, and has probably been slowly altered from it. It is known that the English pointer has been greatly changed within the last century, and in this case the change has, it is believed, been chiefly effected by crosses with the foxhound; but what concerns us is, that the change has been effected unconsciously and gradually, and yet so effectually, that, though the old Spanish pointer certainly came from Spain, Mr. Borrow[3] has not seen, as I am informed by him, any native dog in Spain like our pointer.

2   By a similar process of selection, and by careful training, English racehorses have come to surpass in fleetness and size the parent Arabs, so that the latter, by the regulations for the Goodwood Races, are favoured in the weights which they carry. Lord Spencer[4] and others have shown how the cattle of England have increased in weight and in early maturity, compared with the stock formerly kept in this country. By comparing the accounts given in various old treatises of the former and present state of carrier and tumbler pigeons in Britain, India, and Persia, we can trace the stages through which they have insensibly passed, and come to differ so greatly from the rock-pigeon.

3   Youatt[5] gives an excellent illustration of the

---

[1]Bakewell, Collins, &c.: Robert Bakewell (1725–95) was known for perfecting breeds of cattle and sheep.
[2]Charles: Charles 1 (1600–49), king of England from 1625 to 1649.

---

[3]Borrow: George Borrow (1803–81), who wrote romantic books about his travels in Spain (*Gipsies in Spain* [1841] and *Bible in Spain* [1843]).
[4]Spencer: Herbert Spencer (1820–1903), the English philosopher and evolutionist.
[5]Youatt: William Youatt (1776–1849), a veterinarian and author of several books on breeding, including *Sheep, Their Breeds, Management, and Diseases* (1837).

effects of a course of selection, which may be considered as unconscious, in so far that the breeders could never have expected, or even wished, to produce the result which ensued—namely, the production of two distinct strains. The two flocks of Leicester sheep kept by Mr. Buckley and Mr. Burgess, as Mr. Youatt remarks, "have been purely bred from the original stock of Mr. Bakewell for upwards of fifty years. There is not a suspicion existing in the mind of any one at all acquainted with the subject, that the owner of either of them has deviated in any one instance from the pure blood of Mr. Bakewell's flock, and yet the difference between the sheep possessed by these two gentlemen is so great that they have the appearance of being quite different varieties."

4   If there exist savages so barbarous as never to think of the inherited character of the offspring of their domestic animals, yet any one animal particularly useful to them, for any special purpose, would be carefully preserved during famines and other accidents, to which savages are so liable, and such choice animals would thus generally leave more offspring than the inferior ones; so that in this case there would be a kind of unconscious selection going on. We see the value set on animals even by the barbarians of Tierra del Fuego, by their killing and devouring their old women, in times of dearth, as of less value than their dogs.

5   In plants the same gradual process of improvement, through the occasional preservation of the best individuals, whether or not sufficiently distinct to be ranked at their first appearance, as distinct varieties, and whether or not two or more species or races have become blended together by crossing, may plainly be recognised in the increased size and beauty which we now see in the varieties of the heartsease, rose, pelargonium, dahlia, and other plants, when compared with the older varieties or with their parent-stocks. No one would ever expect to get a first-rate heartsease or dahlia from the seed of a wild plant. No one would expect to raise a first-rate melting pear from the seed of the wild pear, though he might succeed from a poor seedling growing wild, if it had come from a garden-stock. The pear though cultivated in classical

times, appears, from Pliny's[6] description, to have been a fruit of very inferior quality. I have seen great surprise expressed in horticultural works at the wonderful skill of gardeners, in having produced such splendid results from such poor materials; but the art has been simple, and, as far as the final result is concerned, has been followed almost unconsciously. It has consisted in always cultivating the best-known variety, sowing its seeds, and, when a slightly better variety chanced to appear, selecting it, and so onwards. But the gardeners of the classical period, who cultivated the best pears which they could procure, never thought what splendid fruit we should eat; though we owe our excellent fruit in some small degree, to their having naturally chosen and preserved the best varieties they could anywhere find.

6   A large amount of change, thus slowly and unconsciously accumulated, explains, as I believe, the well-known fact, that in a number of cases we cannot recognise, and therefore do not know, the wild parent-stocks of the plants which have been longest cultivated in our flower and kitchen gardens. If it has taken centuries or thousands of years to improve or modify most of our plants up to their present standard of usefulness to man, we can understand how it is that neither Australia, the Cape of Good Hope, nor any other region inhabited by quite uncivilised man, has afforded us a single plant worth culture. It is not that these countries, so rich in species, do not by a strange chance possess the aboriginal stocks of any useful plants, but that the native plants have not been improved by continued selection up to a standard of perfection comparable with that acquired by the plants in countries anciently civilised.

7   In regard to the domestic animals kept by uncivilised man, it should not be overlooked that they almost always have to struggle for their own food, at least during certain seasons. And in two countries very differently circumstanced, individuals of the same

---

[6]Pliny: Pliny the Elder (A.D. 23–79), historian and scientific encyclopedist best known for his thirty-seven-volume *Natural History*.

species, having slightly different constitutions or structure would often succeed better in the one country than in the other; and thus by a process of "natural selection," as will hereafter be more fully explained, two sub-breeds might be formed. This, perhaps, partly explains why the varieties kept by savages, as has been remarked by some authors, have more of the character of true species than the varieties kept in civilised countries.

8   On the view here given of the important part which selection by man has played, it becomes at once obvious, how it is that our domestic races show adaptation in their structure or in their habits to man's wants or fancies. We can, I think, further understand the frequently abnormal characters of our domestic races, and likewise their differences being so great in external characters, and relatively so slight in internal parts or organs. Man can hardly select, or only with much difficulty, any deviation of structure excepting such as is externally visible; and indeed he rarely cares for what is internal. He can never act by selection, excepting on variations which are first given to him in some slight degree by nature. No man would ever try to make a fantail till he saw a pigeon with a tail developed in some slight degree in an unusual manner, or a pouter till he saw a pigeon with a crop of somewhat unusual size; and the more abnormal or unusual any character was when it first appeared, the more likely it would be to catch his attention. But to use such an expression as trying to make a fantail, is, I have no doubt, in most cases, utterly incorrect. The man who first selected a pigeon with a slightly larger tail, never dreamed what the descendants of that pigeon would become through long-continued, partly unconscious and partly methodical, selection. Perhaps the parent-bird of all fantails had only fourteen tail-feathers somewhat expanded, like the present Java fantail, or like individuals of other and distinct breeds, in which as many as seventeen tail-feathers have been counted. Perhaps the first pouter-pigeon did not inflate its crop much more than the turbit now does the upper part of its œsophagus,—a habit which is disregarded by all fanciers, as it is not one of the points of the breed.

Nor let it be thought that some great deviation of structure would be necessary to catch the fancier's eye: he perceives extremely small differences, and it is in human nature to value any novelty, however slight, in one's own possession. Nor must the value which would formerly have been set on any slight differences in the individuals of the same species, be judged of by the value which is now set on them, after several breeds have fairly been established. It is known that with pigeons many slight variations now occasionally appear, but these are rejected as faults or deviations from the standard of perfection in each breed. The common goose has not given rise to any marked varieties; hence the Toulouse and the common breed, which differ only in colour, that most fleeting of characters, have lately been exhibited as distinct at our poultry-shows.

10   These views appear to explain what has sometimes been noticed—namely, that we know hardly anything about the origin or history of any of our domestic breeds. But, in fact, a breed, like a dialect of a language, can hardly be said to have a distinct origin. A man preserves and breeds from an individual with some slight deviation of structure, or takes more care than usual in matching his best animals, and thus improves them, and the improved animals slowly spread in the immediate neighbourhood. But they will as yet hardly have a distinct name, and from being only slightly valued, their history will have been disregarded. When further improved by the same slow and gradual process, they will spread more widely, and will be recognised as something distinct and valuable, and will then probably first receive a provincial name. In semi-civilised countries, with little free communication, the spreading of a new sub-breed would be a slow process. As soon as the points of value are once acknowledged, the principle, as I have called it, of unconscious selection will always tend,—perhaps more at one period than at another, as the breed rises or falls in fashion,—perhaps more in one district than in another, according to the state of civilisation of the inhabitants,—slowly to add to the characteristic features of the breed, whatever they may be. But the chance will be infinitely small of any record having

been preserved of such slow, varying, and insensible changes. . . .

In order to make it clear how, as I believe, natural selection acts, I must beg permission to give one or two imaginary illustrations. Let us take the case of a wolf, which preys on various animals, securing some by craft, some by strength, and some by fleetness; and let us suppose that the fleetest prey, a deer for instance, had from any change in the country increased in numbers, or that other prey had decreased in numbers, during that season of the year when the wolf was hardest pressed for food. Under such circumstances the swiftest and slimmest wolves would have the best chance of surviving and so be preserved or selected,—provided always that they retained strength to master their prey at this or some other period of the year, when they were compelled to prey on other animals. I can see no more reason to doubt that this would be the result, than that man should be able to improve the fleetness of his greyhounds by careful and methodical selection, or by that kind of unconscious selection which follows from each man trying to keep the best dogs without any thought of modifying the breed. I may add, that, according to Mr Pierce,[7] there are two varieties of the wolf inhabiting the Catskill Mountains, in the United States, one with a light greyhound-like form, which pursues deer, and the other more bulky, with shorter legs, which more frequently attacks the shepherd's flocks. . . .

12 It may be worth while to give another and more complex illustration of the action of natural selection. Certain plants excrete sweet juice, apparently for the sake of eliminating something injurious from the sap: this is effected, for instance,[8] by glands at the base of the stipules in some Leguminosæ, and

at the backs of the leaves of the common laurel. This juice, though small in quantity, is greedily sought by insects; but their visits do not in any way benefit the plant. Now, let us suppose that the juice or nectar was excreted from the inside of the flowers of a certain number of plants of any species. Insects in seeking the nectar would get dusted with pollen, and would often transport it from one flower to another. The flowers of two distinct individuals of the same species would thus get crossed; and the act of crossing, as can be fully proved, gives rise to vigorous seedlings which consequently would have the best chance of flourishing and surviving. The plants which produced flowers with the largest glands or nectaries, excreting most nectar, would oftenest be visited by insects, and would oftenest be crossed; and so in the long-run would gain the upper hand and form a local variety. The flowers, also, which had their stamens and pistils placed, in relation to the size and habits of the particular insects which visited them, so as to favour in any degree the transportal of the pollen, would likewise be favoured. We might have taken the case of insects visiting flowers for the sake of collecting pollen instead of nectar; and as pollen is formed for the sole purpose of fertilisation, its destruction appears to be a simple loss to the plant; yet if a little pollen were carried, at first occasionally and then habitually, by the pollen-devouring insects from flower to flower, and a cross thus effected, although ninetenths of the pollen were destroyed it might still be a great gain to the plant to be thus robbed; and the individuals which produced more and more pollen, and had larger anthers, would be selected. . . .

Let us now turn to the nectar-feeding insects; we 13 may suppose the plant, of which we have been slowly increasing the nectar by continued selection, to be a common plant; and that certain insects depended in main part on its nectar for food. I could give many facts showing how anxious bees are to save time: for instance, their habit of cutting holes and sucking the nectar at the bases of certain flowers, which, with a very little more trouble, they can enter by the mouth.

[7]Pierce: James Pierce, whose comments appear in "A Memoir on the Catskill Mountains," *American Journal of Science* 6 (1823).
[8]Leguminosæ: family name of the legumes, such as peas and some beans.

Bearing such facts in mind, it may be believed that under certain circumstances individual differences in the curvature or length of the proboscis, &c., too slight to be appreciated by us, might profit a bee or other insect, so that certain individuals would be able to obtain their food more quickly than others; and thus the communities to which they belonged would flourish and throw off many swarms inheriting the same peculiarities. The tubes of the corolla of the common red and incarnate clovers (Trifolium pratense and incarnatum) do not on a hasty glance appear to differ in length; yet the hive-bee can easily suck the nectar out of the incarnate clover, but not out of the common red clover, which is visited by humble-bees alone; so that whole fields of red clover offer in vain an abundant supply of precious nectar to the hive-bee. That this nectar is much liked by the hive-bee is certain; for I have repeatedly seen, but only in the autumn, many hive-bees sucking the flowers through holes bitten in the base of the tube by humble-bees. The difference in the length of the corolla in the two kinds of clover, which determines the visits of the hive-bee, must be very trifling; for I have been assured that when red clover has been mown, the flowers of the second crop are somewhat smaller, and that these are visited by many hive-bees. I do not know whether this statement is accurate; nor whether another published statement can be trusted, namely, that the Ligurian bee which is generally considered a mere variety of the common hive-bee, and which freely crosses with it, is able to reach and suck the nectar of the red clover. Thus, in a country where this kind of clover abounded, it might be a great advantage to the hive-bee to have a slightly longer or differently constructed proboscis. On the other hand, as the fertility of this clover absolutely depends on bees visiting the flowers, if humble-bees were to become rare in any country, it might be a great advantage to the plant to have a shorter or more deeply divided corolla, so that the hive-bees should be enabled to suck its flowers. Thus I can understand how a flower and a bee might slowly become, either simultaneously or one after the other, modified and adapted to each other in the most perfect manner, by the continued preservation of all the individuals which presented slight deviations of structure mutually favourable to each other.

I am well aware that this doctrine of natural selection, exemplified in the above imaginary instances, is open to the same objections which were first urged against Sir Charles Lyell's[9] noble views on "the modern changes of the earth, as illustrative of geology"; but we now seldom hear the agencies which we see still at work, spoken of as trifling or insignificant, when used in explaining the excavation of the deepest valleys or the formation of long lines of inland cliffs. Natural selection acts only by the preservation and accumulation of small inherited modifications, each profitable to the preserved being; and as modern geology has almost banished such views as the excavation of a great valley by a single diluvial wave, so will natural selection banish the belief of the continued creation of new organic beings, or of any great and sudden modification in their structure. ◆

---

[9]Lyell: Sir Charles Lyell (1797–1875), a British geologist whose Principles of Geology (1838) greatly influenced Darwin.

ARGUING WHEN THE RULES ARE DISPUTED

N CHAPTER 6 WE DEALT WITH ARGUMENTS ABOUT DISPUTED FACTS. In this chapter we deal with disputes where everyone agrees on the principal facts, but there is disagreement about what rules to apply to those facts and what consequences should follow from the application of the rules. The flag-burning case mentioned in Chapter 1 is a good example of such a dispute. Both sides agree that Gregory Johnson burned an American flag during the Republican Convention in 1984. But what rule should the Supreme Court apply to this fact? Should it apply the rule that the state should punish those whose conduct "profoundly offends the majority of people," in which case Johnson would be fined and jailed? Or should it apply the rule that the state should not interfere with the free expression of ideas, in which case Johnson would be released without punishment?

Our model for arguments about rules will be the trial, where people argue cases before a court presumed to be fair-minded. We aren't concerned solely with what happens at the courthouse, however. "Courts" don't necessarily include lawyers and black-robed judges. When a high school teacher protests the superintendent's decision not to renew her contract, the school board becomes a court. When a newspaper runs a series of letters on a controversial issue, the readers become the "court of public opinion." When an employer resolves a dispute between employees, he serves as a one-person court. Think of a "court" as any person or group with the power to decide which argument will prevail, and you will realize that all of us have our days in court.

A MODEL ARGUMENT ANALYZED

A clear example of a courtroom argument about rules occurs in Robert Bolt's *A Man for All Seasons,* a play about the prosecution of Sir Thomas More on a charge that "he did conspire traitorously and maliciously" to deny King Henry VIII's claim to be the Supreme Head of the Church of England.

In case sixteenth-century English history is not your strong suit, let me remind you that Henry VIII was frustrated because the Roman Catholic Church would not grant him a divorce from his first wife. With the help of his

adviser Thomas Cromwell, Henry set out to break the power of the Catholic church in England. This campaign culminated in the Act of Supremacy (1534), which declared that the King, not the Pope, was the head of the Church in England. This done, Henry obtained his divorce from the Church of England despite the Pope's objections and married Anne Boleyn, who became Queen.

Conspicuously absent from Anne's coronation, however, was Sir Thomas More, the chancellor of England. Though More made no statement opposing the Act of Supremacy or denying the validity of the King's divorce, he would not say that he approved of Henry's actions or thought them legal. It was this *silence* that led to the charge of treason. In Bolt's play, Cromwell serves as prosecutor; we will examine a passage in which he questions Sir Thomas:

CROMWELL. (*Moving to left of MORE.*) Now, Sir Thomas, you stand upon your silence.

MORE.   I do.

CROMWELL. (*Turning to the Jury.*) But, Gentlemen of the Jury, there are many kinds of silence. Consider first the silence of a man when he is dead. Let us say we go into the room where he is lying: and let us say it is the dead of night—there's nothing like darkness for sharpening the ear—and we listen. What do we hear? (*He listens intently.*) Silence. What does it betoken, this silence? Nothing. This is silence pure and simple. But consider another case. Suppose I were to draw a dagger from my sleeve and make to kill the prisoner with it; and suppose their lordships there,[1] instead of crying out for me to stop or crying out for help to stop me, maintained their silence. That would *betoken*. It would betoken a willingness that I should do it, and under the law they would be guilty with me. So silence can, according to the circumstances, speak. Consider now the circumstances of the prisoner's silence. The oath was put to good and faithful subjects up and down the country and they had declared His Grace's title to be just and good. And when it came to the prisoner, he refused. He calls this silence. Yet is there a man in this court, is there a man in this

---

[1]Cromwell refers to the two judges in the case, seated on a platform in sight of the jury.

country, who does not *know* Sir Thomas More's opinion of this title? Of course not. But how can that be? Because this silence betokened—nay, this silence *was*—not silence at all, but most eloquent denial.

MORE. (*With some of the academic's impatience for a shoddy line of reasoning.*) Not so, Mr. Secretary, the maxim is *"qui tacet consentire"*. (*He turns to the Foreman.*) The maxim of the law is— (*Very carefully.*) "Silence gives consent." If therefore, you wish to construe what my silence "betoken," you must construe that I consented, not that I denied.

CROMWELL. Is that what the world, in fact, construes from it? Do you pretend that is what you *wish* the world to construe from it?

MORE. The world must construe according to its wits. This court must construe according to the law.

This scene contains all the key elements of the type of argument that we are considering and that you will soon be writing. First, there is a court, in this case two judges and a jury. Second, there is an opponent[2]: More for Cromwell's argument, Cromwell for More's. Third, there is a fact that the opponents both acknowledge to be beyond dispute: More's silence on the subject of the King's title as Supreme Head of the Church. Fourth, for both Cromwell's argument and More's there are definite conclusions they wish the jury to draw (More's denial of the King's title, or his consent). Fifth, the route to each of these conclusions passes through a rule.

A SIMPLE MAP OF A DISPUTE CONTAINING TWO ARGUMENTS

We can visualize a dispute and the arguments that go with it as a road that forks just before it reaches two gates. The dispute between More and Cromwell is shaped as in the diagram at the top of the next page. From the undisputed fact of More's silence, Cromwell would lead the court along the left-hand route. His rule is that silence can mean *anything* according to the circumstances and that the court should use common sense to understand the meaning of an accused man's silence. He tries to hold this gate of interpretation open, and if the court passes through it, More is a step closer to being convicted of treason. More, of course, attempts to close this gate of interpreta-

---

[2]I say "an opponent" for simplicity's sake. In some cases there are several parties in a dispute, all proposing different rules or different reasons. Among these parties there are alliances as well as oppositions. But there is always at least *one* opponent.

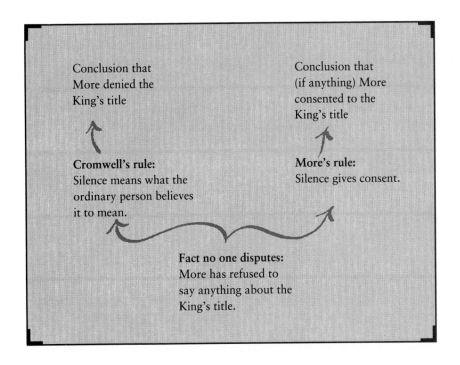

Conclusion that
More denied the
King's title

Conclusion that
(if anything) More
consented to the
King's title

Cromwell's rule:
Silence means what the
ordinary person believes
it to mean.

More's rule:
Silence gives consent.

Fact no one disputes:
More has refused to
say anything about the
King's title.

tion and open another. His rule is a centuries-old maxim of the law: "Silence gives consent." If the court follows the maxim, More is a step nearer acquittal and release. Ultimately, the court is free to pass through either gate. The aguments of the lawyers can only *incline* it toward one rule or another.

ABOUT RULES

Sir Thomas More's citation of a Latin legal maxim might suggest that all rules come from books and have an official status. This is not so. A rule is any general statement that *would* logically lead the "court" from the undisputed fact to the conclusion. A *successful* rule is one that *does* lead it to the desired conclusion.

Suppose, for example, that a brother and sister take their dispute about the ownership of a goldfish to their parents (the family court). The sister might argue that she bought the fish with her own money six months ago (a fact her brother can't deny) and that *whoever buys something owns it*. The brother might argue that he, not she, has been feeding the goldfish ever since it arrived (a fact she can't deny) and that *whoever feeds a pet owns it*. These are well-formed arguments based on rules that come partly from custom and partly from the fertile brains of the disputants.

Or suppose that one morning you drive to school and find that every marked place in the lot for which you have purchased a parking sticker is filled, some of them by cars that have no parking stickers. You have to get to class quickly, so you park against a tree in what you know perfectly well is not an official parking place. When you return to the car, you discover under your windshield wiper a $15 ticket for "parking in a nondesignated area." You've no intention of paying the ticket, so you send a letter to parking operations arguing that *a person who has bought a parking sticker shouldn't be fined for parking irregularly in a lot where cars with no parking stickers are taking up the designated spaces.* In effect, you have made up a rule that interprets your "violation" as "excusable behavior."

The key here is that the rule is a general statement, a maxim of sorts. That is, it applies to a category of cases. In this respect, it is like the major premise of a syllogism.[3] All men are mortal. All buyers are owners. All feeders are owners. All crowded-out-sticker-owners are justified in parking in odd places.

The general statements in the goldfish and parking ticket cases are clearly not indisputable; if they were, there would be no argument. But the arguers are urging the court to treat their rules *as if* they were universal truths, applicable whenever a similar situation arises. If the director of parking operations accepts your argument and tears up your ticket, she will presumably have to void future tickets issued when a sticker-holder is forced to park in an odd place.

EXERCISE 1

Practice Inventing and Stating Rules. An essential skill for the successful arguer is the ability to identify or invent rules that, if accepted, will lead inevitably from the undisputed facts to the disputable conclusion. To exercise this skill, state rules that will lead to each of the conclusions listed in each of the cases that follow. Though the examples are based on actual legal cases, assume that you, unlike a lawyer or judge, are free to use any rules that seem pertinent. Try, however, to make your rule narrow enough that its application to the particular case is obvious. "A person's silence indicates consent rather than objection to what is said or done in the person's presence" is an appropriately narrow rule for the case of Sir Thomas More. "Everybody should do the right thing or else pay the consequences" is too broad to be useful, and you would have difficulty getting it accepted by any court.

1. *Facts beyond dispute:* Tom Piltney, a schoolboy eleven years old, was sitting across the aisle from his friend John Verberg. When he saw John

---

[3] For a discussion of syllogisms and their limitations, see page 157.

falling asleep during a grammar lesson, he kicked him lightly on the shin, intending only to wake him up. Unfortunately, and unbeknownst to Tom, John's leg has been seriously injured some years before. The kick caused a nick, the nick caused an infection, the infection affected the bone of John's leg, and John was forced to have expensive medical treatments that didn't succeed. He was lamed for life.

Conclusion 1: The Piltneys owe John and his family compensation for the injury.

Conclusion 2: The Verbergs have to bear the cost of the injury themselves, as Tom and his parents can't be held responsible.

2. *Facts beyond dispute:* Henry Brawny and his wife, Mary, owned an old, boarded-up farmhouse on a piece of property some miles from the town in which they lived. In the farmhouse they stored old bottles and fruit jars, some of which they considered antiques. Several times over the years the house had been vandalized. The Brawnys posted "no trespassing" signs, but the break-ins continued. Finally, they placed a shotgun trap in one of the bedrooms. At first Henry aimed the gun so that the shot would hit an intruder in the stomach, but Mary insisted that he lower the aim so that it would strike an intruder's legs. A few days after the trap was set, Bill Karko broke into the house intending to steal some of the Brawnys' jars. A blast from the shotgun seriously injured Karko, who will probably never recover the full use of his legs.

Conclusion 1: The Brawnys owe Karko compensation for his injuries.

Conclusion 2: The Brawnys owe Karko no compensation.

3. *Facts beyond dispute:* Ellen Mayer, who was feeling some pain in her right ear, had it examined by Dr. Albert Wilson, who found evidence of disease and recommended an operation. Mayer agreed and signed a form consenting to surgery on the right ear only. On the appointed day she received an anesthetic that rendered her unconscious. Wilson then reexamined the right ear of the unconscious Mayer and decided that its condition was not serious enough to require the surgery. He took the opportunity to examine her left ear closely and discovered that it had a more serious condition than the right, though not one that put her in immediate danger. Without waiting for Mayer to recover consciousness in order to ask her permission, he proceeded to operate on the left ear. The operation was a success. Mayer, however, was not pleased, and sued Wilson.

Conclusion 1: Wilson owes Mayer compensation for performing an operation she did not authorize.

Conclusion 2: Wilson owes Mayer no compensation.

Thomas More (1478–1535; shown in a portrait by Hans Holbein the Younger) was a brilliant public servant even as he maintained intense religious conviction in an age of strife between church and state. He was trained early as a lawyer, though he contemplated joining religious orders. Henry VIII appointed him to a series of increasingly important positions, culminating in the Lord Chancellorship. Just and honest, More was nonetheless merciless in dealing with heretics. For maintaining silence over the Act of Supremacy, he was thrown into the Tower of London in 1534; after fifteen months he was brought to trial on a charge of high treason and was convicted. Five days later he was executed by beheading. Kneeling before the block, More told the onlooking crowd that he died "the king's good servant—but God's first." In 1935 he was named a saint of the Roman Catholic Church.

WAYS TO PERSUADE THE "COURT" TO ACCEPT YOUR RULE

As we noted earlier, rules may come from anywhere, including the mind of an arguer desperate to make his or her case. Why should a "court" prefer one rule to another? How does an arguer justify the rule he or she is proposing?

There is no simple answer to these questions. Courts are made up of human beings, and the motives of human beings can be unfathomable. In general, we can say that they will reject any rule that sounds manifestly unfair or unwise and prefer one that is clearly fair and wise. When the fairness or wisdom is not immediately apparent, successful arguers often use three appeals: references to *authority,* calls for *consistency,* and consideration of larger *consequences.*

First, arguers can show that the rule they favor has an authority behind it, that it is not merely a personal opinion, invented in order to make the argument work. This is precisely what Sir Thomas More does when he refers to the maxim *"qui tacet consentire."* The maxim existed in the law for some centuries before More cited it; it has the weight of authority. When both sides can cite an authority, arguers attempt to show that their rule is derived from a better authority than the one favored by opponents. Thus, a lawyer may argue that where the state Constitution provides one rule and the state legislature another, the Constitution's rule should prevail. Or in ethics, a person might argue that a rule endorsed by Moses, Buddha, Jesus, and Mohammed is preferable to one endorsed by P. T. Barnum or Ivan Boesky.

Second, arguers can show that the rule they favor has consistently been applied to similar situations in the past, so that it would be illogical or unjust to apply a different rule in the present case. Thus a student suspended from high school for a week for wearing a T-shirt with a message the principal found offensive might argue that in seven previous cases involving similar T-shirts students had merely been sent home to change. To switch from the rule that "students wearing offensive shirts will be required to change them" to the rule that "students wearing offensive shirts will be suspended for a week" therefore seems arbitrary and unfair. The student might argue that she would not have risked wearing the shirt if she had known how severe the penalty would be. She had relied on the principal's being consistent in his behavior. The call for consistency obviously makes most sense when it is addressed to an administrator or judge, someone whose decisions in the past people accept as "law" in the present. But then every parent and every employer is sometimes a judge or administrator.

Third, arguers can point to the bad consequences of a general application of the rule they oppose or the good consequences of general application of the rule they favor. Consider the argument about the parking ticket, for example. To show that your rule is preferable, you might point out that fining people who have bought parking stickers is no way to encourage lawful behavior: people who know that they can be fined even if they have a sticker will very likely stop buying one. Or you might point out that if the present policy is enforced, it could create a "chain reaction" of unauthorized parking. People who find their own "authorized" lots full will conclude that they might as well park in whatever lot they choose, since they are at least as likely to be ticketed in their own lot as in someone else's. Since they will take spaces that properly belong to others, the others will also park in someone else's lot. Eventually, the chance of finding a place in one's proper lot could become very slim, creating just the sort of musical-chairs parking situation directors are hired to avoid.

Of course, this argument may fail. The director may feel that her present rule that *all* illegally parked cars should be ticketed may be crude, but at least it is workable. To change to your more complicated rule would require the ticketing officer to determine whether legal places were open *at the time you parked,* a virtually impossible task. It would also seem to authorize parking in

At the time that he tried Sir Thomas More for treason in 1535, Thomas Cromwell (1485–1540; shown in a portrait by Hans Holbein the Younger) was Henry VIII's most powerful advisor. A significant force in establishing Protestantism in England, Cromwell had drafted the parliamentary acts that severed the English Church from the control of Rome and made the king supreme head of that church. From 1536 to 1539 he closed all monasteries in England and Wales, confiscating their property for the Crown. But his fortune reversed in 1540, when he arranged Henry's marriage to a German princess, Anne of Cleves. Repelled by his new wife, Henry turned against Cromwell and allowed him to be accused of treason. There was no trial; Cromwell was beheaded on Tower Hill five summers after the execution of Thomas More.

any odd place—beside hydrants, in fire lanes, blocking exits. If you think the situation over, you may find that the arguments for the present rule are quite strong, and you may decide to write a $15 check rather than a fruitless letter.

THE APPEAL TO CONSISTENCY BY WAY OF ANALOGY

Very often we are forced to plead our case before people who have never passed judgment on a case exactly like it. Under these circumstances an analogy may be an important tool of persuasion. The arguer points to a clearer case (perhaps one already decided), where only one conclusion seems justifiable. He or she then tries to show that the rule that led to that inevitable conclusion also applies to the case at hand.

Consider, for example, an argument made on behalf of Florence Whittaker, a woman who belonged briefly to a religious sect with a colony in Jaffa, Syria. Ms. Whittaker lost her faith in the sect and decided to return to America. She intended to book passage on the next available steamer, but the cult's leader, Frank Sanford (the "second Elijah"), offered to sail her home in his yacht, *Kingdom*. When she expressed a fear that Sanford might refuse to let her off the yacht until she agreed to rejoin the sect, he assured her repeatedly that he would not detain her. On December 28, 1909, she voluntarily boarded the *Kingdom*. When the yacht anchored in the harbor at Portland, Maine, on May 10, however, Sanford would not order a boat to take her ashore. For a month she was unable to escape and had to listen to the preacher's urgings that she return to the flock. Eventually, she was able to get a message to shore and was freed by a court order.

Not surprisingly, Whittaker sued, alleging that Sanford had unjustly imprisoned her and that he owed her compensation for the wrong he had done. Sanford's lawyer argued that there had been no imprisonment. After all, he said, Whittaker had come on board voluntarily, and Sanford had used no violence or physical force to prevent her leaving again. He had merely failed to offer her a means of transportation, and surely the law did not require him to provide boats to anyone who asked. Against this argument, Whittaker's lawyer offered an argument that surrounding a person by a physical barrier like the ocean *was* using "physical force" to imprison her. He developed a compelling analogy, here summarized by Albert R. Savage, Chief Justice of the Maine Supreme Court:

> If one should, without right, turn the key in a door, and thereby prevent a person in the room from leaving, it would be the simplest form of unlawful imprisonment. The restraint is physical. The four walls and the locked door are physical impediments to escape. Now is it different when one who is in control of a vessel at anchor, within practical rowing distance from the shore, who has agreed that a guest on board shall be free to leave, there being no means to leave except by

rowboats, wrongfully refuses the guest the use of a boat? The boat is the key. By refusing the boat he turns the key. The guest is as effectively locked up as if there were walls along the side of the vessel. The restraint is physical. The impassable sea is the physical barrier.

As you can see, the analogy is effective because it neatly matches the case at hand. The difference between imprisonment on a boat and imprisonment in a room is not significant with regard to the rule involved: that under ordinary circumstances no private citizen has a right to physically restrain the movements of another citizen by surrounding him or her with an impassable barrier.

In the case of the parking ticket, you might argue that there is an analogy between buying a parking sticker and buying a theater ticket. A person who buys a theater ticket and then discovers that all the seats are taken is presumably entitled to a refund, not a fine. The director of parking operations, however, might argue that the analogy is a bad one: no theater owner faces her problem of keeping control over an area without walls, doors, or locks. She might argue that your parking fee bought only her *effort* to have space available to you.

An Extended Example of Persuasive Justification of a Rule

Judges in appellate courts in the United States write "opinions" in which they give the reasoning behind their rulings. Such opinions reflect the arguments made by the lawyers in the case, but they are also arguments in their own right, addressed to other judges on the court and to the legal community at large. These written opinions are often excellent examples of the reasoning one offers to persuade a "court" to adopt a rule.

Consider, for example, the opinion written by Judge Ward Hunt of the New York Court of Appeals in an 1866 case involving a fire that destroyed the house of James Ryan. A spark from a steam engine operated by the New York Central Railroad had set fire to one of the company's woodsheds and to the wood stored in it. Ryan's house, though it was 130 feet from the shed, "soon took fire from the heat and sparks, and was entirely consumed, notwithstanding diligent efforts were made to save it." By the time Judge Hunt heard the case, a lower court had established the "fact" that the railroad's negligence had caused the fire in the shed. Ryan and his lawyers argued that if someone's negligence causes a fire (or other catastrophe), then the negligent party should pay for *all* the resulting damage. The railroad's lawyers (and later Judge Hunt) argued for another rule, that negligent people are responsible only for the "natural" or "ordinary" results of their negligence; they are not responsible for consequences no one could foresee.

Diagrammed as a forking path, the dispute between Ryan and the railroad looks like this:

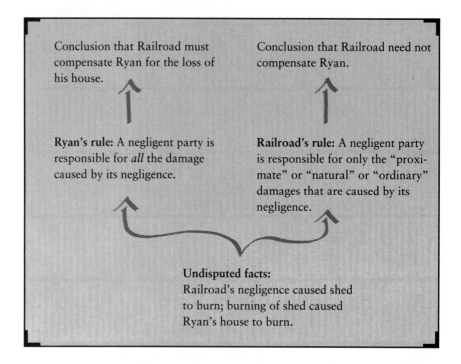

Conclusion that Railroad must compensate Ryan for the loss of his house.

Conclusion that Railroad need not compensate Ryan.

Ryan's rule: A negligent party is responsible for *all* the damage caused by its negligence.

Railroad's rule: A negligent party is responsible for only the "proximate" or "natural" or "ordinary" damages that are caused by its negligence.

Undisputed facts: Railroad's negligence caused shed to burn; burning of shed caused Ryan's house to burn.

"Opinion"
—Judge Ward Hunt

The judge's first statement of the railroad's rule appears in the second sentence.

The judge gives a rule and cites three cases that have been decided according to it: this is the appeal to consistency at work.

It is a general principle that every person is liable for the consequences of his own acts. He is thus liable in damages for the proximate results of his own acts, but not for remote damages. It is not easy at all times to determine what are proximate and what are remote damages. In *Thomas v. Winchester* (2 Seld., 408),[4] Judge Ruggles defines the damages for which a party is liable as those which are the natural or necessary consequences of his acts. Thus, the owner of a loaded gun, who puts it in the hands of a child, by whose indiscretion it is discharged, is liable for the injury sustained by a third person from such discharge. (5 Maule & Sel., 198.) The injury is a natural and ordinary result of the folly of placing a loaded gun in the hands of one ignorant of the manner of using it, and incapable of appreciating its effects. The owner of a horse and cart, who leaves them unattended in the street, is liable for an injury done to a person, or his property, by the running away of the horse (*Lynch v. Nurdin*, 1 Adol. & Ellis, N.S., 29; *Illidge v. Goodin*, 5 Car. & P., 190), for the same reason. The injury is the natural result of the negligence. If the party thus injured had, however, by the delay or confinement from his injury, been prevented

---

[4]Following standard form for judicial opinions, Hunt cites his sources in parentheses. These parenthetical citations usually refer the reader to pertinent cases decided by other courts.

from completing a valuable contract, from which he expected to make large profits, he could not recover such expected profits from the negligent party, in the cases supposed. Such damages would not be the necessary or natural consequences, nor the results ordinarily to be anticipated, from the negligence committed. (6 Hill, 522; 13 Wend., 601; 3 E. D. Smith, 144.) So if an engineer upon a steamboat or locomotive, in passing the house of A., so carelessly manages its machinery that the coals and sparks from its fires fall upon and consume the house of A., the railroad company or the steamboat proprietors are liable to pay the value of the property thus destroyed. (*Field v. N.Y. Central R.R.,* 32 N.Y., 339.) Thus far the law is settled and the principle is apparent. If, however, the fire communicates from the house of A. to that of B., and that is destroyed, is the negligent party liable for his loss? And if it spreads thence to the house of C., and thence to the house of D., and thence consecutively through the other houses, until it reaches and consumes the house of Z., is the party liable to pay the damages sustained by these twenty-six sufferers? The counsel for the plaintiff does not distinctly claim this, and I think it would not be seriously insisted that the sufferers could recover in such case. Where, then, is the principle upon which A. recovers and Z. fails?

> Notice the judge's frequent use of analogy.

> Hunt prepares us to see the bad consequences of using Ryan's rule.

I . . . place my opinion upon the ground that, in the one case, to wit, the destruction of the building upon which the sparks were thrown by the negligent act of the party sought to be charged, the result was to have been anticipated the moment the fire was communicated to the building; that its destruction was the ordinary and natural result of its being fired. In the second, third, or twenty-sixth case, as supposed, the destruction of the building was not a natural and expected result of the first firing. That a building upon which sparks and cinders fall should be destroyed or seriously injured must be expected, but that the fire should spread and other buildings be consumed, is not a necessary or an usual result. That it is possible, and that it is not unfrequent, cannot be denied. The result, however, depends, not upon any necessity of a further communication of the fire, but upon a concurrence of accidental circumstances, such as the degree of the heat, the state of the atmosphere, the condition and materials of the adjoining structures and the direction of the wind. These are accidental and varying circumstances. The party has no control over them, and is not responsible for their effects.

> The judge clarifies the distinction between "proximate" and "remote."

My opinion, therefore, is, that this action cannot be sustained, for the reason that the damages incurred are not the immediate but the remote result of the negligence of the defendants. The immediate result was the destruction of their own wood and sheds; beyond that, it was remote.

To sustain such a claim as the present, and to follow the same to its legitimate consequences, would subject to a liability against which no prudence could guard, and to meet which no private fortune would be adequate. Nearly all fires are caused by negligence, in its extended sense. In a country where wood, coal, gas and oils are universally used, where men are crowded into cities and villages, where servants are employed, and where children find their home in all houses, it is impossible that the most vigilant prudence should guard against the occurrence of accidental or negligent fires. A man may insure his own house or his own furniture, but he cannot

> An elaboration of the bad consequences that would come from following Ryan's rule.

insure his neighbor's building or furniture, for the reason that he has no interest in them. To hold that the owner must not only meet his own loss by fire, but that he must guarantee the security of his neighbors on both sides, and to an unlimited extent, would be to create a liability which would be the destruction of all civilized society. No community could long exist, under the operation of such a principle. In a commercial country, each man, to some extent, runs the hazard of his neighbor's conduct, and each, by insurance against such hazards, is enabled to obtain a reasonable security against loss. To neglect such precaution, and to call upon his neighbor, on whose premises a fire originated, to indemnify him instead, would be to award a punishment quite beyond the offense committed.

The remoteness of the damage, in my judgment, forms the true rule on which the question should be decided, and which prohibits a recovery by the plaintiff in this case.

EXERCISE 2 ◆ *Practice Justifying a Rule.* Look again at the three cases beginning on page 220 (Practice Inventing and Stating Rules). Select one case for which you and your classmates have developed plausible rules for both sides. Briefly state the conflicting rules, then write a persuasive case that one rule is preferable. Discuss the bad consequences of following the rule you reject or the good consequences of accepting the rule you favor. Make appeals to consistency and authority by assuming that the court before which you are arguing has made the following statements in earlier cases:

1. In Devlin versus Anglen, the court noted that its "highest goal was to shape the character of the citizenry by rewarding behavior that is socially productive and punishing behavior that is socially destructive."

2. In the case of Molar versus Bump, the court decided that "a person who deliberately touches another person in an offensive or harmful way is liable for whatever physical damage that touching causes." At a cocktail party Fred Bump had given Bob Molar, a total stranger, a hearty slap on the back that dislodged a loose tooth that found its way into the back of Molar's throat, from which it had to be removed surgically.

3. In the case of Scar versus Striker, the court decided that the rule in Molar versus Bump "applies whether the touching is direct or indirect." Striker had propped a bucket of water above a door so that it would fall on the next person to enter the room.

4. In the case of Guard versus Center, the court held that "if the person touched gives the person who does the touching reason to believe that the touch is acceptable, the toucher cannot be held liable for the consequences of the touching." George Center, age 15, had tackled John Guard, age 14, in a backyard football game, breaking his leg in the process.

5. In the case of Blush versus Lips, the court decided that "a person who is deliberately touched in an offensive way by another person is entitled

GEORGE WILL

"The people who read op-ed pages are not blank slates to be written upon. They are people who have an interest in public affairs and hold settled opinions about them. And that is good. Who would want to live in a country where journalists had real power . . . ?"

© UPI/Bettmann Newsphotos

George Will may be right about the difficulty of changing people's political opinions, but he may also be an example of a journalist whose power is quite real. His syndicated column is published in 450 newspapers, he writes a regular essay for *Newsweek,* and he often appears on television talk shows. His audience is an estimated twenty million.

The evolution of Will's own thought shows that not all political opinions are settled and unchangeable. He grew up a liberal Democrat, but during his graduate work at Oxford University he looked closely at the British "welfare state," which insured its citizens against unemployment, accidents, ill-health, and old age, and controlled the nation's key industries. Affected by what he saw and by the arguments of Conservatives at the University, Will became convinced that liberal social policies—however well intentioned—created a stagnant economy and a citizenry too dependent on government for its own good.

Returning to the United States, Will completed his Ph.D. in political science at Princeton in 1967, undergoing in the process another transformation. Influenced by the work of the eminent scholar Leo Strauss, Will realized that the problems created by British socialism were matched by problems with America's system of free enterprise. America's uncontrolled economic growth, he later wrote, levies "a severe toll against small towns, small enterprises, local governments, craftsmanship, environmental values, a sense of community, and other aspects of humane living." He began to argue that government must do more than encourage business: it must, directly or indirectly, legislate morality.

After a short academic career, Will moved to Washington as a speech-writer and soon became a journalist. At *The Washington Post* he showed he could squeeze an argument into a 750-word column that was witty and readable. In 1977 his columns won a Pulitzer Prize, and in 1983 he published his first book-length essay, *Statecraft as Soulcraft.* Politics have not consumed Will entirely, however. In 1990 he published a best-seller on a subject that interested him long before politics did: *Men at Work: The Craft of Baseball.* ◆

to compensation for an offense to his or her dignity, even if no physical damage is done." Fred Lips, a casual friend of Beverly Blush, had given her a noisy, wet, and unsolicited kiss at a meeting of the school board.

6. In the case of Standpat versus Brushby, the court held that "some touching which the person touched may find offensive is so inevitable and customary that it is unreasonable for the toucher to be responsible for its consequences." Professor Standpat had been standing at the front of an elevator. Dr. Brushby had jostled him slightly on the way out and had aggravated the professor's back condition.

7. In the case of Sleeper versus Blade, the court had noted that "a physician has a positive duty to take whatever steps are necessary to preserve the life of a patient, regardless of how offensive and unsolicited the touching involved may be."

THE IMPORTANCE AND NATURE OF "FACTS NO ONE DISPUTES"

The model of argument we have used in this chapter begins in "facts that no one disputes" and leads by way of a rule to a conclusion by the court. This model naturally raises the question of where "facts no one disputes" come from. The simple answer is that some are accepted by general consent and some are arrived at by a process of argument.

General consent is the most significant source of undisputed facts. When all sides in a dispute agree to a fact, it is by definition undisputed. In our imagined argument over ownership of the goldfish, for example, the brother did not deny that the sister had paid for the fish, nor did the sister deny that the brother had fed it. Agreement on these facts created a solid foundation on which the arguments for both sides could be built. In the parking case, you do not deny parking in the illegal space, and the director of parking operations is not likely to deny that the legal spaces were full. In Florence Whittaker's lawsuit against Frank Sanford, Whittaker did not deny that she had boarded the *Kingdom* voluntarily. In most disputes a good many facts are accepted by general consent.

When general consent fails, facts must be established by argument. In Chapter 6, we dealt with one kind of fact established by argument—the probable fact. An audience (or court) can be convinced that Shakespeare probably wrote *Hamlet*. A court may be convinced that the sparks from the New York Central Railroad's engine very probably (or almost certainly) caused the fire that burned Ryan's house.

In addition to such probable facts, there are "facts" established by the application of rules. Indeed, most of the arguments we have examined in this chapter set out to prove such "facts." If the sister wins the goldfish argument, for example, she will have established the "fact" that she owns the goldfish. When the court decided that Ms. Whittaker *had* been held prisoner, this conclusion became a "fact" that allowed her suit to be successful. These facts are created not by an appeal to our sense of what is probable but by an appeal to our sense of what is just or logical.

Obviously, once a fact is established by argument, it can become the starting point for another argument. Suppose, for example, that in the goldfish argument the sister is an enthusiastic amateur biologist and that the reason she wants to establish ownership is so that she can vivisect the pet in order to see how its heart works. Winning the argument about ownership might get her only partway to her goal because her brother might argue that even if she does own the fish, she has no right to cut up a living creature to satisfy her curiosity. Now we have a dispute that looks like this:

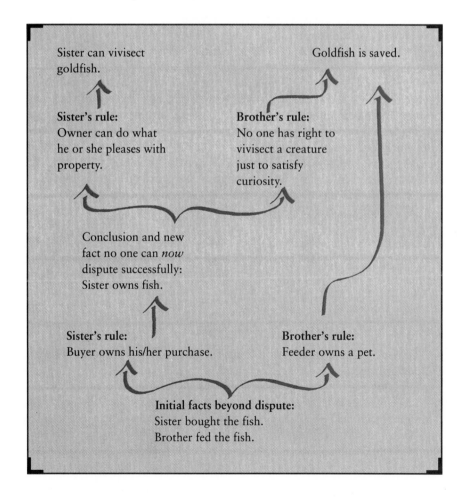

Sister can vivisect goldfish.

Goldfish is saved.

Sister's rule:
Owner can do what he or she pleases with property.

Brother's rule:
No one has right to vivisect a creature just to satisfy curiosity.

Conclusion and new fact no one can *now* dispute successfully: Sister owns fish.

Sister's rule:
Buyer owns his/her purchase.

Brother's rule:
Feeder owns a pet.

Initial facts beyond dispute:
Sister bought the fish.
Brother fed the fish.

As you can imagine, arguments about issues more complex than the fate of a pet goldfish often involve longer ladders of reasoning. Each level of the argument stands, so to speak, on the shoulders of the level before. Such acrobatics can be perilous. If the court rejects any stage of the argument, all stages above it come tumbling down.

WRITING AN ARGUMENT WHEN RULES ARE DISPUTED: POINTS TO CONSIDER

The nature of an argument about rules tells us a good deal about the process you must go through in order to write a successful one. Let's assume that you know from the outset which side you intend to advocate. The first thing you must do is identify very accurately the beginning and ending elements of the dispute. What facts do both sides concede to be true? *Exactly* what conclusions are the two sides trying to reach? If, for example, you are the sister arguing for the right to vivisect the goldfish, you must prepare an argument that establishes not only your ownership but your right to cut open a living creature that you own.

With the beginning and end points of the dispute clearly established, attempt to anticipate the rule (or rules) your opponent will offer and attempt to find a more compelling rule. In general you should choose a narrow rule rather than a broad one. Florence Whittaker's lawyer did not argue that *any* confinement of a person constituted imprisonment—a rule that would include confining someone by threatening her with eternal damnation if she left. He merely argued that confinement by physical barriers constituted imprisonment. An argument based on the broader rule would presumably have failed.

With the rule defined as clearly and narrowly as possible, attempt to find persuasive backing for it, looking especially for appeals to authority, consistency, and consequences. In many cases, developing an analogy to a more clear-cut case can be an effective strategy, but you should not rely on analogy alone, since your case cannot match the comparable case in every detail.

QUESTIONS FOR PEER REVIEW

When you have completed a draft, ask your reviewer to give both general advice (page 65) and reactions to four particular questions:

1. Are the facts that I treat as undisputed actually undisputed? If I rely on a disputed fact, do I establish it by appealing to the reader's sense of what is probable, just, or logical? Does that argument lead back to facts that are *actually* undisputed?

2. Can you identify the general rule from which I am arguing? Does it seem to you to be a valid rule? Is the support I offer for it persuasive? Can you think of other support that would be valuable?

3. If you were my opponent in this argument, what would your argument be? Has my argument taken yours adequately into consideration?

4. Would any bad consequences come from the adoption of my rule in all similar cases? If so, have I persuaded you that the bad consequences are limited enough to make the rule acceptable?

Your reviewer's comments should prepare you to write your final draft.

In some cases, the process of writing the argument will shake your confidence that you are on the right side. If your side is assigned (by the court or by your instructor), you must proceed to make the best argument you can, trusting that the wisdom of the court will insure that the right side prevails. If you are free to change sides, you should do so with enthusiasm, realizing that you have accomplished one of the great goals of a liberal education by losing an argument with yourself.

ASSIGNMENT 1: *PARAGRAPH-LENGTH ARGUMENTS*

Each of the following cases involves one friend who loses or destroys property owned by another friend. Decide in each case what compensation, if any, the loser or destroyer owes to the owner; then make an argument that you believe would persuade a neutral party to agree with you. After you have written paragraphs for each of the four cases, formulate the general "law" (expressed in no more than three sentences) that you think should govern all cases where one friend loses or destroys the property of another.

CASE 1. Gina Davis borrowed Sally Seymore's chemistry notes for the midterm exam and, partly to show her gratitude, offered to take care of Sally's aquarium while Sally was away for spring break. She promised to feed the fish every day and make sure that nothing was amiss. Unfortunately for the fish, Gina was busy during spring break and forgot to check on them for four days. When she finally remembered, she found that the aerator was not working and that the Trinidad guppy (valued at $5) and the Balinese fighting fish (valued at $15) were dead.

CASE 2. Alan Norton, a serious cyclist, lent the expensive mountain bike that he keeps locked in his dormitory room at night to Jim Curry, who said that he wanted to ride it to the shopping mall. When Curry arrived at the mall, he locked the bike securely to a bicycle rack, but he didn't look into the carry-all bag that was attached to the bike's seat. The bag contained Norton's small tool kit worth about $15 and his gold wristwatch worth about $1,500. A thief unzipped the bag, which had no lock, and took both the kit and the watch.

CASE 3. Bill Dawson borrowed chemistry class notes for the entire semester from Sally Seymore while they were standing near the campus bookstore. Seymore's notes were in a rather shabby three-ring binder that Dawson did not open immediately because he was on his way to the bookstore to buy some aspirin. Customers are not allowed to take notebooks or other parcels into the bookstore. Dawson considered putting the binder into one of the coin-operated lockers at the entrance, but he didn't have a quarter and was in a hurry. Instead he put the binder on one of the open shelves that are also used for holding customers' possessions. When he returned, the notebook was gone. Seymore says, and Dawson believes her, that inside the binder was a plastic pocket containing a calculator worth about $25.

CASE 4. Betty Jorgenson was recently at a shopping mall where she ran into a friend, JoAnn Hinkel. Hinkel was looking for her two-year-old son who had slipped into the crowd. She asked Jorgenson to hold two shopping bags for her for a moment while she "chased Freddy down." Freddy was hard to find, and Jorgenson was left holding the bags for about twenty minutes. She decided to buy an ice-cream cone while she was waiting. After she made her purchase and sat down to eat, she realized she had left the bags on the counter. By the time she returned both were gone. One contained a paperback book worth $5, one a silk blouse that cost $95.

ASSIGNMENTS 2–7: *ARGUMENTS ABOUT SCHOOL POLICY*

Assignments 2–7 assume that it is next April and that you are a resident of River City, a town with a population of 2,200 where every citizen can recognize every other citizen at a glance. The town contains a high school (John Dewey High) with 300 students in it, some bussed in from outlying farms. Ninety percent of the school budget is supported by local taxes, and, as there is never money to spare, expenditures are closely monitored. Teachers are not well paid, and in some areas (math, science, and foreign language) it is hard for the town to retain well-qualified teachers. The school is administered by a principal (Dr. Patricia Stokes) who tends to consult the school board on all issues that might provoke controversy.

Near the front door of the high school is a plaque containing some quotations from John Dewey's essay "My Pedagogic Creed" (1897):

I believe that the only true education comes through the stimulation of the child's powers by the demands of the social situations in which he finds himself.

I believe that education, therefore, is a process of living and not a preparation for future living.

I believe that . . . the best and deepest moral training is precisely that which one gets through having to enter into proper relations with others in a unity of work and thought.

I believe, finally, that the teacher is engaged, not simply in the training of individuals, but in the formation of the proper social life.

Jerry Foster, who graduated from the high school two years ago, has been working at a local service station ever since. Foster was not enthusiastic about studying when he was in school and spent a good deal of his time playing football and partying. His report cards were strings of C's and D's, but he graduated with his class. The service station owner, Fred Johnson, recently discovered that Foster cannot read even the headlines of the newspaper. He expressed a good deal of shock at this and persuaded Foster that the high school, by failing to do its job properly, has saddled Foster with a handicap that will limit his earning capacity for life and will also deprive him of the pleasure of reading. Foster, after stewing over Johnson's comments, decides to "demand his rights." With the assistance of Johnson, he drafts a letter to the principal, demanding that the school "arrange for special classes in the evening where I can get the education that the school failed to give me the first time around." Evening classes, he says, are necessary because he works at the service station from its opening at 7:00 A.M. to its closing at 6:00 P.M., and he needs all of this income because his parents can no longer support him. There are at present no adult literacy classes in town and no evening classes at the high school. No volunteer has offered to tutor Foster without charge.

ASSIGNMENT 2: Assume the role of someone who is opposed to Foster's demands. Make an argument in a letter about 500 words long addressed to the principal. Your argument should show that the school has no obligation to offer the classes.

ASSIGNMENT 3: Assume the role of someone sympathetic to Foster's cause. Make an argument in a letter about 500 words long addressed to the principal. Show that the school has an obligation to offer Foster further instruction.

Ms. Francine Knightly, an untenured thirty-year-old physics teacher, is in her second year at John Dewey High. No one disputes her mastery of the subject matter or her effectiveness as a teacher. In fact, her classes have recently been videotaped as models of effective education by members of the National Task Force on Scientific Literacy. Many of the students at the high school and some of the adults in the town are, as the principal once put it, "under the Knightly spell." A growing faction in the town, however, is furious about Knightly's extracurricular activity. She spends most of her evenings in the bar at the bowling alley directly across from the high school. There she is often surrounded by students, none of whom have ever been seen drinking alcohol in her presence. Discussion at the table is sometimes about the foolishness of religion: Knightly is a vociferous atheist. Sometimes the talk is about the incompetence of other teachers at the high school: Knightly is open in her criticism of her colleagues and often mimics their expression of what she calls "wooden-headed ideas." Though Knightly says she is not a communist, there are rumors that some of her statements are distinctly antibusiness and anti-American. Recently, several adults in the bar heard her describe the school's antidrug campaign as "debased Puritanism" and say that marijuana was less dangerous than tobacco and "far less dangerous than sexual abstinence."

In the last two months, the principal has received three requests from teachers that Ms. Knightly's contract not be renewed because her comments about her fellow teachers have led to discipline problems in their classrooms. A minister in the town has written to request that her contract not be renewed because a girl in his congregation (Jenny Brereton) has told him that she and several of her classmates have been experimenting with marijuana "because Ms. Knightly seemed to think it was all right." The principal has brought these letters to the attention of the school board, and a leak from the school board has brought them to the attention of virtually everyone in town.

ASSIGNMENT 4: Assume the role of one of Knightly's detractors. Write a 500-word letter to the school board making an argument that there is good reason for ending her employment at the high school.

ASSIGNMENT 5: Assume the role of one of Knightly's champions. Write a 500-word letter to the school board making an argument that it would be unjust and imprudent not to renew her contract.

Jenny Brereton, a senior at the high school, took College Preparatory English last semester and received a failing grade. In a note to Brereton's parents, her English teacher, Peter Quince, said that the reason for the grade was "Jenny's failure to hand in the two main essays for the course, one on 'A Memorable Vacation' and one on 'London Coffeehouses in the Eighteenth Century.' " In the same semester Jenny received the highest scores in the school's history on the Scholastic Aptitude Test and sold two stories to magazines. Both stories were about the renewal of the local vineyards which had been ruined in the 1930s as a result of the passage of the Eighteenth Amendment to the U.S. Constitution. The first story was about 2,000 words long and was published in *Midwest Now*. The second was 5,000 words long and was featured in an airline magazine. The photos for both stories were taken by Jerry Foster. Brereton and her parents suggested to Peter Quince that he accept these stories in lieu of the two papers required for the course, but Quince refused. The Breretons are now appealing this decision to the principal and the school board. Once again, as will happen in a small town, rumor has spread these facts to the general population.

ASSIGNMENT 6: Assume the role of Peter Quince. Write a 500-word letter to the principal defending your refusal to change Brereton's grade. Once again, your argument should be based on one or more carefully articulated and supported rules. Use your imagination and experience to provide necessary details about Quince's educational philosophy and the way that he plans and conducts his classes.

ASSIGNMENT 7: Assume the role of Jenny Brereton. Write a 500-word argument addressed to the principal, requesting a change in grade. Use your imagination and experience to provide details about the nature of the articles Brereton wrote and the process she followed in writing them.

ASSIGNMENT 8: *AN ARGUMENT OF YOUR CHOICE*

Identify a dispute in which you are interested and write a 1,500- to 2,000-word paper in which you

1. Describe the undisputed facts in the case in such a way that someone unfamiliar with them can understand them. (The explanatory paragraphs in the assignment above can serve as models.)

2. Briefly outline a well-formed argument your opponents have made or might make. Be sure that your identification of their rule or rules is clear.

3. Develop your own argument, advocating a rule or rules that contrast with your opponents' and lead to a different conclusion.

Your paper should be written with a "court" in mind. Your teacher may ask you to identify the nature of this court.

MILLER V. CALIFORNIA
413 US 15[1] (1973)

In 1969, Marvin Miller promoted the sale of four "adult" books and one "adult" movie by mass-mailing brochures that included photographs and drawings suitable to one of the titles: Sex Orgies Illustrated. *An envelope containing the five brochures was addressed to a restaurant in Newport Beach, California, where it was opened by the manager of the restaurant and his mother. Not having requested these brochures, the two complained to police, and Miller was arrested under a California law making it a misdemeanor to distribute obscene material. After Miller was convicted, he appealed. Eventually his appeal reached the U.S. Supreme Court, which upheld the conviction by a 5 to 4 vote.*

In order to follow the legal arguments made by Chief Justice Burger in the majority opinion and Justice Douglas in a dissenting opinion, you need some information on the constitutional and legal issues involved. At the center of the controversy is the First Amendment to the U.S. Constitution: "Congress shall make no law respecting an establishment of religion, or prohibiting the free exercise thereof; or abridging the freedom of speech, or of the press; or the right of the people peaceably to assemble, and to petition the Government for a redress of grievances." The Fourteenth Amendment, by forbidding states to "make or enforce any law which shall abridge the privileges or immunities of citizens of the United States," made the First Amendment apply to state laws as well.

But is the distribution of obscene material protected under the First Amendment? In Roth v. United States *[354 US 476], the majority of the court said no and defined obscenity as "material which deals with sex in a manner appealing to prurient interest." It said that such material was not covered by the First Amendment because it was "utterly without redeeming social importance." The precise meaning of "prurient" in the* Roth *case was to be defined by "contemporary community standards." The minority of the court and many advocates of civil liberties found this decision alarming for several reasons. One was vagueness: someone who published material dealing with sex might be arrested and discover to his or her surprise that (in the opinion of the*

---

[1]By convention, Supreme Court cases are named by stating the name of the party making the appeal (Marvin Miller) and the name of the party on the other side (State of California). The *v.* between is an abbreviation of *versus*. The numbers and letters below tell the reader where the opinions can be found: Volume 413 of the *United States Reports*, page 15.

judge or jury) he had offended community standards. Thus the publisher might be convicted for a crime he could not have known he was violating.

Subsequent cases altered the meaning of obscenity somewhat. Memoirs v. Massachusetts [383 US 413] said that only material "utterly without redeeming social value" could be subject to criminal prosecution. But it was so difficult for prosecutors to prove that a work was utterly without redeeming social value that it became nearly impossible to prosecute obscenity cases. In Ginzberg v. New York [383 US 463] the Court decided that some material might be considered obscene if it were distributed to children, even though it would not be obscene if distributed to adults.

This confusion on the Court about how to define obscenity set the stage for the Miller case, in which Chief Justice Burger and the majority of the court attempted to create a clear legal test for obscenity. Justice Douglas found this new definition no more adequate than those that came before, as you will see.

A case mentioned in Douglas's dissenting opinion also needs explanation. Bouie v. City of Columbia [378 US 347] involved a 1960 sit-in protest in South Carolina. After two protesters were arrested for trespass, the South Carolina courts reinterpreted the trespass statute in a way that made the charges stick. The U.S. Supreme Court, however, threw the conviction out, saying that the Carolina courts had made the sit-in illegal ex post facto (after the fact). In the United States, people can only be punished for actions that were illegal at the time they were committed.

Mr. Chief Justice Burger,
for the majority

1 THIS CASE INVOLVES THE APPLICATION OF A State's criminal obscenity statute to a situation in which sexually explicit materials have been thrust by aggressive sales action upon unwilling recipients who had in no way indicated any desire to receive such materials. This Court has recognized that the States have a legitimate interest in prohibiting dissemination or exhibition of obscene material when the mode of dissemination carries with it a significant danger of offending the sensibilities of unwilling recipients or of exposure to juveniles.[2] It is in this context that we are called on to define the standards which must be used to identify obscene material that a State may regulate

without infringing on the First Amendment. . . . In Roth v. United States the court sustained a conviction under a federal statute punishing the mailing of "obscene, lewd, lascivious or filthy . . ." materials. The key to that holding was the Court's rejection of the claim that obscene materials were protected by the First Amendment. Five Justices joined in the opinion stating:

> All ideas having even the slightest redeeming social importance—unorthodox ideas, controversial ideas, even ideas hateful to the prevailing climate of opinion—have the full protection of the [First Amendment] guaranties, unless excludable because they encroach upon the limited area of more important interests. But implicit in the history of the First Amendment is the rejection of obscenity as utterly

2

[2] At this point, Burger cites twelve cases, including Ginzberg v. New York.

without redeeming social importance. . . . There are certain well-defined and narrowly limited classes of speech, the prevention and punishment of which have never been thought to raise any Constitutional problem. *These include the lewd and obscene. . . . It has been well observed that such utterances are no essential part of any exposition of ideas, and are of such slight social value as a step to truth that any benefit that may be derived from them is clearly outweighed by the social interest in order and morality.*

3   This much has been categorically settled by the Court, that obscene material is unprotected by the First Amendment.[3] We acknowledge, however, the inherent dangers of undertaking to regulate any form of expression. State statutes designed to regulate obscene materials must be carefully limited.[4] As a result, we now confine the permissible scope of such regulation to works which depict or describe sexual conduct. That conduct must be specifically defined by the applicable state law, as written or authoritatively construed. A state offense must also be limited to works which, taken as a whole, appeal to the prurient interest in sex, which portray sexual conduct in a patently offensive way, and which, taken as a whole, do not have serious literary, artistic, political, or scientific value. . . .

4   Under the holdings announced today, no one will be subject to prosecution for the sale or exposure of obscene materials unless these materials depict or describe patently offensive "hard core" sexual conduct specifically defined by the regulating state law, as written or construed. We are satisfied that these specific prerequisites will provide fair notice to a dealer in such materials that his public and commercial activities may bring prosecution.[5] If the inability to define regulated materials with ultimate, god-like precision altogether removes the power of the States or the

Congress to regulate, then "hard core" pornography may be exposed without limit to the juvenile, the passerby, and the consenting adult alike, as, indeed, Mr. Justice Douglas contends. . . .

The dissenting Justices sound the alarm of repression. But, in our view, to equate the free and robust exchange of ideas and political debate with commercial exploitation of obscene material demeans the grand conception of the First Amendment and its high purpose in the historical struggle for freedom. It is a "misuse of the great guarantees of free speech and free press. . . ."[6] The First Amendment protects works which, taken as a whole, have serious literary, artistic, political, or scientific value, regardless of whether the government or the majority of the people approve of the ideas these works represent. "The protection given speech and press was fashioned to insure unfettered interchange of *ideas* for the bringing about of political and social changes desired by the people."[7] But the public portrayal of hard core sexual conduct for its own sake, and for the ensuing commercial gain, is a different matter.

6   There is no evidence, empirical or historical, that the stern 19th-century American censorship of public distribution and display of material relating to sex, see Roth *v.* United States, 482–485, in any way limited or affected expression of serious literary, artistic, political, or scientific ideas. On the contrary, it is beyond any question that the era following Thomas Jefferson to Theodore Roosevelt was an "extraordinarily vigorous period," not just in economics and politics, but in belles lettres and in "the outlying fields of social and political philosophies."[8] We do not see the harsh hand of censorship of ideas—good or bad, sound or unsound—and "repression" of political liberty lurking in every state regulation of commercial exploitation of human interest in sex.

---

[3] Here Burger cites six cases, including Roth *v.* United States.
[4] Burger cites Interstate Circuit, Inc. *v.* Dallas, 390 US 682–685.
[5] Burger cites Roth *v.* United States and Ginzberg *v.* New York.

[6] Burger cites Breard *v.* Alexandria, 341 US 645.
[7] Burger cites Roth *v.* United States. The emphasis on *"ideas"* is his.
[8] V. Parrington, *Main Currents in American Thought,* ix ff. Burger's original footnote quotes Parrington and also cites several books and articles by other historians.

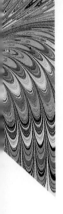

Mr. Justice Brennan finds [that once censorship is introduced] "it is hard to see how state-ordered regimentation of our minds can ever be forestalled."[9] These doleful anticipations assume that courts cannot distinguish commerce in ideas, protected by the First Amendment, from commercial exploitation of obscene material. Moreover, state regulation of hard core pornography so as to make it unavailable to non-adults, a regulation which Mr. Justice Brennan finds constitutionally permissible, has all the elements of "censorship" for adults; indeed even more rigid enforcement techniques may be called for with such dichotomy of regulation.[10] One can concede that the "sexual revolution" of recent years may have had useful byproducts in striking layers of prudery from a subject long irrationally kept from needed ventilation. But it does not follow that no regulation of patently offensive "hard core" materials is needed or permissible; civilized people do not allow unregulated access to heroin because it is a derivative of medicinal morphine.

Mr. Justice Douglas, dissenting

8   Today we leave open the way for California to send a man to prison for distributing brochures that advertise books and a movie under freshly written standards defining obscenity which until today's decision were never the part of any law.

9   The Court has worked hard to define obscenity and concededly has failed. [Douglas here reviews a number of contradictory definitions from earlier Supreme Court rulings.] Today the Court retreats from the earlier formulations and undertakes to make new definitions. This effort, like the earlier ones, is earnest and well intentioned. The difficulty is that we do not deal with constitutional terms, since "obscenity" is not mentioned in the Constitution or Bill of Rights. And the First Amendment makes no such exception from "the press" which it undertakes to protect nor, as I have said on other occasions, is an exception necessarily implied, for there was no recognized exception to the free press at the time the Bill of Rights was adopted which treated "obscene" publications differently from other types of papers, magazines, and books. So there are no constitutional guidelines for deciding what is and what is not "obscene." The Court

is at large because we deal with tastes and standards of literature. What shocks me may be sustenance for my neighbor. What causes one person to boil up in rage over one pamphlet or movie may reflect only his neurosis, not shared by others. We deal here with a regime of censorship which, if adopted, should be done by constitutional amendment after full debate by the people.

Obscenity cases usually generate tremendous   10
emotional outbursts. They have no business being in the courts. If a constitutional amendment authorized censorship, the censor would probably be an administrative agency. Then criminal prosecutions could follow as, if, and when publishers defied the censor and sold their literature. Under that regime a publisher would know when he was on dangerous ground. Under the present regime—whether the old standards or the new ones are used—the criminal law becomes a trap. A brand-new test would put a publisher behind bars under a new law improvised by the courts after the publication. That was done in Ginzburg and has all the evils of an ex post facto law.

My contention is that until a civil proceeding   11
has placed a tract beyond the pale, no criminal prose-

---

[9]Burger cites Brennan's dissenting opinion in Paris Adult Theatre I *v.* Slaton.

[10]Burger cites Interstate Circuit, Inc. *v.* Dallas, 390 US 690.

cution should be sustained. For no more vivid illustration of vague and uncertain laws could be designed than those we have fashioned. As Mr. Justice Harlan has said:

12   The upshot of all this divergence in viewpoint is that anyone who undertakes to examine the Court's decisions since Roth which have held particular material obscene or not obscene would find himself in utter bewilderment.[11]

13   In Bouie v. City of Columbia,[12] we upset a conviction for remaining on property after being asked to leave, while the only unlawful act charged by the statute was entering. We held that the defendants had received no "fair warning, at the time of their conduct" while on the property "that the act for which they now stand convicted was rendered criminal" by the state statute. The same requirement of "fair warning" is due here, as much as in Bouie. The latter involved racial discrimination; the present case involves rights earnestly urged as being protected under the First Amendment. In any case—certainly when constitutional rights are concerned—we should not allow men to go to prison or be fined when they had no "fair warning" that what they did was criminal conduct.

14   If a specific book, play, paper, or motion picture has in a civil proceeding been condemned as obscene and review of that finding has been completed, and thereafter a person publishes, shows, or displays that particular book or film, then a vague law has been made specific. There would remain the underlying question whether the First Amendment allows an implied exception in the case of obscenity. I do not think it does and my views on the issue have been stated over and over again. But at least a criminal prosecution brought at that juncture would not violate the time-honored void-for-vagueness test.

15   No such protective procedure has been designed by California in this case. Obscenity—which even we cannot define with precision—is a hodgepodge. To send men to jail for violating standards they can-

not understand, construe, and apply is a monstrous thing to do in a Nation dedicated to fair trials and due process. . . .

    There is no "captive audience" problem in these obscenity cases. No one is being compelled to look or listen. Those who enter news stands or bookstalls may be offended by what they see. But they are not compelled by the State to frequent those places; and it is only state or governmental action against which the First Amendment, applicable to the States by virtue of the Fourteenth, raises a ban.

17   The idea that the First Amendment permits government to ban publications that are "offensive" to some people puts an ominous gloss on freedom of the press. That test would make it possible to ban any paper or any journal or magazine in some benighted place. The First Amendment was designed "to invite dispute," to induce "a condition of unrest," to "create dissatisfaction with conditions as they are," and even to stir "people to anger."[13] The idea that the First Amendment permits punishment for ideas that are "offensive" to the particular judge or jury sitting in judgment is astounding. No greater leveler of speech or literature has ever been designed. To give the power to the censor, as we do today, is to make a sharp and radical break with the traditions of a free society. The First Amendment was not fashioned as a vehicle for dispensing tranquilizers to the people. Its prime function is to keep debate open to "offensive" as well as "staid" people. The tendency throughout history has been to subdue the individual and exalt the power of government. The use of the standard "offensive" gives authority to government that cuts the very vitals out of the First Amendment.[14] As is intimated by the Court's opinion, the materials before us may be garbage. But so is much of what is said in political campaigns, in the daily press, on TV, or over

---

[11]Douglas cites Interstate Circuit, Inc. v. Dallas, 390 US 676.
[12]378 US 347.

[13]Douglas cites Terminiello v. Chicago, 337 US 1, 4.
[14]Obscenity law has had a capricious history: "The white slave traffic was first exposed by W. T. Snead in a magazine article, 'The Maiden Tribute.' The English law did absolutely nothing to the profiteers in vice, but put Stead in prison for a year for writing about an indecent subject." Z. Chafee, *Free Speech in the United States*, page 151. [Douglas's note, shortened]

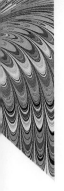

the radio. By reason of the First Amendment—and solely because of it—speakers and publishers have not been threatened or subdued because their thoughts and ideas may be "offensive" to some.

The standard "offensive" is unconstitutional in yet another way. In Coates *v*. City of Cincinnati[15] we had before us a municipal ordinance that made it a crime for three or more persons to assemble on a street and conduct themselves "in a manner annoying to persons passing by." We struck it down, saying: "If three or more people meet together on a sidewalk or street corner, they must conduct themselves so as not to annoy any police officer or other person who should happen to pass by. In our opinion this ordinance is unconstitutionally vague because it subjects the exercise of the right of assembly to an unascertainable standard, and unconstitutionally broad because it authorizes the punishment of constitutionally protected conduct.

19   Conduct that annoys some people does not annoy others. Thus the ordinance is vague, not in the sense that it requires a person to conform his conduct to an imprecise but comprehensive normative standard, but rather in the sense that no standard of conduct is specified at all.

How can we deny Ohio the convenience of   20
punishing people who "annoy" others and allow California power to punish people who publish materials "offensive" to some people is difficult to square with constitutional requirements.

If there are to be restraints on what is obscene,   21
then a constitutional amendment should be the way of achieving the end. There are societies where religion and mathematics are the only free segments. It would be a dark day for America if that were our destiny. But the people can make it such if they choose to write obscenity into the Constitution and define it.

We deal with highly emotional, not rational,   22
questions. To many the Song of Solomon is obscene. I do not think that we, the judges, were ever given the constitutional power to make definitions of obscenity. If it is to be defined, let the people debate and decide by a constitutional amendment what they want to ban as obscene and what standards they want the legislatures and the courts to apply. Perhaps the people will decide that the path towards a mature, integrated society requires that all ideas competing for acceptance must have no censor. Perhaps they will decide otherwise. Whatever the choice, the courts will have some guidelines. Now we have none except our predilections. ◆

LET'S PUT PORNOGRAPHY BACK IN THE CLOSET

Susan Brownmiller

Journalist Susan Brownmiller is one of the founders of Women Against Pornography *and an organizer of the New York Radical Feminists. In 1975, after four years of research, she published* Against Our Will, *a study of the causes of rape and its effects. She published the following essay in* Newsday *in 1979 as part of her well-publicized crusade against pornography.*

---

[15] 402 US 611.

1   *F*REE SPEECH IS ONE OF THE GREAT FOUNDA-
tions on which our democracy rests. I am old enough
to remember the Hollywood Ten, the screenwriters
who went to jail in the late 1940s because they refused to testify before a congressional committee
about their political affiliations. They tried to use the
First Amendment as a defense, but they went to jail
because in those days there were few civil liberties
lawyers around who cared to champion the First
Amendment right to free speech, when the speech
concerned the Communist Party.

2   The Hollywood Ten were correct in claiming
the First Amendment. Its high purpose is the protection of unpopular ideas and political dissent. In the
dark, cold days of the 1950s, few civil libertarians
were willing to declare themselves First Amendment
absolutists. But in the brighter, though frantic, days of
the 1960s, the principle of protecting unpopular political speech was gradually strengthened.

3   It is fair to say now that the battle has largely
been won. Even the American Nazi Party has found
itself the beneficiary of the dedicated, tireless work of
the American Civil Liberties Union. But—and please
notice the quotation marks coming up—"To equate
the free and robust exchange of ideas and political debate with commercial exploitation of obscene material
demeans the grand conception of the First Amendment and its high purposes in the historic struggle for
freedom. It is a misuse of the great guarantees of free
speech and free press."

4   I didn't say that, although I wish I had, for I
think the words are thrilling. Chief Justice Warren
Burger said it in 1973, in the United States Supreme
Court's majority opinion in *Miller* v. *California*. During the same decades that the right to political free
speech was being strengthened in the courts, the nation's obscenity laws also were undergoing extensive
revision.

5   It's amazing to recall that in 1934 the question
of whether James Joyce's *Ulysses* should be banned as
pornographic actually went before the Court. The battle to protect *Ulysses* as a work of literature with re-

deeming social value was won. In later decades, Henry
Miller's *Tropic* books, *Lady Chatterley's Lover* and
the *Memoirs of Fanny Hill* also were adjudged not
obscene. These decisions have been important to me.
As the author of *Against Our Will*, a study of the
history of rape that does contain explicit sexual material, I shudder to think how my book would have
fared if James Joyce, D. H. Lawrence and Henry Miller hadn't gone before me.

6   I am not a fan of *Chatterley* or the *Tropic*
books, I should quickly mention. They are not to my
literary taste, nor do I think they represent female sex-
uality with any degree of accuracy. But I would
hardly suggest that we ban them. Such a suggestion
wouldn't get very far anyway. The battle to protect
these books is ancient history. Time does march on,
quite methodically. What, then, is unlawfully obscene,
and what does the First Amendment have to do
with it?

7   In the Miller case of 1973 (not Henry Miller,
by the way, but a porn distributor who sent unsolicited stuff through the mails), the Court came up
with new guidelines that it hoped would strengthen
obscenity laws by giving more power to the states.
What it did in actuality was throw everything into
confusion. It set up a three-part test by which materials can be adjudged obscene. The materials are obscene if they depict patently offensive, hard-core sexual conduct; lack serious scientific, literary, artistic or
political value; and appeal to the prurient interest of
an average person—as measured by contemporary
community standards.

8   "Patently offensive," "prurient interest" and
"hard-core" are indeed words to conjure with. "Contemporary community standards" are what we're trying to redefine. The feminist objection to pornography
is not based on prurience, which the dictionary defines
as lustful, itching desire. We are not opposed to sex
and desire, with or without the itch, and we certainly
believe that explicit sexual material has its place in literature, art, science and education. Here we part company rather swiftly with old-line conservatives who

don't want sex education in the high schools, for example.

No, the feminist objection to pornography is based on our belief that pornography represents hatred of women, that pornography's intent is to humiliate, degrade and dehumanize the female body for the purpose of erotic stimulation and pleasure. We are unalterably opposed to the presentation of the female body being stripped, bound, raped, tortured, mutilated and murdered in the name of commercial entertainment and free speech.

10 These images, which are standard pornographic fare, have nothing to do with the hallowed right of political dissent. They have everything to do with the creation of a cultural climate in which a rapist feels he is merely giving in to a normal urge and a woman is encouraged to believe that sexual masochism is healthy, liberated fun. Justice Potter Stewart once said about hard-core pornography, "You know it when you see it," and that certainly used to be true. In the good old days, pornography looked awful. It was cheap and sleazy, and there was no mistaking it for art.

11 Nowadays, since the porn industry has become a multimillion dollar business, visual technology has been employed in its service. Pornographic movies are skillfully filmed and edited, pornographic still shots using the newest tenets of good design artfully grace the covers of *Hustler, Penthouse* and *Playboy,* and the public—and the courts—are sadly confused.

12 The Supreme Court neglected to define "hard-core" in the Miller decision. This was a mistake. If "hard-core" refers only to explicit sexual intercourse, then that isn't good enough. When women or children or men—no matter how artfully—are shown tortured or terrorized in the service of sex, that's obscene. And "patently offensive," I would hope, to our "contemporary community standards."

13 Justice William O. Douglas wrote in his dissent to the Miller case that no one is "compelled to look." This is hardly true. To buy a paper at the corner newsstand is to subject oneself to a forcible immersion in pornography, to be demeaned by an array of dehumanized, chopped-up parts of the female anatomy,

packed like cuts of meat at the supermarket. I happen to like my body and I work hard at the gym to keep it in good shape, but I am embarrassed for my body and for the bodies of all women when I see the fragmented parts of us so frivolously, and so flagrantly, displayed.

14 Some constitutional theorists (Justice Douglas was one) have maintained that any obscenity law is a serious abridgement of free speech. Others (and Justice Earl Warren was one) have maintained that the First Amendment was never intended to protect obscenity. We live quite compatibly with a host of free-speech abridgements. There are restraints against false and misleading advertising or statements—shouting "fire" without cause in a crowded movie theater, etc.—that do not threaten, but strengthen, our societal values. Restrictions on the public display of pornography belong in this category.

15 The distinction between permission to publish and permission to display publicly is an essential one and one which I think consonant with First Amendment principles. Justice Burger's words which I quoted above support this without question. We are not saying "Smash the presses" or "Ban the bad ones," but simply "Get the stuff out of our sight." Let the legislatures decide—using realistic and humane contemporary community standards—what can be displayed and what cannot. The courts, after all, will be the final arbiters. ◆

JUST LIKE US?

Jack Hitt, Arthur Caplan, Gary Francione, Roger Goldman, Ingrid Newkirk*

In recent years Harper's Magazine *has frequently sponsored and published "forums" on controversial topics. These round-table discussions give readers a sense of the give-and-take among speakers applying different frameworks to the same subject. The following forum appeared in August 1988.*

1 THE RELATIONSHIP OF MAN TO ANIMAL HAS long been one of sympathy, manifested in such welfare organizations as the kindly Bide-A-Wee or the avuncular ASPCA. In the last few years, the politics of that relationship have been questioned by a number of new and vociferous interest groups which hold to the credo that animals are endowed with certain inalienable rights.

2 Typically, when animal rights advocates are called upon by the media to defend their views, they are seated across the table from research scientists. The discussion turns on the treatment of laboratory animals or the illegal efforts of fanatics who smuggle animals out of research facilities via latter-day underground railroads to freedom.

3 Behind these easy headlines, however, stand serious philosophical questions: How should we treat animals? Why do humans have rights and other animals not? If animals had rights, what would they be? To address these questions, *Harper's Magazine* asked two leading animal rights activists to sit down with a philosopher and a constitutional scholar to examine the logic of their opinions.

BUNNIES AND SEWER RATS

4 JACK HITT: Let me ask a question that many readers might ask: Gary, why have you—a former Supreme Court law clerk and now a professor of law at the University of Pennsylvania—devoted your life to animal rights?

5 GARY FRANCIONE: I believe that animals have *rights*. This is not to say that animals have the same rights that we do, but the reasons that lead us to accord certain rights to human beings are equally applicable to animals. The problem is that our value system doesn't permit the breadth of vision necessary to understand that. We currently use the category of "species" as the relevant criterion for determining membership in our moral community, just as we once used race and sex to determine that membership.

6 If you asked white men in 1810 whether blacks had rights, most of them would have laughed at you. What was necessary then is necessary now. We must change the *way* we think: a paradigm shift in the way we think about animals. Rights for blacks and women were *the* constitutional issues of the nineteenth and twentieth centuries. Animal rights, once more people understand the issue, will emerge as *the* civil rights movement of the twenty-first century.

* The following forum is based on a discussion held at the Cooper Union for the Advancement of Science and Art, in New York City. Jack Hitt served as moderator. Jack Hitt is a senior editor at *Harper's Magazine*. Arthur Caplan is director of the Center for Biomedical Ethics at the University of Minnesota. Gary Francione is a professor at the University of Pennsylvania Law School. He frequently litigates animal rights cases. Roger Goldman is a constitutional law scholar and professor at Saint Louis University School of Law. Ingrid Newkirk is the national director of People for the Ethical Treatment of Animals, in Washington. [*Harper's* note]

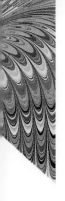

HITT: I want to see where the logic of your beliefs takes us. Suppose I am the head of a company that has invented a dynamite new shampoo. It gives your hair great body; everyone is going to look like Lisa Bonet. But my preliminary tests show that it may cause some irritation or mild damage to the eye. So I've purchased 2,000 rabbits to test this shampoo on their eyes first. Roger, do you find anything offensive about testing shampoo this way?

8   ROGER GOLDMAN: As someone new to the animal rights issue, I don't find it particularly offensive.

9   HITT: What if the only thing new about my shampoo is that it is just a different color?

10   GOLDMAN: If everything else is equal, then I would say the testing is unnecessary.

11   INGRID NEWKIRK: I think Roger hit the nail on the head. The public has absolutely no idea what the tests involve or whether they're necessary. I think Roger might object if he knew that there were alternatives, that a human-skin patch test can be substituted for the rabbit-blinding test. If consumers were informed, then no compassionate consumer would abide such cruelty.

12   FRANCIONE: The problem is that we can use animals in any way we like because they are *property*. The law currently regards animals as no different from that pad of paper in front of you, Roger. If you own that pad, you can rip it up or burn it. By and large we treat animals no differently than glasses, cups, or paper.

13   ARTHUR CAPLAN: I know you lawyers love to talk about the property status of these little creatures, but there are other factors. We treat animals as property because people don't believe that animals have any moral worth. People look at rabbits and say, "There are many rabbits. If there are a few less rabbits, who cares?"

14   NEWKIRK: Not true. Many people, who don't support animal rights, *would* care if you stuck a knife in their rabbit or dog. They're deeply offended by acts of *individual* cruelty.

CAPLAN: Yes, but I suspect that if in your test we   15
substituted ugly sewer rats for button-nosed rabbits, people might applaud the suffering. There are some animals that just don't register in the human consciousness. Rats don't, rabbits might, dogs and horses definitely do.

NEWKIRK: Not always. If the test were done to a   16
sewer rat in *front* of a person, the average person would say, "Don't do that" or "Kill him quickly."

HITT: Why?   17

NEWKIRK: It's institutionalized cruelty, born of our   18
hideous compartmentalized thinking. If the killing is done behind closed doors, if the government says it must be done, or if some man or woman in a white coat assures us that it's for our benefit, we ignore our own ethical good sense and allow it to happen.

HITT: If the frivolity of the original test bothers us,   19
what if we up the ante? What if the product to be tested might yield a cure for baldness?

FRANCIONE: Jack, that is a "utilitarian" argument   20
which suggests that the rightness or wrongness of an action is determined by the *consequences* of that action. In the case of animals, it implies that animal exploitation produces benefits that justify that exploitation. I don't believe in utilitarian moral thought. It's dangerous because it easily leads to atrocious conclusions, both in how we treat humans and how we treat animals. I don't believe it is morally permissible to exploit weaker beings even if we derive benefits.

GOLDMAN: So not even the cancer cure?   21

FRANCIONE: No, absolutely not.   22

CAPLAN: But you miss the point about moral selfishness. By the time you get to the baldness cure, people   23
start to say, "I don't *care* about animals. My interests are a hell of a lot more important than the animals' interests. So if keeping hair on my head means sacrificing those animals, painlessly or not, I want it." It's not utilitarian—it's selfish.

FRANCIONE: But you certainly wouldn't put that forward as a justification, would you?   24

25 CAPLAN: No, it's just a description.

26 FRANCIONE: I can't argue with your assertion that people are selfish. But aren't we morally obliged to assess the consequences of the selfishness? To begin that assessment, people must become aware of the ways in which we exploit animals.

27 Maybe I'm just a hopeless optimist, but I believe that once people are confronted with these facts, they will reassess. The backlash that we're seeing from the exploitation industries—the meat companies and the biomedical research laboratories—is a reaction of fear. They know that the more people learn, the more people will reject this painful exploitation.

28 HITT: But won't your movement always be hampered by that mix of moral utilitarianism and moral egotism? People will say, "Yes, be kind to animals up to a point of utilitarianism (so I can have my cancer cure) and up to a point of moral egotism (so I can have my sirloin)." There may be some shift in the moral center, but it will move only so far.

29 CAPLAN: I agree. Gary can remain optimistic, but confronting people with the facts won't get him very far. Moral egotism extends even into human relations. Let's not forget that we are in a city where you have to step over people to enter this building. People don't say, "Feed, clothe, and house them, and then tax me; I'll pay." We have a limited moral imagination. It may be peculiarly American, but you can show people pictures of starving children or homeless people or animals in leg traps, and many will say, "That's too bad. Life is hard, but I still want my pleasures, my enjoyments."

30 NEWKIRK: There are two answers to that. First, people accept the myth. They were brought up with the illusion that they *must* eat animals to be healthy. Now we know that's not true. Second, because of humankind's lack of moral—or even just plain—imagination, we activists have to tell people exactly what they *should* do. Then we must make it easier for them to do it. If we put a moral stepladder in front of people, a lot of them will walk up it. But most people feel powerless as individuals and ask, "Who am I? I'm only one person. What can I do?" We must show them.

HITT: Roger, I'm wondering whether your moral center has shifted since we began. Originally you weren't offended by my using 2,000 rabbits to test a new shampoo. Are you now?

GOLDMAN: I am still a utilitarian. But if the test is unnecessary or just repetitive, clearly, I'm persuaded that it should be stopped.

33 NEWKIRK: Precisely Gary's point. Armed with the facts, Roger opts not to hurt animals.

ENFRANCHISING ALL CREATURES

34 HITT: Art, what makes human beings have rights and animals not have rights?

35 CAPLAN: Some would argue a biblical distinction. God created humans in his image and did not create animals that way. That's one special property. Another philosophical basis is natural law, which holds that inalienable rights accrue to being human—that is a distinguishing feature in and of itself.

36 Personally I reject both those arguments. I subscribe to an entitlement view, which finds these rights grounded in certain innate properties, such as the ability to reason, the ability to suffer—

37 FRANCIONE: Let's take the ability to suffer and consider it more carefully. The ability to use language or to reason is irrelevant to the right to be free from suffering. Only the ability to feel pain is relevant. Logically, it doesn't follow that you should restrict those rights to humans. On this primary level, the question must be *who* can feel pain, *who* can suffer? Certainly animals must be included within the reach of this fundamental right.

38 If you don't, then you are basing the right not to suffer pain on "intelligence." Consider the grotesque results if you apply that idea exclusively to human beings. Would you say that a smart person has a right to suffer less pain than a stupid person? That is effectively just what we say with animals. Even though

they can suffer, we conclude that their suffering is ir-relevant because we think we are smarter than they are.

CAPLAN: The ability to suffer does count, but the level of thinking and consciousness also counts. What makes us human? What grants us the right to life? It is not just a single attribute that makes us human. Rather, there is a cluster of properties: a sense of place in the world, a sense of time, a sense of self-awareness, a sense that one *is* somebody, a sense that one is morally relevant. When you add up these features, you begin to get to the level of entitlement to rights.

40   FRANCIONE: And I am going to push you to think specifically about rights again. What must you possess in order to have a right to life? I think the most obvious answer is simply a *life!*

41   But let's play this question out in your terms. To have a right to life, you must possess a sense of self, a recollection of the past, and an anticipation of the future, to name a few. By those standards, the chimpanzee—and I would argue, the entire class of Mammalia—would be enfranchised to enjoy a right to life.

42   NEWKIRK: The question is, do they have an interest in living? If they do, then one has an obligation to recognize their natural rights. The most fundamental of these is a desire to live. They *are* alive, therefore they want to *be* alive, and therefore we should *let* them live.

43   The more profound question, though, is what distinguishes humans from other animals. Most scientists, at first, thought that what separates us from the other animals is that human beings use tools. So ethnologists went out into the field and returned with innumerable examples of tool use in animals. The scientists then concluded that it's not tool use but the *making* of tools. Ethnologists, such as Geza Teleki, came back with lots of different examples, everything from chimpanzees making fishing poles to ants making boats to cross rivers. One might think they would then elevate the criterion to making tools in *union* workshops, but they switched to "language." Then there was a discussion about what *is* language. Linguists, among them

Noam Chomsky and Herbert Terrace, said language possessed certain "components." But when various ethnologists were able to satisfy each of these components, the Cartesian scientists became desperate and kept adding more components, including some pretty complicated ones, such as the ability to recite events in the distant past and to create new words based on past experiences. Eventually the number of components was up to sixteen! The final component was teaching someone else the language. But when Roger Fouts gave the signing ape, Washoe, a son, she independently taught him some seventy American hand-language signs.

CAPLAN: One of the sad facts of the literature of   44
both animal and human rights is that everyone is eager to identify the magic property that separates humans from animals. Is it the ability to suffer? The ability to say something? The ability to say something *interesting?* I think the philosophers are all looking in the right place but are missing something. We have rights because we are *social.*

NEWKIRK: Since all animals are social, then you   45
would extend rights to non-humans?

CAPLAN: It's not just sociability. Of course, all ani-   46
mals interact, but there is something about the way humans need to interact.

Suppose we were little Ayn Rands[1] who marched   47
about, self-sufficient, proud, and arrogant. If we were able to chop our own wood, cook our own meals, and fend off those who would assault us, then we wouldn't need any rights. You wouldn't need to have a right to free speech if there was no one to talk to!

My point is that our fundamental rights are not ex-   48
clusively intellectual properties. They are the natural result of the unique way humans have come together to form societies, *dependent* on each other for survival and therefore respectful of each other's rights.

---

[1] Rands: Ayn Rand (1905–82), the Russian-born American writer, was known for challenging Christian ethics by believing that selfishness was a virtue and altruism a vice, and for other extreme opinions.

NEWKIRK: None of this differentiates humans from the other animals. You cannot find a relevant attribute in human beings that doesn't exist in animals as well. Darwin said that the only difference between humans and other animals was a difference of degree, not kind. If you ground any concept of human rights in a particular attribute, then animals will have to be included. Animals have rights.

CAPLAN: That brings up another problem I have with your entire argument. Throughout this discussion, I have argued my position in terms of *ethics*. I have spoken about our moral imagination and animal *interests* and human decency. Why? Because I don't want our relationship with animals to be cast as a battle of rights. Only in America, with its obsession for attorneys, courts, judges, and lawsuits, is the entire realm of human relationships reduced to a clash of rights.

So I ask you: Is our relationship with animals best conceived of under the rubric of rights? I don't think so. When I am dispensing rights, I'm relatively chintzy about it. Do embryos have rights? In my opinion, no. Do irretrievably comatose people have rights? I doubt it. Do mentally retarded people below some level of intellectual functioning have rights? Probably not.

There is a wide range of creatures—some of them human—for whom our rights language is not the best way to deal with them. I want people to deal with them out of a sense of fairness or a sense of humanity or a sense of duty, but not out of a claim to rights.

NEWKIRK: I don't like your supremacist view of a custodial responsibility that grants you the luxury to be magnanimous to those beneath you. The rights of animals are not peripheral interests. In this case, we are talking about blood, guts, pain, and death.

FRANCIONE: Art, when you start talking about obligations without rights, you can justify violations of those obligations or intrusions more easily by spinning airy notions of utility. The reason many of our battles are played out in rights language is because our culture has evolved this notion that a right is something that stands between me and an intrusion. A right doesn't yield automatically because a stronger party might benefit.

If a scientist could cure cancer—without fail—by subjecting me against my will to a painful experiment, it wouldn't matter. I have a right not to be used that way.

CAPLAN: Ironically, I agree with you. That's exactly the role that rights language plays. It defines the barriers or lines that can't be crossed. But if you hand out rights willy-nilly, you lose that function.

NEWKIRK: When should we stop?

CAPLAN: I'm not sure I know the answer, but if you cheapen the currency of rights language, you've got to worry that rights may not be taken seriously. Soon you will have people arguing that trees have rights and that embryos have rights. And the tendency would be to say, "Sure, they have rights, but they are not *important* rights."

NEWKIRK: Art, wouldn't you rather err on the side of giving out too many rights rather than too few?

CAPLAN: No.

NEWKIRK: So, according to your view, maybe we should take away some of the rights we've already granted. After all, granting rights to blacks and women has deprived society of very important things, such as cheap labor. That a society evolves and expands its protective shield should not daunt us. That's like saying, if I continue to be charitable, my God, where will it ever end?

CAPLAN: It may not be rights or bust. There may be other ways to get people to conduct themselves decently without hauling out the heavy artillery of rights language every time.

NEWKIRK: People have to be pushed; society has to be pushed. Those who care deeply about a particular wrong have to pressure the general population. Eventually a law is passed, and then adjustments are made to correct past injustices. You have to bring these matters to a head.

HITT: Roger, from a constitutional perspective, do you think that rights are cheapened when they are broadened?

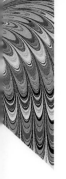

GOLDMAN: When you put it in a constitutional context, you invite conflict. That's inevitable. If you have a free press, you're going to have fair trial problems. If you start expanding rights of liberty, you run up against rights of equality. I don't think expansion cheapens them, but by elevating animal rights to a constitutional issue, you certainly multiply the difficulties.

66 HITT: You could argue that conflict strengthens rights. If you had no conflict over free speech, would we have the solid right to free speech that we have today?

67 GOLDMAN: It depends on who wins. What would happen if free speech lost?

68 FRANCIONE: Roger, you will have conflict and difficulties whether you cast our relationship with animals as one of obligations *or* rights. The real question is, are those obligations enforceable by state authority? If they are, there will be clashes and we will turn to the courts for resolution.

69 CAPLAN: Gary, I would like those obligations enforced by the authority, if you like, of empathy, by the power of character. What matters is how people view animals, how their feelings are touched by those animals, what drives them to care about those animals, not what rights the animals have.

70 FRANCIONE: I agree that you don't effect massive social change exclusively through law, but law can certainly help. That's a classic law school debate: Do moral perceptions shape law or does law shape moral perceptions? It probably goes both ways. I have no doubt that we could effect a great change if animals were included within our constitutional framework.

71 NEWKIRK: Great changes often begin with the law. Remember the 1760s case of the West Indian slave Jonathan Strong. Strong's master had abandoned him in England after beating him badly. The judge in that case feared the consequences of emancipating a slave. But the judge freed Strong and declared, "Let justice prevail, though the heavens may fall."

MOJO, THE TALKING CHIMPANZEE

HITT: Meet Mojo, the signing chimpanzee. Mojo is female and has learned more words than any other chimpanzee. One day you're signing away with Mojo, and she signs back, "I want a baby." Roger, are we under any obligation to grant her wish? 72

GOLDMAN: Since I am not persuaded animals have any rights, I don't believe there is any obligation. 73

HITT: Doesn't it follow that if this chimpanzee can articulate a desire to have a child—a primal desire and one that we would never forbid humans—we have some obligation to fulfill it? 74

CAPLAN: You are alluding to a foundation for rights that we haven't yet discussed. Is the requirement for possessing a right the ability to *claim* it? That is, in order to hold a right to life, one must be able to articulate a claim to life, to be able to say, "I want to live." 75

There may be animals that can get to that level, and Mojo may be one of them. Nevertheless, I don't buy into that argument. Simply being able to claim a right does not necessarily entail an obligation to fulfill it. 76

FRANCIONE: But Mojo does have the right to be left alone to pursue her desires, the right *not* to be in that cage. Aren't we violating some right of Mojo's by confining her so that she cannot satisfy that primal desire? 77

HITT: Is this a fair syllogism? Mojo wants to be free; a right to freedom exists if you can claim it; ergo, Mojo has a right to be free. Does the ability to lay claim to a right automatically translate into the *possession* of such a right? 78

CAPLAN: You don't always generate obligations and duties from a parallel set of rights, matching one with another. 79

Look at the relationship that exists between family members. Some people might argue that children have certain rights to claim from their parents. But there is something wrong with that assumption. Parents have many obligations to their children, but it seems mor- 80 ally weird to reduce this relationship to a contractual model. It's not a free-market arrangement where you put down a rights chit, I put down an obligation chit, and we match them up.

81 My kid might say to me, "Dad, you have an obligation to care for my needs, and my need today is a new car." I don't enter into a negotiation based on a balancing of his rights and my duties. That is not the proper relationship.

82 NEWKIRK: But having a car is not a fundamental right, whereas the right not to be abused is. For example, children have a right not to be used in factories. That right had to be fought for in exactly the same way we are fighting for animal rights now.

83 CAPLAN: Gary, I want to press you further. A baby needs a heart, and some scientist believes the miniature swine's heart will do it.

84 FRANCIONE: Would I take a healthy pig, remove its heart, and put it into the child? No.

85 CAPLAN: I am stymied by your absolutist position that makes it impossible even to consider the pig as a donor.

86 FRANCIONE: What if the donor were a severely retarded child instead of a pig?

87 CAPLAN: No, because I've got to worry about the impact not only on the donor but on society as well.

88 FRANCIONE: Art, assume I have a three-year-old prodigy who is a mathematical wizard. The child has a bad heart. The only way to save this prodigy is to take the heart out of another child. Should we *consider* a child from a low socioeconomic background who has limited mental abilities?

89 CAPLAN: You're wandering around a world of slopes, and I want to wander around a world of steps. I have argued strongly in my writing that it is possible for a human being—specifically an infant born with anencephaly, that is, without most of its brain—to drop below the threshold of a right to life. I think it would be ethical to use such a baby as a source for organ transplants. I do not believe there is a slippery slope between the child born with most of its brain missing and the retarded. There are certain thresholds below which one can make these decisions. At some point along the spectrum of life—many people would say a pig, and I would go further to include the anencephalic baby—we are safely below that threshold.

90 FRANCIONE: You can't equate the pig with the anencephalic infant. The anencephalic child is not the subject of a life in any meaningful sense. That is to say, it does not possess that constellation of attributes—sense of self-awareness, anticipation of the future, memory of the past—that we have been discussing. The pig is clearly the subject of a meaningful life.

91 CAPLAN: But if it's a matter of saving the life of the baby, then I want a surgeon to saw out the pig's heart and put it in the baby's chest.

92 NEWKIRK: The pig can wish to have life, liberty, and the pursuit of happiness, and the anencephalic baby cannot.

93 CAPLAN: But you must also consider the effect on others. I don't think it's going to matter very much what the pig's parents think about that pig. Whereas the child's parents care about the baby, and they don't care about the pig.

94 FRANCIONE: Then you change their reaction.

95 CAPLAN: I don't want to change their reaction. I want human beings to care about babies.

96 NEWKIRK: Like racism or sexism, that remark is pure speciesism.

97 CAPLAN: Speciesism! Mine is a legitimate distinction. The impact of this transplant is going to be different on humans than on lower animals.

98 NEWKIRK: "Lower animals." There comes speciesism rearing its ugly head again. Look, Art, I associate with the child; I don't associate with the pig. But we can't establish why that matters *except* that you are human and I am human.

99 If a building were burning and a baby baboon, a baby rat, and a baby child were inside, I'm sure I

would save the child. But if the baboon mother went into the building, I'm sure she would take out the infant baboon. It's just that there is an instinct to save yourself first, then your immediate family, your countrymen, and on to your species. But we have to recognize and reject the self-interest that erects these barriers and try to recognize the rights of others who happen not to be exactly like ourselves.

100 CAPLAN: I think you can teach humans to care about the pig. The morally relevant factor here is that you will never get the pig to care about *me*.

101 NEWKIRK: Not true, Art. Read John Robbins's book, *Diet for a New America,* in which he lists incidents of altruism by animals outside their own species. Everybody knows about dolphins rescuing sailors. Recently a pig rescued a child from a frozen lake and won an award!

102 CAPLAN: To the extent to which you can make animals drop *their* speciesism, perhaps you will be persuasive on this point.

103 NEWKIRK: Art, if you don't recognize my rights, that's tough for me. But that doesn't mean my rights don't exist.

104 FRANCIONE: If blacks, as a group, got together and said, "We're going to make a conscious decision to dislike non-blacks," would you say that black people no longer had rights?

105 CAPLAN: No, but I would hold them accountable for their racism. I could never hold a pig accountable for its speciesism. And I am never going to see a meeting of pigs having that kind of conversation.

106 NEWKIRK: That happens when the Ku Klux Klan meets, and the ACLU upholds their rights.

107 CAPLAN: The difference is that there are certain things I expect of blacks, whites, yellows—of all human beings and maybe a few animals. But I am not going to hold the vast majority of animals to those standards.

108 NEWKIRK: So the punishment for their perceived deficiencies—which, incidentally, is shared by the human baby—is to beat them to death.

109 CAPLAN: I didn't say that. I am trying to reach for something that isn't captured by the speciesist charge. The difference between people and animals is that I can persuade people. I can *stimulate* their moral imaginations. But I can't do that with most animals, and I want that difference to count.

A WORLD WITH NO DANCING BEARS

110 HITT: How would you envision a society that embraced animal rights? What would happen to pets?

111 NEWKIRK: I don't use the word "pet." I think it's speciesist language. I prefer "companion animal." For one thing, we would no longer allow breeding. People could not create different breeds. There would be no pet shops. If people had companion animals in their homes, those animals would have to be refugees from the animal shelters and the streets. You would have a protective relationship with them just as you would with an orphaned child. But as the surplus of cats and dogs (artificially engineered by centuries of forced breeding) declined, eventually companion animals would be phased out, and we would return to a more symbiotic relationship—enjoyment at a distance.

112 FRANCIONE: Much more than that would be phased out. For example, there would be no animals used for food, no laboratory experiments, no fur coats, and no hunting.

113 GOLDMAN: Would there be zoos?

114 FRANCIONE: No zoos.

115 HITT: Circuses?

116 FRANCIONE: Circuses would have to change. Look, right now we countenance the taking of an animal from the wild—a bear—dressing that bear in a *skirt* and parading it in front of thousands of people while it balances a ball on its nose. When you think about it, that is perverted.

117 HITT: Let's say that your logic prevails. People are

sickened by dancing bears and are demanding a constitutional amendment. What would be the language of a Bill of Rights for animals?

118 NEWKIRK: It already exists. It's "life, liberty, and the pursuit of happiness." We just haven't extended it far enough.

119 GOLDMAN: I am assuming your amendment would restrict not only government action but private action as well. Our Constitution restricts only government action. The single exception is the Thirteenth Amendment, which prohibits both the government and the individual from the practice of slavery.

120 HITT: To whom would these rights apply? Would they apply among animals themselves? Does the lion have to recognize the gazelle's right to life?

121 NEWKIRK: That's not our business. The behavior of the lion and the gazelle is a "tribal" issue, if you will. Those are the actions of other nations, and we cannot interfere.

122 GOLDMAN: What if we knew the lion was going to kill the gazelle—would we have an obligation to stop it?

123 NEWKIRK: It's not our business. This amendment restricts only our code of behavior.

124 HITT: But what Roger is asking is, should the amendment be so broad as to restrict both individual and government action?

125 FRANCIONE: It should be that broad. Of course, it would create a lot of issues we would have to work out. First, to whom would we extend these rights? I have a sneaking suspicion that any moment someone in this room will say, "But what about cockroaches? Will they have these rights? Do they have the right to have credit cards?" Hard questions would have to be answered, and we would have to determine which animals would hold rights and how to translate these rights into concrete protections from interference.

126 NEWKIRK: The health pioneer W. K. Kellogg limited it to "all those with faces." If you can look into the eyes of another, and that other looks back, that's one measure.

So the amendment shouldn't be limited, as some animal rights advocates think, to mammals, because we know that birds, reptiles, insects, and fishes all feel pain. They are capable of wanting to be alive. As long as we know that they have these primal interests, then I think we need to explore down the line—if we think it is down.

128 GOLDMAN: Let me go up the line. What about humans?

129 NEWKIRK: They would be just another animal in the pack.

130 GOLDMAN: But your amendment would massively expand the reach of the Constitution for humans. For example, the Constitution does not require states to provide rights for victims of crime. Under your proposal, if a state decriminalized adultery, shoplifting, or even murder, the victim's *constitutional* rights would be violated.

131 CAPLAN: And if we take the face test, how is that going to affect the way we treat the unborn? Must we enfranchise our fetuses? That's going to be the end of abortion.

132 FRANCIONE: Not necessarily. I am fairly comfortable with the notion that a fetus does not have a right to life. But that is not to say that a fetus doesn't have a right to be free from suffering. Fetuses do feel pain and they *ought* to be free from suffering. But it doesn't make sense to talk about a fetus having a sense of the past, anticipation of the future, and a sense of interaction with others.

133 CAPLAN: But a mouse?

134 FRANCIONE: Sure.

135 CAPLAN: I guess we can experiment on and eat all the animal fetuses we want.

136 FRANCIONE: I didn't say you had a right to inflict pain on animal fetuses. I don't think you have a right to inflict pain on human fetuses.

CAPLAN: Are you suggesting that we can't inflict pain, but we can kill them?

NEWKIRK: You are talking about the manner in which abortions are currently performed, not whether they should be performed. Our standard of lack of suffering holds up if you apply it across the board, for human and non-human fetuses.

139 GOLDMAN: Let me see if I can bring together those whose advocate animal welfare with those who believe animals hold rights. What about a different amendment, similar to the difference between the Thirteenth Amendment, which is an absolute ban on slavery, and the Fourteenth Amendment, which bans discrimination, but not absolutely. In fact, the Fourteenth allows us to take race into account sometimes, such as affirmative action. Do the animals rights activists see a role for a limited amendment similar to the Fourteenth? It would broadly protect animals from unnecessary suffering, but allow for some medical experiments.

140 FRANCIONE: Does your amendment simply expand the word "persons" in the Fourteenth Amendment to include animals?

141 GOLDMAN: No, but it is modeled on Fourteenth Amendment jurisprudence. It would not permit experimentation on animals unless necessary for a compelling need.

142 FRANCIONE: I would favor this approach if the experimenter had the burden to show the compelling need. I would have only one problem with adjudication under this compelling-need standard. My fear is that the balance would always favor the biomedical research community. Everyone agrees that no one should needlessly use animals in experimentation. Yet we all know that millions of animals are being used for frivolous purposes. That is because the biomedical researchers have persuaded enough people that their experiments are so important they have become "compelling" by definition.

143 GOLDMAN: Of course the difference with this constitutional amendment is that it wouldn't pass unless

two-thirds of Congress and three-fourths of the states backed it. So if we're projecting a hundred years from now, you won't have the problem of science experts always prevailing.

FRANCIONE: Roger, I would retire tomorrow if I   144
could get your amendment. The problem is that our society economically *benefits* from exploitation. The animal industries are so strong that they have shaped an entire *value* system that justifies and perpetuates exploitation. So I am not sure your compelling-need test would result in anything substantially different from what we have now. That's why I favor a hard rights notion, to protect the defenseless absolutely. As soon as you let in the "balancers," people such as Art Caplan, you've got trouble.

CAPLAN: The problem with your constitutional   145
amendment is that, finally, it is irrelevant to human behavior. When the lawyers, the constitutional adjudicators, and the Supreme Court justices aren't there, when it's just me and my companion animal or my bug in the woods, where are the animal's rights then?
    There was a time when I was a little boy running   146
around in the woods in New England. It was just a bunch of Japanese beetles in a jar and me. The question was: How is little Art going to deal with those Japanese beetles? Pull their wings off? Never let them out of the jar? Step on them? What do I do with those bugs? What do I think of bugs? No Supreme Court justice is going to tell me what to do with them.

NEWKIRK: A lot of these conflicts of moral obligation   147
result from the wide variety of *unnatural* relationships we have with animals in the first place—whether it's little Art with his jar of Japanese beetles, or the scientist in the lab with his chimpanzee, or any one of us at home with a cat. Just take the single issue of the sterilization of pets. We now have burdened ourselves with the custodial obligation to sterilize thousands of animals because we have screwed up their reproductive cycles so much through domestication and in-

breeding that they have many more offspring than they normally would. What would happen if we just left animals alone, to possess their own dignity? You know, you mentioned earlier that there is something cruel in the lion chasing down and killing the gazelle. Well, nature *is* cruel, but man is crueler yet. ◆

VIVISECTION

C. S. Lewis

C(live) S(taples) Lewis (1898–1963), professor of medieval and Renaissance English at Cambridge University, was also a novelist, a writer of children's books, and a popular speaker on moral and religious questions. Perhaps because of his own transformation from an atheist to a defender of Christian faith, Lewis is especially adept at seeing an issue from more than one angle. "Vivisection" was originally published as a pamphlet in 1947.

1   *I*T IS THE RAREST THING IN THE WORLD TO hear a rational discussion of vivisection. Those who disapprove of it are commonly accused of 'sentimentality', and very often their arguments justify the accusation. They paint pictures of pretty little dogs on dissecting tables. But the other side lie open to exactly the same charge. They also often defend the practice by drawing pictures of suffering women and children whose pain can be relieved (we are assured) only by the fruits of vivisection. The one appeal, quite as clearly as the other, is addressed to emotion, to the particular emotion we call pity. And neither appeal proves anything. If the thing is right—and if right at all, it is a duty—then pity for the animal is one of the temptations we must resist in order to perform that duty. If the thing is wrong, then pity for human suffering is precisely the temptation which will most probably lure us into doing that wrong thing. But the real question—whether it is right or wrong—remains meanwhile just where it was.

2   A rational discussion of this subject begins by inquiring whether pain is, or is not, an evil. If it is

not, then the case against vivisection falls. But then so does the case for vivisection. If it is not defended on the ground that it reduces human suffering, on what ground can it be defended? And if pain is not an evil, why should human suffering be reduced? We must therefore assume as a basis for the whole discussion that pain is an evil, otherwise there is nothing to be discussed.

3   Now if pain is an evil then the infliction of pain, considered in itself, must clearly be an evil act. But there are such things as necessary evils. Some acts which would be bad, simply in themselves, may be excusable and even laudable when they are necessary means to a greater good. In saying that the infliction of pain, simply in itself, is bad, we are not saying the pain ought never to be inflicted. Most of us think that it can rightly be inflicted for a good purpose—as in dentistry or just and reformatory punishment. The point is that it always requires justification. On the man whom we find inflicting pain rests the burden of showing why an act which in itself would be simply bad is, in those particular circumstances, good. If we

find a man giving pleasure it is for us to prove (if we criticize him) that his action is wrong. But if we find a man inflicting pain it is for him to prove that his action is right. If he cannot, he is a wicked man.

Now vivisection can only be defended by showing it to be right that one species should suffer in order that another species should be happier. And here we come to the parting of the ways. The Christian defender and the ordinary 'scientific' (i.e., naturalistic) defender of vivisection, have to take quite different lines.

5   The Christian defender, especially in the Latin countries, is very apt to say that we are entitled to do anything we please to animals because they 'have no souls'. But what does this mean? If it means that animals have no consciousness, then how is this known? They certainly behave as if they had, or at least the higher animals do. I myself an inclined to think that far fewer animals than is supposed have what we should recognize as consciousness. But that is only an opinion. Unless we know on other grounds that vivisection is right we must not take the moral risk of tormenting them on a mere opinion. On the other hand, the statement that they 'have no souls' may mean that they have no moral responsibilities and are not immortal. But the absence of 'soul' in that sense makes the infliction of pain upon them not easier but harder to justify. For it means that animals cannot deserve pain, nor profit morally by the discipline of pain, nor be recompensed by happiness in another life for suffering in this. Thus all the factors which render pain more tolerable or make it less totally evil in the case of human beings will be lacking in the beasts. 'Soullessness', in so far as it is relevant to the question at all, is an argument against vivisection.

6   The only rational line for the Christian vivisectionist to take is to say that the superiority of man over beast is a real objective fact, guaranteed by Revelation, and that the propriety of sacrificing beast to man is a logical consequence. We are 'worth more than many sparrows',[1] and in saying this we are not merely expressing a natural preference for our own

---

[1] Matthew x. 31. [author's note]

species simply because it is our own but conforming to a hierarchical order created by God and really present in the universe whether any one acknowledges it or not. The position may not be satisfactory. We may fail to see how a benevolent Deity could wish us to draw such conclusions from the hierarchical order He has created. We may find it difficult to formulate a human right of tormenting beasts in terms which would not equally imply an angelic right of tormenting men. And we may feel that though objective superiority is rightly claimed for man, yet that very superiority ought partly to *consist in* not behaving like a vivisector: that we ought to prove ourselves better than the beasts precisely by the fact of acknowledging duties to them which they do not acknowledge to us. But on all these questions different opinions can be honestly held. If on grounds of our real, divinely ordained, superiority a Christian pathologist thinks it right to vivisect, and does so with scrupulous care to avoid the least dram or scruple of unnecessary pain, in a trembling awe at the responsibility which he assumes, and with a vivid sense of the high mode in which human life must be lived if it is to justify the sacrifices made for it, then (whether we agree with him or not) we can respect his point of view.

7   But of course the vast majority of vivisectors have no such theological background. They are most of them naturalistic and Darwinian. Now here, surely, we come up against a very alarming fact. The very same people who will most contemptuously brush aside any consideration of animal suffering if it stands in the way of 'research' will also, on another context, most vehemently deny that there is any radical difference between man and the other animals. On the naturalistic view the beasts are at bottom just the same *sort* of thing as ourselves. Man is simply the cleverest of the anthropoids. All the grounds on which a Christian might defend vivisection are thus cut from under our feet. We sacrifice other species to our own not because our own has any objective metaphysical privilege over others, but simply because it is ours. It may be very natural to have this loyalty to our own species, but let us hear no more from the naturalists about the 'sentimentality' of anti-vivisectionists. If loy-

alty to our own species, preference for man simply because we are men, is not a sentiment, then what is? It may be a good sentiment or a bad one. But a sentiment it certainly is. Try to base it on logic and see what happens!

8   But the most sinister thing about modern vivisection is this. If a mere sentiment justifies cruelty, why stop at a sentiment for the whole human race? There is also a sentiment for the white man against the black, for a *Herrenvolk*[2] against the non-Aryans, for 'civilized' or 'progressive' peoples against 'savage' or 'backward' peoples. Finally, for our own country, party, or class against others. Once the old Christian idea of a total difference in kind between man and beast has been abandoned, then no argument for experiments on animals can be found which is not also an argument for experiments on inferior men. If we cut up beasts simply because they cannot prevent us and because we are backing our own side in the struggle for existence, it is only logical to cut up imbeciles, criminals, enemies, or capitalists for the same reasons. Indeed, experiments on men have already begun. We all hear that Nazi scientists have done them. We all suspect that our own scientists may begin to do so, in secret, at any moment.

9   The alarming thing is that the vivisectors have won the first round. In the nineteenth and eighteenth century a man was not stamped as a 'crank' for protesting against vivisection. Lewis Carroll protested, if I remember his famous letter correctly, on the very same ground which I have just used.[3] Dr Johnson[4]—a man whose mind had as much *iron* in it as any man's—protested in a note on *Cymbeline* which is worth quoting in full. In Act I, scene v, the Queen explains to the Doctor that she wants poisons to experi-

ment on 'such creatures as We count not worth the hanging,—but none human.'[5] The Doctor replies:

Your Highness
Shall from this practice but make hard your heart.[6]

Johnson comments: 'The thought would probably have been more amplified, had our author lived to be shocked with such experiments as have been published in later times, by a race of men that have practised tortures without pity, and related them without shame, and are yet suffered to erect their heads among human beings.'[7]

10   The words are his, not mine, and in truth we hardly dare in these days to use such calmly stern language. The reason why we do not dare is that the other side has in fact won. And though cruelty even to beasts is an important matter, their victory is symptomatic of matters more important still. The victory of vivisection marks a great advance in the triumph of ruthless, non-moral utilitarianism over the old world of ethical law; a triumph in which we, as well as animals, are already the victims, and of which Dachau and Hiroshima mark the more recent achievements. In justifying cruelty to animals we put ourselves also on the animal level. We choose the jungle and must abide by our choice.

11   You will notice I have spent no time in discussing what actually goes on in the laboratories. We shall be told, of course, that there is surprisingly little cruelty. That is a question with which, at present, I have nothing to do. We must first decide what should be allowed: after that it is for the police to discover what is already being done. ◆

---

[2] *Herrenvolk:* A group of people believed to have the right to dominate and exploit other groups.
[3] 'Vivisection as a Sign of the Times', *The Works of Lewis Carroll,* ed. Roger Lancelyn Green (London, 1965), pp. 1089–92. See also 'Some Popular Fallacies about Vivisection', *ibid.,* pp. 1092–1100. [author's note]
[4] British moralist and scholar Samuel Johnson (1709–84) published an edition of Shakespeare's plays in 1765.

[5] Shakespeare, *Cymbeline,* I, v, 19–20. [author's note]
[6] *Ibid.,* 23. [author's note]
[7] *Johnson on Shakespeare: Essays and Notes Selected and Set Forth with an Introduction* by Sir Walter Raleigh (London, 1908), p. 181. [author's note]

PART III

PROFESSIONAL & ACADEMIC

plications

Training is everything.
The peach was once a bitter almond;
cauliflower is nothing
but cabbage with a college education.

MARK TWAIN

PROPOSALS

N THIS CHAPTER WE WILL FOCUS ON ESSAYS THAT ATTEMPT TO PER-suade readers to take certain actions in the future or to endorse actions taken in the past. The two types of writing resemble each other so closely that we will call both "proposals," though we stretch the word somewhat by using it this way. Proposals involve the writer in all the difficulties (and opportunities) mentioned in Chapters 6 and 7: the writer often has to establish the credibility of disputed facts and the wisdom of disputed rules. What makes a proposal different from other arguments about facts or rules is that the heart of the proposal is a problem to be solved by action.

The professional worker in government, business, and science lives in a world of proposals accepted or rejected: proposals for changes in the law or the budget, proposals to supply a product or provide a service, research proposals, and proposals to garner government grants. We will touch on a few of these more elaborate types of proposals, but we will begin by examining a simpler kind of problem-centered writing.

THE ADVICE COLUMN

A t its simplest, a proposal is no more than the presentation of a problem and the recommendation of a course of action. In most formal proposals one writer both articulates the problem and presents the solution, but in some cases this labor is divided, allowing us to study one at a time the two central parts of the proposal. In her nationally syndicated column *Miss Manners,* Judith Martin produces one or more of these short question-and-answer proposals each week.

Ms. Martin often writes as if she were merely the secretary of the imaginary Miss Manners, Victorian expert on etiquette. The advice, however, is usually very down to earth. Consider the following example:

"Gift Giving"
—JUDITH MARTIN

Dear Miss Manners:

My boyfriend and I are getting ready to celebrate our six-month going steady anniversary. He's giving me a present. The problem is that I don't know whether I am "supposed" to give him one also. My mother says that it is incorrect for me to because, as a girl, I am not obliged. I feel somewhat awkward since he has already

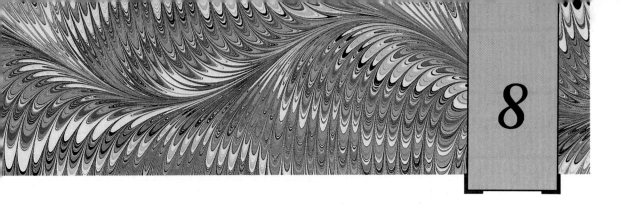

let me know that he has a gift for me. I don't want to seem ill-mannered. Please let me know the proper thing to do.

Gentle Reader:

Would you and your mother please stop thinking along the lines of "as a girl, I am not obliged"? There really is no such thing as obligatory present giving. One goes by one's instincts, and yours obviously are to commemorate this momentous occasion. The general rule about presents between unmarried people is that one gives or accepts only what can suitably be returned during a breakup. (Married couples have the courts to help them decide this.) "Take back your mink" is, for example, impossible to say, and therefore it would be inadvisable to give your boyfriend a mink coat. Books, records, and small leather goods such as wallets and keycases are considered to be a proper type of present to be exchanged by those in temporary arrangements.

The question here is hardly the stuff headlines are made of, but it gives us a good opportunity to note that the question that provokes a proposal has two parts. The questioner has a *goal:* "I don't want to seem ill-mannered." She also has a *problem* that hinders her achieving that goal: she doesn't know whether she is "supposed" to give her boyfriend a gift. The problem solver must accept the goal as a valid one and propose a solution more expert or ingenious than the questioner herself is capable of devising. Miss Manners, of course, has problems of her own: she must not only propose a sensible solution for the questioner but produce a column that will enlighten or entertain a much wider group of readers. Her answer in this case seems to divide its energy about equally between the two goals.

When the questioner poses a more intricate problem, Miss Manners produces a more serious and elaborate answer:

Dear Miss Manners:

Our son is planning to marry a girl from another city, a distance of four hundred miles. What are our responsibilities? We have met his fiancée, but not her parents. Do we (a) call them and invite them to visit us? (b) call first and then visit them? (c) wait for them to call us? Any visits must be overnight stays because of the distance. However, we have three other children at home and cannot offer house guests a

"Daffodil's Parents"
—JUDITH MARTIN

private bath and other conveniences conducive to privacy. If they come to visit, would it be proper to accommodate them in a nearby hotel? If yes, should we pay the bill? Also, if we visit them, should we expect to stay with them or arrange our own accommodations?

Gentle Reader:

If you choose (c), you may wait forever. Society has changed since the rule about the parents of engaged couples was invented, and no one has bothered to revise it to meet such outrageous situations as engagements between couples whose parents live four hundred miles apart. This has resulted in a great deal of confusion and hurt feelings that are better saved for the wedding.

Miss Manners will now come to the rescue. Here is the old rule: The young man's parents call on the young woman's parents. ("Calling" referred to the now defunct custom of arriving at their doorstep for a short surprise visit that would not inconvenience them because everybody was always calling on everyone else all the time, and therefore it was no surprise at all.)

Here is the new rule: The young man's parents initiate the relationship by telephoning or writing the young woman's parents and expressing their desire of becoming acquainted. The details of the two meetings are then worked out with the help of the two people who are in a position to know what would be most convenient for each household—the young couple. All you have to do, then, is call or write the other parents and say, "We're so pleased. Daffodil is such a lovely girl. We're anxious to meet you, and would love to have the pleasure of entertaining you here." Assuming that Daffodil has warned them about your limited bathroom facilities, they can accept or counterinvite you to their hometown. In either case, saying "I'm afraid we don't have room to make you comfortable, so I've made a hotel reservation for you nearby" is proper. Paying the hotel bill of your guests is charming if you can easily afford it but if not, don't worry about it.

This longer exchange between a reader and Miss Manners allows us to examine the etiquette of proposing and solving a problem. The questioner must *make his or her goal clear, either by naming it outright or by implying it unmistakably*. In this case, the questioners' goal is to get the relationship between themselves and Daffodil's parents off on the right foot. The questioner must also *make clear the nature of the problem that prevents his or her reaching the goal, giving all the pertinent details with as few irrelevancies as possible*. In this case and in many others, the problem involves a set of *constraints* that make achievement of the goal difficult: 400 miles to be traveled, a crowded home, and no direct acquaintance with the other couple. Clearly, these constraints create a genuine problem, since inviting Daffodil's parents to visit is asking them to travel 400 miles and stay either in a crowded home or in a hotel room that they may feel obliged to pay for. The etiquette of the etiquette column also demands that the questioner *describe a problem challenging enough to create interest*. The young man's parents have clearly held up their end: they are caught in the sort of danger that invites rescue. Judith

Martin is extremely fortunate; she seems to have an endless supply of readers who become entangled in social difficulties complex enough to produce not only tension, but suspense. One reads the question and wonders briefly whether even Miss Manners will be able to solve this difficulty. The presentation of a significant problem is, as we will see, one of the keys to writing excellent proposals.

The columnist's first job is usually to discuss the problem in a way that (1) *gives readers insight by putting it into a framework the questioner had not considered* and (2) *opens the way toward a solution*. The framework Miss Manners brings to this problem is one of her familiar themes: "Society has changed since the rule . . . was invented." Since young people now move farther from home than their ancestors did, and since the custom of "calling" has vanished, we need a new custom for this situation. As you read through the various proposals collected in this chapter, you will see that the writer often reframes a problem by giving an expert or ingenious explanation of its cause. Even though the new framework can't eliminate the constraints (Daffodil's parents remain four hundred miles away), it allows the reader to see them from a fresh perspective and to begin to hope that there is a way around them. An engineer analyzing a failing bridge may discuss the problem in the same way Miss Manners does when she analyzes a failing custom. "Surfacing materials have changed," the engineer may report, "since the original deck was built, and the problem we face is how to introduce new materials compatible with the old steel plates."

The columnist's next job is, of course, to present a solution that truly fits the problem. You'll notice that the new rule Miss Manners proposes exactly matches the constraints that the questioner listed. It takes into account the travel distance, the "limited bathroom facilities," and the lack of knowledge each couple has of the other. Only if all the constraints are dealt with adequately will the proposal seem satisfying and feasible.

◆ *Responding as Miss Manners.* The following letter elicited from Miss Manners a sixty-one-word reply. Try your hand as an etiquette columnist by providing your own answer of about the same length:

EXERCISE 1

Dear Miss Manners:

One of the things I do for a living is to give lectures. I don't get rich on it, but I give audiences their money's worth, and I have worked up some good speeches that people seem to enjoy.

Word gets around, of course, and I am often asked by small groups, such as clubs and professional organizations, to give luncheon speeches or answer questions at their meetings. But often, when I accept, I find that they have no intention of paying me!

Perhaps I should bring it up when they invite me, but I assume that they know I am a professional, and it seems crass to demand payment while they are telling me how wonderful they've heard I am, how much everyone is looking forward to hearing me, and so on. These same people wouldn't dream of offering me the services or goods they sell for free, of course.

EXERCISE 2

◆ *Writing to Miss Manners.* The following answer was elicited by a sixty-nine-word question to Miss Manners. Like many of her answers, it painstakingly responds to the particulars of the questioner's situation. After reading the answer, try to write a matching question.

> Gentle Reader:
>   Miss Manners is a cucumber sandwich eater in a doughnut world, so don't think she doesn't sympathize with you. But if one wishes to stress one's willingness to work with other people, regardless of gender, one keeps special requests to a minimum, or presents them as if one were the spokeswoman for a faction, as in, "Perhaps we should provide tea at the next meeting for people who would prefer it."

EXERCISE 3

◆ *Writing to and Responding as Miss Manners.* Write a brief question to and answer from Miss Manners. Attempt not only to fulfill each role properly, but to interest a wide readership. In your answer, you may want to imitate not only Miss Manners' way of dealing with substance but her style and her tone.

THE PROBLEM/SOLUTION ESSAY: AN EXAMPLE FROM SCIENCE

The transition from Miss Manners to scientific writing may seem to you an unlikely one, but publishing scientists know that their business consists largely of asking intriguing questions and then proposing ways to answer them. The research proposal, the lab report, and the article in a scientific journal are all built on a basic problem/solution pattern every reader of an advice column should recognize.

Often this basic pattern is obscured for the nonscientific reader by technical language and the presentation of data in unfamiliar forms, but in the more popular writings of accomplished scientists we can find examples that show the layperson how the scientist adopts both the role of questioner (stating a goal and problem as most researchers have conceived it) and problem solver (reframing the problem and presenting a matching solution). The following example is taken from entomologist Vincent Dethier's popular book *To Know a Fly* (1962).

"Extracting Information from a Fly"
—VINCENT DETHIER

The kind of question asked of nature is a measure of a scientist's intellectual stature. Too many research workers have no questions at all to ask, but this does not deter them from doing experiments. They become enamored of a new instrument, acquire it, and then ask only, "What can I do with this beauty?" Others ask such questions as "How many leaves are there this year on the ivy at the zoology building." And having counted them do not know what to do with the information. But some questions can be useful and challenging. And meaningful questions can be asked of a fly.

Between the fly and the biologist, however, there is a language barrier that makes getting direct answers to questions difficult. With a human subject it is only necessary to ask: what color is this? does that hurt? are you hungry? The human subject may, of course, lie; the fly cannot. However, to elicit information from him it is necessary to resort to all kinds of trickery and legerdemain. This means pitting one's brain against that of the fly—a risk some people are unwilling to assume. But then, experimentation is only for the adventuresome, for dreamers, for the brave. . . .

Extracting information from a fly can be . . . challenging. Take the question of taste, for example. Does a fly possess a sense of taste? Is it similar to ours? How sensitive is it? What does it prefer?

The first fruitful experimental approach to this problem began less than fifty years ago with a very shrewd observation; namely, that flies (and bees and butterflies) walked about in their food and constantly stuck out their tongues. The next time you dine with a fly (and modern sanitary practice has not greatly diminished the opportunities), observe his behavior when he gavots across the top of the custard pie. His proboscis, which is normally carried retracted into his head like the landing gear of an airplane, will be lowered, and like a miniature vacuum cleaner he will suck in food. . . .

Proboscis extension has been seen thousands of times by thousands of people but few have been either struck by the sanitary aspects of the act or ingenious enough to figure out how they might put the observation to use to learn about fly behavior.

The brilliant idea conceived by the biologist[1] who first speculated on why some insects paraded around in their food was that they tasted with their feet. In retrospect it is the simplest thing in the world to test this idea. It also makes a fine parlor trick for even the most blasé gathering.

The first step is to provide a fly with a handle since Nature failed to do so. Procure a stick about the size of a lead pencil. (A lead pencil will do nicely. So will an applicator stick, the kind that a physician employs when swabbing a throat.) Dip one end repeatedly into candle wax or paraffin until a fly-sized gob accumulates. Next anesthetize a fly. The least messy method is to deposit him in the freezing compartment of a refrigerator for several minutes. Then, working very rapidly, place him backside down onto the wax and seal his wings onto it with a hot needle.

Now for the experimental proof. Lower the fly gently over a saucer of water until his feet just touch. Chances are he is thirsty. If so, he will lower his proboscis as soon as his feet touch and will suck avidly. When thirst has been allayed, the proboscis will be retracted compactly into the head. This is a neat arrangement

In this case, the writer states the problem before he states the goal.

To answer these questions is the goal.

How does Dethier make his report on a scientific procedure easily comprehensible by nonscientists?

The solution section begins here.

---

[1]The scientist referred to is Dwight E. Minnich. You can read his original article in *Biological Bulletin* (July 1926).

because a permanently extended proboscis might flop about uncomfortably during flight or be trod upon while walking.

Next, lower the fly into a saucer of sugared water. In a fraction of a second the proboscis is flicked out again. Put him back into water (this is the control), and the proboscis is retracted. Water, in; sugar, out. The performance continues almost indefinitely. Who can doubt that the fly can taste with his feet? By taking advantage of its automatism, one can learn very subtle things about a fly's sense of taste.

For example, who has the more acute sense of taste, you or the fly? As the cookbooks say, take ten saucers. Fill the first with water and stir in one teaspoon of sugar. Now pour half the contents of the saucer into another which should then be filled with water. After stirring pour half the contents of the second saucer into a third and fill it with water. Repeat this process until you have a row of ten saucers. Now take a fly (having made certain that he is not thirsty) and lower him gradually into the most dilute mixture. Then try him in the next and so on up the series until his proboscis is lowered. This is the weakest sugar solution that he can taste.

Now test yourself. If you are the sort of person who does not mind kissing the dog, you can use the same saucers as the fly. Otherwise make up a fresh series. You will be surprised, perhaps chagrined, to discover that the fly is unbelievably more sensitive than you. In fact, a starving fly is ten million times more sensitive.

What is a "control"? Why is it important to give the fly water until he stops lowering proboscis when his feet touch it?

How would you describe the tone of this passage?

Dethier's account here carefully avoids the special vocabulary of the laboratory and the tone of a typical article in a scientific journal. Those who know science, however, will recognize that it presents the key components of a scientific paper: an analysis of the problem, a careful description of materials and methods used in the solution to the problem, a statement of results, and a discussion of their significance.

The parallel to an advice column is fairly clear. In the role of *questioner,* the scientist states a goal (to understand the fly's sense of taste) and a problem achieving that goal (an inability to ask the fly directly). Once again, the best problems are the challenging ones, ones that require "all kinds of trickery and legerdemain." Discussing the problem as a *solver* (Mr. Wizard in place of Miss Manners), the scientist reframes it in order to open a way to a solution. The problem is not really an inability to get the fly to talk, in which case it would be impossible to overcome. The problem as a scientist sees it is our inability (until now) to identify precisely the nature of the stimulus that leads to feeding and the location of the organs that receive this stimulus. The layperson thinks of taste as a subjective experience; the scientist redefines it in terms of measurable stimuli and observable behavior.

EVALUATING THE QUALITY OF A PROPOSED EXPERIMENT

To some degree, the success of a scientific paper is measured in the same terms as the success of an advice column: Has the writer managed to present a truly satisfactory solution to an intriguing difficulty? Most of us, when we read Dethier's account of this experimental procedure will say, "Of course he has." At first glance, the proof that flies taste with their feet seems irrefutable.

Scientists, however, are carefully trained skeptics: they learn to examine very carefully the match between the problem and the solution. Do these experiments in fact prove that the fly tastes with its feet? Isn't it possible, for example, that the fly is not *tasting* the sugar water at all, but *smelling* it, and that the organs for smelling are somewhere in the head (or body or wings) rather than the feet? Couldn't we explain the proboscis extension either of the following ways?:

1. Only when the fly's feet touch the water is its nose close enough to the surface to detect the scent; when the *scent* is detected, the fly lowers the proboscis.

2. The fly's proboscis, as Dethier points out, is retracted while the insect is flying. Suspended by its glob of wax, the fly "believes" it is flying and keeps its proboscis tucked up, even though it smells the sugar water below. When the fly's feet touch the water, though, it "believes" it has landed and immediately extends its proboscis.

On close analysis, it appears that the experimenter may have been guilty of jumping to an oversimple conclusion about the relationship between a cause and an effect. And, as it turns out, another entomologist criticized his paper for faults of this kind, producing a dispute too technical for us to consider here—one eventually resolved by new experiments. In the scientific problem/ solution paper, as Dethier points out, the great danger is asserting a badly tested cause-and-effect relationship: ". . . there is the well-known case of the chap who wondered which component in his mixed drink caused his inevitable intoxication. He tried bourbon and water, rum and water, rye and water, gin and water, and concluded, since every drink had water as a constant, the water caused his drunkenness."

Proposing an Experiment. Describe an experiment that could be conducted to solve the problem mentioned above: that the fly might be smelling the sugar water rather than tasting the water with its feet.

PROPOSALS TO THE GENERAL PUBLIC: A LETTER TO THE EDITOR

The difficulty of linking cause to effect is compounded when the subject is human affairs. Now the writer who sets out to write a problem/solution paper must speculate about the cause of a problem too untidy to study in the laboratory. Then he or she must propose a solution, the effects of which are also largely a matter of speculation. The key, of course, is for the writer to establish that there is a high probability of correctness, using methods like those we studied in Chapter 6.

Consider, for example, the following letter to the editor of *The New York Times,* written by Barbara Tuchman in 1973, when the Watergate scandal had convinced millions of Americans that Presidential power had gotten out of control. As you read her proposal, note the ways that she supports her statements about both the problem and the solution.

"Should We Abolish the Presidency?"
—BARBARA TUCHMAN

In the limited space of a letter, and with a well-known goal and problem, Tuchman moves quickly to her proposed solution.

Why would Tuchman insert this sentence about the Constitution?

Do the mentions of Russia and China strengthen the proposal or weaken it?

How might the tone of this paragraph have affected the reception of the proposal?

Owing to the steady accretion of power in the executive over the last forty years, the institution of the Presidency is not now functioning as the Constitution intended, and this malfunction has become perilous to the state. What needs to be abolished, or fundamentally modified, I believe, is not the executive power as such but the executive power as exercised by a single individual.

We could substitute true Cabinet government by a directorate of six, to be nominated as a slate by each party and elected as a slate for a single six-year term with a rotating chairman, each to serve for a year as in the Swiss system. The Chairman's vote would carry the weight of two to avoid a tie. (Although a five-man Cabinet originally seemed preferable when I first proposed the plan in 1968, I find that the main departments of government, one for each member of the Cabinet to administer, cannot be rationally arranged under fewer than six headings—see below.)

Expansion of the Presidency in the twentieth century has dangerously altered the careful tripartite balance of governing powers established by the Constitution. The office has become too complex and its reach too extended to be trusted to the fallible judgment of any one individual. In today's world no one man is adequate for the reliable disposal of power that can affect the lives of millions—which may be one reason lately for the notable non-emergence of great men. Russia no longer entrusts policy-making to one man. In China governing power resides, technically at least, in the party's central executive committee, and when Mao goes the inheritors are likely to be more collective than otherwise.

In the United States the problem of one-man rule has become acute for two reasons. First, Congress has failed to perform its envisioned role as safeguard against the natural tendency of an executive to become dictatorial, and equally failed to maintain or even exercise its own rights through the power of the purse.

It is clear, moreover, that we have not succeeded in developing in this country an organ of representative democracy that can match the Presidency in positive action or prestige. A Congress that can abdicate its right to ratify the act of war, that can obediently pass an enabling resolution on false information and remain helpless to remedy the situation afterward,[2] is likewise not functioning as the Constitution

---

[2] Tuchman refers to the Gulf of Tonkin resolution (1964) authorizing bombing of North Vietnam. The Johnson administration forced passage of this resolution by giving an apparently fictional account of a North Vietnamese attack on a U.S. destroyer.

intended. Since the failure traces to the lower house—the body most directly representing the citizenry and holding the power of the purse—responsibility must be put where it belongs: in the voter. The failure of Congress is a failure of the people.

The second reason, stemming perhaps from the age of television, is the growing tendency of the Chief Executive to form policy as a reflection of his personality and ego needs. Because his image can be projected before fifty or sixty or a hundred million people, the image takes over; it becomes an obsession. He must appear firm, he must appear dominant, he must never on any account appear "soft," and by some magic transformation which he has come to believe in, he *must* make history's list of "great" Presidents.

While I have no pretensions to being a psychohistorian, even an ordinary citizen can see the symptoms of this disease in the White House since 1960, and its latest example in the Christmas bombing of North Vietnam.[3] That disproportionate use of lethal force becomes less puzzling if it is seen as a gesture to exhibit the Commander-in-Chief ending the war with a bang, not a whimper.

Personal government can get beyond control in the U.S. because the President is subject to no advisers who hold office independently of him. Cabinet ministers and agency chiefs and national-security advisers can be and are—as we have lately seen—hired and fired at whim, which means that they are without constitutional power. The result is that too much power and therefore too much risk has become subject to the idiosyncrasies of a single individual at the top, whoever he may be.

Spreading the executive power among six eliminates dangerous challenges to the ego. Each of the six would be designated from the time of nomination as secretary of a specific department of government affairs, viz:

1. Foreign, including military and CIA. (Military affairs should not, as at present, have a Cabinet-level office because the military ought to be solely an instrument of policy, never a policy-making body.)

2. Financial, including Treasury, taxes, budget, and tariffs.

3. Judicial, covering much the same as present.

4. Business (or Production and Trade), including Commerce, Transportation, and Agriculture.

5. Physical Resources, including Interior, Parks, Forest, Conservation, and Environment Protection.

6. Human Affairs, including HEW, Labor, and the cultural endowments.

It is imperative that the various executive agencies be incorporated under the authority of one or another of these departments.

Cabinet government is a perfectly feasible operation. While this column was being written, the Australian Cabinet, which governs like the British by collective

Explain the logic that leads Tuchman to say that the people have failed.

How convincing do you find Tuchman's discussion of the effect of television on politics?

How plausible is Tuchman's view of the effect of unchecked power on the individual who possesses it?

Notice Tuchman's direct discussion of feasibility. How convincing do you find it to be?

---

[3] In December 1972, President Nixon ended a moratorium on bombing North Vietnam by suddenly ordering the heaviest bombing of the war.

responsibility, overrode its Prime Minister on the issue of exporting sheep to China, and the West German Cabinet took emergency action on foreign-exchange control.

The usual objection one hears in this country that a war emergency requires quick decision by one man seems to me invalid. Even in that case, no President acts without consultation. If he can summon the Joint Chiefs, so can a Chairman summon his Cabinet. Nor need the final decision be unilateral. Any belligerent action not clearly enough in the national interest to evoke unanimous or strong majority decision by the Cabinet ought not to be undertaken.

How the slate would be chosen in the primaries is a complication yet to be resolved. And there is the drawback that Cabinet government could not satisfy the American craving for a father-image or hero or superstar. The only solution I can see to that problem would be to install a dynastic family in the White House for ceremonial purposes, or focus the craving entirely upon the entertainment world, or else to grow up.

Though, like most political proposals, this one is not packaged as tidily as an advice column or a scientific paper, it follows essentially the same logical path.

1. It identifies a *"larger" goal*—larger, that is, than the problem itself. We find this goal embedded in the first sentence of Tuchman's essay, where she says that "the Presidency is not now functioning as the Constitution intended, and this malfunction has become perilous to the state." Tuchman's largest stated goal is to preserve the state from the peril of a constitutional breakdown, a goal that most readers of *The New York Times* surely share. We will talk in a minute about the importance of identifying a goal that readers approve of.

2. The *problem* that blocks the way to that goal is also stated in the first sentence: the "accretion of power in the executive." When she states the problem this way, she is saying no more than every news commentator of the day was saying, that the executive branch of government has grown too strong for the legislative or the judicial branch to control in the American system of "checks and balances." In her *discussion of the problem,* Tuchman reframes it: "What needs to be abolished . . . is not the executive power as such but the executive power as exercised by a single individual." She devotes paragraphs 3, 6, 7, and 8 to justifying this reframing, attempting to convince us that the true cause of the difficulty is that few individuals are intellectually or psychologically capable of bearing the burdens of the presidency without drifting toward tyranny. By presenting the problem this way, Tuchman opens the way to a solution.

3. If human psychology is such that no one individual is suited to wield such power, then the *solution* is to move to collective leadership, and Tuchman devotes the second half of her essay to presenting the details of

How greatly is the proposal hurt by not resolving this complication?

Does the tone of the final sentence strengthen or weaken the proposal?

her plan for such a scheme of leadership and to demonstrating that the plan is feasible.

Obviously, we have here a reasonably complete and well-written proposal by a talented writer, and yet it is a proposal that has failed (thus far) to persuade Congress or the people to abolish the presidency.

WHY PROPOSALS FAIL

The great difficulty of writing a successful proposal is that unless it is persuasive in all of its parts, the whole proposal will fail. The reader unwilling to accept the proposer's goal, for instance, may reject the proposal before reaching the problem and solution. Writing a successful proposal requires, therefore, intelligent analysis of the audience's attitudes. Judith Martin can assume that most of her readers accept courteous behavior as an important goal: people who don't value courtesy are unlikely to read a column entitled "Miss Manners." An entomologist writing in a scientific journal can assume that, for most readers, knowing how nature works is a higher goal than preserving the quality or length of an insect's life, so he or she can propose procedures (like Dethier's) that some religious groups and some advocates of animal rights would find appalling.

UNACCEPTABLE GOALS

When the audience is more diverse, the writer is forced to think harder about how to state the goal of the proposal. Suppose, for example, that Barbara Tuchman had begun her proposal this way:

> Owing to the steady accretion of power in the executive and the tendency for voters who may be Democrats on local or state issues to vote Republican in national elections, the institution of the presidency generally concentrates power in the hands of the head of the Republican party. What needs to be abolished, or fundamentally modified, I believe, is not the executive power as such but the executive power as exercised by a single individual.

Now Tuchman's goal would seem to be entirely partisan—an attempt to diminish Republican power—and many readers who did not share this goal would want to read no further. In general, then, the wise proposal writer begins by stating a goal that the overwhelming majority of readers will accept without question. For a general audience, a proposal intended to protect liberty will be listened to more sympathetically than a proposal intended to give Democrats an edge over Republicans. A proposal to improve medical care will be read more sympathetically than a proposal to lower the rates for medical malpractice insurance, even though the two advocate precisely the same course of action. I don't mean to suggest that you alter your goal merely to gain a rhetorical edge, but I do want to suggest that you express it in broad terms that reflect values you share with your audience rather than in narrow, partisan terms that encourage divisiveness. Many proposals fail because the writer *has* a goal the readers could accept enthusiastically but fails to *name* it.

NONPROBLEMS

Even when readers share the writer's goal, they may not agree that he or she has identified an important problem in achieving it. In the 1920s, for example, the NAACP and its allies in Congress proposed a federal law against lynching. To stop lynching was a goal that few members of Congress would have opposed, yet the bill failed in the Senate because many senators felt that the NAACP had not identified a valid problem. Lynching, they reasoned, was murder, and murder was against the law in every state; therefore, the cause of lynching was not the absence of a law, and no additional law could help prevent it. The NAACP argued that the absence of a *federal* law was a problem, since some state courts simply would not convict a white lynch mob of murdering a black man. Federal laws and federal courts, they argued, would better protect civil rights. History has shown that the NAACP's analysis was correct, but the analysis didn't convince key senators at the time. Every writer of proposals can take a lesson here. It is not enough to identify a problem correctly. You must persuade a sometimes resistant audience that you have identified a problem that is real and pressing and deserves their attention.

INFEASIBLE SOLUTIONS

Once readers are convinced that the problem is significant, there still remains the need to convince them that the solution is feasible and doesn't create problems more serious than the one it solves. The feasibility of a solution depends on many factors, some highly technical, as in the case of Vincent Dethier's experiments with the flies. In most cases, the reader will at least need to be convinced that the solution truly matches the problem and that it can be achieved in a reasonable period of time with a reasonable expenditure of resources. If Dethier had presented the amateur scientist with a surefire method of testing the fly's sense of taste that required $10,000 worth of equipment and six months of hard labor, his solution would have been technically feasible but practically impossible. If the reader were a high school teacher with a family to support, she might decide that though such a procedure would help her achieve her goal of understanding the fly's method of tasting, it would interfere with the more important goal of keeping food on the table.

GEORGE ORWELL

"What I have most wanted to do throughout the past ten years is to make political writing into an art. My starting point is always a feeling of partisanship, a sense of injustice. . . . But I could not do the work of writing a book, or even a long magazine article, if it were not also an aesthetic experience."

*E*ric Arthur Blair (who later adopted the pseudonym George Orwell) was born in Bengal, India, where his father was a minor British colonial official. His parents were not wealthy (Orwell described them as "lower-upper-middle class") but apparently had ambitions for their son: they sent him to an expensive preparatory school and then to Eton—the exclusive "public" school that has served for generations as a stepping stone to Cambridge University. Orwell was miserable at these schools, where his relative poverty made him feel like an outsider, but they put him in a position to achieve a status and wealth beyond his parents'. He could have become an insider.

Instead of entering Cambridge, however, Orwell made a series of decisions that kept him outside the comfortable, respectable classes of British society. He joined the Indian Imperial Police in Burma, but quit his job after five years, disgusted by the "evil despotism" England imposed on its colonies. He then lived among the poor in Paris and London, working as a dishwasher and day laborer. In 1933 he published *Down and Out in Paris and London,* an account of these years, and four years later he published *The Road to Wigan Pier,* a comparable account of life among unemployed coal miners. In these and other books, he forced his readers to face unpleasant problems: the rise of fascism, the plight of the working class, the decline of Soviet communism into Stalinist tyranny, the ugliness of racism and colonialism. He also reminded his many upper-middle-class readers that their comfortable way of life was made possible by the suffering of others.

Orwell's most popular works are novels—the satirical *Animal Farm* and the grim *1984.* But it was his essays, which combined some of the century's most brilliant prose with a reformer's anger, that made him the conscience of his generation. ◆

The proposer who sees that the solution is bound to create new problems will often devote a part of the proposal to showing that these problems are far less important than the benefits. Barbara Tuchman, for example, devotes her last two paragraphs to dealing with problems her proposal would create. One, that collective leadership would break down in a war emergency, she attempts to prove a nonproblem. Another, that a cabinet government would be psychologically unsatisfactory to the American people, she dismisses as trivial. Perhaps she dismissed these problems too quickly; for some reason, her proposal never gained much support.

REFUTING A PROPOSAL

Obviously, an opponent can refute a proposal at any of the points just mentioned: by showing that the goal is unacceptable, the problem a nonproblem, the solution infeasible or fraught with unwanted consequences. A good place to study the craft of criticizing proposals is in the columns of George Will, a writer who devotes perhaps half of his syndicated columns to presenting or opposing various plans for political and social change.

In the example reprinted below, Will—who was usually very supportive of President Reagan's political positions—disagrees with the President's proposal on prayer in public schools. In presenting his proposal Reagan had told the nation that his goal was "to reawaken America's religious and moral heart, recognizing that a deep and abiding faith in God is the rock upon which this great nation was founded." The problem standing between him and this goal was a 1962 Supreme Court ruling that organized prayer in public schools was unconstitutional under the First Amendment prohibition of a state-sponsored religion. In his discussion of the problem, the President implied the nation was suffering from a bad court decision: ". . . current interpretation of our Constitution holds that the minds of our children cannot be free to pray to God in the public schools. No one will ever convince me that a moment of voluntary prayer will harm a child or threaten a school or state." His proposed solution was a new amendment stating that "nothing in this Constitution shall be construed to prohibit individual or group prayer in public schools or other public institutions." Will respectfully disagrees.

"Against Prefabricated Prayer"
—GEORGE WILL

How does Will's opening paragraph affect the way most readers will hear his case?

I stand foursquare with the English ethicist who declared: "I am fully convinced that the highest life can only be lived on a foundation of Christian belief—or some substitute for it." But President Reagan's constitutional amendment concerning prayer in public schools is a mistake.

His proposal reads: "Nothing in the Constitution shall be construed to prohibit individual or group prayer in public schools or other public institutions. No person shall be required by the United States or by any state to participate in prayer." This would restore the *status quo ante* the 1962 Supreme Court ruling that public school prayers violate the ban on "establishment" of religion. The amendment would not settle the argument about prayer; it would relocate the argument. All 50 states, or perhaps all 3,041 county governments, or all 16,214 school districts would have to decide whether to have "voluntary" prayers. But the issue is not really voluntary prayers for individuals. The issue is organized prayers for groups of pupils subject to compulsory school attendance laws. In a 1980 resolution opposing "government authored or sponsored religious exercises in public schools," the Southern Baptist Convention noted that "the Supreme Court has not held that it is illegal for any individual to pray or read his or her Bible in public schools."

Notice that Will and Reagan state the problem differently.

This nation is even more litigious than religious, and the school prayer issue has prompted more, and more sophisticated, arguments about constitutional law than about the nature of prayer. But fortunately Senator Jack Danforth is an ordained Episcopal priest and is the only person ever to receive degrees from the Yale Law School and the Yale Divinity School on the same day. Danforth is too polite to pose the question quite this pointedly, but the question is: Is public school prayer apt to serve authentic religion, or is it apt to be mere attudinizing, a thin gruel of vague religious vocabulary? Religious exercises should arise from a rich tradition, and reflect that richness. Prayer, properly understood, arises from the context of the praying person's particular faith. So, Danforth argues, "for those within a religious tradition, it simply is not true that one prayer is as good as any other."

On what principle does Will seem to select sources to quote?

One person's prayer may not be any sort of prayer to another person whose devotion is to a different tradition. To children from certain kinds of Christian families, a "nondenominational" prayer that makes no mention of Jesus Christ would be incoherent. The differences between Christian and Jewish expressions of piety are obvious; the differences between Protestants and Roman Catholics regarding, for example, Mary and the saints are less obvious, but they are not trivial to serious religious sensibilities. And as Danforth says, a lowest-common-denominator prayer would offend all devout persons. "Prayer that is so general and so diluted as not to offend those of most faiths is not prayer at all. True prayer is robust prayer. It is bold prayer. It is almost by definition sectarian prayer."

Why, precisely, would the devout be offended by such prayer?

Liturgical reform in the Roman Catholic and Episcopal churches has occasioned fierce controversies that seem disproportionate, if not unintelligible, to persons who are ignorant of or indifferent about those particular religious traditions. But liturgy is a high art and a serious business because it is designed to help turn minds from worldly distractions, toward transcendent things. Collective prayer should express a shared inner state, one that does not occur easily and spontaneously. A homogenized religious recitation, perfunctorily rendered by children who have just tumbled in from a bus or playground, is not apt to arise from the individual wills, as real prayer must.

Is this picture of school prayer pertinent to the question?

Buddhists are among the almost 90 religious organizations in America that have at least 50,000 members. Imagine, Danforth urges, the Vietnamese Buddhist in a fourth-grade class in, say, Mississippi. How does that child deal with "voluntary" prayer that is satisfactory to the local Baptists? Or imagine a child from America's growing number of Muslims, for whom prayer involves turning toward Mecca and prostrating oneself. Muslim prayer is adoration of Allah; it involves no requests and asks no blessing, as most Christian prayers do. Reagan says: "No one will ever convince me that a moment of voluntary prayer will harm a child . . ." Danforth asks: How is America—or religion—served by the embarrassment of children who must choose between insincere compliance with, or conscientious abstention from, a ritual?

How accurate is Will's view of the psychology of peer pressure in grade school?

Do you find the analogy persuasive?

In a nation where millions of adults (biologically speaking) affect the Jordache look or whatever designer's whim is *de rigueur,* peer pressure on children is not a trivial matter. Supporters of Reagan's amendment argue that a nine-year-old is "free" to absent himself or otherwise abstain from a "voluntary" prayer—an activity involving his classmates and led by that formidable authority figure, his teacher. But that argument is akin to one heard a century ago from persons who said child labor laws infringed the precious freedom of children to contract to work 10-hour days in coal mines.

What more might Will have said? Why didn't he say it?

Is it illogical for people who are not religious to support Reagan's proposal?

To combat the trivializing of religion and the coercion of children who take their own religious traditions seriously, Danforth suggests enacting the following distinction: "The term 'voluntary prayer' shall not include any prayer composed, prescribed, directed, supervised, or organized by an official or employee of a state or local government agency, including public school principals and teachers." When religion suffers the direct assistance of nervous politicians, the result is apt to confirm the judgment of the child who prayed not to God but for God because "if anything happens to Him, we're properly sunk."

It is, to say no more, curious that, according to some polls, more Americans favor prayers in schools than regularly pray in church. Supermarkets sell processed cheese and instant mashed potatoes, so many Americans must like bland substitutes for real things. But it is one thing for the nation's palate to tolerate frozen waffles; it is another and more serious thing for the nation's soul to be satisfied with add-water-and-stir instant religiosity. When government acts as liturgist for a pluralistic society, the result is bound to be a puree that is tasteless, in several senses.

What is the nature of Will's criticism here? It seems from the first sentence that he agrees, at least in a general way, with President Reagan's goal of fostering religion, but he rejects the proposal as a mistake. One *unwanted consequence* of "non-denominational" prayer in the schools, he tells us, would be the "trivializing of religion." These prayers would have to be written by, or approved by, authorities who would ensure that they were sufficiently non-denominational to keep the school system out of court: in effect, they would have to be lawyers' prayers or principals' prayers rather than the "robust" prayers of the devout. Another unwanted consequence cited by both Will and Danforth is the "embarrassment of children who must choose between insincere compliance with, or conscientious abstention from, a ritual." This embarrassment is closely tied to Will's questioning of the *feasibility* of Reagan's plan, which depends on the ability of schoolchildren to choose freely to participate in or abstain from the group prayer. Will simply doesn't believe that the average grade-schooler is capable of resisting the combination of peer pressure and adult leadership in the classroom: as a practical matter, "voluntary" prayer would become required prayer.

The heart of Will's critique of President Reagan's proposal is a quite sharp disagreement about the nature of the problem. Reagan saw the Supreme Court's decision on school prayer as an obstacle to the free exercise of religion. Will takes the opposite view. The court's decision, he argues, actually prevents the required exercise of "add-water-and-stir religiosity" in the schools, and preventing this does no damage to true religion. The problem Reagan raises is, in Will's view, a *nonproblem,* and if we accept Will's analysis, Reagan's proposal will not persuade us.

WRITING PROPOSALS: POINTS TO CONSIDER

When you write a proposal, bear in mind that each of its parts corresponds to a response you hope to elicit from the reader, and that each of these responses is a step toward the decision that you hope the reader will make. In general, the proposal's parts and the reader's path match up as follows:

Parts of Proposal	Reader's Path Toward Decision
Statment of larger goal:	I share this goal.
Identification and discussion of the problem:	I recognize that the problem(s) stated are serious enough to hinder our achieving the goal.
Solution:	I see that the proposed solution fits the problem(s), is feasible, and does not create more serious problems than it solves.

Effective proposal writing requires good judgment about how the parts will actually affect the intended audience.

When you have completed the draft of your proposal, a good practice is to tell a peer reviewer who the intended readers are and have the reviewer read the draft as if through their eyes. Ask your reviewer how confident she is that the audience's responses will be those listed in the right-hand column of the diagram on the previous page.

If you are refuting a proposal, you should once again ask your reviewer to read through the eyes of the intended audience. After she reads, ask her whether the audience will understand precisely what the original proposal was. Ask whether you have persuaded the audience to reject the proposer's goal, the analysis of the problem, or the solution.

In addition to this analysis, you may want to ask the reviewer to consider the three questions about persuasiveness that we discussed in Chapter 6:

1. Is my essay entirely free of logical fallacies?

2. Is my evidence, including my use of authorities, always unimpeachable?

3. Do I present myself as a reasonable person whose judgment can be trusted in an area of uncertainty?

And, of course, you may want your reader to respond to the general peer-review questions listed on pages 65–66.

ASSIGNMENT 1: *A SUMMARY OF A PROPOSAL*

One of the best ways to understand the logic of a proposal is to rephrase it in a compressed form, neatly dividing your summary into parts concentrating on

1. The goal.

2. The problem or problems (identification and discussion or reframing).

3. The solution (including comments the author may make about feasibility and unwanted consequences).

Attempt such a three-part summary of one of the following essays:

1. Chief Justice Warren's argument in Miranda *v.* Arizona (page 285).

2. Martin Luther King, Jr.'s "Letter from Birmingham Jail" (page 301).

3. George Orwell's "Politics and the English Language" (page 293).

4. Lewis Thomas's "How to Fix the Premedical Curriculum" (page 313).

In the process of writing the summary, you will probably rearrange the author's material considerably and change its emphasis. An essay like King's, for instance, is a proposal, but is many other things as well. Your summary will extract the proposal only, making its pattern clearly visible.

ASSIGNMENT 2: *A SUMMARY AND ANALYSIS OF A PROPOSAL*

Summarize a proposal as in Assignment 1, but pause after each of the three parts to analyze the tactics the author uses to make the proposal persuasive. What does the author do to establish common ground with the reader and to establish credibility? What sort of evidence and arguments does the author use? Do you find logical fallacies; if so, do they seriously damage the argument? Has the author failed to meet any obvious criticisms of his or her proposal? Your aim in this analysis is not to refute the author's argument but to examine it closely.

ASSIGNMENT 3: *A REFUTATION OF A PROPOSAL*

Find a proposal that you feel contains serious weaknesses and write a refutation of it comparable to George Will's response to President Reagan's school prayer amendment (page 276) or Theodore White's response to the proposal for direct presidential elections (page 311). You may use any proposal printed in this book or any proposal you find published in such sources as the opinion-editorial page of your local newspaper, the *My Turn* column in *Newsweek,* or the pages of any recent periodical, scholarly or popular. Your refutation will necessarily include an adequate summary of the proposal so that your reader can understand what the argument is about.

ASSIGNMENT 4: *A PROPOSAL SUITABLE FOR PUBLICATION*

Write your own proposal on a topic of current interest. Undertake this proposal as a professional might, planning from the outset to see it published in a particular newspaper or magazine. Make its style, form, and argument appropriate for the audience that reads this publication. For comparison's sake, your teacher may ask you to submit a copy of an article printed in the publication to which your article would be submitted.

ASSIGNMENT 5: *A COMPETITIVE PROPOSAL*

Assume that the trustees of your college have announced a competition with the following rules.

> The Board of Trustees is pleased to announce its seventeenth annual competition for proposed improvements to college life. Proposals are invited in three categories:
>
> 1. Improving the Classroom Atmosphere. The trustees invite proposals that enhance the effectiveness of classroom teaching not by altering equipment or textbooks, but by improving the interaction between students and teachers. The winning proposal will be distributed to all faculty members and discussed at the faculty preschool seminar next fall. Proposals will be evaluated on clarity of purpose, feasibility, and capacity to improve learning in a wide range of classes.
>
> 2. Improving the Campus Environment. The trustees invite proposals that enhance the campus as a learning and living environment.

Proposals should involve costs of no more than $10,000 to the college. The winning proposal will be studied by the Campus Facilities Committee: five winning proposals in the last ten years have been recommended by this committee and undertaken by the college. Proposals will be evaluated on clarity of purpose, feasibility, and capacity to benefit an important segment of the student body.

3. Improving the Community. The trustees invite proposals that allow students or student organizations to perform valuable services for the community. Proposals should involve voluntary contribution of student labor; they may also involve solicitation of funds from the community. The college will contribute up to $1,000 to aid in the implementation of the winning proposal if the proposal demonstrates a need for such funding. Proposals will be evaluated on clarity of purpose, feasibility, and benefit to the community.

Authors of winning proposals will receive $500 in scholarship aid and will be recognized at the annual awards banquet. Proposals are limited to four double-spaced pages.

Write an entry to this competition.

MIRANDA V. ARIZONA
384 US 436 (1966)

Millions of Americans who have never been arrested have heard their "Miranda rights" read to them by television detectives: "You have a right to remain silent," etc. The law that requires this warning was never passed by Congress. It was created by the Supreme Court's interpretation of the Fifth Amendment to the U.S. Constitution: "No person shall . . . be compelled in any criminal case to be a witness against himself, nor be deprived of life, liberty, or property without due process of law. . . ."

The Miranda case is, as Justice White noted in his dissenting opinion, an example of the Court's proposing and implementing "new law and new public policy." Reviewing cases in which accused men were taken into custody and isolated from legal or other advice until they had confessed to a crime, the court created a new standard to insure that such confessions were not "compelled." Three dissenting justices and some politicians and law enforcement officials objected strenuously to the proposal. Billboards saying "Impeach Earl Warren" appeared in some parts of the country. Nonetheless, the Miranda rule is now the law of the land.

Chief Justice Warren, for the majority

1   *T*HE CONSTITUTIONAL ISSUE WE DECIDE IN each of these cases is the admissibility of statements obtained from a defendant questioned while in custody or otherwise deprived of his freedom of action in any significant way. In each, the defendant was questioned by police officers, detectives, or a prosecuting attorney in a room in which he was cut off from the outside world. In none of these cases was the defendant given a full and effective warning of his rights at the outset of the interrogation process. In all the cases, the questioning elicited oral admissions, and in three of them, signed statements as well were admitted at their trials. They all thus share salient features—incommunicado interrogation of individuals in a police-dominated atmosphere, resulting in self-incriminating statements without full warning of constitutional rights.

2   An understanding of the nature and setting of this in-custody interrogation is essential to our decisions today. The difficulty in depicting what transpires at such interrogations stems from the fact that in this country they have largely taken place incommunicado. From extensive factual studies undertaken in the early 1930's, including the famous Wickersham Report to

Congress by a Presidential Commission, it is clear that police violence and the "third degree" flourished at that time. In a series of cases decided by this Court long after these studies, the police resorted to physical brutality—beating, hanging, whipping—and to sustained and protracted questioning incommunicado in order to extort confessions. The Commission on Civil Rights in 1961 found much evidence to indicate that "some policemen still resort to physical force to obtain confessions."[1] The use of physical brutality and violence is not, unfortunately, relegated to the past or to any part of the country. Only recently in Kings County, New York, the police brutally beat, kicked and placed lighted cigarette butts on the back of a potential witness under interrogation for the purpose of securing a statement incriminating a third party.[2]

3   The examples given above are undoubtedly the exception now, but they are sufficiently widespread to be the object of concern. Unless a proper limitation upon custodial interrogation is achieved—such as these decisions will advance—there can be no assurance that practices of this nature will be eradicated in the foreseeable future.

4   Again we stress that the modern practice of in-custody interrogation is psychologically rather than physically oriented. . . . Interrogation still takes place in privacy. Privacy results in secrecy and this in turn results in a gap in our knowledge as to what in fact goes on in the interrogation rooms. A valuable source of information about present police practices, however, may be found in various police manuals and texts which document procedures employed with success in the past, and which recommend various other effective tactics. These texts are used by law enforcement agencies themselves as guides. It should be noted that these texts professedly present the most enlightened and effective means presently used to obtain statements through custodial interrogation. By considering these texts and other data, it is possible to describe procedures observed and noted around the country.

The officers are told by the manuals that the "principal psychological factor contributing to a successful interrogation is *privacy*—being alone with the person under interrogation."[3] The efficacy of this tactic has been explained as follows:

5

> If at all practicable, the interrogation should take place in the investigator's office or at least in a room of his own choice. The subject should be deprived of every psychological advantage. In his own home he may be confident, indignant, or recalcitrant. He is more keenly aware of his rights and more reluctant to tell of his indiscretions or criminal behavior within the walls of his home. Moreover his family and other friends are nearby, their presence lending moral support. In his own office, the investigator possesses all the advantages. The atmosphere suggests the invincibility of the forces of the law.[4]

6

To highlight the isolation and unfamiliar surroundings, the manuals instruct the police to display an air of confidence in the suspect's guilt and from outward appearances to maintain only an interest in confirming certain details. The guilt of the subject is to be posited as a fact. The interrogator should direct his comments toward the reasons why the subject committed the act, rather than court failure by asking the subject whether he did it. Like other men, perhaps the subject has had a bad family life, had an unhappy childhood, had too much to drink, had an unrequited desire for women. The officers are instructed to minimize the moral seriousness of the offense,[5] to cast blame on the victim or on society.[6] These tactics are designed to put the subject in a psychological state where his story is but an elaboration of what the police purport to know already—that he is guilty. Explanations to the contrary are dismissed and discouraged. [Warren goes on to quote texts recommending relentless psychological pressure, suggestions

7

---

[1] Inbau and Reid, *Criminal Investigations and Confessions* (1962), p. 1.
[2] *Commission on Civil Rights Report* (1961), part 5, p. 17.

[3] People *v.* Portelli, 15 NY 2d 235, 205.
[4] O'Hara, *Fundamentals of Criminal Investigation* (1956), p. 99.
[5] Inbau and Reid, pp. 34–43, 87.
[6] Inbau and Reid, pp. 43–65.

that the criminal behavior may be legally justified, and the "good cop/bad cop" or "Mutt and Jeff" strategy.]

8   The interrogators sometimes are instructed to induce a confession out of trickery. The technique here is quite effective in crimes which require identification or which run in series. In the identification situation, the interrogator may take a break in his questioning to place the subject among a group of men in a line-up. "The witness or complainant (previously coached, if necessary) studies the line-up and confidently points out the subject as the guilty party."[7] Then the questioning resumes "as though there were now no doubt about the guilt of the subject." A variation on this technique is called the "reverse line-up":

9   The accused is placed in a line-up, but this time he is identified by several fictitious witnesses or victims who associate him with different offenses. It is expected that the subject will become desperate and confess to the offense under investigation in order to escape from the false accusations.[8]

10   The manuals also contain instructions for police on how to handle the individual who refuses to discuss the matter entirely, or who asks for an attorney or relatives. The examiner is to concede him the right to remain silent. "This usually has a very undermining effect. First of all, he is disappointed in his expectation of an unfavorable reaction on the part of the interrogator. Secondly, a concession of this right to remain silent impresses the subject with the apparent fairness of his interrogator."[9] After this psychological conditioning, however, the officer is told to point out the incriminating significance of the suspect's refusal to talk:

11   Joe, you have a right to remain silent. That's your privilege and I'm the last person in the world who'll try to take it away from you. If that's the way you want to leave this, O.K. But let me ask you this. Suppose you were in my shoes and I were

in yours and you called me in to ask me about this and I told you, "I don't want to answer any of your questions." You'd probably think I had something to hide, and you'd probably be right in thinking that. That's exactly what I'll have to think about you, and so will everybody else. So let's sit here and talk this whole thing over.[10]

Few will persist in their initial refusal to talk, it is said, if this monologue is employed correctly.   12

In the event that the subject wishes to speak to a relative or an attorney, the following advice is tendered: 13

[T]he interrogator should respond by suggesting that the subject first tell the truth to the interrogator himself rather than get anyone else involved in the matter. If the request is for an attorney, the interrogator may suggest that the subject save himself or his family the expense of any such professional service, particularly if he is innocent of the offense under investigation. The interrogator may also add, "Joe, I'm only looking for the truth, and if you're telling the truth, that's it. You can handle this by yourself."[11]   14

From these representative samples of interrogation techniques, the setting prescribed by the manuals and observed in practice becomes clear. In essence, it is this: To be alone with the subject is essential to prevent distraction and to deprive him of any outside support. The aura of confidence in his guilt undermines his will to resist. He merely confirms the preconceived story the police seek to have him describe. . . .   15

It is obvious that such an interrogation environment is created for no purpose other than to subjugate the individual to the will of his examiner. This atmosphere carries its own badge of intimidation. To be sure, this is not physical intimidation, but it is equally destructive of human dignity. The current practice of incommunicado interrogation is at odds with one of our Nation's most cherished principles—   16

---

[7] O'Hara, pp. 105–106.
[8] O'Hara, p. 106
[9] Inbau and Reid, p. 111.

[10] p. 111.
[11] p. 112.

that the individual may not be compelled to incriminate himself. Unless adequate protective devices are employed to dispel the compulsion inherent in custodial surroundings, no statement obtained from the defendant can truly be the product of his free choice. . . .

We have concluded that without proper safeguards the process of in-custody interrogation of persons suspected or accused of crime contains inherently compelling pressures which work to undermine the individual's will to resist and to compel him to speak where he would not otherwise do so freely. In order to combat these pressures and to permit a full opportunity to exercise the privilege against self-incrimination, the accused must be adequately and effectively apprised of his rights and the exercise of those rights must be fully honored. . . .

18   At the outset, if a person in custody is to be subjected to interrogation, he must first be informed in clear and unequivocal terms that he has the right to remain silent. For those unaware of the privilege, the warning is needed simply to make them aware of it— the threshold requirement for an intelligent decision as to its exercise. . . .

19   The warning of the right to remain silent must be accompanied by the explanation that anything said can and will be used against the individual in court. This warning is needed in order to make him aware not only of the privilege, but also of the consequences of forgoing it. It is only through an awareness of these consequences that there can be any assurance of real understanding and intelligent exercise of the privilege. Moreover, this warning may serve to make the individual more acutely aware that he is faced with a phase of the adversary system—that he is not in the presence of persons acting solely in his interest.

20   The circumstances surrounding in-custody interrogation can operate very quickly to overbear the will of one merely made aware of his privilege by his interrogators. Therefore, the right to have counsel present at the interrogation is indispensable to the protection of the Fifth Amendment privilege under the system we delineate today. . . .

Accordingly we hold that an individual held for interrogation must be clearly informed that he has the right to consult with a lawyer and to have the lawyer with him during interrogation under the system for protecting the privilege we delineate today. As with the warnings of the right to remain silent and that anything stated can be used in evidence against him, this warning is an absolute prerequisite to interrogation. No amount of circumstantial evidence that the person may have been aware of this right will suffice to stand in its stead. Only through such a warning is there ascertainable assurance that the accused was aware of this right.

21   If an individual indicates that he wishes the assistance of counsel before any interrogation occurs, the authorities cannot rationally ignore or deny his request on the basis that the individual does not have or cannot afford a retained attorney. The financial ability of the individual has no relationship to the scope of the rights involved here. The privilege against self-incrimination secured by the Constitution applies to all individuals. The need for counsel in order to protect the privilege exists for the indigent as well as the affluent. . . .

22   In order fully to apprise a person interrogated of the extent of his rights under this system then, it is necessary to warn him not only that he has the right to consult with an attorney, but also that if he is indigent a lawyer will be appointed to represent him. Without this additional warning, the admonition of the right to consult with counsel would often be understood as meaning only that he can consult with a lawyer if he has one or has the funds to obtain one. The warning of a right to counsel would be hollow if not couched in terms that would convey to the indigent—the person most often subjected to interrogation—the knowledge that he too has a right to have counsel present. As with the warnings of the right to remain silent and of the general right to counsel, only by effective and express explanation to the indigent of this right can there be assurance that he was truly in a position to exercise it.

23   Once warnings have been given, the subsequent procedure is clear. If the individual indicates in any manner, at any time prior to or during questioning,

that he wishes to remain silent, the interrogation must cease. At this point he has shown that he intends to exercise his Fifth Amendment privilege; any statement taken after the person invokes his privilege cannot be other than the product of compulsion, subtle or otherwise. Without the right to cut off questioning, the setting of in-custody interrogation operates on the individual to overcome free choice in producing a statement after the privilege has been once invoked. If the individual states that he wants an attorney, the interrogation must cease until an attorney is present. At that time, the individual must have an opportunity to confer with the attorney and to have him present during any subsequent questioning. If the individual cannot obtain an attorney and he indicates that he wants one before speaking to police, they must respect his decision to remain silent. . . .

24   To summarize, we hold that when an individual is taken into custody or otherwise deprived of his freedom by authorities in any significant way and is subjected to questioning, the privilege against self-incrimination is jeopardized. Procedural safeguards must be employed to protect the privilege, and unless other fully effective means are adopted to notify the person of his right of silence and to assure that the exercise of the right will be scrupulously honored, the following measures are required. He must be warned prior to any questioning that he has the right to remain silent, that anything he says can be used against him in a court of law, that he has the right to the presence of an attorney, and that if he cannot afford an attorney one will be appointed for him prior to any questioning if he so desires. Opportunity to exercise these rights must be afforded to him throughout the interrogation. After such warnings have been given, and such opportunity afforded him, the individual may knowingly and intelligently waive these rights and agree to answer questions or make a statement. But unless and until such warnings and waiver are demonstrated by the prosecution at trial, no evidence obtained as a result of interrogation can be used against him.

Justice White, dissenting

25   • • • The Court has not discovered or found the law in making today's decision, nor has it derived it from some irrefutable sources; what it has done is to make new law and new public policy in much the same way that it has in the course of interpreting other great clauses of the Constitution. This is what the Court historically has done. Indeed, it is what it must do and will continue to do until and unless there is some fundamental change in the constitutional distribution of governmental powers.

26   But if the Court is here and now to announce new and fundamental policy to govern certain aspects of our affairs, it is wholly legitimate to examine the mode of this or any other constitutional decision in this Court and to inquire into the advisability of its end product in terms of the long-range interest of the country. At the very least the Court's text and reasoning should withstand analysis and be a fair exposition of the constitutional provision which its opinion interprets. Decisions like these cannot rest alone on syllogism, metaphysics or some ill-defined notions of natural justice, although each will perhaps play its part. In proceeding to such constructions as it now announces, the Court should also duly consider all the factors and interests bearing upon the cases, at least insofar as the relevant materials are available; and if the necessary considerations are not treated in the record or obtainable from some other reliable source, the Court should not proceed to formulate fundamental policies based on speculation alone.

First, we may inquire what are the textual and factual bases of this new fundamental rule. To reach the result announced on the grounds it does, the Court must stay within the confines of the Fifth Amendment, which forbids self-incrimination only if *compelled*. Hence the core of the Court's opinion is that because of the "compulsion inherent in custodial surroundings, no statement obtained from [a] defendant [in custody] can truly be the product of his free choice," absent the use of adequate protective devices as described by the Court. However, the Court does not point to any sudden inrush of new knowledge requiring the rejection of 70 years' experience. . . . Rather than asserting new knowledge, the Court concedes that it cannot truly know what occurs during custodial questioning, because of the innate secrecy of such proceedings. It extrapolates a picture of what it conceives to be the norm from police investigatorial manuals, published in 1959 and 1962 or earlier, without any attempt to allow for adjustments in police practices that may have occurred in the wake of more recent decisions of state appellate tribunals or this Court. But even if the relentless application of the described procedures could lead to involuntary confessions, it most assuredly does not follow that each and every case will disclose this kind of interrogation or this kind of consequence. Insofar as appears from the Court's opinion, it has not examined a single transcript of any police interrogation, let alone the interrogation that took place in any one of these cases which it decides today. Judged by any of the standards for empirical investigation utilized in the social sciences the factual basis for the Court's premise is patently inadequate. . . .

28   Today's result would not follow even if it were agreed that to some extent custodial interrogation is inherently coercive. The test has been whether the totality of circumstances deprived the defendant of a "free choice to admit, to deny, or to refuse to answer,"[12] and whether physical and psychological coercion was of such a degree that "the defendant's will was overborne at the time he confessed."[13] The duration and nature of incommunicado custody, the presence or absence of advice concerning the defendant's constitutional rights, and the granting or refusal of requests to communicate with lawyers, relatives, or friends have all been rightly regarded as important data bearing on the basic inquiry. But it has never been suggested, until today, that such questioning was so coercive and accused persons so lacking in hardihood that the very first response to the very first question following the commencement of custody must be conclusively presumed to be the product of an overborne will. . . .

On the other hand, even if one assumed that   29 there was an adequate factual basis for the conclusion that all confessions obtained during in-custody interrogation are the product of compulsion, the rule propounded by the Court would still be irrational, for, apparently, it is only if the accused is also warned of his right to counsel and waives both that right and the right against self-incrimination that the inherent compulsiveness of interrogation disappears. But if the defendant may not answer without a warning a question such as "Where were you last night?" without having his answer be a compelled one, how can the Court ever accept his negative answer to the question of whether he wants to consult his retained counsel or counsel whom the Court will appoint? And why if counsel is present and the accused nevertheless confesses, or counsel tells the accused to tell the truth, and that is what the accused does, is the situation any less coercive insofar as the accused is concerned? . . .

By considering any answers to any interrogation   30 to be compelled regardless of the content and course of examination and by escalating the requirements to prove waiver, the Court not only prevents the use of compelled confessions but for all practical purposes forbids interrogation except in the presence of counsel. That is, instead of confining itself to protection of the right against compelled self-incrimination the Court

----

[12]White cites Lisenba *v.* California, 314 US 219, 241.

[13]White cites Haynes *v.* Washington, 373 US 503, 513, and Lynumn *v.* Illinois, 372 US 528, 534.

has created a limited Fifth Amendment right to counsel—or, as the Court expresses it, a "need for counsel to protect the Fifth Amendment privilege. . . ." The focus then is not on the will of the accused but on the will of counsel and how much influence he can have on the accused. Obviously there is no warrant in the Fifth Amendment for thus installing counsel as the arbiter of the privilege.

31   In sum, for all the Court's expounding on the menacing atmosphere of police interrogation procedures, it has failed to supply any foundation for the conclusions it draws or the measures it adopts.

32   Criticism of the Court's opinion, however, cannot stop with a demonstration that the factual and textual bases for the rule it propounds are, at best, less than compelling. Equally relevant is an assessment of the rule's consequences measured against community values. The Court's duty to assess the consequences of its action is not satisfied by the utterance of the truth that a value of our system of criminal justice is "to respect the inviolability of the human personality" and to require government to produce the evidence against the accused by its own independent labors. More than the human dignity of the accused is involved; the human personality of others in the society must also be preserved. Thus the values reflected by the privilege are not the sole desideratum;[14] society's interest in the general security is of equal weight.

33   The obvious underpinning of the Court's decision is a deep-seated distrust of all confessions. As the Court declares that the accused may not be interrogated without counsel present, absent a waiver of the right to counsel, and as the Court all but admonishes the lawyer to advise the accused to remain silent, the result adds up to a judicial judgment that evidence from the accused should not be used against him in any way, whether compelled or not. This is the not so subtle overtone of the opinion—that it is inherently wrong for the police to gather evidence from the accused himself. And this is precisely the nub of this dissent. I see nothing wrong or immoral, and certainly nothing unconstitutional, in the police's asking a suspect whom they have reasonable cause to arrest whether or not he killed his wife or in confronting him with the evidence on which the arrest was based, at least where he has been plainly advised that he may remain completely silent. Until today, "the admissions or confessions of the prisoner, when voluntarily and freely made, have always ranked high in the scale of incriminating evidence."[15] Particularly when corroborated, as where the police have confirmed the accused's disclosure of the hiding place of implements or fruits of a crime, such confessions have the highest reliability and significantly contribute to the certitude with which we may believe the accused is guilty. Moreover, it is by no means certain that the process of confessing is injurious to the accused. To the contrary it may provide psychological relief and enhance the prospects for rehabilitation.

34   This is not to say that the value of respect for the inviolability of the accused's individual personality should be accorded no weight or that all confessions should be indiscriminately admitted. This Court has long read the Constitution to proscribe compelled confessions, a salutary rule from which there should be no retreat. But I see no sound basis, factual or otherwise, and the Court gives none, for concluding that the present rule against the receipt of coerced confessions is inadequate for the task of sorting out inadmissible evidence and must be replaced by the *per se*[16] rule which is now imposed. Even if the new concept can be said to have advantages of some sort over the present law, they are far outweighed by its more likely undesirable impact on other very relevant and important interests.

35   The most basic function of any government is to provide for the security of the individual and of his property. These ends of society are served by the criminal laws which for the most part are aimed at the prevention of crime. Without the reasonably effective performance of the task of preventing private violence

---

[14] Latin, "thing to be desired."

[15] White cites Brown *v*. Walker, 161 US 591, 596, and Hopt *v*. Utah, 110 US 574, 584–585.

[16] Latin, "in or by itself." White uses the phrase to point out that the new rule would make the fact of captivity by itself evidence of coercion.

and retaliation, it is idle to talk about human dignity and civilized values.

The modes by which the criminal laws serve the interest in general security are many. First the murderer who has taken the life of another is removed from the streets, deprived of his liberty and thereby prevented from repeating his offense. . . . Secondly, the swift and sure apprehension of those who refuse to respect the personal security and dignity of their neighbor unquestionably has its impact on others who might be similarly tempted. . . . Thirdly, the law concerns itself with those whom it has confined. The hope and aim of modern penology, fortunately, is as soon as possible to return the convict to society a better and more law-abiding man than when he left. . . .

37   The rule announced today will measurably weaken the ability of the criminal law to perform these tasks. It is a deliberate calculus to prevent interrogations, to reduce the incidence of confessions and pleas of guilty and to increase the number of trials.[17] Criminal trials, no matter how efficient the police are, are not sure bets for the prosecution, nor should they be if the evidence is not forthcoming. Under the present law, the prosecution fails to prove its case in about 30% of the criminal cases actually tried in the federal courts.[18] But it is something else again to remove from the ordinary criminal case all those confessions which heretofore have been held to be free and voluntary acts of the accused and to thus establish a new constitutional barrier to the ascertainment of truth by the judicial process. There is, in my view, every reason to believe that a good many criminal defendants who otherwise would have been convicted on what this Court has previously thought to be the most satisfactory kind of evidence will now, under this new version of the Fifth Amendment, either not be tried at all or will be acquitted if the State's evidence, minus the confession, is put to the test of litigation.

38   I have no desire whatsoever to share the responsibility for any such impact on the present criminal process.

39   In some unknown number of cases the Court's rule will return a killer, a rapist or other criminal to the streets and to the environment which produced him, to repeat his crime whenever it pleases him. As a consequence, there will not be a gain, but a loss, in human dignity. The real concern is not the unfortunate consequences of this new decision on criminal law as an abstract, disembodied series of authoritative proscriptions, but the impact on those who rely on the public authority for protection and who without it can only engage in violent self-help with guns, knives and the help of their neighbors similarly inclined. ◆

---

[17] In a long footnote, White cites statistics indicating that in 1964, only one crime in four was solved and that about 90 percent of convictions in federal courts were secured by confessions and guilty pleas.

[18] *Federal Offenders in the United States District Courts: 1964,* p. 6 (Table 4), p. 59 (Table 1). *Federal Offenders in the United States District Courts: 1963,* p. 5 (Table 3). *District of Columbia Offenders: 1963,* p. 2 (Table 1).

POLITICS AND THE ENGLISH LANGUAGE

George Orwell

It would be possible to put together a long book of proposals to reform the English language or the way that people use it, but difficult to show that any of these proposals have led to great changes. George Orwell's "Politics and the English Language," however, must be counted as an exceptionally successful essay of its kind. Nearly a half century after it was written, it continues to appear in dozens of anthologies every year, making the case for a few simple rules that could create a "deep change in attitude," affecting not only language but political thought. The essay was originally published in the journal Horizon *in April 1946 and later reprinted in* Shooting an Elephant *(1950).*

1   MOST PEOPLE WHO BOTHER WITH THE matter at all would admit that the English language is in a bad way, but it is generally assumed that we cannot by conscious action do anything about it. Our civilization is decadent and our language—so the argument runs—must inevitably share in the general collapse. It follows that any struggle against the abuse of language is a sentimental archaism, like preferring candles to electric light or hansom cabs to aeroplanes. Underneath this lies the half-conscious belief that language is a natural growth and not an instrument which we shape for our own purposes.

2   Now, it is clear that the decline of a language must ultimately have political and economic causes: it is not due simply to the bad influence of this or that individual writer. But an effect can become a cause, reinforcing the original cause and producing the same effect in an intensified form, and so on indefinitely. A man may take to drink because he feels himself to be a failure, and then fail all the more completely because he drinks. It is rather the same thing that is happening to the English language. It becomes ugly and inaccurate because our thoughts are foolish, but the slovenliness of our language makes it easier for us to have foolish thoughts. The point is that the process is reversible. Modern English, especially written English, is full of bad habits which spread by imitation and which can be avoided if one is willing to take the necessary trouble. If one gets rid of these habits one can think more clearly, and to think clearly is a necessary first step towards political regeneration: so that the fight against bad English is not frivolous and is not the exclusive concern of professional writers. I will come back to this presently, and I hope that by that time the meaning of what I have said here will have become clearer. Meanwhile, here are five specimens of the English language as it is now habitually written.

3   These five passages have not been picked out because they are especially bad—I could have quoted far worse if I had chosen—but because they illustrate various of the mental vices from which we now suffer. They are a little below the average, but are fairly representative samples. I number them so that I can refer back to them when necessary:

"(1) I am not, indeed, sure whether it is not true to say that the Milton who once seemed not unlike a seventeenth-century Shelley had not become, out of

an experience ever more bitter in each year, more alien [*sic*] to the founder of that Jesuit sect which nothing could induce him to tolerate."

> Professor Harold Laski
> (Essay in *Freedom of Expression*).

"(2) Above all, we cannot play ducks and drakes with a native battery of idioms which prescribes such egregious collocations of vocables as the Basic *put up with* for *tolerate* or *put at a loss* for *bewilder*."

> Professor Lancelot Hogben
> *(Interglossa)*.

"(3) On the one side we have the free personality: by definition it is not neurotic, for it has neither conflict nor dream. Its desires, such as they are, are transparent, for they are just what institutional approval keeps in the forefront of consciousness; another institutional pattern would alter their number and intensity; there is little in them that is natural, irreducible, or culturally dangerous. But *on the other side,* the social bond itself is nothing but the mutual reflection of these self-secure integrities. Recall the definition of love. Is not this the very picture of a small academic? Where is there a place in this hall of mirrors for either personality or fraternity?"

> Essay on psychology in *Politics* (New York).

"(4) All the 'best people' from the gentlemen's clubs, and all the frantic fascist captains, united in common hatred of Socialism and bestial horror of the rising tide of the mass revolutionary movement, have turned to acts of provocation, to foul incendiarism, to medieval legends of poisoned wells, to legalize their own destruction of proletarian organizations, and rouse the agitated petty-bourgeoisie to chauvinistic fervour on behalf of the fight against the revolutionary way out of the crisis."

> Communist pamphlet.

"(5) If a new spirit *is* to be infused into this old country, there is one thorny and contentious re-

form which must be tackled, and that is the humanization and galvanization of the B.B.C. Timidity here will bespeak cancer and atrophy of the soul. The heart of Britain may be sound and of strong beat, for instance, but the British lion's roar at present is like that of Bottom in Shakespeare's *Midsummer Night's Dream*—as gentle as any sucking dove. A virile new Britain cannot continue indefinitely to be traduced in the eyes or rather ears, of the world by the effete languors of Langham Place, brazenly masquerading as 'standard English'. When the Voice of Britain is heard at nine o'clock, better far and infinitely less ludicrous to hear aitches honestly dropped than the present priggish, inflated, inhibited, schoolma'amish arch braying of blameless bashful mewing maidens!"

> Letter in *Tribune*.

4 Each of these passages has faults of its own, but, quite apart from avoidable ugliness, two qualities are common to all of them. The first is staleness of imagery: the other is lack of precision. The writer either has a meaning and cannot express it, or he inadvertently says something else, or he is almost indifferent as to whether his words mean anything or not. This mixture of vagueness and sheer incompetence is the most marked characteristic of modern English prose, and especially of any kind of political writing. As soon as certain topics are raised, the concrete melts into the abstract and no one seems able to think of turns of speech that are not hackneyed: prose consists less and less of *words* chosen for the sake of their meaning, and more and more of *phrases* tacked together like the sections of a prefabricated hen-house. I list below, with notes and examples, various of the tricks by means of which the work of prose-construction is habitually dodged:

DYING METAPHORS

5 A newly invented metaphor assists thought by evoking a visual image, while on the other hand a metaphor which is technically "dead" (e.g., *iron resolu-*

tion) has in effect reverted to being an ordinary word and can generally be used without loss of vividness. But in between these two classes there is a huge dump of worn-out metaphors which have lost all evocative power and are merely used because they save people the trouble of inventing phrases for themselves. Examples are: *Ring the changes on, take up the cudgels for, toe the line, ride roughshod over, stand shoulder to shoulder with, play into the hands of, no axe to grind, grist to the mill, fishing in troubled waters, rift within the lute, on the order of the day, Achilles' heel, swan song, hotbed.* Many of these are used without knowledge of their meaning (what is a "rift," for instance?), and incompatible metaphors are frequently mixed, a sure sign that the writer is not interested in what he is saying. Some metaphors now current have been twisted out of their original meaning without those who use them even being aware of the fact. For example, *toe the line* is sometimes written *tow the line.* Another example is *the hammer and the anvil,* now always used with the implication that the anvil gets the worst of it. In real life it is always the anvil that breaks the hammer, never the other way about: a writer who stopped to think what he was saying would be aware of this, and would avoid perverting the original phrase.

OPERATORS OR VERBAL FALSE LIMBS

6   These save the trouble of picking out appropriate verbs and nouns, and at the same time pad each sentence with extra syllables which give it an appearance of symmetry. Characteristic phrases are: *render inoperative, militate against, make contact with, be subject to, give rise to, give grounds for, have the effect of, play a leading part (rôle) in, make itself felt, take effect, exhibit a tendency to, serve the purpose of, etc., etc.* The keynote is the elimination of simple verbs. Instead of being a single word, such as *break, stop, spoil, mend, kill,* a verb becomes a *phrase,* made up of a noun or adjective tacked on to some general-purposes verb such as *prove, serve, form, play, render.* In addition, the passive voice is wherever possible used in preference to the active, and noun constructions are

used instead of gerunds (*by examination of* instead of *by examining*). The range of verbs is further cut down by means of the *-ize* and *de-* formation, and the banal statements are given an appearance of profundity by means of the *not un-* formation. Simple conjunctions and prepositions are replaced by such phrases as *with respect to, having regard to, the fact that, by dint of, in view of, in the interests of, on the hypothesis that;* and the ends of sentences are saved from anticlimax by such resounding commonplaces as *greatly to be desired, cannot be left out of account, a development to be expected in the near future, deserving of serious consideration, brought to a satisfactory conclusion,* and so on and so forth.

PRETENTIOUS DICTION

Words like *phenomenon, element, individual* (as noun), *objective, categorical, effective, virtual, basic, primary, promote, constitute, exhibit, exploit, utilize, eliminate, liquidate,* are used to dress up simple statements and give an air of scientific impartiality to biased judgments. Adjectives like *epoch-making, epic, historic, unforgettable, triumphant, age-old, inevitable, inexorable, veritable,* are used to dignify the sordid processes of international politics, while writing that aims at glorifying war usually takes on an archaic colour, its characteristic words being: *realm, throne, chariot, mailed fist, trident, sword, shield, buckler, banner, jackboot, clarion.* Foreign words and expressions such as *cul de sac, ancien régime, deus ex machina, mutatis mutandis, status quo, gleichschaltung, weltanschauung,* are used to give an air of culture and elegance. Except for the useful abbreviations *i.e., e.g.,* and *etc.,* there is no real need for any of the hundreds of foreign phrases now current in English. Bad writers, and especially scientific, political and sociological writers, are nearly always haunted by the notion that Latin or Greek words are grander than Saxon ones, and unnecessary words like *expedite, ameliorate, predict, extraneous, deracinated, clandestine, subaqueous* and hundreds of others constantly gain ground from their Anglo-Saxon opposite num-

7

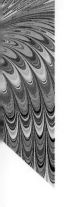

bers.[1] The jargon peculiar to Marxist writing (*hyena, hangman, cannibal, petty bourgeois, these gentry, lacquey, flunkey, mad dog, White Guard,* etc.) consists largely of words and phrases translated from Russian, German or French; but the normal way of coining a new word is to use a Latin or Greek root with the appropriate affix and, where necessary, the *-ize* formation. It is often easier to make up words of this kind (*deregionalize, impermissible, extramarital, nonfragmentatory* and so forth) than to think up the English words that will cover one's meaning. The result, in general, is an increase in slovenliness and vagueness.

MEANINGLESS WORDS

8   In certain kinds of writing, particularly in art criticism and literary criticism, it is normal to come across long passages which are almost completely lacking in meaning.[2] Words like *romantic, plastic, values, human, dead, sentimental, natural, vitality,* as used in art criticism, are strictly meaningless in the sense that they not only do not point to any discoverable object, but are hardly ever expected to do so by the reader. When one critic writes, "The outstanding feature of Mr. X's work is its living quality", while another writes, "The immediately striking thing about Mr. X's work is its peculiar deadness", the reader accepts this as a simple difference of opinion. If words like *black* and *white* were involved, instead of the jargon words *dead* and

---

[1] An interesting illustration of this is the way in which the English flower names which were in use till very recently are being ousted by Greek ones, *snapdragon* becoming *antirrhinum, forget-me-not* becoming *myosotis,* etc. It is hard to see any practical reason for this change of fashion: it is probably due to an instinctive turning-away from the more homely word and a vague feeling that the Greek word is scientific. [author's note]

[2] Example: "Comfort's catholicity of perception and image, strangely Whitmanesque in range, almost the exact opposite in aesthetic compulsion, continues to evoke that trembling atmospheric accumulative hinting at a cruel, an inexorably serene timelessness . . . Wrey Gardiner scores by aiming at simple bull's-eyes with precision. Only they are not so simple, and through this contented sadness runs more than the surface bitter-sweet of resignation" (*Poetry Quarterly*). [author's note]

living, he would see at once that language was being used in an improper way. Many political words are similarly abused. The word *Fascism* has now no meaning except in so far as it signifies "something not desirable." The words *democracy, socialism, freedom, patriotic, realistic, justice,* have each of them several different meanings which cannot be reconciled with one another. In the case of a word like *democracy,* not only is there no agreed definition, but the attempt to make one is resisted from all sides. It is almost universally felt that when we call a country democratic we are praising it: consequently the defenders of every kind of régime claim that it is a democracy, and fear that they might have to stop using the word if it were tied down to any one meaning. Words of this kind are often used in a consciously dishonest way. That is, the person who uses them has his own private definition, but allows his hearer to think he means something quite different. Statements like *Marshall Pétain was a true patriot, The Soviet Press is the freest in the world, The Catholic Church is opposed to persecution,* are almost always made with intent to deceive. Other words used in variable meanings, in most cases more or less dishonestly, are: *class, totalitarian, science, progressive, reactionary, bourgeois, equality.*

9   Now that I have made this catalogue of swindles and perversions, let me give another example of the kind of writing that they lead to. This time it must of its nature be an imaginary one. I am going to translate a passage of good English into modern English of the worst sort. Here is a well-known verse from *Ecclesiastes:*

> "I returned and saw under the sun, that the race is not to the swift, nor the battle to the strong, neither yet bread to the wise, nor yet riches to men of understanding, nor yet favour to men of skill; but time and chance happeneth to them all."

10   Here it is in modern English:

> "Objective consideration of contemporary phenomena compels the conclusion that success or failure in competitive activities exhibits no tendency to be

commensurate with innate capacity, but that a considerable element of the unpredictable must invariably be taken into account."

11   This is a parody, but not a very gross one. Exhibit (3), above, for instance, contains several patches of the same kind of English. It will be seen that I have not made a full translation. The beginning and ending of the sentence follow the original meaning fairly closely, but in the middle the concrete illustrations—race, battle, bread—dissolve into the vague phrase "success or failure in competitive activities." This had to be so, because no modern writer of the kind I am discussing—no one capable of using phrases like "objective consideration of contemporary phenomena"—would ever tabulate his thoughts in that precise and detailed way. The whole tendency of modern prose is away from concreteness. Now analyse the two sentences a little more closely. The first contains forty-nine words but only sixty syllables, and all its words are those of everyday life. The second contains thirty-eight words of ninety syllables: eighteen of its words are from Latin roots, and one from Greek. The first sentence contains six vivid images, and only one phrase ("time and chance") that could be called vague. The second contains not a single fresh, arresting phrase, and in spite of its ninety syllables it gives only a shortened version of the meaning contained in the first. Yet without a doubt it is the second kind of sentence that is gaining ground in modern English. I do not want to exaggerate. This kind of writing is not yet universal, and outcrops of simplicity will occur here and there in the worst-written page. Still, if you or I were told to write a few lines on the uncertainty of human fortunes, we should probably come much nearer to my imaginary sentence than to the one from *Ecclesiastes*.

12   As I have tried to show, modern writing at its worst does not consist in picking out words for the sake of their meaning and inventing images in order to make the meaning clearer. It consists in gumming together long strips of words which have already been set in order by someone else, and making the results presentable by sheer humbug. The attraction of this way of writing is that it is easy. It is easier—even quicker, once you have the habit—to say *In my opinion it is a not unjustifiable assumption that* than to say *I think*. If you use ready-made phrases, you not only don't have to hunt about for words; you also don't have to bother with the rhythms of your sentences, since these phrases are generally so arranged as to be more or less euphonious. When you are composing in a hurry—when you are dictating to a stenographer, for instance, or making a public speech—it is natural to fall into a pretentious, Latinized style. Tags like *a consideration which we should do well to bear in mind* or *a conclusion to which all of us would readily assent* will save many a sentence from coming down with a bump. By using stale metaphors, similes and idioms, you save much mental effort, at the cost of leaving your meaning vague, not only for your reader but for yourself. This is the significance of mixed metaphors. The sole aim of a metaphor is to call up a visual image. When these images clash—as in *The Fascist octopus has sung its swan song, the jackboot is thrown into the melting pot*—it can be taken as certain that the writer is not seeing a mental image of the objects he is naming; in other words he is not really thinking. Look again at the examples I gave at the beginning of this essay. Professor Laski (1) uses five negatives in fifty-three words. One of these is superfluous, making nonsense of the whole passage, and in addition there is the slip *alien* for akin, making further nonsense, and several avoidable pieces of clumsiness which increase the general vagueness. Professor Hogben (2) plays ducks and drakes with a battery which is able to write prescriptions, and, while disapproving of the everyday phrase *put up with,* is unwilling to look *egregious* up in the dictionary and see what it means. (3), if one takes an uncharitable attitude towards it, is simply meaningless: probably one could work out its intended meaning by reading the whole of the article in which it occurs. In (4), the writer knows more or less what he wants to say, but an accumulation of stale phrases chokes him like tea leaves blocking a sink. In (5), words and meaning have almost parted company. People who write in this manner usually have a general emotional meaning—they dislike one thing and

want to express solidarity with another—but they are not interested in the detail of what they are saying. A scrupulous writer, in every sentence that he writes, will ask himself at least four questions, thus: What am I trying to say? What words will express it? What image or idiom will make it clearer? Is this image fresh enough to have an effect? And he will probably ask himself two more: Could I put it more shortly? Have I said anything that is avoidably ugly? But you are not obliged to go to all this trouble: You can shirk it by simply throwing your mind open and letting the ready-made phrases come crowding in. They will construct your sentences for you—even think your thoughts for you, to a certain extent—and at need they will perform the important service of partially concealing your meaning even from yourself. It is at this point that the special connection between politics and the debasement of language becomes clear.

13   In our time it is broadly true that political writing is bad writing. Where it is not true, it will generally be found that the writer is some kind of rebel, expressing his private opinions and not a "party line." Orthodoxy, of whatever colour, seems to demand a lifeless, imitative style. The political dialects to be found in pamphlets, leading articles, manifestos, White Papers and the speeches of under-secretaries do, of course, vary from party to party, but they are all alike in that one almost never finds in them a fresh, vivid, home-made turn of speech. When one watches some tired hack on the platform mechanically repeating the familiar phrases—*bestial atrocities, iron heel, bloodstained tyranny, free peoples of the world, stand shoulder to shoulder*—one often has a curious feeling that one is not watching a live human being but some kind of dummy: a feeling which suddenly becomes stronger at moments when the light catches the speaker's spectacles and turns them into blank discs which seem to have no eyes behind them. And this is not altogether fanciful. A speaker who uses that kind of phraseology has gone some distance towards turning himself into a machine. The appropriate noises are coming out of his larynx, but his brain is not involved as it would be if he were choosing his words for him-

self. If the speech he is making is one that he is accustomed to make over and over again, he may be almost unconscious of what he is saying, as one is when one utters the responses in church. And this reduced state of consciousness, if not indispensable, is at any rate favourable to political conformity.

In our time, political speech and writing are largely the defence of the indefensible. Things like the continuance of British rule in India, the Russian purges and deportations, the dropping of the atom bombs on Japan, can indeed be defended, but only by arguments which are too brutal for most people to face, and which do not square with the professed aims of political parties. Thus political language has to consist largely of euphemism, question-begging and sheer cloudy vagueness. Defenceless villages are bombarded from the air, the inhabitants driven out into the countryside, the cattle machine-gunned, the huts set on fire with incendiary bullets: this is called *pacification*. Millions of peasants are robbed of their farms and sent trudging along the roads with no more than they can carry: this is called *transfer of population* or *rectification of frontiers*. People are imprisoned for years without trial, or shot in the back of the neck or sent to die of scurvy in Arctic lumber camps: this is called *elimination of unreliable elements*. Such phraseology is needed if one wants to name things without calling up mental pictures of them. Consider for instance some comfortable English professor defending Russian totalitarianism. He cannot say outright, "I believe in killing off your opponents when you can get good results by doing so." Probably, therefore, he will say something like this:

"While freely conceding that the Soviet régime exhibits certain features which the humanitarian may be inclined to deplore, we must, I think, agree that a certain curtailment of the right to political opposition is an unavoidable concomitant of transitional periods, and that the rigours which the Russian people have been called upon to undergo have been amply justified in the sphere of concrete achievement."

The inflated style is itself a kind of euphemism. A mass of Latin words falls upon the facts like soft

14

15

16

snow, blurring the outlines and covering up all the details. The great enemy of clear language is insincerity. When there is a gap between one's real and one's declared aims, one turns as it were instinctively to long words and exhausted idioms, like a cuttlefish squirting out ink. In our age there is no such thing as "keeping out of politics." All issues are political issues, and politics itself is a mass of lies, evasions, folly, hatred and schizophrenia. When the general atmosphere is bad, language must suffer. I should expect to find—this is a guess which I have not sufficient knowledge to verify—that the German, Russian and Italian languages have all deteriorated in the last ten or fifteen years, as a result of dictatorship.

17   But if thought corrupts language, language can also corrupt thought. A bad usage can spread by tradition and imitation, even among people who should and do know better. The debased language that I have been discussing is in some ways very convenient. Phrases like *a not unjustifiable assumption, leaves much to be desired, would serve no good purpose, a consideration which we should do well to bear in mind,* are a continuous temptation, a packet of aspirins always at one's elbow. Look back through this essay, and for certain you will find that I have again and again committed the very faults I am protesting against. By this morning's post I have received a pamphlet dealing with conditions in Germany. The author tells me that he "felt impelled" to write it. I open it at random, and here is almost the first sentence that I see: "(The Allies) have an opportunity not only of achieving a radical transformation of Germany's social and political structure in such a way as to avoid a nationalistic reaction in Germany itself, but at the same time of laying the foundations of a co-operative and unified Europe." You see, he "feels impelled" to write—feels, presumably, that he has something new to say—and yet his words, like cavalry horses answering the bugle, group themselves automatically into the familiar dreary pattern. This invasion of one's mind by ready-made phrases (*lay the foundations, achieve a radical transformation*) can only be prevented if one is constantly on guard against them, and

every such phrase anesthetizes a portion of one's brain.

I said earlier that the decadence of our language is probably curable. Those who deny this would argue, if they produced an argument at all, that language merely reflects existing social conditions, and that we cannot influence its development by any direct tinkering with words and constructions. So far as the general tone or spirit of a language goes, this may be true, but it is not true in detail. Silly words and expressions have often disappeared, not through any evolutionary process but owing to the conscious action of a minority. Two recent examples were *explore every avenue* and *leave no stone unturned,* which were killed by the jeers of a few journalists. There is a long list of flyblown metaphors which could similarly be got rid of if enough people would interest themselves in the job; and it should also be possible to laugh the *not un-* formation out of existence,[3] to reduce the amount of Latin and Greek in the average sentence, to drive out foreign phrases and strayed scientific words, and, in general, to make pretentiousness unfashionable. But all these are minor points. The defence of the English language implies more than this, and perhaps it is best to start by saying what it does *not* imply.

To begin with it has nothing to do with archaism, with the salvaging of obsolete words and turns of speech, or with the setting up of a "standard English" which must never be departed from. On the contrary, it is especially concerned with the scrapping of every word or idiom which has outworn its usefulness. It has nothing to do with correct grammar and syntax, which are of no importance so long as one makes one's meaning clear, or with the avoidance of Americanisms, or with having what is called a "good prose style." On the other hand it is not concerned with fake simplicity and the attempt to make written English colloquial. Nor does it even imply in

19

---

[3] One can cure oneself of the *not un-* formation by memorizing this sentence: *A not unblack dog was chasing a not unsmall rabbit across a not ungreen field.* [author's note]

every case preferring the Saxon word to the Latin one, though it does imply using the fewest and shortest words that will cover one's meaning. What is above all needed is to let the meaning choose the word, and not the other way about. In prose, the worst thing one can do with words is to surrender to them. When you think of a concrete object, you think wordlessly, and then, if you want to describe the thing you have been visualizing you probably hunt about till you find the exact words that seem to fit. When you think of something abstract you are more inclined to use words from the start, and unless you make a conscious effort to prevent it, the existing dialect will come rushing in and do the job for you, at the expense of blurring or even changing your meaning. Probably it is better to put off using words as long as possible and get one's meaning as clear as one can through pictures or sensations. Afterwards one can choose—not simply *accept*—the phrases that will best cover the meaning, and then switch round and decide what impression one's words are likely to make on another person. This last effort of the mind cuts out all stale or mixed images, all prefabricated phrases, needless repetitions, and humbug and vagueness generally. But one can often be in doubt about the effect of a word or a phrase, and one needs rules that one can rely on when instinct fails. I think the following rules will cover most cases:

(i) Never use a metaphor, simile or other figure of speech which you are used to seeing in print.
(ii) Never use a long word where a short one will do.
(iii) If it is possible to cut a word out, always cut it out.
(iv) Never use the passive where you can use the active.
(v) Never use a foreign phrase, a scientific word or a jargon word if you can think of an everyday English equivalent.
(vi) Break any of these rules sooner than say anything outright barbarous.

These rules sound elementary, and so they are, but they demand a deep change of attitude in anyone who has grown used to writing in the style now fashionable. One could keep all of them and still write bad English, but one could not write the kind of stuff that I quoted in those five specimens at the beginning of this article.

I have not here been considering the literary use of language, but merely language as an instrument for expressing and not for concealing or preventing thought. Stuart Chase and others have come near to claiming that all abstract words are meaningless, and have used this as a pretext for advocating a kind of political quietism. Since you don't know what Fascism is, how can you struggle against Fascism? One need not swallow such absurdities as this, but one ought to recognize that the present political chaos is connected with the decay of language, and that one can probably bring about some improvement by starting at the verbal end. If you simplify your English, you are freed from the worst follies of orthodoxy. You cannot speak any of the necessary dialects, and when you make a stupid remark its stupidity will be obvious, even to yourself. Political language—and with variations this is true of all political parties, from Conservatives to Anarchists—is designed to make lies sound truthful and murder respectable, and to give an appearance of solidity to pure wind. One cannot change this all in a moment, but one can at least change one's own habits, and from time to time one can even, if one jeers loudly enough, send some worn-out and useless phrase—some *jackboot, Achilles' heel, hotbed, melting pot, acid test, veritable inferno* or other lump of verbal refuse—into the dustbin where it belongs. ◆

20

LETTER FROM BIRMINGHAM JAIL

Martin Luther King, Jr.

Since his assassination in 1968, Martin Luther King, Jr., has received so much official praise that we sometimes forget how controversial a figure he was when alive. Among the sources of this controversy was King's advocacy of the techniques of nonviolent resistance to unjust laws practiced by Mohandas Gandhi (see Orwell's "Reflections on Gandhi, page 143). In 1963, Dr. King was arrested during a civil rights demonstration in Birmingham, Alabama, and charged with violating a law forbidding parades without permits. While in jail, King read an open letter issued by eight Birmingham clergymen who opposed the illegal demonstrations and urged "both our white and Negro citizenry to observe the principles of law and order and common sense."

King's now classic response is a justification of nonviolent resistance to unjust laws and a proposal that such resistance continue. It received national attention when it was printed in The Christian Century *and in* The Atlantic Monthly. *The following version is from King's* Why We Can't Wait *(1964).*

April 16, 1963[1]

MY DEAR FELLOW CLERGYMEN:

While confined here in the Birmingham city jail, I came across your recent statement calling my present activities "unwise and untimely." Seldom do I pause to answer criticism of my work and ideas. If I sought to answer all the criticisms that cross my desk, my secretaries would have little time for anything other than such correspondence in the course of the day, and I would have no time for constructive work. But since I feel that you are men of genuine good will and that your criticisms are sincerely set forth, I want to try to answer your statement in what I hope will be patient and reasonable terms.

I think I should indicate why I am here in Birmingham, since you have been influenced by the view which argues against "outsiders coming in." I have the honor of serving as president of the Southern Christian Leadership Conference, an organization operating in every southern state, with headquarters in Atlanta, Georgia. We have some eighty-five affiliated organizations across the South, and one of them is the Alabama Christian Movement for Human Rights. Frequently we share staff, educational and financial resources with our affiliates. Several months ago the affiliate here in Birmingham asked us to be on call to engage in a nonviolent direct-action program if such were deemed necessary. We readily consented, and when the hour came we lived up to our promise. So I, along with several members of my staff, am here because I was invited here. I am here because I have organizational ties here.

---

[1]This response to a published statement by eight fellow clergymen from Alabama (Bishop C. C. J. Carpenter, Bishop Joseph A. Durick, Rabbi Hilton L. Grafman, Bishop Paul Hardin, Bishop Holan B. Harmon, the Reverend George M. Murray, the Reverend Edward V. Ramage and the Reverend Earl Stallings) was composed under somewhat constricting circumstances. Begun on the margins of the newspaper in which the statement appeared while I was in jail, the letter was continued on scraps of writing paper supplied by a friendly Negro trusty, and concluded on a pad my attorneys were eventually permitted to leave me. Although the text remains in substance unaltered, I have indulged in the author's prerogative of polishing it for publication. [author's note]

But more basically, I am in Birmingham because injustice is here. Just as the prophets of the eighth century B.C. left their villages and carried their "thus saith the Lord" far beyond the boundaries of their home towns, and just as the Apostle Paul left his village of Tarsus and carried the gospel of Jesus Christ to the far corners of the Greco-Roman world, so am I compelled to carry the gospel of freedom beyond my own home town. Like Paul, I must constantly respond to the Macedonian call for aid.

4 Moreover, I am cognizant of the interrelatedness of all communities and states. I cannot sit idly by in Atlanta and not be concerned about what happens in Birmingham. Injustice anywhere is a threat to justice everywhere. We are caught in an inescapable network of mutuality, tied in a single garment of destiny. Whatever affects one directly, affects all indirectly. Never again can we afford to live with the narrow, provincial "outside agitator" idea. Anyone who lives inside the United States can never be considered an outsider anywhere within its bounds.

5 You deplore the demonstrations taking place in Birmingham. But your statement, I am sorry to say, fails to express a similar concern for the conditions that brought about the demonstrations. I am sure that none of you would want to rest content with the superficial kind of social analysis that deals merely with effects and does not grapple with underlying causes. It is unfortunate that demonstrations are taking place in Birmingham, but it is even more unfortunate that the city's white power structure left the Negro community with no alternative.

6 In any nonviolent campaign there are four basic steps: collection of the facts to determine whether injustices exist; negotiation; self-purification; and direct action. We have gone through all these steps in Birmingham. There can be no gainsaying the fact that racial injustice engulfs this community. Birmingham is probably the most thoroughly segregated city in the United States. Its ugly record of brutality is widely known. Negroes have experienced grossly unjust treatment in the courts. There have been more unsolved bombings of Negro homes and churches in Birmingham than in any other city in the nation. These are the hard, brutal facts of the case. On the basis of these conditions, Negro leaders sought to negotiate with the city fathers. But the latter consistently refused to engage in good-faith negotiation.

7 Then, last September, came the opportunity to talk with leaders of Birmingham's economic community. In the course of the negotiations, certain promises were made by the merchants—for example, to remove the stores' humiliating racial signs. On the basis of these promises, the Reverend Fred Shuttlesworth and the leaders of the Alabama Christian Movement for Human Rights agreed to a moratorium on all demonstrations. As the weeks and months went by, we realized that we were the victims of a broken promise. A few signs, briefly removed, returned; the others remained.

8 As in so many past experiences, our hopes had been blasted, and the shadow of deep disappointment settled upon us. We had no alternative except to prepare for direct action, whereby we would present our very bodies as a means of laying our case before the conscience of the local and the national community. Mindful of the difficulties involved, we decided to undertake a process of self-purification. We began a series of workshops on nonviolence, and we repeatedly asked ourselves: "Are you able to accept blows without retaliating?" "Are you able to endure the ordeal of jail?" We decided to schedule our direct-action program for the Easter season, realizing that except for Christmas, this is the main shopping period of the year. Knowing that a strong economic-withdrawal program would be the by-product of direct action, we felt that this would be the best time to bring pressure to bear on the merchants for the needed change.

9 Then it occurred to us that Birmingham's mayoral election was coming up in March, and we speedily decided to postpone action until after election day. When we discovered that the Commissioner of Public Safety, Eugene "Bull" Connor, had piled up enough votes to be in the runoff, we decided again to postpone action until the day after the runoff so that the demonstrations could not be used to cloud the issues. Like many others, we waited to see Mr. Connor de-

feated, and to this end we endured postponement after postponement. Having aided in this community need, we felt that our direct-action program could be delayed no longer.

10   You may well ask: "Why direct action? Why sit-ins, marches and so forth? Isn't negotiation a better path?" You are quite right in calling for negotiation. Indeed, this is the very purpose of direct action. Nonviolent direct action seeks to create such a crisis and foster such a tension that a community which has constantly refused to negotiate is forced to confront the issue. It seeks so to dramatize the issue that it can no longer be ignored. My citing the creation of tension as part of the work of the nonviolent-resister may sound rather shocking. But I must confess that I am not afraid of the word "tension." I have earnestly opposed violent tension, but there is a type of constructive, nonviolent tension which is necessary for growth. Just as Socrates felt that it was necessary to create a tension in the mind so that individuals could rise from the bondage of myths and half-truths to the unfettered realm of creative analysis and objective appraisal, so must we see the need for nonviolent gadflies to create the kind of tension in society that will help men rise from the dark depths of prejudice and racism to the majestic heights of understanding and brotherhood.

11   The purpose of our direct-action program is to create a situation so crisis-packed that it will inevitably open the door to negotiation. I therefore concur with you in your call for negotiation. Too long has our beloved Southland been bogged down in a tragic effort to live in monologue rather than dialogue.

12   One of the basic points in your statement is that the action that I and my associates have taken in Birmingham is untimely. Some have asked: "Why didn't you give the new city administration time to act?" The only answer that I can give to this query is that the new Birmingham administration must be prodded about as much as the outgoing one, before it will act. We are sadly mistaken if we feel that the election of Albert Boutwell as mayor will bring the millennium to Birmingham. While Mr. Boutwell is a much more gentle person than Mr. Connor, they are both segregationists, dedicated to maintenance of the status quo. I have hope that Mr. Boutwell will be reasonable enough to see the futility of massive resistance to desegregation. But he will not see this without pressure from devotees of civil rights. My friends, I must say to you that we have not made a single gain in civil rights without determined legal and nonviolent pressure. Lamentably, it is an historical fact that privileged groups seldom give up their privileges voluntarily. Individuals may see the moral light and voluntarily give up their unjust posture; but, as Reinhold Niebuhr has reminded us, groups tend to be more immoral than individuals.

13   We know through painful experience that freedom is never voluntarily given by the oppressor; it must be demanded by the oppressed. Frankly, I have yet to engage in a direct-action campaign that was "well-timed" in the view of those who have not suffered unduly from the disease of segregation. For years now I have heard the word "Wait!" It rings in the ear of every Negro with piercing familiarity. This "Wait" has almost always meant "Never." We must come to see, with one of our distinguished jurists, that "justice too long delayed is justice denied."

14   We have waited for more than 340 years for our constitutional and God-given rights. The nations of Asia and Africa are moving with jetlike speed toward gaining political independence, but we still creep at horse-and-buggy pace toward gaining a cup of coffee at a lunch counter. Perhaps it is easy for those who have never felt the stinging darts of segregation to say, "Wait." But when you have seen vicious mobs lynch your mothers and fathers at will and drown your sisters and brothers at whim; when you have seen hate-filled policemen curse, kick and even kill your black brothers and sisters; when you see the vast majority of your twenty million Negro brothers smothering in an airtight cage of poverty in the midst of an affluent society; when you suddenly find your tongue twisted and your speech stammering as you seek to explain to your six-year-old daughter why she can't go to the public amusement park that has just been advertised on television, and see tears welling up in her eyes when she is told that Funtown is closed to colored children, and see ominous clouds of inferiority

beginning to form in her little mental sky, and see her beginning to distort her personality by developing an unconscious bitterness toward white people; when you have to concoct an answer for a five-year-old son who is asking: "Daddy, why do white people treat colored people so mean?"; when you take a cross-country drive and find it necessary to sleep night after night in the uncomfortable corners of your automobile because no motel will accept you; when you are humiliated day in and day out by nagging signs reading "white" and "colored"; when your first name becomes "nigger," your middle name becomes "boy" (however old you are) and your last name becomes "John," and your wife and mother are never given the respected title "Mrs."; when you are harried by day and haunted by night by the fact that you are a Negro, living constantly at tiptoe stance, never quite knowing what to expect next, and are plagued with inner fears and outer resentments; when you are forever fighting a degenerating sense of "nobodiness"—then you will understand why we find it difficult to wait. There comes a time when the cup of endurance runs over, and men are no longer willing to be plunged into the abyss of despair. I hope, sirs, you can understand our legitimate and unavoidable impatience.

15   You express a great deal of anxiety over our willingness to break laws. This is certainly a legitimate concern. Since we so diligently urge people to obey the Supreme Court's decision of 1954 outlawing segregation in the public schools, at first glance it may seem rather paradoxical for us consciously to break laws. One may well ask: "How can you advocate breaking some laws and obeying others?" The answer lies in the fact that there are two types of laws: just and unjust. I would be the first to advocate obeying just laws. One has not only a legal but a moral responsibility to obey just laws. Conversely, one has a moral responsibility to disobey unjust laws. I would agree with St. Augustine that "an unjust law is no law at all."

16   Now, what is the difference between the two? How does one determine whether a law is just or unjust? A just law is a manmade code that squares with the moral law or the law of God. An unjust law is a code that is out of harmony with the moral law. To put it in the terms of St. Thomas Aquinas: An unjust law is a human law that is not rooted in eternal law and natural law. Any law that uplifts human personality is just. Any law that degrades human personality is unjust. All segregation statutes are unjust because segregation distorts the soul and damages the personality. It gives the segregator a false sense of superiority and the segregated a false sense of inferiority. Segregation, to use the terminology of the Jewish philosopher Martin Buber, substitutes an "I–it" relationship for an "I–thou" relationship and ends up relegating persons to the status of things. Hence segregation is not only politically, economically and sociologically unsound, it is morally wrong and sinful. Paul Tillich has said that sin is separation. Is not segregation an existential expression of man's tragic separation, his awful estrangement, his terrible sinfulness? Thus it is that I can urge men to obey the 1954 decision of the Supreme Court, for it is morally right; and I can urge them to disobey segregation ordinances, for they are morally wrong.

17   Let us consider a more concrete example of just and unjust laws. An unjust law is a code that a numerical or power majority group compels a minority group to obey but does not make binding on itself. This is *difference* made legal. By the same token, a just law is a code that a majority compels a minority to follow and that it is willing to follow itself. This is *sameness* made legal.

18   Let me give another explanation. A law is unjust if it is inflicted on a minority that, as a result of being denied the right to vote, had no part in enacting or devising the law. Who can say that the legislature of Alabama which set up that state's segregation laws was democratically elected? Throughout Alabama all sorts of devious methods are used to prevent Negroes from becoming registered voters, and there are some counties in which, even though Negroes constitute a majority of the population, not a single Negro is registered. Can any law enacted under such circumstances be considered democratically structured?

19   Sometimes a law is just on its face and unjust in

its application. For instance, I have been arrested on a charge of parading without a permit. Now, there is nothing wrong in having an ordinance which requires a permit for a parade. But such an ordinance becomes unjust when it is used to maintain segregation and to deny citizens the First-Amendment privilege of peaceful assembly and protest.

20   I hope you are able to see the distinction I am trying to point out. In no sense do I advocate evading or defying the law, as would the rabid segregationist. That would lead to anarchy. One who breaks an unjust law must do so openly, lovingly, and with a willingness to accept the penalty. I submit that an individual who breaks a law that conscience tells him is unjust, and who willingly accepts the penalty of imprisonment in order to arouse the conscience of the community over its injustice, is in reality expressing the highest respect for law.

21   Of course, there is nothing new about this kind of civil disobedience. It was evidenced sublimely in the refusal of Shadrach, Meshach and Abednego to obey the laws of Nebuchadnezzar,[2] on the ground that a higher moral law was at stake. It was practiced superbly by the early Christians, who were willing to face hungry lions and the excruciating pain of chopping blocks rather than submit to certain unjust laws of the Roman Empire. To a degree, academic freedom is a reality today because Socrates practiced civil disobedience. In our own nation, the Boston Tea Party represented a massive act of civil disobedience.

22   We should never forget that everything Adolf Hitler did in Germany was "legal" and everything the Hungarian freedom fighters did in Hungary was "illegal." It was "illegal" to aid and comfort a Jew in Hitler's Germany. Even so, I am sure that, had I lived in Germany at the time, I would have aided and comforted my Jewish brothers. If today I lived in a Communist country where certain principles dear to the Christian faith are suppressed, I would openly advocate disobeying that country's antireligious laws.

23   I must make two honest confessions to you, my Christian and Jewish brothers. First, I must confess

----
[2] King refers to the Biblical story recorded in Daniel, chapter 3.

that over the past few years I have been gravely disappointed with the white moderate. I have almost reached the regrettable conclusion that the Negro's great stumbling block in his stride toward freedom is not the White Citizen's Counciler or the Ku Klux Klanner, but the white moderate, who is more devoted to "order" than to justice; who prefers a negative peace which is the absence of tension to a positive peace which is the presence of justice; who constantly says: "I agree with you in the goal you seek, but I cannot agree with your methods of direct action"; who paternalistically believes he can set the timetable for another man's freedom; who lives by a mythical concept of time and who constantly advises the Negro to wait for a "more convenient season." Shallow understanding from people of good will is more frustrating than absolute misunderstanding from people of ill will. Lukewarm acceptance is much more bewildering than outright rejection.

24   I had hoped that the white moderate would understand that law and order exist for the purpose of establishing justice and that when they fail in this purpose they become the dangerously structured dams that block the flow of social progress. I had hoped that the white moderate would understand that the present tension in the South is a necessary phase of the transition from an obnoxious negative peace, in which the Negro passively accepted his unjust plight, to a substantive and positive peace, in which all men will respect the dignity and worth of human personality. Actually, we who engage in nonviolent direct action are not the creators of tension. We merely bring to the surface the hidden tension that is already alive. We bring it out in the open, where it can be seen and dealt with. Like a boil that can never be cured so long as it is covered up but must be opened with all its ugliness to the natural medicines of air and light, injustice must be exposed, with all the tension its exposure creates, to the light of human conscience and the air of national opinion before it can be cured.

25   In your statement you assert that our actions, even though peaceful, must be condemned because they precipitate violence. But is this a logical assertion? Isn't this like condemning a robbed man because

his possession of money precipitated the evil act of robbery? Isn't this like condemning Socrates because his unswerving commitment to truth and his philosophical inquiries precipitated the act by the misguided populace in which they made him drink hemlock? Isn't this like condemning Jesus because his unique God-consciousness and never-ceasing devotion to God's will precipitated the evil act of crucifixion? We must come to see that, as the federal courts have consistently affirmed, it is wrong to urge an individual to cease his efforts to gain his basic constitutional rights because the quest may precipitate violence. Society must protect the robbed and punish the robber.

26   I had also hoped that the white moderate would reject the myth concerning time in relation to the struggle for freedom. I have just received a letter from a white brother in Texas. He writes: "All Christians know that the colored people will receive equal rights eventually, but it is possible that you are in too great a religious hurry. It has taken Christianity almost two thousand years to accomplish what it has. The teachings of Christ take time to come to earth." Such an attitude stems from a tragic misconception of time, from the strangely irrational notion that there is something in the very flow of time that will inevitably cure all ills. Actually, time itself is neutral; it can be used either destructively or constructively. More and more I feel that the people of ill will have used time much more effectively than have the people of good will. We will have to repent in this generation not merely for the hateful words and actions of the bad people but for the appalling silence of the good people. Human progress never rolls in on wheels of inevitability; it comes through the tireless efforts of men willing to be coworkers with God, and without this hard work, time itself becomes an ally of the forces of social stagnation. We must use time creatively, in the knowledge that the time is always ripe to do right. Now is the time to make real the promise of democracy and transform our pending national elegy into a creative psalm of brotherhood. Now is the time to lift our national policy from the quicksand of racial injustice to the solid rock of human dignity.

You speak of our activity in Birmingham as extreme. At first I was rather disappointed that fellow clergymen would see my nonviolent efforts as those of an extremist. I began thinking about the fact that I stand in the middle of two opposing forces in the Negro community. One is a force of complacency, made up in part of Negroes who, as a result of long years of oppression, are so drained of self-respect and a sense of "somebodiness" that they have adjusted to segregation; and in part of a few middle-class Negroes who, because of a degree of academic and economic security and because in some ways they profit by segregation, have become insensitive to the problems of the masses. The other force is one of bitterness and hatred, and it comes perilously close to advocating violence. It is expressed in the various black nationalist groups that are springing up across the nation, the largest and best-known being Elijah Muhammad's Muslim movement. Nourished by the Negro's frustration over the continued existence of racial discrimination, this movement is made up of people who have lost faith in America, who have absolutely repudiated Christianity, and who have concluded that the white man is an incorrigible "devil."   27

I have tried to stand between these two forces,   28
saying that we need emulate neither the "do-nothingism" of the complacent nor the hatred and despair of the black nationalist. For there is the more excellent way of love and nonviolent protest. I am grateful to God that, through the influence of the Negro church, the way of nonviolence became an integral part of our struggle.

If this philosophy had not emerged, by now   29
many streets of the South would, I am convinced, be flowing with blood. And I am further convinced that if our white brothers dismiss as "rabble-rousers" and "outside agitators" those of us who employ nonviolent direct action, and if they refuse to support our nonviolent efforts, millions of Negroes will, out of frustration and despair, seek solace and security in black-nationalist ideologies—a development that would inevitably lead to a frightening racial nightmare.

30 Oppressed people cannot remain oppressed forever. The yearning for freedom eventually manifests itself, and that is what has happened to the American Negro. Something within has reminded him of his birthright of freedom, and something without has reminded him that it can be gained. Consciously or unconsciously, he has been caught up by the *Zeitgeist*,[3] and with his black brothers of Africa and his brown and yellow brothers of Asia, South America and the Caribbean, the United States Negro is moving with a sense of great urgency toward the promised land of racial justice. If one recognizes this vital urge that has engulfed the Negro community, one should readily understand why public demonstrations are taking place. The Negro has many pent-up resentments and latent frustrations, and he must release them. So let him march; let him make prayer pilgrimages to the city hall; let him go on freedom rides—and try to understand why he must do so. If his repressed emotions are not released in nonviolent ways, they will seek expression through violence; this is not a threat but a fact of history. So I have not said to my people: "Get rid of your discontent." Rather, I have tried to say that this normal and healthy discontent can be channeled into the creative outlet of nonviolent direct action. And now this approach is being termed extremist.

31 But though I was initially disappointed at being categorized as an extremist, as I continued to think about the matter I gradually gained a measure of satisfaction from the label. Was not Jesus an extremist for love: "Love your enemies, bless them that curse you, do good to them that hate you, and pray for them which despitefully use you, and persecute you." Was not Amos an extremist for justice: "Let justice roll down like waters and righteousness like an ever-flowing stream." Was not Paul an extremist for the Christian gospel: "I bear in my body the marks of the Lord Jesus." Was not Martin Luther an extremist: "Here I stand; I cannot do otherwise, so help me God." And John Bunyan: "I will stay in jail to the

---

[3] The spirit of the age.

end of my days before I make a butchery of my conscience." And Abraham Lincoln: "This nation cannot survive half slave and half free." And Thomas Jefferson: "We hold these truths to be self-evident, that all men are created equal . . ." So the question is not whether we will be extremists, but what kind of extremists we will be. Will we be extremists for hate or for love? Will we be extremists for the preservation of injustice or for the extension of justice? In that dramatic scene on Calvary's hill three men were crucified. We must never forget that all three were crucified for the same crime—the crime of extremism. Two were extremists for immorality, and thus fell below their environment. The other, Jesus Christ, was an extremist for love, truth and goodness, and thereby rose above his environment. Perhaps the South, the nation and the world are in dire need of creative extremists.

32 I had hoped that the white moderate would see this need. Perhaps I was too optimistic; perhaps I expected too much. I suppose I should have realized that few members of the oppressor race can understand the deep groans and passionate yearnings of the oppressed race, and still fewer have the vision to see that injustice must be rooted out by strong, persistent and determined action. I am thankful, however, that some of our white brothers in the South have grasped the meaning of this social revolution and committed themselves to it. They are still all too few in quantity, but they are big in quality. Some—such as Ralph McGill, Lillian Smith, Harry Golden, James McBride Dabbs, Ann Braden and Sarah Patton Boyle—have written about our struggle in eloquent and prophetic terms. Others have marched with us down nameless streets of the South. They have languished in filthy, roach-infested jails, suffering the abuse and brutality of policemen who view them as "dirty nigger-lovers." Unlike so many of their moderate brothers and sisters, they have recognized the urgency of the moment and sensed the need for powerful "action" antidotes to combat the disease of segregation.

33 Let me take note of my other major disappointment. I have been so greatly disappointed with the white church and its leadership. Of course, there are

some notable exceptions. I am not unmindful of the fact that each of you has taken some significant stands on this issue. I commend you, Reverend Stallings, for your Christian stand on this past Sunday, in welcoming Negroes to your worship service on a nonsegregated basis. I commend the Catholic leaders of this state for integrating Spring Hill College several years ago.

34   But despite these notable exceptions, I must honestly reiterate that I have been disappointed with the church. I do not say this as one of those negative critics who can always find something wrong with the church. I say this as a minister of the gospel, who loves the church; who was nurtured in its bosom; who has been sustained by its spiritual blessings and who will remain true to it as long as the cord of life shall lengthen.

35   When I was suddenly catapulted into the leadership of the bus protest in Montgomery, Alabama, a few years ago, I felt we would be supported by the white church. I felt that the white ministers, priests and rabbis of the South would be among our strongest allies. Instead, some have been outright opponents, refusing to understand the freedom movement and misrepresenting its leaders; all too many others have been more cautious than courageous and have remained silent behind the anesthetizing security of stained-glass windows.

36   In spite of my shattered dreams, I came to Birmingham with the hope that the white religious leadership of this community would see the justice of our cause and, with deep moral concern, would serve as the channel through which our just grievances could reach the power structure. I had hoped that each of you would understand. But again I have been disappointed.

37   I have heard numerous southern religious leaders admonish their worshipers to comply with a desegregation decision because it is the law, but I have longed to hear white ministers declare: "Follow this decree because integration is morally right and because the Negro is your brother." In the midst of blatant injustices inflicted upon the Negro, I have watched white churchmen stand on the sideline and mouth pious irrelevancies and sanctimonious trivialities. In the midst of a mighty struggle to rid our nation of racial and economic injustice, I have heard many ministers say: "Those are social issues, with which the gospel has no real concern." And I have watched many churches commit themselves to a completely otherworldly religion which makes a strange, un-Biblical distinction between body and soul, between the sacred and the secular.

38   I have traveled the length and breadth of Alabama, Mississippi and all the other southern states. On sweltering summer days and crisp autumn mornings I have looked at the South's beautiful churches with their lofty spires pointing heavenward. I have beheld the impressive outlines of her massive religious-education buildings. Over and over I have found myself asking: "What kind of people worship here? Who is their God? Where were their voices when the lips of Governor Barnett[4] dripped with words of interposition and nullification? Where were they when Governor Wallace[5] gave a clarion call for defiance and hatred? Where were their voices of support when bruised and weary Negro men and women decided to rise from the dark dungeons of complacency to the bright hills of creative protest?"

39   Yes, these questions are still in my mind. In deep disappointment I have wept over the laxity of the church. But be assured that my tears have been tears of love. There can be no deep disappointment where there is not deep love. Yes, I love the church. How could I do otherwise? I am in the rather unique position of being the son, the grandson and the great-grandson of preachers. Yes, I see the church as the body of Christ. But, oh! How we have blemished and scarred that body through social neglect and through fear of being nonconformists.

---

[4] Ross Barnett, governor of Mississippi, in 1962 ordered resistance to the registration of a black student, James Meredith, at the University of Mississippi.
[5] George Wallace, governor of Alabama, stood in a doorway of the University of Alabama in a symbolic effort to block the registration of two black students in 1963.

40   There was a time when the church was very powerful—in the time when the early Christians rejoiced at being deemed worthy to suffer for what they believed. In those days the church was not merely a thermometer that recorded the ideas and principles of popular opinion; it was a thermostat that transformed the mores of society. Whenever the early Christians entered a town, the people in power became disturbed and immediately sought to convict the Christians for being "disturbers of the peace" and "outside agitators." But the Christians pressed on, in the conviction that they were "a colony of heaven," called to obey God rather than man. Small in number, they were big in commitment. They were too God-intoxicated to be "astronomically intimidated." By their effort and example they brought an end to such ancient evils as infanticide and gladiatorial contests.

41   Things are different now. So often the contemporary church is a weak, ineffectual voice with an uncertain sound. So often it is an archdefender of the status quo. Far from being disturbed by the presence of the church, the power structure of the average community is consoled by the church's silent—and often even vocal—sanction of things as they are.

42   But the judgment of God is upon the church as never before. If today's church does not recapture the sacrificial spirit of the early church, it will lose its authenticity, forfeit the loyalty of millions, and be dismissed as an irrelevant social club with no meaning for the twentieth century. Every day I meet young people whose disappointment with the church has turned into outright disgust.

43   Perhaps I have once again been too optimistic. Is organized religion too inextricably bound to the status quo to save our nation and the world? Perhaps I must turn my faith to the inner spiritual church, the church within the church, as the true *ekklesia*[6] and the hope of the world. But again I am thankful to God that some noble souls from the ranks of organized religion have broken loose from the paralyzing chains of conformity and joined us as active partners in the struggle for freedom. They have left their secure con-

---

[6] Literally, "assembly of the people."

gregations and walked the streets of Albany, Georgia, with us. They have gone down the highways of the South on tortuous rides for freedom. Yes, they have gone to jail with us. Some have been dismissed from their churches, have lost the support of their bishops and fellow ministers. But they have acted in the faith that right defeated is stronger than evil triumphant. Their witness has been the spiritual salt that has preserved the true meaning of the gospel in these troubled times. They have carved a tunnel of hope through the dark mountain of disappointment.

44   I hope the church as a whole will meet the challenge of this decisive hour. But even if the church does not come to the aid of justice, I have no despair about the future. I have no fear about the outcome of our struggle in Birmingham, even if our motives are at present misunderstood. We will reach the goal of freedom in Birmingham and all over the nation, because the goal of America is freedom. Abused and scorned though we may be, our destiny is tied up with America's destiny. Before the pilgrims landed at Plymouth, we were here. Before the pen of Jefferson etched the majestic words of the Declaration of Independence across the pages of history, we were here. For more than two centuries our forebears labored in this country without wages; they made cotton king; they built the homes of their masters while suffering gross injustice and shameful humiliation—and yet out of a bottomless vitality they continued to thrive and develop. If the inexpressible cruelties of slavery could not stop us, the opposition we now face will surely fail. We will win our freedom because the sacred heritage of our nation and the eternal will of God are embodied in our echoing demands.

45   Before closing I feel impelled to mention one other point in your statement that has troubled me profoundly. You warmly commended the Birmingham police force for keeping "order" and "preventing violence." I doubt that you would have so warmly commended the police force if you had seen its dogs sinking their teeth into unarmed, nonviolent Negroes. I doubt that you would so quickly commend the policemen if you were to observe their ugly and inhumane treatment of Negroes here in the city jail; if you were

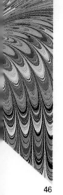

to watch them push and curse old Negro women and young Negro girls; if you were to see them slap and kick old Negro men and young boys; if you were to observe them, as they did on two occasions, refuse to give us food because we wanted to sing our grace together. I cannot join you in your praise of the Birmingham police department.

46   It is true that the police have exercised a degree of discipline in handling the demonstrators. In this sense they have conducted themselves rather "nonviolently" in public. But for what purpose? To preserve the evil system of segregation. Over the past few years I have consistently preached that nonviolence demands that the means we use must be as pure as the ends we seek. I have tried to make clear that it is wrong to use immoral means to attain moral ends. But now I must affirm that it is just as wrong, or perhaps even more so, to use moral means to preserve immoral ends. Perhaps Mr. Connor and his policemen have been rather nonviolent in public, as was Chief Pritchett in Albany, Georgia, but they have used the moral means of nonviolence to maintain the immoral end of racial injustice. As T. S. Eliot has said: "The last temptation is the greatest treason: To do the right deed for the wrong reason."

47   I wish you had commended the Negro sit-inners and demonstrators of Birmingham for their sublime courage, their willingness to suffer and their amazing discipline in the midst of great provocation. One day the South will recognize its real heroes. They will be the James Merediths, with the noble sense of purpose that enables them to face jeering and hostile mobs, and with the agonizing loneliness that characterizes the life of the pioneer. They will be old, oppressed, battered Negro women, symbolized in a seventy-two-year-old woman in Montgomery, Alabama, who rose up with a sense of dignity and with her people decided not to ride segregated buses, and who responded with ungrammatical profundity to one who inquired about her weariness: "My feets is tired, but my soul is at rest." They will be the young high school and college students, the young ministers of the gospel and a host of their elders, courageously and nonviolently sitting in at lunch counters and willingly going to jail for

conscience' sake. One day the South will know that when these disinherited children of God sat down at lunch counters, they were in reality standing up for what is best in the American dream and for the most sacred values in our Judaeo-Christian heritage, thereby bringing our nation back to those great wells of democracy which were dug deep by the founding fathers in their formulation of the Constitution and the Declaration of Independence.

48   Never before have I written so long a letter. I'm afraid it is much too long to take your precious time. I can assure you that it would have been much shorter if I had been writing from a comfortable desk, but what else can one do when he is alone in a narrow jail cell, other than write long letters, think long thoughts and pray long prayers?

49   If I have said anything in this letter that overstates the truth and indicates an unreasonable impatience, I beg you to forgive me. If I have said anything that understates the truth and indicates my having a patience that allows me to settle for anything less than brotherhood, I beg God to forgive me.

50   I hope this letter finds you strong in the faith. I also hope that circumstances will soon make it possible for me to meet each of you, not as an integrationist or a civil-rights leader but as a fellow clergyman and a Christian brother. Let us all hope that the dark clouds of racial prejudice will soon pass away and the deep fog of misunderstanding will be lifted from our fear-drenched communities, and in some not too distant tomorrow the radiant stars of love and brotherhood will shine over our great nation with all their scintillating beauty.

    Yours for the cause of Peace and Brotherhood,
    MARTIN LUTHER KING, JR. ◆

DIRECT ELECTIONS: AN INVITATION TO NATIONAL CHAOS

Theodore H. White

Many people have said that the United States' system of electing a President is anti-quated and eccentric. Rather than deciding the election by a direct popular vote, we have, in effect, fifty separate presidential elections—one in each state. Whichever candidate wins a state actually "wins" a certain number of "electors" pledged to vote for him or her at the meeting of the Electoral College.

The system can produce unsatisfactory results: electors sometimes violate their oaths and vote as they please, and in a close race, the winner of the popular vote might lose the election. In 1968 the system nearly produced a situation in which no candidate received the majority of electoral votes, in which case the President would have been elected by the House of Representatives. In 1969–70 Congress considered a proposal to abolish the old system and replace it with a direct election by popular vote. White's argument against the proposal appeared in Life *on January 30, 1970.*

1   *L*AST SEPTEMBER, IN A TRIUMPH OF NOBLE purpose over common sense, the House passed and has sent to the Senate a proposal to abolish the Federal System.

2   It is not called that, of course. Put forth as an amendment to the Constitution, the new scheme offers a supposedly better way of electing Presidents. Advanced with the delusive rhetoric of *vox populi, vox Dei,*[1] it not only wipes out the obsolete Electoral College but abolishes the sovereign states as voting units. In the name of The People, it proposes that a giant plebiscite pour all 70,000,000 American votes into a single pool whose winner—whether by 5,000 or 5,000,000—is hailed as National Chief.

3   American elections are a naked transaction in power—a cruel, brawling yearlong adventure swept by profound passion and prejudice. Quite naturally, therefore, Constitution and tradition have tried to limit the sweep of passions, packaging the raw votes within each state, weighing each state's electoral vote proportionately to population, letting each make its own rules and police its own polls.

4   The new theory holds that an instantaneous direct cascade of votes offers citizens a more responsible choice of leadership—and it is only when one tests high-minded theory against reality that it becomes nightmare.

5   Since the essence of the proposal is a change in the way votes are counted, the first test must be a hard look at vote-counting as it actually operates. Over most of the United States votes are cast and counted honestly. No one anymore can steal an election that is not close to begin with, and in the past generation vote fraud has diminished dramatically.

6   Still, anyone who trusts the precise count in Gary, Ind.; Cook County, Ill.; Duval County, Texas; Suffolk County, Mass.; or in half a dozen border and

---

[1]*vox populi, vox Dei:* "the voice of the people is the voice of God."

Southern states is out of touch with political reality. Under the present electoral system, however, crooks in such areas are limited to toying with the electoral vote of one state only; and then only when margins are exceptionally tight. Even then, when the dial riggers, ballot stuffers, late counters and recounters are stimulated to play election-night poker with the results, their art is balanced by crooks of the other party playing the same game.

7   John F. Kennedy won in 1960 by the tissue-thin margin of 118,550—less than ⅕ of one percent of the national total—in an election stained with outright fraud in at least three states. No one challenged his victory, however, because the big national decision had been made by electoral votes of honest-count states, sealed off from contamination by fraud elsewhere—and because scandal could as well be charged to Republicans as to Democrats. But if, henceforth, all the raw votes from Hawaii to Maine are funneled into one vast pool, and popular results are as close as 1960 and 1968, the pressure to cheat or call recounts must penetrate everywhere—for any vote stolen anywhere in the Union pressures politicians thousands of miles away to balance or protest it. Twice in the past decade, the new proposal would have brought America to chaos.

8 ▶   To enforce honest vote-counting in all the nation's 170,000 precincts, national policing becomes necessary. So, too, do uniform federal laws on voter qualifications. New laws, for example, will have to forbid any state from increasing its share of the total by enfranchising youngsters of 18 (as Kentucky and Georgia do now) while most others limit voting to those over 21. Residence requirements, too, must be made uniform in all states. The centralization required breaches all American tradition.

9 ▶   Reality forces candidates today to plan campaigns on many levels, choosing groups and regions to which they must appeal, importantly educating themselves on local issues in states they seek to carry.

10   But if states are abolished as voting units, TV becomes absolutely dominant. Campaign strategy changes from delicately assembling a winning coalition of states and becomes a media effort to capture the largest share of the national "vote market." Instead of courting regional party leaders by compromise, candidates will rely on media masters. Issues will be shaped in national TV studios, and the heaviest swat will go to the candidate who raises the most money to buy the best time and most "creative" TV talent.

11 ▶   The most ominous domestic reality today is race confrontation. Black votes count today because blacks vote chiefly in big-city states where they make the margin of difference. No candidate seeking New York's 43 electoral votes, Pennsylvania's 29, Illinois' 26 can avoid courting the black vote that may swing those states. If states are abolished as voting units, the chief political leverage of Negroes is also abolished. Whenever a race issue has been settled by plebiscite—from California's Proposition 14 (on Open Housing) in 1964 to New York's Police Review Board in 1966—the plebiscite vote has put the blacks down. Yet a paradox of the new rhetoric is that Southern conservatives, who have most to gain by the new proposal, oppose it, while Northern liberals, who have the most to lose, support it because it is hallowed in the name of The People.

12   What is wrong in the old system is not state-by-state voting. What is wrong is the anachronistic Electoral College and the mischief anonymous "electors" can perpetrate in the wake of a close election. Even more dangerous is the provision that lets the House, if no candidate has an electoral majority, choose the President by the undemocratic unit rule—one state, one vote. These dangers can be eliminated simply by an amendment which abolishes the Electoral College but retains the electoral vote by each state and which, next, provides that in an election where there is no electoral majority, senators and congressmen, individual voting in joint session and hearing the voices of the people in their districts, will elect a President.

13   What is right about the old system is the sense of identity it gives Americans. As they march to the polls, Bay Staters should feel Massachusetts is speaking, Hoosiers should feel Indiana is speaking; blacks and other minorities should feel their votes count; so,

too, should Southerners from Tidewater to the Gulf. The Federal System has worked superbly for almost two centuries. It can and should be speedily improved. But to reduce Americans to faceless digits on an enor-mous tote board, in a plebiscite swept by demagogu-ery, manipulated by TV, at the mercy of crooked counters—this is an absurdity for which goodwill and noble theory are no justification. ◆

HOW TO FIX THE PREMEDICAL CURRICULUM

Lewis Thomas

Though he achieved sudden literary fame with the publication of The Lives of a Cell: Notes of a Biology Watcher *(1974), Lewis Thomas is primarily a physician, medical researcher, and educator. He has been dean of the medical schools at New York University and Yale and is currently Emeritus President of the Sloan-Kettering Cancer Center in New York City. The proposal below was originally published in* The New England Journal of Medicine *and later reprinted in* The Medusa and the Snail *(1979).*

1   THE INFLUENCE OF THE MODERN MEDICAL school on liberal-arts education in this country over the last decade has been baleful and malign, nothing less. The admission policies of the medical schools are at the root of the trouble. If something is not done quickly to change these, all the joy of going to college will have been destroyed, not just for that growing majority of undergraduate students who draw breath only to become doctors, but for everyone else, all the students, and all the faculty as well.

2   The medical schools used to say they wanted applicants as broadly educated as possible, and they used to mean it. The first two years of medical school were given over entirely to the basic biomedical sci-ences, and almost all entering students got their first close glimpse of science in those years. Three chemis-try courses, physics, and some sort of biology were all

that were required from the colleges. Students were encouraged by the rhetoric of medical-school cata-logues to major in such nonscience disciplines as his-tory, English, philosophy. Not many did so; almost all premedical students in recent generations have had their majors in chemistry or biology. But anyway, they were authorized to spread around in other fields if they wished.

3   There is still some talk in medical deans' offices about the need for general culture, but nobody really means it, and certainly the premedical students don't believe it. They concentrate on science.

4   They concentrate on science with a fury, and they live for grades. If there are courses in the hu-manities that can be taken without risk to class standing they will line up for these, but they will not get into anything tough except science. The so-called

social sciences have become extremely popular as stand-ins for traditional learning.

The atmosphere of the liberal-arts college is being poisoned by premedical students. It is not the fault of the students, who do not start out as a necessarily bad lot. They behave as they do in the firm belief that if they behave any otherwise they won't get into medical school.

6   I have a suggestion, requiring for its implementation the following announcement from the deans of all the medical schools: henceforth, any applicant who is self-labeled as a "premed," distinguishable by his course selection from his classmates, will have his dossier placed in the third stack of three. Membership in a "premedical society" will, by itself, be grounds for rejection. Any college possessing something called a "premedical curriculum," or maintaining offices for people called "premedical advisers," will be excluded from recognition by the medical schools.

7   Now as to grades and class standing. There is obviously no way of ignoring these as criteria for acceptance, but it is the grades *in general* that should be weighed. And, since so much of the medical-school curriculum is, or ought to be, narrowly concerned with biomedical science, more attention should be paid to the success of students in other, nonscience disciplines before they are admitted, in order to assure the scope of intellect needed for a physician's work.

8   Hence, if there are to be MCAT tests,[1] the science part ought to be made the briefest, and weigh the least. A knowledge of literature and languages ought to be the major test, and the scariest. History should be tested, with rigor.

9   The best thing would be to get rid of the MCATs, once and for all, and rely instead, wholly, on the judgment of the college faculties.

10   You could do this if there were some central, core discipline, universal within the curricula of all the colleges, which could be used for evaluating the free range of a student's mind, his tenacity and resolve, his innate capacity for the understanding of human be-

---

[1]MCAT: Medical College Admission Test.

ings, and his affection for the human condition. For this purpose, I propose that classical Greek be restored as the centerpiece of undergraduate education. The loss of Homeric and Attic Greek from American college life was one of this century's disasters. Putting it back where it once was would quickly make up for the dispiriting impact which generations of spotty Greek in translation have inflicted on modern thought. The capacity to read Homer's language closely enough to sense the terrifying poetry in some of the lines could serve as a shrewd test for the qualities of mind and character needed in a physician.

11   If everyone had to master Greek, the college students aspiring to medical school would be placed on the same footing as everyone else, and their identifiability as a separate group would be blurred, to everyone's advantage. Moreover, the currently depressing drift on some campuses toward special courses for prelaw students, and even prebusiness students, might be inhibited before more damage is done.

12   Latin should be put back as well, but not if it is handled, as it ought to be, by the secondary schools. If Horace has been absorbed prior to college, so much for Latin. But Greek is a proper discipline for the college mind.

13   English, history, the literature of at least two foreign languages, and philosophy should come near the top of the list, just below Classics, as basic requirements, and applicants for medical school should be told that their grades in these courses will count more than anything else.

14   Students should know that if they take summer work as volunteers in the local community hospital, as ward aides or laboratory assistants, this will not necessarily be held against them, but neither will it help.

15   Finally, the colleges should have much more of a say about who goes on to medical school. If they know, as they should, the students who are generally bright and also respected, this judgment should carry the heaviest weight for admission. If they elect to use criteria other than numerical class standing for recommending applicants, this evaluation should hold.

16   The first and most obvious beneficiaries of this

new policy would be the college students themselves. There would no longer be, anywhere where they could be recognized as a coherent group, the "pre-meds," that most detestable of all cliques eating away at the heart of the college. Next to benefit would be the college faculties, once again in possession of the destiny of their own curriculum, for better or worse. And next in line, but perhaps benefiting the most of all, are the basic-science faculties of the medical schools, who would once again be facing classrooms of students who are ready to be startled and excited by a totally new and unfamiliar body of knowledge, eager to learn, unpreoccupied by the notions of rele-vance that are paralyzing the minds of today's first-year medical students already so surfeited by science that they want to start practicing psychiatry in the first trimester of the first year.

Society would be the ultimate beneficiary. We could look forward to a generation of doctors who have learned as much as anyone can learn, in our colleges and universities, about how human beings have always lived out their lives. Over the bedrock of knowledge about our civilization, the medical schools could then construct as solid a structure of medical science as can be built, but the bedrock would always be there, holding everything else upright. ◆

EVALUATIONS

ARY MCCARTHY, WHO HAD A LONG AND STORMY CAREER AS A THEATER and book reviewer, once wrote that most reviews that appear in newspapers are not truly evaluations. Newspaper publishers, she pointed out, depend on advertising revenue from the book publishers, so they encourage reviewers to write plot summaries and vague compliments.

I pass McCarthy's comment along because we will be dealing in this chapter with reviews of products—products of all kinds, including ice cream bars, buildings, books, and movies. Product reviews that we encounter in newspapers and magazines may or may not be true evaluations. Some are merely announcements and descriptions of new products; some seem to be (and perhaps are) rewritten press releases from the manufacturer or producer.

The difference between such announcements and a genuine evaluation is that the evaluation sorts out the various elements that determine the product's quality and takes a critical stance toward them. The logic of a true evaluation concedes from the outset that there is rarely a simple answer to the question "How good is X?" or "Is X better than Y?" Even among simple pencil sharpeners, Model X may be "best" because it is least expensive, Model Y because its mechanism is the most reliable, and Model Z because it deals most efficiently with the pencil shavings. The company accountant, for whom every decision involves primarily dollars and cents, may favor Model X. The secretaries, who have no idea how much the old model cost but remember its irritating tendency to jam, may favor Model Y. The janitor will vote for Model Z. Often an evaluator's most challenging work is to reveal the way that different frames of reference demand that different elements be evaluated. After sorting out the competing elements, the writer can either mediate among them ("The best compromise among cost, reliability, and tidiness is Model Z") or can advocate one viewpoint ("Pencil sharpeners are cheap; good secretaries are rare. Buy Model Y").

Learning to recognize the logic of evaluations may not only make you a better writer of them, but a sharper observer of the way humans behave (and misbehave) when they try to decide questions of quality.

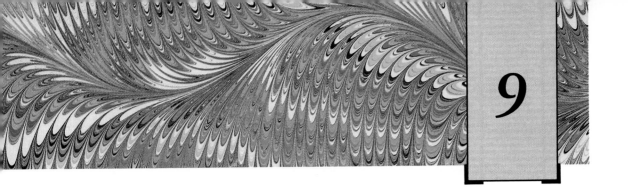

THE RANGE OF EVALUATIONS:
FROM TECHNICAL TO INTERPRETIVE

A useful way to look at the various types of evaluations is to imagine them arranged along a continuum. At the left of the line are technical evaluations that devote most of their space to presenting information new to the reader and are relatively objective in their tone. Think of reviews of automobiles, computers, or appliances as examples. At the right are interpretive evaluations. These may give bits of new information, but their primary business is to encourage the reader to see the subject from a particular perspective. In these evaluations the tone is less objective: the writer is making a distinctly personal statement about the thing evaluated. Think of reviews of films, books, and record albums—ones that seriously discuss the artistic merit or social significance of the work.

Most reviews lie between the extremes, and all must deal with both the subject being reviewed and the reviewer's frame of reference. If a review were *purely* technical, it would not be an evaluation at all, merely a description: evaluations necessarily involve a frame of reference, a value system, that makes judgment possible. Conversely, if a review were *purely* interpretive, it would be nothing but a personal statement of values, casting no clear light on the product reviewed.

In this chapter, we will work along the continuum from technical to interpretive evaluations, sampling a Consumers Union report on ice cream bars at the beginning and a controversial critique of the movie *E.T. The Extra-Terrestrial* at the end. As we examine these evaluations, we'll note ways that the writers present:

1. *Background* showing what is being evaluated and why it deserves attention.

2. *Elements* to be judged.

3. *Analysis* of the subject according to these elements.

4. A *critical stance* that establishes priorities among elements.

A TECHNICAL EVALUATION

"Ice Cream Bars for Big Kids" appeared in *Consumer Reports*, August 1989, as a five-page article with charts, diagrams, photographs, and a boxed mini-article on "novelties" that combine ice cream with candy and cookies. We'll examine the article's main line of development briefly here, omitting some parts and rearranging others.

SECTION 1: BACKGROUND INFORMATION

Because a *Consumer Reports* article must engage readers as well as inform them, "Ice Cream Bars" begins with a lead intended to draw the reader into the article by recalling pleasant memories:

"Ice Cream Bars for Big Kids"
—CONSUMER REPORTS

> Thirtysomething summers ago, the sound of bells coming down the street heralded the arrival of the Good Humor man. From every door, kids poured forth, eagerly proferring their dimes and nickels to this pied piper of *Popsicles* in anticipation of a few minutes of fast-melting pleasure on a stick.
>
> Those kids grew up, but they didn't outgrow their love of ice-cream bars. They buy more than a billion dollars worth of frozen novelties (the trade's term for single-serving goodies) each year.
>
> That's just fine with ice-cream makers: Adult-oriented frozen novelties fetch profits of 30 percent, compared with margins of 20 percent for products aimed at children. Eager to spur impulse sales, some supermarket managers have added special freezer displays right at the checkout.
>
> The products in the freezer cases range from bite-sized bonbons to bars so big and rich they might do for two. Amidst the sandwiches, cones, and sundaes, you'll find fairly plain (if rich) bars—chocolate or vanilla ice cream covered with chocolate. That's what we tested. . . .

The lead quickly takes us to statistics demonstrating that "frozen novelties" are, economically speaking, important enough to deserve some attention. The fourth paragraph looks at first like an unnecessary (or merely amusing) description of what we find in freezer cases, but from a technical point of view it serves the important purpose of defining precisely what is to be evaluated by distinguishing "plain (if rich) bars" from "bite-sized bonbons . . . sandwiches, cones, and sundaes," which lie outside the scope of the investigation. Other paragraphs in the background section discuss government standards for butterfat content and the industry's practice of fluffing up the ice cream until it is as much as 50 percent air.

Consumers Union, the publisher of *Consumer Reports,* employs a large staff of highly trained product testers. Their reports follow a reliable pattern, including an explicit identification of the elements they have investigated, the special criteria (if any) they have applied to each element, and the method of testing they used.

Taste-testing ice cream isn't one long slurpfest, though we encountered few complaints from our panel of trained tasters. For two months, those panelists sampled portions of the bars, whose identity had been concealed, under red lights to keep appearance out of the judgments. The panelists compared the bars with a host of flavor and texture benchmarks that they rechecked before each session. (Example: The benchmark for vanilla intensity was one-half teaspoon of vanilla extract dissolved in a cup of milk, heated to drive off the alcohol, and then cooled.) Our statisticians then compared the panel's descriptions to CU's criteria for excellence. . . .

The bars the panelists sampled included pricey, heavily advertised brands like *Dove Bar* and *Haagen-Dazs;* entries from such perennials as *Good Humor, Eskimo Pie, Dolly Madison,* and *Polar Bar,* and a couple of supermarket economy brands.

For the ice cream bar tests, Consumers Union adopted cost, size, calorie content, fat content, and taste as the principal elements. For the first four, the testers had no need to develop special criteria: everyone expects that lower cost will be preferable to higher and that fewer grams of fat will be preferable to more. Taste, however, creates thorny problems, especially for an organization that strives to be "objective" in its reports. To achieve objectivity, the testers created specific criteria—the desirable level of sweetness, for example, and the desirable texture. Often they associated a specific criterion with a "benchmark." Such "benchmarking" has the advantage of helping to define almost undefinable qualities. Tell me that you like a flower to smell sweet, and I may not know how sweet. Tell me that it should smell as sweet as a hyacinth, and I think I know what you mean. Benchmarks are not used in every evaluation; they are far commoner in technical reviews than in interpretive ones.

For the taste element in evaluating ice cream bars, Consumers Union established the following criteria (which I have paraphrased):

1. *Dense texture.* CU's testers note that all ice cream makers pump some air into their product to keep the ice cream from being a "thick, solidly frozen mass, not very refreshing to eat," but they object to ice cream that is too airy. They set as a standard a mixture of about 20 percent air, which "feels dense and substantial when it melts in your mouth."

2. *Thick coating.* CU deducted points for "paper-thin coating."

3. *Quick-melting coating.* The quicker the better, in CU's opinion, since quick melting delivers "a sharp burst of flavor."

4. *Intense, but not overwhelming, flavor.* The benchmark for vanilla is described above. The benchmark for chocolate in the ice cream or the coating is "the intensity of an ordinary milk chocolate bar," unless the coating is dark chocolate, in which case it might "approach the intensity of semisweet baking chocolate" without losing points. The cream flavor CU adopted as a standard was "somewhere between whole milk and cream."

5. *Moderate sweetness.* The benchmark was "four to six teaspoons of sugar dissolved in a cup of water."

6. *Absence of interfering flavors.* CU deducted points for "saltiness," "freezer taste," and other peculiarities.

7. *Absence of bitterness.* Allowing some latitude for dark chocolate coatings, CU deducted points for bitterness.

8. *Absence of iciness.* CU deducted points for "coarse, icy texture."

9. *Absence of gumminess.* CU deducted points for anything that approached the gumminess of marshmallow creme.

A wise consumer of technical evaluations learns to examine criteria carefully, since rigorous application of wrongheaded criteria will only give rigorously wrongheaded results. If Consumers Union is wrong in assuming that we like our ice cream sweet at the level of "four to six teaspoons of sugar dissolved in a cup of water" and our chocolate coating thick and free of bitterness, then their evaluation will be invalid as far as we are concerned.

EXERCISE 1

◆ *Identifying Elements and Criteria.* Suggest a set of elements appropriate to evaluating each of the following items. Name criteria where possible and appropriate:

1. Pencils for note taking.

2. Video cassette recorders.

3. Mountain bikes.

4. College-level history textbooks.

SECTION 3: ANALYSIS ACCORDING TO ELEMENTS

Consumer Reports gives its analysis of test results in both tabular form and in a written summary. The complete table for the ice cream bar tests is shown on pages 322–323. Here is the summary:

Four varieties of *Dove Bar* and three of *Haagen-Dazs* earned a rating of excellent. In fact, while a taster or two may have demurred, by the time we'd averaged all the numbers, five of those bars actually emerged with scores of 100. But if you care about your purse or your poundage, beware. Those bars cost about a dollar apiece and carry a calorie payload of over 300.

At the other end of the scale were the seven bars we rated only fair. Those products—smaller than the premium bars, sometimes by a lot—cost between 16 and 38 cents each; calories range from about 130 to 225. All three supermarket products landed in the sensory cellar.

Notice that this analysis is merely a summary of data. It is no more reliable than the criteria themselves are, and it doesn't solve the problem of which bar is best. Instead, it clarifies the conflict between elements: what is cheapest and best for us is also least flavorful. To resolve this conflict, the evaluator must leap to another level of thinking, which we are calling critical stance.

SECTION 4: CRITICAL STANCE

In a very few cases, the reviewer will find no conflict among the elements: one product will be superior in every respect. Ordinarily, however, analysis uncovers the need to make a choice among conflicting values. The *Consumer Reports* article presents its conflict directly and quickly imposes a framework of values that makes a recommendation possible.

The same stuff that makes an ice cream bar delicious also makes it fattening. Lots of butterfat and cocoa butter. Lots of sugar. Coconut oil, a tropical oil high in saturated fat, is used in the coatings to help keep the chocolate shell from falling off. Clearly, these are not desserts for the calorie-conscious or for those worried about dietary fats.

Or are they? It all depends on how you look at these products. If you're trying to limit your daily fat intake to 30 percent of all calories, as CU's medical consultants recommend, you should aim to eat no more than 67 grams of fat, evenly divided among saturated, monounsaturated, and polyunsaturated fats.

The superpremium ice cream bars each contain 20 to 31 grams of fat, most of it saturated and all of it loaded with calories. To the one out of 10 Americans who eats ice cream every day, all that fat makes the 30 percent goal well nigh impossible to achieve. To the once-a-month splurger, however, the extra fat and the extra few hundred calories may not matter. . . .

Recommendations: As long as you don't eat one every day, there's little point in economizing on adult ice cream bars, either in money or calories. You might as well do it right: Pick one of the *Dove* or *Haagen-Dazs* bars we rated excellent. While we hesitate to call them "perfect," they met every test we expected of them. If ice cream is part of your daily diet, though, look to a brand that's more moderate in calories, fat, and price. Or change your diet.

The writer here is moving so fast that readers may not notice the frameworks that are quickly rejected or accepted. First, the writer constructs what we might call the "absolute health and nutrition" framework. Within this framework, strictly applied, all ice cream bars, especially Dove and Haagen-Dazs, are unacceptable for the majority of Americans who have reason to worry about their arteries and waistlines. But this entirely rational framework is rejected by our writer. So is the "cheapest is best" framework. So, with only a slight nod, is the "least possible damage framework," which would have made Dove and Haagen-Dazs losers once more on the principle that the rational consumer who cannot resist ice cream bars should at least choose ones low in fat and calories. Instead, the writer adopts the "occasional splurge" framework, the only one likely to push Dove and Haagen-Dazs to the top. Taste is given priority over nutrition and expense. Disciplined, moderate consumption of an expensive product is presented as superior to undisciplined consumption of cheaper (and somewhat healthier) products.

I'm not sure that I disagree with the writer's choices, and I don't want to fret too much about ice cream bars, but we should pause to note two things about the nature of critical stance. First, it involves free choice: the writer takes a stand when information ceases to tell its own story. And second, like all stances involving free choice, it connects with larger systems of values. In the process of telling us that Dove and Haagen-Dazs are the best bars, Consumers Union also tells us that we should be able to control our appetitites. The step from taste-testing to moral philosophy can be sur-

Ice-cream bars

1 Product. Listed in order of sensory score; products rated equally listed alphabetically. If a product comes with a choice of chocolate coatings, we note whether it's **dark** or **milk** chocolate. All but the *Baskin Robbins* are sold in supermarkets.
2 Sensory index. Based on tests by a panel of trained tasters. We compared the

1 Product

Chocolate

Dove Bar Dark

Haagen-Dazs Dark

Dove Bar Milk

Klondike Milk

Nestle Quik Milk

Vanilla

Dove Bar Milk

Haagen-Dazs Dark

Haagen-Dazs Milk

Dove Bar Dark

Dreyer's Dark

Polar Bar Milk

Klondike Milk

Nestle Milk

Haagen-Dazs Milk with Almonds

Eskimo Pie Original Dark

Baskin Robbins Dark

Steve's Milk

Weight Watchers (ice milk)

Good Humor

Eskimo Pie Sugar Free

Dolly Madison

Eskimo Pie Dark

Freezer Pleezer

Nestle Crunch Milk

A & P

Pathmark

A & P (ice milk)

panelists' assessments of flavor and texture with CU's criteria for excellence.

3 Cost per bar. The average, based on what CU shoppers paid in New York, Georgia, Texas, and California. The expensive brands typically come only two or three to a package. Cheaper products may come as many as 10 or 12 to a package.

4 Size. Ice cream is measured by volume, in fluid ounces. Because of varying amounts of air pumped into ice cream dur-ing processing (known as overrun), this measurement is not a good guide to the weight of the ice cream.

5 Calories per bar. As measured by CU. The ingredients that make some ice-cream bars taste better than others are, sadly, the ones that add the most calories.

6 Fat per fluid ounce. The fat comes mostly from the cream, but also from coconut oil and cocoa butter used in the coating. All three contain highly saturated fats.

7 Sensory comments. The ice cream was expected to be flavorful—rich in dairy and cream flavor with distinct vanilla or chocolate notes as appropriate. The coating was also expected to be appropriately flavored, with the dairy-chocolate blend of milk chocolate or the slightly bitter, more intense taste of dark chocolate if the label so specified. We've noted the sweetness level for each bar. If you find "very sweet" too sweet, try a "sweet."

2 Sensory index (0 Poor—Excellent 100; P F G VG E)	3 Cost per bar	4 Size	5 Calories per bar	6 Fat per fl. oz.	7 Sensory comments
	$ .99	4 fl.oz.	358	6 g	Dense, flavorful ice cream; thick, intense, slightly bitter coating melts quickly. Sweet.
	1.07	3.7	385	7	Very dense, very chocolaty ice cream; thick, intense, slightly bitter coating melts quickly. Sweet.
	1.00	4	352	6	Dense, flavorful ice cream; thick, distinct milk-chocolate coating melts quickly. A bit too sweet.
	.50	5	287	4	Somewhat dense, icy ice cream; thin, somewhat coarse coating with a hint of butterscotch melts a bit slowly. Slight freezer taste. Sweet.
	.37	3	225	6	Airy, gummy, icy ice cream low in flavor; thin, somewhat coarse coating a bit low in flavor and melts a bit slowly. Freezer taste. Sweet.
	1.03	4	342	5	Dense flavorful ice cream; thick, smooth, distinct milk-chocolate coating melts quickly. Very sweet.
	1.07	3.7	377	7	Very dense, flavorful ice cream; thick, smooth, slightly bitter, intense coating melts quickly. Sweet.
	1.07	3.7	319	6	Very dense, flavorful ice cream; thick, smooth, distinct milk-chocolate coating melts quickly. Very sweet.
	.97	4	353	6	Dense, flavorful ice cream; thick, smooth, slightly bitter, intense coating melts quickly and falls off in pieces. Sweet.
	.63	4	295	5	Dense, slightly icy, flavorful ice cream; very thick, slightly bitter, intense coating melts quickly. Sweet.
	.33	3.5	234	5	Somewhat dense, slightly icy, flavorful ice cream; somewhat thick coating. Sweet.
	.50	5	294	4	Dense, slightly icy, flavorful ice cream; somewhat thick coating with a hint of butterscotch but a bit low in chocolate flavor, melts a bit slowly. Sweet.
	.97	3.7	286	5	Dense, slightly icy, flavorful ice cream; thick coating with a hint of caramel melts quickly. Very sweet.
	1.08	3.7	377	8	Very dense, flavorful ice cream; thick coating melts quickly. Almonds have intense roasted flavor but leave particles behind. Very sweet.
	.47	2.3	182	6	Somewhat dense, slightly icy ice cream a bit low in flavor; thick, slightly bitter, intense coating. Sweet.
	.84	3.5	310	6	Somewhat dense, slightly icy and gummy ice cream a bit low in dairy flavor; thick, slightly bitter, intense coating melts quickly. Slight freezer taste. Sweet.
	1.23	4.8	439	6	Dense, slightly icy, flavorful ice cream; thick, slightly rough coating a bit low in flavor, melts a bit slowly, and tends to fall off in pieces. Very sweet.
	.25	1.7	111	4	Somewhat dense, icy, gummy ice milk a bit low in flavor; thin, slightly bitter coating low in flavor. Slight freezer taste.
	.50	3	201	5	Somewhat dense, slightly icy, slightly gummy ice cream a bit low in flavor; thin, somewhat intense coating. Slight freezer taste. Sweet.
	.40	2.5	182	5	Somewhat dense, icy ice cream a bit gummy and low in flavor; thin, slightly coarse, gritty, bitter, somewhat intense coating. Slight freezer taste. Sweet.
	.33	3	197	4	Somewhat dense, icy, gummy ice cream a bit low in dairy flavor; thin, slightly bitter, somewhat intense coating melts a bit slowly. Sweet.
	.35	3	209	5	Airy, icy, gummy ice cream a bit low in flavor; thin, slightly bitter, slightly rough, somewhat intense coating. Slight freezer taste. Sweet.
	.17	2.5	147	4	Airy, icy, gummy ice cream a bit low in flavor; thin, somewhat intense coating melts a bit slowly. Slight freezer taste. Somewhat sweet.
	.38	3	190	4	Somewhat dense, icy, gummy ice cream a bit low in flavor; thin, somewhat intense coating melts a bit slowly. Slight freezer taste. Sweet.
	.20	2.5	151	4	Somewhat dense, icy, gummy ice cream a bit low in flavor; thin coating a bit low in flavor. slight freezer taste. Sweet.
	.18	2.5	151	4	Airy, very icy, slightly gummy ice cream a bit low in flavor; thin coating with low flavor. Slight freezer taste. Somewhat sweet.
	.16	2.5	131	3	Airy, very icy, gummy, slightly salty ice milk a bit low in flavor, thin coating a bit low in flavor, melts a bit slowly. Freezer taste. Sweet.

prisingly small. The step from movie criticism to moral philosophy is smaller still, as we shall soon see.

EXERCISE 2

◆ *Altering the Assumptions Used in an Evaluation.* Assume that you are writing a review of ice cream bars and that you have the same data Consumers Union did (see the chart on pages 322–323). Assume that most people eat ice cream at least twice a week and are unlikely to change their habits. Assume that you drink skim or low-fat milk and have come to find even whole milk (4 percent butterfat) unpleasantly rich. Assume that you believe this change in taste is typical of the nation. Assume that you and everyone you know prefers a slightly bitter taste in chocolate and that you have no reason to doubt this to be the general opinion. Change the ranking of the ice cream bars to fit these assumptions.

A MIDDLE CASE: CRITICAL NOTICES

We are now leaving the technical evaluation behind and moving to a middle case, one where the product reviewed is not (and perhaps cannot be) so carefully tested and benchmarked and where the writer's critical stance becomes both more obvious and more crucial. Because it is important for us to concentrate from this point forward on the critical stance of our reviewers, we will be looking at conflicting evaluations of a single product: the movie *E.T. The Extra-Terrestrial*. If you haven't seen the movie, or if your memory of it has faded, you might consider making some popcorn and doing a couple of hours of video homework.

Before we look at particular reviews, we should think in a general way about the situation of film reviewers. To begin with, the reviewer needs to consider his audience and purpose. The most common type of movie review is written largely for people who have not seen the film and want to know whether they should. Such reviews are essentially notices: they tell the reader what the film is about and give the critic's evaluation with very little explanation. An elaborate analysis would bore and would confuse those who haven't seen the film.

Pauline Kael's short review of *E.T. The Extra-Terrestrial* for the *New Yorker* is a good example of such a critical notice:

E.T.
—PAULINE KAEL

E.T. The Extra-Terrestrial—Steven Spielberg's movie is bathed in warmth and it seems to clear all the bad thoughts out of your head. It's the story of a ten-year-old boy, Elliott, who feels fatherless and lost because his parents have separated, and who finds a miraculous friend—an alien inadvertently left on Earth by a visiting spaceship. This fusion of science fiction and mythology is emotionally rounded and complete; it reminds you of the goofiest dreams you had as a kid. It puts a spell on the audience; it's genuinely entrancing. The stars are Henry Thomas, as Elliott, and

E.T., who was designed by Carlo Rambaldi. With Drew Barrymore, Robert Mac-Naughton, Dee Wallace, and Peter Coyote. The script is by Melissa Mathison.

The elements of an evaluation are present here in a very truncated form. Kael's summary of the plot and identification of the director, cast, and script writer correspond to the *background* section of "Ice Cream Bars." In this very brief review, she concentrates on a single *element* of the movie: its emotional impact. Her compact *analysis* mentions "warmth," escape from "bad thoughts," emotional completeness, and capacity to bring back the dreams of childhood: the criteria by which Kael gauges the film's emotional impact. By elevating the emotional element above all others, she has taken her *critical stance:* for her, a movie with this emotional impact, this enchantment, shouldn't be faulted for lack of social significance. Other critics, as we will see, disagree strongly.

If such reviews are written largely for the benefit of those who have not seen the film, they are also designed to be interesting to those who have. They give at least the same sort of pleasure we get from reading a newspaper account of a ball game we have watched the night before: we see the same event from a slightly different angle and relive our first experience of it. Sometimes reviews give the additional pleasure of confirming or challenging our judgment.

Consider, for example, another review of *E.T.,* this one by Robert Asahina for *The New Leader:*

E.T.
—ROBERT ASAHINA

Spielberg is . . . represented this summer by *E.T. The Extra-Terrestrial,* a film he directed and produced from Melissa Mathison's script. Again the setting is one of those nameless California suburbs that all look alike—white man's land, with two-car garages and split-level houses as far as the eyes can see. No big-city problems here, no crime, no poverty, no pollution. Children ride bikes safely in the streets; cars are used mostly for driving the kids to school and for shopping at the local mall; neighbors are friendly; families get together for pizza parties on weekend nights.

It's a pleasant fantasy, maybe actually a reality somewhere. There are, to be sure, some shadings to Spielberg and Mathison's sunny picture of suburban life: The family in question is headed by a woman, Mary (Dee Wallace, one of my favorite lost causes), whose husband has left her and their three children. Still, that seems merely a convenient way of dispensing with a dominant male who would have no place in the childlike tale that is to unfold.

For *E.T.* is really *Lassie* in science fiction drag. Elliott (Henry Thomas), Mary's younger son, finds a strange animal in the backyard, in this case not a dog but a stranded alien that looks like a cross between Yoda and a canister vacuum cleaner. Elliott takes the creature home, gives him a name ("E.T."), hides him from Mom and the mysterious, unidentified adults who are tracking him, teaches him lots of neat tricks (such as how to speak English), and loses him in a final parting that shouldn't leave a dry eye in the theater.

It nevertheless did. I was so flabbergasted by Spielberg and Mathison's transparent manipulativeness that I didn't have time to react with the mindless emotionalism that has clouded the acuity of supposedly sharp-eyed critics like Pauline Kael, who found the film "enchanting."[1] "Sappy" or "simple-minded" would be more accurate. I fail to see what is so wonderful about filming the adults (except dear Mom and a kindly scientist near the end) in half-light, from waist level, so they appear menacing. That's looking at the story from the point of view of a small child. If you're pre-teen, or have the mind of a kid, then *E.T.* is for you.

Discussing Asahina's review with a friend, I found myself saying that it is as if he and Kael had gone to different movies, but on second thought this statement misses the point entirely. What is remarkable is that the two have seen the same things and evaluated them very differently. Both saw a dreamy film: Kael pronounced this dreaminess "enchanting"; Asahina pronounced it "sappy." Both saw a "sunny" film that avoided stubborn social and psychological conflicts: Kael judged this avoidance warm and reassuring; Asahina judged it irresponsible and childish.

In terms of the four elements we have been discussing, we could characterize Asahina's review this way. His *critical stance* is inherent in everything he says: without an honest facing of the world, he implies, enchantment is no more than a refusal to grow up. Given this critical stance, a socially significant theme, one that reflects the conflicts of real life, becomes a key *element,* and the avoidance of clichéd situations and emotions becomes an important criterion for excellence. Asahina's *analysis* declares the film to be essentially one long cliché: "*Lassie* in science fiction drag." *Background* information is given throughout the review, but it is often worked in as evidence to support Asahina's view of the film: "Again the setting is one of those nameless California suburbs that all look alike—white man's land, with two-car garages and split-level houses as far as the eyes can see." Spielberg fans must have flinched when they read Asahina's sentence about the suburbs, but who could deny the accuracy of it? Asahina has played by the rules, not ignoring or distorting what actually happens in the film. He has, however, presented it in a very different framework from Kael's.

EXERCISE 3

◆ *Identifying Key Elements and Criteria.* The three passages that follow are all excerpted from positive reviews of *E.T.* The reasoning behind the reviews, however, varies—sometimes dramatically. Read each passage closely and decide what element or elements of the film are singled out as important. Identify criteria used in the discussion of these elements.

To begin with the solid foundations, screenwriter Melissa Mathison seems to know the newly separated young family, that sad American statistic, from its

---

[1] Asahina is quoting from a longer review by Kael.

cracked heart out. And at the center of this family is Elliott (the amazing young Henry Thomas, the older brother of "Raggedy Man"). At 10, he is excess baggage to his older brother Michael (Robert MacNaughton), busy with his lofty teen-age friends. He is also infinitely too old to play with his four-year-old sister, Gertie (a true enchantress, the no-nonsense Drew Barrymore), although he treats her decently enough. Of the three children, Elliott is possibly the most deeply affected by his father's recent departure; however, he is lonely and sturdy in equal parts.

The setting which director/coproducer Spielberg has picked for "E.T." is the beginning of the magic. The family lives in Spielberg's beloved, intimately understood suburbs, yet at the same time on the last frontier. Redwood forests and damp, unfolding ferns are only a bike ride away for these lucky kids. And these are magical forests: they could hold all of "Midsummer Night's Dream," or King Arthur—magic mushrooms and faerie rings.

Sheila Benson, *Los Angeles Times*

"E.T." is an affectionate anthropological document about American suburban life—thanks to the precision of each behavioral tic in the children: trading insults at the dinner table, faking a fever by holding a thermometer to the lightbulb, playing dress-up with the amiable alien. The domestic comedy . . . is observed with such fidelity it is, on its own, worth the admission price. You don't have to suspend disbelief to get involved. The three children (indistinguishable from the actors who play them) are funny and true, the Disney version of American middle-class kids brought up to date.

Their mother (Dee Wallace), recently deserted by dad, runs the household in a slightly dazed, slightly tearful, unfalteringly loving manner. Keeping unsuspecting mother and alien apart offers an opportunity for some delightful comic choreography—mother moving around the kitchen unpacking the groceries so intently she doesn't notice E.T. and knocks him flat with the refrigerator door.

Every detail adds believability to the action. Carlo Rambaldi's mechanical alien is as real as any of the other characters. A frenetic episode in which a medical team struggles to save a life is harrowing because the doctors and nurses are not actors, but the real thing.

Joseph Gelmis, *Newsday*

. . . children are the natural audience for "E.T.," which establishes Spielberg as the most amiably childlike director on the current scene. More than any other moviemaker, he understands what makes kids tick, and uses his savvy in scene after scene.

For proof, go to a daytime show and listen to pre-teens howl with glee when the friendly spaceman hides from an earthbound mother by masquerading as a stuffed animal. The glee comes partly from the harmless ruse and partly from the audience's delighted recognition of a mom—just like a real one!—who's too preoccupied with grownup affairs to keep track of her children's toys.

As the story unfolds, her obliviousness to the existence of E.T. becomes one of the movie's funniest themes. But typically for a Spielberg film, the ribbing is always goodnatured, and stops before it has time to become grating or snide.

David Sterritt, *Christian Science Monitor*

THE INTERPRETIVE EVALUATION: INCREASED ATTENTION TO THE CRITIC'S FRAME OF REFERENCE

The evaluations we have examined so far devote most of their space and attention to presenting information about the thing (ice cream bar or movie) being reviewed. But some reviews are intended more to persuade the audience to take a particular view of a thing than to inform the audience about the thing itself. Often these "interpretive" reviews address an audience already acquainted with the subject and prepared for a more challenging discussion of what its meaning and value are.

In interpretive reviews, what we have been calling the author's framework or frame of reference becomes a dominant concern. Often the writer sees the subject in light of some larger issue and produces an essay that is at least as much about the issue as about the thing reviewed. Such evaluations are not appropriate in all circumstances: a reader who picked up *Consumer Reports* to read a review of ice cream bars would be understandably irritated if the writer concentrated instead on the evils of American merchandising, using ice cream bars as an example.

Even when the thing evaluated invites interpretation (as literature, film, and architecture do) some people are irritated by reviewers who "read between the lines" or "have an ax to grind" or "don't take the thing in the spirit in which it was intended." If you are yourself inclined to feel such irritation, let me ask you to set it aside for a time and remember two things:

1. "Objectivity" in a review is probably impossible and is not always desirable. Even a carefully benchmarked review of ice cream bars, as we have seen, ultimately involves the reviewer's system of values. In the technical review these values may be hidden. In the interpretive review, they are open to inspection. This openness allows us to compare the reviewer's values to our own and to understand how the subject looks from a different perspective.

2. There is no reason to assume that the spirit in which a work is intended must always be the spirit in which it is evaluated. The person who tells a racist joke presumably intends it to be funny, but we aren't obliged to judge

Some Elements and Criteria
Commonly Used in Evaluating Films

The distinction between elements and criteria is sometimes difficult to make, and the language of critics sometimes blurs the distinction between the aspect of a film being analyzed (the element) and the standards by which that element will be evaluated (the criteria).

The following list of elements and criteria commonly used by film critics should help you keep the distinction clear. It should also be a practical help to you in completing Exercise 3 (page 326) and some of the assignments at the end of this chapter.

♦ **Theme—what the work means.** *Significance* tends to be the major criterion for this element, but critics vary greatly in what they view as significant. Some look for *psychological significance,* the revelation of important truths about our individual and private lives. Some look for *social significance,* exploration of relations among groups in society.

♦ **Emotional Impact—what the work makes us feel.** For some critics *strength* of emotion (whether comic or tragic) is the key criterion for this element; others emphasize *honesty* of emotion and may value understatement.

♦ **Story Line (or Plot)—the way the story unfolds.** Criteria include *interest, suspensefulness,* and *credibility.* These criteria may be at odds, since interest and suspense are sometimes created by manipulating events in a way that makes them seem improbable.

♦ **Characterization—the presentation of personalities.** Criteria include *realism, consistency, clarity,* and *depth.* Again, there may be conflict among these criteria, since in reality every human character is full of inconsistencies.

♦ **Acting—the projection of personality by the actor.** Criteria here are particularly hard to define. Once again, many critics value *realism* above all things. Others value a strong *"presence"* (or "star quality") that holds the audience's interest. (These criteria may be in conflict when actors have more "presence" than is realistically appropriate to the character. An actress playing a shy schoolteacher shouldn't dazzle the audience.

♦ **Cinematography—the camerawork and editing.** Cinematography includes such matters as camera angles, framing, fast- and slow-motion, lighting, and pace of the movement from scene to scene. Criteria include *visual variety coherence,* and *continuity.* There is sometimes a conflict between variety and the other two criteria. Films may be coherent but visually dull or visually varied but incomprehensible.

♦ **Sound track—the use of sound and music.** *Clarity* and *realism* are generally important criteria for the use of sound in general. Music is often discussed in terms of *appropriateness* to the situation in which it is used as well as inherent *quality.* The quality of music can, of course, be a large separate area of evaluation with its own elements and criteria. ♦

it solely on the success or failure of its humor. The medieval sculptor who created a gargoyle may have intended it as a device for warding off evil spirits, but we may judge it by standards other than magical effectiveness. The *effect* of a work may be something quite different from the *intention,* and it is not illogical for reviewers to concentrate their attention on the effect they perceive.

AN EXAMPLE OF AN INTERPRETIVE EVALUATION

Phyllis Deutsch's rather long review of *E.T.* for the film journal *Jump Cut* is clearly interpretive. It concentrates on an aspect of the movie that may have hardly crossed Spielberg's mind: its depiction of sex roles. Because I will interrupt the review to make comments, you may want to read it straight through first to follow the thread of her argument.

"*E.T.*"
—PHYLLIS DEUTSCH

Steven Spielberg's film *E.T.* is this year's biggest money-maker. T-shirts and posters all over the country celebrate the space creature, and Neil Diamond has written a song using E.T.'s memorable "phone home" as its theme. Reviews of the movie are mostly positive, and reviewers generally cite the film's make-believe ambiance and happy ending as causes for its enormous success. In doing so, they—and most of the American public—have overlooked the sexist backbone of Spielberg's superficially engaging fairytale.

Writing almost a year after the film's release, Deutsch assumes that virtually everyone reading her essay will have seen it. By emphasizing the film's overwhelming success, she accomplishes two things. First, she shows that it is a subject worthy of our consideration: a film this successful must be getting some messages across to millions of viewers, and it is worthwhile examining what they are. Second, she turns *E.T.* into a benchmark of American social attitudes: whatever attitudes it expresses are apparently acceptable to the vast majority of Americans. When Deutsch tells us that we all love this film *and* it is sexist, she creates a tension that keeps us (or at least kept me) reading.

The two paragraphs that follow are devoted to one aspect of the film's alleged sexism: its sexual stereotyping.

How convincing do you find Deutsch's argument that E.T. is "male-identified"?

Robert Asahina says that Elliott teaches E.T. to talk. Who is right? How important is the detail?

The film is explicit in the sexual stereotyping of its characters. E.T. is male-identified, even though the creature has no genitals. It is continuously referred to as "he." The first link between E.T. and Elliott is a baseball tossed back and forth; what better symbol of male bonding exists? Elliott, of course, is a little boy, his brother is a big boy, and all the children in the movie who have adventures (tinkering with telecommunications devices, fooling cops, riding flying bicycles) are boys. Elliott's sister is spunky and bright (*she* at least asks whether E.T. is a boy or girl), but she dresses up the creature, brings him flowers, and stays close to mama. Gertie also teaches E.T. to talk, but this deed (which makes the film possible) is seen as far less important than the physical machinations of the boys.

Elliott's mother, another sexist creation, represents Spielberg's traditional view of the nuclear family as a sex-segregated enterprise. Mary has moments of humor and animation, but she spends most of her time bustling over concerns of everyday life. She worries about her job, her shopping, cleaning up, cooking, and taking care of the kids. She's so intent on arranging the groceries that she disregards Gertie's attempts to introduce her to E.T., who stands just a few feet away. Later, in a Halloween costume, Mary is cute and sexy (she's dressed as some kind of catlike animal) and as giddy as ever. While photographing her three children, she fails to realize that the one in the middle has a funny voice and a flat head. Like the buffoon in a comic opera, poor Mary constantly misses the obvious.

David Sterritt says that the "ribbing" of Mary is never snide. Deutsch disagrees. Who do you think is more accurate?

Some of you who are reading this book will have been among the millions of children who crowded neighborhood theaters to watch *E.T.* in the summer of 1982. You may be saying to yourself that Phyllis Deutsch has missed the point of the movie, at least as far as its juvenile audience is concerned. *You* didn't notice this supposed stereotyping at the time; you thought that the scenes where Elliott's mother fails to notice E.T. were simply hilarious; and you are fairly certain that you have interpreted the movie the way that Spielberg intended it. But Deutsch's argument doesn't depend on your consciousness of the stereotyping or on Spielberg's intention. Her point is that, for whatever reason, the stereotyping was there, and you and your grade-school classmates were drinking it in along with the movie's humor and adventure.

The next two paragraphs extend Deutsch's point about stereotyped sex roles, in this case shifting the focus to Elliott's missing father and adult males generally.

Obviously her husband's departure exacerbates Mary's confusion. He has left the family and taken his mistress to Mexico. But Spielberg so steadily emphasizes Mary's inadequacy by caricaturing her as a frazzled housewife that the father seems to play a negligible role in the familial disaster. Following the disappearance of Elliott, a policeman grills Mary trying to find out if anything has happened in the family that might have caused her son to run away. Mary tearfully replies that her husband has gone and that "it hasn't been easy on the children." Clearly, she's the one at fault: she's at home and not doing a proper job of raising the kids. Meanwhile, daddy is free in Latin America. In the viewer's mind, daddy's departure is subliminally excusable: would you want to live with such an unstable woman?

Can you recall your own feelings about the mother and father when you first saw the movie? Do they match Deutsch's picture of the movie's effect?

The children's complete idolization of their missing father is another nail in Mary's coffin. Mike and Elliott yearn for dad ("remember how he used to take us to the ballgames?") but are not angry with him. Surely children respond to a parent's departure more complexly than this. But when Mike and Gertie tease Elliott about his goblin stories, he pouts and says, "Daddy would understand." He implies that mommy would not. In fact, Mary does grab the kids and run like hell when she first sees E.T. turning grey on her bathroom floor. This act, which strikes me as eminently sensible, immediately casts her with the other "bad" adults in the film. When she finally comes around at the end, there are intimations that it has something to do with that nice male scientist who watches over her with great sympathy. Mary gets a man, but it's unlikely she'll work any less hard, for in Spielberg's universe men don't do dishes. In this film particularly, they serve two mythological functions, both of which are embodied in the characterization of E.T.

Before we go on to those two mythological functions, let's consider the way that Deutsch deploys her evidence and her arguments. As we noted in Chapter 6, most arguments about facts, causes, and effects are essentially probabilistic arguments. That is, the author is trying to convince us that something is *likely* or *very likely* to be true, even though she can't present it as a certainty. Some of Deutsch's assertions in this paragraph may strike you as less than *very likely*. How can we be sure, for example, that Spielberg makes the departure of Elliott's father "subliminally excusable" to the average viewer? How confident are we that the "nice male scientist" won't do dishes or otherwise carry his weight in the family? When we discuss subconscious suggestions or hypothetical futures, we are generally making judgments that go beyond the data.

On the other hand, Deutsch is careful to point to the parts of the movie that her assertions are based on, particularly in the paragraph about the idolization of the father. Interpretive reviews may lack the clear criteria and benchmarks we associate with technical evaluations, but they ought not to be based on vague impressions. Evaluators should point out parts of the film (or book, or record album, or building) that are the bases of their judgments.

Now back to those "two mythological functions" that men serve and E.T. embodies.

E.T. is first of all an orphan, completely helpless being on an unknown planet. Left alone, childlike E.T. will surely get into trouble (remember his drunken stumbling around the house) or perhaps die. Casting E.T. as a little (male) child in need of help enables the director to cast his audience as mothers . . . Eternal Mothers willing to give unconditional love to a completely dependent creature. While eternal mothers are generally women, Spielberg continues his sexist motif by denying Mary that role; instead, Elliott plays Eternal Mother to E.T.'s Eternal Infant. And Elliott's treatment of E.T. nearly damns the motherhood myth by revealing its destructive underside. Elliott is extremely territorial and speaks of E.T. as his special possession and pet. The boy expends a great deal of love on the creature, but he also controls him. Elliott's love—and Elliott's control—make it unnecessary for E.T. to ever learn more than garbled English. Why grow up if mama is always there? Spielberg shows the motherhood myth—embodied in Elliott and E.T.'s relationship—as a symbiotic power game in which both parties play impossible roles. Mother suffers eternally from unrequited martyrdom and child suffers eternally from stunted growth; Spielberg may cart out the Eternal Mother to tug at our heart strings, but he quickly dissects her and puts her to rest.

But Spielberg gives the Eternal Father resounding applause. When E.T. is not a clinging infant, making mothers of us all, he is the flipside of the fantasy: the ultimate patriarch who has come to mend the fractured family and restore order in

Since Elliott is male, it would seem natural to assume that his protection and education of E.T. represents fatherhood rather than motherhood. Why do you think Deutsch links Elliott to the "Eternal Mother"?

the kingdom. Although Spielberg portrays E.T. as a comic drunk in the first part of the film, in the end he inspires reverence and awe. After all, he is a creature of profound intelligence and wisdom. He even dies and comes back to life. Is this King Arthur, Christ, and maybe even God Himself? Yes, says Spielberg, and we all cry some more, blinded by the power of a different myth, one that moves from father to king to God with sweeping grandeur and leaves a lot of troubled women in its wake. In the film, as in life, the ambiguous Eternal Mother cannot compete with the purity, serenity, and wisdom of the Eternal Father, who gracefully casts a spell and quietly resolves all. Never mind that underneath is a whimpering boy-child, incapable of growing up. Never mind that underneath is Elliott's real father, who skips town when the going gets rough.

In these two paragraphs Deutsch views Spielberg's movie in light of myths concerning sex roles: Eternal Mother, Eternal Infant, Eternal Father. Anthropologists tell us that all cultures have myths that create patterns of behavior and belief, and that such myths often seem so "natural" to the members of their culture that they do not notice them. Are the myths Deutsch mentions at work in our culture and in the movie? She would have great difficulty proving absolutely that they are. She can only report Spielberg's presentation of E.T. and Elliott in a way that helps us see the connections that *she* sees between th' character and the archetypes. She can suggest what she couldn't positiv' prove to a skeptical reader: that Spielberg is relying on and strengthenir' mythology that justifies male domination. Notice that in the "Eternal F' paragraph, Deutsch's concerns spread well beyond this particular mo' is troubled by the tales of King Arthur and the Knights of the Rou' which certainly do present a society dominated by men, and she is ' Christian theology, which traditionally presents God as a mal' a male the savior of the world. It is all, Deutsch implies, pa' story.

Not all readers will accept every aspect of Deutsch's 'ed when she "archetypal" criticism. I find myself more irritated than ' nyone who has tells us that Elliott is presented as a nagging Mother. 'ted mythologies heard and understood feminist criticism of male-d' they are present should now be at least willing to consider the possib' to present a male-in Spielberg's film. Spielberg may never have in' noticed that one was dominated mythology, and most viewers may n' r's intention or the pub-presented. Deutsch is not concerned with the ' hat she perceives to be the lic's conscious reaction. She is concerned wi' of children.
movie's effect, particularly its effect on the ' ents for the positive aspects of

Deutsch's conclusion balances com' in her introduction:
the film with a return to the ideas prese'

Spielberg knows his stuff, no doubt ' ut that. Reviewers have praised the film's
inventiveness and originality, but it's ' hoax. The movie moves so fast, the images
are so dramatic, and the sound tra' is so loud that we miss the sexist fireworks on

display. What's really a shame is that there is much in these mythologies worth preserving: the emphasis on love, benevolence, and trust; the belief that wonder still exists, as do miracles; the implication that there are meeting grounds for strangers of all kinds. Spielberg could be a true visionary but is hampered by his passion for mythologies that separate human beings according to sex and perpetuate unequal power (and hence, love) relations among them. E.T. as characterized is a "he" who will always be taken care of by some loving mother because of his obvious vulnerability but who, at the same time, maintains the whip of control by dint of greater wisdom.

Movies like this are not a balm in our impossible times; they simply make matters worse by repeating the crimes that got us here in the first place. We should all stop believing in fairies until someone makes a film in which little girls have adventures on bicycles, too.

Deutsch's review is obviously highly partisan: it tells us at least as much about her frame of reference, her ideology, as it does about the movie. To use a term often heard in academic and intellectual circles, it is a feminist "reading" of the movie. If you searched hard, you might also find Marxist, psychoanalytical, theological, environmentalist, civil libertarian, and neoconservative "readings" of it. Any film, book, building, muscial composition, or public statement that attracts a great deal of attention will be "read" from angles that would surprise the writer or creator. The artist who believes himself to be producing a comedy may be surprised to find it reviewed as a political statement or a revelation of his psyche.

To some, this is a distressing state of affairs, but it is also a stimulating writing an interpretive evaluation, a critic like Deutsch allows us to see subject from a fresh perspective. By bringing her strong convictions the subject she evaluates, she enriches the public debate about what we should live in. She gives our minds a workout. By its nature, evaluation is unlikely to change the opinion of the world we agree with some aspects of it, it will begin to change the which we view events. If we disagree with it, we have a iting an interpretation of our own.

EXERCISE 4

◆ *Evaluating the controversial assertions in an Interpretive Evaluation.* List at least six assertions as being (iDeutsch makes about *E.T.* Classify each of these r opinion)

0. Impossible to evalu

1. Almost certainly false.

2. Probably false.

3. About as likely to be true as false.

4. Probably true.

5. Almost certainly true.

Give your reasons for placing each sertion where you do.

MARY McCARTHY

". . . the writer must be, first of all, a listener and observer, who can pay attention to reality, like an obedient pupil, and who is willing, always, to be surprised by the messages reality is sending through to him."

Mary McCarthy was orphaned at the age of six and for several years was "cared for" by pious relatives who were capable of disciplining children by making them stand for three hours in the snow or beating them regularly with a razor strop. Such abuses in the name of charity may have sharpened McCarthy's eye for hypocrisies of every kind—for every discrepancy between what people say and what they do.

As a writer, she became known for a frankness that sometimes became combativeness. She initially made a name for herself as a book and theater reviewer, praising and criticizing without any attention to the reputation of writers or actors. She accused other reviewers of timidity and also of lacking what we are here calling a "critical stance." Of critics writing for *The Saturday Review* and *The New York Times Book Review* she said, "they have been occupied in reducing the mountainous land of literature to a smooth, horizontal surface."

Critic Edmund Wilson, the second of her four husbands, encouraged her to write fiction, but her frankness seemed incompatible with the practice of writing about made-up worlds. As a result, she adopted a literary style that took, as she said, "real plums and put them in an imaginary cake." Her seven novels are filled with satirical, thinly disguised portraits of people she knew, including herself. In her memoirs, *Memories of a Catholic Girlhood* and *How I Grew,* she used her novelistic talent, her humor, and her habit of honest self-scrutiny to give a remarkably clear picture of her coming of age.

Critics of McCarthy often talked about her "cold eye" and "acid tongue," and in the 1960s and 1970s she put both of these to work in reports that condemned the Vietnam War and excoriated the Nixon administration during the Watergate hearings. Age did not tame her. Toward the end of her life she was sued for libel after calling her old friend Lillian Hellman an "utter liar." Hellman's death before the trial commenced deprived McCarthy of an eagerly awaited opportunity to do battle once again for her version of the truth. ◆

WRITING EVALUATIONS: POINTS TO CONSIDER

Two questions you will face early in the process of writing an evaluation are (1) what sort of readers you are trying to reach and (2) how you hope your review will affect them. Do you, like the typical writer of a technical evaluation, intend primarily to present information to the reader who is not acquainted with the product you are evaluating? Or do you, like the typical writer of an interpretive evaluation, intend to review something familiar to your readers from an angle they may not have considered?

If your evaluation is essentially a technical review (of a new product, for instance), then you will need to think about such questions as the following:

1. How much background do I need to give readers so that they can understand the nature and significance of the product? Will I need to do research before I can write a background section?

2. What are the elements the reader will expect to see evaluated? Is it safe to ignore some of these, or must they all be dealt with before my evaluation is complete?

3. For the elements that I include in the evaluation, are there established criteria or benchmarks of quality? If so, can I use them? If not, what criteria shall I use?

4. Would my evaluation be more convincing if I constructed tests similar to those used in *Consumer Reports?* If so, are such tests feasible? Can they be constructed scientifically enough to produce credible data?

5. If there is a conflict between elements evaluated, what stance will I adopt to justify favoring one element over others? If there is no conflict, am I merely stating the obvious rather than producing an evaluation that someone would want to read?

If your review is less technical than interpretive, you will face a somewhat different set of questions:

1. How much background or summary is necessary to refresh or improve the reader's knowledge of the subject itself?

2. Among the elements that might be used to evaluate a product or creation of this kind, which will I feature and which will I ignore or minimize? Will readers feel that this selection is justified by my purpose, or will they feel that I have selected elements at random?

3. In evaluating the elements I select, are there any criteria or benchmarks that I can use? Can I, for instance, compare my subject to another subject of the same sort ("*E.T.*'s stereotyping of sex roles is as absolute as that in the 1942 classic *Casablanca*")? Or can I mention the reactions of the audience ("Everyone in the audience, including mothers, laughed when Mary smashed E.T. with the refrigerator door")?

4. Is the critical stance that I will take a significant one, socially or artistically? Am I sufficiently committed to it to write with conviction?

QUESTIONS FOR PEER REVIEW

When you have completed a draft of your evaluation, you may describe your intended audience to your peer reviewer and ask the following questions:

1. Have I given enough background on the subject to keep my reader from being lost? Does the background establish the subject's significance?

2. Do you feel that I have focused on the pertinent elements to be evaluated? Have I omitted elements that you feel should be included?

3. Have I persuaded you to accept my evaluation for each of the elements discussed? Where I have provided criteria or benchmarks, do they seem to be sensible ones? Where I have not provided them, do you feel that I should? If I have constructed tests for an element, do the tests seem valid?

4. Have I identified conflicts between the elements? If not, have I simply missed a conflict that you can point out to me?

5. Is my critical stance clear and consistent? Does it justify my elevating the importance of the element or elements I emphasize in the evaluation?

6. Have I given my audience useful information or given them a fresh perspective on the subject?

You may also want your reader to respond to the general peer-review questions listed on pages 65–66.

ASSIGNMENTS FOR CHAPTER 9

ASSIGNMENT 1: *A Technical Evaluation*

Examine the reviews of new products that appear in such magazines as *Consumer Reports* and *Consumer Digest*. Write an evaluation that resembles these in format. Be explicit about the elements evaluated and the criteria or benchmarks used. To keep from becoming mired in difficult-to-interpret facts and figures or technically complex tests, you may want to evaluate a very simple group of products, such as

1. Two or three types of ballpoint pens.

2. Two or three types of disposable cups.

3. The hamburgers or fries served at two fast-food restaurants.

4. Backpacks, briefcases, or other carryalls for students.

5. Two or three varieties of apples.

While these may strike you as trivial subjects, it is worth remembering that the design or development of each of them was a matter of importance to someone's career and that each must make its way in a competitive market.

ASSIGNMENT 2: *A Brief "Notice" Review of a Movie, Book, or Record Album*

Remembering that the writer of a "notice" review is simultaneously introducing a product and evaluating it, write a brief review of a record, book, or film, appropriate for publication in a national magazine. Gene Santoro's review of *Graceland* (page 344), Robert Asahina's of *E.T.* (page 325), or any of the reviews of *The Writing Life* (page 354) can serve as models for balancing information and evaluation.

ASSIGNMENT 3: *An Interpretive Evaluation of an Advertisement*

Advertisements, as many commentators have pointed out, do much more than sell a particular product. Like books, films, and television programs, they can be seen as self-contained works of art telling (or implying) stories to millions

How do you spin stories about the ones that got away now that you're miles apart?

Get your best friend on the line.

Growing up meant sharing every moment. Every childhood dream. Like the size of the fish you didn't catch, or what was the best excuse for being late for supper.

Even moving away didn't keep you apart because you count on AT&T Long Distance Service to keep you close. You can share your thoughts on everything from getting a raise to raising children of your own. And with AT&T's clear connections, you'll feel like you're right back home again.

Reach out and touch someone.®

AT&T
The right choice.

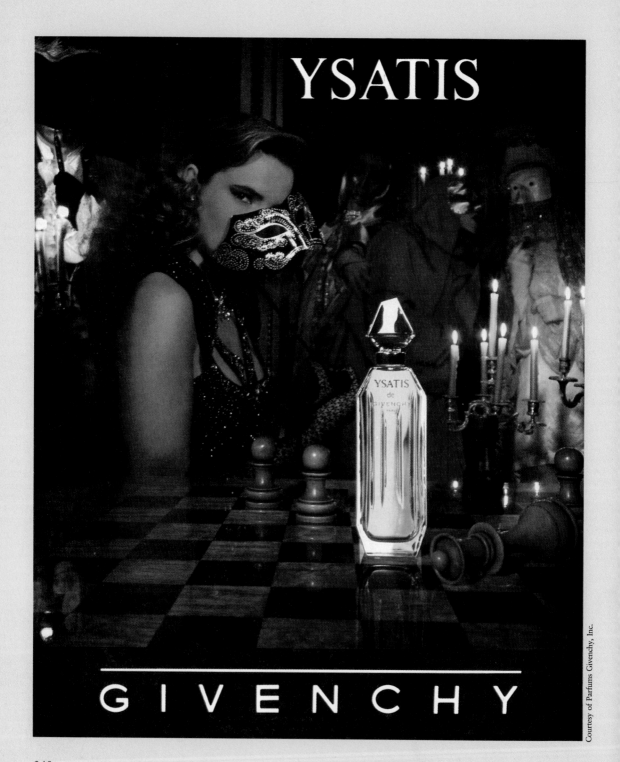

YSATIS

GIVENCHY

of people. Assume that you are a writer for a monthly journal called *Messages*. You write a short column (about 350 words) in which you evaluate one advertisement currently running in a popular magazine. Your purpose is not to evaluate the product, but to evaluate the social content of the advertisement: what it says about how we live or how we should live. Some months your review features an ad you applaud, sometimes one you condemn. On pages 339 and 340, you will find two advertisements that are potentially reviewable. Write a column about one of them or about an ad you choose yourself.

ASSIGNMENT 4: *AN INTERPRETIVE REVIEW OF A MOVIE, POEM, OR STORY*

Remembering that the purpose of the interpretive review is to alter your reader's understanding or evaluation of a subject, write such a review of a film, poem, or story you believe your teacher and classmates are familiar with. You may find a subject among poems and stories collected on pages 381–403 of this book.

ASSIGNMENT 5: *A STUDY OF THE CRITICAL RECEPTION OF A BOOK OR FILM*

Choose a major book or film: one for which you can find at least three interpretive evaluations that take critical stances significantly different from each other. Write an essay in which you review these reviews, explaining as clearly as you can how and why the critics differ. (*Book Review Digest* and *Film Review Annual*, both available in most college libraries, can serve as starting points for research.)

MARKET RESEARCH IN THE GENERAL STORE

Noel Perrin

Noel Perrin teaches English at Dartmouth College, ranches, farms, and writes essays for a variety of publications. Simply reading the titles of his collections of essays gives some sense of his commitment to country living: A Passport Secretly Green *(1961),* First Person Rural *(1978),* Second Person Rural *(1980), and* Third Person Rural *(1983). The essay below is from* First Person Rural.

1   ABOUT FIFTEEN MONTHS AGO, THE BEST Foods Company made a big splash with a series of TV ads about pancake syrup. They filmed the ads in Vermont. In them, native after native was shown tucking into two samples of pancake, and then saying that he or she preferred the one soaked in a Best Foods product called Golden Griddle to the one soaked in Vermont maple syrup.

2   These ads upset a lot of people in Vermont, including the Attorney General, who got an injunction against them. They also upset me. Because if Golden Griddle was really better, why was I working so hard every spring? Why was I hanging sap buckets, gathering, boiling, falling into snow drifts, when I could just as well be down working at a Best Foods factory in New Jersey? So I decided to check this matter out.

3   The first thing I did was to buy a bottle of Golden Griddle. That is, I bought a plastic container filled with a mixture of sugar, dextrose syrup, corn syrup, sodium benzoate, potassium sorbate, natural and artificial flavors, and caramel coloring. Plus 3%

maple syrup. The next Sunday morning I had my wife serve me two identical pancakes, just as in the TV ads. One was covered with Golden Griddle and one with my own maple syrup.

4   I had no trouble telling them apart. The Golden Griddle had a nice color, and it's certainly sweet enough. But it had quite a perceptible chemical taste. I voted the maple syrup first by a wide margin. Then I gave the test to her and our daughters. Same results.

5   This was such fun that the following Sunday morning we decided to do it again. We invited two couples to breakfast, old friends who happen to be fellow sugarers. Four more votes for maple syrup. Maple syrup now ahead eight to nothing.

6   By now it looked pretty suspicious. How come all the Vermonters in the TV ads like Golden Griddle better, and all the ones we tried like maple syrup better? But before deciding that Best Foods was pulling a fast one, we decided to wait one more Sunday. This time we invited some other old friends—father, mother, and two teenage children—who must be

something like eighth and ninth generation Vermonters. We were not expecting the result. Three votes for Golden Griddle, one for maple syrup.

7   The three who had picked Golden Griddle were pretty unhappy about it, being good Vermonters. Naturally we spent the rest of breakfast discussing what made them choose it, and doing more tasting. All three finally decided it was because Golden Griddle has such a strong flavor.

8   At this point I developed a theory. As anyone who has read this far knows, maple syrup comes in three grades called Fancy, A, and B, with progressively stronger tastes. There's also a fourth variety, stronger still, which never appears in retail stores. Officially, it's called 'ungraded syrup,' but locally everyone calls it Grade C.

9   I had been using Fancy at the three Sunday breakfasts. What if I had used B or C? Would the father and the two kids in that family have still preferred Golden Griddle? I decided I would run a much bigger test, this time using two kinds of maple syrup as well as Golden Griddle. But first I would find out exactly what Best Foods had done, so I could compare my results to theirs as accurately as possible.

10   After quite a lot of writing and phoning, I learned that they had hired a New York market research company called Decisions Center, Inc., to come to Vermont and do the whole thing. Decisions Center had done a good and careful job. They spent three days testing 223 people, of whom 58% had preferred Golden Griddle, 40% had chosen maple syrup, and 2% hadn't been able to decide. And, sure enough, they had used a mild Grade A syrup from a big producer down in Windsor County. I know him. The only possibly sneaky thing in the whole operation was done by Best Foods itself, not the market researchers. The tests were given in a shopping center in the little industrial city of Springfield, Vermont. The people tested were naturally mostly from Springfield. But when it came time to make the folksy commercials, all these city people were taken over to Newfane, a picture-postcard village, so the background would look more rural and authentic. But that's probably normal advertising technique.

The first free day I had, I hustled down to Windsor County and bought a quart of the identical Grade A syrup they had used. Then I opened an old mayonnaise jar of my own Grade C, picked up the bottle of Golden Griddle, and set off for the shopping center in my town. That is, I walked over to the general store. All one morning, my daughter Amy and I sat at a table in the Village Store in Thetford Center and ran tests. Forty people tried our three samples. That represents everyone who came into the store that morning, except a few on diets and two who have diabetes.

12   What we found was fascinating. About a quarter of the human race have naturally good palates— or, at any rate, a quarter of the people in our test did. That is, about a quarter of the people we tested not only had a preference, but could identify the different syrups by taste. After the test they'd say Sample 1 is early-run maple, Sample 2 ain't maple syrup at all, and Sample 3 must be end of the season. They were right.

13   All nine people who could identify the samples put the Grade A first. All but one of them put the Golden Griddle last. They hated it. Elmer Brown, for example, who runs Brown's Nursery, and is a native of northern Vermont. The minute he tasted Sample 2, he looked at me accusingly and said, 'Why, Noel, that one's got Karo in it.'

14   Of the other 31, three liked the Grade A best, thirteen liked Grade C best, and fifteen liked Golden Griddle best. So my test results are as follows. One hundred per cent of the people with good palates preferred maple syrup, and so did 52% of the people without good palates.

15   But I don't see any great surprise in that. Why wouldn't they? Maple syrup is free from potassium sorbate and sodium benzoate; it has absolutely no synthetic smell. The important finding, as I see it, is that 90.3% of the people with untrained palates wanted a powerful flavor. Something really strong. What I interpret this to mean is that if you're a gourmet, it's well worth getting Fancy or Grade A maple syrup. Maybe even if you just *want* to be one. But if you're not and don't care whether you ever are,

you're wasting your money. Being a maple producer, I am hardly going to suggest that you therefore get Golden Griddle or Log Cabin or Vermont Maid (which seems actually to be made in Winston-Salem, North Carolina). Instead I suggest you get a good hearty grade B, and save $2 a gallon. Or since you won't find it in any store, write to some farmer and get a gallon of Grade C direct from him. It currently costs about $9 a gallon, which isn't all that much more than the supermarket stuff. Golden Griddle, Log Cabin, etc., if you ever bought a whole gallon at once, would run you between $6.50 and $7.50.

You don't know a farmer to write? I know lots, and I have an obliging publisher. If you write me care of him, I will undertake to pass orders on. For Fancy, A, B, or C. After all, I'm not plugging my own syrup. What with those tests and my regular customers, not to mention making 300 maple sugar hearts for our village fair last summer,[1] I'm sold out. ◆

PAUL SIMON'S GRACELAND

Gene Santoro

Reviews of record albums or concerts present special problems for both the reader and the writer. A book reviewer can easily quote a passage in order to clarify a point, but (unless the review is to be broadcast) music reviewers cannot replay musical passages. Nonetheless, they can put musical works into larger frameworks. This is what Gene Santoro, a regular reviewer for The Nation, Rolling Stone, *and* Down Beat, *does in his review of* Graceland *(*Down Beat, *December 1986).*

1   TOWARD THE END OF SIMON AND GARFUN-kel's long career, Paul Simon began dabbling in different sounds to color that rather monochromatic duo's music: *El Condor Pasa* drew on Andean panpiping, while *Bridge Over Troubled Waters* elaborated on gospel changes and a key religious image. On his own over the years, Simon extended his attempts to refract his ideas through a prism of styles: jubilee spirituals (*Loves Me Like A Rock*), salsa (*Me And Julio Down By The Schoolyard*), second-line soul (*Take Me To the Mardi Gras*).

2   But none of these previous dips into generic crosscurrents matches the total immersion on *Graceland,* a release that's as catchy and danceable as its implications are provocative. Deftly juggling a variety of South African styles, American r&b and c&w, zydeco (courtesy of Rockin' Dopsie on *That Was Your Mother*), Tex-Mex-flavored rock & roll (via Los Lobos on *All Around The World Or The Myth Of Fingerprints*), and Tin Pan Alley tunesmithing, Simon hasn't so much fused his elements as he has created a musical space they all inhabit as neighbors. And they interact, just like in the real world, where latin polyrhythms collide with American r&b to produce zydeco, or with eastern European polkas to spawn Texas two-steps, where congas and talking drums nestle next to c&w in Sunny Ade's juju, where funk gives birth to Afrobeat. It's a process as old as the hills.

3   The various ironic tensions Simon sets up, however, are very much of our time. "These are the days of miracle and wonder/This is the long-distance call,"

---

[1] I made them out of the rest of my Grade C. Personally, I wouldn't dream of putting C on pancakes. As syrup, I only like Fancy, A, and B. [author's note]

he sings over the loping lead bass of *The Boy in The Bubble,* but the miracles include lasers in the jungle, babies with baboon hearts, and modern terrorism ("The bomb in the baby carriage/was wired to the radio"). For the title track, the Nashville-via-Nigeria pedal steel of Sunny Ade's Demola Adepoju entwines with the Everly Brothers' harmonies to float behind lyrics that first metaphorically relate the bottleneck Delta blues and the Civil War—the opening struggle against American apartheid—and then seek to transcend the glitzy reality of Elvis' residence under the pressure of loss: "Losing love is like a window in your heart/Everybody sees you're blown apart/Everybody sees the wind blow."

That dialog—or lack of it—between the historical and the introspective powers the lyrics over a collection of dance grooves that chatter with guitar crosstalk while the lead vocal spouts inconclusive cocktail party exchanges (*I Know What I Know*), stride to a ska-ish Zulu walking beat tickled by accordion (*Gumboots,* which are the shoes worn by South African miners), or sway to a gentle guitar lick stung on the chorus by the stuttering Tower of Power horns (*Diamonds On The Soles Of Her Shoes*), as New York City street scenes commingle with reminders of one of South Africa's prime money-making industries.

And so on. Without ever making any direct political statements, without ever abandoning the infectious musicality that first drew him into this project, Simon demonstrates that apartheid—apartness—is not only racist and stupid but ultimately untenable in a shrinking world whose confluent cultures create cross-currents as rich as these. And by returning home for the last two cuts with Dopsie and Los Lobos, he brings us face to face with the implications of the music—and ourselves. ◆

SLAVERY, FREEDOM, AND ARCHITECTURE

John Ruskin

As we saw in the case of the Consumer Reports *evaluation of ice cream bars, even the most carefully "objective" evaluation tends at some point to become involved with more general issues of how people should live. John Ruskin (1819–1900), probably the most influential English art critic of his time, was also one of the most outspoken critics of the selfishness and greed he saw in modern society. The following passage from his multivolume* The Stones of Venice *(1851–53) begins with an allusion to an earlier section of the work, in which he says that the nature of a building's ornamentation is inextricably connected with politics.*

*I*N THE 13TH AND 14TH PARAGRAPHS OF CHAPter XXI. of the first volume of this work, it was noticed that the systems of architectural ornament, properly so called, might be divided into three:—1. Servile ornament, in which the execution or power of the inferior workman is entirely subjected to the intellect of the higher;—2. Constitutional ornament, in which the executive inferior power is, to a certain point, emancipated and independent, having a will of its own, yet confessing its inferiority and rendering

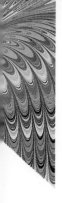

obedience to higher powers;—and 3. Revolutionary ornament, in which no executive inferiority is admitted at all. I must here explain the nature of these divisions at somewhat greater length.

Of Servile ornament, the principal schools are the Greek, Ninevite, and Egyptian; but their servility is of different kinds. The Greek master-workman was far advanced in knowledge and power above the Assyrian or Egyptian. Neither he nor those for whom he worked could endure the appearance of imperfection in anything; and, therefore, what ornament he appointed to be done by those beneath him was composed of mere geometrical forms,—balls, ridges, and perfectly symmetrical foliage,— which could be executed with absolute precision by line and rule, and were as perfect in their way, when completed, as his own figure sculpture. The Assyrian and Egyptian, on the contrary, less cognizant of accurate form in anything, were content to allow their figure sculpture to be executed by inferior workmen, but lowered the method of its treatment to a standard which every workman could reach, and then trained him by discipline so rigid, that there was no chance of his falling beneath the standard appointed. The Greek gave to the lower workman no subject which he could not perfectly execute. The Assyrian gave him subjects which he could only execute imperfectly, but fixed a legal standard for his imperfection. The workman was, in both systems, a slave.

Rozine Mazin, Agence TOP

3   But in the mediæval, or especially Christian, system of ornament, this slavery is done away with altogether; Christianity having recognized, in small things as well as great, the individual value of every soul. But it not only recognizes its value; it confesses its imperfection, in only bestowing dignity upon the acknowledgment of unworthiness. That admission of lost power and fallen nature, which the Greek or Ninevite felt to be intensely painful, and, as far as

might be, altogether refused, the Christian makes daily and hourly contemplating the fact of it without fear, as tending, in the end, to God's greater glory. Therefore, to every spirit which Christianity summons to her service, her exhortation is: Do what you can, and confess frankly what you are unable to do; neither let your effort be shortened for fear of failure, nor your confession silenced for fear of shame. And it is, perhaps, the principal admirableness of the Gothic schools of architecture, that they thus receive the results of the labour of inferior minds; and out of fragments full of imperfection, and betraying that imperfection in every touch, indulgently raise up a stately and unaccusable whole.

But the modern English mind has this much in common with that of the Greek, that it intensely desires, in all things, the utmost completion or perfection compatible with their nature. This is a noble character in the abstract, but becomes ignoble when it causes us to forget the relative dignities of that nature itself, and to prefer the perfectness of the lower nature to the imperfection of the higher; not considering that as, judged by such a rule, all the brute animals would be preferable to man, because more perfect in their functions and kind, and yet are always held inferior to him, so also in the works of man, those which are more perfect in their kind are always inferior to those which are, in their nature, liable to more faults and shortcomings. For the finer the nature, the more flaws it will show through the clearness of it; and it is a law of this universe, that the best things shall be seldomest seen in their best form. The wild grass grows well and strongly, one year with another; but the wheat is, according to the greater nobleness of its nature, liable to the bitterer blight. And therefore, while in all things that we see or do, we are to desire perfection, and strive for it, we are nevertheless not to set the meaner thing, in its narrow accomplishment, above the nobler thing, in its mighty progress; not to esteem smooth minuteness above shattered majesty; not to prefer mean victory to honourable defeat; not to lower the level of our aim, that we may the more surely enjoy the complacency of success. But, above all, in our dealings with the souls of other men, we are to take care how we check, by severe requirement or narrow caution, efforts which might otherwise lead to a noble issue; and, still more, how we withhold our admiration from great excellencies, because they are mingled with rough faults. Now, in the make and nature of every man, however rude or simple, whom we employ in manual labour, there are some powers for better things: some tardy imagination, torpid capacity of emotion, tottering steps of thought, there are, even at the worst; and in most cases it is all our own fault that they *are* tardy or torpid. But they cannot be strengthened, unless we are content to take them in their feebleness, and unless we prize and honour them in their imperfection above the best and most perfect manual skill.

Rozine Mazin, Agence TOP

And this is what we have to do with all our labourers; to look for the *thoughtful* part of them, and get that out of them, whatever we lose for it, whatever faults and errors we are obliged to take with it. For the best that is in them cannot manifest itself, but in company with much error. Understand this clearly: You can teach a man to draw a straight line, and to cut one; to strike a curved line, and to carve it; and to copy and carve any number of given lines or forms, with admirable speed and perfect precision; and you find his work perfect of its kind: but if you ask him to think about any of those forms, to consider if he

cannot find any better in his own head, he stops; his execution becomes hesitating; he thinks, and ten to one he thinks wrong; ten to one he makes a mistake in the first touch he gives to his work as a thinking being. But you have made a man of him for all that. He was only a machine before, an animated tool.

And observe, you are put to stern choice in this matter. You must either make a tool of the creature, or a man of him. You cannot make both. Men were not intended to work with the accuracy of tools, to be precise and perfect in all their actions. If you will have that precision out of them, and make their fingers measure degrees like cog-wheels, and their arms strike curves like compasses, you must unhumanize them. All the energy of their spirits must be given to make cogs and compasses of themselves. All their attention and strength must go to the accomplishment of the mean act. The act of the soul must be bent upon the finger-point, and the soul's force must fill all the invisible nerves that guide it, ten hours a day, that it may not err from its steely precision, and so soul and sight be worn away, and the whole human being be lost at last—a heap of sawdust, so far as its intellectual work in this world is concerned; saved only by its Heart, which cannot go into the form of cogs and compasses, but expands, after the ten hours are over, into fireside humanity. On the other hand, if you will make a man of the working creature, you cannot make a tool. Let him but begin to imagine, to think, to try to do anything worth doing; and the engine-turned precision is lost at once. Out come all his roughness, all his dulness, all his incapability; shame upon shame, failure upon failure, pause after pause: but out comes the whole majesty of him also; and we know the height of it only when we see the clouds settling upon him. And, whether the clouds be bright or dark, there will be transfiguration behind and within them.

6 And now, reader, look round this English room of yours, about which you have been proud so often, because the work of it was so good and strong, and the ornaments of it so finished. Examine again all those accurate mouldings, and perfect polishings, and unerring adjustments of the seasoned wood and tempered steel. Many a time you have exulted over them,

and thought how great England was, because her slightest work was done so thoroughly. Alas! if read rightly, these perfectnesses are signs of a slavery in our England a thousand times more bitter and more degrading than that of the scourged African, or helot Greek. Men may be beaten, chained, tormented, yoked like cattle, slaughtered like summer flies, and yet remain in one sense, and the best sense, free. But to smother their souls within them, to blight and hew into rotting pollards the suckling branches of their human intelligence, to make the flesh and skin which, after the worm's work on it, is to see God,[1] into leathern thongs to yoke machinery with,—this it is to be slave-masters indeed; and there might be more freedom in England, though her feudal lords' lightest words were worth men's lives, and though the blood of the vexed husbandman dropped in the furrows of her fields, than there is while the animation of her multitudes is sent like fuel to feed the factory smoke, and the strength of them is given daily to be wasted into the fineness of a web, or racked into the exactness of a line.

And, on the other hand, go forth again to gaze 7 upon the old cathedral front, where you have smiled so often at the fantastic ignorance of the old sculptors: examine once more those ugly goblins, and formless monsters, and stern statues, anatomiless and rigid; but do not mock at them, for they are signs of the life and liberty of every workman who struck the stone; a freedom of thought, and rank in scale of being, such as no laws, no charters, no charities can secure; but which it must be the first aim of all Europe at this day to regain for her children. ◆

---

[1] Job xix, 26. [author's note]

LEARNING TO LOVE MA BELL'S NEW BUILDING

Ellen Posner

As the architecture critic for The Wall Street Journal, *Ellen Posner faces the difficult task of writing evaluations suitable for a very mixed audience, some of whom know a great deal about architecture, but most of whom know very little. Her technique in the following review (published in the* Journal, *October 12, 1983) is to explain the critical elements in the controversy over the building, to represent both sides fairly, and then to pronounce her own judgment. This technique can be useful whenever the reviewer is asking a reader to explore unfamiliar territory.*

1 NEARLY SIX YEARS AGO, WHEN PHILIP Johnson and John Burgee first made public their design for American Telephone and Telegraph Co.'s new corporate headquarters on Madison Avenue, critics responded with alarm, calling the proposed building any number of unkind names, including a grandfather's clock, a Renaissance Revival pay phone, and a Chippendale highboy.[1] When built, they warned, it would be a post-modern joke at the city's expense. Today, the building itself, 42 stories of finely worked pinkish-beige granite, topped by a pediment that is decidedly more Greek than Chippendale, is nearly complete. It already has tenants on three floors, and should be formally open and fully occupied by January.

2 Viewed from the middle distance of the Queensboro Bridge among the clustered towers on the Manhattan skyline, AT&T looks relatively small (it is about half the height of the Empire State Building and hundreds of feet shorter than the nearby Chrysler and Citicorp buildings), yet it stands out immediately with a strong personality of its own, both dignified and exciting. At street level, the AT&T building already is

[1] Chippendale highboy: a tall chest of drawers with an ornamental crown, based on furniture designed by Thomas Chippendale (1718–79).

drawing crowds: People stop frequently to look at it and to walk with obvious pleasure through the Italianate lobby.

3 Some members of New York's architectural community have still not been won over. One well-known architect, unwilling to offend Mr. Johnson by speaking on the record, called AT&T an environmental mistake. Most skyscrapers, he said, contribute to our experience of a city as a public environment by conforming to zoning regulations that require buildings to be set back as they rise in height in order to let light reach the street. But AT&T (because of a special permit from the City Planning Commission) rises straight up on all sides, without a setback. The same architect commented that it was "no accident" that Mr. Johnson appeared on the cover of the *New York Times Magazine* "fondling the model" as if it were an independent sculptural object, not a part of the city. "It was presented as if it were a Greek temple," he said. "And it is not."

4 The AT&T building is, however, relatively narrow. The space behind it is a pedestrian area open to the side streets and covered by a barrel-vaulted glass roof that connects the building to a four-story annex. Since part of the lot remains virtually unoccupied by

architecture and part contains only a very small building, the configuration does seem to respect the scale of the side streets (perhaps even to enhance them by contributing visual diversity) and to make allowances for light.

It was the pedimented top, though, that was the focus of most of the early criticisms. At the time it could only be judged by the way it appeared on an eye-level plastic model or in small-scale two-dimensional renderings. Some critics were incapable of imagining what the actual building would look like at full scale, got the wrong impression and, in many cases, are now recanting. James Stewart Polshek, dean of the School of Architecture at Columbia, says this kind of misjudgment is a constant problem, for architects as well as laymen. He calls it "modelitis." Although everyone was "yelling and screaming" about the top of the building after the initial presentation of the model, he observes, it has turned out to be a rather inconsequential feature, now that it has been seen at full scale.

6   It is standard practice, of course, for architects to present designs to clients by means of models and drawings and for developers to rent buildings based on this sort of presentation. But the fact is that no one will ever be standing over the pediment of the actual building and looking down at it, or down on his or her knees in front of it in order to peer into the entrance, or directly in front of it and able to see it from top to bottom all at once. In fact, the top of the AT&T building can barely be seen from Madison Avenue.

7   Now that AT&T is an actual physical presence on the street, it is not at all surprising that some of the original negative votes have been recast as positive, since the building has turned out to be almost a "classic" New York skyscraper. Mr. Johnson takes this process of reassessment in stride, calling it perfectly natural.

C. Griffiths/MAGNUM PHOTOS

8   He says that he probably would not have liked the building himself if he had seen only the model. "John Burgee and I always envisioned it as two buildings," he said, "which is the way it is actually seen. There is the far view and the street view. Sometimes when we showed it, we would cover up one part with our hands." But now, he says, he has the opportunity to say, "I told you so."

9   Michael Graves, an architect known for his own controversial post-modern designs, says that it is unrealistic to expect people to grasp more than the basic idea of a building at an initial presentation. But

C. Griffiths/MAGNUM PHOTOS

architects commented that dark streets are, to them, wonderfully urban and that density (in the right places) is exciting. In Mr. Stern's opinion, Wall Street, dark and cavernous even for New York, is the "most exciting street" in the world. If he wanted light and space he would "stand in a parking lot in White Plains."

What certainly could not be seen at the presentation of the AT&T Building six years ago was the texture of materials used, the level of craftsmanship and the expense that the client would go to ($200 million) to ensure first-rate work. But now, at street level, everyone can enjoy the sensuous qualities of the rough-cut granite, the smooth, elegant bronze and the polished marble. And then there are the changing vistas that appear as one moves through the colonnade and the lobby, gazing in and then out of gridded windows and eye-like cutouts in the walls.

The lobby has been derided for its excessive showmanship, and it probably was not necessary to gild the vaulted ceiling. But it is an elegantly composed space that has, because of the fine materials and attention to detail, the glamorous urban quality of some of the city's early skyscrapers. The only questionable element is the 20,000-pound bronze statue, "The Genius of Electricity," usually nicknamed "Golden Boy," which has been moved uptown from its original niche atop AT&T's old headquarters at 195 Broadway.

In 1980 the New York Landmarks Conservancy attempted to persuade Charles Brown, AT&T's chairman, that the statue should be left where it was. The conservancy argued that the statue was one of the best-known symbols in the lower Manhattan skyline and that it was meant to be seen from a great distance. In the new lobby, close up, Golden Boy can be seen for what he always really was: a naked man wrapped grotesquely in telephone wire. He should be

he's happy if they want to call names at that stage or any other. When people said it reminded them of a clock or a radio, at least they meant it evoked some association with something. "After all," he says, "can you imagine anyone calling the IBM building anything?"

Along with his fellow architect Robert A. M. Stern, Mr. Graves is not concerned that AT&T rises straight up rather than being set back. Mr. Graves says he would much rather have darkness caused by a building of AT&T's caliber than the light and space of the "dead plazas" that haunt Sixth Avenue. Both

standing free outdoors, glistening in the sun, abstract and far away.

After all the fuss, AT&T is a rather simple structure, with an identifiable roof, windows, entrance, and materials that a great many people can understand. And instead of being an affront to the city, AT&T is well on its way to becoming a truly public building. ◆

WELL, I DON'T LOVE YOU, E.T.

George Will

George Will was among the many parents who sat through E.T. *elbow-to-elbow with a son or daughter during the summer of 1982. His report on the movie was published in the* Washington Post *(July 19, 1982) and reprinted in* The Morning After: American Successes and Excesses 1981–1986.

1   THE HOT BREATH OF SUMMER IS ON America, but few children feel it. They are indoors, in the dark, watching the movie *E.T.* and being basted with three subversive ideas:

2   Children are people.

3   Adults are not.

4   Science is sinister.

5   The first idea amounts to counting chickens before they are hatched. The second is an exaggeration. The third subverts what the movie purports to encourage: a healthy capacity for astonishment.

6   The yuckiness of adults is an axiom of children's cinema. And truth be told, adults are, more often than not, yucky. That is because they are human, a defect they share with their pint-size detractors. (A wit once said that children are natural mimics who act like their parents in spite of all efforts to teach them good manners.) Surely children are unmanageable enough without gratuitously inoculating them with anti-adultism. Steven Spielberg, the perpetrator of *E.T.*, should be reminded of the charge that got Socrates condemned to drink hemlock: corrupting the youth of Athens.

7   It is not easy to corrupt American youth additionally. Geoffrey Will, 8, like all younger brothers in the theater, swooned with pleasure while sitting next to his censorious father watching the little boy in *E.T.* shout across the dinner table at the big brother; "Shut up, penis breath!" *E.T.* has perfect pitch for child talk at its gamiest. Convincing depictions of a child's-eye view of the world are rare. George Eliot's "The Mill on the Floss" and Henry James's "What Maisie Knew" are two. But those delicate sensibilities could not have captured the scatological sounds of young American male siblings discussing their differences.

8   I feel about children expressing themselves the way Wellington felt about soldiers. He even disapproved of soldiers cheering, because cheering is too nearly an expression of opinion. The little boy in *E.T.* did say something neat: "How do you explain school to a higher intelligence?" The children who popped through C. S. Lewis's wardrobe into Narnia never said anything that penetrating. Still the proper way to converse with a young person is:

9   Young person: What's that bird?

10   Older person: It's a guillemot.

11   Young person: That's not my idea of a guillemot.

12   Older person: It's God's idea of a guillemot.

13   I assume every American has spent the last

month either in line to see, or seeing, *E.T.* In the first month it earned $100 million—$17.5 million during the Fourth of July weekend. But in case you have been spelunking beneath Kentucky since May, *E.T.* is about an extraterrestrial creature left behind in a California suburb when his buddies blast off for home. He is befriended by a boy in the American manner: The boy tosses a ball to E.T. and E.T. chucks it back.

14 It is, I suppose, illiberal and—even more unforgivable—ethnocentric (or, in this case, speciescentric) to note that E.T. is not just another pretty face. E.T. looks like a stump with a secret sorrow. (Except to another E.T. As Voltaire said, to a toad, beauty is popeyes, a yellow belly and spotted back.) E.T. is a brilliant, doe-eyed, soulful space elf who waddles into the hearts of the boy, his big brother and little sister. But a wasting illness brings E.T. to death's door just as a horde of scary scientists crashes through the door of the boy's house.

15 Throughout the movie they have been hunting the little critter, electronically eavesdropping on the house and generally acting like Watergate understudies. They pounce upon E.T. with all the whirring, pulsing, blinking paraphernalia of modern medicine. He dies anyway, then is inexplicably resurrected. He is rescued from the fell clutches of the scientists by a posse of kid bicyclists and boards a spaceship for home. This variant of the boy-sundered-from-dog theme leaves few eyes dry. But what is bothersome is the animus against science, which is seen as a morbid calling for callous vivisectionists and other unfeeling technocrats.

16 A childish (and Rousseau-ist) view of children as noble savages often is part of a belief that nature is a sweet garden and science and technology are spoilsome intrusions. But nature is, among other things, plagues and pestilences, cholera and locusts, floods and droughts. Earlier ages thought of nature in terms of such afflictions. As Robert Nisbet[1] says, this age can take a sentimental view of nature because science has done so much to ameliorate it.

Disdain for science usually ends when the disdainer gets a toothache, or his child needs an operation. But hostility to science is the anti-intellectualism of the semi-intellectual. That is in part because science undercuts intellectual vanity: Measured against what is unknown, the difference between what the most and least learned persons know is trivial. *E.T.* is, ostensibly, an invitation to feel what we too rarely feel: wonder. One reason we rarely feel wonder is that science has made many things routine that once were exciting, even terrifying (travel, surgery). But science does more than its despisers do to nurture the wonderful human capacity for wonder.

18 U.S. missions have revealed that Saturn has braided rings and a ring composed of giant snowballs. The space program is the greatest conceivable adventure; yet the government scants it and Philistine utilitarians justify it because it has yielded such marvels as nonstick frying pans. We live in (let us say the worst) an age of journalism: an age of skimmed surfaces, of facile confidence that reality is whatever can be seen and taped and reported. But modern science teaches that things are not what they seem: Matter is energy; light is subject to gravity; the evidence of gravity waves suggests that gravitic energy is a form of radiation; to increase the speed of an object is to decrease the passage of its time. This is science; compared with it, space elves are dull as ditchwater.

19 The epigram that credulity is an adult's weakness but a child's strength is true. Victoria Will (21 months) croons ecstatically at the sight of a squirrel; she sees, without thinking about it, that a squirrel is a marvelous piece of work—which, come to think about it, it is. For big people, science teaches the truth that a scientist put this way: The universe is not only queerer than we suppose, it is queerer than we can suppose. ◆

---

[1] Nisbet: Robert Nisbet (1913–   ), American sociologist whose writings cover intellectual history, political science, and philosophy as well as sociology.

REVIEWS OF THE WRITING LIFE

Some of the twelve members of the "panel" for The Riverside Guide to Writing *are more controversial politically than Annie Dillard, but none is more controversial as a stylist. It isn't surprising, therefore, that when she published her 1989 book* The Writing Life *(see excerpt, page 70), it received a very mixed set of reviews. What is interesting, as usual, is how much the reviews reveal about the differing perspectives of the reviewers.*

'SPEND IT ALL, SHOOT IT, PLAY IT, LOSE IT'[1]

1   THIS IS A TRICKY REVIEW FOR ME TO write. Annie Dillard is one of my favorite contemporary authors. Over and over again, beyond the point of wonder, I have not only enjoyed reading her work, but have found that it nourishes—inspires—my imagination and my own work. An impressive number of copies of both "Pilgrim at Tinker's Creek" and "Holy the Firm" have passed through my study, continually repurchased after I have pressed one into someone's hands, squeaking, "But you *must* read this."

2   So how am I to say that "The Writing Life" irritates me, that I find it overwritten, self-important and, therefore, unrevealing? This may of course say more about me than it does about the book.

3   In the first place, I do not often enjoy books about writing (I cannot stand novels about the writing of novels either)—other writers always seem to take it so deadly seriously. Does no one else write because it is the most agreeable way of earning a modest living without having to dress up and go out at crack of dawn? Does no one except me enjoy being a writer, find it fun, feel lucky, privileged, amused? Ms. Dillard says of the writer: "He is careful of what he reads, for that is what he will write. He is careful of what he learns, because that is what he will know."

4   I cannot treat myself, as a writer, so preciously, and doubt that anyone else either should or does.

Then of course I feel frivolous and worldly, guilty even. Because I fritter my time and do not take it seriously enough, I will never be such a good writer, not just as Ms. Dillard is, but as I could be. Feeling guilty makes me cross, and my eyes sharpen to every mauve passage, which deepens into hues of royal purple under my malignant stare, and (until I have to review the book) I am the only loser and what I lose is joy. For Annie Dillard is a wonderful writer and "The Writing Life" is full of joys. These are clearest to me when she comes at her subject tangentially, talking not of herself at her desk but of other parallel cases—the last chapter, a story about a stunt pilot who was an artist of air, is, quite simply, breathtaking.

6   There are so many bits like this, Ms. Dillard at her best, taking the easily overlooked, the mundane, and revealing it as the beautiful, the important, the meaningful truth that it certainly is. She knows so many things—stories and histories and facts and scraps—and she probes them for meaning so surely. As admiration mounts, you really do have to ask yourself: Is she being honest when she tells us to take care about what we read? Because no one could know in advance that there is worthwhile material to be found in as many strange byways as she finds them.

7   Unfortunately, the bits do not add up to a book. Near the beginning of "The Writing Life," Ms. Dillard states categorically: "Writing a book, full time, takes between two and ten years. . . . Thomas Mann was a prodigy of production. Working full time, he wrote a page a day. That is 365 pages a year, for he did write every day—a good-sized book a year. At a

---

[1]*Source: New York Times Book Review*, September 17, 1989, p. 15.

page a day, he was one of the most prolific writers who ever lived. Flaubert wrote steadily, with only the usual, appalling, strains. For twenty-five years he finished a big book every five to seven years. My guess is that full-time writers average a book every five years: seventy-three usable pages a year, or a usable fifth of a page a day. . . . On plenty of days the writer can write three or four pages, and on plenty of other days he concludes he must throw them away."

8   I don't know if I can face these gloomy statistics. I don't know if they are true. But if Ms. Dillard believes them, then perhaps that explains the problem with "The Writing Life." It has not been given its necessary time; it is not a full two years younger than "An American Childhood," her wonderful autobiography. Are these the scraps that she concluded must be thrown out of that work, or are they notes toward a book that might have been?

9   To be fair, later she also writes: "One of the few things I know about writing is this: spend it all, shoot it, play it, lose it, all, right away, every time. Do not hoard what seems good for a later place in the book, or for another book; give it, give it all, give it now. . . . Something more will arise for later, something better. These things fill from behind, from beneath, like well water. Similarly, the impulse to keep to yourself what you have learned is not only shameful, it is destructive. Anything you do not give freely and abundantly becomes lost to you. You open your safe and find ashes."

10   That flamboyant energy and generosity are at the heart of Ms. Dillard's craft. It is not her fault that I am not really interested in how writers write, but in what they write. In real books about real things. ◆

—Sara Maitland

MOTHBALLED[1]

1   FIFTEEN YEARS AGO, IN *PILGRIM AT TINKER Creek,* Annie Dillard wrote that she had "no intention of inflicting all my childhood memories on anyone";

[1]*Source: The Nation,* October 16, 1989, p. 435.

in her last book, *An American Childhood,* she did exactly that. She wasn't wrong, really, to break that promise—*Childhood* was a very good book, almost a great one—but still, it indicated how attenuated and self-obsessed her work was becoming. Now, in *The Writing Life,* Dillard has gone one step farther down that path: She has moved from writing about herself to writing about writing about herself.

2   *The Writing Life* isn't a bad book, exactly,— I don't think Dillard is capable of writing anything awful—but it's thin and fragmented, and self-pitying. Nothing comes more easily to a writer than moaning about the creative agony of the artist, but Dillard has always had such perfect, poetic taste and such a fine sense of the ridiculous that I would never have expected it of her. Though her work has probably never sold in proportion to its merit, she does have a Pulitzer Prize and at least one best seller under her belt. So it's just plain embarrassing when she whines that writing is "work . . . so meaningless, so fully for yourself alone, and so worthless to the world, that no one except you cares whether you do it well, or ever." Ten minutes at a job that really is meaningless might change her mind.

3   I have called the book fragmented, but anecdotal might be a kinder term—though it implies the same limitations. Several of the anecdotes in *The Writing Life* deal with Dillard's work on *Holy the Firm,* "a favorite, difficult book," though she's too shy to mention it by title. Dillard is horrified when she discovers that two neighbor children, 6 and 7 years old, have read the book, or perhaps have had part of it read to them. "'WHAT?' I said." And "WHAT?" she cries, in capital-letter anguish, when they ask her a question about the moth. (*Holy the Firm* opens with a description of a moth caught in a candle flame, simultaneously being consumed in and illuminated by the fire.) Apparently, Dillard considers the book beyond the comprehension of even adult mortals. "No one had understood [it] but a Yale critic," she tells us, grandly, and there it was, approached by mere children! The 7-year-old offers his professional opinion of the work ("I liked that story"), and she chokes on that, too. "Why," she asks, "did it seem to console

me to repeat to myself, 'Oh well, he's older'?" Dillard apparently means this to be amusing, in an ominous sort of way (out of the mouths of babes you will learn how shallow or misunderstood you are). And it *is*, but not in the way that she intends. In one of the funniest parts of *An American Childhood*, Dillard wrote about herself as a precocious grade-schooler, reading the Modern Library classics in search of something as good as *Mad* magazine. "*The Interpretation of Dreams* was okay," she said, but Joyce's *Ulysses* was just "awful." Is Dillard really so vain that she can't see the humor in it when one of her own books gets the same sort of treatment?

4   Even on a subject as barren as this one, though, Dillard's prose style remains amazing. Reviewers tend to use adjectives such as "luminous" and "radiant" in describing her writing. That usually means vague and sentimental and pseudopoetic—but she's not. Her prose is rich when it needs to be, but she never merely assembles conglomerations of syllables for their own sake. The nature writing in Dillard's *Pilgrim at Tinker Creek* can take the reader's breath away with its beauty, but she never yields to the temptation to be falsely pretty. I grew up in southwest Virginia, probably not far from what was then her Tinker Creek home; when I saw how many pages of *Pilgrim* were devoted to starlings and copperhead snakes, I knew she wasn't afraid to report the fauna of the area as it actually exists. More important, everything in that book, and in most of her others, has a meaning beyond the literal. I sometimes believe that Dillard took Blake's "To see a world in a grain of sand/and a heaven in a wild flower" as her job description.

5   Most of Dillard's books have moments of immense beauty and power—that is why it is so jarring how silly some of the metaphors in *The Writing Life* are. Writing desks hover "thirty feet from the ground"; the writer, she says, must crank "the engine of belief that keeps you and your desk in midair." (Trust your feelings, Luke. The Force will be with you.) A two-page chapter is devoted to a typewriter that turns volcanic, "exploding with fire and ash." It shakes the walls and floor of her house in its fury; she grabs a bucket of water to douse it, but decides to leave it be, though the eruptions recur randomly through the night. A couple of days later, it works just fine. I know Dillard wants us to think deep mystical thoughts about creative fire, but the only deep thought I had was this: Could one of the most brilliant writers of our time be dumb enough to want to pour water in a burning electrical appliance?

6   One could be cynical and argue that there's a reason *The Writing Life* seems mostly self-obsessed: that Dillard has been navel-gazing so long that her chin has become permanently attached to her chest. But I don't really think that's the problem. Yes, most of her books are ultimately about herself, but they are really about how she transforms what she perceives. (To return to one of the controlling metaphors of *Holy the Firm*, it is the body of the moth that is illuminated in the candle flame, but the beauty is in the glow of the light.) Dillard's books, whatever their nominal subjects, constitute her spiritual autobiography, and that's the riskiest kind of writing—her books work only if every sentence is an epiphany. That's a word critics have debased beyond recognition, but Dillard's best work honestly provides something that can only be called revelation, and that something cannot be faked. So there may be a good reason that her last couple of books have been merely about the inside of her head: What else can you write when the epiphanies don't come? ◆

—*Michael Edens*

[REVIEW OF] THE WRITING LIFE[1]

W HEN ASKED IN A 1987 INTERVIEW WITH *People* magazine about the book she was writing, Annie Dillard responded: "It's about what something feels like. . . . As far as I know, it has never been written about before." Whether or not the subject of the writing life has been written about before, Dillard's new book provides an articulate account of "what it feels like" to be a writer as well as an un-

[1] *Source: The Christian Century*, November 15, 1989, pp. 1063–4.

usual look into her own life as an award-winning writer and an unapologetic mystic.

2   The form and style of the book is familiar to anyone who has read her other works. It is full of penetrating metaphors, lucid stories about sacrifice and struggle and keen bits of humor, which add to the image she paints of the life of the writer. One gets the feeling that Dillard has a love-hate relationship with the craft and profession of writing. She warns the reader who may be thinking about being a writer that the writer's life "is colorless to the point of sensory deprivation," which may come as a shock to those who have read *Pilgrim at Tinker Creek,* that Pulitzer Prize–winning marvel of detail, imagination and mystical insight. She even incriminates herself as a writer by saying that people who want to be writers must lack "material footing" in their lives. Furthermore, the metaphors she employs to describe the struggle of writing—cutting off a piece of one's thigh, taming lions, sitting up with a sick person, tending a weed-filled garden—gives the initial impression that she is sorry she took up the profession.

3   But the most interesting and significant detail about the language Dillard uses to describe the "dark side" of the writing life is that it is almost exactly the same as the language she uses in her other works to describe the spiritual life, the life in quest of God. She even tells some of the same stories that she told in *Teaching a Stone to Talk,* stories about Hasidic Jews who, while having what she considers a healthy fear of God, still desire the presence of God, even if it were to kill them. Stories such as these, stories that emphasize struggling, fighting, and even dying for the sake of something greater, something wonderful, are very familiar to the experienced reader of Dillard. The difference is that, in this book, these stories refer to the writing life itself as being that "something" that is wonderful to be sought for at all costs.

4   Such notions may seem to contradict earlier comments about the horrors of writing. But the underlying idea of the book is that writing and all that it involves is a sign and possibly even a part of the substance of Dillard's spiritual life. Writing is a way of purity by virtue of its "deeper penetration into the universe." Of course, in Dillard's thought, the universe and the Absolute are often synonymous and, apparently, the event of writing is one way in which Dillard and God, as she understands God, communicate. A life of writing for Dillard parallels the life of the spirit; often the two are worked out together, and always with fear and trembling.

5   Commenting on teaching, Dillard has said, "When I teach, I preach. I thump the Bible. I exhort my students morally. I talk to them about the dedicated life . . . The dedicated life is the life worth living. You must give with your whole heart." Apparently it is the writing life that is the dedicated one and the one worth living. *The Writing Life* is valuable as a nontechnical description and guide to the writing profession. But it is more valuable as a metaphor for the life in pursuit of something greater than the finite, possibly something to which only art can do justice, something that is well worth all the attention given it—namely, God and the pursuit of God. ◆

—B. Jill Carroll

WRITING ABOUT LITERATURE

T O PRODUCE A CHAPTER ON WRITING ABOUT LITERATURE IS A FOOL'S errand. There are so many types of literature and so many different approaches that can be taken to it that no chapter can do the job. What this one will attempt is more modest: to present you with an approach to writing one type of paper about one type of literature.

The type of literature will be the narrative, the story. As a member of a society that produces a constant stream of stories—in print, on film, on videotape, and in conversation—you probably know a good deal more about narrative techniques than you are *aware* of knowing. Until we are asked to write about narratives carefully, most of us read them with unconscious ease, just as we ride a bicycle without precisely knowing how we do it. Unconscious ease has its advantages, but it doesn't allow you to hold things up to scrutiny, to analyze or improve your understanding. Writing about narratives is, among other things, an exercise in raising your level of awareness of the storyteller's techniques and your responses to them.

The type of paper that we will be discussing (and that you will be writing) is grounded in a careful analysis of six elements of a narrative: setting (including place and time), character, point of view, plot, theme, and symbolism. Analyzing the way that these elements work in a story often helps you understand the story better. More important, it can help you become conscious of what you *don't* understand. Discovering a *problem* that could prevent readers from understanding a narrative fully is a crucial step toward writing the kind of paper we are discussing here, a paper that presents a solution to a difficulty. The pattern is like the problem-solution pattern we discussed in Chapter 8.

By identifying a problem of interpretation in a narrative and by proposing a solution, you show that you have arrived at an understanding of the work. *An understanding* is not the same thing as *the truth,* of course. Literary works are not puzzles to be solved once and for all, and if your problem is an intriguing one, you can be certain that other readers would arrive at other solutions. Each intelligent solution has its virtues; each teaches us something new about the story or places the emphasis on a new facet. This is not to say, however, that all views of a literary work are equally valuable. An understanding is not the same as an uninformed or slipshod opinion. It is formed

10

from close study and takes into account all significant aspects of the work. It doesn't leave obvious questions unexplored, and it can be listened to with respect by people who disagree with it strongly. Literature teachers often give A's to papers that reveal an *understanding* of a story that is different from their own. Sometimes they are even persuaded to alter their own understandings. But they may give F's to papers that express an unsupported *opinion* about a story, even if that opinion matches their own.

A STORY FOR ANALYSIS

Since analysis is an important step toward understanding, we will begin by analyzing "The Blue Eyes," a very short story by Isak Dinesen.[1]

"The Blue Eyes"
—ISAK DINESEN

I have heard a story . . . of a skipper who named his ship after his wife. He had the figure-head of it beautifully carved, just like her, and the hair of it gilt. But his wife was jealous of the ship. "You think more of the figure-head than of me," she said to him. "No," he answered, "I think so highly of her because she is like you, yes, because she is you yourself. Is she not gallant, full-bosomed; does she not dance in the waves, like you at our wedding? In a way she is really even kinder to me than you are. She gallops along where I tell her to go, and she lets her long hair hang down freely, while you put up yours under your cap. But she turns her back to me, so that when I want a kiss I come home to Elsinore." Now once, when this skipper was trading at Trankebar, he chanced to help an old native King to flee from traitors in his own country. As they parted the King gave him two big blue, precious stones, and these he had set into the face of his figure-head, like a pair of eyes to it. When he came home he told his wife of his adventure, and said: "Now she has your blue eyes too." "You had better give me the stones for a pair of earrings," she said. "No," he said again, "I cannot do that, and you would not ask me to if you understood." Still the wife could not stop fretting about the blue stones, and one

---

[1]The pen name of Baroness Karen Blixen (1885–1962), the Danish-born author of such notable books as *Seven Gothic Tales, Out of Africa,* and *Winter's Tales,* from which "The Blue Eyes" is taken. "The Blue Eyes" is actually a tale within the tale "Peter and Rosa." See Assignment 4 at the chapter's end.

day, when her husband was with the skippers' corporation, she had a glazier of the town take them out, and put two bits of blue glass into the figure-head instead, and the skipper did not find out, but sailed off to Portugal. But after some time the skipper's wife found that her eyesight was growing bad, and that she could not see to thread a needle. She went to a wise woman, who gave her ointments and waters, but they did not help her, and in the end the old woman shook her head, and they told her that this was a rare and incurable disease, and that she was going blind. "Oh, God," the wife then cried, "that the ship was back in the harbor of Elsinore. Then I should have the glass taken out, and the jewels put back. For did he not say that they were my eyes?" But the ship did not come back. Instead, the skipper's wife had a letter from the Consul of Portugal, who informed her that she had been wrecked, and gone to the bottom with all hands. And it was a very strange thing, the Consul wrote, that in broad daylight she had run straight into a tall rock, rising out of the sea.

ANALYSIS OF A STORY: SIX ELEMENTS OF THE NARRATIVE

1. Setting: Place and Time. Setting is a good starting point in the analysis of a narrative because paying attention to the *place* and *time,* the two subelements of setting, helps us get our bearings. For both of these subelements, I like to begin with a broad identification and then to narrow as much as possible.

Let's begin with place, then. Where shall we say, broadly, that the story is set? Three places are mentioned by name. Elsinore, the skipper's home port; Trankebar, where he assists the native King and is given the blue stones; and Portugal, where he drowns. A few minutes of research in your library's reference section will tell you that Elsinore (or Helsingore) is a city in Denmark and that Trankebar (or Tranquebar) is a city in southeast India. Elsinore, however, is the story's principal setting, and is (for Dinesen and other Danes, at least) an ordinary enough place: it was virtually Dinesen's hometown. If Trankebar sounds like the setting for a romance, Elsinore is as solid as Baltimore.

In many cases the setting can be more exactly identified: the story may be set not only in a particular city but on a particular street, in a particular house, perhaps in a particular room. In this case it is hard to define a setting narrower than the whole of Elsinore. We may suspect that most of the conversations happen inside the skipper's house, but there is no clear evidence.

And in what *time,* broadly, did the story take place? In her first sentence, Dinesen puts the story vaguely in the past: the narrator has heard this story but does not claim to be acquainted personally with any of the people in it. Apparently the story takes place in a time of sailing ships and a time when a person with failing eyes would consult not a physician but a "wise woman." We could say that the date is earlier than, say, 1880, but such literalness seems silly. The general time is the distant past invoked by the "once upon a time" beginning of fairy tales. In some stories we know the day and the hour of each scene. Here we cannot say precisely, but the story must stretch over a period of months or years: even in a fairy tale, there must be time for the voyage to Trankebar and the voyage to Portugal.

2. Character. In *Aspects of the Novel* E. M. Forster draws a useful distinction between *flat* characters and *round*. A flat character, he tells us, is one constructed around "a single idea or quality," and the very flattest "can be expressed in one sentence." Round characters more nearly resemble the people we encounter in everyday life. Their personalities have many qualities, and the mixture of qualities sometimes makes them behave so that they surprise us, as Forster puts it, "in a convincing way."

We can begin our analysis of the characters in "The Blue Eyes" by ranging them along the continuum from flat to round. The flattest of all surely are the hands on the skipper's ship, so flat that they are not even mentioned separately and so can't be counted characters at all. Next, perhaps, is the "old native King," whose entire "personality" is his gratitude for being saved. But the "wise woman" is perhaps just as flat: her only personality trait is the regret she expresses by shaking her head as she pronounces the wife's eye disease incurable.

Relative to these very flat characters, the skipper seems slightly rounded. We know him to be

1. Adventurous (as shown by the voyage to Trankebar).

2. Deeply in love with his wife.

3. Poetic in speech and artistic in temperament (as shown by his attitude toward the figure-head).

The wife is slightly more rounded still. We know her to be

1. Jealous (of the figure-head).

2. Unimaginative (incapable of understanding the significance of the figure-head).

3. Capable of deceit.

We also know her to be *capable of change*. Once her eyes begin to fail she *sees* the significance of the figure-head and appears to repent of her deception and jealousy. To use two more useful terms borrowed from Forster, she is a *dynamic* (changing) character rather than a *static* (unchanging) one. In my view, but perhaps not in yours, she is a more interesting character than her impossibly wise and virtuous husband: she is recognizably human, and, like most humans, she grows wiser only when she pays dearly for her errors. Her capacity to change is one thing that gives her character roundness.

By comparison to the principal characters of a longer piece of realistic fiction, of course, even the wife is relatively flat. If you have read Toni Cade Bambara's "The Hammer Man" (page 394), for example, you know that Manny and the narrator are far rounder characters than the skipper and his wife.

3. Point of View. One of the most important tools of the storyteller is the ability to choose the point of view from which events will be described. In their pure form, the principal points of view can be seen as the vertices of a triangle.

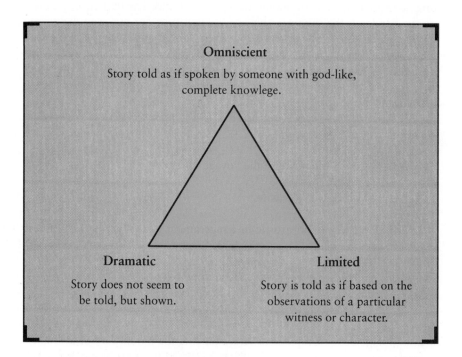

At one corner is the *omniscient* (all-knowing) point of view, in which the author (or the narrator) places no apparent limit on what is revealed to the audience. Like God, the omniscient narrator can look at will into the minds of all the characters in the story. Often the narrator reveals a knowledge of things that no character involved in the story could possibly have. When the point of view is omniscient, the reader has the impression that the story is being told by someone whose judgments and generalizations are unchallengeable because they are based on a complete knowledge of the world of the story. One sign of omniscient narration is the use of *summaries* of actions or conversations to which no one claims to have been a witness. The creation story in Genesis is told from an omniscient point of view: "In the beginning, God created the heavens and the earth." The author doesn't claim to have been there but does write as someone who *knows* and whose knowledge is not to be questioned.

At another corner of the triangle is the *dramatic* or *objective* point of view, in which everything is viewed as if with a motion picture camera. The actions and words of the characters are recorded but not their unspoken thoughts, and the reader is left with the impression of having witnessed the story as it occurred, with no narrator making judgments or generalizations or summarizing the action. The method here is sometimes called *scenic* to distinguish it from the *summarizing* method available to the omniscient narrator.

At the third corner of the triangle is the *limited* point of view, which restricts itself to the observations of a single witness to the story.[2] The reader seems to view everything from inside the skull of this witness, who becomes the story's *center of consciousness*. Stories with first-person[3] narrators are often restricted in this way: we inhabit the mind of the "I" who speaks in the story. The character who serves as the center of consciousness is direct witness to events and conversations and may be a participant as well:

> I was glad to hear that Manny had fallen off the roof. I had put out the tale that I was down with yellow fever, but nobody paid me no mind, least of all Dirty Red who stomped right in to announce that Manny had fallen off the roof and that I could come out of hiding now. My mother dropped what she was doing, which was the laundry, and got the whole story out of Red. "Bad enough you gots to hang around with boys," she said. "But fight with them too. And you would pick the craziest one at that."

This is the voice of the narrator in "The Hammer Man," and when we hear it we realize that what it tells us is neither an objective rendering of appearances (as in the dramatic point of view) nor an authoritative statement of reality, including both surface appearances and deeper truths (as in the omniscient point of view). Instead, it is a *version* of reality *as perceived by one individual*, who may sometimes be mistaken.

Except for some first-person narratives, few stories are told purely from any one of the three points of view. Usually, some material is presented from an omniscient point of view, some dramatically, and some from the limited perspective of a single character. One way of dealing with this mixture is to say that a story may blend points of view in any proportion and that if we want to characterize its *general* point of view, we might have to locate it somewhere other than at the triangle's corners—perhaps inside, perhaps along

---

[2]Or one witness at a time. Sometimes the author leaps from one limited point of view to another.
[3]Using, that is, the first-person singular pronoun: "*I* saw," "*I* have heard."

one edge. As I discuss the point of view in a story, I will insert a diagram showing where on the triangle it seems to belong.

In "The Blue Eyes," the narrator knows the whole story without having witnessed it, and he begins by summarizing a good deal of action. Though he "heard" the story from someone else, he serves here essentially as if he were the all-knowing author: whatever he says must be taken as the truth. It appears, then, that the narration is from the omniscient point of view. But this classification oversimplifies the situation. Some parts of the story use dialogue, an essentially dramatic technique, and allow us to draw our own conclusions about the characters of the skipper and his wife. At other times in the story we dip into the consciousness of the wife: "his wife was jealous of the ship," "the wife could not stop fretting," and so forth. Never do we dip into the consciousness of the skipper or any other character. On balance, most literary scholars would probably describe the point of view of "The Blue Eyes" as *limited omniscient,* a hybrid form that allows authors to establish one character as the story's center of consciousness but also allows them to escape that consciousness to make observations the character would not.

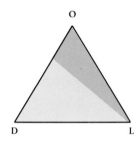

EXERCISE 1

◆ *Identifying Point of View.* Identify the point of view of each of the following passages, and be prepared to discuss the reasons that you classify it as you do.

1. Now once, when this skipper was trading at Trankebar, he chanced to help an old native King to flee from traitors in his own country.

2. When he came home he told his wife of his adventure, and said: "Now she has your blue eyes too." "You had better give me the stones for a pair of earrings," said she. "No," he said again, "I cannot do that, and you would not ask me to if you understood."

3. But after some time the skipper's wife found that her eyesight was growing bad, and that she could not see to thread a needle.

4. Plot. In *Aspects of the Novel* Forster tells us that "the king died and the queen died" is not a plot. "The king died and the queen died of grief," however, Forster does call a plot. What is the difference? A plot is not merely a collection of unconnected events; it is a series of events connected by *causation.* Event 1 causes Event 2, which causes Event 3, and so on until the story ends.[4] A plot synopsis of "The Blue Eyes" stressing causation might read as follows:

A skipper named his ship after his wife and had a figure-head for it carved in her image; into the eyes of the figure-head, he placed precious blue stones. Because she

---

[4]Complex stories may have several plots, several separate lines of causally connected events.

364   PROFESSIONAL AND ACADEMIC APPLICATIONS

was jealous of the figure-head, the wife had the stones cut out to keep for herself. Because the stones had magically become her eyes, she went blind, and because they had also become the ship's eyes, the ship crashed on a rock in broad daylight, drowning the skipper.

There is, however, another traditional method of analyzing plot. Rather than causation, this method emphasizes a *protagonist* pursuing a goal and confronted with a *problem* or *conflict*. In the case of "The Blue Eyes," this second method presents us with a dilemma. We must decide who the protagonist is, whose problem the story is primarily concerned with. Partly because of the story's point of view, my own feeling is that the wife is the protagonist, and I would summarize the plot as follows:

A wife wanted her husband to love her completely [the goal], but he seemed to lavish his affection on the figure-head of his ship instead, saying that the figure-head *was* her, an explanation that she could not accept [conflict]. When he acquired some precious blue stones, she wanted them for earrings, but he would not take them out of the eyes of the figure-head where he had placed them, so she cut them out herself [heightened recurrences of the conflict]. When her eyesight began to fail, she realized she had blinded herself by blinding the figure-head. She wished that the ship were in port so that she could replace the stones, but news came that the ship had smashed into a huge rock in broad daylight and her husband had drowned.

It is possible to view the skipper as the story's protagonist, but I think the wife is the more likely choice. We understand the wife's goal better than we do the husband's, and the story seems to center on her struggle.

◆ **Summarizing the Plot from Another Perspective.** Assume that the skipper, not the wife, is the protagonist of the story. Write a plot summary that stresses his goal and his struggles.

EXERCISE 2

5. Theme. The theme is the dominant idea of a literary work, corresponding to what we have been calling the framework of an essay. Generally, literature textbooks define the theme as a general statement about the human condition, expressible in a sentence. By this definition, "jealousy" cannot be the theme of a story, though "jealousy leads to ruin" might be: jealousy might be the subject of a story but cannot be a theme because a theme needs to be a complete statement, a complete sentence. Nor can "the wife betrays her husband" be a theme: it is a statement about two particular people, not a general statement about the human condition.

This rather fussy textbook definition makes the relationship of the theme to the story seem fairly simple: one theme per story, and every competent reader should be able to identify it. In practice, theme is a more difficult element to pin down. When I asked six people with degrees in English, including two Ph.D.'s with considerable teaching experience, what the theme of "The Blue Eyes" is, I got the following answers:

1. Altering someone's means of expressing love will result in tragedy, *or* we must allow those around us to express their love as they will.

2. The clash of the real and the ideal results in destruction, *or* lack of trust leads to destruction.

3. Jealousy leads to ruin, *or* life is full of mystery.

4. Some objects have a power, either intrinsically or assigned to them by humans, that is undeniable and dangerous.

5. By betraying others, we betray ourselves.

6. Sometimes love should be blind.

Though some of these statements of the theme may be preferable to others, each could be supported in an essay about the story. Like most literary works, "The Blue Eyes" suggests many themes. The difficult question for the person analyzing the story is which of these to treat as dominant, and on that question there is room for reasonable disagreement. Identifying the theme is, therefore, precisely the sort of problem that might produce a good essay.

You'll notice that three of the six respondents above simply couldn't be content with a single theme, apparently feeling that no single one does the story justice. If you follow the convention of assigning a single theme to the story (often a good idea for simplicity's sake), then you will want to choose the one that in your view best holds the story together. And if you are writing an essay on the subject, you will want to show why you take this view, arguing your case as carefully as you would in any other argument.

EXERCISE 3

◆ *Evaluating Arguments About Theme.* Each of the following one-paragraph essays attempts to identify an important theme in "The Blue Eyes" and convince readers that the theme is truly implied in the story. Decide which argument you find most convincing and which you find least convincing. Be prepared to explain the reasons behind your ranking.

1. The theme of "The Blue Eyes" is that there is more mystery in the world than the average person believes possible. The wife in the story represents the average person. Her husband represents the extraordinary person. The wife lives in Elsinore, a small port city near Dinesen's birthplace. Unlike Dinesen, who lived for seventeen years in Africa, however, the wife never leaves home. Her attitude

toward life is what we might expect of a middle-class housewife. She tucks her hair respectably under her cap and wants the blue stones for her earrings. She can't understand why they should be placed in the eyes of the figure-head (an apparently extravagant and poetic gesture), and she can't understand why her husband should be so delighted by a figure made of wood. It never occurs to her that the figure and the stones might have magical powers, and she never comprehends the skipper's romantic and artistic nature. Perhaps it is the skipper's knowledge of a wider world, a world of wonders and adventures, that makes him extraordinary. At any rate, his more poetic, magical view of life turns out to correspond more closely to the truth than her narrow vision does. And by not understanding or at least accepting the mysteries that he knows, she brings disaster to them both.

2. The theme of "The Blue Eyes" is that Karen Blixen wants to be Isak Dinesen; in other words, women often want to be men. This theme is first apparent in the roles Dinesen assigns to her characters. The woman is unimaginative and unadventurous and is ignorant, jealous, and petty. She stays at home, primarily *because* she is a woman, and spends her time finding fault with her husband. Her husband, on the other hand, is full of adventurousness and imagination, and is also loving, courageous, and wise. He travels the world and rescues an old King, but he also shows his wife his devotion by naming the ship after her and carving the figure-head in her image. Throughout her life, Dinesen chose to live like the skipper. Not only did she travel to Africa and manage a coffee plantation for over ten years, she also changed her name to the male name, Isak. And by writing in English instead of her native language, she both gave up her identity even more and showed her romantic devotion to her English lover who died in a plane crash just before she began her writing career. The message of the story is clearly that the male life is the one worth living. In fact, when the woman says she wishes to put the eyes back in the ship, she proves that she realizes that her husband really meant that the ship *was* her, and by accepting that fact, she "buys into" the male life of magic and adventure. Furthermore, we can assume that Dinesen's life influenced this story because she set the story in Elsinore; Dinesen grew up, and escaped from, a place very near this city. Also, Dinesen often writes autobiographically, clearly seen in her *Out of Africa* which tells the story of her life in Africa. Finally, Dinesen's sexual confusion has a very real source: she lost her father to suicide and her lover to an accident, and this pattern of dying men and suffering women is reflected in the story, which ends with the woman finally seeing that the male life is the only one worth dying for.

3. The theme of "The Blue Eyes," that trust between a husband and wife must be absolute, is supported by the characters, plot, and symbolism of the story. The characters contrast sharply in their trust for one another. While the husband finds a creative way of trusting his wife—making her image the figure-head on his ship so that she would guide him in all his travels—the wife stays at home and frets, doubting her husband's love because he enjoys his journeys and his

ship so much. So while the skipper maintains his devotion to his wife, his wife grows more and more unhappy, resorting to deception to get back at her husband. The conflict that shapes the plot, then, is caused by the wife's inability to trust her husband's love. The story ends tragically when the wife suffers for her lack of trust: her husband drowns and she goes blind. Finally, the figure-head itself stands for the ideal love that would have included absolute trust. It is a symbol of the wife as she might be, freed of her imperfections. But it is also a symbol of the guiding force that a loving and trusting spouse can be.

6. Symbolism.   Probably no element of literature produces more anxiety in the classroom than symbolism. Yet in ordinary life, we are comfortable with the idea that people, places, and objects may signify meanings beyond themselves. Thanks partly to millions of dollars spent on advertising, the "golden arches" have come to symbolize the following things to various people:

1. A McDonald's restaurant.

2. Fast food generally.

3. Wholesomeness (think of all those American-way-of-life advertisements).

4. Mass marketing generally.

5. Mass production of a bland product.

6. The replacement of mom-and-pop businesses by franchises.

7. The ugliness of commercial "strips" in American cities.

The list begins, I think, with the most common meaning of the arches. It could be continued indefinitely with meanings that are strongly present for a few people but not present for others. But which meanings are most present in our minds depends partly on context. Meaning number 2 could be reinforced by a series of photographs showing the logos of McDonald's, Burger King, and Kentucky Fried Chicken. Meaning number 6 could also be reinforced by a series of photographs: one showing a traditional diner on a street corner, one showing the diner being destroyed by bulldozers, one showing a sign (with the "golden arches" logo conspicuously present) announcing the construction of a new McDonald's on the now vacant corner, one showing the newly constructed restaurant with its arches glowing.

   Three points are worth making here. The first is that we seem to be inclined by nature to attach meanings to objects: symbolism is not a purely literary phenomenon. The second is that the meaning we attach most strongly to an object will be affected by the context in which the object appears. In a literary work, therefore, the meanings that are most strongly present in the reader's mind ought logically to be those determined by the context of the whole story or poem. The third point is that the meanings of symbols are not mutually exclusive. The golden arches do not stop signifying a McDonald's restaurant at the moment they begin to signify the decline of mom-and-pop businesses.

In "The Blue Eyes," the figure-head with its blue gemstone eyes is the most conspicuous symbol. I asked the same six people who gave us themes for "The Blue Eyes" to tell me what they thought this symbol meant. If they could not be content with a single meaning, they could list more than one. Here are the meanings they listed:

1. The wife.

2. The wife *and* the ship.[5]

3. The love the skipper had for his wife *or* the wife that the skipper wanted to have.[6]

4. The skipper's desire to have his wife with him even when his occupation demanded that he be separated from her.

5. The human tendency to idealize the loved one, to project on him or her the qualities one most desires.

6. A guiding force, similar to the assistance spouses give each other as they "sail through the seas of life."

7. The ideal of beauty *or* love *or* both.

8. The power of imagination *or* of art.

Once again, I have tried to arrange the meanings from the narrowest and most obvious to the broadest and most interpretive. In general, the readers who chose meanings near the top of the list said that they saw the points of people who chose the later meanings, but they were themselves uncomfortable with such speculations. The readers who chose meanings near the bottom of the list felt that those who chose near the top were right "as far as they went" but that they didn't go nearly far enough: they had not *interpreted* the symbol.

---

[5] This interpreter refused to rank the two meanings, saying that they are intertwined.
[6] This interpreter said that the figure-head simultaneously symbolized one thing in the skipper's eyes and another in the wife's.

How speculative should one be in assigning a meaning to a literary symbol? There is no fixed rule, but the goal is ordinarily a *plausible interpretation*. To be *plausible* you must be able to develop a strong argument, based on the details of the story, that will support your position. To create an *interpretation*, as was pointed out in Chapter 1, you need to go beyond facts that speak for themselves and take a position with which some reasonable people would disagree. On the list above, I am not convinced that meanings 1 and 2 are interpretations that require argument. The other meanings, however, need demonstration and so might produce interesting essays.

EXERCISE 4   ◆ *Writing Short Arguments for an Interpretation of a Symbol.* Choose a meaning for the figure-head from the list above or suggest a meaning of your own. In a paragraph 100–150 words long, explain why you believe your meaning fits the context of the story well.

A POEM FOR ANALYSIS

The analysis of poetry *as poetry* involves many elements that we will not consider in this chapter, including meter, assonance, consonance, and other aspects of sound. Cramped for space and time, we will concentrate on narrative poems and will treat them essentially as we would other stories. Much is lost by this method, but something is gained. When we examine a poem as a narrative, we may learn things about it that would have escaped our notice had we been concentrating specifically on poetic elements.

A 1986 poem by Sharon Olds[7] is particularly suited to such an analysis.

SUMMER SOLSTICE, NEW YORK CITY

By the end of the longest day of the year he could not stand it,
he went up the iron stairs through the roof of the building
and over the soft, tarry surface
to the edge, put one leg over the complex green tin cornice
5   and said if they came a step closer that was it.
Then the huge machinery of the earth began to work for his life,
the cops came in their suits blue-grey as the sky on a cloudy evening,
and one put on a bulletproof vest, a
black shell around his own life,
10   life of his children's father, in case
the man was armed, and one, slung with a
rope like the sign of his bounden duty,

---

[7]Sharon Olds, born in 1942, won major awards for both her first two volumes of poetry. "Summer Solstice, New York City" first appeared in *The New Yorker* and was later reprinted in her third volume, *The Gold Cell* (1987).

came up out of a hole in the top of the neighboring building,
like the gold hole they say is in the top of the head,
15 and began to lurk toward the man who wanted to die.
The tallest cop approached him directly,
softly, slowly, talking to him, talking, talking,
while the man's leg hung over the lip of the next world,
and the crowd gathered in the street, silent, and the
20 dark hairy net with its implacable grid was
unfolded near the curb and spread out and
stretched as the sheet is prepared to receive at birth.
Then they all came a little closer
where he squatted next to his death, his shirt
25 glowing its milky glow like something
growing in a dish at night in the dark in a lab, and then
everything stopped
as his body jerked and he
stepped down from the parapet and went toward them
30 and they closed on him, I thought they were going to
beat him up, as a mother whose child has been
lost will scream at the child when it's found, they
took him by the arms and held him up and
leaned him against the wall of the chimney and the
35 tall cop lit his cigarette
in his own mouth, and gave it to him, and
then they all lit cigarettes, and the
red glowing ends burned like the
tiny campfires we lit at night
40 back at the beginning of the world.

In the following pages, you'll see first an analysis of the poem and then a short essay discussing the relation of theme and setting in the poem. Both are intended as models for the assignments at the chapter's end. The analysis is, by nature, a rather disjointed set of observations. Such analyses are often written as preparations for more unified, coherent essays. The essay selects some ideas turned up in the analysis and expands on them, leaving other ideas behind. It is less complete, but within its narrowed range, more thorough and (one hopes) more persuasive.

ANALYSIS: THE SIX NARRATIVE ELEMENTS IN "SUMMER SOLSTICE"

1. Setting: Place and Time. The general *place* is New York City. More narrowly, it is a building in the city, the street below (where the crowd gathers) and an adjacent building (from the top of which one policeman emerges). In fact, most of the action is confined to one edge of the building's roof. The *time,* generally, is our century (the century of bulletproof vests), perhaps 1986, the year the poem was published. More specifically, it is June 21, the longest day of the year, and it is dusk: the net and the man emerging from the nearby building are still visible in the early part of the narrative, but later the man's white shirt has a "milky glow," and by the time the story ends, the glowing ends of the cigarettes are very visible. The entire story takes place in a very limited time, perhaps an hour.

One curiosity related to setting is Olds's sudden mention, in the last lines of the poem, of a very different place and time: the campsites of prehistoric men.

2. Character. The poem includes two groups of people that are not separated into individual characters: the crowd in the street and most of "the cops." Three or four characters in the story do have separate identities: the man who threatens suicide, the "tall cop" who talks to him and eventually gives him a cigarette, the policeman who emerges from the top of a neighboring building with a rope on his shoulder, and the policeman who puts on the bulletproof vest (but the man in the vest may be the "tall cop"). All of these characters are *flat.* The man in the bulletproof vest, for example, has a single trait, the desire to protect his life for his children's sake. We know almost nothing about the near suicide, only that "he could not stand it." Whether he is *static* or *dynamic* is impossible to say. He comes back from the parapet, but whether he has by then decided that he *can* stand it we will never know.

3. Point of View. The point of view is difficult to characterize. Only twice do we come close to entering the mind of any character directly involved in the story: when we hear that the man on the roof "could not stand it" and when we are told that one of the policemen puts on the bulletproof vest to protect the "life of his children's father." Neither of these instances seems truly to be a descent into the consciousness of a character, however. Both seem to be the sort of suppositions any observer might draw: isn't a man about to jump from a building likely to be someone who "can't stand it"? And isn't it probable that the man strapping on a bulletproof vest does so partly for the sake of his children? The narrator does not tell the story from the point of view of the suicidal man or the policeman in the vest. Instead, as we discover with a slight shock when the word "I" appears in line 30, she seems to be telling it from her own perspective, as a witness. It now appears that the point of view is *limited* and that the narrator serves as the *center of consciousness.*

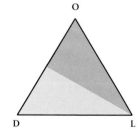

This analysis is not strictly accurate, however, since the narrator has shown us at least one thing she could not have observed from any conceivable vantage point: the man walking up the stairs to the roof. Perhaps the best statement that we can make is that the point of view is *limited omniscient,* with more stress on limitation than in "The Blue Eyes."

4. Plot. The plot of "Summer Solstice" can be stated fairly simply as a series of events linked by causation, though we have to speculate somewhat about the causes:

> Because he could not stand his life, a man climbed to the top of a building and stepped to the edge, prepared to jump. Because he was seen on the parapet, the police were called. Because one of the policemen talked reassuringly to him, the man stepped back from the parapet, rescued or at least reprieved.

Was the man actually prepared to jump? Were the "tall cop's" words reassuring, and was it them that brought the man back from the edge? I am not entirely certain, but the conjectures seem plausible.

A *protagonist-conflict* summary is more difficult because it is hard to identify a protagonist. This does not appear to be the story of a man's struggle to kill himself but the story of "the cops'" struggle to prevent his doing so. Somewhat uneasily, therefore, I would offer this as a possible summary:

> The cops [the collective protagonist] want to save [their goal] the life of a man who is poised to commit suicide. He warns them away, saying that he will jump if they come one step closer [the conflict]. They take the usual measures to protect him, including the spreading of a safety net, and attempt to persuade him not to jump. After a time, the persuasion works. He steps back from the parapet; they surround him and share a cigarette with him.

5. Theme. Among the possible themes of this story, the one that strikes me most forcibly is this: the despair we sometimes feel in isolation is weaker than the common bond of humanity that helps us endure. That despair is present in the poem is obvious: the man "could not stand it." But something brings him back from the brink, and the intriguing difficulty of interpreting the poem is to identify the force that counters the despair. It is partly the setting that makes me call the force the "common bond of humanity." New York City has, after all, a reputation for being a gigantic, impersonal, spiritless place. But in Olds's poem, it notices this one man on a ledge, it watches him from the street, it climbs out of a nearby building with a rope to save him, it stretches out a safety net, it approaches him "softly, slowly" in the person of "the tallest cop . . . talking to him, talking, talking." And finally, when the man steps down from the parapet, it encloses him, holds him, lights a cigarette for him, and passes it from mouth to mouth. The poem seems to assert that when the chips are down, we can care for each other as if we were members of one large family.

6. Symbolism. Like many poems, "Summer Solstice" is so dense with meanings that many things in it acquire a symbolic importance. The police might be seen as symbols of the city or the society, for instance, or even as symbols of something larger yet, "the huge machinery of the earth" that works to save each human. New York City might be seen as a symbol of modern life, with its pressures and its apparent lack of concern for the individual. The fire that glows on the ends of the cigarettes when the rescuers and the would-be suicide share a smoke might be a symbol of the bond that holds us together and has held us together since we lit "tiny campfires . . . back at the beginning of the world."

A SAMPLE ESSAY

"Summer Solstice, New York City" presents several difficulties, several obstacles to understanding, and so is a good subject for an essay. Among the difficulties are these:

1. Because of the story's point of view, we don't know what the motivations of the suicidal man are. We don't know what, precisely, he couldn't stand at the poem's beginning, and we don't know what persuaded him to step back from the parapet at the story's end.

2. The theme of the poem is not self-evident. Reasonable people could certainly disagree about it.

3. It is not immediately clear why Olds sets the poem in time as she does. Is there some special significance to the sunset hour of the summer solstice?

4. The sixth line of the poem—"Then the huge machinery of the earth began to work for his life"—sounds especially important, but its meaning is vague. Readers may wonder what, precisely, this "huge machinery" includes.

5. Olds repeatedly introduces similes and metaphors that compare things in the setting to rather unlikely things outside the setting. The police uniforms are compared to "the sky on a cloudy evening," for example, and the glow of the cigarettes is compared to the glow of "tiny campfires" in prehistoric times. The reader may wonder if there is a pattern to these comparisons.

You'll notice that not all these problems are precisely correlated to the six elements used in analyzing narratives. Problems often present themselves in unexpected forms, and part of the challenge of writing a good essay about literature is to relate a nonstandard problem to the standard terms of analysis.

The following short paper focuses on the fifth problem listed above. It attempts to "solve" the problem of Olds's comparisons by showing that they are related to the theme of the poem. The paper handles in a fairly conventional fashion the practical problems of an essay about a literary work: how to introduce quotations, what balance to strike between quotations and commentary, how much summary to include, and other matters of form. To that extent, you may find it useful as a pattern for your own essay. No pattern, however, should be followed slavishly. In practice, essays by literary critics vary tremendously in form, and some assignments will require you to produce a paper of a very different sort.

THE FIRE IN SHARON OLDS'S "SUMMER SOLSTICE, NEW YORK CITY"

At the end of Sharon Olds's "Summer Solstice, New York City," a man who has been coaxed back from the parapet of the building from which he had threatened to jump is surrounded by a group of policemen. The poem's narrator says, "I thought they were going to/ beat him up, as a mother whose child has been/ lost will scream at the child when it's found . . ." (30–32). Instead, the police "took him by the arms" to a safe place,

and the
tall cop lit a cigarette
in his own mouth, and gave it to him, and
then they all lit cigarettes, and the
red glowing ends burned like the
tiny campfires we lit at night
back at the beginning of the world. (34–40)

The fire is a symbol of love, of community. It links prehistoric men and the men gathered on the roof of a New York building. In a sense, this link comes as a complete surprise since no mention of prehistoric times has preceded it. But in another sense the link between prehistoric and modern times is implied throughout the poem: in fact, this link points directly to the theme.

The poem's New York City setting would seem to be as far removed from "the beginning of the world" as it is possible to be, but Olds reminds us repeatedly that underneath contemporary life are the ancient experiences of all humanity. The title's mention of the summer solstice, for example, calls to mind astronomical observations older than Stonehenge, older than ancient Greece, older than history. The calculation of the solstices and equinoxes is one of the earliest great human accomplishments, one of the cornerstones of agriculture and so of civilization. It takes us back—in imagination at least—to the time when there were not cities, but tribes; not strangers living in close proximity, but extended families. The New Yorker who recognizes that this is the longest day of the year is echoing a thought his ancestors had several thousand years ago.

Olds also links the present time to prehistory by comparing objects from the poem's present time to objects and events that are relatively timeless parts of human life. The policemen's suits are "blue-grey as the sky on a cloudy evening" (7). The bulletproof vest is "a/ black shell" (8–9) that may remind the reader of ancient armor. The safety net is "stretched as the sheet is prepared to receive at birth" (22). She repeatedly refers to the timeless relations of family life and the unchanging realities of the body. The man who puts on the vest is protecting the "life of his children's father" (10). The man with the rope comes "out of a hole in the top of the

Sample Paper

The title indicates the essay's focus.

The summary is minimal; just enough to make the essay comprehensible to someone unfamiliar with the poem.

Quotations longer than four lines are indented.

The thesis shows the problem—to explain the presence of the campfires. It also uses an element stressed in literary analysis: theme.

"Calls to whose mind?" you may ask. If this reaction is purely personal, if no other readers share it, then this interpretation is not useful.

The use of very short quotations ties the interpretation to the text. It shows that the assertions have a basis.

neighboring building,/ like the gold hole they say is in the top of the head" (13–14), a reference to folklore about the fontanel, the soft spot in a baby's skull. And, as we saw, the cops who surround the man at the poem's end are compared to a mother who finds her lost child.

Only once does Olds introduce a jarringly modern image—when she compares the man's shirt "glowing its milky glow" to "something/ growing in a dish at night in the dark in a lab" (25–26). But even this image may fit the pattern. The policemen who save the man are always linked with timeless things, with the family or with nature. But the man in danger, the man "squatted next to his death" (24), is linked to something new and vaguely sinister.

The pattern seems to point the way to the poem's theme: that the strongest bond of human life, the love that holds the family or tribe together, is still with us. It may sometimes be obscured. The city may produce isolation or despair, but it is still possible for "the huge machinery of the earth" to work for us. The men sharing their cigarettes on top of a building in New York City are made of essentially the same stuff as the men who gathered around campfires "back at the beginning of the world" (40).

The interpreter should attempt to account for parts of the work that don't seem to fit the interpretation.

The conclusion reminds the reader of the problem raised in the introduction.

WRITING ESSAYS ABOUT LITERATURE: POINTS TO CONSIDER

Showing an understanding of a work, which is the most common purpose for essays written in college literature classes, requires that you begin with careful reading and analysis. The analysis need not be written for any audience other than yourself, but you will probably find that the process of writing element-by-element notes forces you to see aspects of the work that otherwise would escape your attention.

The following questions can guide you through your analysis of a narrative:

SETTING

Place

Where generally is the story set? (If the story is science fiction, you may need to begin with the planet. Ordinarily the country or city is a good starting point.)

What are the more specific settings? (You may find locations as specific as particular rooms.)

Which is the principal setting?

How does awareness of place affect the way you read the story?

Time

What is the general time period of the story? (The century might be a good starting point.)

What is the more specific time period? (You may be able to narrow to an hour.)

How does awareness of time affect the way you read the story?

CHARACTER

Who are the characters in the story?

Which characters are relatively *round*? Which are relatively *flat*?

What are the qualities or characteristics of the characters?

Are any of the characters ambiguous, hard to figure?

Which characters are *static*? Which are *dynamic*?

What change do you see in the dynamic characters?

POINT OF VIEW

If there is a first-person narrator, is he or she essentially inside the story (a character) or outside it? Does the narrator serve essentially as a witness or as a substitute author?

What passages are presented from an *omniscient* point of view? Which from a *dramatic*? Which from a *limited*?

Does one character serve as the story's *center of consciousness*?

On balance, how would you characterize the point of view? Where would you put it on the point-of-view triangle?

How does consciousness of the point of view affect the way you read the story?

PLOT

How would you summarize the plot as a sequence of causes and effects?

Who is the protagonist of the story?

How would you summarize the plot in terms of the protagonist's *goal* and the *conflicts* he or she becomes involved with?

THEME

What are some statements about the human condition that seem to be suggested by the story?

Which of these statements seems best to match your understanding of the story?

SYMBOLISM

What are the principal symbols in the story?

What do you understand their meaning to be?

Answering these questions will not automatically give you an understanding of the story but will focus your attention on matters that may aid your understanding.

More important, the analysis may reveal a problem that makes your understanding of the narrative incomplete. With thought, such a problem can become an excellent topic for an essay. In fact, one way to search for a topic is to make a list of problems and then discuss the list with a classmate or other person who knows the narrative. If your classmate also finds one of your problems difficult, and if you think you can propose a solution that will improve his or her understanding, then you have probably found a promising paper topic. In writing your draft, remember that your essay is essentially an argument, that you must assemble evidence to back your assertions.

QUESTIONS FOR PEER REVIEW

When your draft is complete, you may benefit by having a peer reviewer answer the following questions:

1. Do I identify a problem that you, too, recognize as a problem? That is, have I found something in the narrative that has been an obstacle to your understanding?

2. Do I propose a solution to the problem that you find plausible? What aspects of my solution are most convincing? What aspects are least convincing?

3. Can you propose a better solution to the problem?

4. Is my argument based on a sound analysis of the narrative elements? If I have made mistakes about elements, what are they?

In addition to these questions, you may want your peer reviewer to answer the general questions on pages 65–66.

ASSIGNMENT 1: *AN ANALYSIS OF A NARRATIVE*

Choose one of the short stories or poems collected on pages 381–403. Write a detailed analysis using the six narrative elements as outlined above.

ASSIGNMENT 2: *AN ESSAY ON A PROBLEM OF INTERPRETATION*

After analyzing the narrative elements, write a 500- to 750-word paper in which you describe a problem of interpretation in a narrative and propose a solution to that problem. The following questions may serve as problems in themselves, or they may point you to related problems:

1. Can we understand the true character of the Duchess in "My Last Duchess"?

2. What is the most important conflict in "The Chicago Defender Sends a Man to Little Rock"?

3. Can we account for the suicide in "Richard Cory"?

4. Who (or what) is Arnold Friend in "Where Are You Going, Where Have You Been?".

5. What is the theme of "Day of the Butterfly"?

6. Who is the protagonist in "The Hammer Man," and what is the struggle?

7. What are the sources of conflict in "Star Food"?

Your analysis of any of these stories should reveal reasons that such questions cannot be answered easily or certainly.

ASSIGNMENT 3: *A PROBLEM ESSAY WITH SOURCES*

A common assignment in literature classes requires you to refer to "outside" or "secondary" sources in a paper that interprets a story or poem. One way to approach such an essay is to begin with a statement of how a previous interpreter or interpreters have attempted to solve the problem you discuss, then describe your own solution. This is the approach taken by Robert Miller in "Mark Twain's Jim" (page 413) and by Charles R. Woodard in "Wilbur's 'Still, Citizen Sparrow' " (page 416).

Write an essay on this pattern, addressing a problem in "My Last Duchess," "Richard Cory," or "Where Are You Going, Where Have You Been?" These three works have received enough critical attention that you should be able to find at least one critic interested in a problem you also find interesting. Valuable sources for locating such criticism are the *MLA International Bibliography of Books and Articles on the Modern Languages and Literatures, Contemporary Literary Criticism, Poetry Explication,* and *Twentieth-Century Short Story Explication.*

ASSIGNMENT 4: *A STUDY OF THE EFFECT OF CONTEXT*

"The Blue Eyes," though Isak Dinesen sometimes recited it (from memory) as a separate story, was originally embedded in a larger story "Peter and Rosa" from *Winter's Tales.* Read "Peter and Rosa" and write an essay on the following question: how is our understanding of "The Blue Eyes" affected by its placement inside "Peter and Rosa"?

MY LAST DUCHESS

Robert Browning

Robert Browning (1812–89) was one of the dominant English poets of the Victorian era. His most remarkable poems are dramatic monologues—poems in which a single speaker reveals setting, conflict, and character. Since the character is talking to another character rather than to the audience, the reader seems to overhear the monologue, and interpreting it presents the reader with the challenge of recreating the context in which it would have taken place. "My Last Duchess" first appeared in Dramatic Lyrics *(1842).*

Ferrara[1]

1 THAT'S MY LAST DUCHESS PAINTED ON
   the wall,
Looking as if she were alive. I call
That piece a wonder, now: Frà Pandolf's[2] hands
Worked busily a day, and there she stands.
5 Will't please you sit and look at her? I said
"Fra Pandolf" by design, for never read
Strangers like you that pictured countenance,
The depth and passion of its earnest glance,
But to myself they turned (since none puts by
10 The curtain I have drawn for you, but I)
And seemed as they would ask me, if they durst,
How such a glance came there; so, not the first
Are you to turn and ask thus. Sir, 'twas not
Her husband's presence only, called that spot
15 Of joy into the Duchess' cheek: perhaps
Frà Pandolf chanced to say "Her mantle laps
Over my lady's wrist too much," or "Paint
Must never hope to reproduce the faint

Half-flush that dies along her throat": such stuff
Was courtesy, she thought, and cause enough 20
For calling up that spot of joy. She had
A heart—how shall I say?—too soon made glad,
Too easily impressed; she liked whate'er
She looked on, and her looks went everywhere.
Sir, 'twas all one! My favor at her breast, 25
The dropping of the daylight in the West,
The bough of cherries some officious fool
Broke in the orchard for her, the white mule
She rode with round the terrace—all and each
Would draw from her alike the approving speech, 30
Or blush, at least. She thanked men—good! but
   thanked
Somehow—I know not how—as if she ranked
My gift of a nine-hundred-years-old name
With anybody's gift. Who'd stoop to blame
This sort of trifling? Even had you skill 35
In speech—which I have not—to make your will
Quite clear to such an one, and say, "Just this
Or that in you disgusts me; here you miss,
Or there exceed the mark"—and if she let
Herself be lessoned so, nor plainly set 40
Her wits to yours, forsooth, and made excuse,
—E'en then would be some stooping; and I
   choose

---

[1] *Ferrara:* a center of culture during the early Italian Renaissance.
[2] Frà Pandolf: an imaginary artist, intended to represent a number of early Renaissance painters; "Fra" (brother) was the title given to monks and friars.

Never to stoop. Oh sir, she smiled, no doubt,
Whene'er I passed her; but who passed without
Much the same smile? This grew; I gave com-
    mands;
Then all smiles stopped together. There she stands
As if alive. Will 't please you rise? We'll meet
The company below, then. I repeat,
The Count your master's known munificence

Is ample warrant that no just pretense   50
Of mine for dowry will be disallowed;
Though his fair daughter's self, as I avowed
At starting, is my object. Nay, we'll go
Together down, sir. Notice Neptune,[3] though,
Taming a sea-horse, thought a rarity,   55
Which Claus of Innsbruck[4] cast in bronze for
    me! ◆

---

[3] Neptune: in Roman mythology, the god of the sea.
[4] Claus of Innsbruck: another imaginary artist.

RICHARD CORY

Edwin Arlington Robinson

*Edwin Arlington Robinson (1869–1935), an American poet best known for his long
narrative poems and for his shorter psychological portraits of New England characters,
published "Richard Cory" in his book* The Children of the Night *(1897).*

1   WHENEVER RICHARD CORY WENT DOWN
        town,
    We people on the pavement looked at him:
    He was a gentleman from sole to crown,
        Clean favored, and imperially slim.

5   And he was always quietly arrayed,
        And he was always human when he talked;
    But still he fluttered pulses when he said,
        "Good-morning," and he glittered when he walked.

    And he was rich—yes, richer than a king,
10   And admirably schooled in every grace:
    In fine, we thought that he was everything
        To make us wish that we were in his place.

So on we worked, and waited for the light,
    And went without the meat, and cursed the
        bread;
And Richard Cory, one calm summer night,   15
    Went home and put a bullet through his head. ◆

THE CHICAGO DEFENDER SENDS A MAN TO LITTLE ROCK

Gwendolyn Brooks

Gwendolyn Brooks, an American poet and novelist, is best known for her portrayal of the lives of the black citizens of her native city, Chicago. She won the Pulitzer prize for Poetry early in her career (for her 1949 work Annie Allen*), but most critics agree that her later work is more significant, politically and artistically. "The Chicago Defender," first published in 1960, was reprinted in Brooks's* Selected Poems *(1963).*

Fall, 1957

1   IN LITTLE ROCK[1] THE PEOPLE BEAR
Babes, and comb and part their hair
And watch the want ads, put repair
To roof and latch. While wheat toast burns
5   A woman waters multiferns.

Time upholds or overturns
The many, tight, and small concerns.

In Little Rock the people sing
Sunday hymns like anything,
10 Through Sunday pomp and polishing.

And after testament and tunes,
Some soften Sunday afternoons
With lemon tea and Lorna Doones.

I forecast
15 And I believe
Come Christmas Little Rock will cleave
To Christmas tree and trifle, weave,
From laugh and tinsel, texture fast.

In Little Rock is baseball; Barcarolle.
That hotness in July . . . the uniformed figures raw   20
    and implacable
And not intellectual,
Batting the hotness or clawing the suffering dust.
The Open Air Concert, on the special twilight
    green. . . .
When Beethoven is brutal or whispers to lady-like
    air.
Blanket-sitters are solemn, as Johann troubles to lean 25
To tell them what to mean. . . .

There is love, too, in Little Rock. Soft women softly
Opening themselves in kindness.
Or, pitying one's blindness,
Awaiting one's pleasure   30
In azure
Glory with anguished rose at the root. . . .
to wash away old semi-discomfitures.
They re-teach purple and unsullen blue.
The wispy soils go. And uncertain   35
Half-havings have they clarified to sures.

In Little Rock they know
Not answering the telephone is a way of rejecting
    life,
That it is our business to be bothered, is our business
To cherish bores or boredom, be polite   40
To lies and love and many-faceted fuzziness.

[1]Little Rock: the desegregation of Central High in Little Rock, Arkansas, in 1957 was resisted by both the local population and state authorities. President Eisenhower eventually had to send in federal troops to maintain order.

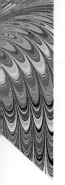

I scratch my head, massage the hate-I-had.
I blink across my prim and pencilled pad.
The saga I was sent for is not down.
Because there is a puzzle in this town.
The biggest News I do not dare
Telegraph to the Editor's chair:
"They are like people everywhere."

The angry Editor would reply
50 In hundred harryings of Why.

And true, they are hurling spittle, rock,
Garbage and fruit in Little Rock.
And I saw coiling storm a-writhe
On bright madonnas. And a scythe
Of men harassing brownish girls.   55
(The bows and barrettes in the curls
And braids declined away from joy.)

I saw a bleeding brownish boy. . . .

The lariat lynch-wish I deplored.

The loveliest lynchee was our Lord. ◆

WHERE ARE YOU GOING, WHERE HAVE YOU BEEN?

Joyce Carol Oates

Joyce Carol Oates, a professor of English at Princeton University, is a prolific novelist, short-story writer, poet, and critic. "Where Are You Going, Where Have You Been?" is from her 1970 book The Wheel of Love and Other Stories.

To Bob Dylan

1 HER NAME WAS CONNIE. SHE WAS FIFTEEN and she had a quick nervous giggling habit of craning her neck to glance into mirrors or checking other people's faces to make sure her own was all right. Her mother, who noticed everything and knew everything and who hadn't much reason any longer to look at her own face, always scolded Connie about it. "Stop gawking at yourself, who are you? You think you're so pretty?" she would say. Connie would raise her eyebrows at these familiar complaints and look right through her mother, into a shadowy vision of herself as she was right at that moment: she knew she was pretty and that was everything. Her mother had been

pretty once too, if you could believe those old snapshots in the album, but now her looks were gone and that was why she was always after Connie.

2 "Why don't you keep your room clean like your sister? How've you got your hair fixed—what the hell stinks? Hair spray? You don't see your sister using that junk."

3 Her sister June was twenty-four and still lived at home. She was a secretary in the high school Connie attended, and if that wasn't bad enough—with her in the same building—she was so plain and chunky and steady that Connie had to hear her praised all the time by her mother and her mother's sisters. June did this, June did that, she saved money and helped clean the house and cooked and Connie couldn't do a thing,

her mind was all filled with trashy daydreams. Their father was away at work most of the time and when he came home he wanted supper and he read the newspaper at supper and after supper he went to bed. He didn't bother talking much to them, but around his bent head Connie's mother kept picking at her until Connie wished her mother were dead and she herself were dead and it were all over. "She makes me want to throw up sometimes," she complained to her friends. She had a high, breathless, amused voice which made everything she said sound a little forced, whether it was sincere or not.

4   There was one good thing: June went places with girlfriends of hers, girls who were just as plain and steady as she, and so when Connie wanted to do that her mother had no objections. The father of Connie's best girlfriend drove the girls the three miles to town and left them off at a shopping plaza, so that they could walk through the stores or go to a movie, and when he came to pick them up again at eleven he never bothered to ask what they had done.

5   They must have been familiar sights, walking around that shopping plaza in their shorts and flat ballerina slippers that always scuffed the sidewalk, with charm bracelets jingling on their thin wrists; they would lean together to whisper and laugh secretly if someone passed by who amused or interested them. Connie had long dark blond hair that drew anyone's eye to it, and she wore part of it pulled up on her head and puffed out and the rest of it she let fall down her back. She wore a pullover jersey blouse that looked one way when she was at home and another way when she was away from home. Everything about her had two sides to it, one for home and one for anywhere that was not home: her walk that could be childlike and bobbing, or languid enough to make anyone think she was hearing music in her head, her mouth which was pale and smirking most of the time, but bright and pink on these evenings out, her laugh which was cynical and drawling at home—"Ha, ha, very funny"—but high-pitched and nervous anywhere else, like the jingling of the charms on her bracelet.

6   Sometimes they did go shopping or to a movie, but sometimes they went across the highway, ducking fast across the busy road, to a drive-in restaurant where older kids hung out. The restaurant was shaped like a big bottle, though squatter than a real bottle, and on its cap was a revolving figure of a grinning boy who held a hamburger aloft. One night in midsummer they ran across, breathless with daring, and right away someone leaned out a car window and invited them over, but it was just a boy from high school they didn't like. It made them feel good to be able to ignore him. They went up through the maze of parked and cruising cars to the bright-lit, fly-infested restaurant, their faces pleased and expectant as if they were entering a sacred building that loomed out of the night to give them what haven and what blessing they yearned for. They sat at the counter and crossed their legs at the ankles, their thin shoulders rigid with excitement, and listened to the music that made everything so good: the music was always in the background like music at a church service, it was something to depend upon.

7   A boy named Eddie came in to talk with them. He sat backward on his stool, turning himself jerkily around in semicircles and then stopping and turning again, and after a while he asked Connie if she would like something to eat. She said she did and so she tapped her friend's arm on her way out—her friend pulled her face up into a brave droll look—and Connie said she would meet her at eleven, across the way. "I just hate to leave her like that," Connie said earnestly, but the boy said that she wouldn't be alone for long. So they went out to his car and on the way Connie couldn't help but let her eyes wander over the windshields and faces all around her, her face gleaming with a joy that had nothing to do with Eddie or even this place; it might have been the music. She drew her shoulders up and sucked in her breath with the pure pleasure of being alive, and just at that moment she happened to glance at a face just a few feet from hers. It was a boy with shaggy black hair, in a convertible jalopy painted gold. He stared at her and then his lips widened into a grin. Connie slit her eyes at him and turned away, but she couldn't help glancing back and there he was still watching her. He wagged a finger and laughed and said, "Gonna get

you, baby," and Connie turned away again without Eddie noticing anything.

She spent three hours with him, at the restaurant where they ate hamburgers and drank Cokes in wax cups that were always sweating, and then down an alley a mile or so away, and when he left her off at five to eleven only the movie house was still open at the plaza. Her girlfriend was there, talking with a boy. When Connie came up the two girls smiled at each other and Connie said, "How was the movie?" and the girl said, "*You* should know." They rode off with the girl's father, sleepy and pleased, and Connie couldn't help but look at the darkened shopping plaza with its big empty parking lot and its signs that were faded and ghostly now, and over at the drive-in restaurant where cars were still circling tirelessly. She couldn't hear the music at this distance.

9   Next morning June asked her how the movie was and Connie said, "So-so."

10   She and that girl and occasionally another girl went out several times a week that way, and the rest of the time Connie spent around the house—it was summer vacation—getting in her mother's way and thinking, dreaming, about the boys she met. But all the boys fell back and dissolved into a single face that was not even a face, but an idea, a feeling, mixed up with the urgent insistent pounding of the music and the humid night air of July. Connie's mother kept dragging her back to the daylight by finding things for her to do or saying, suddenly, "What's this about the Pettinger girl?"

11   And Connie would say nervously, "Oh, her. That dope." She always drew thick clear lines between herself and such girls, and her mother was simple and kindly enough to believe her. Her mother was so simple, Connie thought, that it was maybe cruel to fool her so much. Her mother went scuffling around the house in old bedroom slippers and complained over the telephone to one sister about the other, then the other called up and the two of them complained about the third one. If June's name was mentioned her mother's tone was approving, and if Connie's name was mentioned it was disapproving. This did not really mean she disliked Connie and actually Connie thought that her mother preferred her to June because she was prettier, but the two of them kept up a pretense of exasperation, a sense that they were tugging and struggling over something of little value to either of them. Sometimes, over coffee, they were almost friends, but something would come up—some vexation that was like a fly buzzing suddenly around their heads—and their faces went hard with contempt.

12   One Sunday Connie got up at eleven—none of them bothered with church—and washed her hair so that it could dry all day long, in the sun. Her parents and sisters were going to a barbecue at an aunt's house and Connie said no, she wasn't interested, rolling her eyes to let her mother know just what she thought of it. "Stay home alone then," her mother said sharply. Connie sat out back in a lawn chair and watched them drive away, her father quiet and bald, hunched around so that he could back the car out, her mother with a look that was still angry and not at all softened through the windshield, and in the back seat poor old June all dressed up as if she didn't know what a barbecue was, with all the running yelling kids and the flies. Connie sat with her eyes closed in the sun, dreaming and dazed with the warmth about her as if this were a kind of love, the caresses of love, and her mind slipped over onto thoughts of the boy she had been with the night before and how nice he had been, how sweet it always was, not the way someone like June would suppose but sweet, gentle, the way it was in movies and promised in songs; and when she opened her eyes she hardly knew where she was, the back yard ran off into weeds and a fence line of trees and behind it the sky was perfectly blue and still. The asbestos "ranch house" that was now three years old startled her—it looked small. She shook her head as if to get awake.

13   It was too hot. She went inside the house and turned on the radio to drown out the quiet. She sat on the edge of her bed, barefoot, and listened for an hour and a half to a program called XYZ Sunday Jamboree, record after record of hard, fast, shrieking songs she sang along with, interspersed by exclama-

tions from "Bobby King": "An' look here you girls at Napoleon's—Son and Charley want you to pay real close attention to this song coming up!"

14 And Connie paid close attention herself, bathed in a glow of slow-pulsed joy that seemed to rise mysteriously out of the music itself and lay languidly about the airless little room, breathed in and breathed out with each gentle rise and fall of her chest.

15 After a while she heard a car coming up the drive. She sat up at once, startled, because it couldn't be her father so soon. The gravel kept crunching all the way in from the road—the driveway was long— and Connie ran to the window. It was a car she didn't know. It was an open jalopy, painted a bright gold that caught the sunlight opaquely. Her heart began to pound and her fingers snatched at her hair, checking it, and she whispered "Christ, Christ," wondering how bad she looked. The car came to a stop at the side door and the horn sounded four short taps as if this were a signal Connie knew.

16 She went into the kitchen and approached the door slowly, then hung out the screen door, her bare toes curling down off the step. There were two boys in the car and now she recognized the driver: he had shaggy, shabby black hair that looked crazy as a wig and he was grinning at her.

17 "I ain't late, am I?" He said.

18 "Who the hell do you think you are?" Connie said.

19 "Toldja I'd be out, didn't I?"

20 "I don't even know who you are."

21 She spoke sullenly, careful to show no interest or pleasure, and he spoke in a fast bright monotone. Connie looked past him to the other boy, taking her time. He had fair brown hair, with a lock that fell onto his forehead. His sideburns gave him a fierce, embarrassed look, but so far he hadn't even bothered to glance at her. Both boys wore sunglasses. The driver's glasses were metallic and mirrored everything in miniature.

22 "You wanta come for a ride?" he said.

23 Connie smirked and let her hair fall loose over one shoulder.

"Don'tcha like my car? New paint job," he said. "Hey."

"What?"

"You're cute."

She pretended to fidget, chasing flies away from the door.

"Don'tcha believe me, or what?" he said.

29 "Look, I don't even know who you are," Connie said in disgust.

30 "Hey, Ellie's got a radio, see. Mine's broke down." He lifted his friend's arm and showed her the little transistor the boy was holding, and now Connie began to hear the music. It was the same program that was playing inside the house.

31 "Bobby King?" she said.

32 "I listen to him all the time. I think he's great."

33 "He's kind of great," Connie said reluctantly.

34 "Listen, that guy's *great*. He knows where the action is."

35 Connie blushed a little, because the glasses made it impossible for her to see just what this boy was looking at. She couldn't decide if she liked him or if he was just a jerk, and so she dawdled in the doorway and wouldn't come down or go back inside. She said, "What's all that stuff painted on your car?"

36 "Can'tcha read it?" He opened the door very carefully, as if he was afraid it might fall off. He slid out just as carefully, planting his feet firmly on the ground, the tiny metallic world in his glasses slowing down like gelatine hardening and in the midst of it Connie's bright green blouse. "This here is my name, to begin with," he said. ARNOLD FRIEND was written in tarlike black letters on the side, with a drawing of a round grinning face that reminded Connie of a pumpkin, except it wore sunglasses. "I wanta introduce myself, I'm Arnold Friend and that's my real name and I'm gonna be your friend, honey, and inside the car's Ellie Oscar, he's kinda shy." Ellie brought his transistor radio up to his shoulder and balanced it there. "Now these numbers are a secret code, honey," Arnold Friend explained. He read off the numbers, 33, 19, 17 and raised his eyebrows at her to see what she thought of that, but she didn't think much of it.

The left rear fender had been smashed and around it was written, on the gleaming gold background: DONE BY CRAZY WOMAN DRIVER. Connie had to laugh at that. Arnold Friend was pleased at her laughter and looked up at her. "Around the other side's a lot more—you wanta come and see them?"

"No."

38 "Why not?"

39 "Why should I?"

40 "Don'tcha wanta see what's on the car? Don'tcha wanta go for a ride?"

41 "I don't know."

42 "Why not?"

43 "I got things to do."

44 "Like what?"

45 "Things."

46 He laughed as if she had said something funny. He slapped his thighs. He was standing in a strange way, leaning back against the car as if he were balancing himself. He wasn't tall, only an inch or so taller than she would be if she came down to him. Connie liked the way he was dressed, which was the way all of them dressed: tight faded jeans stuffed into black, scuffed boots, a belt that pulled his waist in and showed how lean he was, and a white pullover shirt that was a little soiled and showed the hard small muscles of his arms and shoulders. He looked as if he probably did hard work, lifting and carrying things. Even his neck looked muscular. And his face was a familiar face, somehow: the jaw and chin and cheeks slightly darkened, because he hadn't shaved for a day or two, and the nose long and hawklike, sniffing as if she were a treat he was going to gobble up and it was all a joke.

47 "Connie, you ain't telling the truth. This is your day set aside for a ride with me and you know it," he said, still laughing. The way he straightened and recovered from his fit of laughing showed that it had been all fake.

48 "How do you know what my name is?" she said suspiciously.

49 "It's Connie."

50 "Maybe and maybe not."

51 "I know my Connie," he said, wagging his finger. Now she remembered him even better, back at the restaurant, and her cheeks warmed at the thought of how she sucked in her breath just at the moment she passed him—how she must have looked at him. And he had remembered her. "Ellie and I come out here especially for you," he said. "Ellie can sit in back. How about it?"

52 "Where?"

53 "Where what?"

54 "Where're we going?"

55 He looked at her. He took off the sunglasses and she saw how pale the skin around his eyes was, like holes that were not in shadow but instead in light. His eyes were like chips of broken glass that catch the light in an amiable way. He smiled. It was as if the idea of going for a ride somewhere, to some place, was a new idea to him.

56 "Just for a ride, Connie sweetheart."

57 "I never said my name was Connie," she said.

58 "But I know what it is. I know your name and all about you, lots of things," Arnold Friend said. He had not moved yet but stood still leaning back against the side of his jalopy. "I took a special interest in you, such a pretty girl, and found out all about you like I know your parents and sister are gone somewheres and I know where and how long they're going to be gone, and I know who you were with last night, and your best girlfriend's name is Betty. Right?"

59 He spoke in a simple lilting voice, exactly as if he were reciting the words to a song. His smile assured her that everything was fine. In the car Ellie turned up the volume on his radio and did not bother to look around at them.

60 "Ellie can sit in the back seat," Arnold Friend said. He indicated his friend with a casual jerk of his chin, as if Ellie did not count and she should not bother with him.

61 "How'd you find out all that stuff?" Connie said.

62 "Listen: Betty Schultz and Tony Fitch and Jimmy Pettinger and Nancy Pettinger," he said, in a chant. "Raymond Stanley and Bob Hutter—"

63 "Do you know all those kids?"

64 "I know everybody."

65 "Look, you're kidding, You're not from around here."

66 "Sure."

67 "But—how come we never saw you before?"

68 "Sure you saw me before," he said. He looked down at his boots, as if he were a little offended. "You just don't remember."

69 "I guess I'd remember you," Connie said.

70 "Yeah?" he looked up at this, beaming. He was pleased. He began to mark time with the music from Ellie's radio, tapping his fists lightly together. Connie looked away from his smile to the car, which was painted so bright it almost hurt her eyes to look at it. She looked at that name. ARNOLD FRIEND. And up at the front fender was an expression that was familiar—MAN THE FLYING SAUCERS. It was an expression kids had used the year before, but didn't use this year. She looked at it for a while as if the words meant something to her that she did not yet know.

71 "What're you thinking about? Huh?" Arnold Friend demanded. "Not worried about your hair blowing around in the car, are you?"

72 "No."

73 "Think I maybe can't drive good?"

74 "How do I know?"

75 "You're a hard girl to handle. How come?" he said. "Don't you know I'm your friend? Didn't you see me put my sign in the air when you walked by?"

76 "What sign?"

77 "My sign." And he drew an X in the air, leaning out toward her. They were maybe ten feet apart. After his hand fell back to his side the X was still in the air, almost visible. Connie let the screen door close and stood perfectly still inside it, listening to the music from her radio and the boy's blend together. She stared at Arnold Friend. He stood there so stiffly re-laxed, pretending to be relaxed, with one hand idly on the door handle as if he were keeping himself up that way and had no intention of ever moving again. She recognized most things about him, the tight jeans that showed his thighs and buttocks and the greasy leather

boots and the tight shirt, and even that slippery friendly smile of his, that sleepy dreamy smile that all the boys used to get across ideas they didn't want to put into words. She recognized all this and also the singsong way he talked, slightly mocking, kidding, but serious and a little melancholy, and she recognized the way he tapped one fist against the other in homage of the perpetual music behind him. But all these things did not come together.

78 She said suddenly, "Hey, how old are you?"

79 His smile faded. She could see then that he wasn't a kid, he was much older—thirty, maybe more. At this knowledge her heart began to pound faster.

80 "That's a crazy thing to ask. Can'tcha see I'm your own age?"

81 "Like hell you are."

82 "Or maybe a coupla years older, I'm eighteen."

83 "Eighteen?" she said doubtfully.

84 He grinned to reassure her and lines appeared at the corners of his mouth. His teeth were big and white. He grinned so broadly his eyes became slits and she saw how thick the lashes were, thick and black as if painted with a black tarlike material. Then he seemed to become embarrassed, abruptly, and looked over his shoulder at Ellie. "*Him*, he's crazy," he said. "Ain't he a riot, he's a nut, a real character." Ellie was still listening to the music. His sunglasses told nothing about what he was thinking. He wore a bright orange shirt unbuttoned halfway to show his chest, which was a pale, bluish chest and not muscu-lar like Arnold Friend's. His shirt collar was turned up all around and the very tips of the collar pointed out past his chin as if they were protecting him. He was pressing the transistor radio up against his ear and sat there in a kind of daze, right in the sun.

85 "He's kinda strange," Connie said.

86 "Hey, she says you're kinda strange! Kinda strange!" Arnold Friend cried. He pounded on the car to get Ellie's attention. Ellie turned for the first time and Connie saw with shock that he wasn't a kid either—he had a fair, hairless face, cheeks reddened slightly as if the veins grew too close to the surface of

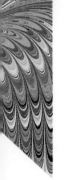

his skin, the face of a forty-year-old baby. Connie felt a wave of dizziness rise in her at this sight and she stared at him as if waiting for something to change the shock of the moment, make it all right again. Ellie's lips kept shaping words, mumbling along with the words blasting in his ear.

"Maybe you two better go away," Connie said faintly.

88 "What? How come?" Arnold Friend cried. "We come out here to take you for a ride. It's Sunday." He had the voice of the man on the radio now. It was the same voice, Connie thought. "Don'tcha know it's Sunday all day and honey, no matter who you were with last night today you're with Arnold Friend and don't you forget it!—Maybe you better step out here," he said, and this last was in a different voice. It was a little flatter, as if the heat was finally getting to him.

89 "No. I got things to do."

90 "Hey."

91 "You two better leave."

92 "We ain't leaving until you come with us."

93 "Like hell I am—"

94 "Connie, don't fool around with me. I mean, I mean, don't fool *around*," he said, shaking his head. He laughed incredulously. He placed his sunglasses on top of his head, carefully, as if he were indeed wearing a wig, and brought the stems down behind his ears. Connie stared at him, another wave of dizziness and fear rising in her so that for a moment he wasn't even in focus but was just a blur, standing there against his gold car, and she had the idea that he had driven up the driveway all right but had come from nowhere before that and belonged nowhere and that everything about him and even about the music that was so familiar to her was only half real.

95 "If my father comes and sees you—"

96 "He ain't coming. He's at a barbecue."

97 "How do you know that?"

98 "Aunt Tillie's. Right now they're—uh—they're drinking. Sitting around," he said vaguely, squinting as if he were staring all the way to town and over to Aunt Tillie's back yard. Then the vision seemed to get clear and he nodded energetically. "Yeah. Sitting around. There's your sister in a blue dress, huh? And

high heels, the poor sad bitch—nothing like you, sweetheart! And your mother's helping some fat woman with the corn, they're cleaning the corn—husking the corn—"

99 "What fat woman?" Connie cried.

100 "How do I know what fat woman, I don't know every goddam fat woman in the world!" Arnold laughed.

101 "Oh, that's Mrs. Hornby . . . Who invited her?" Connie said. She felt a little light-headed. Her breath was coming quickly.

102 "She's too fat. I don't like them fat. I like them the way you are, honey," he said, smiling sleepily at her. They stared at each other for a while, through the screen door. He said softly, "Now what you're going to do is this: you're going to come out that door. You're going to sit up front with me and Ellie's going to sit in the back, the hell with Ellie, right? This isn't Ellie's date. You're my date. I'm your lover, honey."

103 "What? You're crazy—"

104 "Yes, I'm your lover. You don't know what that is, but you will," he said. "I know that too. I know all about you. But look: it's real nice and you couldn't ask for nobody better than me, or more polite. I always keep my word. I'll tell you how it is. I'm always nice at first, the first time. I'll hold you so tight you won't think you have to try to get away or pretend anything because you'll know you can't. And I'll come inside you where it's all secret and you'll give in to me and you'll love me—"

105 "Shut up! You're crazy!" Connie said. She backed away from the door. She put her hands against her ears as if she'd heard something terrible, something not meant for her. "People don't talk like that, you're crazy," she muttered. Her heart was almost too big now for her chest and its pumping made sweat break out all over her. She looked out to see Arnold Friend pause and then take a step toward the porch lurching. He almost fell. But, like a clever drunken man, he managed to catch his balance. He wobbled in his high boots and grabbed hold of one of the porch posts.

106 "Honey?" he said. "You still listening?"

107   "Get the hell out of here!"

108   "Be nice, honey. Listen."

109   "I'm going to call the police—"

110   He wobbled again and out of the side of his mouth came a fast spat curse, an aside not meant for her to hear. But even this "Christ!" sounded forced. Then he began to smile again. She watched this smile come, awkward as if he were smiling from inside a mask. His whole face was a mask, she thought wildly, tanned down onto his throat but then running out as if he had plastered makeup on his face but had forgotten about his throat.

111   "Honey—? Listen, here's how it is. I always tell the truth and I promise you this: I ain't coming in that house after you."

112   "You better not! I'm going to call the police if you—if you don't—"

113   "Honey," he said, talking right through her voice, "honey, I'm not coming in there but you are coming out here. You know why?"

114   She was panting. The kitchen looked like a place she had never seen before, some room she had run inside but which wasn't good enough, wasn't going to help her. The kitchen window had never had a curtain, after three years, and there were dishes in the sink for her to do—probably—and if you ran your hand across the table you'd probably feel something sticky there.

115   "You listening, honey? Hey?"

116   "—going to call the police—"

117   "Soon as you touch the phone I don't need to keep my promise and can come inside. You won't want that."

118   She rushed forward and tried to lock the door. Her fingers were shaking. "But why lock it," Arnold Friend said gently, talking right into her face. "It's just a screen door. It's just nothing." One of his boots was at a strange angle, as if his foot wasn't in it. It pointed out to the left, bent at the ankle. "I mean, anybody can break through a screen door and glass and wood and iron or anything else if he needs to, anybody at all and specially Arnold Friend. If the place got lit up with a fire honey you'd come runnin' out into my arms, right into my arms an' safe at home—like you knew I was your lover and'd stopped fooling around. I don't mind a nice shy girl but I don't like no fooling around." Part of those words were spoken with a slight rhythmic lilt, and Connie somehow recognized them—the echo of a song from last year, about a girl rushing into her boyfriend's arms and coming home again—

119   Connie stood barefoot on the linoleum floor, staring at him. "What do you want?" she whispered.

120   "I want you," he said.

121   "What?"

122   "Seen you that night and thought, that's the one, yes sir. I never needed to look anymore."

123   "But my father's coming back. He's coming to get me. I had to wash my hair first—" She spoke in a dry, rapid voice, hardly raising it for him to hear.

124   "No, your Daddy is not coming and yes, you had to wash your hair and you washed it for me. It's nice and shining and all for me. I thank you, sweetheart," he said, with a mock bow, but again he almost lost his balance. He had to bend and adjust his boots. Evidently his feet did not go all the way down; the boots must have been stuffed with something so that he would seem taller. Connie stared out at him and behind him Ellie in the car, who seemed to be looking off toward Connie's right into nothing. This Ellie said, pulling the words out of the air one after another as if he were just discovering them, "You want me to pull out the phone?"

125   "Shut your mouth and keep it shut," Arnold Friend said, his face red from bending over or maybe from embarrassment because Connie had seen his boots. "This ain't none of your business."

126   "What—what are you doing? What do you want?" Connie said. "If I call the police they'll get you, they'll arrest you—"

127   "Promise was not to come in unless you touch that phone, and I'll keep that promise," he said. He resumed his erect position and tried to force his shoulders back. He sounded like a hero in a movie, declaring something important. He spoke too loudly and it was as if he were speaking to someone behind Connie. "I ain't made plans for coming in that house where I don't belong but just for you to come out to

me, the way you should. Don't you know who I am?"

"You're crazy," she whispered. She backed away from the door but did not want to go into another part of the house, as if this would give him permission to come through the door. "What do you . . . You're crazy, you . . ."

129 "Huh? What're you saying, honey?"

130 Her eyes darted everywhere in the kitchen. She could not remember what it was, this room.

131 "This is how it is, honey; you come out and we'll drive away, have a nice ride. But if you don't come out we're gonna wait till your people come home and then they're all going to get it."

132 "You want that telephone pulled out?" Ellie said. He held the radio away from his ear and grimaced, as if without the radio the air was too much for him.

133 "I toldja shut up, Ellie," Arnold Friend said, "you're deaf, get a hearing aid, right? Fix yourself up. This little girl's no trouble and's gonna be nice to me, so Ellie keep to yourself, this ain't your date—right? Don't hem in on me. Don't hog. Don't crush. Don't bird dog. Don't trail me," he said in a rapid meaningless voice, as if he were running through all the expressions he'd learned but was no longer sure which one of them was in style, then rushing on to new ones, making them up with his eyes closed, "Don't crawl under my fence, don't squeeze in my chipmunk hole, don't sniff my glue, suck my popsicle, keep your own greasy fingers on yourself!" He shaded his eyes and peered in at Connie, who was backed against the kitchen table. "Don't mind him honey he's just a creep. He's a dope. Right? I'm the boy for you and like I said you come out here nice like a lady and give me your hand, and nobody else gets hurt, I mean, your nice old bald-headed daddy and your mummy and your sister in her high heels. Because listen: why bring them in this?"

134 "Leave me alone," Connie whispered.

135 "Hey, you know that old woman down the road, the one with the chickens and stuff—you know her?"

136 "She's dead!"

137 "Dead? What? You know her?" Arnold Friend said.

138 "She's dead—"

139 "Don't you like her?"

140 "She's dead—she's—she isn't there anymore—"

141 "But don't you like her, I mean, you got something against her? Some grudge or something?" Then his voice dipped as if he were conscious of a rudeness. He touched the sunglasses perched on top of his head as if to make sure they were still there. "Now you be a good girl."

142 "What are you going to do?"

143 "Just two things, or maybe three," Arnold Friend said. "But I promise it won't last long and you'll like me the way you get to like people you're close to. You will. It's all over for you here, so come on out. You don't want your people in any trouble, do you?"

144 She turned and bumped against a chair or something, hurting her leg, but she ran into the back room and picked up the telephone. Something roared in her ear, a tiny roaring, and she was so sick with fear that she could do nothing but listen to it—the telephone was clammy and very heavy and her fingers groped down to the dial but were too weak to touch it. She began to scream into the phone, into the roaring. She cried out, she cried for her mother, she felt her breath start jerking back and forth in her lungs as if it were something Arnold Friend were stabbing her with again and again with no tenderness. A noisy sorrowful wailing rose all about her and she was locked inside it the way she was locked inside this house.

145 After a while she could hear again. She was sitting on the floor with her wet back against the wall.

146 Arnold Friend was saying from the door, "That's a good girl. Put the phone back."

147 She kicked the phone away from her.

148 "No, honey. Pick it up. Put it back right."

149 She picked it up and put it back. The dial tone stopped.

150 "That's a good girl. Now you come outside."

151 She was hollow with what had been fear, but what was now just an emptiness. All that screaming had blasted it out of her. She sat, one leg cramped

under her, and deep inside her brain was something like a pinpoint of light that kept going and would not let her relax. She thought, I'm not going to see my mother again. She thought, I'm not going to sleep in my bed again. Her bright green blouse was all wet.

152   Arnold Friend said, in a gentle-loud voice that was like a stage voice. "The place where you came from ain't there any more, and where you had in mind to go is canceled out. This place you are now—inside your daddy's house—is nothing but a cardboard box I can knock down any time. You know that and always did know it. You hear me?"

153   She thought, I have got to think. I have to know what to do.

154   "We'll go out in a nice field, out in the country here where it smells so nice and it's sunny," Arnold Friend said. "I'll have my arms tight around you so you won't need to try to get away and I'll show you what love is like, what it does. The hell with this house! It looks solid all right," he said. He ran a fingernail down the screen and the noise did not make Connie shiver, as it would have the day before. "Now put your hand on your heart, honey. Feel that? That feels solid too, but we know better, be nice to me, be sweet like you can because what else is there for a girl like you but to be sweet and pretty and give in?—and get away before her people come back?"

155   She felt her pounding heart. Her hand seemed to enclose it. She thought for the first time in her life that it was nothing that was hers, that belonged to her, but just a pounding, living thing inside this body that wasn't really hers either.

156   "You don't want them to get hurt," Arnold Friend went on. "Now get up, honey. Get up all by yourself."

157   She stood.

158   "Now turn this way. That's right. Come over here to me—Ellie, put that away, didn't I tell you? You dope. You miserable creepy dope," Arnold Friend said. His words were not angry but only part of an incantation. The incantation was kindly. "Now come out through the kitchen to me honey, and let's see a smile, try it, you're a brave sweet little girl and now they're eating corn and hot dogs cooked to

bursting over an outdoor fire, and they don't know one thing about you and never did and honey you're better than them because not a one of them would have done this for you."

Connie felt the linoleum under her feet; it was cool. She brushed her hair back out of her eyes. Arnold Friend let go of the post tentatively and opened his arms for her, his elbows pointing in toward each other and his wrists limp, to show that this was an embarrassed embrace and a little mocking, he didn't want to make her self-conscious.

160   She put out her hand against the screen. She watched herself push the door slowly open as if she were safe back somewhere in the other doorway, watching this body and this head of long hair moving out into the sunlight where Arnold Friend waited.

161   "My sweet little blue-eyed girl," he said, in a half-sung sigh that had nothing to do with her brown eyes but was taken up just the same by the vast sunlit reaches of the land behind him and on all sides of him, so much land that Connie had never seen before and did not recognize except to know that she was going to it. ◆

THE HAMMER MAN

Toni Cade Bambara

Toni Cade Bambara was born in New York City in 1939 and raised in Harlem and Bedford-Stuyvesant. A graduate of Queens College (B.A.) and City College of New York (M.A.), she began publishing stories in 1960. "The Hammer Man" first appeared in The Negro Digest *in 1966 and was reprinted in* Gorilla, My Love *(1972).*

1   *I* WAS GLAD TO HEAR THAT MANNY HAD FALlen off the roof. I had put out the tale that I was down with yellow fever, but nobody paid me no mind, least of all Dirty Red who stomped right in to announce that Manny had fallen off the roof and that I could come out of hiding now. My mother dropped what she was doing, which was the laundry, and got the whole story out of Red. "Bad enough you gots to hang around with boys," she said. "But fight with them too. And you would pick the craziest one at that."

2   Manny was supposed to be crazy. That was his story. To say you were bad put some people off. But to say you were crazy, well, you were officially not to be messed with. So that was his story. On the other hand, after I called him what I called him and said a few choice things about his mother, his face did go through some piercing changes. And I did kind of wonder if maybe he sure was nuts. I didn't wait to find out. I got in the wind. And then he waited for me on my stoop all day and all night, not hardly speaking to the people going in and out. And he was there all day Saturday, with his sister bringing him peanut-butter sandwiches and cream sodas. He must've gone to the bathroom right there cause every time I looked out the kitchen window, there he was. And Sunday, too. I got to thinking the boy was mad.

3   "You got no sense of humor, that's your trouble," I told him. He looked up, but he didn't say nothing. All at once I was real sorry about the whole thing. I should've settled for hitting off the little girls in the school yard, or waiting for Frankie to come in

so we could raise some kind of hell. This way I had to play sick when my mother was around cause my father had already taken away my BB gun and hid it.

4   I don't know how they got Manny on the roof finally. Maybe the Wakefield kids, the ones who keep the pigeons, called him up. Manny was a sucker for sick animals and things like that. Or maybe Frankie got some nasty girls to go up on the roof with him and got Manny to join him. I don't know. Anyway, the catwalk had lost all its cement and the roof always did kind of slant downward. So Manny fell off the roof. I got over my yellow fever right quick, needless to say, and ventured outside. But by this time I had already told Miss Rose that Crazy Manny was after me. And Miss Rose, being who she was, quite naturally went over to Manny's house and said a few harsh words to his mother, who, being who she was, chased Miss Rose out into the street and they commenced to get with it, snatching bottles out of the garbage cans and breaking them on the johnny pumps and stuff like that.

5   Dirty Red didn't have to tell us about this. Everybody could see and hear all. I never figured the garbage cans for an arsenal, but Miss Rose came up with sticks and table legs and things, and Manny's mother had her share of scissor blades and bicycle chains. They got to rolling in the streets and all you could see was pink drawers and fat legs. It was something else. Miss Rose is nutty but Manny's mother's crazier than Manny. They were at it a couple of times during my sick spell. Everyone would congregate on the window sills or the fire escape, commenting that it

was still much too cold for this kind of nonsense. But they watched anyway. And then Manny fell off the roof. And that was that. Miss Rose went back to her dream books and Manny's mother went back to her tumbled-down kitchen of dirty clothes and bundles and bundles of rags and children.

6   My father got in on it too, cause he happened to ask Manny one night why he was sitting on the stoop like that every night. Manny told him right off that he was going to kill me first chance he got. Quite naturally this made my father a little warm, me being his only daughter and planning to become a doctor and take care of him in his old age. So he had a few words with Manny first, and then he got hold of the older brother, Bernard, who was more his size. Bernard didn't see how any of it was his business or my father's business, so my father got mad and jammed Bernard's head into the mailbox. Then my father started getting messages from Bernard's uncle about where to meet him for a showdown and all. My father didn't say a word to my mother all this time; just sat around mumbling and picking up the phone and putting it down, or grabbing my stickball bat and putting it back. He carried on like this for days till I thought I would scream if the yellow fever didn't have me so weak. And then Manny fell off the roof, and my father went back to his beer-drinking buddies.

7   I was in the school yard, pitching pennies with the little boys from the elementary school, when my friend Violet hits my brand-new Spaudeen over the wall. She came running back to tell me that Manny was coming down the block. I peeked beyond the fence and there he was all right. He had his head all wound up like a mummy and his arm in a sling and his legs in a cast. It looked phony to me, especially that walking cane. I figured Dirty Red had told me a tale just to get me out there so Manny could stomp me, and Manny was playing it up with costume and all till he could get me.

8   "What happened to him?" Violet's sisters whispered. But I was too busy trying to figure out how this act was supposed to work. Then Manny passed real close to the fence and gave me a look.

9   "You had enough, Hammer Head," I yelled.

"Just bring your crummy self in this yard and I'll pick up where I left off." Violet was knocked out and the other kids went into a huddle. I didn't have to say anything else. And when they all pressed me later, I just said, "You know that hammer he always carries in his fatigues?" And they'd all nod waiting for the rest of a long story. "Well, I took it away from him." And I walked off nonchalantly.

10   Manny stayed indoors for a long time. I almost forgot about him. New kids moved into the block and I got all caught up with that. And then Miss Rose finally hit the numbers and started ordering a whole lot of stuff through the mail and we would sit on the curb and watch these weird-looking packages being carried in, trying to figure out what simpleminded thing she had thrown her money away on when she might just as well wait for the warm weather and throw a block party for all her godchildren.

11   After a while a center opened up and my mother said she'd increase my allowance if I went and joined because I'd have to get out of my pants and stay in skirts, on account of that's the way things were at the center. So I joined and got to thinking about everything else but old Hammer Head. It was a rough place to get along in, the center, but my mother said that I needed to be be'd with and she needed to not be with me, so I went. And that time I sneaked into the office, that's when I really got turned on. I looked into one of those not-quite-white folders and saw that I was from a deviant family in a deviant neighborhood. I showed my mother the word in the dictionary, but she didn't pay me no mind. It was my favorite word after that. I ran it in the ground till one day my father got the strap just to show how deviant he could get. So I gave up trying to improve my vocabulary. And I almost gave up my dungarees.

12   Then one night I'm walking past the Douglas Street park cause I got thrown out of the center for playing pool when I should've been sewing, even though I had already decided that this was going to be my last fling with boy things, and starting tomorrow I was going to fix my hair right and wear skirts all the time just so my mother would stop talking about her gray hairs, and Miss Rose would stop call-

ing me by my brother's name by mistake. So I'm walking past the park and there's ole Manny on the basketball court, perfecting his lay-ups and talking with himself. Being me, I quite naturally walk right up and ask what the hell he's doing playing in the dark, and he looks up and all around like the dark had crept up on him when he wasn't looking. So I knew right away that he'd been out there for a long time with his eyes just going along with the program.

13   "There was two seconds to go and we were one point behind," he said, shaking his head and staring at his sneakers like they was somebody. "And I was in the clear. I'd left the man in the backcourt and there I was, smiling, you dig, cause it was in the bag. They passed the ball and I slid the ball up nice and easy cause there was nothing to worry about. And . . ." He shook his head. "I muffed the goddamn shot. Ball bounced off the rim . . ." He stared at his hands. "The game of the season. Last game." And then he ignored me altogether, though he wasn't talking to me in the first place. He went back to the lay-ups, always from the same spot with his arms crooked in the same way, over and over. I must've gotten hyp-notized cause I probably stood there for at least an hour watching like a fool till I couldn't even see the damn ball, much less the basket. But I stood there anyway for no reason I know of. He never missed. But he cursed himself away. It was torture. And then a squad car pulled up and a short cop with hair like one of the Marx Brothers came out hitching up his pants. He looked real hard at me and then at Manny.

14   "What are you two doing?"

15   "He's doing a lay-up. I'm watching." I said with my smart self.

16   Then the cop just stood there and finally turned to the other one who was just getting out of the car.

17   "Who unlocked the gate?" the big one said.

18   "It's always unlocked," I said. Then we three just stood there like a bunch of penguins watching Manny go at it.

19   "This on the level?" the big guy asked, tilting his hat back with the thumb the way big guys do in hot weather. "Hey you," he said, walking over to Manny. "I'm talking to you." He finally grabbed the ball to get Manny's attention. But that didn't work. Manny just stood there with his arms out waiting for the pass so he could save the game. He wasn't paying no mind to the cop. So, quite naturally, when the cop slapped him upside his head it was a surprise. And when the cop started counting three to go, Manny had already recovered from the slap and was just tick-ing off the seconds before the buzzer sounded and all was lost.

20   "Gimme the ball, man." Manny's face was all tightened up and ready to pop.

21   "Did you hear what I said, black boy?"

22   Now, when somebody says that word like that, I gets warm. And crazy or no crazy, Manny was my brother at that moment and the cop was the enemy.

23   "You better give him back his ball," I said. "Manny don't take no mess from no cops. He ain't bothering nobody. He's gonna be Mister Basketball when he grows up. Just trying to get a little practice in before the softball season starts."

24   "Look here, sister, we'll run you in too," Harpo said.

25   "I damn sure can't be your sister seeing how I'm a black girl. Boy, I sure will be glad when you run me in so I can tell everybody about that. You must think you're in the South, mister."

26   The big guy screwed his mouth up and let one of them hard-day sighs. "The park's closed, little girl, so why don't you and your boyfriend go on home."

27   That really got me. The "little girl" was bad enough but that "boyfriend" was too much. But I kept cool, mostly because Manny looked so pitiful waiting there with his hands in a time-out and there being no one to stop the clock. But I kept my cool mostly cause of that hammer in Manny's pocket and no telling how frantic things can get what with a big-mouth like me, a couple of wise cops, and a crazy boy too.

28   "The gates are open," I said real quiet-like, "and this here's a free country. So why don't you give him back his ball?"

29   The big cop did another one of those sighs, his specialty I guess, and then he bounced the ball to Manny who went right into his gliding thing clear up

to the backboard, damn near like he was some kind
of very beautiful bird. And then he swooshed that
ball in, even if there was no net, and you couldn't really hear the swoosh. Something happened to the
bones in my chest. It was something.

30   "Crazy kids anyhow," the one with the wig
said and turned to go. But the big guy watched
Manny for a while and I guess something must've
snapped in his head, cause all of a sudden he was hot
for taking Manny to jail or court or somewhere and
started yelling at him and everything, which is a bad
thing to do to Manny, I can tell you. And I'm standing there thinking that none of my teachers, from kin-
dergarten right on up, none of them knew what they
were talking about. I'll be damned if I ever knew one
of them rosy-cheeked cops that smiled and helped you
get to school without neither you or your little raggedy dog getting hit by a truck that had a smile on its
face, too. Not that I ever believed it. I knew Dick and
Jane was full of crap from the get-go, especially them
cops. Like this dude, for example, pulling on Manny's
clothes like that when obviously he had just done
about the most beautiful thing a man can do and not
be a fag. No cop could swoosh without a net.

31   "Look out, man," was all Manny said, but it
was the way he pushed the cop that started the real
yelling and threats. And I thought to myself, Oh God
here I am trying to change my ways, and not talk
back in school, and do like my mother wants, but just
have this last fling, and now this—getting shot in the
stomach and bleeding to death in Douglas Street park
and poor Manny getting pistol-whipped by those bas-
tards and whatnot. I could see it all, practically crying
too. And it just wasn't no kind of thing to happen to
a small child like me with my confirmation picture in
the paper next to my weeping parents and schoolmates. I could feel the blood sticking to my shirt and
my eyeballs slipping away, and then that confirmation
picture again; and my mother and her gray hair; and
Miss Rose heading for the precinct with a shotgun;
and my father getting old and feeble with no one to
doctor him up and all.

32   And I wished Manny had fallen off the damn
roof and died right then and there and saved me all

this aggravation of being killed with him by these
cops who surely didn't come out of no fifth-grade
reader. But it didn't happen. They just took the ball
and Manny followed them real quiet-like right out
of the park into the dark, then into the squad car
with his head drooping and his arms in a crook. And
I went on home cause what the hell am I going to
do on a basketball court, and it getting to be nearly
midnight?

33   I didn't see Manny no more after he got into
that squad car. But they didn't kill him after all cause
Miss Rose heard he was in some kind of big house
for people who lose their marbles. And then it was
spring finally, and me and Violet was in this very boss
fashion show at the center. And Miss Rose bought
me my first corsage—yellow roses to match my
shoes. ◆

DAY OF THE BUTTERFLY

Alice Munro

Alice Munro is a Canadian writer of novels and short stories. Her works often reflect her own upbringing in rural Ontario. "Day of the Butterfly" is from Munro's first collection of stories, Dance of the Happy Shades *(1968).*

1 *I* DO NOT REMEMBER WHEN MYRA SAYLA CAME to town, though she must have been in our class at school for two or three years. I start remembering her in the last year, when her little brother Jimmy Sayla was in Grade One. Jimmy Sayla was not used to going to the bathroom by himself and he would have to come to the Grade Six door and ask for Myra and she would take him downstairs. Quite often he would not get to Myra in time and there would be a big dark stain on his little button-on cotton pants. Then Myra had to come and ask the teacher, "Please may I take my brother home, he has wet himself?"

2 That was what she said the first time and everybody in the front seats heard her—though Myra's voice was the lightest singsong—and there was a muted giggling which alerted the rest of the class. Our teacher, a cold gentle girl who wore glasses with thin gold rims and in the stiff solicitude of certain poses resembled a giraffe, wrote something on a piece of paper and showed it to Myra. And Myra recited uncertainly: "My brother has had an accident, please, teacher."

3 Everybody knew of Jimmy Sayla's shame and at recess (if he was not being kept in, as he often was, for doing something he shouldn't in school) he did not dare go out on the school grounds, where the other little boys, and some bigger ones, were waiting to chase him and corner him against the back fence and thrash him with tree branches. He had to stay with Myra. But at our school there were the two sides, the Boys' Side and the Girls' Side, and it was believed that if you so much as stepped on the side

that was not your own you might easily get the strap. Jimmy could not go out on the Girls' Side and Myra could not go out on the Boys' Side, and no one was allowed to stay in the school unless it was raining or snowing. So Myra and Jimmy spent every recess standing in the little back porch between the two sides. Perhaps they watched the baseball games, the tag and skipping and building of leaf houses in the fall and snow forts in the winter; perhaps they did not watch at all. Whenever you happened to look at them their heads were slightly bent, their narrow bodies hunched in, quite still. They had long smooth oval faces, melancholy and discreet—dark, oily, shining hair. The little boy's was long, clipped at home, and Myra's was worn in heavy braids coiled on top of her head so that she looked, from a distance, as if she was wearing a turban too big for her. Over their dark eyes the lids were never fully raised; they had a weary look. But it was more than that. They were like children in a medieval painting, they were like small figures carved of wood, for worship or magic, with faces smooth and aged, and meekly, cryptically uncommunicative.

4 Most of the teachers at our school had been teaching for a long time and at recess they would disappear into the teachers' room and not bother us. But our own teacher, the young woman of the fragile gold-rimmed glasses, was apt to watch us from a window and sometimes come out, looking brisk and uncomfortable, to stop a fight among the little girls or start a running game among the big ones, who had been huddled together playing Truth or Secrets. One

day she came out and called, "Girls in Grade Six, I want to talk to you!" She smiled persuasively, earnestly, and with dreadful unease, showing fine gold rims around her teeth. She said, "There is a girl in Grade Six called Myra Sayla. She *is* in your grade, isn't she?"

5   We mumbled. But there was a coo from Gladys Healey. "Yes, Miss Darling!"

6   "Well, why is she never playing with the rest of you? Every day I see her standing in the back porch, never playing. Do you think she looks very happy standing back there? Do you think you would be very happy, if *you* were left back there?"

7   Nobody answered; we faced Miss Darling, all respectful, self-possessed, and bored with the unreality of her question. Then Gladys said, "Myra can't come out with us, Miss Darling. Myra has to look after her little brother!"

8   "Oh," said Miss Darling dubiously. "Well you ought to try to be nicer to her anyway. Don't you think so? Don't you? You will try to be nicer, won't you? I *know* you will." Poor Miss Darling! Her campaigns were soon confused, her persuasions turned to bleating and uncertain pleas.

9   When she had gone Gladys Healey said softly, "You will try to be nicer, won't you? I *know* you will!" and then drawing her lip back over her big teeth she yelled exuberantly, "I don't care if it rains or freezes." She went through the whole verse and ended it with a spectacular twirl of her Royal Stuart tartan skirt. Mr. Healey ran a Dry Goods and Ladies' Wear, and his daughter's leadership in our class was partly due to her flashing plaid skirts and organdie blouses and velvet jackets with brass buttons, but also to her early-maturing bust and the fine brutal force of her personality. Now we all began to imitate Miss Darling.

10   We had not paid much attention to Myra before this. But now a game was developed; it started with saying, "Let's be nice to Myra!" Then we would walk up to her in formal groups of three or four and at a signal, say together, "Hel-lo Myra, Hello *My*-ra!" and follow up with something like, "What do you wash your hair in, Myra, it's so nice and shiny,

My-ra." "Oh she washes it in cod-liver oil, don't you, Myra, she washes it in cod-liver oil, can't you smell it?"

And to tell the truth there was a smell about Myra, but it was a rotten-sweetish smell as of bad fruit. That was what the Saylas did, kept a little fruit store. Her father sat all day on a stool by the window, with his shirt open over his swelling stomach and tufts of black hair showing around his belly button; he chewed garlic. But if you went into the store it was Mrs. Sayla who came to wait on you, appearing silently between the limp print curtains hung across the back of the store. Her hair was crimped in black waves and she smiled with her full lips held together, stretched as far as they would go; she told you the price in a little rapping voice, daring you to challenge her and, when you did not, handed you the bag of fruit with open mockery in her eyes.

12   One morning in the winter I was walking up the school hill very early; a neighbour had given me a ride into town. I lived about half a mile out of town, on a farm, and I should not have been going to the town school at all, but to a country school nearby where there were half a dozen pupils and a teacher a little demented since her change of life. But my mother, who was an ambitious woman, had prevailed on the town trustees to accept me and my father to pay the extra tuition, and I went to school in town. I was the only one in the class who carried a lunch pail and ate peanut-butter sandwiches in the high, bare, mustard-coloured cloakroom, the only one who had to wear rubber boots in the spring, when the roads were heavy with mud. I felt a little danger, on account of this; but I could not tell exactly what it was.

13   I saw Myra and Jimmy ahead of me on the hill; they always went to school very early—sometimes so early that they had to stand outside waiting for the janitor to open the door. They were walking slowly, and now and then Myra half turned around. I had often loitered in that way, wanting to walk with some important girl who was behind me, and not quite daring to stop and wait. Now it occurred to me that

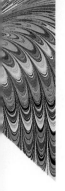

Myra might be doing this with me. I did not know what to do. I could not afford to be seen walking with her, and I did not even want to—but, on the other hand, the flattery of those humble, hopeful turnings was not lost on me. A role was shaping for me that I could not resist playing. I felt a great pleasurable rush of self-conscious benevolence; before I thought what I was doing I called, "Myra! Hey, Myra, wait up, I got some Cracker Jack!" and I quickened my pace as she stopped.

14   Myra waited, but she did not look at me; she waited in the withdrawn and rigid attitude with which she always met us. Perhaps she thought I was playing a trick on her, perhaps she expected me to run past and throw an empty Cracker Jack box in her face. And I opened the box and held it out to her. She took a little. Jimmy ducked behind her coat and would not take any when I offered the box to him.

15   "He's shy," I said reassuringly. "A lot of little kids are shy like that. He'll probably grow out of it."

16   "Yes," said Myra.

17   "I have a brother four," I said. "He's awfully shy." He wasn't. "Have some more Cracker Jack," I said. "I used to eat Cracker Jack all the time but I don't any more. I think it's bad for your complexion."

18   There was a silence.

19   "Do you like Art?" said Myra faintly.

20   "No. I like Social Studies and Spelling and Health."

21   "I like Art and Arithmetic." Myra could add and multiply in her head faster than anyone else in the class.

22   "I wish I was as good as you. In Arithmetic," I said, and felt magnanimous.

23   "But I am no good at Spelling," said Myra. "I make the most mistakes, I'll fail maybe." She did not sound unhappy about this, but pleased to have such a thing to say. She kept her head turned away from me staring at the dirty snowbanks along Victoria Street, and as she talked she made a sound as if she was wetting her lips with her tongue.

24   "You won't fail," I said. "You are too good in Arithmetic. What are you going to be when you grow up?"

25   She looked bewildered. "I will help my mother," she said. "And work in the store."

26   "Well I am going to be an airplane hostess," I said. "But don't mention it to anybody. I haven't told many people."

27   "No, I won't," said Myra. "Do you read Steve Canyon in the paper?"

28   "Yes." It was queer to think that Myra, too, read the comics, or that she did anything at all, apart from her role at the school. "Do you read Rip Kirby?"

29   "Do you read Orphan Annie?"

30   "Do you read Betsy and the Boys?"

31   "You haven't had hardly any Cracker Jack," I said. "Have some. Take a whole handful."

32   Myra looked into the box. "There's a prize in there," she said. She pulled it out. It was a brooch, a little tin butterfly, painted gold with bits of coloured glass stuck onto it to look like jewels. She held it in her brown hand, smiling slightly.

33   I said, "Do you like that?"

34   Myra said, "I like them blue stones. Blue stones are sapphires."

35   "I know. My birthstone is sapphire. What is your birthstone?"

36   "I don't know."

37   "When is your birthday?"

38   "July."

39   "Then yours is ruby."

40   "I like sapphire better," said Myra. "I like yours." She handed me the brooch.

41   "You keep it," I said. "Finders keepers."

42   Myra kept holding it out, as if she did not know what I meant, "Finders keepers," I said.

43   "It was your Cracker Jack," said Myra, scared and solemn. "You bought it."

44   "Well, you found it."

45   "No—" said Myra

46   "Go on!" I said. "Here, I'll *give* it to you." I took the brooch from her and pushed it back into her hand.

47   We were both surprised. We looked at each other; I flushed but Myra did not. I realized the pledge as our fingers touched; I was panicky, but *all*

right. I thought, I can come early and walk with her other mornings. I can go and talk to her at recess. Why not? *Why not?*

48 Myra put the brooch in her pocket. She said, "I can wear it on my good dress. My good dress is blue."

49 I knew it would be. Myra wore out her good dresses at school. Even in midwinter among the plaid wool skirts and serge tunics, she glimmered sadly in sky-blue taffeta, in dusty turquoise crepe, a grown woman's dress made over, weighted by a big bow at the v of the neck and folding empty over Myra's narrow chest.

50 And I was glad she had not put it on. If someone asked her where she got it, and she told them, what would I say?

51 It was the day after this, or the week after, that Myra did not come to school. Often she was kept at home to help. But this time she did not come back. For a week, then two weeks, her desk was empty. Then we had a moving day at school and Myra's books were taken out of her desk and put on a shelf in the closet. Miss Darling said, "We'll find a seat when she comes back." And she stopped calling Myra's name when she took attendance.

52 Jimmy Sayla did not come to school either, having no one to take him to the bathroom.

53 In the fourth week or the fifth, that Myra had been away, Gladys Healey came to school and said, "Do you know what—Myra Sayla is sick in the hospital."

54 It was true. Gladys Healey had an aunt who was a nurse. Gladys put up her hand in the middle of Spelling and told Miss Darling. "I thought you might like to know," she said. "Oh yes," said Miss Darling. "I do know."

55 "What has she got?" we said to Gladys.

56 And Gladys said, "Akemia,[1] or something. And she has blood transfusions." She said to Miss Darling, "My aunt is a nurse."

---

[1] That is, leukemia, a usually fatal disease of the blood.

So Miss Darling had the whole class write Myra a letter, in which everybody said, "Dear Myra, We are all writing you a letter. We hope you will soon be better and be back to school, Yours truly . . ." and Miss Darling said, "I've thought of something. Who would like to go up to the hospital and visit Myra on the twentieth of March, for a birthday party?"

58 I said, "Her birthday's in July."

59 "I know," said Miss Darling. "It's the twentieth of July. So this year she could have it on the twentieth of March, because she's sick."

60 "But her *birthday* is in July."

61 "Because she's sick," said Miss Darling, with a warning shrillness. "The cook at the hospital could make a cake and you could all give a little present, twenty-five cents or so. It would have to be between two and four, because that's visiting hours. And we couldn't all go, it'd be too many. So who wants to go and who wants to stay here and do supplementary reading?"

62 We all put up our hands. Miss Darling got out the spelling records and picked out the first fifteen, twelve girls and three boys. Then the three boys did not want to go so she picked out the next three girls. And I do not know when it was, but I think it was probably at this moment that the birthday party of Myra Sayla became fashionable.

63 Perhaps it was because Gladys Healey had an aunt who was a nurse, perhaps it was the excitement of sickness and hospitals, or simply the fact that Myra was so entirely, impressively set free of all the rules and conditions of our lives. We began to talk of her as if she were something we owned, and her party became a cause; with womanly heaviness we discussed it at recess, and decided that twenty-five cents was too low.

64 We all went up to the hospital on a sunny afternoon when the snow was melting, carrying our presents, and a nurse led us upstairs, single file, and down a hall past half-closed doors and dim conversations. She and Miss Darling kept saying, "Sh-sh," but we were going on tiptoe anyway; our hospital demeanor was perfect.

At this small country hospital there was no children's ward, and Myra was not really a child; they had put her in with two grey old women. A nurse was putting screens around them as we came in.

Myra was sitting up in bed, in a bulky stiff hospital gown. Her hair was down, the long braids falling over her shoulders and down the coverlet. But her face was the same, always the same.

67 She had been told something about the party, Miss Darling said, so the surprise would not upset her; but it seemed she had not believed, or had not understood what it was. She watched us as she used to watch in the school grounds when we played.

68 "Well, here we are!" said Miss Darling. "Here we are!"

69 And we said, "Happy birthday, Myra! Hello, Myra, happy birthday!" Myra said, "My birthday is in July." Her voice was lighter than ever, drifting, expressionless.

70 "Never mind when it is, really," said Miss Darling. "Pretend it's now! How old are you, Myra?"

71 "Eleven," Myra said. "In July."

72 Then we all took off our coats and emerged in our party dresses, and laid our presents, in their pale flowery wrappings, on Myra's bed. Some of our mothers had made immense, complicated bows of fine satin ribbon, some of them had even taped on little bouquets of imitation roses and lillies of the valley. "Here Myra," we said, "here Myra, happy birthday." Myra did not look at us, but at the ribbons, pink and blue and speckled with silver, and the miniature bouquets; they pleased her, as the butterfly had done. An innocent look came into her face, a partial, private smile.

73 "Open them, Myra," said Miss Darling. "They're for you!"

74 Myra gathered the presents around her, fingering them, with this smile, and a cautious realization, an unexpected pride. She said, "Saturday I'm going to London to St. Joseph's Hospital."

75 "That's where my mother was at," somebody said. "We went and saw her. They've got all nuns there."

76 "My father's sister is a nun," said Myra calmly.

77 She began to unwrap the presents, with an air that not even Gladys could have bettered, folded the tissue paper and the ribbons, and drawing out books and puzzles and cutouts as if they were all prizes she had won. Miss Darling said that maybe she should say thank you, and the person's name with every gift she opened, to make sure she knew whom it was from, and so Myra said, "Thank you, Mary Louise, thank you, Carol," and when she came to mine she said, "Thank you, Helen." Everyone explained their presents to her and there was talking and excitement and a little gaiety, which Myra presided over. Though she was not gay. A cake was brought in with *Happy Birthday Myra* written on it, pink on white, and eleven candles. Miss Darling lit the candles and we all sang Happy Birthday to You, and cried, "Make a wish, Myra, make a wish—" and Myra blew them out. Then we all had cake and strawberry ice cream.

78 At four o'clock a buzzer sounded and the nurse took out what was left of the cake, and the dirty dishes, and we put on our coats to go home. Everybody said, "Goodbye, Myra," and Myra sat in the bed watching us go, her back straight, not supported by any pillow, her hands resting on the gifts. But at the door I heard her call; she called "Helen!" Only a couple of the others heard; Miss Darling did not hear, she had gone out ahead. I went back to the bed.

79 Myra said, "I got too many things. You take something."

80 "What?" I said. "It's for your birthday. You always get a lot at a birthday."

81 "Well you take something," Myra said. She picked up a leatherette case with a mirror in it, a comb and a nail file and a natural lipstick and a small handkerchief edged with gold thread. I had noticed it before. "You take that," she said.

82 "Don't you want it?"

83 "You take it." She put it into my hand. Our fingers touched again.

84 "When I come back from London," Myra said, "you can come and play at my place after school."

85

"Okay," I said. Outside the hospital window there was a clear carrying sound of somebody playing in the street, maybe chasing with the last snowballs of the year. This sound made Myra, her triumph and her bounty, and most of her future in which she had found this place for me, turn shadowy, turn dark. All the presents on the bed, the folded paper and ribbons, those guilt-tinged offerings, had passed into this shadow, they were no longer innocent objects to be touched, exchanged, accepted without danger. I didn't want to take the case now but I could not think how to get out of it, what lie to tell. I'll give it away, I thought, I won't ever play with it. I would let my little brother pull it apart.

86

The nurse came back, carrying a glass of chocolate milk.

"What's the matter, didn't you hear the buzzer?"

So I was released, set free by the barriers which now closed about Myra, her unknown, exalted, ether-smelling hospital world, and by the treachery of my own heart. "Well, thank you," I said. "Thank you for the thing. Goodbye."

Did Myra ever say goodbye? Not likely. She sat in her high bed, her delicate brown neck rising out of a hospital gown too big for her, her brown carved face immune to treachery, her offering perhaps already forgotten, prepared to be set apart for legendary uses, as she was even in the back porch at school. ◆

STAR FOOD

Ethan Canin

Ethan Canin, a graduate of Stanford University and of the Iowa Writer's Workshop, is presently a physician-in-training. "Star Food," originally published in the magazine Chicago, *was reprinted in* Best American Stories 1986 *and in Canin's 1987 collection* Emperor of the Air.

1   THE SUMMER I TURNED EIGHTEEN I DISAPpointed both my parents for the first time. This hadn't happened before, since what disappointed one usually pleased the other. As a child, if I played broom hockey instead of going to school, my mother wept and my father took me outside later to find out how many goals I had scored. On the other hand, if I spent Saturday afternoon on the roof of my parents' grocery store staring up at the clouds instead of counting cracker cartons in the stockroom, my father took me to the back to talk about work and disci-

pline, and my mother told me later to keep looking for things that no one else saw.

This was her theory. My mother felt that men like Leonardo da Vinci and Thomas Edison had simply stared long enough at regular objects until they saw new things, and thus my looking into the sky might someday make me a great man. She believed I had a worldly curiosity. My father believed I wanted to avoid stock work.   2

Stock work was an issue in our family, as were all the jobs that had to be done in a grocery store.   3

Our store was called Star Food and above it an incandescent star revolved. Its circuits buzzed, and its yellow points, as thick as my knees, drooped with the slow melting of the bulb. On summer nights flying insects flocked in clouds around it, droves of them burning on the glass. One of my jobs was to go out on the roof, the sloping, eaved side that looked over the western half of Arcade, California, and clean them off the star. At night, when their black bodies stood out against the glass, when the wind carried in the marsh smell of the New Jerusalem River, I went into the attic, crawled out the dormer window onto the peaked roof, and slid across the shingles to where the pole rose like a lightning rod into the night. I reached with a wet rag and rubbed away the June bugs and pickerel moths until the star was yellow-white and steaming from the moisture. Then I turned and looked over Arcade, across the bright avenue and my dimly lighted high school in the distance, into the low hills where oak trees grew in rows on the curbs and where girls drove to school in their own convertibles. When my father came up on the roof sometimes to talk about the store, we fixed our eyes on the red tile roofs or the small clouds of blue barbecue smoke that floated above the hills on warm evenings. While the clean bulb buzzed and flickered behind us, we talked about loss leaders or keeping the elephant-ear plums stacked in neat triangles.

4   The summer I disappointed my parents, though, my father talked to me about a lot of other things. He also made me look in the other direction whenever we were on the roof together, not west to the hills and their clouds of barbecue smoke, but east toward the other part of town. We crawled up one slope of the roof, then down the other so that I could see beyond the back alley where wash hung on lines in the moonlight, down to the neighborhoods across Route 5. These were the neighborhoods where men sat on the curbs on weekday afternoons, where rusted, wheel-less cars lay on blocks in the yards.

5   "You're going to end up on one of those curbs," my father told me.

6   Usually I stared farther into the clouds when he said something like that. He and my mother argued about what I did on the roof for so many hours at a time, and I hoped that by looking closely at the amazing borders of clouds I could confuse him. My mother believed I was on the verge of discovering something atmospheric, and I was sure she told my father this, so when he came upstairs, made me look across Route 5, and talked to me about how I was going to end up there, I squinted harder at the sky.

"You don't fool me for a second," he said.   7

He was up on the roof with me because I had   8
been letting someone steal from the store.

From the time we first had the star on the   9
roof, my mother believed her only son was destined for limited fame. Limited because she thought that true vision was distilled and could not be appreciated by everybody. I discovered this shortly after the star was installed, when I spent an hour looking out over the roofs and chimneys instead of helping my father stock a shipment of dairy. It was a hot day and the milk sat on the loading dock while he searched for me in the store and in our apartment next door. When he came up and found me, his neck was red and his footfalls shook the roof joists. At my age I was still allowed certain mistakes, but I'd seen the dairy truck arrive and knew I should have been downstairs, so it surprised me later, after I'd helped unload the milk, when my mother stopped beside me as I was sprinkling the leafy vegetables with a spray bottle.

"Dade, I don't want you to let anyone keep you   10
from what you ought to be doing." — mom

"I'm sorry," I said. "I should have helped with   11
the milk earlier."

"No," she said, "that's not what I mean." Then   12
she told me her theory of limited fame while I sprayed the cabbage and lettuce with the atomizer. It was the first time I had heard her idea. The world's most famous men, she said, presidents and emperors, generals and patriots, were men of vulgar fame, men who ruled the world because their ideas were obvious and could be understood by everybody. But there was also limited fame. Newton and Galileo and Enrico Fermi

were men of limited fame, and as I stood there with the atomizer in my hand my mother's eyes watered over and she told me she knew in her heart that one day I was going to be a man of limited fame. I was twelve years old.

13   After that day I found I could avoid a certain amount of stock work by staying up on the roof and staring into the fine layers of stratus clouds that floated above Arcade. In the *Encyclopedia Americana* I read about cirrus and cumulus and thunderheads, about inversion layers and currents like the currents at sea, and in the afternoons I went upstairs and watched. The sky was a changing thing, I found out. It was more than a blue sheet. Twirling with pollen and sunlight, it began to transform itself.

14   Often as I stood on the roof my father came outside and swept the sidewalk across the street. Through the telephone poles and crossed power lines he looked up at me, his broom strokes small and fierce as if he were hoeing hard ground. It irked him that my mother encouraged me to stay on the roof. He was a short man with direct habits and an understanding of how to get along in the world, and he believed that God rewarded only two things, courtesy and hard work. God did not reward looking at the sky. In the car my father acknowledged good drivers and in restaurants he left good tips. He knew the names of his customers. He never sold a rotten vegetable. He shook hands often, looked everyone in the eye, and on Friday nights when we went to the movies he made us sit in the front row of the theater. "Why should I pay to look over other people's heads?" he said. The movies made him talk. On the way back to the car he walked with his hands clasped behind him and greeted everyone who passed. He smiled. He mentioned the fineness of the evening as if he were the admiral or aviator we had just seen on the screen. "People like it," he said. "It's good for business." My mother was quiet, walking with her slender arms folded in front of her as if she were cold.

15   I liked the movies because I imagined myself doing everything the heroes did—deciding to invade at daybreak, swimming half the night against the seaward current—but whenever we left the theater I was disappointed. From the front row, life seemed like a clear set of decisions, but on the street afterward I realized that the world existed all around me and I didn't know what I wanted. The quiet of evening and the ordinariness of human voices startled me.

16   Sometimes on the roof, as I stared into the layers of horizon, the sounds of the street faded into the same ordinariness. One afternoon when I was standing under the star my father came outside and looked up at me. "You're in a trance," he called. I glanced down at him, then squinted back at the horizon. For a minute he waited, and then from across the street he threw a rock. He had a pitcher's arm and could have hit me if he wanted, but the rock sailed past me and clattered on the shingles. My mother came right out of the store anyway and stopped him. "I wanted him off the roof," I heard my father tell her later in the same frank voice in which he explained his position to vegetable salesmen. "If someone's throwing rocks at him he'll come down. He's no fool."

17   I was flattered by this, but my mother won the point and from then on I could stay up on the roof when I wanted. To appease my father I cleaned the electric star, and though he often came outside to sweep, he stopped telling me to come down. I thought about limited fame and spent a lot of time noticing the sky. When I looked closely it was a sea with waves and shifting colors, wind seams and denials of distance, and after a while I learned to look at it so that it entered my eye whole. It was blue liquid. I spent hours looking into its pale wash, looking for things, though I didn't know what. I looked for lines or sectors, the diamond shapes of daylight stars. Sometimes, silver-winged jets from the air force base across the hills turned the right way against the sun and went off like small flash bulbs on the horizon. There was nothing that struck me and stayed, though, nothing with the brilliance of white light or electric explosion that I thought came with discovery, so after a while I changed my idea of discovery. I just stood on the roof and stared. When my mother asked me, I told her that I might be seeing new things but that seeing change took time. "It's slow," I told her. "It may take years."

The first time I let her steal I chalked it up to surprise. I was working the front register when she walked in, a thin, tall woman in a plaid dress that looked wilted. She went right to the standup display of cut-price, nearly expired breads and crackers, where she took a loaf of rye from the shelf. Then she turned and looked me in the eye. We were looking into each other's eyes when she walked out the front door. Through the blue-and-white LOOK UP TO STAR FOOD sign on the window I watched her cross the street.

19   There were two or three other shoppers in the store, and over the tops of the potato chip packages I could see my mother's broom. My father was in back unloading chicken parts. Nobody else had seen her come in; nobody had seen her leave. I locked the cash drawer and walked to the aisle where my mother was sweeping.

20   "I think someone just stole."

21   My mother wheeled a trash receptacle when she swept, and as I stood there she closed it, put down her broom, and wiped her face with her handkerchief. "You couldn't get him?"

22   "It was a her."

23   "A lady?"

24   "I couldn't chase her. She came in and took a loaf of rye and left."

25   I had chased plenty of shoplifters before. They were kids usually, in sneakers and coats too warm for the weather. I chased them up the aisle and out the door, then to the corner and around it while ahead of me they tried to toss whatever it was—Twinkies, freeze-pops—into the sidewalk hedges. They cried when I caught them, begged me not to tell their parents. First time, my father said, scare them real good. Second time, call the law. I took them back with me to the store, held them by the collar as we walked. Then I sat them in the straight-back chair in the stockroom and gave them a speech my father had written. It was printed on a blue index card taped to the door. DO YOU KNOW WHAT YOU HAVE DONE? it began. DO YOU KNOW WHAT IT IS TO STEAL? I learned to pause between the questions, pace the room, check

the card. "Give them time to get scared," my father said. He was expert at this. He never talked to them until he had dusted the vegetables or run a couple of women through the register. "Why should I stop my work for a kid who steals from me?" he said. When he finally came into the stockroom he moved and spoke the way policemen do at the scene of an accident. His manner was slow and deliberate. First he asked me what they had stolen. If I had recovered whatever it was, he took it and held it up to the light, turned it over in his fingers as if it were of large value. Then he opened the freezer door and led the kid inside to talk about law and punishment amid the frozen beef carcasses. He paced as he spoke, breathed clouds of vapor into the air.

26   In the end, though, my mother usually got him to let them off. Once when he wouldn't, when he had called the police to pick up a third-offense boy who sat trembling in the stockroom, my mother called him to the front of the store to talk to a customer. In the stockroom we kept a key to the back door hidden under a silver samovar that had belonged to my grandmother, and when my father was in front that afternoon my mother came to the rear, took it out, and opened the back door. She leaned down to the boy's ear. "Run," she said.

27   The next time she came in it happened the same way. My father was at the vegetable tier, stacking avocados. My mother was in back listening to the radio. It was afternoon. I rang in a customer, then looked up while I was putting the milk cartons in the bottom of the bag, and there she was. Her gray eyes were looking into mine. She had two cans of pineapple juice in her hands, and on the way out she held the door for an old woman.

28   That night I went up to clean the star. The air was clear. It was warm. When I finished wiping the glass I moved out over the edge of the eaves and looked into the distance where little turquoise squares—lighted swimming pools—stood out against the hills.

29   "Dade—"

30   It was my father's voice from behind the peak of the roof.

31   "Yes?"

32   "Come over to this side."

33   I mounted the shallow-pitched roof, went over the peak, and edged down the other slope to where I could see his silhouette against the lights on Route 5. He was smoking. I got up and we stood together at the edge of the shingled eaves. In front of us trucks rumbled by on the interstate, their trailers lit at the edges like the mast lights of ships.

34   "Look across the highway," he said.

35   "I am."

36   "What do you see?"

37   "Cars."

38   "What else?"

39   "Trucks."

40   For a while he didn't say anything. He dragged a few times on his cigarette, then pinched off the lit end and put the rest back in the pack. A couple of motorcycles went by, a car with one headlight, a bus.

41   "Do you know what it's like to live in a shack?" he said.

42   "No."

43   "You don't want to end up in a place like that. And it's damn easy to do if you don't know what you want. You know how easy it is?"

44   "Easy," I said.

45   "You have to know what you want."

46   For years my father had been trying to teach me competence and industry. Since I was nine I had been squeeze-drying mops before returning them to the closet, double-counting change, sweeping under the lip of the vegetable bins even if the dirt there was invisible to customers. On the basis of industry, my father said, Star Food had grown from a two-aisle, one-freezer corner store to the largest grocery in Arcade. When I was eight he had bought the failing gas station next door and built additions, so that now Star Food had nine aisles, separate coolers for dairy, soda, and beer, a tiered vegetable stand, a glass-fronted butcher counter, a part-time butcher, and, under what used to be the rain roof of the failing gas station, free parking while you shopped. When I started high school we moved into the apartment next door, and at meals we discussed store improvements. Soon my father invented a grid system for easy location of foods. He stayed up one night and painted, and the next morning there was a new coordinate system on the ceiling of the store. It was a grid, A through J, 1 through 10. For weeks there were drops of blue paint on his eyelashes.

47   A few days later my mother pasted up fluorescent stars among the grid squares. She knew about the real constellations and was accurate with the ones she stuck to the ceiling. Even though she also knew that the aisle lights in Star Food stayed on day and night, so that her stars were going to be invisible. We saw them only once, in fact, in a blackout a few months later, when they lit up in hazy clusters around the store.

48   "Do you know why I did it?" she asked me the night of the blackout as we stood beneath their pale light.

49   "No."

50   "Because of the idea."

51   She was full of ideas, and one was that I was accomplishing something on the shallow-pitched section of our roof. Sometimes she sat at the dormer window and watched me. Through the glass I could see the slender outlines of her cheekbones. "What do you see?" she asked. On warm nights she leaned over the sill and pointed out the constellations. "They are the illumination of great minds," she said.

52   After the woman walked out the second time I began to think a lot about what I wanted. I tried to discover what it was, and I had an idea it would come to me on the roof. In the evenings I sat up there and thought. I looked for signs. I threw pebbles down into the street and watched where they hit. I read the newspaper, and stories about ballplayers or jazz musicians began to catch my eye. When he was ten years old, Johnny Unitas strung a tire from a tree limb and spent afternoons throwing a football through it as it swung. Dizzy Gillespie played with an

orchestra when he was seven. There was an emperor who ruled China at age eight. What could be said about me? He swept the dirt no one could see under the lip of the vegetable bins.

The day after the woman had walked out the second time, my mother came up on the roof while I was cleaning the star. She usually wore medium heels and stayed away from the shingled roof, but that night she came up. I had been over the glass once when I saw her coming through the dormer window, skirt hem and white shoes lit by moonlight. Most of the insects were cleaned off and steam was drifting up into the night. She came through the window, took off her shoes, and edged down the roof until she was standing next to me at the star. "It's a beautiful night," she said.

54   "Cool."

55   "Dade, when you're up here do you ever think about what is in the mind of a great man when he makes a discovery?"

56   The night was just making its transition from the thin sky to the thick, the air was taking on weight, and at the horizon distances were shortening. I looked out over the plain and tried to think of an answer. That day I had been thinking about a story my father occasionally told. Just before he and my mother were married he took her to the top of the hills that surround Arcade. They stood with the New Jerusalem River, western California, and the sea on their left, and Arcade on their right. My father has always planned things well, and that day as they stood in the hill pass a thunderstorm covered everything west, while Arcade, shielded by hills, was lit by the sun. He asked her which way she wanted to go. She must have realized it was a test, because she thought for a moment and then looked to the right, and when they drove down from the hills that day my father mentioned the idea of a grocery. Star Food didn't open for a year after, but that was its conception, I think, in my father's mind. That afternoon as they stood with the New Jerusalem flowing below them, the plains before them, and my mother in a cotton

skirt she had made herself, I think my father must have seen right through to the end of his life.

57   I had been trying to see right through to the end of my life, too, but these thoughts never led me in any direction. Sometimes I sat and remembered the unusual things that had happened to me. Once I had found the perfect, shed skin of a rattlesnake. My mother told my father that this indicated my potential for science. I was on the roof another time when it hailed apricot-sized balls of ice on a summer afternoon. The day was hot and there was only one cloud, but as it approached from the distance it spread a shaft of darkness below it as if it had fallen through itself to the earth, and when it reached the New Jerusalem the river began throwing up spouts of water. Then it crossed onto land and I could see the hailstones denting parked cars. I went back inside the attic and watched it pass, and when I came outside again and picked up the ice balls that rolled between the corrugated roof spouts, their prickly edges melted in my fingers. In a minute they were gone. That was the rarest thing that had ever happened to me. Now I waited for rare things because it seemed to me that if you traced back the lives of men you arrived at some sort of sign, rainstorm at one horizon and sunlight at the other. On the roof I waited for mine. Sometimes I thought about the woman and sometimes I looked for silhouettes in the blue shapes between the clouds.

58   "Your father thinks you should be thinking about the store," said my mother.

59   "I know."

60   "You'll own the store some day."

61   There was a carpet of cirrus clouds in the distance, and we watched them as their bottom edges were gradually lit by the rising moon. My mother tilted back her head and looked up into the stars. "What beautiful names," she said. "Cassiopeia, Lyra, Aquila."

62   "The Big Dipper," I said.

63   "Dade?"

64   "Yes?"

65   "I saw the lady come in yesterday."

66   "I didn't chase her."

67   "I know."

68 "What do you think of that?"

69 "I think you're doing more important things," she said. "Dreams are more important than rye bread." She took the bobby pins from her hair and held them in her palm. "Dade, tell me the truth. What do you think about when you come up here?"

70 In the distance there were car lights, trees, aluminum power poles. There were several ways I could have answered.

71 I said, "I think I'm about to make a discovery."

72 After that my mother began meeting me at the bottom of the stairs when I came down from the roof. She smiled expectantly. I snapped my fingers, tapped my feet. I blinked and looked at my canvas shoe-tips. She kept smiling. I didn't like this so I tried not coming down for entire afternoons, but this only made her look more expectant. On the roof my thoughts piled into one another. I couldn't even think of something that was undiscovered. I stood and thought about the woman.

73 Then my mother began leaving little snacks on the sill of the dormer window. Crackers, cut apples, apricots. She arranged them in fan shapes or twirls on a plate, and after a few days I started working regular hours again. I wore my smock and checked customers through the register and went upstairs only in the evenings. I came down after my mother had gone to sleep. I was afraid the woman was coming back, but I couldn't face my mother twice a day at the bottom of the stairs. So I worked and looked up at the door whenever customers entered. I did stock work when I could, stayed in back where the air was refrigerated, but I sweated anyway. I unloaded melons, tuna fish, cereal. I counted the cases of freeze-pops, priced the cans of All-American ham. At the swinging door between the stockroom and the back of the store my heart went dizzy. The woman knew something about me.

74 In the evenings on the roof I tried to think what it was. I saw mysterious new clouds, odd combinations of cirrus and stratus. How did she root me into the linoleum floor with her gray stare? Above me on the roof the sky was simmering. It was blue gas. I knew she was coming back.

It was raining when she did. The door opened and I felt the wet breeze, and when I looked up she was standing with her back to me in front of the shelves of cheese and dairy, and this time I came out from the counter and stopped behind her. She smelled of the rain outside.

76 "Look," I whispered, "why are you doing this to me?"

77 She didn't turn around. I moved closer. I was gathering my words, thinking of the blue index card, when the idea of limited fame came into my head. I stopped. How did human beings understand each other across huge spaces except with the lowest of ideas? I have never understood what it is about rain that smells, but as I stood there behind the woman I suddenly realized I was smelling the inside of clouds. What was between us at that moment was an idea we had created ourselves. When she left with a carton of milk in her hand I couldn't speak.

78 On the roof that evening I looked into the sky, out over the plains, along the uneven horizon. I thought of the view my father had seen when he was a young man. I wondered whether he had imagined Star Food then. The sun was setting. The blues and oranges were mixing into black, and in the distance windows were lighting up along the hillsides.

79 "Tell me what I want," I said then. I moved closer to the edge of the eaves and repeated it. I looked down over the alley, into the kitchens across the way, into living rooms, bedrooms, across slate rooftops. "Tell me what I want," I called. Cars pulled in and out of the parking lot. Big rigs rushed by on the interstate. The air around me was as cool as water, the lighted swimming pools like pieces of the daytime sky. An important moment seemed to be rushing up. "Tell me what I want," I said again.

80 Then I heard my father open the window and come out onto the roof. He walked down and stood

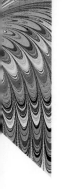

next to me, the bald spot on top of his head reflecting the streetlight. He took out a cigarette, smoked it for a while, pinched off the end. A bird fluttered around the light pole across the street. A car crossed below us with the words JUST MARRIED on the roof.

"Look," he said, "your mother's tried to make me understand this." He paused to put the unsmoked butt back in the pack. "And maybe I can. You think the gal's a little down and out; you don't want to kick her when she's down. Okay, I can understand that. So I've decided something, and you want to know what?"

82 He shifted his hands in his pockets and took a few steps toward the edge of the roof.

83 "You want to know what?"

84 "What?"

85 "I'm taking you off the hook. Your mother says you've got a few thoughts, that maybe you're on the verge of something, so I decided it's okay if you let the lady go if she comes in again."

86 "What?"

87 "I said it's okay if you let the gal go. You don't have to chase her."

88 "You're going to let her steal?"

89 "No," he said. "I hired a guard."

90 He was there the next morning in clothes that were all dark blue. Pants, shirt, cap, socks. He was only two or three years older than I was. My father introduced him to me as Mr. Sellers. "Mr. Sellers," he said, "this is Dade." He had a badge on his chest and a ring of keys the size of a doughnut on his belt. At the door he sat jingling them.

91 I didn't say much to him, and when I did my father came out from the back and counted register receipts or stocked impulse items near where we sat. We weren't saying anything important, though. Mr. Sellers didn't carry a gun, only the doughnut-size key ring, so I asked him if he wished he did.

92 "Sure," he said.

93 "Would you use it?"

94 "If I had to."

95 I thought of him using his gun if he had to. His hands were thick and their backs were covered with hair. This seemed to go along with shooting somebody if he had to. My hands were thin and white and the hair on them was like the hair on a girl's cheek.

96 During the days he stayed by the front. He smiled at customers and held the door for them, and my father brought him sodas every hour or so. Whenever the guard smiled at a customer I thought of him trying to decide whether he was looking at the shoplifter.

97 And then one evening everything changed.

98 I was on the roof. The sun was low, throwing slanted light. From beyond the New Jerusalem and behind the hills, four air force jets appeared. They disappeared, then appeared again, silver dots trailing white tails. They climbed and cut and looped back, showing dark and light like a school of fish. When they turned against the sun their wings flashed. Between the hills and the river they dipped low onto the plain, then shot upward and toward me. One dipped, the others followed. Across the New Jerusalem they turned back and made two great circles, one inside the other, then dipped again and leveled off in my direction. The sky seemed small enough for them to fall through. I could see the double tails, then the wings and the jets. From across the river they shot straight toward the store, angling up so I could see the V-wings and camouflage and rounded bomb bays, and I covered my ears, and in a moment they were across the water and then they were above me, and as they passed over they barrel-rolled and flew upside down and showed me their black cockpit glass so that my heart came up into my mouth.

99 I stood there while they turned again behind me and lifted back toward the hills, trailing threads of vapor, and by the time their booms subsided I knew I wanted the woman to be caught. I had seen a sign. Suddenly the sky was water-clear. Distances moved in, houses stood out against the hills, and it seemed to me that I had turned a corner and now looked over a rain-washed street. The woman was a thief. This was a simple fact and it presented itself to me simply. I felt the world dictating its course.

100 I went downstairs and told my father I was ready to catch her. He looked at me, rolling the chew-

ing gum in his cheek. "I'll be damned."

101   "My life is making sense," I said.

102   When I unloaded potato chips that night I laid the bags in the aluminum racks as if I were putting children to sleep in their beds. Dust had gathered under the lip of the vegetable bins, so I swept and mopped there and ran a wet cloth over the stalls. My father slapped me on the back a couple of times. In school once I had looked through a microscope at the tip of my own finger, and now as I looked around the store everything seemed to have been magnified in the same way. I saw cracks in the linoleum floor, speckles of color in the walls.

103   This kept up for a couple of days, and all the time I waited for the woman to come in. After a while it was more than just waiting; I looked forward to the day when she would return. In my eyes she would find nothing but resolve. How bright the store seemed to me then when I swept, how velvety the skins of the melons beneath the sprayer bottle. When I went up to the roof I scrubbed the star with the wet cloth and came back down. I didn't stare into the clouds and I didn't think about the woman except with the thought of catching her. I described her perfectly for the guard. Her gray eyes. Her plaid dress.

104   After I started working like this my mother began to go to the back room in the afternoons and listen to music. When I swept the rear I heard the melodies of operas. They came from behind the stockroom door while I waited for the woman to return, and when my mother came out she had a look about her of disappointment. Her skin was pale and smooth, as if the blood had run to deeper parts.

105   "Dade," she said one afternoon as I stacked tomatoes in a pyramid, "it's easy to lose your dreams."

106   "I'm just stacking tomatoes."

107   She went back to the register. I went back to stacking, and my father, who'd been patting me on the back, winking at me from behind the butcher counter, came over and helped me.

108   "I notice your mother's been talking to you."

109   "A little."

110   We finished the tomatoes and moved on to the lettuce.

   "Look," he said, "it's better to do what you have to do, so I wouldn't spend your time worrying frontwards and backwards about everything. Your life's not so long as you think it's going to be."

   We stood there rolling heads of butterball lettuce up the shallow incline of the display cart. Next to me he smelled like Aqua Velva.

   "The lettuce is looking good," I said.

114   Then I went up to the front of the store. "I'm not sure what my dreams are," I said to my mother. "And I'm never going to discover anything. All I've ever done on the roof is look at the clouds."

115   Then the door opened and the woman came in. I was standing in front of the counter, hands in my pockets, my mother's eyes watering over, the guard looking out the window at a couple of girls, everything revolving around the point of calm that, in retrospect, precedes surprises. I'd been waiting for her for a week, and now she came in. I realized I never expected her. She stood looking at me, and for a few moments I looked back. Then she realized what I was up to. She turned around to leave, and when her back was to me I stepped over and grabbed her.

116   I've never liked fishing much, even though I used to go with my father, because the moment a fish jumps on my line a tree's length away in the water I feel as if I've suddenly lost something, I'm always disappointed and sad, but now as I held the woman beneath the shoulder I felt none of this disappointment. I felt strong and good. She was thin, and I could make out the bones and tendons in her arm. As I led her back toward the stockroom, through the bread aisle, then the potato chips that were puffed and stacked like a row of pillows, I heard my mother begin to weep behind the register. Then my father came up behind me. I didn't turn around, but I knew he was there and I knew the deliberately calm way he was walking. "I'll be back as soon as I dust the melons," he said.

117   I held the woman tightly under her arm but despite this she moved in a light way, and suddenly, as we paused before the stockroom door, I felt as if I were leading her onto the dance floor. This flushed me with remorse. Don't spend your whole life looking

backwards and forwards, I said to myself. Know what you want. I pushed the door open and we went in. The room was dark. It smelled of my whole life. I turned on the light and sat her down in the straight-back chair, then crossed the room and stood against the door. I had spoken to many children as they sat in this chair. I had frightened them, collected the candy they had tried to hide between the cushions, presented it to my father when he came in. Now I looked at the blue card. DO YOU KNOW WHAT YOU HAVE DONE? it said. DO YOU KNOW WHAT IT IS TO STEAL? I tried to think of what to say to the woman. She sat trembling slightly. I approached the chair and stood in front of her. She looked up at me. Her hair was gray around the roots.

118   "Do you want to go out the back?" I said.

119   She stood up and I took the key from under the silver samovar. My father would be there in a moment, so after I let her out I took my coat from the hook and followed. The evening was misty. She crossed the lot, and I hurried and came up next to her. We walked fast and stayed behind cars, and when we had gone a distance I turned and looked back. The stockroom door was closed. On the roof the star cast a pale light that whitened the aluminum-sided eaves.

120   It seemed we would be capable of a great communication now, but as we walked I realized I didn't know what to say to her. We went down the street without talking. The traffic was light, evening was approaching, and as we passed below some trees the streetlights suddenly came on. This moment has always amazed me. I knew the woman had seen it too, but it is always a disappointment to mention a thing like this. The streets and buildings took on their night shapes. Still we didn't say anything to each other. We kept walking beneath the pale violet of the lamps, and after a few more blocks I just stopped at one corner. She went on, crossed the street, and I lost sight of her.

121   I stood there until the world had rotated fully into the night, and for a while I tried to make myself aware of the spinning of the earth. Then I walked back toward the store. When they slept that night, my mother would dream of discovery and my father would dream of low-grade crooks. When I thought of this and the woman I was sad. It seemed you could never really know another person. I felt alone in the world, in the way that makes me aware of sound and temperature, as if I had just left a movie theater and stepped into an alley where a light rain was falling, and the wind was cool, and, from somewhere, other people's voices could be heard. ◆

Mark Twain's Jim

Robert Keith Miller

Robert Keith Miller is a professor of English at the University of Wisconsin—Stevens Point. He is a frequent contributor to scholarly journals, newspapers, and popular magazines. He is also the author of books on Oscar Wilde and Mark Twain. The following selection from Mark Twain *(1983) deals with the question of how Twain has portrayed Jim, the runaway slave and faithful companion in* Huckleberry Finn.

Drawing by Kemble, from Huckleberry Finn *(1885).*

IF MODERN CRITICS HAVE BEEN APT TO TAKE Huck too seriously, they have tended to do the same with Jim, celebrating him as a larger-than-life figure. According to Roger Salomon, both Huck and Jim "are related to the demigods of the river, to the barbarous primitivism of the Negro, and beyond that to the archetypal primitives of the Golden Age, instinctively good, uncorrupted by reason, living close to nature and more influenced by its portents than by the conventions of civilization." James Cox is only slightly more moderate. Describing Jim as "the conscience of the novel, the spiritual yardstick by which all men are measured," Cox also turns Jim into a walking myth— the "great residue of primitive, fertile force." So pervasive is this trend that other critics have even praised Jim for being superstitious. Walter Blair believes that when Jim speaks of witches, his "soaring improvisations prove his mastery of supernatural lore." And Gladys Bellamy sounds almost infatuated, admiring Jim for his "manly qualities" and the "dark knowledge that lies in his blood and his nerve ends." [1]

There can be no question that Twain intended his readers to feel sympathetic toward Jim. The runaway slave plays a vital role in helping Huck survive. Although it is Huck who discovers the cave on Jackson's Island, it is Jim who insists that they make their camp within it, pointing out that it is going to rain. Jim is proved right; it soon begins to rain "like all fury," and Huck is delighted to be comfortably settled in the cave. "Jim, this is nice," he says. "I wouldn't [2] want to be nowhere else but here." And Jim responds by reminding Huck—and the reader—that he is responsible for their well being:

> Well, you wouldn't a ben here, 'f it hadn't a ben for Jim. You'd a ben down dah in de woods widout any dinner, en gittin' mos' drownded, too, dat you would, honey.

3 In a manner of speaking, Jim has provided a home for Huck—something he does once again, after they have left the island for the raft. It is Jim who builds a shelter on the raft, protecting them from bad weather and the lapping of the waves. He knows how to do things and is experienced in the art of survival.

4 Moreover, his loyalty and kindness are remarkable in a book populated mostly with scoundrels. He remains faithful to Huck throughout the book—and, at the end, he is loyal even to Tom Sawyer, a boy who has done nothing but injure him during the last several weeks. And the text makes it clear that Jim is deeply attached to his children. Huck tells us:

> I went to sleep, and Jim didn't call me when it was my turn. He often done that. When I waked up, just at day-break, he was setting there with his head down betwixt his knees, moaning and mourning to himself. I didn't take notice, nor let on. I knowed what it was about. He was thinking about his wife and his children, away up yonder, and he was low and homesick; because he hadn't ever been away from home before in his life; and I do believe he cared just as much for his people as white folks does for their'n. It does not seem natural, but I reckon it's so. He was often moaning and mourning, that way, nights, when he judged I was asleep, and saying, "Po' little 'Lizabeth! po' little Johnny! it's mighty hard; I spec' I ain't ever gwyne to see you no mo'!" He was a mighty good nigger, Jim was.

5 The carefully controlled understatement of Huck's closing line helps drive the point home. Jim is indeed "mighty good."

6 Nonetheless, Jim is portrayed as being extraordinarily gullible and something of a comic figure. Back in St. Petersburg, Jim had been a local celebrity by virtue of his account of how witches had put him in a trance and rode him all over the state. Every time Jim tells his story, it becomes increasingly dramatic. The origin of the tale could hardly be more trivial: Jim had wakened one night to find his hat hanging from a tree—where it had been placed by Tom Sawyer as a practical joke. But he seems to believe his own, more colorful version:

> Jim was monstrous proud about it, and he got so he wouldn't hardly notice the other niggers. Niggers would come from miles to hear Jim tell about it, and he was more looked up to than any nigger in that country. . . . Niggers is always talking about witches in the dark by the kitchen fire; but whenever one was talking and letting on to know all about such things, Jim would happen in and say, "Hm! What you know 'bout witches?" and that nigger was corked up and had to take a back seat. . . . Jim was most ruined, for a servant, because he got so stuck up on account of having seen the devil and been rode by witches.

7 Surely there is nothing admirable about believing in witchcraft and turning one's delusions into a source of pride. So far from being some sort of wonderful "dark knowledge" worthy of our respect, Jim's belief in witches makes him look foolish. It also links him to the slave on the Phelps plantation who brings him his meals, a pathetic character, with a "chuckle-headed face, and his wool . . . all tied up in little bunches with thread," who is convinced that witches are always after him. Twain's humor is at Jim's expense.

8 More seriously, Jim's passive acceptance of his imprisonment on the Phelps plantation, and his foolish toleration of the punishment the boys inflict upon him, are both perfectly consistent with his behavior throughout the novel. He seems to have been exhausted by his one bold action—his flight to Jackson's Island. Thereafter, he drifts down the river, taking orders from a fourteen-year-old boy and willingly dressing up as "a sick Arab" when told to do so. Although he knows how to cook catfish and make corn bread, he is ultimately helpless when it comes to as-

serting himself and realizing his own escape from bondage. He entrusts himself to Huck, and when they drift past Cairo—all too significantly—he accepts the situation with disappointing ease.

9   Jim's willingness to go along with the absurdities of Tom Sawyer's grand "evasion" should therefore come as no surprise to critics. Jim has been "going along" throughout most of the book. Had Twain meant Jim to be the hero of the novel, he would have allowed him to escape as the result of his own ingenuity—or at least through Huck's, since Huck is, to an extent, his adopted son. But the ending of *Huckleberry Finn* makes it clear that Jim's flight down the Mississippi lacked any real meaning. Jim has been free for months—not by virtue of his own action, but by the unexpected generosity of Miss Watson. Here is the ultimate indignity. To picture Jim in the last few scenes of the novel is to picture a man dressed in woman's clothing who is about to discover that he owes his life to the kindness of the mistress he betrayed. But Jim shows no resentment, not even any embarrassment. When Tom Sawyer pays him forty dollars for his trouble, he is absolutely delighted. "I *tole* you I bin rich wunst," he happily proclaims, "en gwineter to be rich *agin;* en it's come true; en heah she *is!*" The modern reader may be forgiven for wishing that Jim had told all those nice white folk to go to hell. Instead, he dances off the stage like a jolly buffoon, the comic Negro from a nineteenth-century minstrel show.

10   This conclusion would have been inconceivable if Twain had intended the work to celebrate Jim. It is true that Twain was bitterly opposed to slavery. But by the time he wrote *Huckleberry Finn,* he had come to think little of men in general, referring frequently to "the damned human race." Because he considered slavery to be cruel and unjust, it does not follow that he believed the slave superior to the master. Jim has definite limitations. And when Huck bestows upon him his highest praise, saying that he knew Jim was "white inside," it comes as a distinctly mixed blessing in a novel populated with extraordinarily disagreeable whites. Rather than reading *Huckleberry Finn* as a tribute to "the barbarous primitivism of the Negro,"

and then complaining that Twain wrote a conclusion that betrayed this interpretation, it would be more accurate to see the work as denying any fundamental difference between white and black, by revealing that both are subject to the same follies. . . . ◆

WILBUR'S "STILL, CITIZEN SPARROW"

Charles R. Woodard

Richard Wilbur is one of America's leading contemporary poets, a winner of both the Pulitzer Prize and the National Book Award. "Still, Citizen Sparrow" is from his 1950 book, Ceremony and Other Poems. *Charles R. Woodard, a professor at the University of Alabama in Huntsville, published the following essay on Wilbur's poem in* The Explicator, *February 1976.*

STILL, CITIZEN SPARROW

Still, citizen sparrow, this Vulture which you call
Unnatural, let him but lumber again to air
Over the rotten office, let him bear
The carrion ballast up, and at the tall

Tip of the sky lie cruising. Then you'll see
That no more beautiful bird is in heaven's height,
No wider more placid wings, no watchfuller flight;
He shoulders nature there, the frightfully free,

The naked-headed one. Pardon him, you
Who dart in the orchard aisles, for it is he
Devours death, mocks mutability,
Has heart to make an end, keeps nature new.

Thinking of Noah, childheart, try to forget
How for so many bedlam hours his saw
Soured the song of birds with its wheezy gnaw,
And the slam of his hammer all the day beset

The people's ears. Forget that he could bear
to see the towns like coral under the keel,
And the fields so dismal deep. Try rather to feel
How high and weary it was, on the waters where

He rocked his only world, and everyone's.
Forgive the hero, you who would have died
Gladly with all you knew; he rode that tide
To Ararat; all men are Noah's sons.

—RICHARD WILBUR

RICHARD WILBUR'S "STILL, CITIZEN SPARrow" has given great difficulty to a majority of those readers who have discussed it in print. By general agreement the poem has come to be seen as in some way a commentary upon politics, with the vulture taken to be representative of rotten politicians who are yet somehow superior to the tame "citizen sparrows" who elect them. A careful scrutiny of the language, however, makes it difficult to sustain such an interpretation. The chief stumbling block in the first half of the poem is the phrase "rotten office," which has regularly been taken to refer to corrupt political office. Donald L. Hill, in his book *Richard Wilbur* (New York: Twayne Publishers, 1967), sees the vulture as "a certain political leader, now out of office," who is "unnatural, a monster." The poet, he continues, "defends this vulture, arguing that if he can be given a chance to climb again to the altitude where he is at home, he will be both beautiful and powerful" (p. 72).

2   Such a reading leads one immediately into difficulty with the phrase "carrion ballast," however; Hill is puzzled but assumes that it is to be equated with "rotten office" (p. 72). In fact the poem is best understood if we take the word *office* to mean not a post or position but "performance of a duty or function, service, etc." (*The Shorter Oxford English Dictionary*). Wilbur, who has repeatedly affirmed his dedication to the "things of this world," has his eye on the vulture *as* vulture, not as symbol. It is its "office" or function to consume the "rotten," quite literally carrion, with which it is laden or "ballasted" in flight; the image in the first stanza is the quite explicit one of the ungainly vulture's cumbersome launching of himself into the air after feeding. Despite this unsavory function, as the home-keeping bourgeois "citizen" sparrow sees it, the vulture once aloft is a bird of surpassing beauty and freedom, superior to the sparrow in that its function as scavenger is to "keep nature new" through its digestion of carrion.

3   The second part of the poem, seemingly without transition, switches to Noah. That Wilbur is drawing an implied comparison between Noah and the vulture seems inescapable; as the vulture's wings rock on the buoying air far above the range of the disapproving sparrows, so Noah's ark rocked, borne up by water, far above the towns and fields of his disapproving neighbors. The attempt to read an exclusively political import into the poem is most likely to break down here, for Noah is in no sense a politician, certainly not a corrupt one, nor is he simply representative of some Carlylean[1] "hero" or strong man. The vulture and Noah are not characters in an allegory; rather they are the two terms in a comparison sufficiently far-fetched to constitute a conceit. An object of displeasure to his sparrow-like neighbors, Noah had the courage to endure loneliness, to "mock mutability" and keep nature's species alive. We are all his copies, bearing the saved essence of the past on the rising flood of time. If Noah's heroism must be seen in symbolic terms, it is not that of the politician but of the artist, attempting through his work to hold off the flood of man's mortality. ◆

---

[1]Carlylean: in *On Heroes, Hero-Worship and the Heroic in History* (1841), Thomas Carlyle (1795–1881) suggests that the strongest and best will rise to the top and should serve as the leaders in war, society, religion, education, and the arts.

Some Advice on Research

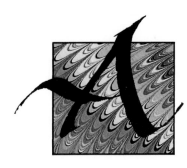

LMOST ALL WRITING INVOLVES RESEARCH. EVEN MEMOIRISTS, IF THEY take their jobs seriously, generally consult some source besides their own recollections. Mary McCarthy, in the process of writing *Memories of a Catholic Girlhood,* interviewed members of her family and searched for newspaper accounts of her mother and father's lives. In writing his autobiography, James Weldon Johnson used reference books, family photographs, and letters; he even found and quoted from a book of children's stories that he had read as a child. Rather than treating "the research paper" as a separate type of assignment, this chapter will suggest techniques useful for short papers and long, "personal" essays and formal term papers. We will discuss field notebooks, interviews, and questionnaires as well as library research. The formal research paper, with its special problems of manuscript and citation form, will be the subject of Chapter 12.

Though it is easy for a textbook writer to suggest that research is an orderly process, a matter of working systematically through card catalogues and indexes and eventually collecting a neat pile of note cards, this is far from true. Effective research requires a clear vision of an intellectual goal, the ability to distinguish quickly between information useful in pursuing that goal and information that can safely be ignored, and a cool head in the face of stubborn and unpredictable problems—temperamental interviewees, magazines with missing pages, books not on the shelves, indexes put together by people who clearly didn't have your problem in mind. A good portion of a researcher's time is spent working around obstacles, and it is often in the process of improvising an alternative route that the alert researcher happens onto information better than anything he or she could have imagined.

The hints below should, therefore, be taken only as hints, intended to save you some time. In practice, research is a skill that you learn on the job, first as a student writer, then as a member of a profession. Hint 10, you will notice, tells you that not every source needs to be read word for word. You will probably find that the best way to use this chapter is to skim the whole of it, reading closely only those parts for which you can see an immediate use. You may return to other parts when the need arises.

11

HINT 1

Develop hypotheses early.

The very word *research* suggests to some people that the truth about a given subject is out there somewhere and that the researcher's task is essentially to find and record it. But as this book stresses repeatedly, writing and thinking involve interpretation: the joining of a subject and a framework. Unless you have a framework, a thesis, your research is likely to produce a mass of data that says nothing.

Objectivity seems to demand that you form no thesis before your research is complete. But if you have no thesis, you have no way of formulating questions for interviews or evaluating the importance of what you read. A better approach is to form a thesis—perhaps it would be better to call it a hypothesis—as early as possible, and then be prepared to change it as often as an honest interpretation of the data demands. In fact, you may find it useful to begin work on a project by drafting a one-page summary, based on entirely imaginary research, of what you hope your final essay will be. This exercise focuses your search for authentic information. Sometimes you may find that your final paper reverses the thesis of your anticipatory summary. The flexibility that allows such a reversal is far more valuable in research than mere objectivity is.

HINT 2

If you plan to write from direct observation, keep a journal or field notebook.

Field notebooks are standard equipment for newspaper and magazine reporters, sociologists and anthropologists, and natural scientists who do their work out-of-doors. A mammalogist at my university, for example, makes systematic daily observations of mammal behavior in the field, beginning each entry by carefully noting the location, the time and date, and the weather conditions, then describing with as much precision as he can anything that strikes him as novel or thought-provoking about the animals he is watching. For practical reasons, he prefers spiral-bound notebooks (from which no pages can escape) with backs stiff enough to serve as a firm working surface.

Spiral notebooks were not invented when Charles Darwin sailed as a naturalist on the *Beagle* in 1831–1836, but he had similar habits of observation and writing. In the field, he carried a pocket notebook to record information and observations. Aboard the ship or in camp he kept a journal in which he wrote every day and which he subsequently published as *The Voyage of the Beagle,* one of the great travel books of all time. Here is a fairly typical passage from the unrevised journal, describing the effects of the thin atmosphere high in the Cordilleras, the "Alps" of South America:

"The Cordilleras"
—CHARLES DARWIN

> Now that the clouds were dispersed it froze severely: but as there was no wind we were very comfortable. The increased brilliancy of the moon & stars at this elevation is very striking & is clearly owing to the great transparency of the Air. All travellers have remarked on the difficulty of judging of heights & distances in mountainous districts & generally attribute it to the want of objects of comparison. It appears to me that it is full as much owing to the extreme transparency, confounding different distances; & partly likewise to the novel degree of fatigue from a little exertion opposing habit to the evidence of the senses. I am sure this transparency gives a peculiar aspect to the landscape; to a certain extent all the objects are brought in one plane as in a drawing. The cause of this state of the atmosphere is, I presume, owing to the equal dryness. The skin & some of the flesh of the Carcases of dead animals are preserved. Articles of food, such as bread & sugar, become very hard; woodwork shrinks, as I found with my Geological hammer. All of which shows the extreme dryness. Another curious effect is the facility with which Electricity is excited. My flannel waistcoat appeared in the dark when rubbed as if washed with Phosphorus; every hair on a dog's back crackled, the sheets & leather gear of the saddle in handling all sent out sparks.

Observations as close as those Darwin made are perishable, and only someone who writes daily can expect to preserve them. A good night's sleep can be fatal to the memory of details.

Besides aiding the memory, daily journal writing improves the writer's powers of observation, just as a pencil in hand seems to improve the artist's. There is in Darwin's descriptions an alertness of mind that must be created in part by the very act of recording what he sees. A similar alertness can be seen in the entries Joan Didion makes in her daily notebook: "'That woman Estelle . . . is partly the reason why George Sharp and I are separated today.' *Dirty crêpe-de-Chine wrapper, hotel bar, Wilmington RR, 9:45 a.m. August Monday morning.*" Unlike Darwin, Didion does not attempt to make her notebook a comprehensible record. Instead she uses it to collect the odd details that bring back to *her* mind an experience, a time. Though Didion says that she does not mine this notebook when she writes an essay or novel, no doubt the practice it has given her in noticing unexpected details produces some of the rich texture of her writing. For the writer who works directly from life rather than from books, the daily notebook is one of the principal sources of such details.

HINT 3

If you interview, plan questions in advance, put your subject at ease, and verify your notes when possible.

The interview—an important source of information for reporters, social scientists, and some businesspeople—ought to be used by student writers more often than it is. A skillfully conducted interview gives you fresh information to work with, information that no other writer has touched. Unfortunately, television has created an image of the interview as something that derives its interest from the fame of the person interviewed. In fact, interviews with relatively unknown people uncover information odder and more interesting than anything you are likely to hear from a celebrity, as Joan Didion proves in such essays as "Marrying Absurd" and "Amado Vazquez."

What makes interviews hard is precisely what makes them valuable: they involve face-to-face contact with people. Since the person you are interviewing is donating time to be helpful, you are under a stronger-than-normal obligation to observe the ordinary courtesies, making an appointment at a time convenient for the interviewee, not overstaying your welcome, being generous with your thanks. At the same time, the interview is not an entirely social occasion; you need to be as prepared and focused as you would be for an important business meeting.

One of the most accomplished interviewers of the century is Jessica Mitford, author of books and articles that uncovered abuses in the Famous Writers School, the funeral industry, prison management, and the criminal justice system. Her advice on interviewing is valuable.

from
Poison Penmanship
—JESSICA MITFORD

The individuals to be interviewed will usually fall into two categories. Friendly Witnesses, those who are sympathetic to your point of view, such as the victim of a racket you are investigating, or an expert who is clarifying for you technical matters within his field of knowledge; and Unfriendlies, whose interests may be threatened by your investigation and who therefore will be prone to conceal rather than reveal the information you are seeking.

While your approach to each of these will differ, some general rules hold good for *all* interviews. Prepare your approach as a lawyer would for an important cross-examination. Take time to think through exactly what it is that you want to learn from the interview; I write out and number in order the questions I intend to ask. That way I can number the answer, keyed to the number of the question, without interrupting the flow of conversation, and if the sequence is disturbed (which it probably will be, in the course of the interchange), I have no problem reconstructing the Q. and A. as they occurred. Naturally other questions may arise that I had not foreseen, but I will still have my own outline as a guide to the absolute essentials.

Immediately after the interview, I type up the Q.s and A.s before my notes get cold. If, in the course of doing this, I discover that I have missed something, or another question occurs to me, I call up the person immediately while the subject is still freshly in mind.

In the case of the Friendly Witness, it often helps to send him a typescript of the interview for correction or elaboration. I did this to good effect after interviews with defense lawyers from whom I was seeking information about the conspiracy law for *The Trial of Dr. Spock,* and with Dr. Margen and other physicians who revealed the nature of drug experiments on prisoners for *Kind and Usual Punishment.* In each case the expert whom I had consulted not only saved me from egregious error but in correcting my transcription of the interview enriched and strengthened the points to be made.

For Unfriendly Witnesses—which in my experience have included undertakers, prosecutors, prison administrators, Famous Writers—I list the questions in graduated form from Kind to Cruel. Kind questions are designed to lull your quarry into a conversational mood: "How did you first get interested in funeral directing as a career?" "Could you suggest any reading material that might help me to understand more about problems of Corrections?" and so on. By the time you get to the Cruel questions—"What is the wholesale cost of your casket retailing for three thousand dollars?" "How do you justify censoring a prisoner's correspondence with his lawyer in violation of the California law?"—your interlocutor will find it hard to duck and may blurt out a quotable nugget.

The portable tape recorder can obviously be useful to interviewers, allowing them to capture the interviewee's precise words. It has not, however, replaced the notebook. Some people are reluctant to talk in the presence of a tape recorder, and some portions of even a carefully taped interview may turn out inaudible. Should you have the good fortune to get ninety minutes of audible tape, you will face the difficult task of finding and transcribing the key quotations. Experienced reporters who use tape recorders generally take notes to serve as a backup and as a visual reminder of the key points of the conversation. Some treat the tape as the backup and rely primarily on the notebook.

HINT 4

If you use a questionnaire, design it carefully and justify your interpretation of its results.

Interviews are useful in situations where the opinions of an individual or a few individuals count. They are cumbersome in situations where the opinions of large numbers of people are important. Suppose that a student on a twenty-thousand-student campus is writing a proposal that the library should be kept open around the clock, except for Friday and Saturday nights. She believes, from conversations with her friends, that a large portion of the student body has been inconvenienced by the present policy, and she would like to prove the extent of this inconvenience to the administration. A questionnaire seems to be the best solution: if she could produce data indicating that the closing of the library was having an adverse effect on a large number of students, her case would surely be strengthened.

But administering a questionnaire properly is not an easy task. There is, in the first place, the difficulty of constructing the questions properly. Consider the following alternatives:

1. Do you believe that as many as 25 percent of students lose ten or more hours of research each semester because of the library's being closed from midnight to 8:00 A.M. on weekday (Sunday through Thursday) nights?

2. Should the library be open at night on weekdays?

3. The university library closes from midnight to 8:00 A.M. Monday through Thursday. If the library were open all night these nights, how many more hours would you have spent there this week?

Each of these questions is flawed. Number 1 is unnecessarily difficult and asks respondents about the lives of people they have never met. Number 2 is ambiguous. Not every respondent will take "at night" to mean "midnight to 8:00 A.M." and "weekdays" to mean Monday through Thursday. Some will say that the library should (or should not) be open at nights for their *personal* benefit. Some will say that it *should* be open for the sake of others or even for the university's reputation, even though they would never use it themselves. Still others may understand the question to be asking them to estimate a probability, as in "*Should* the Cardinals win the pennant this year?" When the question is this ambiguous, the results are almost impossible to interpret.

Number 3 has things to be said for it. It gives respondents the essential information in short, clear sentences, and it asks them to examine only their own behavior and opinions rather than the opinions of others. By limiting the time frame to the week immediately past, it avoids speculation about the future and doesn't ask for impossible feats of memory. Even this question has weaknesses, however. Different respondents may interpret "week" differently: Does it mean the last seven days, including today? Does it mean the seven days prior to this one? Does it mean last calendar week? Perhaps the questioner should specify a range of dates. Even then, there would be problems to consider. Not every week in a school term, for example, produces the same level of library use. Such difficulties can (and should) be discussed in any report that uses survey data.

I don't mean to exaggerate the difficulty of framing good questions for surveying groups of people, but I do want to warn that the difficulties are considerable—so considerable that one ought to be skeptical about the validity of even professionally constructed questionnaires. A wise researcher will at least have each question scrutinized by several readers attuned to the sort of problems we have been discussing.

As crucial as the writing of good questions is the selection of people who will complete the questionnaire. On some occasions it is possible to survey everyone in a given group, but in the example we are working with, this would clearly be impossible. Even if our investigator could afford to mail questionnaires to twenty thousand students, only a fraction of them would respond, and this fraction would probably not be very representative of the whole population. Presumably, people irritated by the library's closing would be more likely to return the form than those who have never even considered going to a library at night. Researchers who can't afford mass mailings ordinarily must hand their questionnaires directly to respondents, then hover in the area until a significant[1] number of questionnaires is returned. But such handing and hovering must happen somewhere. Suppose the researcher on the library question decides to poll students as they enter or leave the library. Would the sample be representative? No, because students in the library at any given time are probably more-frequent-than-average users of the library. Suppose the researcher does a 2:00 A.M. survey or an 8:00 A.M. survey in a twenty-four-hour diner near campus. Would the sample be representative? Probably not. The 2:00 survey of night owls would exaggerate the inconvenience of the library's closing and the 8:00 survey of breakfast eaters would probably underestimate it. A better time and place might be the snack bar at the student union at noon.

If you intend to use questionnaires extensively in your research, I suggest that you consult a faculty member (perhaps from the sociology or psychology department) who can discuss with you such issues as the form of questions, the format of responses, and the appropriate size and composition of your sample of respondents. A good short discussion of these issues can be found in chapter 9 of *The Practice of Social Research* (Earl Babbie), in chapters 9 and 10 of *The Science of Educational Research* (George J. Mouly), and in *The Survey Research Handbook* (Pamela L. Alreck and Robert B. Settle).

HINT 5

Do not commit yourself to a long library research paper on a subject where too few sources are available.

In the academic world, the aim of a research project is to make new knowledge, not to reproduce old knowledge. In this respect, library research seems

---

[1] "Statistical significance," an important concept in survey research, is too complex to discuss here. Common sense should tell you, however, that a large sample is more likely to produce credible data than a small one. When samples smaller than twenty are offered as representative of large populations, statisticians tend to show acute anxiety or downright amusement.

almost to be a contradiction in terms, since everything found on the shelves is known to at least one earlier researcher. The new knowledge produced by library research is really a novel combination of materials not novel in themselves: the research-based essay is like a "new" dish created from groceries anyone could have purchased but that no one has brought together precisely *this* way with precisely *this* effect.

Obviously, the opportunities for novel combinations are greatly reduced if the researcher (or the cook) works with a very few ingredients. If you attempt to do a library research paper on the Flat Earth Society's denial that men have landed on the moon, for example, and discover after some hours of research that your library can offer you only one magazine article of moderate length and two ten-line newspaper stories repeating information found in the article, you will be in a difficult position. Unless you redefine your topic or find a way to do some nonlibrary research (perhaps an interview with a local member of the society), what you will probably produce is a paraphrase of the magazine article.

The problem of finding adequate sources is not merely one of finding a large enough number of them. In some cases, you may find ten or fifteen sources that all seem to say the same thing. What you need are sources that differ from each other *or from you* in their perspective or in the data they collect. In most academic subjects, a difference in perspective (framework) is an especially valuable find since it allows the researcher to develop the arguments and counterarguments by which scholars attempt to reveal the truth. In "Mark Twain's Jim" (page 413), Robert Keith Miller uses library research in his introduction to "situate himself" (as critics say) among other readers of *Huckleberry Finn,* to show that he has identified a problem on which reasonable people can and do disagree. He uses only five sources (the novel and four critics), but we feel that these are enough because they show a range of differing opinions.

HINT 6

Where it is feasible, begin library research at the encyclopedia level.

You may have learned in high school that no respectable research paper would cite a general reference encyclopedia as a source, and it is certainly true that a supposed research paper that gets most of its information from encyclopedia articles suggests a writer unable or unwilling to locate other (probably more interesting) material. But great encyclopedias (such as *Encyclopædia Britannica,* available in almost every library) should not be dismissed lightly, particularly in the early stages of research. The longer articles, often written by internationally recognized experts, survey an area of knowledge ("Shakespeare" or "Mitochondria"), giving background information that will be useful to you when you read other sources. They define areas of dispute that may be topics for lively papers. And they usually conclude with a bibliography that can lead you to important scholarly sources.

Though they are in many ways less impressive than *Britannica,* the following general-interest encyclopedias are often worth consulting:

Chambers's Encyclopædia is useful because it presents subjects from a European and British perspective. It is published in England (unlike *Britannica,* which is—despite its name—American).

Collier's Encyclopedia devotes a higher percentage of its space to modern subjects than *Britannica* does.

The Encyclopedia Americana devotes a good deal of attention to scientific and technical subjects.

Larger libraries will ordinarily include a number of specialized encyclopedias you may find useful. An exhaustive list here would be impossible, but the following titles will give you a sense of what is available:

Encyclopedia of Education.
The Encyclopedia of Philosophy.
Encyclopedia of Psychology.
International Encyclopedia of the Social Sciences.
McGraw-Hill Dictionary of Art.
McGraw-Hill Dictionary of Science and Technology.

While encyclopedias usually offer good biographical information on major figures from the past, they are less useful for minor figures or—especially—for individuals who are still alive. For additional biographical information, the following sources are particularly valuable:

Current Biography.
Contemporary Authors.
Who's Who (with several variations, including *Who's Who in America*).

If encyclopedia-level research turns up no information on a topic on which you had planned to do a long research paper, see Hint 5. You may need to alter your topic or your approach.

HINT 7

If you are doing extensive library research,
save time by locating existing bibliographies.

One of the keys to effective research is learning how to exploit the labors of others. If you are researching a topic that has produced a good deal of earlier research and comment—the sort of topic that gets a full article in *Encyclopædia Britannica*, for example—there is a good chance that someone else has gone to the trouble of compiling a bibliography for you. The ends of encyclopedia articles and other general reference sources often contain such bibliographies, and some of the works listed there, such as biographies, will in turn contain their own bibliographies.

This route from encyclopedia-level research to bibliographies will not always lead to the most valuable sources. A second course of action is to start with what we might call "general bibliographies," catalogues (usually compiled by scholars) of important works in a given area. Among the heavily used general bibliographies are

Guide to Historical Literature.
Cambridge Bibliography of English Literature.
Research Guide for Psychology.
A Guide to Philosophical Bibliography and Research.

Topics that have received a good deal of scholarly attention often produce more focused bibliographies. Someone researching a paper on Robert Browning, for example, might start with *The Victorian Poets: A Guide to Research* or *Readers' Guide to Robert Browning.*

You can locate both general and focused bibliographies in the card catalogue (or, in this computerized age, the on-line catalogue) of your library. For this purpose, search *by subject.* If the subject heading you choose is a major one, there will be a subheading that lists bibliographies. If you find no bibliographies or are otherwise disappointed in the card catalogue's listings, you may need to try another subject heading. The card catalogue may produce nothing under *religion and evolution,* for instance, but may have several entries under *Bible and evolution.* The choice of headings is not arbitrary; almost all libraries in the United States now use the Library of Congress's system of headings. If you have trouble finding a productive heading, therefore, you can consult the *Library of Congress Subject Headings,* a three-volume reference work that is probably kept very near the catalogue. Or ask your librarian for help.

HINT 8

Use indexes and digests to search for articles in magazines, newspapers, and other periodicals.

Tens of thousands of magazines, scholarly publications, and newspapers print millions of articles each year in the United States alone. The total output of information is so great that indexing has become a considerable business in its own right. Indexes and bibliographies overlap somewhat in their definition and function, but when research librarians talk about indexes, they usually mean publications that sort the output of articles from current periodicals. Don't be confused by the fact that some indexes are also bibliographies and vice versa. There are now so many indexes available in large libraries that it would be foolish to attempt to list them all, but we will discuss at least three representative ones: *Readers' Guide to Periodical Literature, New York Times Index,* and *Essay and General Literature Index.*

Readers' Guide indexes more than 180 periodicals and manages to do so at remarkable speed. Every two weeks it publishes a slim paperback of publications for the two weeks before, arranged by author, title, and subject. These biweekly accumulations are combined to produce thicker paperback accumulations by month and still thicker ones by quarter (three months). At the end of a publication year, all the citations are combined in a single bound volume. Many libraries have the complete set of yearly indexes, stretching back to 1905. This is a truly remarkable resource. For material published in popular (as opposed to scholarly) magazines, it allows the researcher both a long reach back into time and an opportunity to bring research very near the present moment. Someone interested in the growing "professionalization" of college sports, for example, can trace the story through hundreds of articles and essays distributed over more than eight decades and extending to the current month. There are now dozens of indexes like *Readers' Guide,* most of them somewhat more specialized in their coverage. Some typical titles are

Applied Science and Technology Index, which specializes in scientific, technical, and engineering journals.

Bibliographic Index, an annual publication that lists major bibliographies published during the previous year.

Humanities Index, which covers scholarly periodicals in such fields as philosophy, history, anthropology, and religion.

Social Sciences Index, which covers scholarly periodicals in such fields as psychology, sociology, economics, and law.

Public Affairs Information Service Bulletin, which lists articles by public and private agencies on social, economic, and political topics.

MLA International Bibliography of Books and Articles on the Modern Languages and Literatures, an index whose title speaks for itself.

New York Times Index would at first seem to be a limited tool, since it indexes only a single newspaper. The publication has, however, covered current affairs thoroughly since 1851, and the indexing is unusually complete. Like *Readers' Guide, New York Times Index* is issued initially in small pamphlets covering two weeks and eventually accumulated into annual volumes.

Subject heading ———

Abstract of a
news story

News stories of
special interest
are printed in
boldface.

Note on length of article:
(L) means over three
columns, (M) means one to
two, and (S)means less than
one column.

Publication information:
month, day, section number,
page number, and column
number.

**UNITED STATES POLITICS AND GOVERNMENT-
Cont**
Jl 1.I7:1

Russell Baker Op-Ed column on Pres. Bush's demand for constitutional amendment to prohibit flag-buring: wonders why he is not fighting for amber waves of grain, spacious skies and shining seas, all threatened by profit-making schemers (S) Jl 1.1.23:1

Ken Philmus, manager of George Washington Bridge, says that when American flag is lowered into position on bridge on Fourth of July, maintenance crew and staff are filled with pride; 60-by-90 foot flag, reputedly largest free-flying banner in world, has hung from bridge's western arch on national holidays since 1947 (S) Jl 2.1.6:6

Congressional leaders and some Bush Administration officials say President's popularity will be put to serious test when he makes some hard decisions on budget and cloud of other issues now facing him (M). Jl 2.1 17:1

Supreme Court ruling that burning American flag as politcal protest is protected by First Amendment produces patriotic uproar and demands for constitutional amendment; cartoon (M) Jl 2.IV. 1:1

Editorial on American attachment to the flag, its virtues and the sad extreme to which it is being pushed in aftermath of Supreme Court decision extending First Amendment protection to those who would burn flag as act of political protest. Jl 2.IV.12:1

Anthony Lewis column opposes Pres. Bush's call for constitutional amendment to prevent desecration of the American flag, saying it would amount to an exception to Bill of Rights Jl 2.IV.13:1

Garrision Keillor Op-Ed article attacking Pres. Bush's proposal for constitutional amendment to outlaw buring the flag. Jl 2.IV.13.4

These volumes create, as the publishers say, "A Book of Record," in which newsworthy events can be traced day by day, sometimes in the most minute detail. A researcher needing to know when and where President Ford bumped his head on the doorjamb of Air Force One could find the answer in the *New York Times Index*. Other important newspaper indexes are *Christian Science Monitor Index, The* [London] *Times Index*, and *Wall Street Journal Index*.

The *Essay and General Literature Index* deserves special mention because it indexes essays and articles that are collected in books. Without such an index, being "collected in" a book would amount almost to being "hidden in" one, since sections of books do not receive special listings in either periodical indexes or the card catalogue.

Included in your library's research collection will be many volumes of *digests* or *abstracts*, which are essentially indexes expanded to include substantial information about the items indexed. *Book Review Digest*, for example, reprints short extracts from book reviews and gives the locations of complete reviews. It is a valuable resource for those who want to learn quickly whether a book they are considering (perhaps as a source for a research paper) has been well or ill received by critics. *Facts on File* summarizes press coverage of major news stories. *Biological Abstracts, Psychology Abstracts*, and other similarly titled volumes summarize the articles they index and are great aids for the busy researcher.

In recent years, computer technology has had a dramatic impact on indexing. Some of the resources listed above (like the *MLA Bibliography*) are now available in an electronic form that lets you use the machine's capacity to sort rapidly. Several new indexes, including the *National Newspaper Index*, are available only on CD-ROM or via modem. Your library will have information on computerized bibliographies and indexes available to you.

HINT 9

Choose a convenient system for keeping bibliographical references and notes, and stick to it.

"I had it in my hands just the other day," I find myself saying too frequently. "It" will be a book from which I copied a passage without noting the page number. Or it will be an article that I know would be useful to me today, even though I can't quite remember which issue of which magazine I read it in. The result of letting a source out of your hands without recording the pertinent information could be a loss of vital information but will more likely be a waste of time. An unnecessary trip to the library and the frustration of finding that the book is now checked out to someone else or that the magazine has gone to the bindery: these difficulties take time that would be better spent writing.

More efficient researchers develop and follow a system for keeping track of bibliographic information and notes. For full-scale research projects, a standard operating procedure is to carry two sets of index cards: a 3″ × 5″ set for bibliographic information and a 4″ × 6″ set for notes. As soon as you discover a book or magazine (mentioned in a bibliography, let's say) that *may* be useful, you write down all the information that would be necessary to cite it in the final essay. For safety's sake, your bibliography card for a journal or magazine article ought to include the following:

1. The author.
2. The title of the article.
3. The title of the magazine or journal.
4. The volume number (if there is one).
5. The issue number (if there is one).
6. The date of publication (sometimes given only as a year).
7. The pages where the article begins and ends.

A complete book produces a simple bibliography card:

1. The author.
2. The title.
3. The place of publication.
4. The publisher.
5. The date of publication.

An article contained within an edited book produces a slightly more complex one:

1. The name of the author of the article.
2. The title of the article.
3. The title of the book.
4. The name of the editor of the book.
5. The place of publication.
6. The publisher.
7. The date of publication.
8. The pages where the article begins and ends.

All this information is noted in highly compressed form in a standard bibliography or index or in the card catalogue. There is no easier time to write it down than when you are looking at such a source. If you are standing at the card catalogue, you may want to write the call number on the 3″ × 5″ bibliography card.

You will not, however, want to write notes on this small card. Instead, you will file it safely away and write notes on your larger 4″ × 6″'s. Since you know that you have complete bibliographic information safely filed, you can begin each note card by placing the shortest possible identification of the book in the upper-right-hand corner of your note card—perhaps only the author's

BIBLIOGRAPHY CARD

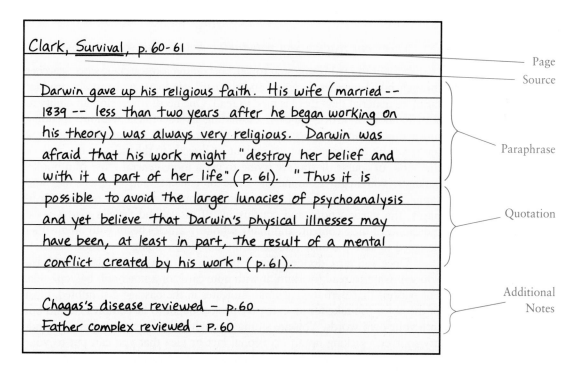

QH 31 ———————————————— Call Number

D2 C57 ———————————————— Complete name
                                        of author

1984

     Clark, Ronald W. The Survival ——— Title of work

of Charles Darwin: A Biography of ——— Complete publication
                                                    information

a Man and an Idea. New York:

Random House, 1984.

NOTE CARD

Clark, Survival, p. 60-61 ———————————

                                                   — Page
                                                 — Source

Darwin gave up his religious faith. His wife (married --

1839 -- less than two years after he began working on

his theory) was always very religious. Darwin was

afraid that his work might "destroy her belief and   Paraphrase

with it a part of her life" (p. 61). "Thus it is

possible to avoid the larger lunacies of psychoanalysis

and yet believe that Darwin's physical illnesses may   Quotation

have been, at least in part, the result of a mental

conflict created by his work" (p. 61).

Chagas's disease reviewed — p. 60   Additional
                                                              Notes
Father complex reviewed - p. 60

Some Advice on Research   433

last name, perhaps this plus a key word from the title: "Johnson, <u>Way</u>" or "Twain, <u>Mississippi</u>."

Barbara Tuchman describes her own approach to note cards, which is a sensible one:

> As to the mechanics of research, I take notes on four-by-six index cards, reminding myself about once an hour of a rule I read long ago in a research manual, "Never write on the back of anything." Since copying is a chore and a bore, use of the cards, the smaller the better, forces one to extract the strictly relevant, to distill from the very beginning, to pass the material through the grinder of one's own mind, so to speak. Eventually, as the cards fall into groups according to subject or person or chronological sequence, the pattern of my story will emerge. Besides, they are convenient, as they can be filed in a shoebox and carried around in a pocketbook. When ready to write I need only take along a packet of them, representing a chapter, and I am equipped to work anywhere; whereas if one writes surrounded by a pile of books, one is tied to a single place, and furthermore likely to be too much influenced by other authors.

The system using two sizes of index cards has great practical advantages for major projects. For minor projects, you may prefer to keep all your notes and bibliographic entries in a spiral notebook. The important thing is to keep the information safely and systematically.

HINT 10

Vary your reading and note-taking style to suit your purpose.

Learning *not* to read is one step toward becoming a researcher, since searches through bibliographies, indexes, and the card catalogue will usually produce far more material than there is time to read. One needs to develop an ability to scan a book or article quickly, estimating its usefulness without spending much time poring over its individual paragraphs. If you are looking for a particular bit of information, you might go directly to the index at the back of the book, of course. If you are trying to get a more general sense of a book's contents, you might examine the table of contents and chapter titles and sample a few paragraphs before committing yourself to serious reading. Ordinarily, the introductions and conclusions of essays and articles give a good indication of their content, and many scholarly articles begin with an abstract designed to save the busy researcher the time lost reading irrelevant material.

Once you have decided that a source is worth a second glance, at least, you will want to read (or skim) it with note cards or a notebook by your side. For reasons that Barbara Tuchman indicates in the passage just quoted, most of the notes you take for an extensive project ought to be compressed and put into your own words. You are sifting through what researchers call "secondary sources," picking up an occasional fact or idea that you can put to your own use and phrase according to your purpose. Occasionally, you may use a

BARBARA TUCHMAN

"Historians who stuff in every item of research they have found, every shoe-lace and telephone call of a biographical subject, are not doing the hard work of selecting and shaping a readable story."

© 1990 Rand Hendrix

Barbara Tuchman, daughter of a prosperous New York family, graduated from Radcliffe College in 1933 with a history major and an enthusiasm for research. One might have expected her to become an academic historian, but her interest was journalism. After an apprenticeship as a researcher and editorial assistant for the Institute of Pacific Relations, she became a correspondent for *The Nation,* and during World War II she served with the Office of War Information.

After the war, she discovered that she had become "a Park Avenue matron" with a husband, three children, "and no status whatever." But she also had time to work, and she set herself the task of writing history that would be read by non-historians. Her formula was simple: "There should be a beginning, a middle, and an end, plus an element of suspense to keep the reader turning the pages." Tuchman's first success was *The Zimmerman Telegram* (1958), a best-seller about Germany's attempt to lure Mexico into World War I by offering it a part of the southwestern United States. This book showed Tuchman's ability to integrate thorough research and exciting storytelling.

Her next book, *The Guns of August* (1962), earned her a Pulitzer Prize, as did her 1971 work *Stillwell and the American Experience in China, 1911–1945.* Tuchman produced ten books, covering historical periods from the Bronze Age to the Vietnam War years. Some academic historians have criticized her methods, but many readers agree with Bruce Bliven of *The New Yorker:* ". . . her control of her material is so certain and her opinions are so passionate that it would be risky to argue with her." ◆

source because the author's authority adds weight to your argument. In such a case, you will want direct quotations on your note cards. To avoid unintentional plagiarism, be certain to mark such quotations as quotations. Occasionally, you will find a source so broadly significant to your essay that you know you *will* use it, but you can't yet foresee where or in how many ways. In such a case, you will probably want to photocopy it so it will always be on hand.

Inexperienced researchers tend to make the following mistakes: they either read sources laboriously or skip them entirely; they exhaust themselves copying long passages from books rather than attempting to separate essential from inessential material; they photocopy everything, not even pausing to skim it first, and so end up at home with a briefcase full of bad material as their only resource. I confess to having made all of these errors. Experienced researchers end up with a lighter briefcase and a clearer mind. They scan and skim far more material than they read, and they leave the library with a small cache of high-quality xeroxes and note cards. I seem to be getting somewhat better at this, but confess that it is a skill one learns slowly.

HINT 11

Do not become a slave to your research.

On this subject Barbara Tuchman is once again well worth quoting:

> The most important thing about research is to know when to stop. How does one recognize the moment? When I was eighteen or thereabouts, my mother told me that when out with a young man I should always leave a half-hour before I wanted to. Although I was not sure how this might be accomplished, I recognized the advice as sound, and exactly the same rule applies to research. One must stop *before* one has finished; otherwise, one will never stop and never finish. I had an object lesson in this once in Washington at the Archives. . . . The Archives people introduced me to a lady professor who had been doing research in United States relations with Morocco all her life. She had written her Ph.D. thesis on the subject back in, I think, 1936, and was still coming for six months each year to work in the Archives. She was in her seventies and, they told me, had recently suffered a heart attack. When I asked her what year was her cut-off point, she looked at me in surprise and said she kept a file of newspaper clippings right up to the moment. I am sure she knew more about United States–Moroccan relations than anyone alive, but would she ever leave off her research in time to write that definitive history and tell the world what she knew? I feared the answer. Yet I knew how she felt. I too feel compelled to follow every lead and learn everything about a subject, but fortunately I have an even more overwhelming compulsion to see my work in print. That is the only thing that saves me.

Like art, research may have value for its own sake, but as a writer, you need to be a pragmatist. In the course of writing an undergraduate research paper, you cannot expect to become a world-class expert on your subject. You can, however, become well enough informed to be listened to with respect, and you can ordinarily do this in a period of time that will allow you to meet your deadline.

HINT 12

Cite sources when you owe an intellectual debt.

Though the mechanics of acknowledging sources can become quite complex in formal research papers (see Chapter 12), the general principles are simple enough. You need only remember that the words and ideas of other writers are their property—legally and ethically. We needn't concern ourselves here with the legal dimension of their ownership since you are not likely to violate the copyright of any of the sources you use. But the ethical question is always with us. In our society, and particularly in an academic community, people expect to be paid for their intellectual labors—if not in money, at least by the increase in reputation that comes from becoming a source for other researchers.

The ethical rule for the acknowledgment of sources, then, is simply this: when you know whose *ideas, facts, or words* you are using, give that person credit. If you know that an idea or fact is not your own (if you got it from a book, for instance), you need to ask yourself whether it belongs to anyone else in particular. It may not. Many ideas belong to the rather vague body of information called "general knowledge." *You* may not have known until you started your research that Darwin published the *Origin of Species* in 1859 or that Darwin was not the first to conceive the idea that species might change gradually over the ages, but both these facts are general knowledge. No one could name a particular person who "came up" with them, and so no one is deprived of due credit if they are worked into your paper without a citation. But if you said that (contrary to the speculations of many psychiatrists) Darwin's ill health was not psychosomatic but was caused by the bite of a South American beetle, you would be benefiting from the work of a particular scholar, Saul Adler. To use this idea without mentioning his name is to deprive him of due credit.

How do you know whether an idea or fact belongs to the body of general knowledge? A useful test is to see how the information is treated in standard reference sources, such as encyclopedias. Information that appears in an *unsigned* encyclopedia entry and is not attributed to a particular source is being treated by the editors of the encyclopedia as general knowledge. You may treat it the same way. Information in a *signed* encyclopedia article cannot automatically be assumed to be general knowledge: Bettyanne Kevles's initials appear at the end of the 1990 *Encyclopædia Britannica* article on Charles Darwin, and some of the opinions expressed in it are distinctly hers, differing sharply from the opinions expressed by Sir Gavin de Beer, whose initials appeared in the 1974 edition of *Britannica*. Information that appears without attribution in *several* reference sources, signed or unsigned—that Martin Luther King, Jr., was killed on April 4, 1968, for example—is clearly general knowledge.

If you are unable to decide whether a piece of information is general knowledge or is the property of some previous researcher, err on the side of courtesy and honesty: give credit to the source you are using.

When you put the words of another author into your paper, even one who is stating ideas you have thought of yourself, you owe that author full credit for the work. That is, you must enclose the imported passage in quotation marks *and* name the person who wrote or said the words. To give the name of the author without the quotation marks would imply that you are paraphrasing the passage, putting it into your own words. If the words are not yours, this constitutes a sort of theft. Writing on the same subject as another author, you will, of course, sometimes use identical words and phrases for a few words at a stretch. But when the stretch exceeds about a dozen words, or when the organization of whole paragraphs seems virtually identical and the verbal similarity strong, you may well be accused of plagiarism.

Most colleges and universities have stringent policies punishing plagiarism, whether it happens in the form of taking ideas, facts, or words without giving credit. The penalties may include failure in the course, suspension, and expulsion. But, finally, the best reason to avoid plagiarism is to be able to face yourself in the mirror.

HINT 13

Whenever possible, work necessary acknowledgments of your sources economically into the text of your essay.

While the scholarly apparatus of parenthetical citations and a "Works Cited" section are important in academic works, they can be cumbersome for the general reader. Most readers, seeing a surprising fact or opinion in your essay, will want to know its source immediately, without pausing to look at your list of works cited. If someone is being quoted, they will want to know immediately who this person is and what his or her credentials are. Consider the following examples drawn from essays in this book.

> Some constitutional theorists (Justice Douglas was one) have maintained that any obscenity law is a serious abridgment of free speech. Others (and Justice Earl Warren was one) have maintained that the First Amendment was never intended to protect obscenity.
>
> —Susan Brownmiller, "Let's Put Pornography Back in the Closet"

> Chivalry's famous celebrator Ramon Lull, a contemporary of St. Louis, could now state as his thesis that "God and chivalry are in concord."
>
> —Barbara Tuchman, "Chivalry"

Writing a book, full time, takes between two and ten years. The long poem, John Berryman said, takes between five and ten years.

–Annie Dillard, *The Writing Life*

You'll notice that the three writers are forced to make assumptions about their readers' level of background knowledge. Brownmiller, writing for *Newsday*, assumes that most of her readers know what a justice of the Supreme Court is and the names of two of the most famous justices. Tuchman, writing a book about the fourteenth century for a general audience, pauses to give some information about Ramon Lull but assumes that most readers will know perfectly well who St. Louis is. Annie Dillard, assuming, apparently, that most readers of *The Writing Life* will be people interested in literature, does not pause to identify John Berryman as a modern American poet. Deciding how much information to give in an in-text citation can be difficult. Your goal is to give the minimum information your audience needs to understand the significance of the source.

In formal research papers, you will often use too many sources to allow an in-text citation for every bit of information. Even there, however, you should mention particularly significant sources as you go, supplementing these acknowledgments with the more formal apparatus discussed in Chapter 12.

HINT 14

Consult (and cultivate) your librarian.

Professional librarians, trained in research techniques and familiar with the peculiarities of their own libraries, are a valuable resource. If your campus library conducts tours, attend one so that you can hear from your local experts such information as what computerized indexes are available to you, how your computer–card catalogue works, and how the reference area is arranged. When you find yourself at wit's end on a research project, go to the librarian for help and treat him or her well: this is a relationship worth cultivating.

My favorite research librarian, Wayne Barnes, recommended Jean Key Gates's *Guide to the Use of Books and Libraries* as my best resource when I undertook this chapter. I can, in turn, recommend it to you as a thoroughly useful book. But I want to end by recommending Mr. Barnes himself, or whichever of his colleagues sits at the reference desk of your own library.

WRITING THE RESEARCH PAPER

"RESEARCH PAPER" CAN MEAN ANYTHING FROM AN ESSENTIALLY PERsonal essay supplemented by interviews to a paper that cites a source after virtually every sentence. Several of the essays included earlier in this book might, therefore, be called research papers. Justice Earl Warren's written decision in *Miranda* v. *Arizona* includes citations of police training manuals and court decisions, for example, and Robert Keith Miller's discussion of the character Jim in *Huckleberry Finn* cites articles and books written by four other critics. These might, therefore, be called research papers.

In this chapter, however, we will be dealing with essays that rely more heavily on research than Miller's does, ones that cite the work of several earlier writers and support virtually every assertion by showing the source of the information it is based on. Such essays serve as reviews of previous scholarship on a subject, but they can and should do more. Ideally, they should not only review the findings of other researchers but put those findings into a framework that allows the reader to see a significant pattern in them. As an undergraduate, you are most likely to undertake such essays as "term papers" or "term projects." These names convey an indirect warning: such essays are very time-consuming. The research may take several weeks, the drafting is often laborious and uncovers a need for further research, and the time required to get the manuscript into the correct form frequently surprises even experienced writers.

The long labor does have its rewards since the effort of researching and writing makes you an apprentice scholar, the possessor of at least a small area where your knowledge is far greater than that of most students or—for that matter—most professors. The key is to do the job right, which means among other things that you must:

1. Select a problem that is likely to be interesting to both yourself and your readers and that is *limited* enough that you can read the most important works already published on it. "Charles Darwin" would obviously be too broad a topic: you would have to study dozens of books and hundreds of articles to pretend to any sort of expertise. "Darwin and Religion" would also be too broad for anyone with only a semester or quarter to read and write. "Darwin's illness" is more like it, a topic that is briefly mentioned in

almost every biography but that has been the subject of only two complete books and about twenty articles. And once you begin to read, you could find a way to narrow the topic still further: "Theories about the cause of Darwin's illness."

2. Read as many of the major works on the subject as you can. A good way to start is to locate a bibliography on your subject (see page 426). Often you will find a recent book or article on the subject that can serve as a cornerstone for your research. This cornerstone source will contain a bibliography that will direct you to other sources, some of which will contain their own useful bibliographies. Eventually, you will identify a cluster of sources that are referred to by scholar after scholar: these are the ones you need to be familiar with. If your subject were Darwin's illness, Ralph Colp's book *To Be an Invalid* would certainly be a key source and might well be your cornerstone. Because the book was published in 1977, however, you would need to update your research by consulting indexes that include more recent works (see page 428).

3. Work your way back to primary sources whenever possible. The precise definition of "primary" (as opposed to "secondary") varies with your subject matter, but a good colloquial definition of a primary source is one that gives information "from the horse's mouth." On the subject of Darwin's symptoms, for example, his letters and diaries are primary sources. On the subject of what psychiatrists in the 1920s thought to be the source of Darwin's disease, articles by the psychiatrists are primary sources. You should try to get your hands on the primary sources whenever they are available, since secondary sources are inherently less reliable. On the subject of Darwin's symptoms, a biographer's summary cannot be as reliable as Darwin's own words. On psychiatric theories of the 1920s, a summary written in the 1980s may be filled with distortions and oversimplifications. Above all, you must adopt the attitude of an investigator rather than that of a research drudge. If you lose sight of what you hope to prove, your research will produce nothing but a collection of lifeless facts.

CHARLES DARWIN

"I had, also, during many years, followed a golden rule, namely, that whenever a published fact, a new observation or thought came across me, which was opposed to my general results, to make a memorandum of it without fail and at once; for I had found by experience that such facts and thoughts were far more apt to escape from the memory than favourable ones."

Darwin Museum, Down House

"You will be a disgrace to yourself and your family," Charles Darwin's father once told him. The prediction had some basis. As a schoolboy Darwin neglected his books, and though the Darwins had been physicians for two generations, he was a mediocre medical student at Edinburgh University. Sent to Cambridge to prepare himself for a career in the church, Darwin spent his time hunting, fishing, and talking with scientists.

One of these scientists recommended Darwin for the post of naturalist aboard H.M.S. *Beagle,* soon to sail on a surveying expedition to South America. His father reluctantly consented, and in December 1831 Darwin began the voyage that changed his life. For five years, aboard ship and on land, he studied specimens and wrote observations on geography, local customs, botany, and zoology. He also studied Charles Lyell's *Principles of Geology,* which argued the "uniformitarian" hypothesis that great changes in the surface of the earth come less often from sudden cataclysms than from the gradual operation of everyday forces over millennia.

After returning to England he published his *Journal of Researches* (or *Voyage of the Beagle*) and three other books based on the *Beagle* data. Meanwhile, he had begun in his "transmutation notebooks" to develop the reasoning that eventually produced *The Origin of Species* (1859). This brilliant book applied Lyell's uniformitarian principles to biology, arguing that species were not separately created but evolved over the course of centuries by the gradual operation of the everyday force of "natural selection" (see the excerpt on page 210). The *Origin* ignited the debate on evolution that raged throughout the world in the nineteenth century and changed the course of modern thought. Darwin himself, however, stayed out of the public eye, continuing to write significant scientific studies in his secluded country house almost to the day of his death. ◆

The bulk of this chapter will be given over to a sample research paper, annotated to point out its key features. I believe that you will learn more by scrutinizing this paper than by reading more generalizations. As you look at the paper, notice the way that the author defines her topic and divides it into its subordinate parts. Notice how she uses sources and how she cites them. The comments on the facing pages will point out some of the paper's features.

Following the paper, you will find a brief reference section explaining the two principal forms used to cite sources used in college research papers: the MLA (Modern Language Association) style used in the sample and the APA (American Psychological Association) style often used for papers in the social and natural sciences. For a more detailed description of these styles see the most recent edition of *The MLA Handbook for Writers of Research Papers,* the *Publication Manual of the American Psychological Association,* or Kate Turabian's *A Manual for Writers of Term Papers, Theses, and Dissertations.*

Carolyn Douglas

Prof. Gene Joy

Humanities 104

24 May 1990

Changing Theories of Darwin's Illness

From 1831-36, Charles Darwin explored South America and several Pacific islands as the naturalist aboard the <u>Beagle</u>. Though he suffered from seasickness, he was healthy and energetic on land. In 1833 he undertook a horseback journey of 400 miles through an unsettled region of Argentina, climbing mountains along the way, hunting with gauchos, and going for "several days without tasting anything besides meat" (C. Darwin, <u>Works</u> 1: 106-21). Soon after his return to England, however, his health broke, and by 1842, at the age of 33, he was living in seclusion in the English countryside, so easily exhausted that he could work for only a few hours each day and could manage only short walks (F. Darwin, <u>Life</u> 1: 87-102). He was so ill that he could barely cope with a visit from friends: ". . . my health always suffered from the excitement, violent shivering and vomiting attacks being thus brought on" (C. Darwin, <u>Autobiography</u> 115).

"Many of my friends, I believe, think me a hypochondriac," Darwin wrote in 1845 (F. Darwin, <u>Life</u> 1: 318), and Sir Peter Medawar[1] has suggested that Darwin's inability to find a physical cause for his disease was "surely a great embarrassment for a man whose whole intellectual life was a marshalling and assay of hard evidence" (67). About 1857, Darwin told his physician that he

1. Rather than use a cover sheet (which some teachers may require and others dislike), Douglas gives her name, the professor's name, the course, and the date at the head of her paper.

2. Douglas summarizes material from an entire chapter of the first volume of Darwin's collected works to give evidence of his good health. Notice that she paraphrases almost everything but includes one brief quotation. This is a good technique for showing that her comments are closely connected with what Darwin actually said in the book. Notice that the parenthetical citation specifies C. (Charles) Darwin, to avoid confusion with F. (Francis) Darwin, the author of another source listed under Works Cited. The citation also includes *Works* (the briefest convenient form of the title) to avoid confusion since two works by Charles Darwin appear under Works Cited.

3. Francis Darwin is a primary source here. He reported what he saw with his own eyes. Douglas condenses into one sentence material from sixteen pages of her source.

4. Douglas avoids quoting secondary (distant) sources on the state of Darwin's health, choosing instead Darwin's own words, the primary source.

5. The raised number indicates that there is an endnote (see page 462) with explanatory matter that may interest the reader but is not essential.

6. Since the reader will assume that these are Medawar's words, there is no need to give his name in the citation, and since he is the author of only one work under Works Cited, there is no need to give a title. The page number is sufficient.

7. believed the illness had been caused by "the extreme sea-sickness he underwent in H.M.S. 'Beagle.'"[2] His son and biographer, Francis Darwin, reported that the "ill health was of a dyspeptic kind, and may probably have been allied to gout, which was to some extent an hereditary malady" ("Darwin" 525). Modern medi-

8. cine, however, does not recognize long-term effects of seasick-ness (Berkow 1: 1450), and it does not associate gout with shiv-ering and vomiting (Berkow 1: 975-76). The precise cause of

9. Darwin's illness remains a mystery, but the best evidence now available suggests that it was caused by the psychological stress of advocating the theory of evolution. The persistent attempt to find a physical cause reveals at least as much about society's reluctance to consider mental disease "real" as it does about what was wrong with Charles Darwin.

    The first argument for a psychological origin other than hypochondria was made in 1901, nearly two decades after Darwin's

10. death, by physician William W. Johnston. Using evidence in Francis Darwin's The Life and Letters of Charles Darwin, Johnston demonstrated that the illness grew more severe when Darwin worked on his theory of evolution and that it subsided when he did other things. Johnston identified the illness as "chronic neurasthe-

11. nia," caused by a "continued overstrain of exhausted nerve cells" and the resulting "loss of normal nerve supply to the digestive organs and the heart" (157-58). The notion of neurasthenia, exhaustion of nerve cells as a result of strong emotions, has

12. essentially been abandoned by modern medicine (Diamond 8: 27-28),

7. Darwin said this to Dr. Lane; Lane repeated it in a letter to Dr. Richardson; Dr. Richardson repeated it in a lecture; Dr. Colp, who had seen a printed form of the lecture, quoted it in his book, *To Be an Invalid.* Since Douglas can't go back to any source earlier than Colp's book, she puts in an explanatory note to explain that she is quoting indirectly, through Colp. It is always best to quote a source directly, but Douglas's technique is good if direct quotation is impossible.

8. Douglas cites a standard medical reference book, *The Merck Manual,* on the present understanding of seasickness and gout.

9. Douglas has a two-part thesis, expressed in two sentences. She aims to show both that the disease had a psychological cause *and* that the reluctance or willingness of people to admit this fact is an indication of changing attitudes toward psychosomatic illness.

10. Notice that throughout the paper Douglas is careful to give relevant credentials for her sources. The reader now knows that Johnston is a physician but that his training dates from the nineteenth century.

11. Douglas learned of the existence of Johnston's article by reading another source (Colp's *To Be an Invalid*). Rather than accept Colp's characterization of the article, however, she found it on the library shelf and read it herself.

12. Once again, Douglas went to a standard reference book to verify the present state of thinking about a disease. In this case the book was the *International Encyclopedia of Psychiatry, Psychology, and Neurology,* where she found a signed article on neurasthenia by Leon Diamond.

but the correlation between Darwin's research on evolution and his illness has continued to fuel speculation.

For about fifty years, from World War I through the early 1960s, psychoanalytic theories dominated the discussion of Darwin's illness. Dr. Edward J. Kempf wrote the first study of this kind for the <u>Psychoanalytic</u> <u>Review</u> in 1918. Arguing from evidence in <u>The</u> <u>Life</u> <u>and</u> <u>Letters</u>, Kempf suggests that Darwin suffered from an "anxiety neurosis" caused by his "complete submission to his father" (191). Kempf believed that this submission prevented Darwin from expressing anger, first toward his father and then toward others. Darwin, according to Kempf, feared "being offensive, ungrateful, and unappreciative" and so he became, on the surface, "hyperappreciative" and extraordinarily kind. Anger, however, was "a repressed emotional impulse that he had to be incessantly on guard against and which, perhaps, contributed to wearying him into invalidism" (174).

In 1954, Dr. Rankine Good published an influential explanation of Darwin's psychology, apparently based on the same sources used by Kempf. Good believed that Darwin felt "aggression, hate, and resentment . . . at an unconscious level" for his "tyrannical" father. By "reaction-formation," however, his conscious feeling was a "reverence for his father which was boundless and most touching." Darwin's illness, according to Good, was

> . . . in part, the punishment Darwin suffered for
> harbouring such thoughts about his father. For Darwin <u>did</u>
> revolt against his father. He did so in a typical

13. Douglas's own research has shown her that most of the publications about Darwin from 1918 through about 1963 were either psychoanalytic or reacted to psychoanalytic theories. She therefore opens her paragraph with a generalization she does not attribute to any source. It is her own thought. Several sources told her that Kempf wrote the first psychoanalytic study, so she treats this information as common knowledge.

14. The Kempf article is very long. Douglas summarizes it and includes a few key quotations. Since the quotations are widely separated in the text (seventeen pages apart), she pinpoints them with page numbers. Such pinpoint citations are a scholarly courtesy, useful to a reader who may want to examine the quotations in context.

15. Douglas calls Good's explanation "influential" because several of her sources refer to it.

16. Good wrote, "Further, there is a wealth of evidence that unmistakably points to these symptoms as a distorted expression of the aggression, hate, and resentment felt, at an unconscious level, by Darwin towards his tyrannical father, although, at a conscious level, we find the reaction-formation of the reverence for his father which was boundless and most touching." Notice how Douglas shortens and simplifies this material in her paper. The summarized material comes from the same page of Good's article as the extended quotation that follows, so Douglas delays her parenthetical notation until after the long quotation.

17. Quotations longer than four lines are indented.

obsessional way (and like most revolutionaries) by transpos-
ing the unconscious emotional conflict to a conscious
intellectual one--concerning evolution. Thus, if Darwin did
not slay his father in the flesh, then in his The Origin of
Species . . . he certainly slew the Heavenly Father in the
realm of natural history. (106)

Like Oedipus,[3] Darwin suffered greatly for this "unconscious
patricide." Good believes that it accounts for his "almost forty
years of severe and crippling neurotic suffering" (107).

Speculations of this sort irritated some of Darwin's admirers. In 1958 George Gaylord Simpson, an eminent paleontologist
and expert on Darwin's life, disagreed with the "psychiatrists
and psychoanalysts" who "have considered the disease to be purely
psychological." The "psychoneurotic theory," said Simpson, "is
an easy way out with any undiagnosed illness." A great many
illnesses were undiagnosed in Victorian times, Simpson pointed
out, including brucellosis, "an infectious, long-continuing
disease that frequently produces exactly Darwin's symptoms," and
one to which he was "undoubtedly exposed" (121). Soon after, Dr.
Saul Adler, an internationally recognized expert on diseases
transmitted by parasites, also argued against a "purely psychological aetiology." He pointed out that in the Voyage of the
Beagle, Darwin records being attacked by "the great black bug of
the Pampas," a blood-sucking insect Adler believed to be "no
other than Triatoma infestans . . . the causative agent of
Chagas's disease." Chagas's disease, Adler pointed out, matches

18.

19.

20.

18. Good's article actually reads "in his *The Origin of Species, The Descent of Man,* &c., he certainly slew . . . ." To shorten the quotation, Douglas cuts a few words and indicates the cut with three periods, the standard way to mark an ellipsis within a sentence.

19. Since Simpson's entire discussion of the illness is confined to one page of an article, Douglas does not put in a citation after each short quotation. The citation after "undoubtedly exposed" gives the location of all the preceding information and quotation from Simpson. It shows only the page number because the context makes it clear that Simpson is being quoted, and there is only one work by Simpson under Works Cited.

20. Again, Douglas is careful to show that the authority she quotes has good credentials.

many of Darwin's symptoms, including exhaustion and stomach trouble (<u>Nature</u> 1102). Sir Gavin de Beer's 1963 biography of Darwin embraced Adler's theory and dismissed the psychoanalytic theories with contempt, especially one (clearly Good's, though Good is not named) suggesting that "Darwin's theories of evolution and natural selection killed the Heavenly Father, and that Darwin suffered the remorse of Oedipus." De Beer treated this diagnosis as if it were an accusation of weakness and attempted to refute it by showing that Darwin was, after all, a <u>man</u>:

> It must remain a matter of opinion whether this is sufficient explanation of the reduction to semi-invalidism of a man with the physical stamina, courage, fortitude, healthy mind, and good judgment that Darwin showed during the voyage of the <u>Beagle</u>, when for five years he cheerfully endured the hardships of life at sea in a little ship and ashore, when he roughed it with the gauchos, ate coarse food and enjoyed it, climbed mountains, made numerous, lengthy, arduous, and dangerous journeys on foot and on horseback, slept out, caught venomous snakes, fished, admired Spanish ladies, cracked jokes, and took everything in his stride.
> (115)

De Beer was in a position to make his opinions known. Writing for <u>Encyclopaedia</u> <u>Britannica</u>, he briefly mentioned the psychoanalytic theories and announced that "all this specious and special pleading is unnecessary" in light of Adler's discovery ("Darwin" 496). At this point, it certainly appeared that the

21. The tone of de Beer's comments interests Douglas because it suggests that he finds psychosomatic illness unmanly and disgraceful. Therefore she introduces the quotation in a way that draws attention to the tone.

22. Douglas's quotation from de Beer is long. Quotations this long are justifiable only when the precise wording is crucial to making a point. In this case, the wording is important because it reveals the tone of de Beer's discussion.

case for psychological causation was weakening. And the case for physical causation gained still more strength in 1971, when John H. Winslow published a book demonstrating that Darwin, like other Victorians, may have taken arsenic for medical reasons and that there is "a very close match" between his symptoms and the symptoms of chronic arsenic poisoning (26-34).

But the case for physical causation had weaknesses, and doubt was soon cast on both the theory of Chagas's disease and the arsenic theory. Dr. A. W. Woodruff, a British expert on tropical diseases, questioned Adler's diagnosis. He pointed out that many of Darwin's symptoms (heart palpitations, undue fatigue, and trembling fingers) appeared before Darwin sailed on the Beagle, and that when they recurred after his return, they were associated not with physical strain (as would have been expected with Chagas's disease) but with "mental stress." He also pointed out that no other member of the Beagle crew suffered from Chagas's symptoms, and he questioned the accuracy of Professor Adler's statistics about the high rate of infection with Chagas's disease in the province of Mendoza, where Darwin was attacked by the "black bug" (745-50). Woodruff's diagnosis of Darwin's illness was "an anxiety state with obsessive features and psychosomatic manifestations" (749). After reading Woodruff's article, Professor Adler continued to believe in the theory of Chagas's disease, but he pointed out the possibility that Darwin suffered both from it and from "an innate or acquired neurosis" (Journal 1250). The "black bug" theory therefore lies

23. Once again, Douglas paraphrases many pages and quotes only briefly. The phrase "a very close match" sums up Winslow's point, and Douglas wants to quote it to make the quotation from Colp two paragraphs later comprehensible.

24. Notice again the care with which Douglas notes the credentials of the people she quotes or paraphrases.

25. Because the quotations from Woodruff are spread through a long article, Douglas pinpoints them with citations to particular pages.

in limbo, and even its chief proponent did not argue that it excluded psychological causation of some of Darwin's symptoms.

The arsenic theory has been answered by Dr. Ralph Colp, a physician and psychiatrist who studied Darwin's _Diary_ of _Health_, his letters, and other relevant documents thoroughly. Colp points out that, unlike arsenic poisoning, Darwin's disease was intermittent: ". . . acute nausea and vomiting would sometimes abruptly cease, and his stomach would return to normal, or near-normal, function." In addition, with chronic arsenic poisoning the patient ordinarily loses weight and suffers from "disturbances of the lower part of the bowel," but even during his acute periods of illness Darwin maintained his weight and his bowels were unaffected (133). These and other discrepancies between the symptoms of arsenic poisoning and Darwin's actual symptoms led Colp to conclude that "there is not 'a very close match' between the two groups of symptoms" (137).

Dr. Colp's 1977 book _To_ _Be_ _an_ _Invalid_, which carefully correlates fluctuations in Darwin's health with records of Darwin's activities, confirms what William W. Johnston noted in 1901: work on the theory of evolution made the illness worse, and practically any relief from that work made it better. It was not merely the strain of mental work that brought on a bout of illness; Darwin's health flourished while he wrote a difficult book on a non-evolutionary topic (52) but suffered as _The_ _Origin_ _of_ _Species_ neared completion (65-66). Colp draws a cautious but firm conclusion: "I believe that the evidence shows that Darwin's

26. Douglas has used past tense to refer to the works of other writers because she views these works as bits of past history. Beginning with Colp, she uses present tense ("has been answered," "points out") because she views his theory as current. When the history of ideas is not an issue, most writers use present tense in referring to works by other writers.

27. Douglas chooses a key quotation from Colp that exactly matches one she used from Winslow.

28. Douglas's references to Johnston and later to Good help the reader see the connections between parts of the paper.

feelings about his evolutionary theory were a major cause for his illness." He does not commit himself to a psychoanalytic view like Good's, but instead emphasizes some of the stresses in Darwin's life: his awareness that his theories offended some of his few friends, his knowledge that other friends who were eminent scientists doubted some of his conclusions, his awareness that time spent in society was time taken away from his great work, and an "obsessional" concern with problems in the theory that he could not solve. Darwin did "have a neurotic side," Colp concludes. He sometimes felt "an excessive and inappropriate anxiety" and he "was tortured by obsessional thoughts," many of them related to his work (141-43). Colp's book is clearly the most complete study of Darwin's illness ever published, and his conclusion seems difficult to refute.

The consensus opinion among experts today seems to be that psychological illness could and did reduce the once vigorous Darwin to semi-invalidism, or at least contributed to his suffering. In the most recent book-length biography, Ronald W. Clark reviews earlier theories and rejects both Chagas's disease and Oedipal conflict. He believes, however, that there was a more "straightforward and likely" psychological cause. Darwin's wife Emma was deeply religious, and Darwin feared that his scientific work might "destroy her belief and with it a part of her life." He also must have sensed that his theory would do damage to the "confident world" of the Victorians. "Thus," Clark concludes, "it is possible to avoid the larger lunacies of psychoanalysis

29. Douglas is stating her own opinion when she says that Colp's conclusion seems hard to refute. Notice, however, that the next paragraph supports her opinion by showing that views like Colp's, to some degree based on his work, now seem to form a "consensus."

30. Notice that Douglas is echoing the words of de Beer, quoted on page 5. She is also reminding us of the first part of her thesis.

31. Douglas is careful to bring her research up to date, quoting the latest biography and two current encyclopedia articles to check current views.

and yet believe that Darwin's illnesses may have been, at least
in part, the result of a mental conflict created by his work"

32.   (61). The 1989 article on Darwin in Encyclopedia Americana,
surprisingly, continues to advocate the theory of Chagas's disease, but the article has not been revised in at least 17 years.
Its author is Sir Gavin de Beer, who died in 1972. The 1990
edition of Encyclopaedia Britannica reports that "a careful

33.   analysis of the attacks [of illness] in the context of his
[Darwin's] activities points to psychogenic origins" (Kevles
980). Clearly, the author is referring to Colp's book.

     In the process of giving his now accepted conclusions, Colp
comments that "maturity and neurosis can coexist in the same
person" (142). In the context of the history of the controversy
over Darwin's illness, this sentence seems especially significant. It appears that in Darwin's own time, psychological dis-

34.   ease was considered not "disease" at all but mere hypochondria.
In the twentieth century, psychiatrists and psychologists (though
their theories have sometimes sounded bizarre) have gradually
established the reality of psychological illness. Though we can
see in many of Darwin's "defenders" during the 1950s and 1960s a
tendency to treat psychologically caused illness as though it
were some sort of defect in the character of the sufferer, this
view seems to be losing ground--at least in Darwin's case. Most
writers, and perhaps most readers, seem willing to acknowledge
that psychological illness can coexist not only with maturity but

35.   with a greatness like Darwin's.

32. Here is a good example of the danger of assuming that an encyclopedia article will give you the indisputable "facts."

33. To make the meaning of the quotation clear, Douglas inserts words of her own. Square brackets mark such editorial insertions.

34. In this paragraph, Douglas turns to the second part of her thesis, showing that attitudes to psychosomatic illness have changed through time.

35. The final sentence directly addresses the thesis and has a note of finality.

36.

Notes

[1] Winner of the Nobel Prize for Medicine, 1960. Medawar believed that Darwin's illness was partly organic and partly psychological.

[2] The source of this quotation is a letter from Darwin's physician, Dr. Edward Lane, to Dr. B. W. Richardson. Because the letter is not available, I have quoted it from Colp's <u>To Be an Invalid</u>, page 59.

[3] Good is clearly thinking of Freud's famous "Oedipus complex."

36. Not every research paper needs a page of Notes. When it is used, it contains only the exploratory notes that the writer feels compelled to add to the text of the paper. Exploratory notes give additional information or clarify something obscure within the text. They should not be used to give the sort of bibliographical information given under Works Cited. Notice that both the Notes section and the Works Cited section begin with a centered heading, then have a double space between heading and first line.

Works Cited

37.

Adler, Saul. "Darwin's Illness." Nature 10 Oct. 1959: 1102-03.

---. "Darwin's Illness." British Medical Journal 8 May 1965:
1249-50.

38.

Berkow, Robert, ed. The Merck Manual of Diagnosis and Therapy
15th ed. 2 vols. Rahway, NJ: Merck, 1987.

Clark, Ronald W. The Survival of Charles Darwin: The Biography
of a Man and an Idea. New York: Random, 1984.

39.

Colp, Ralph. To Be an Invalid: The Illness of Charles Darwin.
Chicago: U of Chicago P, 1977.

40.

Darwin, Charles. The Autobiography of Charles Darwin, 1809-1882.
With Original Omissions Restored. Ed. Nora Barlow. New
York: Harcourt, 1958.

41.

---. Journal of Researches, 1839. Vol. 1 of The Works of
Charles Darwin. 18 vols. New York: AMS Press, 1972.

Darwin, Francis. "Darwin, Charles Robert." Dictionary of
National Biography. 1888. 1973 ed.

42.

---, ed. The Life and Letters of Charles Darwin. 2 vols. New
York: Basic, 1959.

De Beer, Gavin. Charles Darwin: A Scientific Biography. 1963.
Garden City, NY: Doubleday, 1965.

43.

---. "Darwin, Charles." Encyclopedia Americana. 1989 ed.

---. "Darwin, Charles." Encyclopaedia Britannica: Macropaedia.
1974 ed.

44.

Diamond, Leon. "Neurasthenia." International Encyclopedia of
Psychiatry, Psychology, and Neurology. Ed. Benjamin B.

37. In citing weekly or biweekly publications, use the date rather than the volume number.

38. In citing a work of two or more volumes, give the total number of volumes even if you use only one. Indicate in the text of the paper which volume you are citing (see page 446).

39. Notice the abbreviation for University Press.

40. Use this form for a book written by one person and edited by another.

41. If each volume in a series (like *The Works of Charles Darwin*) has its own title, include the title in the citation and indicate which volume it is.

42. When you are focusing more on the editor's words (from the introduction, preface, or notes, for example) than on those of the original author, you may list the work under the editor's name.

43. Notice the brief citation form for standard encyclopedias; include only the name of the encyclopedia and the edition used. Although these articles are signed, many are not; if the article is unsigned, begin with the title of the article.

44. If you are citing a reference work that is not well known, use the form for books in the series and include the editor, the number of volumes, and the complete publication information.

Wolman. 12 vols. New York: Aesculapius, 1977.

Good, Rankine. "The Life of the Shawl." The Lancet 9 Jan.
1954: 106-07.

45. Johnston, William W. "The Ill Health of Charles Darwin: Its
Nature and Its Relation to His Work." American
Anthropologist, n.s. 3 (1901): 139-58.

Kempf, Edward J. "Charles Darwin--The Affective Sources of His
Inspiration and Anxiety-Neurosis." Psychoanalytic Review 5
(1918): 151-92.

Kevles, Barbara. "Darwin, Charles." Encyclopaedia Britannica:
Macropaedia. 1990 ed.

46. Medawar, Peter. "Darwin's Illness." The Art of the Soluble.
London: Methuen, 1967. 61-67.

47. Simpson, George Gaylord. "Charles Darwin in Search of Himself."
Scientific American Aug. 1958: 117-22.

Winslow, John H. Darwin's Victorian Malady: Evidence for Its
Medically Induced Origin. Philadelphia: American
Philosophical Society, 1971.

Woodruff, A. W. "Darwin's Health in Relation to His Voyage to
South America." British Medical Journal 20 March 1965:
745-50.

45. Occasionally a publication is issued in more than one series; "n.s." indicates a new series.

46. When using a titled chapter from a book, list the name of the chapter before providing the title and publication information for the whole book.

47. Monthly and bimonthly publications are listed by date rather than by volume number.

GENERAL COMMENTS ON CITATION FORM

The technicalities of citation form take some getting used to—more getting used to, in fact, than most people will do in their lifetimes. Even experienced scholars routinely consult manuals or samples when they compose their Works Cited section: almost no one *knows,* without some assistance, precisely how to list a translated article by two authors appearing in a journal with continuous pagination. You should, however, learn the general method of citation well enough to be able to read the citations in scholarly articles. If you learn this much, you will be able to cite sources in your own paper by finding parallel examples in published sources or in handbooks.

In general, citation in scholarly papers uses a two-part system. The major part is the Works Cited section (called in scientific papers the References section). This alphabetical list at the back of the paper contains the bibliographic information necessary to allow readers to identify precisely the sources that a writer has used. The minor part of the system of citation is the series of parenthetical notations in the text of the paper. Each notation follows a quotation, paraphrase, or summary and tells readers (1) which of the sources from the Works Cited section is involved and (2) what pages of that source are referred to. The sometimes complicated rules of citation form are created to allow the writer to use this two-part system as economically and clearly as possible.

THE MLA CITATION STYLE

The style of documentation described at length in *The MLA Handbook for Writers of Research Papers* assumes that the reader who wants to identify, evaluate, or locate a source needs answers to the following questions:

1. Who wrote the work?

2. What is its title?

3. If it appears between the covers of a larger journal or book, what is the title of the larger work?

4. If the work was prepared by a named editor or translator, who is he or she?

5. If the work is available in more than one edition or revision, or if it is part of a multivolume work, which edition or volume is used?

6. What is the place of publication and the publisher's name?

7. When was the work published?

8. If the work is included in a larger work, what pages are involved?

It is possible to find (but easier to invent) an example of a Works Cited listing that answers all these questions in order:

```
Doe, Jane.  "Her Article."  Her Book.  Trans.
    John Q. Public.  2nd edition.  Baltimore,
    Md.: Trankebar Press, 1990.  10-20.
```

The carefully prescribed form allows the writer to compress a great deal of information into this brief citation.

Many variations in citation form are essentially omissions of unnecessary information or slight necessary additions. Consider the following examples of citations for complete books.

```
Dubois, Kenneth P., and E. M. K. Geiling.  Text-
    book of Toxicology.  New York: Oxford UP,
    1959.
Dobzhansky, Theodosius.  Genetics and the Origin
    of Species.  1937.  3rd ed., rev.  New York:
    Columbia UP, 1951.
Krause, Ernst.  Erasmus Darwin.  Trans. W. S.
    Dallas.  With a preliminary notice by
    Charles Darwin.  London: John Murray, 1879.
```

In the first example, no article or chapter title is needed; there is no editor or translator; there is no other edition, volume, or revision; and there is no need to give page numbers (since we are not dealing with a separate article inside the book). The example shows us how much can be left out of the form in a simple case. The second example is slightly more complicated. It tells the reader that Dobzhansky's book was first published in 1937 but that the paper refers to the "third edition, revised in 1951." Such citations avoid confusion. For instance, it may be possible to find an edition of Darwin's *Origin of Species* that was published in 1990, but it is important to show that the original publication was 1859. In the third example, a comment is added to note that the book includes a section written by Charles Darwin.

When the source cited is not the book but a single article or chapter inside it, more information is needed:

```
Darlington, Cyril D.  "Purpose and Particles in
    the Study of Heredity."  Science, Medicine
    and History.  Ed. E. Ashworth Underwood.  2
    vols.  London: Oxford UP, 1953.  472-81.
Simpson, George Gaylord.  Foreword.  The Life and
    Letters of Charles Darwin.  Ed. Francis
    Darwin.  2 vols.  New York: Basic Books,
    1959.  v-xvi.
```

Notice that in the first example, it is necessary to name both the author of the article and the editor of the whole book. The "Ed." before E. Ashworth Underwood's name can be read "edited by." Notice, too, that the citation ends with a listing of the first and last pages of the article. In the second example, Simpson's foreword has no title, so it is simply listed as "Foreword." Introductions, prefaces, appendixes, and other such parts of books ordinarily have Roman-numeral page numbers.

Many academic journals are issued at infrequent intervals—quarterly (four times per year)—or even annually. Such journals are treated essentially as if they were books, so the citation form for them looks very like what we have just discussed:

> Kempf, Edward J. "Charles Darwin--The Affective
>   Sources of His Inspiration and Anxiety-
>   Neurosis." Psychoanalytic Review 5 (1918):
>   151-92.
> Sulloway, Frank. "Darwin's Conversion: The
>   Beagle Voyage and Its Aftermath." Journal
>   of the History of Biology Fall 1982: 325-96.

The first of the above examples is from a journal that numbers its pages continuously through the year. That is, if the first issue of the year ends on page 121, the second issue starts at page 122 rather than page 1. "*Psychoanalytic Review* 5 (1918): 151–92" means "pages 151–92 of Volume 5 of *Psychoanalytic Review,* published in 1918." The second example above is for a journal that starts page numbering anew with each issue: it directs the reader to pages 325–96 of the Fall issue.

Journals, magazines, and newspapers that are issued more frequently use a somewhat different form:

> Provine, W. B. Review of To Be an Invalid, by
>   Ralph Colp. Science 24 June 1977: 1431-32.
> Silver, John. "Darwin, too, Saw the Ocean in the
>   Andes." New York Times 30 March 1987: A18.

The first example above is from *Science,* a weekly publication, and you'll notice that it gives the date of publication in just the same place our earlier example had said "Fall 1982." Since such dates clearly identify which issue is being talked about, there is no need to give other identifiers that may show on the cover (such as "Volume 33, number 1"). Notice, too, that a book review can be listed by a description if it doesn't have a specific title. The second example is from a daily newspaper. Notice that the page number is A18— Section A, page 18. Had the article been printed without an author's name, the citation would have begun with the title.

Unpublished sources follow forms loosely like those used for published sources:

```
Golomb, Miriam.  Lecture on Misapplications of
     Natural Selection.  Campus Writing Program
     Workshop.  Columbia, Missouri, 10 Jan. 1989.
Perry, Carolyn.  Telephone interview.  21 August
     1989.
```

Obviously, these sources are not available to readers of a research paper, but they *are* sources and should be listed in the Works Cited section.

Parenthetical notations in the text.   In the MLA style, parenthetical notations in the text of the paper give the minimal amount of information needed to identify the pertinent listing in the Works Cited section (call this the *identifier*), then give the page numbers referred to. The form is "*identifier,* space, page numbers."

How much identification is necessary will vary. If, for example, your parenthetical notation follows a sentence in which you have identified Edward J. Kempf as your source, and if there is only one Kempf listing in your Works Cited section, then *no* further identification is necessary. Your notation might be simply (**163–64**). If you had quoted without naming Kempf, your notation might be (**Kempf 163–64**). If you had named Kempf in the text, but there are two articles by him, your notation might be **"Darwin" 163–64**. If you had not named Kempf and there are two articles, your citation might be **Kempf, "Darwin" 163–64**. The key is to consider the purpose of the parenthetical citation, which is to point the reader to the appropriate listing on the Works Cited page with as little fuss as possible. See the sample research paper in this chapter for additional information on and examples of parenthetical notations and Works Cited entries.

THE APA CITATION STYLE

The style of citation described in the *Publication Manual of the American Psychological Association* is more commonly used for papers in the natural sciences or social sciences than for those in the humanities. Rather than describe it at length here, I will give you examples of some typical citations:

A book with two or three authors:

```
Dubois, K. P., & Geiling, E. M. K. (1959).  Text-
     book of toxicology. New York: Oxford University
     Press.
```

A book written by one author and edited by another:

>Darwin, C. (1958). <u>The autobiography of Charles Darwin, 1809-1882. With original omissions restored</u> (N. Barlow, Ed.). New York: Harcourt.

A translation:

>Krause, E. (1879). <u>Erasmus Darwin</u> (W. S. Dallas, Trans.). London: John Murray.

A work in several volumes:

>Darwin, C. (1972). <u>Journal of researches, 1839</u>. Vol. 1 of <u>The works of Charles Darwin</u> (Vols. 1-18). New York: AMS Press.

A new edition and/or revision of a book:

>Dobzhansky, T. (1951). <u>Genetics and the origin of species</u> (3rd ed., rev.). New York: Columbia University Press. (Original work published 1937)

An article from a reference book:

>Kevles, B. (1990). Darwin, Charles. In <u>Encyclopaedia Britannica: Macropaedia</u>.

An article collected in a book:

>Darlington, C. D. (1953). Purpose and particles in the study of heredity. In E. A. Underwood, (Ed.), <u>Science, medicine and history</u> (pp. 472-81). London: Oxford University Press.

An article in a periodical with continuous pagination:

>Kempf, E. J. (1918). Charles Darwin--the affective sources of his inspiration and anxiety-neurosis. <u>Psychoanalytic Review</u>, 5, 151-92.

An article in a periodical that paginates each issue separately:

>Sulloway, F. (1982, Fall). Darwin's conversion: the <u>Beagle</u> voyage and its aftermath. <u>Journal of the History of Biology</u>, 15(3), 325-96.

An article from a weekly or biweekly periodical:

```
Adler, S. (1959, Oct. 10). Darwin's illness.
    Nature, pp. 1102-03.
```

Parenthetical notations in the text. In APA style, the year of publication is considered more important than it is in the MLA style. Thus a typical parenthetical notation might be (**1982, p. 326**). Notice that there is a comma between the date and the page, and that a **p.** is used to indicate the page number. A **pp.** is used to indicate a group of pages. If the author is not indicated in the text, his or her name precedes the year: (**Sulloway, 1982, p. 326**). Should you have two articles by the same author in the same year, they are distinguished by a letter following the year: (**Sulloway, 1982b, pp. 326–33**). Sometimes the year and page number are noted in separate sets of parentheses, thus: Sulloway (**1982**) has shown that Darwin's conversion to evolutionary views was completed only after his return from the voyage of the *Beagle* (**pp. 326–33**).

PART IV

MATTERS OF
m & Style

No writer can improve his work
  until he discards the dulcet notion
that the reader is feeble-minded,
  for writing is an act of faith,
    not a trick of grammar.

E. B. WHITE

ORGANIZING THE EXPOSITORY ESSAY

SKED TO DESCRIBE RULES OF WRITING LEARNED IN HIGH SCHOOL, A student in the first class to use *The Riverside Guide to Writing* presented this complete formula for organizing a five-paragraph theme:

> First, you write a funnel-shaped introduction that starts with a very broad generality that narrows down to your thesis statement. Then you divide your thesis into three parts and make the three parts topic sentences for the next three paragraphs. Then you restate your thesis in different words at the beginning of the concluding paragraph, and you relate it to a larger context. That's your web conclusion; then you're done.

The formula is familiar to many students and most composition instructors. It gives essays what one of my colleagues calls the well-ironed look: crisp to the point of brittleness.

Unfortunately, the formula has two weaknesses. First, we seldom find a professionally written essay that follows it. Second, students following it slavishly tend to produce papers that are dull exercises. See, for example, "Seat Belts" on page 514. As it turned out, the student who recited the formula was an able writer with an interesting mind; he could produce engaging papers that followed the formula closely. He soon decided that his success was coming despite the formula rather than because of it, however, and began every serious writer's search for a "formula" that is less artificial and restrictive. This chapter will be a part of that search, concentrating on the body of the essay. The next chapter will be another part, concentrating on introductions and conclusions.

To avoid confusion, I should say that our investigation will be limited to *expository* prose—prose that explains or argues. Narrative prose, prose that tells a story without explanation or argument, is organized quite differently and is discussed in Chapter 10.

FIRM AND FLEXIBLE APPROACHES TO ORGANIZATION

We saw in Chapter 1 that writing involves interpretation and that interpretation implies not only subjects but frameworks, not only things talked about but assertions. The primary reason writers struggle with organization is that they want to help readers understand the relationships among

the larger and smaller frameworks of an essay. For generations, students in composition classes have learned that the best way to accomplish this goal is to write explicit framework statements and put them in particular places: the "thesis statement" should be the final sentence of the introductory paragraph; a topic sentence should begin each paragraph and control it in the same way that the thesis controls the whole essay.

This firm approach to organization can produce satisfying results, as in the following paragraph by Theodore White:

> (1) The Latin School[1] taught the mechanics of learning with very little pretense of culture, enrichment or enlargement of horizons. (2) Mr. Russo, who taught English in the first year, had the face of a prizefighter—a bald head which gleamed, a pug nose, a jut jaw, hard and sinister eyes which smiled only when a pupil scored an absolute triumph in grammar. (3) He was less interested in the rhymes of *The Idylls of the King* or "Evangeline," or in the story in *Quentin Durward,* than in drubbing into us the structure of paragraph and sentence. (4) The paragraph began with the "topic sentence"—that was the cornerstone of all teaching in composition. (5) And sentences came with "subjects," "predicates," "metaphors," "similes," and "analogies." (6) Verbs were transitive, intransitive, and sometimes subjunctive. (7) He taught the English language as if he were teaching us to dismantle an automobile engine or a watch and then assemble it again correctly. (8) We learned clean English from him. (9) Mr. Graetsch taught German in the same way, mechanically, so that one remembered all the rest of one's life that six German prepositions take the dative case—*aus-bei-mit, nach-von-zu,* in alphabetical order. (10) French was taught by Mr. Scully. (11) Not only did we memorize passages (*D'un pas encore vaillant et ferme, un vieux prêtre marche sur la route poudreuse*), but we memorized them so well that long after one had forgotten the title of the work, one remembered its phrases; all irregular French verbs were mastered by the end of the second year.

from
In Search of History
—THEODORE WHITE

Just as Mr. Russo would have wished, White begins this paragraph with a topic sentence. Once the topic sentence establishes the framework ("mechanics . . . with little pretense of culture, enrichment or enlargement of horizons"), White keeps it in front of his readers constantly, reminding us of it as he adds

---

[1] The Boston Public Latin School.

the corroborating details. Consider the second sentence. It tells us that Russo looked like a "prizefighter" with a "pug nose," reminding us of the framework by showing that he does not appear to be a cultured man. It tells us that Russo's head gleams and his jaw juts, details that refresh our sense of the framework by reminding us of the oily, squared-off surfaces of machines. It tells us that only one thing made Russo smile, and that was a triumph in "grammar," the most mechanical aspect of an English class.

And so White works, sentence after sentence, reinforcing the paragraph's interpretation of reality. Look at the contrast of "rhymes" (cultural) and "drubbing" (mechanical) in sentence 3, or the use of "cornerstone" (mechanical) in sentence 4. Look at the number of times that White links teaching to memorization of lists and passages; and look—especially—at the comparison to automobile engines and watches in sentence 7. White wants his paragraph to leave a single strong impression on the mind, and it certainly does so. Though we may forget many details, we can hardly fail to get the gist.

THE FLEXIBLE APPROACH

Theodore White generally followed Mr. Russo's advice and took the firm course. Most paragraphs in his books and essays have a framework, explicitly stated in a topic sentence. Subsequent sentences very deliberately bring the topic sentence back to mind. Not every writer engineers an essay in this way, however. Consider the following passage from Annie Dillard's *Encounters with Chinese Writers,* recalling what she saw and heard at a conference in China in 1982.

from
Encounters with Chinese Writers
—Annie Dillard

"I believe," says one man, "that after several decades we will be able to lead a good life on our soil." He is speaking of his goals as a writer, and he is addressing the point directly.

He is a handsome man, and an elegant one in his trim gray jacket. He sits erect and relaxed, often with a disdainful expression; when he laughs, his face crumples surprisingly into a series of long dimples. He writes scathing criticism of the government. He is not laughing now, nor is he disdainful. The very contraction and repose of his limbs suggest great passion under great control. He repeats, "I believe that after several decades we will be able to lead a good life on our soil."

Ah, that soil! He has put his finger on it. For the main fact and difficulty of China is its millions of square miles of terrible soil, soil that all the will and cooperation in the world cannot alter. He has put his finger on it, and so have many others—for the soil of his populous region is so clay-like, and the technology for working it is so labor-intensive, that it—the soil—actually has fingerprints on it.

Driving to this meeting we saw fields on the outskirts of the city, and patches of agriculture. There was a field of eggplant. Separating the rows of eggplant were long strips of dried mud, five inches high, like thick planks set on edge. These low walls shield shoots and stems from drying winds. We stopped to look. The walls were patted mud; there were fingerprints. There were fingerprints dried into the loess walls around every building in the western city of Xian. There were fingerprints in the cones of dried mud around every tree's roots in large afforestation plots near Hangzhou, and along the Yangtze river. There is good soil in China, too, on which the peasants raise three and even four crops a year, and there are 2,000-acre fields, and John Deere tractors—but there is not enough. There are only some arable strips in the river valleys—only one-tenth of China's land. If you look at your right palm, you see a map of China: the rivers flow east, and most of the rest is high and dry; the arable land is like dirt collected in the lines of your palm.

Near the eggplant field, two men were pulling a plow. These humans were pulling the iron plow through the baked ground by ropes lashed across their chests. A third man guided the plow's tongue. "The old planet," Maxine Hong Kingston calls China; it is the oldest enduring civilization on earth.

If Dillard had a teacher who insisted that the cornerstone of composition was putting topic sentences at the beginning of paragraphs, she seems to have shaken off his influence. In many cases, Dillard's essays are organized primarily by the use of images that seize the reader's attention and imagination. In this case, the key images are in the fourth paragraph and concern hands and dirt: the fingerprints in the mud strips and in the soil around buildings and new-planted trees; the hand with soil in the palm's lines, offered as a map of China. The direction of the passage is set more by these images than by any "topic sentence" stating a general idea. And the passage is broken into paragraphs for reasons that have less to do with framing a complete idea than with controlling pace and emphasis. When White ends a paragraph, he seems to be telling us, "There's a complete idea, now I'm moving to the next, which is related." When Dillard ends a paragraph, she sometimes seems to mean, "Let that soak in a bit, we're going to look at something else, eventually *you'll* put the pieces of the frame together." A flexible approach to organization like Dillard's demands more of the reader than a firm approach like White's. When used well, it draws readers in, gets them actively involved. But it carries with it the danger of misunderstanding and sheer fatigue. The exasperated reader may throw down the book and say, "So, what's the point?"

EXERCISE 1

◆ *Converting a Passage to a Firmer Organization.* In the middle of the Dillard passage, there is a general statement that corresponds to a topic sentence and makes "the point" perfectly clear: "the main fact and difficulty of China is its millions of square miles of terrible soil, soil that all the will and cooperation in the world cannot alter." Using that sentence as a topic sentence, rewrite the passage as a *single paragraph* of no more than three hundred words that would satisfy Mr. Russo's standard of firm organization. Your rewrite should contain *only material related to the topic sentence,* so you will find yourself either eliminating some of the information from the original passages or changing the way it is presented.

When you have finished, compare your version to Dillard's original. What are the advantages and disadvantages of each?

To say that a writer's approach to organization is either firm or flexible is an oversimplification. These approaches exist as extremes of a continuum:

White's style is closer to the left end than Dillard's, but there are writers far more rigid: Mr. Russo may have been one. Dillard is fairly far to the right, but (in this passage, at least) not so far that her prose ceases to be expository and becomes purely poetic. Most of the writing done by students and by writers on the job—lawyers, executives, engineers, and academics—falls nearer White's position than Dillard's but is not as inflexibly organized as the traditional five-paragraph theme described at the beginning of this chapter.

A good compromise position for writing college papers is one that allows "fully conscious" deviations from firm organization. For a given essay, for instance, you may decide that you do not want to state your thesis in the introduction. You may want to reserve it for the concluding paragraph or avoid any direct statement of it. But if you do so, you will want to be certain that *you know* perfectly well what your thesis is and that *your readers know* as well. If the thesis isn't written into the paper in so many words, you should be able to state it in a sentence or two if asked, and so should your readers. Similarly, you may want to avoid the predictability of putting a topic sentence at the head of each paragraph, but your drift should be clear enough that the reader could supply a topic sentence if asked. Vary your reader's experience by an occasional deviation from the standard "firm" pattern if you like, but be firm enough to avoid confusion.

In situations where you must write quickly, with little or no time to revise, the prudent thing is to be conservative. If I were writing an essay exam, for example, I would use a very firm pattern. In fact, I would wish there were a way to write my thesis statement and topic sentences in bright red ink since I wouldn't want the grader to be even momentarily confused about the framing of my essay.

FOUR COMMON PATTERNS OF ORGANIZATION

Some thesis statements and topic sentences create expectations about the general shape of things to come. When Maya Angelou begins a chapter by saying "In Stamps the segregation was so complete that most Black children didn't really, absolutely know what whites looked like," most of her readers probably expect that she will proceed by giving examples to illustrate this generalization. When Theodore White says that Jimmy Carter's "personality . . . had to be examined as a set of layers of faith, of action, even of unpleasant-ness," readers correctly assume that the paragraphs that follow will deal with these various layers.

There are more such patterns of expectation and organization than we can discuss or even list, but four patterns are worth exploring because you may find them useful as you plan and draft an essay or a section of an essay. These four are (1) illustration, (2) comparison or contrast, (3) classification, and (4) division.

ILLUSTRATION

Illustration is the simplest of the patterns, in its pure form comprising no more than a frame filled with appropriate examples. It is also the most com-mon and most versatile: looking over the essays collected in this book, I found that almost every one used simple illustration at some point. Theodore White's paragraph about the Boston Public Latin School is a good specimen. It could be diagrammed thus:

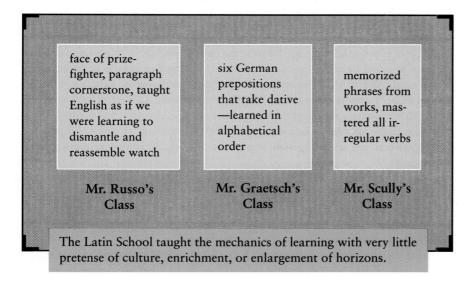

| face of prize-fighter, paragraph cornerstone, taught English as if we were learning to dismantle and reassemble watch | six German prepositions that take dative —learned in alphabetical order | memorized phrases from works, mas-tered all ir-regular verbs |

Mr. Russo's Class **Mr. Graetsch's Class** **Mr. Scully's Class**

The Latin School taught the mechanics of learning with very little pretense of culture, enrichment, or enlargement of horizons.

You'll notice that illustration is in a sense a form of comparison. White is telling us that these three teachers are alike, that they all fit comfortably in one frame. It is possible to develop an entire paragraph or even an entire essay on the basis of a single example, but it is more common (because generally more persuasive) to give more than one. As the White paragraph shows, the examples need not be developed to the same degree. The example of Mr. Russo is virtually a paragraph itself, developed by illustrations of Russo's appearance and behavior.

COMPARISON OR CONTRAST

Illustration is an important pattern of organization because it corresponds to a basic pattern of thought: the fitting of details into a framework. Comparison and contrast are important for the same reason: the patterns correspond to crucial logical moves. The writer who uses comparison is telling readers that two "different" things are in some important ways alike. The writer who uses contrast is telling readers that two "similar" things are in some important ways different.

Consider the following passage from Martin Luther King, Jr.'s "Letter from Birmingham Jail." King is in the difficult position of insisting that state authorities *obey* the law that ordered desegregation of schools, even while he encourages his followers to *disobey* segregationist laws. Obedience to law, his opponents have argued, is not a matter of picking and choosing: a person who disobeys a law he dislikes is in no position to insist that others obey a law they dislike. King answers that there are two types of law—the just and the unjust—and that every person is obliged to obey the former and disobey the latter.

Now, what is the difference between the two? How does one determine whether a law is just or unjust? A just law is a manmade code that squares with the moral law or the law of God. An unjust law is a code that is out of harmony with the moral law. To put it in the terms of St. Thomas Aquinas: An unjust law is a human law that is not rooted in eternal law and natural law. Any law that uplifts human personality is just. Any law that degrades human personality is unjust. All segregation statutes are unjust because segregation distorts the soul and damages the personality. . . .

Let us consider a more concrete example of just and unjust laws. An unjust law is a code that a numerical or power majority group compels a minority group to obey but does not make binding on itself. This is *difference* made legal. By the same token, a just law is a code that a majority compels a minority to follow and that it is willing to follow itself. This is *sameness* made legal.

Let me give another explanation. A law is unjust if it is inflicted on a minority that, as a result of being denied the right to vote, had no part in enacting or devising the law. Who can say that the legislature of Alabama which set up that state's segregation laws was democratically elected? Throughout Alabama all sorts of devious methods are used to prevent Negroes from becoming registered voters, and there are some counties in which, even though Negroes constitute a majority of the population, not a single Negro is registered. Can any law enacted under such circumstances be considered democratically structured?

King's discussion is a good example of what is sometimes called the *point-by-point* method of organizing a contrast. We could diagram it as follows:

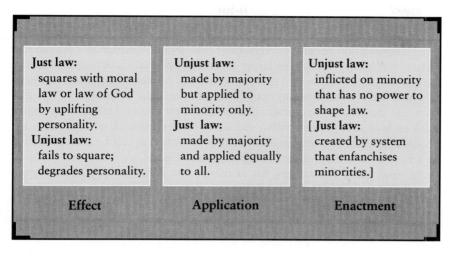

You'll notice that King's words suggest a precise point-by-point contrast but don't conform to it absolutely. He reverses the order in which he takes up the just and the unjust, and he leaves the last part of the last comparison unstated (never saying that laws are just when all parties have a vote). There may be copy editors somewhere who are unhappy with these discrepancies, but few readers will be troubled by them. The aim of organization is not to follow a pattern but to communicate ideas efficiently, which King clearly does.

An alternative to the point-by-point method of comparison or contrast is the *divided* method. Had King used it, he would have given all his information about one type of law first and all his information about the other afterward, thus:

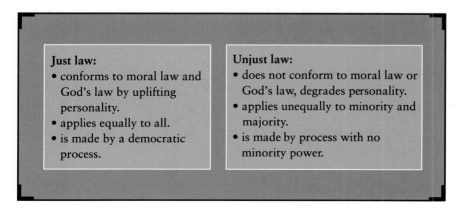

The divided method is more common than the point-by-point because it is usually more convenient. Textbooks tend to suggest that writers use either one method or the other, but two are sometimes mixed.[2]

CLASSIFICATION

Classification requires a very clear and logical distinction between the classes, the frames within the larger frame. In an ideal classification scheme, the classes are defined so that there is no overlap between them and every item to which the system seems to apply falls into one class or another. The most elaborate classification schemes, like the one that allows biologists to distinguish each of the quarter-million species of beetles from all other species, are astonishing feats. The smaller classification systems that can be used to organize an essay or a chapter necessarily have fewer parts. In *A Layman's Guide to Psychiatry and Psychology,* for example, Eric Berne includes a three-page section that divides all humanity into three classes: endomorphs, mesomorphs, and ectomorphs.

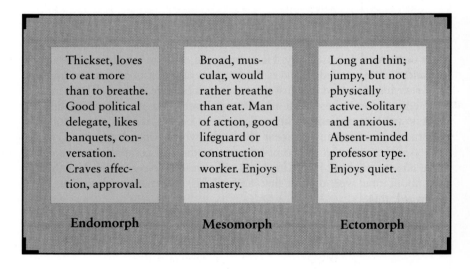

Thickset, loves to eat more than to breathe. Good political delegate, likes banquets, conversation. Craves affection, approval.	Broad, muscular, would rather breathe than eat. Man of action, good lifeguard or construction worker. Enjoys mastery.	Long and thin; jumpy, but not physically active. Solitary and anxious. Absent-minded professor type. Enjoys quiet.
Endomorph	**Mesomorph**	**Ectomorph**

Classification is closely related to contrast, since the writer's task is to distinguish categories so clearly from one another that the reader can easily tell which box to drop a given item or individual into. Logically, the difference is that classification always involves groups of things (categories), while contrast can involve individuals: you can contrast Grant and Lee, but neither of the generals is a category.

---

[2] See John Ruskin's discussion of "Servile ornament," p. 345.

Strict classification is used far less often than illustration or contrast because its logic is at odds with the complexities of the world. The writer can rarely create categories that are perfectly separate and that also correspond with observable reality. Psychologists who use the three-part scheme know very well that few people are perfect ectomorphs, endomorphs, or mesomorphs. Most people combine characteristics of at least two types. Nonetheless, the scheme can simplify and so make discussable a subject that would otherwise be overwhelmingly complex: in place of 4 billion individuals, shaped by hundreds of cultures and millions of genes, Berne gives us three types that we can at least contemplate.

DIVISION: STRICT AND LOOSE

Division can be as rigorous as classification in keeping its frames separate and ensuring that they cover the whole of the subject. An anatomist's division of the human body into its various organ systems has this sort of rigor: ideally, every part of the body is accounted for, and each falls neatly into just one system.

More commonly, the division is loose—more a matter of usefulness than of logic. The subject is divided into facets that may overlap and may have large gaps between them. A critic writing about a short story, for example, may divide her essay into parts dealing with plot, character, setting, and theme. Of course, the characters are not completely separable from the plot or the setting. Nor does the theme exist as something entirely divorced from the other elements. The divisions overlap and interact in a way that might make a pure logician nervous, but they are useful because they allow us to think about one aspect of the story at a time, rather than be overwhelmed by the undivided whole. The writer of a proposal may divide his essay into sections concerning the goal, the problem, and the solution, even though these three parts must overlap to some degree.

The chapters in this book are almost uniformly organized by division. In the case of this chapter the major divisions (to my mind) are

The Weakness of the "School Theme" Formula.
Firm and Flexible Approaches to Organization.
Common Patterns of Organization.
Outlining.

The third of these divisions is in turn divided into four parts, of which you are now reading the last.

◆ *Drawing Box Diagrams to Reveal Organization.* Carolyn Douglas's research paper "Changing Theories of Darwin's Illness" (page 444) is organized rather firmly. Search through it and identify passages that utilize *three*

EXERCISE 2

of the patterns of organization described above. A "passage" may be as short as a few sentences or as long as the whole essay. For each of the three passages you select, draw a box diagram similar to those used throughout this chapter to make the organizational scheme clear.

OUTLINING

The relationship between the box diagrams we have been looking at and outlining should be fairly obvious, especially if you remember that long before the word *outline* referred to a document giving the main points of an essay, it meant the boundary line marking the edge of a drawn figure. An outline is a way of making visible the frameworks that shape the paper.

Because boxes and other such visual schemes are cumbersome, most outlining is done in list form. In the early stages of composing, as we noted in Chapter 2, a simple list may be an entirely adequate outline. The list will mean nothing to a stranger, but each item on it serves the writer as a memory peg on which a number of ideas and details are hung. Some very systematic writers seem to be able to construct elaborate list-outlines before they begin to draft. I once met a woman who claimed that she listed a topic sentence for every paragraph of a long essay before she began to draft any of them. Such a procedure would be useful, but since most of us get our thoughts in order in the process of drafting, there is danger in following such an outline slavishly. A thorough prewriting outline that doesn't change may be the sign of an exceptionally clear mind but is at least as likely to be evidence of a dull one.

On the other hand, when the goal is firm organization, a thorough outline created *after* the essay is drafted can be very useful because the process of making one often uncovers faulty relations among the essay's parts. The conventions of formal outlining are useful here because they make the framing obvious. Each Roman numeral entry represents a major framework, each capital letter a smaller one, each Arabic numeral a still smaller, etc. There is an advantage even in the very artificial rule that there should be no A-entry in an outline without a corresponding B, no 1-entry without a corresponding 2. The rule ensures that the framework is broader than the thing it contains.

A formal outline of your paper should be a complete summary of the whole; it should be detailed enough that a reader could turn to it rather than the paper to refresh her memory. Such outlines are sometimes required on long, formal writing projects. I include one here both as an example and as a way of summarizing the contents of this chapter.

OUTLINE OF CHAPTER 10

I. The traditional formula for organization is artificial and inflexible.
   A. A description of the traditional formula in a student's own words.
   B. The formula's weaknesses.
      1. Does not correspond to professional practice.

2. Often produces dull papers.
C. The search for a "formula" that is less rigid.

II. There are firm and flexible approaches to organization.
    A. The firm approach using predictably placed "framework" statements.
        1. The thesis statement at the end of the introductory paragraph.
        2. The topic sentence at the start of each paragraph.
    B. An example of the firm approach.
        1. Theodore White's paragraph.
        2. Analysis of the paragraph.
            a. Presence and placement of topic sentence.
            b. Reinforcement of central idea of topic sentence throughout paragraph.
    C. An example of the flexible approach.
        1. Annie Dillard's passage.
        2. Analysis of the passage, showing that attention to "framework" statements has been replaced by attention to images.
            a. Advantages of the flexible approach.
            b. Disadvantages of the flexible approach.
    D. The continuum between firm and flexible approaches.
        1. Description of the continuum.
        2. Recommendation of a conservative position on the continuum in the case of college writing.
        3. Recommendation that writing under pressure be more conservative still.

III. Patterns of organization create expectations about the shape of things to come.
    A. Illustration.
        1. Pattern is fundamental: a frame filled with appropriate examples.
        2. Analysis of Theodore White paragraph (with box diagram).
    B. Comparison or contrast.
        1. Pattern corresponds to a key pattern of thought.
        2. Example: Martin Luther King, Jr. passage.
        3. Analysis of passage as example of point-by-point method (with box diagram).
        4. Explanation of the divided method (with box diagram).
    C. Classification.
        1. Pattern requires strict logic.
        2. Analysis of Eric Berne example (with box diagram).
        3. Relation of classification to contrast.
        4. Limitations and advantages of the pattern.
    D. Division.
        1. Pattern may be applied loosely or strictly.
            a. Scientific division schemes are strict.
            b. Others are often loose.
         2. Analysis of this chapter as an example of division.

IV. Outlines can reveal the relations among frameworks in an essay.
  A. Relationship between the traditional list-outline and the box diagram.
  B. Use of scratch outlines before writing.
  C. Use of formal outlines to check relations among the essay's parts.
  D. An outline of this chapter.

EXERCISE 3

◆ *A Formal Outline.* Formal outlines are frequently required for term papers, but "Changing Theories of Darwin's Illness" by Carolyn Douglas (page 444) has none. To gain a clearer view of how she has organized her essay and to practice the conventions of formal outlining, provide an outline that could have been handed in with the paper.

EXERCISE 4

◆ *Re-Paragraphing an Essay.* The following column by Ellen Goodman, about 650 words long, was originally printed in several short paragraphs suitable for the narrow columns of a newspaper. Ignoring the problem of narrow columns, mark the points where you believe paragraph breaks would be most useful to indicate the essay's organization, then answer the questions that follow.

A WORKING COMMUNITY

(1) I have a friend who is a member of the medical community. (2) It does not say that, of course, on the stationery that bears her home address. (3) This membership comes from her hospital work. (4) I have another friend who is a member of the computer community. (5) This is a fairly new subdivision of our economy, and yet he finds his sense of place in it. (6) Other friends and acquaintances of mine are members of the academic community, or the business community, or the journalistic community. (7) Though you cannot find these on any map, we know where we belong. (8) None of us, mind you, was born into these communities. (9) Nor did we move into them, U-Hauling our possessions along with us. (10) None has papers to prove we are card-carrying members of one such group or another. (11) Yet it seems that more and more of us are identified by work these days, rather than by street. (12) In the past, most Americans lived in neighborhoods. (13) We were members of precincts or parishes or school districts. (14) My dictionary still defines community, first of all in geographic terms, as "a body of people who live in one place." (15) But today fewer of us do our living in that one place; more of us just use it for sleeping. (16) Now we call our towns "bedroom suburbs," and many of us, without small children as icebreakers, would have trouble naming all the people on our street. (17) It's not that we are more isolated today. (18) It's that many of us have transferred a chunk of our friendships, a major portion of our everyday social lives, from home to office. (19) As more of our neighbors work away from home, the workplace becomes our neighborhood. (20) The kaffeeklatsch of the fifties is the coffee break of the eighties. (21) The water cooler, the hall, the elevator, and the parking lot are the back fences of these neighborhoods. (22) The people we have

lunch with day after day are those who know the running saga of our mother's operations, our child's math grades, our frozen pipes, and faulty transmissions. (23) We may be strangers at the supermarket that replaced the corner grocer, but we are known at the coffee shop in the lobby. (24) We share with each other a cast of characters from the boss in the corner office to the crazy lady in Shipping, to the lovers in Marketing. (25) It's not surprising that when researchers ask Americans what they like best about work, they say it is "the shmoose [chatter] factor." (26) When they ask young mothers at home what they miss most about work, it is the people. (27) Not all the neighborhoods are empty, nor is every workplace a friendly playground. (28) Most of us have had mixed experiences in these environments. (29) Yet as one woman told me recently, she knows more about the people she passes on the way to her desk than she does about the people she passes on her way around the block. (30) Our new sense of community hasn't just moved from house to office building. (31) The labels that we wear connect us with members from distant companies, cities, and states. (32) We assume that we have something "in common" with other teachers, nurses, city planners. (33) It's not unlike the experience of our immigrant grandparents. (34) Many who came to this country still identified themselves as members of the Italian community, the Irish community, the Polish community. (35) They sought out and assumed connections with people from the old country. (36) Many of us have updated that experience. (37) We have replaced ethnic identity with professional identity, the way we replaced neighborhoods with the workplace. (38) This whole realignment of community is surely most obvious among the mobile professions. (39) People who move from city to city seem to put roots down into their professions. (40) In an age of specialists, they may have to search harder to find people who speak the same language. (41) I don't think that there is anything massively disruptive about this shifting sense of community. (42) The continuing search for connection and shared enterprise is very human. (43) But I do feel uncomfortable with our shifting identity. (44) The balance has tipped and we seem increasingly dependent on work for our sense of self. (45) If our offices are our new neighborhoods, if our professional titles are our new ethnic tags, then how do we separate our selves from our jobs? (46) Self-worth isn't just something to measure in the marketplace. (47) But in these new communities, it becomes harder and harder to tell who we are without saying what we do.

1. Identify the thesis statement of Goodman's essay. If you feel that no single sentence perfectly expresses Goodman's thesis, write your own thesis statement for the essay.

2. Identify a topic sentence for each of the paragraphs you have identified. If you find no adequate topic sentence, write your own.

3. Describe the position of this essay on the continuum of firm and flexible organization. How does it compare to the Dillard passage about China and the White paragraph about the Latin School?

INTRODUCTIONS AND CONCLUSIONS

HAPTER 13 CONCERNED ITSELF WITH ORGANIZING THE BODY OF AN essay. Organizing introductions and conclusions is another matter because they more directly involve the difficult relationship between writers and readers. Readers are free agents, under no obligation to read past the first paragraph of an essay. How can the writer persuade them to continue? They are often strangers. How can the writer gain their trust and sympathy? Being human, they have short memories. How can the writer leave them with the right ideas in their minds, the right attitudes or emotions? The student whose comments begin Chapter 13 and the one whose essay begins Chapter 16 know formulas designed to solve these problems, but formulas can do more harm than good. Eventually readers tire of "funnel-shaped" introductions and "web" conclusions that seem to be pasted onto essays artificially.

Perhaps the best way to learn to write introductions and conclusions is to study closely the methods used by professional writers. That will be the plan for this chapter. We will examine four cases, each drawn from a complete essay included in this book. Just where the writer would draw the lines between the introduction, body, and conclusion isn't clear in every case, but we can at least get a sense of how four writers bring readers into the essay and how they lead them back out.

CASE 1

An Introduction Built on a Scene, Matched with a Conclusion Built on a Parallel Scene

Most of us have a good deal of "dramatic curiosity," the sort of curiosity that makes us stop as we are flipping through television channels to wonder who that man with the package in his arms is, what building's steps he is running up, and why. Essayists often engage this curiosity by beginning with a scene, as Annie Dillard does in "Singing with the Fundamentalists":

> It is early spring. I have a temporary office at a state university on the West Coast. The office is on the third floor. It looks down on the Square, the enormous courtyard at the center of campus. From my desk, I see hundreds of people moving between classes. There is a large circular fountain in the Square's center.
>
> Early in the morning, on the first day of spring quarter, I hear singing. A pack of students has gathered at the fountain in the Square's center.

14

I know who these singing students are; they are the Fundamentalists. The campus has a lot of them. Mornings they sing on the Square; it is their only perceptible activity. What are they singing? Whatever it is, I want to join them, for I like to sing; whatever it is, I want to take my stand with them, for I am drawn to their very absurdity; their innocent indifference to what people think. My colleagues and students here, and my friends everywhere, dislike and fear Christian fundamentalists. You may never have met such people, but you've heard what they do: they pile up money, vote in blocs, and elect right-wing crazies; they censor books; they carry handguns; they fight fluoride in the drinking water and evolution in the schools; probably they would lynch people if they could get away with it. I'm not sure my friends are right. I close my pen and join the singers in the square.

Dillard accomplishes several things in this introduction. The most important for the essay's organization is to let the reader know what the elements of her interpretation will be. The title and the opening paragraphs tell us that the subject will be the fundamentalist students and Dillard's involvement with them. We cannot at this point describe the framework completely, but we can predict that it will oppose the view taken by Dillard's "friends everywhere." By revealing this much about her framework and no more, Dillard gives us cause to read on, wondering what conclusions she will reach.

At the same time that Dillard is introducing her essay, she is introducing herself. She makes a good impression because she writes without pretension; she shows a sense of humor that allows her to parody the opinions of her friends and an independent judgment that allows her to doubt that they are right. She establishes herself as a person whose opinion is worth having, and we are curious to see what she will report when she joins the singers.

Her description of several mornings of singing with the fundamentalists forms the body of the essay. The conclusion alludes to things you will not understand unless you have read the whole essay, but you can get the drift:

The sun is rising higher. We are singing our last song. We are praying. We are alone together.

He is my peace
Who has broken down every wall . . .

When the song is over, the hands go down. The heads lower, the eyes open and blink. We stay still a second before we break up. We have been standing in a broad current; now we have stepped aside. We have dismantled the radar cups: we have closed the telescope's vault. Students gather their book bags and go. The two leaders step down from the fountain's rim and pack away their guitars. Everyone scatters. I am in no hurry, so I stay after everyone is gone. It is after nine-o'clock, and the Square is deserted. The fountain is playing to an empty house. In the pool the cheerful hands are waving over the water, bobbing under the fountain's veil and out again in the current, *hola.*

Dillard's conclusion is set in the same place as her introduction. The parallel scenes give the essay a sense of completeness; she opens her essay with the beginning of a song session and ends with the end of one.

What has changed from the introductory scene to the concluding one is Dillard's perspective. At first she was looking on the fundamentalists from her office and referring to them as "they." In the final paragraphs, she is by the fountain among the fundamentalists, using the pronoun "we." She has also developed a new understanding of what the fundamentalists are doing, an understanding expressed symbolically by the mention of radar cups, the telescope's vault, and the hands waving in the fountain. If you have not read the essay, these references will confuse you, but if you have, they will bring the essence of the essay back to mind, probably more effectively than a standard summarizing conclusion would.

CASE   2

A "Funnel-Shaped" Introduction, Matched with a "Web" Conclusion

Textbooks sometimes refer to openings that begin with a broad generalization and narrow to the subject as "funnel-shaped" or "inverted pyramid" introductions. Conclusions that present the essay's particular topic in the context of larger concerns are sometimes referred to as "web" conclusions. It is very unlikely that George Orwell had these terms on his mind when he wrote "Reflections on Gandhi" (page 143), an essay that reviews Mohandas Gandhi's autobiography *My Experiments with Truth.* Nonetheless, his essay follows a pattern you may have seen diagrammed in a composition text:

> Saints should always be judged guilty until they are proved innocent, but the tests that have to be applied to them are not, of course, the same in all cases. In Gandhi's case the questions one is inclined to ask are: to what extent was Gandhi moved by vanity—by the consciousness of himself as a humble, naked old man, sitting on a praying mat and shaking empires by sheer spiritual power—and to what extent did he compromise his own principles by entering politics, which of their nature are inseparable from coercion and fraud? To give a definite answer, one would have to study Gandhi's acts and writings in immense detail, for his whole life was a sort of pilgrimage in which every act was significant. But this partial autobiography, which ends in the nineteen-twenties, is strong evidence in his favor, all the more because it covers what he would have called the unregenerate part of his

ANNIE DILLARD

"The essay is, and has been, all over the map. There's nothing you cannot do with it; no subject matter is forbidden, no structure is proscribed. You get to make up your own structure every time, a structure that arises from the material and best contains them."

© John Montré

Many writers strive for an understated, almost impersonal style—what George Orwell called prose "like a windowpane" and Theodore White called "clean English." Annie Dillard is not one of these. She fills her essays with her very distinctive voice: exuberant, humorous, sometimes breathtakingly beautiful. Her advice to writers is to hold nothing back: "spend it all, shoot it, play it, lose it."

Dillard's style may originate in the restlessness of her parents: the father who incessantly read Mark Twain's *Life on the Mississippi* and, under its spell, quit his executive job to buy a boat and float downriver toward New Orleans; the mother whose impatience with the role of a middle-class Pittsburgh housewife made her seem to Dillard like a "Samson in chains." Dillard became an avid naturalist at age ten and an amateur theologian at eighteen (when her minister responded to her religious doubts by filling her arms with books by C. S. Lewis). As an undergraduate at Hollins College she majored in English and creative writing but also studied theology "because of the great beauty of it." She went on to write a master's thesis on Henry David Thoreau, another naturalist with a theological bent and an essayist whose style is far from quiet and self-effacing. "I will brag as lustily as chanticleer," Thoreau wrote, "if only to keep my neighbors awake."

Five years after finishing her thesis, Dillard published her first book of poetry—*Tickets for a Prayer Wheel* (1974)—and her Pulitzer Prize-winning *Pilgrim at Tinker Creek,* a prose narrative often compared to Thoreau's *Walden.* Since then, she has published steadily, producing six books: *Holy the Firm* (1978), *Living by Fiction* (1982), *Teaching a Stone to Talk* (1982), *Encounters with Chinese Writers* (1984), *An American Childhood* (1987), and *The Writing Life* (1989). Dillard's subjects are remarkably diverse: they involve religion, literary theory, cultural studies, and distant memories. But, as critic Michael Edens points out, there is a common thread. Dillard's books "constitute her spiritual autobiography" and are "really about how she transforms what she perceives." ◆

life and reminds one that inside the saint, or near-saint, there was a very shrewd, able person who could, if he had chosen, have been a brilliant success as a lawyer, an administrator, or perhaps even a businessman.

Journalists sometimes talk about the need to hook the reader with the first sentence, and Orwell certainly manages to do so here: the suggestion that saints can be guilty of anything is slightly shocking, and that anyone should be judged guilty until proved innocent violates our ordinary sense of justice. What sort of person would write this sentence, we wonder, and what can he be driving at? Orwell's opening sentences often jolt the reader into a state of alertness, if not outright irritation.

From this opening generality about saints, Orwell narrows to one saint—Gandhi—and the "tests" he should be put to. And from these fairly broad tests, he narrows once again to the essay's nominal subject, Gandhi's autobiography. This seems to be a fairly standard funnel-shaped introduction.[1]

Like many other long book reviews, Orwell's essay does not confine itself to evaluating the book. Instead it becomes a discussion of Gandhi's life and philosophy, frequently referring to information found in the book but also referring to other sources. Its early parts concentrate on Gandhi as a private and religious man, the later parts on Gandhi as a politician, particularly his philosophy of nonviolence. Orwell raises such questions as whether nonviolent protest could be effective in a totalitarian state like Hitler's Germany or Stalin's Russia and whether it could be used effectively against a ruthless invading power. The final paragraph is too long to quote in its entirety, but you can see its general pattern in the abbreviated version that follows:

> These and kindred questions need discussion, and need it urgently, in the few years left to us before somebody presses the button and the rockets begin to fly. It seems doubtful whether civilization can stand another major war, and it is at least thinkable that he would have been ready to give honest consideration to the kind of question that I have raised above. . . . One may feel, as I do, a sort of aesthetic distaste for Gandhi, one may reject the claims of sainthood made on his behalf (he never made any such claims himself, by the way), one may also reject sainthood as an ideal and therefore feel that Gandhi's basic aims were antihuman and reactionary: but regarded simply as a politician, and compared with the other leading political figures of our time, how clean a smell he has managed to leave behind!

Orwell begins his final paragraph—his web conclusion—by broadening the perspective, setting the particular case of Gandhi's nonviolence in the larger context of the potential of a violent world to destroy itself. (He was writing in 1949, the year that the Soviet Union became the second nation to explode an atom bomb.) The paragraph ends with a summary of the essay's thesis and its

---

[1]The standard funnel-shaped introduction ends with the thesis statement. In this respect, Orwell's may be nonstandard, though the last sentence of the paragraph at least touches on the thesis.

outline: there are two Gandhis, the saint for whom Orwell has little use and the politician who deserves serious attention. If you read the whole essay, you'll find that Orwell's summary reflects it accurately but avoids being a mere repetition of things said before. Like his introductions, his conclusions are worth studying. When they summarize, they do so with force and freshness.

Consider, too, the way that the conclusion fits with the introduction. Orwell begins by letting us know that he doesn't care for the idea of saint-liness. He tells us that he intends to subject the saint Gandhi to some severe tests. And in his conclusion, he gave the man fairly high marks. One tends to trust Orwell's positive judgment partly because it seems so reluctantly given.

CASE 3

An Introduction That Stresses the Author's Attitude, Matched with a Conclusion That Reflects a Change in That Attitude

Essays that demonstrate a change in the writer's attitudes, ideas, or emotions often begin and end with reports on the author's situation. Maya Angelou uses this technique in "My Sojourn in the Land of My Ancestors" (page 33). Her introductory paragraphs may strike you at first as overloaded with auto-biographical information:

> During the early sixties in New York City, I met, fell in love with, and married a South African Freedom Fighter who was petitioning the United Nations over the issue of apartheid. A year later, my fifteen-year-old son, Guy, and I followed my new husband to North Africa.
>
> I worked as a journalist in Cairo and managed a home that was a haven to Freedom Fighters still trying to rid their countries of colonialism. I was a moderately good mother to a growingly distant teenager and a faithful, if not loving, wife. I watched my romance wane and my marriage end in the shadows of the Great Pyramid.
>
> In 1962, my son and I left Egypt for Ghana, where he was to enter the university and I was to continue to a promised job in Liberia. An automobile accident left Guy with a broken neck and me with the responsibility of securing work and a place for him to recover. Within months I did have a job, a house, and a circle of black American friends who had come to Africa before me. With them I, too, became a hunter for that elusive and much longed-for place the heart could call home.

Angelou could have begun her essay with an immediate statement of her emotional condition. She could, that is, have begun by saying, "I was a hunter for that elusive and much longed-for place the heart could call home." Had she done so, we would have understood immediately the importance of her being an uprooted American in a foreign land, a black American who seems to have no African friends, a one-time wife now separated from her husband, and a mother whose teenage son has become emotionally "distant."

Why does Angelou delay the sentence that establishes the framework for these facts until the very end of the introduction? There may be several reasons, including the importance of first impressions. By beginning with the hard facts stated without a strong emotional reaction, she presents herself as a strong, level-headed woman who can cope with difficulty. When she finally makes her emotional statement, we feel that *even* her strength is not enough to prevent the longing for a true home—a family, a culture, a sense of belonging. The strength helps us to take the longing seriously.

The body of the essay involves her brief stay in the small village of Dunkwa, Ghana, during her journey to Cape Coast Castle, a place once used as a prison for captured slaves. I believe that you will be able to detect the emotional flavor of the visit by reading Angelou's conclusion:

> We ate leftovers from the last night feast, and I said a sad good-bye to my hosts. The children walked me back to my car, with the oldest boy carrying my bag. I couldn't offer money to my hosts, Arkansas had taught me that, but I gave change to the children. They bobbed and jumped and grinned.
>
> "Good-bye, Bambara Auntie."
>
> "Go and come, Auntie."
>
> "Go and come."
>
> I drove into Cape Coast before I thought of the gruesome castle and out of its environs before the ghosts of slavery caught me. Perhaps their attempts had been half-hearted. After all, in Dunkwa, although I let a lie speak for me, I had proved that one of their descendants, at least one, could just briefly return to Africa, and that despite cruel betrayals, bitter ocean voyages, and hurtful centuries, we were still recognizable.

Take the introduction and conclusion together and you have a sense of a need felt and fulfilled. It is clear that Angelou found "just briefly" in Dunkwa many of the things she had felt the absence of in the opening paragraphs. One of the best bits of advice I ever received about writing introductions and conclusions was to "bring the readers in through a door, walk them around the room, and take them out through the same door again." Angelou does precisely this. Her introduction shows (by its absence) the importance of "a place the heart can call home." The conclusion returns to this importance, but now more cheerfully. If the essay works for us, we realize that we are back where we started, but in a very different mood.

CASE 4

An Introduction That Develops a Question, Matched with a Conclusion That Discusses an Answer

When the writer has studied a subject and is writing for a less knowledgeable audience, the introduction may need to cover a great deal of ground quickly, giving readers in compressed form background essential to what will follow.

Eileen O'Brien's introductory paragraph for "What Was the Acheulean Hand Ax?" (page 196) performs this task admirably. In 169 well-chosen words, she manages to introduce nonanthropologists to a number of facts and assumptions they have never encountered before and to present them with the question that her essay will attempt to answer:

About one and one-half million years ago, a new type of large, symmetrically shaped stone implement entered the prehistoric tool kit, signaling both an advance in early craftsmanship and the advent of *Homo erectus,* a small-brained but otherwise fairly recognizable form of human being. The tool was the hand ax, which these ancestral humans faithfully made for well over one-hundred million years. Named for archaeological finds at Saint Acheul, France, examples of the Acheulean hand ax are found from the Vaal River of South Africa to the lakes, bogs, and rivers of Europe, from the shores of the Mediterranean to India and Indonesia. Such continuity over time and space speaks to us of use, success, and reuse—a design integral to some task, a task appropriate or essential to diverse environments. *Homo erectus* needed tools; tools to cut, slice, and chop; to dig, pound, and grind; tools to defend against predators and competitors, to produce and process food or other materials, even tools to make tools. But which task (or tasks) the hand ax performed is still being debated.

In some ways, O'Brien's situation is like that of the newspaper reporter, who is instructed to begin a story by providing the reader as soon as possible the answers to six key questions: *who, what, where, when, why,* and *how?* The first five questions are answered in her opening paragraph; the *how?* ("How was the ax made?") is delayed till the second paragraph.

The body of the essay deals with precisely what the reader would expect, O'Brien's answer to the unsettled question of how *H. erectus* used this prehistoric tool. She suggests that the "hand" ax was in fact a throwing weapon, a hypothesis she tests by having two student athletes—a discus thrower and a javelin thrower—try tossing a replica and observing how it behaves as a projectile. O'Brien concludes the essay with some thoughts that both support this hypothesis and add interest to it:

Homo erectus, like later *Homo sapiens,* was physically defenseless compared with the rest of the animal kingdom. Relatively slow, without canines, claws, tusks, or other natural means of defense, these early humans were easy prey when out of a tree. With handheld weapons they could defend themselves, once attacked. With projectile weapons, they could wound, maim, or kill without making physical contact, avoiding assault or retaliation. Modern humans are notoriously expert at killing from a distance. The hand ax may be proof that this behavioral strategy was refined long ago, at a time when truly "giants strode the earth"—when by dint of size the megamammals of the Pleistocene asserted their dominance, when migrating game might pass by in a continuous parade without a break in ranks, and humankind struggled to survive, both consumer and consumed. At the other end of time, at the dawn of history, is it possible that the ancient Greeks preserved as a sport a tradition handed down from that distant yesterday?

You'll notice that the conclusion of O'Brien's essay is far less cautious than the introduction. This partly reflects the tradition of scientific writing, which ties the early parts of a paper closely to the data, but allows greater freedom in the concluding "discussion" section. O'Brien takes advantage of this freedom by suggesting (in question form, the better to emphasize uncertainty) a connection between the prehistoric hand ax and the discus. She is far beyond her data here, but the suggestion is so striking that it makes her hypothesis memorable. The next time someone asks you what an Acheulean hand ax is, you may say—throwing caution to the wind—that it was the prehistoric ancestor of the ancient Greek discus.

GENERALIZATIONS ABOUT INTRODUCTIONS AND CONCLUSIONS

These four cases have elements in common that we can use to form six generalizations:

1. Introductions and conclusions need not be distinct parts of the essay indicated by such phrases as "before we begin" or "in conclusion." Especially in short essays, the beginning and ending may blend imperceptibly into the body.

2. However its boundary is marked, the introduction should give readers a preview of the essay's subject or framework, or both. In the cases we have studied, Orwell and Dillard indicate both a subject and a framework or frameworks: Gandhi as saint and practical politician, fundamentalist students as *non*members of the lunatic fringe. Angelou presents primarily the framework and O'Brien primarily the subject. An introduction could hardly be called an introduction if it leaves readers clueless about both the subject and the framework.

3. The beginning of the essay introduces not only the interpretation but the interpreter. Writers who want readers to stay with them for several pages need to present themselves as people whose judgments and opinions are likely to be valuable. Angelou, Didion, and Orwell do this business very directly. You can't read their introductions without forming an opinion of their characters. In O'Brien's case, the author's character is perhaps less important than her knowledge, and her introduction leaves us certain that she knows a great deal more on this subject than we do: if we read on, we will learn something from her.

4. "Summarizing" in a broad sense is one of the conclusion's main functions. The summary, particularly of a long or complicated essay, may be a very deliberate review of the subject and principal frameworks, as Orwell's is. Such direct summary is not always necessary, though. A writer like Dillard can bring parts of the essay back to the reader's mind by returning to key images. In a short and informal essay like Angelou's a heavy-handed summary would be awkward. Angelou's solution is to remind us, very delicately, that her visit to Dunkwa was an interlude in her trip to Cape Coast Castle, a prison for slaves. The grimness of her destination reminds us of the darker note on which the essay started.

5. Introductions and conclusions can be more effective if they are thought of as carefully matched pairs. If the introduction raises a question, the conclusion should probably remind the reader of an answer to that question. If the introduction presents the writer's frame of mind, the conclusion might examine his or her frame of mind at a later point. If the introduction presents a scene, the conclusion might present a parallel scene. Returning to the starting point can give a conclusion a satisfying feeling of closure.

6. Introductions and conclusions effective in one context might be catastrophic in others. Maya Angelou's introduction works very well in a magazine like *Ms.*, which contains many personal essays. In a magazine like *Natural History* (for which O'Brien wrote) it would not work so well. Some readers would find its tone inappropriately personal and would want it to get down to business more quickly. In deciding on a strategy for introductions and conclusions, you must consider your audience's expectations. For most college essays, Orwell and O'Brien are better models than Angelou or Dillard, but there are occasions when the Orwell and O'Brien introductions would strike the reader as cold and impersonal.

In Chapter 2, we saw a case of a writer blocked by her attempt to write an introduction that would "grab the reader's attention." Her situation provides us with one more observation. If you have time for revision, don't feel that you need to start writing at the beginning of an essay. Writing an introduction naturally forces you to concentrate your attention on the reader's reactions. Sometimes it is best to concentrate your attention *first* on the body of an essay—its essential content. After that content is somewhat settled, you may find it easier to see how your introduction and conclusion can work together, shaping the reader's perceptions of who you are and what you are saying.

ASSISTING THE READER:

CONNECTION, IMAGERY, SIMPLICITY

RECISELY WHAT GOES ON IN A READER'S MIND IS AS MUCH A MYSTERY as what goes on in a writer's, but research is beginning to give us a picture that is not very encouraging. In one experiment, psychologists[1] programmed a computer to display the words of a passage one at a time. The reader pushed a button to see the next word, and the computer recorded the length of time between button pushes. At the end of the passage, the investigators asked the readers (university undergraduates) questions to see whether they understood the passage correctly. Here is one of the passages used in the test. Read it closely. It may surprise you.

> There was a strange noise emanating from the dark house. Bob had to venture in to find out what was there. He was terrified; rumor had it that this house was haunted. He would feel more secure with a stick to defend himself and so he went and looked among his baseball equipment. He found a bat that was very large and brown and was flying back and forth in the gloomy room. Now he didn't need to be afraid any longer.

As you can imagine, readers paused for some time when the word "flying" appeared on the computer screen. They had imagined Bob grasping a baseball bat, and for many of them this picture was so firmly entrenched that they would not change it. Asked what Bob found in the closet, they responded that he had found a baseball bat. The experimenters comment that these readers had apparently lost both their visual memories of the letters *b, a, t,* and their memories of the word's sound. They couldn't, therefore, reconsider the word itself and interpret it to mean "a fuzzy flying creature." They had only their mental picture of Bob's situation to rely on, and they clung to it, despite the fact that baseball bats don't ordinarily fly back and forth under their own power.

In a variation of the experiment, the psychologists revised the passage by dividing the next-to-last sentence in two: "He found a bat. It was large and

---

[1] Daneman, Meredyth, and Patricia A. Carpenter. "Individual Differences in Integrating Information Between and Within Sentences." *Journal of Experimental Psychology: Learning, Memory, and Cognition* 9 (1983): 561–84.

brown and was flying back and forth in the gloomy room." Now even more readers clung to the idea that Bob had found a baseball bat. Even the placement of a period can have a considerable effect on how the reader understands or misunderstands a passage. Readers pause noticeably at the end of sentences and paragraphs, apparently using the time to consolidate the gist of a passage and clear the precise words for their memory. If they have been misled, they take themselves still further into the wilderness.

From experiments like this one, psychologists have drawn a number of conclusions that should interest writers. The most important is that readers will quickly forget most of the words on the page. Indeed, there is good evidence that the words of one sentence are being forced out of the memory while the words of the next sentence come in,[2] as though the working memory were an overcrowded room. Of course, readers holding a typed or printed page *can* read through a passage several times, as scholars do, to weigh each word. But ordinarily readers rush through a passage once, at a speed exceeding two hundred words per minute. Instead of looking back, they typically "get the gist" of a phrase or sentence and forget the precise wording. This gist then shapes the way they interpret subsequent words. Once readers get the gist of "sporting equipment" and "stick," they will naturally associate "b-a-t" with baseball rather than with caves and vampires.

The limitations of working memory, the inherent difficulty of converting marks on a page into ideas and images, the difficulty of sitting still and thinking, the conflict between the reader's expectations and the writer's intentions—all these keep most readers, as E. B. White once put it, "in trouble about half the time." And when readers are confused, the writer is, of course, the loser. In Chapters 13 and 14 we dealt with organization as a way of helping readers. In this chapter we will deal with three other aids: connection, imagery, and simplicity.

---

[2]In fact, the rate of forgetting words may be far faster than this. It appears that by the time the reader gets to the end of a sentence, some of the words in it will already have vanished from the working memory. Indeed, the reader may be "getting the gist" so fast that he or she skips some words altogether.

CONNECTION: BUILDING BRIDGES

The bat experiment confirms one thing that good writers must suspect intuitively: readers tend to lose their way at the ends of sentences. Their forward progress is halted for an instant while they consolidate what has come before, and when they start to move on to the next sentence, they may be stranded like hikers trying to cross a stream but unable to find the next dry rock. The writer therefore provides bridges to link each sentence to what has come before.

VERBAL BRIDGES

The most common bridge is repetition. In some cases, the author quite literally repeats in a new sentence a key word from an earlier sentence. In other cases, he or she uses a pronoun to recall a key noun without having to repeat it. Or the writer may use "word families" so closely related that the reader can hardly miss their connection. Theodore White's Latin School paragraph, which you saw in Chapter 13, is so dense with these three forms of repetition that we can't mark them all without producing something that looks like a spider's web, but we can mark a few key repetitions in blue, a few pronoun links in red, and a couple of word families in yellow.

(1) The Latin School taught the mechanics of learning with very little pretense of culture, enrichment or enlargement of horizons. (2) Mr. Russo, who taught English in the first year, had the face of a prizefighter—a bald head which gleamed, a pug nose, a jut jaw, hard and sinister eyes which smiled only when a pupil scored an absolute triumph in grammar. (3) He was less interested in the rhymes of *The Idylls of the King* or "Evangeline," or in the story in *Quentin Durward,* than in drubbing into us the structure of paragraph and sentence. (4) The paragraph began with the "topic sentence"—that was the cornerstone of all teaching in composition. (5) And sentences came with "subjects," "predicates," "metaphors," "similes," and "analogies." (6) Verbs were transitive, intransitive, and sometimes subjunctive. (7) He taught the English language as if he were teaching us to dismantle an automobile engine or a watch and then assemble it again correctly. (8) We learned clean English from him. (9) Mr. Graetsch taught German in the same way, mechanically, so that one remembered all the rest of one's life that six German prepositions take the dative case—*aus-bei-mit, nach-von-zu,* in alphabetical order. (10) French was taught by Mr. Scully. (11) Not only did we memorize passages (*D'un pas encore vaillant et ferme, un vieux prêtre marche sur la route poudreuse*), but we memorized them so well that long after one had forgotten the title of the work, one remembered its phrases; all irregular French verbs were mastered by the end of the second year.

It is hard for the reader to get lost in a paragraph where every sentence is tied to what came before by a strong verbal leash.

LOGICAL BRIDGES

In expository prose, however, there is a danger that the reader will misunderstand the logical connection between sentences even when the verbal connection is tight. Expository prose moves in directions that we might label "downward" (↓), "upward" (↑), and "onward" (→). The movement downward takes the reader from a general statement to a more particular one that supports it. The movement upward takes the reader to a more general statement, sometimes to a general conclusion. The movement onward simply adds information at the already established level of generality.

The shift from White's first sentence ("The Latin School taught . . .") to his second ("Mr. Russo, who taught . . .") is definitely downward, from a statement about the school as a whole to a consideration of a particular teacher. The shift from sentence 6 ("Verbs were transitive . . .") to sentence 7 ("He taught the English language . . .") is definitely upward from a very particular lesson Mr. Russo taught to a general observation about the nature of his teaching. Between sentence 8 and sentence 9 we move onward from one major example to another. The progress of White's whole paragraph might be diagrammed roughly as follows:

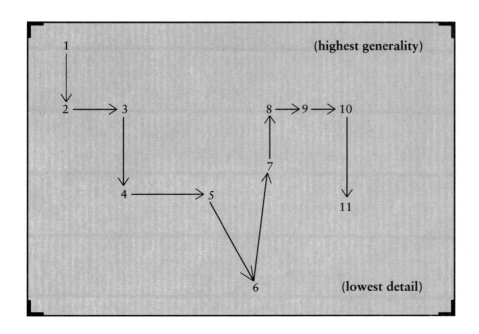

The movement from general to particular and back is, as we noted in Chapter 1, one of the keys to good writing and good thinking, and in most cases the reader can take it in stride. Should a passage be particularly difficult, the writer can help the reader with such transitional expressions as these:

1. To move downward: *for example, for instance, to illustrate, to be more precise.*

2. To move upward: *therefore, in conclusion, in short, thus, accordingly,* or *to sum it up.*

3. To move onward: the writer might use *and, or, second, in the second place, furthermore, next, finally, moreover, in addition, to take another example, also,* or *likewise.*

In addition, the author may sometimes need to signal a brief halt or reverse in the paragraph's logical movement:

4. To mark a reexamination or qualification of a previous statement: *however, but, yet, on the contrary, on the other hand, nevertheless, despite this fact, still,* or *instead.*

5. To mark a brief logical detour: *as a sidelight, while we are on the subject,* or *by the way.*

In informal prose on relatively simple subjects, a writer will use such transitions sparingly, knowing that the reader can usually supply them for herself or himself. When the prose is more formal or more difficult, the writer uses more transitions to make explicit the connection between sentences and between phrases inside sentences. A relatively scholarly essay like Eileen O'Brien's "What Was the Acheulean Hand Ax?" (page 196) may be thick with logical transitions:

> *Accordingly,* except for those hand axes that were misplaced or lost, the hand ax should not be in the archaeological record. Excavators, *however,* recover hand axes in abundance, mostly at sites that are within or alongside what were once (and may still be) watercourse or wetland environments. *For example,* at the Acheulean site of Olorgesailie . . .

There is no absolute rule about when a writer needs to insert a transitional marker. Too many of them can clog a passage and make the writer sound pompous. Too few can make it difficult for the reader to follow the logical movement. Perhaps the best practice is to use transitional expressions liberally in preliminary drafts, where you are yourself discovering logical connections. When you revise, eliminate ones that are unnecessary.

THEODORE WHITE

"A new thought had also crept in in my senior year—the thought that I could, conceivably, write of history as a newspaperman. Both Charlie Duhig and John Fairbank thought I was not really and truly of the stuff of scholarship. Without being specific, both implied that I had the manners, lust and ego of someone who might be a journalist."

Courtesy Harper and Row, Inc.

One of Theodore White's favorite expressions was "it was like playing the bass tuba on the day it rained gold." He was fortunate to win scholarships that allowed him, though poor, to attend Harvard; fortunate that the accident of studying in the Harvard-Yenching library led him to study Chinese; fortunate to be traveling in China early in 1939, where he had a new stroke of luck. He made contact with Chiang Kai-shek's Nationalist government and was immediately offered a job in Chiang's Ministry of Information. Thus he was plunged into what he called "one of the greatest upheavals of the twentieth century," a three-way struggle among the Japanese invaders, the Nationalist government, and Mao Zedong's Communist rebels.

Such circumstances were ideal for a person with White's ambition to be a writer and his ability to produce clear, graceful prose. Soon he was *Time*'s "special correspondent" in China and had been invited to write a book about the war. "There could be no doubt," said White, "that I had made a score."

White's reports from Asia during World War II and from Europe and various parts of the United States afterward kept him in demand as a journalist. He also wrote two moderately successful novels, and in 1959 actor Gary Cooper offered him $80,000 for the film rights to one of them. White accepted and used the money to support himself for two years while he researched and wrote his Pulitzer Prize-winning *The Making of the President 1960*.

White followed this triumph with reports on the 1964, 1968, and 1972 Presidential campaigns, but none of these books were as well-received as the 1960 book—perhaps because readers no longer shared White's patriotism, his "unabashed love" of "the idea that America was the goal and the promise to which all mankind . . . had been marching." In 1976, White abandoned his planned campaign volume and wrote instead a report on his own remarkable life, *In Search of History: A Personal Adventure*. Some reviewers feel it is his finest work. ◆

EXERCISE 1

◆ *Inserting Transitional Markers.* The only explicit transitional word in White's paragraph about the Latin School is the "And" that begins sentence 5. Insert the appropriate transitions into sentences 2, 3, 4, 6, 7, 8, 9, 10, and 11. Evaluate the result. Is it always clear what sort of transition is necessary? Is the passage improved by the insertion of the transitions? Would it be improved by the insertion of *some* additional transitions?

EXERCISE 2

◆ *Unscrambling a Scrambled Paragraph.* The connections and transitions of some writers are so clear that they write an occasional passage that can be dismantled "like an automobile engine or a watch" and put together again in the correct order. The following sentences from Margaret Mead's *Sex and Temperament in Three Primitive Societies* form a paragraph that at least approaches this state of coherence. Return them, if you can, to their original order. Be prepared to discuss the reasons behind your arrangement.

1. In later years, this is the greatest claim that he has upon her.

2. An Arapesh boy grows his wife.

3. And in those exceptional cases when the arranged marriage falls through from the death of the betrothed husband, and the girl is betrothed again after she has attained her growth, the tie is never felt to be so close.

4. Upon the young adolescent husband particularly falls the onus of growing yams, working sago, hunting for meat, with which to feed his wife.

5. A little girl is betrothed when she is seven or eight to a boy about six years her senior, and she goes to live in the home of her future husband.

6. Here the father-in-law, the husband, and all of his brothers combine to grow the little bride.

7. Similarly when a man inherits the widow of a relative, he may have contributed very little food to her growth—especially if she is older than he—and these marriages, lacking the most important sanction that the culture recognizes, are less stable.

8. As a father's claim to his child is not that he has begotten it but rather that he has fed it, so also a man's claim to his wife's attention and devotion is not that he has paid a bride-price for her, or that she is legally his property, but that he has actually contributed the food which has become flesh and bone of her body.

9. If she is dilatory or sulky or unwilling, he can invoke this claim: "I worked the sago, I grew the yams, I killed the kangaroo that made your body. Why do you not bring in the firewood?"

IMAGERY: CAPTURING THE GIST

In "Politics and the English Language" (page 293), George Orwell suggests that the writer with an idea to communicate should not rush to commit it to words: "Probably it is better to put off using words as long as possible and get one's meaning as clear as one can through pictures or sensations." Like many writers, Orwell believed that images are closer to thought than words are and that it is through the communication of images that the writer can best convey the essence of a message. Research in the psychology of reading supports this view: remember how quickly the mental image of a man holding a baseball bat replaced any memory of the word "bat."

Orwell's paragraphs usually contain at least one striking image that is likely to outlast in memory the words that presented it. Some paragraphs in his descriptive essays like "Marrakech" consist of little more than a topic sentence and a parade of crisp, clear images that report his experience. When he deals with a subject that does not naturally provide images, he finds metaphors, similes, and analogies that give the reader a sensory impression to cling to. Consider the following paragraph on political writing from "Politics and the English Language."

(1) In our time it is broadly true that political writing is bad writing. (2) Where it is not true, it will generally be found that the writer is some kind of rebel, expressing his private opinions and not a "party line." (3) Orthodoxy, of whatever colour, seems to demand a lifeless, imitative style. (4) The political dialects to be found in pamphlets, leading articles, manifestos, White Papers and the speeches of under-secretaries do, of course, vary from party to party, but they are all alike in that one almost never finds in them a fresh, vivid, home-made turn of speech. (5) When one watches some tired hack on the platform mechanically repeating the familiar phrases—*bestial atrocities, iron heel, bloodstained tyranny, free peoples of the world, stand shoulder to shoulder*—one often has a curious feeling that one is not watching a live human being but some kind of dummy: a feeling which suddenly becomes stronger at moments when the light catches the speaker's spectacles and turns them into blank discs which seem to have no eyes behind them. (6) And this is not altogether fanciful. (7) A speaker who uses that kind of phraseology has gone some distance towards turning himself into a machine. (8) The appropriate noises are coming out of his larynx, but his brain is not involved as it would be if he were choosing his words for himself. (9) If the speech he is making is one that he is accustomed to make over and over again, he may be almost unconscious of what he is saying, as one is when one utters the responses in church. (10) And this reduced state of consciousness, if not indispensable, is at any rate favorable to political conformity.

We know from our excursion into the psychology of reading that readers will forget most of the words in Orwell's paragraph. At best, Orwell might hope that the reader encountering this paragraph for the first time will (1) get its gist, (2) find the evidence and arguments persuasive, and (3) retain in memory some image or images by which the gist can later be recalled. If you'll look at sentences 5 through 9, you'll see Orwell creating the paragraph's key image: the picture of the political speaker as a kind of machine, mindless and eyeless behind his glinting spectacles. In a sense, Orwell entrusted his idea to that image, wagering that readers would not forget it and that it would carry for them the essence of his idea.

His wager was a good one, as you can confirm by a simple experiment. Have someone who has never read "Politics and the English Language" read Orwell's paragraph aloud so that she will notice every word but not have time to memorize. Tell her before she begins that you are going to ask her to reproduce the paragraph from memory. After she has read, take the book from her immediately and give her time to write. The result will look something like this:

> In our time it is generally supposed that political writing is bad writing. When it is not, it is normally supposed that the writer is some kind of rebel, stating his own opinions, not that of the political establishment. Something about political writing and speakers using hackneyed phrases . . . *bestial atrocities, stand shoulder to shoulder, free peoples of the world.* . . . Often when one hears a political speech, one can imagine that the speaker is not a man but a robot and the feeling becomes stronger when the light catches his glasses and he becomes. . . . This is not altogether fanciful. When a man uses standard political phrases his mind is not engaged to the extent that it would be if he were using his own words to express his thoughts.

In this case, the reader has done a fair job of remembering the first two sentences, but we see *not a single word* of sentence 3, the topic sentence, which is essentially imageless. Sentence 4 is also virtually absent. But the mechanical man with the glaring glasses and the string of clichés is very much present. Notice that this reader used a word for him that Orwell did not: *robot*. Clearly, she remembers the image rather than the words, and she understands its significance. We needn't worry that she cannot remember the words of the topic sentence. She has retained the essence of the paragraph.

I do not mean to suggest that every paragraph should have one key image: many have several strong ones. Nor do I mean to suggest that every paragraph must deliberately include an image for the sake of show. What we need to remember is that the image is a powerful link between the mind of the writer and the mind of the reader.

EXERCISE 3

◆ *An Experiment with Imagery.* Repeat the experiment just outlined, using Theodore White's paragraph about the Latin School (page 502) or Annie Dillard's passage about China (page 478) or Edward Dowden's about Shelley (page 512) instead of the Orwell paragraph. You will, of course, have to find someone who has not yet read these passages to serve as an experimental subject. Report the results of your experiment: What clues does it give about ways that writers can make their paragraphs memorable? If you look closely, you should be able to develop hypotheses that go beyond those suggested in this chapter.

SIMPLICITY: A WINDOWPANE STYLE

Reviewing Professor Edward Dowden's biography of the poet Percy Bysshe Shelley, Mark Twain pauses to describe a cakewalk, "a competition in elegant deportment." If you have watched Miss America contestants walk the runway in their bathing suits and high heels, you have some sense of what a cakewalk is. The main differences are that the true cakewalk contestants may be either men or women and that they wear more clothes.

> All that the competitor knows of fine airs and graces he throws into his carriage, all that he knows of seductive expression he throws into his countenance. He may use all the helps he can devise: watch-chain to twirl with his fingers, cane to do graceful things with, snowy handkerchief to flourish and get artful effects out of, shiny new stovepipe hat to assist in his courtly bows . . .

Professor Dowden's biography, Twain says, "is a literary cake-walk."

> The ordinary forms of speech are absent from it. All the pages, all the paragraphs, walk by sedately, elegantly, not to say mincingly, in their Sunday-best, shiny and sleek, perfumed, with *bouton-nieres* in their button holes; it is rare to find even a chance sentence that has forgotten to dress. If the book wishes to tell us that Mary Godwin, child of sixteen, had known afflictions, the fact saunters forth in this nobby outfit: "Mary was herself not unlearned in the lore of pain"—meaning that she had not always traveled on asphalt; or, as some authorities would frame it, that she had "been there herself," a form which, while preferable to the book's form, is still not to be recommended. If the book wishes to tell us that Harriet Shelley hired a wet nurse, that commonplace fact gets turned into a dancing master, who does his professional bow before us in pumps and knee-breeches, with his fiddle under one arm and his crush-hat under the other, thus: "The beauty of Harriet's motherly relation to her babe was marred in Shelley's eyes by the introduction into his house of a hireling nurse to whom was delegated the mother's tenderest office."

Cakewalk prose draws attention from the subject to the style, hindering readers' understanding and usually irritating them in the bargain. For many writers, such prose is a constant temptation, and for many successful writers, learning to resist the temptation marked a turning point in their careers.

George Orwell, for example, early in his career wanted to write prose "full of detailed descriptions and arresting similes, and also full of purple passages in which words were used partly for the sake of their sound." Later, when he had truly found himself as a writer, he "tried to write less picturesquely and more exactly." Finally, he arrived at an ideal for prose that is precisely opposed to the cakewalk: ". . . one can write nothing readable unless one constantly struggles to efface one's own personality. Good prose is like a windowpane."

Orwell's position is extreme: there are excellent writers who seem not to have struggled to efface their personalities. But the tendency to cakewalk is so strong in most of us that we need the advice he gives in "Politics and the English Language." I recommend the entire essay and give here the six rules with which it ends:

1. Never use a metaphor, simile or other figure of speech which you are used to seeing in print.

2. Never use a long word where a short one will do.

3. If it is possible to cut a word out, always cut it out.

4. Never use the passive where you can use the active.

5. Never use a foreign phrase, a scientific word or a jargon word if you can think of an everyday English equivalent.

6. Break any of these rules sooner than say anything outright barbarous.

Orwell's style has served as a model for many writers in the second half of the twentieth century, but his windowpane ideal addresses only one aspect of the writer's relation to readers—the need to assist them in a difficult task. The other side of the relation, the need to engage them, will be the subject of Chapter 16.

EXERCISE 4

◆ *Active and Passive Voice.* Identify each of the following sentences as either active or passive. If they are passive, convert them to active. If they are active, convert them to passive. The passages are drawn from essays in this book.

1. In the later 19th century a search was made for ciphered messages embedded in the dramatic texts.

2. We ate leftovers from last night's feast, and I said a sad goodbye to my hosts.

3. These hymns seem to have been written just yesterday, apparently by the same people who put out lyrical Christmas greeting cards and bookmarks.

4. They called my uncle by his first name and ordered him around the Store.

5. . . . the King revisited the Countess and, on being again rejected, he villainously raped her . . .

SOME HELP WITH ACTIVE AND PASSIVE VOICE

"Instead of writing, 'My teacher used poor judgment,' you can write, 'Better judgment on my teacher's part could have been used.' The passive voice, indeed, can be used by you in such a way that you are enabled to have the number of words that have been written by you to be increased 100%." (Laurence Perrine)

Almost every writer on style advises us to use the active voice rather than the passive whenever possible. To understand the technical distinction between the two, you need to know a bit of grammar.

In an **active** voice sentence, the grammatical subject does the action described by the verb. There is a direct object (a noun or pronoun that answers the question "whom or what?" after the verb):

The President approved the invasion.
["Who approved?" we ask, and the answer is clearly "the President." "Approved what?" we ask, and the answer is clearly "the invasion." The active voice sentence in normal word order begins by telling us who or what acted and ends by identifying the thing or person acted on.]

In a **passive** voice sentence, the grammatical subject is not the person or thing that acts. To add the actor to the sentence, the writer must add a *by*-phrase:

The invasion was approved.
[The invasion did *not* do the approving, and the sentence does not say who did.]

The invasion was approved by the President.

[The person acting is added in a *by*-phrase. Notice that the sentence begins by naming the thing acted on and ends by naming the actor.]

As you can see, the passive voice sentence that never names the actor can give the impression of evasiveness. The passive voice sentence that adds the subject in a *by*-phrase is not evasive, but is wordier than an active voice sentence and often sounds anticlimactic.

There are, of course, occasions when the passive is preferable: when the actor is unknown, for example, or in a context where the person or thing acted on is clearly more important than the actor.

The President was seen napping during the Ambassador's speech.

The footprints had been carefully raked over.

For those of us who are not good enough grammarians to use the standard tests for active and passive voice, a sensible rule to follow is this: Form the habit of putting the true subject, the person or thing *doing* the action of the sentence, up front—in the sentence's subject position. If you do this, you will generally avoid the passive voice. ◆

◆ *Effective and Ineffective Figures of Speech.* Comment on the effectiveness of the similes and metaphors found in each of the following passages. Some are taken directly from readings in this book; some have been altered (and so damaged).

1. All around me, hands are going up—that tall girl, that blond boy with his head back, the redheaded boy up front, the girl with the McDonald's jacket. Their hands rise as if pulled on strings.

2. Loyalty, meaning the pledged word, was chivalry's heart and soul.

3. When you write, you lay out a line of words. The line of words is a miner's pick, a woodcarver's gouge, a surgeon's probe. You wield it, and it digs a path you follow. Soon you find yourself deep in new territory. Is it a dead end, or have you located a new subject?

4. The average hand ax looks like a giant stone almond, although some are more ovate and others more triangular. . . . Whether roughly finished or as refined as a work of art, the hand ax always has an eccentric center of gravity and a sharp edge around almost all of its perimeter. Thus in cross section lengthwise, it resembles a stretched out teardrop.

5. In addition, the white lie can often actually be beneficial, thus further tipping the scales of utility.

6. One can concede that the "sexual revolution" of recent years may have had useful byproducts in striking layers of prudery from a subject long irrationally kept from ventilation. But it does not follow that no regulation of patently offensive "hard core" materials is needed or permissible; civilized people do not allow unregulated access to heroin because it is a derivative of medicinal morphine.

◆ *Editing Professor Dowden.* Remembering both Mark Twain's observations on cakewalk prose and George Orwell's six rules, revise the following passage from Professor Dowden's *Life of Shelley* to make its prose more efficient. In the process, you should substantially shorten the passage but should not omit any important information. Unless you have traveled in England, three references in the passage may be unfamiliar to you: for "Tory," you may substitute "Republican"; for "Stockton-on-Tees," "River City"; and for "Michaelmas Term," "Fall Semester."

The special charm of Oxford for Shelley lay in the comparative freedom of his student's life. He could pursue his own studies without interruption, and in the citadel of his chambers, be poet, natural philosopher, metaphysician, in turns as it pleased him. If he desired the companionship of some chosen friend, there was all the afternoon free for country rambles, all the endless hours from five till long past midnight for converse and debate.

One such friend, and only one during the months at Oxford, Shelley found. Thomas Jefferson Hogg, son of a gentleman of old family and high Tory politics, residing at Stockton-on-Tees, had entered University College in the early part of the year 1810, a short time before Shelley. Early in Michaelmas Term they met for the first time, and speedily followed a close alliance, which for a season excluded every other friendship, and was momentous in its consequences for each of the inseparable pair. There was little resemblance between the friends. Hogg had intellectual powers of no common order, and all through his life was an ardent lover of literature; but he cared little or nothing for doctrines and abstract principles such as formed the very food on which the revolutionary intellect of Shelley fed; and his interest in literature was that of a man of the world who finds in poetry a refuge from the tedium of common life . . .

◆ *Editing Inflated Prose.* In the original version of the following para-graph, George Orwell discusses the tension between his desire to write poetically about the world and his need to write about politics. The version printed here has been puffed up by the addition of many unnecessary words and the substitution of fancy, long, or pretentious words for his plainer ones. Edit the passage to restore its original windowpane style.

EXERCISE 7

What I have most wanted to do throughout the past ten years is to make political writing into something somehow more ineffable, more artlike in nature. My *point d'appui* is always a feeling of partisanship, a sense of what we might call, for lack of a better word, injustice. When I embark upon the adventure of a book, I do not ruminate to myself, "I am going to produce a work of art." I write it because there is some prevarication that I want to expose, some fact to which I want to draw attention, and my initial concern is to get a hearing. But I could not do the onerous labor of writing a book, or even a protracted magazine article, if it were not also an aesthetic experience. Anyone who cares to put my work under a microscope will see that even when it is downright propaganda it contains much that a full-time politician would consider irrelevant. I am not able, and I do not want, completely to abandon the world view that I acquired in the dreamy, golden-domed years of childhood. So long as I remain sentient and disease-free I shall continue to feel strongly about the manner in which articles, books and other materials are written, to love the surface of the earth, and to take a pleasure in solid objects and scraps of useless information. It is no use trying to suppress that side of myself. The task at hand is to find an equilibrium point between my ingrained likes and dislikes and the essentially public, non-individual activities that this age of man forces on us all.

ENGAGING THE READER

WITHOUT TAKING BACK ANYTHING SAID IN CHAPTER 15, I WANT TO present you with an alternative view of readers. True, "most readers are in trouble about half the time," as E. B. White says. And true, the writer has an obligation to smooth their way by writing direct, connected, well-organized prose. Nonetheless, it is a mistake to underestimate readers, who ordinarily have permanent teeth and considerable knowledge and expect to be treated as adults. An essay is clear in vain if its clarity reveals nothing that engages the reader's attention and intelligence.

Several years ago an experienced composition teacher gave me a copy of the following paper, which he said was the most extreme case he had ever seen of the problem created by ignoring readers' intelligence and assuming that all they care about is a tidy package.

SEAT BELTS

A major problem in the United States is death in traffic accidents. The number of deaths would be diminished if everyone used seat belts. Therefore, everyone should use seat belts.

Young people should use seat belts. People between sixteen and twenty-five are more likely to be in accidents than any other group. Because they are so often in accidents, it is important that they buckle their seat belts.

Older people should also use seat belts. Although they are not in accidents as often as younger people, their lives are very valuable. Older people have responsible jobs and are often parents. If they are killed, others suffer from the loss. Therefore, they too should take the time to fasten their seat belts and protect themselves.

The very young should use seat belts. Children and young teen-agers have their whole lives in front of them. Their parents should teach them to buckle up. Infants should be placed in carriers that can be strapped in with a seat belt.

As we have seen, all people should use seat belts. Young people need to be careful because they are in so many accidents. Older people need to think about how their deaths would affect others. Infants and children need to have their lives protected so that they will not die before they have experienced life.

The paper is flawless in its way. It contains no mechanical errors and reflects perfectly the writer's training in the five-paragraph theme: an introduction

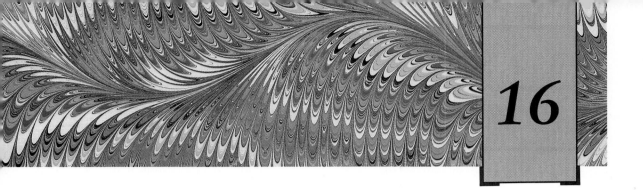

that "tells them what you're going to say," three body paragraphs, each dealing with an aspect of the subject, and a conclusion that "tells them what you've said." And yet when I have read it aloud in front of college professors, they have always responded with groans or laughter. Why?

When I ask them, they tell me that the paper is "limp" or "flat" or "predictable." It argues a thesis that apparently needs no arguing, using the reasoning and language that every reader would expect to find in such a paper. After reading the first two paragraphs, most of us could write the last three ourselves, using almost the same words. No one could complain that the essay is hard to follow, but it doesn't lead anywhere interesting, and it doesn't engage the reader either by its content or by its style.

In this chapter we will be dealing with texture and tone, two aspects of style undeveloped in "Seat Belts." Before beginning a discussion of either, however, I want to warn you that it is dangerous to separate style and substance. People who think of style as a separate aspect of their writing tend to produce what we called "cakewalk" prose in Chapter 15. E. B. White, in *The Elements of Style,* put the case this way:

> Young writers often suppose that style is a garnish for the meat of prose, a sauce by which a dull dish is made palatable. Style has no such separate entity; it is nondetachable, unfilterable. The beginner should approach style warily, realizing that it is himself he is approaching, no other; and he should begin by turning resolutely away from all devices that are popularly believed to indicate style—all mannerisms, tricks, adornments. The approach to style is by way of plainness, simplicity, orderliness, sincerity.

The novelist Booth Tarkington put it more succinctly: "If they ever catch us Writing, we're gone."

The trouble with "Seat Belts" stems at least as much from what it says as how it says it. Chapters 2 and 5 concerned themselves in part with ways to improve the *what* of such a paper, ways to discover the complexities of a subject. This chapter will concentrate on the *how,* ways to keep the mind of the reader (and writer) engaged in individual sentences and paragraphs. Nonetheless, we should remember that *what* and *how* are finally inseparable.

TEXTURE

We will use the word *texture* to mean the antithesis of the dull uniformity we see in "Seat Belts." It would be possible in theory to write an essay made up of uniform paragraphs that present no unexpected details, contain no sentences longer than fourteen words or shorter than twelve, and include not a single word that draws attention to itself. It is even possible that such an essay would be clear and comprehensible, but it is unlikely that most readers would have the stamina to finish it. The texture added by unexpected details, variations of sentence length and structure, and the use of strong verbs are among the things that keep the reader alert and engaged.

UNEXPECTED DETAILS

George Orwell once confessed that he took "pleasure in solid objects and scraps of useless information" and that they found their way into his writing, even when they were not essential to his purpose. Since most of us are, like Orwell, attracted to curiosities for their own sake, these objects and scraps can be a source of pleasure and interest for the reader. Curiosities are not always easy to come by, however. Barbara Tuchman's success as a writer of popular history books comes largely from her skill in uncovering details that are specific, tangible, and surprising. For example, to give her readers a sense of what life was like for the fourteenth-century French nobleman Jean, Duc de Berry, she examined both the work of several previous historians and documents surviving from Berry's lifetime. As you read through the passage below, consider how many times she presents you with an object or piece of information you find interesting in its own right, regardless of its connection with Berry.

"Jean, Duc de Berry"
—Barbara Tuchman

Berry was too absorbed in acquisition and art to be interested in war. He lived for possessions, not glory. He owned two residences in Paris, the Hôtel de Nesle and another near the Temple, and built or acquired a total of seventeen castles in his duchies of Berry and Auvergne. He filled them with clocks, coins, enamels, mosaics, marquetry, illuminated books, musical instruments, tapestries, statues, triptychs painted in bright scenes on dazzling gold ground bordered with gems, gold vessels and spoons, jeweled crosses and reliquaries, relics, and curios. He owned one of Charlemagne's teeth, a piece of Elijah's mantle, Christ's cup from the Last Supper, drops of the Virgin's milk, enough of her hairs and teeth to distribute as gifts, soil from various Biblical sites, a narwhal's teeth, porcupine's quills, the molar tooth of a giant, and enough gold-fringed vestments to robe all the canons of three cathedrals at one time. Agents kept him apprised of curiosities, and when one reported a "giant's bones" dug up near Lyon in 1378, he at once authorized purchase. He kept live swans and bears representing his chosen device, a menagerie with apes and dromedaries, and rare fruit trees in his garden. He ate strawberries with crystal picks mounted in silver and gold, and read by candlelight from six carved ivory candle-holders.

Like most affluent lords, he had a good library of classics and contemporary works; he commissioned translations from the Latin, bought romances from booksellers in Paris, and bound his books in precious bindings, some in red velvet with gold clasps. He commissioned from renowned illuminators at least twenty Books of Hours, among them two exquisite masterpieces, the *Grandes Heures* and *Très Riches Heures*. His pleasure was to see illustrated his favorite scenes and portraits, including his own. Delicate multiple-towered cities and castles, rural occupations, knights and ladies in garden, hunt, and banquet hall, clad in garments of surpassing elegance, ornamented the prayerbooks. The Duke himself usually appears robed in the pure sky blue, whose pigment was so precious that two pots of it were listed in an inventory of Berry's "treasures."

Berry introduced the newly invented pedal organ into his churches and bought a new jacket for four livres so that his cornetist who played so beautifully might perform a solo before Charles V. He had gold and pearls ground together for a laxative, and during enforced idleness when he was bled to relieve the effects of gluttony and an apoplectic tendency, he played at dice, his favorite pastime. In one game with knightly companions, he wagered his coral prayer beads for forty francs. Accompanied by his swans, bears, and tapestries, he moved continually from one of his castles to another, carrying half-finished works of art by artists at one place to be completed by those at another, taking part in local processions and pilgrimages, visiting monasteries, enjoying wine harvests in autumn, and sending home to the Duchess on one occasion in June new peas, cherries, and 78 ripe pears. He collected dogs, always searching for more, no matter how many he had, and when he heard of an unusual variety of greyhound in Scotland, obtained a safe-conduct from Richard II to allow four couriers on horseback to make the round trip to bring him back a pair.

This parade of things and actions gives us a memorable impression of Berry's wealth and his times. But useful as they are in supporting Tuch-

Jean, Duc de Berry (1340–1416), third son of King John II the Good of France, controlled large portions of France during the Hundred Years' War with England. His fame as a patron of the arts has eclipsed his political reputation, however; indeed, Berry spent so much money promoting the arts that his estate was bankrupt at his death and could not pay for his funeral. Of the many illuminated manuscripts Berry commissioned, one of the most famous is the **Belles Heures du Duc de Berry** *by the Limbourg brothers. The illumination shown here, "The Duke on a Journey," illustrates a prayer for a safe journey.*

man's generalizations, we can't help feeling that Tuchman introduces many of them for pure pleasure. Long after we forget who the Duc de Berry was, we may remember the laxatives made up of ground gold and pearls or some of the oddities—"drops of the Virgin's milk," "the molar tooth of a giant"—that testify to the curiosity and gullibility of the Middle Ages but also appeal to our own sense of the fabulous. Tuchman's paragraphs are like glass display cases filled with objects to examine, or like film clips showing her subject in action.

How different it is with "Seat Belts," where the sentences are so general that they take us away from the world of things into a vague, vaporish world where nothing has a hard edge, nothing has weight, texture, color, or smell. The concreteness, the "thinginess," of good writing literally brings us back to our senses. When Theodore White reported on the Nixon-Kennedy debates, he watched workmen paint and repaint the wall behind the podiums from which the candidates would speak, attempting to darken it to a shade of gray that Nixon's advisers thought would be most flattering to their man. The paint always came out too light, and White wrote that it was still "tacky to the touch," when the candidates went on the air. That an accomplished journalist will feel a wall to see whether he can call it tacky shows the importance of an unexpected detail.

EXERCISE 1

◆ *A Paragraph with Unexpected Details.* Write a paragraph that illustrates a simple generalization by collecting details that are both pertinent and curious. Were I writing such a paragraph, I might begin, "My parents, though they are now well off financially, are children of the Great Depression, and they simply can't throw anything away." Or "One thing has to be said about writing under a deadline: it makes you look for any excuse to get away from the keyboard." *Avoid making up details to fill your paragraph.* Most of us, when we try to invent curious details, come up with ones that are either predictable or incredible. Reality is the best source of surprises.

SENTENCE VARIETY

Linguists tell us that virtually all normal people master the sentence structures in their language by the time they reach adolescence. And yet, particularly when we are writing slowly and painstakingly, many of us fall into a monotonous pattern: one or two short clauses to a sentence, almost invariably starting with the principal subject.

> The very young should use seat belts. Children and young teen-agers have their whole lives in front of them. Their parents should teach them to buckle up. Infants should be placed in carriers that can be strapped in with a seat belt.

Two or three pages of this type of prose will wear on the reader's nerves, partly because the uniformity of the sentences does nothing to distinguish important information from unimportant. Compare the first paragraph of a report written by Mary McCarthy during the Watergate hearings in 1973:

This April, when the Watergate revelations broke, I was traveling across America. Almost more amazing than the daily disclosures themselves was the evidence that the story was being told, democratically, to the entire population, which was discussing it, democratically, as if at a town meeting. Leaving New York and flying westward, to Minneapolis, Seattle, then down to Carmel Valley, California, I had expected to lose whole chapters of the story, since this country, on the whole, outside of a few sophisticated cities—New York, Washington, Los Angeles, St. Louis—is poorly informed by its press. Wire service dispatches, usually cut and mangled, a mixed bag of columnists, to give "balance," a tendentious editorial page, prevailingly Republican, compete for space with social news and advertisements of supermarket specials. My first hope, I thought, of getting any real coverage would be when I finally reached an area served by the Los Angeles *Times,* a pro-Administration paper with fair and comprehensive news coverage. But not at all. In every city I arrived at, the local papers were full of Watergate; regardless of their politics and of pressure, if any, from their advertisers, they were keeping their readers in touch with the most minor episodes of this fantastic crime serial.

A full analysis of McCarthy's sentences would require more grammatical terminology than would be useful here, but we can make a few common-sense observations. If we count the names of cities as one word, the sentence lengths are as follows: 12, 34, 44, 32, 32, 4, 42. The average length of 29 is fairly high, but the range is the important thing. Her four-word sentence (actually a sentence fragment) has special force because it alters the rhythm of the passage. In fact, it seems to stop the flow of long sentences dead, just at the point when she is announcing her change of mind. The first eight sentences of "Seat Belts," on the other hand, are far less varied: 11, 11, 5, 5, 16, 15, 6, and 15 words each. The short sentences come too frequently to have any special punch.

The more complex structure of McCarthy's sentences also suggests, rightly or wrongly, that her thought is more thoroughly structured than the thought of the "Seat Belts" writer. Consider the difference between saying

My first hope of getting any real coverage would come later. At least, that's what I thought at the time. I would finally reach an area served by the Los Angeles *Times.* The *Times* is a pro-Administration paper, but its news columns are fair and comprehensive.

and saying

My first hope, I thought, of getting any real coverage would be when I finally reached an area served by the Los Angeles *Times,* a pro-Administration paper with fair and comprehensive news columns.

Besides being wordier, the first version makes it hard for the reader to distinguish the less important thought (the pro-Administration stance of the *Times*) from the more important (the assumption that there would be no "real coverage" in the midsection of the country). Though McCarthy's sentences are often long, they make her prose compact and reveal the structure of her thinking. The idea-to-word ratio is high and keeps us alert.

EXERCISE 2

◆ *Revising for Sentence Variety.* The passage below, taken from a later paragraph of McCarthy's report, has been broken into very short sentences that follow a few simple patterns. Combine and rewrite the sentences to make the style more consistent with that of the first paragraph.

> Nixon is a television creation. He is a sort of gesturing phantom. He is not comfortable with the old-fashioned world of printer's type. In this old-fashioned world, facts can be checked and verified. His aversion to the press is understandable. The Watergate story did not lend itself to the fugitive images of television. It lent itself to the durable columns of newsprint. This is not an accident. Printer's ink and domestic liberty have an old association. Television is a mass medium. It can be controlled and manipulated. Total control of the printed word seems to be all but impossible. This has been shown in the Soviet Union. If newspapers are censored or suppressed, broadsides and leaflets can still circulate. They can pass from hand to hand. The revival of the U.S. press under Nixon is an essential part of the Watergate phenomenon . . .

STRONG VERBS AND VERB FORMS

A writer's choice of words obviously affects the clarity of prose, but it also affects what we are calling texture. When readers encounter a word that they couldn't have foreseen, that they probably wouldn't have thought of themselves, they pay attention. When the word is both unforeseen and effective, they are pleased. Obviously, the writer's choices include every part of speech, but in this chapter we will concentrate on verbs for the simple reason that attention to them is more likely to improve a writer's style than attention to any other part of speech.

Ignoring the linguists' meanings of *strong* and *weak* (which have to do with the formation of the past tense), we will define a weak verb as one that creates no particular image and has no particular emotional overtones. In this respect *be* (and its various forms, including *is, am, was,* and *were*) is probably the weakest verb in the language. If I say, "We were friends," the verb seems very pale compared to the noun that follows it. "Friends" may be a word rich in associations; "were" is not. If I say, "We invaded the library," on the other hand, the verb is (for most readers) stronger than the noun that follows it. I probably don't mean that we crashed through the door in a tank, machine guns blazing, but the verb "invade" is associated with such violence, and the force of that association carries over into a sentence that may mean something like, "A crowd of us entered the library all at once, making a good deal more noise than the librarian wanted to hear."

The weakest verbs are the ones most widely used, the ones we hear in so many contexts that they are not associated with any particular actions or settings. Among the weakest are these: *be, have, do, make, go, come, take, give, get, put, use, seem, show, look, see,* and *say.* For any one of these we can name a set of stronger alternatives. For *go,* for example, we might substitute *walk* as slightly stronger and *saunter, mince, sashay, march, slither, stride,* and *mosey* as stronger still.

Weak verbs serve a valuable function in the language. They are, so to speak, team players. They don't draw attention to themselves and they are as useful as the all-purpose jackknife. We can say that "the President *went* to Camp David this weekend" or that "The beauty queen *went* down the sidewalk, surrounded by reporters." If we were determined to use strong verbs all the time, we would have to decide in each case whether our subject *strode, slithered,* or *minced,* and our readers might feel that they were reading a thesaurus rather than an essay. Invariably, if only to avoid exhausting both themselves and their readers, professional writers use more weak verbs than strong. But the *constant* use of weak verbs becomes tedious. Occasionally readers should encounter verbs more precise than *went* or *walked,* ones richer in associations.

E. B. White's description (from "Education," page 139) of his son's day at a city school demonstrates the way that strong verbs and verb forms[1] can enrich the texture of a paragraph. As you read, identify any verb stronger than *walk* and notice its effect:

> His days were rich in formal experience. Wearing overalls and an old sweater (the accepted uniform of the private seminary), he sallied forth at morn accompanied by a nurse or parent and walked (or was pulled) two blocks to a corner where the school bus made a flag stop. This flashy vehicle was as punctual as death: seeing us waiting at the cold curb, it would sweep to a halt, open its mouth, suck the boy in, and spring away with an angry growl. It was a good deal like a train picking up a bag of mail. At school the scholar was worked on for six or seven hours by half a dozen teachers and a nurse, and was revived on orange juice in midmorning. In a cinder court he played games supervised by an athletic instructor, and in a cafeteria he ate lunch worked out by a dietitian. He soon learned to read with gratifying facility and discernment and to make Indian weapons of a semi-deadly nature. Whenever one of his classmates fell low of a fever the news was put on the wires and there were breathless phone calls to physicians, discussing periods of incubation and allied magic.

---

[1] By "verb forms," I mean participles, gerunds, and infinitives, which are being lumped with finite verbs for the purpose of this discussion.

Some of White's strong verbs are chosen for the humor of juxtaposition. Clearly he likes putting "sallied forth," a construction we might associate with stories of medieval knighthood, with the unheroic "was pulled." I enjoy the way that the boy is "worked on" by the school staff and then "revived" by midmorning orange juice: the language suggests (to me at least) the training of a professional boxer rather than a six-year-old boy. But the most striking verbs are those applied to the bus, which "sees" the boy waiting by the curb, "sweeps" to a halt, "sucks" the boy in, and "springs away." By choosing these verbs, White conjures the image of a giant carnivorous animal swallowing the boy up. This image dominates the passage and expresses White's combination of humor and concern for the boy. Weaken the verbs—have the bus "come" to a halt, "take" the boy in, and "move" away—and the effect is lost.

The effect of substituting a stronger verb for a weaker is not always so spectacular as this. Often the result is only a slight gain in precision. But such gains keep the reader engaged by showing the writer's mind at work, choosing a word that works harder than its weaker synonym.

EXERCISE 3

◆ *Strengthening Verbs.* In the passages below, one or two strong verbs have been replaced by weaker synonyms set inside square brackets. Propose a better alternative for each of these.

1. In *The Innocents Abroad* Mark Twain describes the crowded, fly-infested alleys of an Italian city: "These alleys are paved with stone and [covered] with deceased cats and decayed rags and decomposing vegetable tops and remnants of old boots, and soaked in dishwater, and the people sit around on stools and enjoy it."

2. In *An American Childhood* Annie Dillard points out that it is the old, not the young, who have a sense of wonder: "The busy teacher halts on her way to school and stoops to pick up fine bright leaves 'to show the children'—but it is she, now in her sixties, who is increasingly [surprised] by the leaves, their brightness all so much trash in the gutter."

3. In "Such, Such Were the Joys" George Orwell describes the way that his preparatory school trained boys who might enhance its reputation by winning scholarships: "For a period of two or three years, the scholarship boys were [filled] with learning as cynically as a goose is [filled] for Christmas."

4. In "Comrade Laski, C.P.U.S.A. (M.-L.)" Joan Didion describes the mannerisms of a rigidly orthodox member of the "Communist Party, U.S.A. (Marxist-Leninist), a splinter faction of the Stalinist-Marxists": "He had with him a small book of Mao's poems, and as he talked he [placed] it on the table, [matched] it with the edge first vertically and then horizontally."

TONE

Tone has so many meanings that we need to begin by stipulating one for our purpose here. We will mean by tone the social relationship between the writer and the audience. My mother said to me on more than one occasion, "Don't take that tone with me, young man!" What she meant, of course, was this: "Remember that I am your parent, and that a child owes a parent at least the appearance of respect." Just as there is a tone a child is expected to take in conversations with a parent, there is a tone the writer is expected to take in relation to the audience.

Precisely what this tone is varies from situation to situation, but let's try to define the tone used in most forms of "public" writing, writing that might pass before the eyes of people we know distantly, if at all. The tone is earnest, distant, and deferential. That is, the writer is expected to set playfulness aside and say precisely what she means. She is to speak as if from behind a lectern, not assuming a familiar air and not using the casual expressions she would use among friends. She is to be polite and deferential when she approaches any question that might be controversial: if possible she should find a way to show her readers that she and they are really on the same side of the question.

In public discourse, every departure from this earnest, distant, deferential tone is risky, since a writer who seems frivolous, overly familiar, or confrontational may be dismissed out of hand. Nonetheless, the expected tone may be so inhibiting that it produces an essay like "Seat Belts," so eager to avoid giving offense that it ends up saying nothing at all. In this section, we will look at three ways that writers depart from the expected tone of public discourse in order to engage the reader.

ABANDONING EARNESTNESS

As "Seat Belts" shows us, an earnest discussion of a serious topic is sometimes wasted. The reader has heard it all before, so many times that one more appeal of the same sort is likely to go unheard. In these circumstances, writers with a talent for humor sometimes abandon the attempt to say what they mean directly and resort instead to humor and irony. In 1956, for example, the North Carolina legislature passed a series of laws intended to circumvent the desegregation of schools ordered by the U.S. Supreme Court. Newspaper editor Harry Golden, a liberal and champion of civil rights, did not respond with an earnest plea, but with an ironic proposal:

Those who love North Carolina will jump at the chance to share in the great responsibility confronting our Governor and the State legislature. A special session of the Legislature (July 25–28, 1956) passed a series of amendments to the State

"The Vertical Negro Plan"
—HARRY GOLDEN

Constitution. These proposals submitted by the Governor and his Advisory Education Committee include the following:

(A) The elimination of the compulsory attendance law, "to prevent any child from being forced to attend a school with a child of another race."

(B) The establishment of "Education Expense Grants" for education in a private school, "In the case of a child assigned to a public school attended by a child of another race."

(C) A "uniform system of local option" whereby a majority of the folks in a school district may suspend or close a school if the situation becomes "intolerable."

But suppose a Negro child applies for this "Education Expense Grant" and says he wants to go to a private school too? There are fourteen Supreme Court decisions involving the use of public funds;[2] there are only two "decisions" involving the elimination of racial discrimination in public schools.

The Governor has said that critics of these proposals have not offered any constructive advice or alternatives. Permit me, therefore, to offer an idea for the consideration of the members of the regular sessions. A careful study of my plan, I believe, will show that it will save millions of dollars in tax funds and eliminate forever the danger to our public education system. Before I outline my plan, I would like to give you a little background.

One of the factors involved in our tremendous industrial growth and economic prosperity is the fact that the South, voluntarily, has all but eliminated *VERTICAL SEGREGATION.* The tremendous buying power of the twelve million Negroes in the South has been based wholly on the absence of racial segregation. The white and Negro stand in the same grocery and supermarket counters; deposit money in the same bank teller's window; pay phone and light bills to the same clerk; walk through the same dime and department stores, and stand at the same drugstore counters.

It is only when the Negro "sets" that the fur begins to fly.

Now, since we are not even thinking about restoring *VERTICAL SEGREGATION,* I think my plan would not only comply with the Supreme Court decisions, but would maintain "sitting-down" segregation. Now here is the *GOLDEN VERTICAL NEGRO PLAN.* Instead of all those complicated proposals, all the next session needs to do is pass one small amendment which would provide only desks in the public schools of our state—no seats.

The desks should be those standing-up jobs, like the old-fashioned bookkeeping desk. Since no one in the South pays the slightest attention to a *VERTICAL NEGRO,* this will completely solve our problem. And it is not such a terrible inconvenience for young people to stand up during their classroom studies. In fact, this may be a blessing in disguise. They are not learning to read sitting down,

---

[2]Golden refers to a series of Supreme Court decisions indicating that a state or local government could not discriminate against blacks in the allocation of funding for schools.

anyway; maybe standing up will help. This will save more millions of dollars in the cost of our remedial English course when the kids enter college. In whatever direction you look with the *GOLDEN VERTICAL NEGRO PLAN,* you save millions of dollars, to say nothing of eliminating forever any danger to our public education system upon which rests the destiny, hopes, and happiness of this society.

Far more successful than a frontal assault on segregation, Golden's frequent attacks via humor and irony won him the commendations of such civil rights leaders as Martin Luther King, Jr. These attacks were read and even cherished by some Southerners who would not have listened to an earnest plea in the "Seat Belts" style. As one of Golden's fellow journalists said, "You simply can't lynch a man who makes you laugh."

CLOSING THE DISTANCE BETWEEN WRITER AND READER

By convention, the writer of a public essay or article writes as if she were not herself but some sort of generalized person addressing other people who had no particular identities. In her chapter on "White Lies," for example, Sissela Bok sounds like this:

White lies are at the other end of the spectrum of deception from lies in a serious crisis. They are the most common and the most trivial forms that duplicity can take. The fact that they are so common provides their protective coloring. And their very triviality, when compared to more threatening lies, makes it seem unnecessary or even absurd to condemn them.

The tone here is, as Miss Manners would say, "excruciatingly correct." "White Lies" is a condemnation of forms of deception we all practice, but it is not meant personally. Bok doesn't want to point a finger at her audience or even look them too directly in the eye. She certainly doesn't want to say "Listen, bub, if you think all that lying is harmless, you've got another think coming." She speaks philosophically, generally maintaining a safe psychological distance between herself as an individual and her readers as individuals. In most academic writing and most business writing, maintaining some such distance (not always quite so much) is wise policy. But the distance can become stultifying, and the complete writer needs to know how to diminish it.

In some situations, the writer may want to eliminate it almost entirely in order to make it clear that he is not on his high horse. The humorist Garrison Keillor is a master of this tactic, as you can see from the opening sentences of his essay "Country Golf":

I don't have many friends who have done one thing so well that they're famous for it and could sit on their laurels if they wanted to, although I do know a woman who can touch her nose with her tongue, which she is famous for among all the people who've seen her do it. She doesn't do it often, because she doesn't need to, having proved herself. I also know a man who wrote a forty-one-word palindrome, which is about as far as you can go in the field of writing that reads the same forwards and backwards. And I know Chet Atkins, who is emplaqued in the Country Music Hall of Fame, in Nashville, and has a warm, secure spot in the history of the guitar.

There is very little sense of distance here. We don't feel that Keillor is addressing us from the podium, safe in the armor of an impersonal style. What diminishes the distance is partly content. How can we feel that anyone is standing on his dignity when he begins by telling us about a friend who can stick out her tongue and touch her nose with it? The diction, too, plays a role. Keillor uses the first-person singular pronoun (*I*), contracts his verbs (*don't*), and as a rule uses everyday, conversational words and turns of phrase ("friends" rather than "acquaintances" or "colleagues"; "which is about as far as you can go" instead of "which is a remarkable accomplishment"). Imagine the shift in psychological distance had Keillor begun this way:

> Most of us have few acquaintances who have become famous for their specialties and could rest on their laurels if they wished, although we may know someone who has achieved local prominence for a dubious achievement like touching her nose with her tongue.

This is a perfectly acceptable sentence, more appropriate in tone for most public situations than Keillor's original. But its distance and propriety make it less engaging, and it would be a terrible way to begin an essay like "Country Golf," where the personality of the writer must show through.

Occasionally a writer closes the distance between herself and the reader by addressing him directly, as if face to face. The British novelist and essayist Brigid Brophy, for example, begins a newspaper article called "The Menace of Nature" this way:

> So? Are you just back? Or are you, perhaps, staying on there for the extra week? By "there" I mean, of course, one of the few spots left where the machine has not yet gained the upper hand; some place as yet unstrangled by motorways and unfouled by concrete mixers; a place where the human spirit can still—but for how much longer?—steep itself in natural beauty and recuperate after the nervous tension, the sheer stress, of modern living.
>
> Well (I assume you're *enough* recuperated to stand this information?): I think you've been piously subscribing to a heresy.

When I read this passage, I not only feel that the distance between Brophy and myself has been eliminated but that she has cornered me somewhere and is giving me a good talking-to. Obviously there is a danger of giving offense by such a direct approach to readers, but—used sparingly—the technique keeps them on their toes.

You'll have surmised that Keillor's essay and Brophy's are both personal and informal. Most essays that dramatically decrease the distance between reader and writer are. But it is sometimes useful to diminish the gap even in more formal, academic writing. Describing the size of the city states (singular, *polis,* plural *polei*) in ancient Greece, British scholar H. D. F. Kitto does not hold his reader entirely at arm's length:

"The Polis"
–H. D. F. KITTO

> It is important to realize their size. The modern reader picks up a translation of Plato's *Republic* or Aristotle's *Politics;* he finds Plato ordaining that his ideal city shall have 5,000 citizens, and Aristotle that each citizen should be able to know all the others by sight, and he smiles, perhaps, at such philosophic fantasies. But Plato and Aristotle are not fantasts. Plato is imagining a polis on the normal Hellenic scale; indeed he implies that many existing Greek poleis are too small—for many had less than 5,000 citizens. . . .
>
> To think on this scale is difficult for us, who regard a state of ten million as small, and are accustomed to states which, like the U.S.A. and the U.S.S.R., are so big that they have to be referred to by their initials; but when the adjustable reader has become accustomed to the scale, he will not commit the vulgar error of confusing size with significance. The modern writer is sometimes heard to speak with splendid scorn of "those petty Greek states, with their interminable quarrels." Quite so; Platea, Sicyon, Aegina, and the rest are petty, compared with modern states. The Earth itself is petty, compared with Jupiter—but then, the atmosphere of Jupiter is mainly ammonia, and that makes a difference. We do not like breathing ammonia—and the Greeks would not much have liked breathing the atmosphere of the vast modern State. They knew of one such, the Persian Empire—and thought it very suitable, for barbarians. Difference in scale, when it is great enough amounts to difference in kind.

Unlike Keillor and Brophy, Kitto does not use first- or second-person pronouns, such as *I* and *you,* but the passage doesn't treat the reader impersonally. Kitto addresses himself to a "modern reader" who is certain to share to some degree in the "vulgar error of confusing size with significance." He looks us, so to speak, directly in the eye, and argues with us. Having taken a personal interest in our errors, he does not correct them by a dispassionate account of Greek civilization, but by a rather outrageous analogy (the polis as earth, the modern state as Jupiter) and by a stern dressing-down. Professor Kitto is shaking his finger at us. His attitude is not disengaged, but personal.

REPLACING DEFERENCE WITH EDGE

The tone that Brophy and Kitto adopt doesn't only reduce the traditional psychological distance between the writer and the reader, it also decreases the traditional deference. Both writers assume that they are addressing readers at least half inclined to disagree with them, and neither attempts to hide the disagreement.

The writer's open disagreement with a view the reader is at least partly disposed to accept creates a quality we will call *edge*. The writer says to the reader, in effect, "You are probably inclined to listen to those who view my subject in framework X, but I insist that you consider framework Y." The reader is inclined to view Las Vegas weddings as merely flashy and convenient, but the writer (Joan Didion) tells the reader that they may be bumbling attempts at niceness. The reader may accept the widespread notion that European culture is superior to American culture, but the writer (Mark Twain) presents Europe as a cultural backwater. The reader may be inclined to listen to those who see fundamentalists as part of the lunatic fringe, but the writer (Annie Dillard) sees them as better attuned to the world than their detractors. Obviously, not every subject lends itself to this sort of assertive treatment, and not every writer is comfortable with confrontation. Nonetheless, the acknowledgment of disagreement can give an essay an edge that keeps both the writer and the reader engaged.

At its worst, edge becomes mere quarrelsomeness. At its best, it can be the expression of high purpose. George Orwell, a writer with edge in abundance, once said that each writer had to struggle against the tendency to become "a minor official, working on themes handed down to him from above and never telling what seems to him the whole of the truth." Orwell recommends as an anthem for the writer the words of the old Revivalist hymn:

> Dare to be a Daniel,[3]
> Dare to stand alone;
> Dare to have a purpose firm,
> Dare to make it known.

But, Orwell complains, too few writers have the courage of the prophet: "To bring this hymn up to date one would have to add a 'Don't' at the beginning of each line."

A prophet's courage might serve as the most extreme and ideal form of what we are calling edge. Willingness to parrot a theme "handed down from above" is a good definition of edgelessness. "Seat Belts," though it may be sincerely intended, sounds like such parroting; it is as edgeless as a sponge.

Compare the tone of a newspaper column Orwell wrote during the Royal Air Force's massive bombing of German cities in 1943. Rather than assure the reader that all sensible people see eye to eye on the bombing of civilian targets, he stresses disagreement. He even begins by encouraging the reader to sympathize with the views of his opponents:

> Miss Vera Brittain's pamphlet, *Seeds of Chaos,* is an eloquent attack on indiscriminate or "obliteration" bombing. "Owing to the RAF raids," she says, "thou-

---

[3] The courage of this Hebrew prophet led him to confront the king's ministers and to be thrown into a den of lions.

sands of helpless and innocent people in German, Italian and German-occupied cities are being subjected to agonizing forms of death and injury comparable to the worst tortures of the Middle Ages." Various well-known opponents of bombing, such as General Franco and Major General Fuller, are brought out in support of this. Miss Brittain is not, however, taking the pacifist standpoint. She is willing and anxious to win the war, apparently. She merely wishes us to stick to "legitimate" methods of war and abandon civilian bombing, which she fears will blacken our reputation in the eyes of posterity. Her pamphlet is issued by the Bombing Restriction Committee, which has issued others with similar titles.

Notice how reasonable and moderate Orwell makes Miss Brittain's position sound. I think most of us are at this point nodding in agreement, and that this is precisely what Orwell has in mind. We are now in the proper attitude for the paragraph that follows:

> Now, no one in his senses regards bombing, or any other operation of war, with anything but disgust. On the other hand, no decent person cares tuppence for the opinion of posterity. And there is something very distasteful in accepting war as an instrument and at the same time wanting to dodge responsibility for its more obviously barbarous features. Pacifism is a tenable position, provided you are willing to take the consequences. But all talk of "limiting" or "humanizing" war is sheer humbug. . . .

Having invited us to identify with Brittain's position, he leaps on us with no pretense of deference, no attempt to escape conflict by finding a middle ground. Orwell defies the proverb: he catches his flies with vinegar rather than honey. By confronting us so aggressively he forces us to pay attention. Can he really prove to us that our desire to humanize war by eliminating civilian bombing is humbug?

As it turns out, he makes a strong case, turning mainly on the unfairness of selectively slaughtering the young men who are sent to the front in modern warfare.

> War is not avoidable at this stage of history, and since it has to happen it does not seem to be a bad thing that others should be killed besides young men. I wrote in 1937: "Sometimes it is a comfort to me to think that the aeroplane is altering the conditions of war. Perhaps when the next great war comes we may see that sight unprecedented in all history, a jingo[4] with a bullet hole in him." We haven't yet seen that (it is perhaps a contradiction in terms), but at any rate the suffering of this war has been shared out more evenly than even the last one was. The immunity of civilians, one of the things that have made war possible, has been shattered. Unlike Miss Brittain, I don't regret that. I can't feel that war is "humanized" by being confined to the slaughter of the young and becomes "barbarous" when the old get killed as well.

---

[4] A militaristic nationalist politician; a hawk.

Oddly enough, when Orwell wrote this piece, he was acting the role of "a minor official, working on themes handed down to him from above." That is, he was working for the British government, commissioned to write propaganda to support the war effort. We don't feel, however, that he avoids "telling what seems to him the whole of the truth." By showing us very frankly that he disagrees with a position we must find attractive, he both engages our attention and persuades us that—under most difficult circumstances—he is an honest man writing well.

STYLE AND STYLES

If you began this chapter hoping for simple instructions on how to improve your style, I'm sure you long ago gave up that hope. On some questions of style, there is general consensus: fewer words are better than more, connected sentences are better than disjointed ones, prose that evokes images is preferable to prose that does not. Beyond such principles, style becomes a matter of hard choices, but hard choices can be a pleasure. E. B. White wrote:

> There are as many kinds of essays as there are human attitudes or poses, as many essay flavors as there are Howard Johnson ice creams. The essayist arises in the morning and, if he has work to do, selects his garb from an unusually extensive wardrobe: he can pull on any sort of shirt, be any sort of person, according to his mood or his subject matter—philosopher, scold, jester, raconteur, confidant, pundit, devil's advocate, enthusiast.

Understanding the range of choices available to you is the first step to choosing well.

EXERCISE 4

◆ *A Rewrite of "Seat Belts."* Write an essay about the same length as "Seat Belts" and on the same issue (you need not choose the same side of the issue). Make your essay more engaging than the original.

Handbook

OF GRAMMAR AND USAGE

3

PUNCTUATION AND MECHANICS

SECTION

GRAMMAR AND SENTENCE STRUCTURE

*T*his unit covers the forms and the functions of the eight parts of speech, how to use these basic units to build phrases and clauses, and how to combine these word groups to construct clear, complete, smoothly flowing sentences. Understanding grammar will help you to use the English language more effectively in your writing.

1.1 PARTS OF SPEECH

The eight parts of speech are nouns, pronouns, verbs, adjectives, adverbs, prepositions, conjunctions, and interjections.

1.1A NOUNS

A **noun** names a person, a place, a thing, or an idea.

Persons	operator	contestant	Louisa May Alcott
Places	kitchen	valley	Wyoming
Things	freighter	aardvark	oxygen
Ideas	obsession	realism	quality

Dates and days of the week are also classified as nouns.

A.D. 1100   Tuesday   November 29, 1984

Common and Proper Nouns

A **common noun** names a class of people, places, things, or ideas. Do not capitalize a common noun unless it begins a sentence. A **proper noun** gives the name or title of a particular person, place, thing, or idea, and it always begins with a capital letter.

Common Noun	A **speedway** is a race track for automobiles.
Proper Noun	The **Indianapolis Speedway** is the site of the Indianapolis 500.

Compound Nouns

A **compound noun** consists of two or more words used together to form a single noun. There are four kinds of compound nouns. One kind is formed by joining two or more words: *football*. A second kind consists of words joined by hyphens: *city-state*. A third kind consists of two words that are often used together: *sugar beet*. The fourth kind is a proper noun that consists of more than one word: *Missouri River*.

Collective Nouns

A **collective noun** refers to a *group* of people, places, things, or ideas.

> A **swarm** of bees buzzed around us!

> Phyllis has an **accumulation** of compositions that show her progress as a writer.

Concrete and Abstract Nouns

Concrete nouns refer to material things, to people, or to places. Some concrete nouns name things that you can perceive with your senses: *traffic, seasoning, barking*. Other concrete nouns name things that can be measured or perceived only with the aid of technical devices. Although you cannot see an atom, *atom* is a concrete noun because it names a material substance. In the following sentences, the nouns in boldface type are concrete.

> In **polo** the **players** ride on **horseback** and hit a **ball** with a long-handled **mallet.**

> You can tell that that is Denise's **car** because of the **noise** that it makes.

> **Penicillin,** which was discovered by **Alexander Fleming** in **1929,** is actually a **mold** that combats disease-carrying **germs.** [Even though you cannot see, hear, smell, taste, or feel germs, they have a definite material existence.]

Abstract nouns name ideas, qualities, emotions, or attitudes.

> Many critics consider the **conflict** between **integrity** and **power** to be the **theme** of *Macbeth.*

> **Disappointment** was visible on the faces of the players, but the crowd, moved by the **intensity** of the team's **effort,** applauded loudly.

> Galileo defended the **freedom** to pursue the **truth.**

Using Nouns Effectively

In writing, you usually need to use both concrete nouns and abstract nouns. Abstract nouns are necessary in most forms of writing. However, if you link them with details and examples that include concrete nouns, your writing will be clearer and more interesting.

Read the following paragraph from *Quite Early One Morning* by the Welsh writer Dylan Thomas. Notice how Thomas relies on concrete nouns to express his impressions and ideas. The concrete nouns are in italic type.

I was born in a large Welsh *town* at the beginning of the Great War—an ugly, lovely *town* (or so it was and is to me), crawling, sprawling by a long and splendid curving *shore* where truant *boys* and sandfield *boys* and old *men* from nowhere, beach-combed, idled and paddled, watched the dock-bound *ships* or the ships steaming away into wonder and *India*, magic and *China*, *countries* bright with *oranges* and loud with *lions;* threw *stones* into the *sea* for the barking outcast *dogs;* made *castles* and *forts* and *harbors* and *race tracks* in the *sand;* and on Saturday summer *afternoons* listened to the brass *band,* watched the *Punch and Judy,* or hung about on the fringes of the *crowd* to hear the fierce religious *speakers* who shouted at the *sea,* as though it were wicked and wrong to roll in and out like that, white-horsed and full of *fishes.*

Quite Early One Morning
—Dylan Thomas

Dylan Thomas relies on concrete nouns to evoke certain feelings about childhood. *India, China, oranges,* and *lions* convey a sense of adventure and discovery. *Castles, forts, harbors,* and *race tracks* create a sense of the boys' imaginative play when they were young. Note that Thomas does not completely avoid abstract nouns; *wonder* and *magic* are both abstract.

In your own writing, use concrete nouns to make ideas and impressions more vivid and interesting.

1.1B *PRONOUNS*

A **pronoun** is a word that is used in place of a noun. A pronoun identifies persons, places, things, or ideas without renaming them. The noun that a pronoun replaces is the **antecedent** of that pronoun. There are eight kinds of pronouns: personal, possessive, demonstrative, reflexive, intensive, interrogative, relative, and indefinite.

Personal Pronouns

Personal pronouns require different forms to express person, number, and gender. **Person** refers to the relationship between the speaker or writer (first person), the individual or thing spoken to (second person), and the individual or thing spoken about (third person). The **number** of a personal pronoun indicates whether the antecedent is singular or plural. The **gender** of a personal pronoun indicates whether the antecedent is masculine, feminine, or neuter.

Tricia and Annette will not soon forget Machiavelli's *The Prince,* for **it** greatly astonished **them.** [*It* replaces *The Prince,* and *them* replaces *Tricia and Annette.*]

Critics who try to interpret *The Prince* are perplexed because **they** find inconsistencies and contradictions. [*They* replaces *critics.*]

Possessive Pronouns

Possessive pronouns are personal pronouns that show ownership or belonging.

> Copies of *The Courtier* have arrived at the bookstore, and we can pick up **ours** at any time. [*Ours* replaces *copies.*]

> Georgina is doing **her** term paper on Sir Francis Bacon. [*Her* refers to *Georgina.*]

The following list shows the common personal pronouns; the possessive pronouns are in parentheses.

	Singular	Plural
First Person	I, me (my, mine)	we, us (our, ours)
Second Person	you (your, yours)	you (your, yours)
Third Person	he, him (his)	they, them (their, theirs)
	she, her (her, hers)	
	it (its)	

Demonstrative Pronouns

Demonstrative pronouns specify the individual or the group that is being referred to. The demonstrative pronouns are *this, that, these,* and *those.*

> **This** is a more interesting collection of photographs than **that.**

> **These** are the clippers that I used to trim the hedge; **those** are too rusty to use.

Reflexive Pronouns

Reflexive pronouns indicate that people or things perform actions to, for, or on behalf of themselves. To form a reflexive pronoun, add the suffix *-self* or *-selves* to the personal pronouns.

First Person	myself, ourselves
Second Person	yourself, yourselves
Third Person	himself, herself, itself, oneself, themselves

Example: Cervantes's Don Quixote convinces **himself** that the world is like the romances that he reads. He rides out to find adventure for **himself.**

Intensive Pronouns

Intensive pronouns are the same words as the reflexive pronouns, but they draw special attention to a person or a thing mentioned in the sentence. Intensive pronouns usually come immediately after the nouns or pronouns that they intensify.

We drove around the grounds of the estate but could not visit the *mansion* **itself,** which was locked. [The pronoun *itself* draws special attention to the word *mansion.*]

Following the play, the *playwright* **herself** appeared for a bow. [The pronoun *herself* draws special attention to the word *playwright.*]

Interrogative Pronouns

Interrogative pronouns introduce questions. The most frequently used interrogative pronouns are *who, whom, which, what,* and *whose.*

We can get tickets for two games next week. **Which** would you like to attend?

Whose is this glove that I just found in our closet?

Relative Pronouns

Relative pronouns introduce adjective clauses (pages 571–72), which modify nouns and pronouns. The relative pronouns are *who, whom, whose, which,* and *that.*

Sir Thomas More's home in Chelsea, **which** was known as the "Great House," was a center of political and scholarly inquiry. [*Home* is the antecedent of *which.*]

We read some writings by More **that** were commissioned by Henry VIII. [*Writings* is the antecedent of *that.*]

Erasmus, **whose** *The Praise of Folly* is well known, was a member of More's circle. [*Erasmus* is the antecedent of *whose.*]

Indefinite Pronouns

Indefinite pronouns refer to people, places, or things in general. Often you can use these pronouns without antecedents. The following list contains commonly used indefinite pronouns.

all	either	most	other
another	enough	much	others
any	everybody	neither	plenty
anybody	everyone	nobody	several
anyone	everything	none	some
anything	few	no one	somebody
both	many	nothing	someone
each	more	one	something

Examples: Margaret More Roper's learning astonished **everyone! Few** thought women capable of intellectual endeavors.

Anyone with an interest in political science should read More's *Utopia*. For a time Henry VIII respected **none** of his statesmen more than he did Lord Chancellor Thomas More.

EXERCISE 1   Using Pronouns in Writing

The following paragraph needs pronouns in order to make it read more smoothly and less repetitiously. Rewrite the entire paragraph, replacing nouns with pronouns where suitable. Use any of the kinds of pronouns studied in this section. Underline the pronouns in your rewritten paragraph.

Orson Welles was an influential figure in both American radio and American motion pictures. Although Welles is known best as an actor and as a motion-picture director, Welles first established Welles in the public eye through radio broadcasting. In 1938, Welles produced a broadcast that described a fictional invasion of New Jersey by creatures from Mars. The broadcast by Welles was so realistic that scores of alarmed listeners phoned the local authorities of the listeners. After the sensation of the radio broadcast, Welles went to Hollywood to write, direct, and act in films of Welles's own. Welles made several films, including *Citizen Kane. Citizen Kane* was an immediate critical success. The next films by Welles, *The Magnificent Ambersons* and *Journey into Fear,* failed at the box office when the films were released, although critics admired both *The Magnificent Ambersons* and *Journey into Fear.* After that time, Welles acted in many films, but Welles wrote and directed few. *The Lady from Shanghai, The Trial,* and *Falstaff* are the most notable of the later films that Welles directed. In spite of Welles's relatively few films, Welles had an important and enduring impact on American films.

1.1C   *VERBS*

A **verb** is a word that expresses an action or a state of being. There are three kinds of verbs: action verbs, linking verbs, and auxiliary verbs.

Action Verbs

An **action verb** describes the behavior or action of someone or something. Action verbs may express physical actions or mental activities.

The fire truck **raced** toward the scene of the fire. [*Raced* refers to a physical action.]

A glacier **crawls** forward at a pace of only a few inches a year. [*Crawls* refers to a physical action.]

Philip **memorizes** names and dates easily because he **concentrates** so well. [*Memorizes* and *concentrates* refer to mental activities.]

The archeologist **believed** that the site contained some very interesting artifacts. [*Believed* refers to a mental activity.]

Linking Verbs

A **linking verb** connects a noun or a pronoun with a word or words that identify or describe the noun or pronoun. Many linking verbs are verbs of being, which you form from the word *be.*

> Will Rogers **was** an American humorist of the 1920s and 1930s. [The word *humorist* identifies Will Rogers.]

> The Wilkinsons **were** anxious about encountering heavy traffic on the way to the airport. [The word *anxious* describes the Wilkinsons.]

There are several linking verbs in addition to *be:*

appear	grow	seem	stay
become	look	smell	taste
feel	remain	sound	

> The students standing on the corner **grew** impatient as they waited for the bus. [*Grew* links the descriptive word *impatient* to *students.*]

> The howling of the coyote **sounds** rather distant. [*Sounds* links the descriptive word *distant* to *howling.*]

Some verbs can be either action verbs or linking verbs, depending on their use in a sentence.

Action
> Lynette **felt** along the wall for the light switch.

Linking
> Although Ron studied late all week, he still **felt** energetic by the weekend.

Auxiliary Verbs

Sometimes a verb needs the help of another verb, called an **auxiliary verb** or a **helping verb.** The verb that it helps is called the **main verb.** Together, a main verb and an auxiliary verb form a **verb phrase.** A verb phrase may have more than one auxiliary verb. Common auxiliary verbs appear in the following list:

am, are, be, been, is, was, were	may, might
have, has, had	can, could
do, does, did	will, would
shall, should	must

In the following sentences, the auxiliary verbs are in italic type, and the main verbs are in boldface type. *Still* and *never* are not part of the verb phrase.

When Rhonda left, other cast members *were* still **rehearsing.**

The clerk at the warehouse *could* not *have been* wrong when she said that our package *had* **arrived!**

Will you *be* **waiting** for me at the entrance to the art institute?

Characteristics of Verbs

Verbs have several characteristics that you need to understand in order to use them correctly.

Transitive and Intransitive Verbs.
All action verbs are either transitive or intransitive. A verb is **transitive** when its action is directed toward someone or something, which is called the **object of the verb** (pages 558–59).

      verb   ┌──── obj. ────┐

The Chinese **built** the Great Wall of China over a period of several hundred years. [*Great Wall* is the object of the verb *built. Built* is transitive.]

        verb   obj.   obj.

By using a timer, Mr. Allen **photographed** himself and his family. [*Himself* and *family* are the objects of the verb *photographed. Photographed* is transitive.]

A verb is **intransitive** when the performer of the action does not direct that action toward someone or something. In other words, an intransitive verb does not have a receiver of the action. Some action verbs, such as *go*, are intransitive. All linking verbs are intransitive.

Although Bill **knew** about the surprise party ahead of time, he **acted** surprised. [The verbs *knew* and *acted* do not have objects. They are intransitive.]

The inn at the top of the mountain **seems** empty. [*Seems* is a linking verb. It is intransitive.]

Many verbs can be either transitive or intransitive, depending on whether there is a receiver of the action.

Transitive

    verb obj.

Stop Sheila because she forgot to take this letter to the mailbox. [The object of *stop* is *Sheila.*]

Intransitive

                     verb

The subway train approached the station and **stopped.** [Stopped has no object.]

Changes in Verb Form. An important characteristic of the verb is that its form changes according to how it is used. A verb changes form in order to agree in person and number with its subject. A verb also changes form to express tense and mood. The basic forms of a verb are its **principal parts.** For an explanation of the rules governing changes in verb form, see pages 586–99.

EXERCISE 2

Verbs

Number your paper from 1 to 7. *Step 1:* Next to each number, write the verbs and verb phrases in the corresponding sentence in the following paragraph. There are twelve verbs and verb phrases. *Step 2:* Label each main verb *Action* or *Linking.* *Step 3:* Label each verb or verb phrase *Transitive* or *Intransitive.*

(1) The League of Nations was an international association of countries, and its goal was world peace. (2) After France, Great Britain, Italy, Japan, and the United States wrote a constitution for the League in 1919, the League started operations in January 1920. (3) Although President Woodrow Wilson of the United States was the chief planner of the League, the United States did not join. (4) The Senate disagreed with Wilson's terms for membership. (5) In March 1920, the Senate rejected the treaty that would have brought the United States into the League. (6) Throughout the 1920s, people in the United States took little interest in foreign affairs, and the country never joined the League. (7) In April 1946, the United Nations replaced the League of Nations.

Using Verbs Effectively

Verbs can make the difference between an ordinary piece of writing and one that stirs the reader's imagination. For this reason, good writers use verbs that tell *how* something happened. Consider the verb *ran* and its synonym in the following example.

The dog **ran** across the field.

The dog **scampered** across the field.

When you read that a dog scampered, you form a definite image of how the dog was moving.

The following paragraph is from the short story "The Lagoon" by Joseph Conrad. Notice how Conrad uses specific verbs to describe the action. These verbs are in italic type.

The Malay only *grunted,* and went on looking fixedly at the river. The [other] man *rested* his chin on his crossed arms and *gazed* at the wake of the boat. At the end of the straight avenue of forests cut by the intense glitter of the river, the sun *appeared* unclouded and dazzling, poised low over water that *shone* smoothly like a band of metal.

The forests, somber and dull, *stood* motionless and silent on each side of the broad stream. At the foot of big, towering trees, trunkless nipa palms *rose* from the mud of the bank, in bunches of leaves enormous and heavy, that *hung* unstirring over the brown swirl of eddies. In the stillness of the air every tree, every leaf, every bough, every tendril of creeper and every petal of minute blossoms *seemed to have been bewitched* into an immobility perfect and final.

"The Lagoon"
—Joseph Conrad

With the verb *grunted,* Conrad tells us how the man sounded. The verb *gazed* suggests that the man was lost in thought. Later in the paragraph, the forests *stood,* the palms *rose,* and the leaves *hung.* All of these verbs make the forests seem alive. In your own writing, use verbs that tell the reader *how* an action occurs.

1.1D *ADJECTIVES*

An **adjective** is a word that modifies a noun or a pronoun. To modify means to change, and an adjective changes the meaning of a noun or a pronoun by describing it, limiting it, or making it more specific. An adjective answers one of three questions: *Which? What kind?* or *How many?*

Which?

The course focused on **Western** *civilization.* [Which civilization? *Western* civilization.]

What Kind?

The tennis player has an **unorthodox** *serve.* [What kind of serve? An *unorthodox* serve.]

How Many?

Twenty thousand *people* flocked to the stadium. [How many people? *Twenty thousand.*]

Articles.   The most frequently used adjectives are the three articles: *a, an,* and *the. A* and *an* are **indefinite articles** because they do not specify a particular person, place, thing, or idea. *The* is a **definite article** because it always specifies a particular person, place, thing, or idea.

Indefinite   Tom took **a** large *supply* of food on his camping trip.

Definite   He ate nearly all of **the** *food* that he brought.

Placement of Adjectives

Adjectives usually appear directly before the nouns or pronouns that they modify. Sometimes, a comma separates adjectives from the words that they modify.

Just beyond the hill was a **beautiful** *valley* with **several small** *clusters* of houses.

Illogical and **vague,** the *speech* made the audience restless.

Adjectives may follow linking verbs and modify the subjects of sentences.

The *staff* remained **loyal** throughout the long campaign, and the

candidate was very **proud** of them. [*Remained* and *was* are linking verbs.]

Adjectives sometimes follow the words that they modify and are separated from them by commas.

Our team's offensive *line,* **large** but **mobile,** dominated our opponent's defense during the game.

Proper Adjectives

A **proper adjective** is a name that functions as the modifier of a noun or a pronoun. Proper adjectives are always capitalized.

Last evening we heard a **Brahms** *symphony.*

The **New Orleans** *harbor* is one of the busiest harbors in the country.

To create many proper adjectives, you use the suffixes *-n, -an, -ian, -ese, -ish,* or *-al,* changing the spelling of the noun as needed.

Proper Noun	Proper Adjective
Elizabeth	Elizabethan
Lebanon	Lebanese
Ireland	Irish
Albania	Albanian

Nouns Used as Adjectives

Some nouns function as adjectives without changing form, as in the following examples.

The office contained **mahogany** *paneling* and tables with **glass** *tops*.

The invention of the **jet** *airplane* has diminshed the need for **passenger** *trains*, but **freight** *trains* have had an increase in business.

Possessive Nouns. **Possessive nouns** are nouns that show possession or ownership; they function as adjectives because they modify nouns or pronouns.

The **tunnel's** *lights* suddenly went out, plunging us into darkness.

Everyone admired the **actor's** *costumes*.

Pronouns Used as Adjectives

A pronoun functions as an adjective when it modifies a noun or a pronoun. Indefinite pronouns, demonstrative pronouns, interrogative pronouns, the relative pronoun *whose*, and the possessive pronouns* in the following list may serve as adjectives.

	Singular	Plural
First Person	my	our
Second Person	your	your
Third Person	his, her, its	their

For **her** *class* in computer science, Donna asked the neighbors whether she could use **their** *minicomputer*.

Your *guitar* seems to have lost **its** excellent *tone*. [Notice that the possessive pronoun *its* is spelled without an apostrophe.]

---

* The words in the following list are called *possessive pronouns* throughout this handbook, but some people call them *pronominal adjectives*. Use the term that your teacher prefers.

The following list contains examples of the other kinds of pronouns that can function as adjectives:

Indefinite	few, many, several, some
Demonstrative	that, this, these, those
Interrogative	what, which, whose
Relative	whose

Will the person **whose** *car* is blocking the entrance to the hospital please move it?

I would like to know **which** *newspaper* carried **that** *story* about the new

amusement park, for **several** *friends* are interested in reading it.

Using Adjectives Effectively

Adjectives provide the means for creating a mood or a lasting impression of a person, a place, or a thing. To create mood, use adjectives that appeal to the senses. Examples of such adjectives include *white, black, gigantic, minuscule, tepid,* and *frigid.* However, you can also use adjectives that refer to emotional states and abstract qualities. *Innocent, angry, confusing,* and *hopeful* are examples of such adjectives.

The following passage is from the short story "The Fall of the House of Usher" by Edgar Allan Poe. Notice how Poe uses some adjectives that appeal to the senses and other adjectives that refer to emotional states and abstract qualities. Adjectives that contribute to the mood of the passage are in italic type.

> The room in which I found myself was very *large* and *lofty.* The windows were *long, narrow,* and *pointed,* and at so *vast* a distance from the *black oaken* floor as to be altogether *inaccessible* from within. *Feeble* gleams of *encrimsoned* light made their way through the *trellised* panes and served to render sufficiently *distinct* the more *prominent* objects around; the eye, however, struggled in vain to reach the *remoter* angles of the chamber, or the recesses of the *vaulted* and *fretted* ceiling. *Dark* draperies hung upon the walls. The *general* furniture was *profuse, comfortless, antique,* and *tattered.* Many books and *musical* instruments lay scattered about but failed to give any vitality to the scene. I felt that I breathed an atmosphere of sorrow. An air of *stern, deep,* and *irredeemable* gloom hung over and pervaded all.

Several of Poe's adjectives appeal to the senses: *large, lofty, vast, black, oaken, encrimsoned, trellised, vaulted,* and *dark.* On the other hand, *stern, deep,* and *irredeemable* refer to abstract qualities. The mood is one of gloom and decay.

In your writing, use adjectives that appeal to the senses and those that refer to emotional states or abstract qualities.

1.1E ADVERBS

Like adjectives, adverbs are modifiers. An **adverb** is a word that modifies a verb, an adjective, or another adverb. An adverb answers one of five questions about the word or phrase that it modifies: *How? When? Where? How often?* or *To what extent?*

How?

Tricia *raised* her arms **triumphantly** when she set a school record in the high jump.

When?

The personnel manager *will see* you **now.**

Where?

We *called* **everywhere,** but no room is available for the conference.

How Often?

Sometimes the smoke alarm *sounds* when something on the stove is burning.

To What Extent?

Jeanine is **rather** *doubtful* about getting a part-time job.

Adverbs such as *rather, really, certainly, indeed,* and *truly* are adverbs of extent and are used for emphasis.

Leonardo da Vinci was a **truly** *remarkable* man in both the breadth and the depth of his interests. [To what extent was Leonardo da Vinci remarkable? *Truly* remarkable.]

The words *not* and *never* are adverbs. They tell to what extent *(not at all)* and when *(never)*.

Dennis *will* **not** *build* the kitchen cabinets himself because he *has* **never** *had* experience in carpentry.

Many sentences contain nouns that function as adverbs. Such adverbs usually tell when or where.

Yesterday our boss *informed* us that we have Saturday off.

Adverbs Used to Modify Verbs

Adverbs often modify verbs. An adverb does not have to appear next to the verb that it modifies. Notice the different positions of the adverbs *silently* and *slowly* in the following sentences.

Beginning	**Silently** and **slowly,** the tide *covered* the narrow strip of land.
Middle	The tide **silently** and **slowly** *covered* the narrow strip of land.
End	The tide *covered* the strip of land **silently** and **slowly.**

Adverbs Used to Modify Adjectives

Adverbs may modify adjectives. An adverb usually comes directly before the adjective that it modifies.

In spite of its **very** *forbidding* title, the essay was **fairly** *easy* to read.

The Super Bowl drew an audience of **nearly** *one hundred million* viewers.

Adverbs Used to Modify Other Adverbs

Adverbs can modify other adverbs. Such adverbs usually precede the adverbs that they modify.

Rafael is popular because he listens **so** *well* to other people. [*So* emphasizes the fact that Rafael listens well.]

Although the footbridge over the ravine was considered safe, Ed and Mark

crossed it **quite** *slowly.*

1.1F ***PREPOSITIONS***

A **preposition** is a word that expresses a relationship between a noun or a pronoun and another word in a sentence.

A special pilot **from** *shore* climbed **on** *board* and went **to** the *helm.* [The preposition *from* relates *shore* to *pilot.* The preposition *on* relates *board* to *climbed.* The preposition *to* relates *helm* to *went.*]

The following list contains frequently used prepositions:

along	beyond	off	to
among	by	on	toward
around	despite	onto	under
at	down	out	underneath
before	during	outside	until
behind	except	over	up
below	for	past	upon
beneath	from	since	with
beside	in	through	within
besides	near	till	without
between			

A **compound preposition** is a preposition that consists of more than one word.

> When the Lansings got to the store, they bought two easy chairs **instead of** just *one.*

Frequently used compound prepositions are in the following list:

according to	in addition to	on account of
aside from	in front of	out of
as of	in place of	prior to
as well as	in regard to	with regard to
because of	in spite of	with respect to
by means of	instead of	

A preposition is usually followed by a noun or a pronoun, which is called the **object of the preposition.** Together, the preposition, the object, and the modifiers of that object form a **prepositional phrase.**

> prep.
> The referee called a charging foul **against the opposing team's seven-foot-tall**
> obj.
> **center.** [The prepositional phrase consists of the preposition, *against;* the modifiers, *the, opposing, team's,* and *seven-foot-tall;* and the object, *center.*]

In some sentences, particularly interrogative sentences, the preposition follows the object.

> obj.   prep.
> **Whom** are you rooting **for** this weekend? [**Think:** *For whom* are you rooting this weekend?]

A prepositional phrase functions as an adjective if it modifies a noun or a pronoun. A prepositional phrase functions as an adverb if it modifies a verb, an adjective, or an adverb.

Used as an Adjective

The *road* **on which we live** has a picnic *area* **for the residents.**

Used as an Adverb

The defense attorney *looked* doubtfully **at the witness** and then

began her cross-examination **in a quiet but effective voice.**

Some words can function as prepositions or as adverbs, depending on their use in a sentence.

	prep. obj.
Preposition	Larry saw Marilyn standing **outside the stadium.**
	adv.
Adverb	If you *venture* **outside** in the cold weather, wear a coat.

EXERCISE 3 **Prepositional Phrases**

List the prepositional phrases in the following sentences. Underline the prepositions once and the objects of the prepositions twice.

1. Throughout history individuals have envisioned societies in which people could live in harmony with one another and with nature.
2. Plato, a philosopher who lived during the fourth-century B.C., wrote *The Republic,* which described his concept of the ideal society.
3. In Plato's perfect society, harmony would exist between the three classes: the philosopher-kings, who would be responsible for government; the guardians, who would maintain order in the land; and the artisans, farmers, and merchants, who would supply material needs.
4. According to Plato all people in the society would find satisfaction in their roles, despite the divisions among the classes.
5. Since Plato's era many other people have been intrigued by the idea of building utopian communities.

1.1G *CONJUNCTIONS*

A **conjunction** is a word that connects words or groups of words. In fact, the word *conjunction* literally means "the act of joining" or "combination." There are three kinds of conjunctions: coordinating conjunctions, correlative conjunctions, and subordinating conjunctions.

Coordinating Conjunctions

A **coordinating conjunction** connects individual words or groups of words that perform the same function in a sentence. The coordinating conjunctions are *and, but, for, nor, or, so,* and *yet.* A coordinating conjunction can connect words, phrases, or clauses. For a complete explanation of phrases and clauses, see pages 561–76.

> The dolphin next to our boat *surfaced, jumped,* **and** *dived* as we watched. [connects words]

> The antique dealer, *hoping to find a bargain* **but** *not expecting to find one,* went to the auction. [connects phrases]

> *We may be a few minutes late for the picnic,* **for** *the road crews repairing the expressway have slowed traffic considerably.* [connects clauses]

Correlative Conjunctions

A **correlative conjunction** is a conjunction that consists of two or more words that function together. Like coordinating conjunctions, correlative conjunctions connect words that perform equal functions in a sentence. The following list contains correlative conjunctions:

both . . . and	not only . . . but (also)
either . . . or	whether . . . or
neither . . . nor	

> Julian said that he had read **neither** *this novel* **nor** *that long poem* before. [connects words]

> **Not only** *did we see a funny show at the club,* **but** *we* **also** *watched comedians doing improvisations after the regular show.* [connects clauses]

Subordinating Conjunctions

A **subordinating conjunction** introduces a subordinate clause (pages 570–71), which is a clause that cannot stand by itself as a complete sentence. The subordinating conjunction connects the subordinate clause to an independent clause, which *can* stand by itself as a complete sentence.

> ┌——— sub. clause ———┐ ┌——————— indep. clause ———————┐
> **As** the months went by, the Smiths grew accustomed to their new home. [The subordinating conjunction *as* introduces the subordinate clause and connects the clause to the independent clause.]

Subordinating conjunctions usually express relationships of time, manner, cause, condition, comparison, or purpose.

Time	after, as, as long as, as soon as, before, since, until, when, whenever, while
Manner	as, as if, as though
Cause	because
Condition	although, as long as, even if, even though, if, provided that, though, unless, while
Comparison	as, than
Purpose	in order that, so that, that

Jerry has been practicing the drums constantly and plays **as though** he has had a
——— sub. clause ———
great deal of experience. [*As though* expresses manner.]

The stores are extremely crowded these days **unless** you go early on a
——— sub. clause ———
Saturday morning. [*Unless* expresses condition.]

Conjunction or Preposition?   Certain words can function as either conjunctions or prepositions. However, there are two important differences between a word used as a preposition and one used as a conjunction. First, a preposition always has an object, and a conjunction never has one.

Preposition
> **Before** *me* is a book of Renaissance poetry. [The pronoun *me* is the object of the preposition *before*.]

Conjunction
> **Before** we read it, we should learn something about Renaissance poets' use of myth and allegory. [*Before* has no object. Instead, it introduces the subordinate clause *Before we read it*.]

Second, a preposition introduces a prepositional phrase. A conjunction, on the other hand, connects words or groups of words.

Preposition
> ┌─── prep. phrase ───┐
> **After** much preparation, Renaissance poets made classical allusions with ease. [*After* introduces the prepositional phrase *After much preparation*.]

Conjunction
> Spenser's literary career flourished **after** Sir Walter Raleigh presented him to Queen Elizabeth I. [*After* connects the subordinate clause *after Sir Walter Raleigh presented him to Queen Elizabeth I* to the preceding independent clause.]

Conjunctive Adverbs

A **conjunctive adverb** is an adverb that functions somewhat like a coordinating conjunction because it usually connects independent clauses (page 570). A semicolon precedes the conjunctive adverb, and a comma usually follows it.

Conjunctive Adverb

> An expert on career planning will speak in the auditorium on Friday; **furthermore,** he will answer your questions after the lecture.

Coordinating Conjunction

> An expert on career planning will speak in the auditorium on Friday, **and** he will answer your questions after the lecture.

The following list contains frequently used conjunctive adverbs:

also	furthermore	later	still
besides	however	moreover	then
consequently	indeed	nevertheless	therefore
finally	instead	otherwise	thus

EXERCISE 4   Conjunctions and Conjunctive Adverbs

Rewrite the following paragraphs by using conjunctions and conjunctive adverbs whenever appropriate to connect ideas and to provide variety in your sentences. You may make other changes so that the passage reads smoothly. Underline the conjunctions and the conjunctive adverbs that you use.

Margaret Mead was a psychological anthropologist. She was respected. She was controversial. Mead was born in Philadelphia, Pennsylvania, in 1901. She grew up in a liberal intellectual atmosphere. Her father was a professor. Her mother was a sociologist. Her mother was an early advocate of women's rights. She was a senior in college. She took a course in anthropology. She later said that this was the most influential event in her life. She decided to become an anthropologist. She became known as a tireless field investigator.

Margaret Mead's interests centered on several aspects of psychology and anthropology. She studied childhood and adolescence. She studied cultural change. She studied the contemporary national character. Her first field research was done in Samoa in 1925 and 1926. She went by herself. She studied the lives of adolescent girls. She went to New Guinea to study the young children. She wanted to test some of the psychological theories popular at that time. Twenty-five years later she returned to observe the changes. The children had become adults. In the late 1930s she did field research in Bali. There she pioneered the use of photography in the study of behavior and personality.

During her career she served on several United States government commissions. She was very involved in education. She taught in universities. She interpreted the lessons of anthropology to the general public. She was a curator at the American

Museum of Natural History for most of her professional life. She was involved in programs concerned with mental health and technological change. Margaret Mead died in New York City on November 15, 1978. *Blackberry Winter* is her autobiography.

1.1H *INTERJECTIONS*

An **interjection** is an exclamatory word or phrase that can stand by itself, although it may also appear in a sentence. Many interjections express strong emotions. They are followed by exclamation points.

> **Wow!** That ball was really hit!

When an interjection appears within a sentence, you should set it off with a comma or commas.

> **So,** you didn't find what you were looking for at the corner store.

> **My,** these grapefruits are truly excellent!

1.2 SENTENCE STRUCTURE

1.2A *FOUR SENTENCE PURPOSES*

A **sentence** is a group of words that has a subject and a predicate and that expresses a complete thought. It describes an action or states a condition of a person, a place, or a thing. There are four categories of sentences: declarative, interrogative, exclamatory, and imperative.

A **declarative sentence** makes a statement and ends with a period. An **interrogative sentence** asks a question and ends with a question mark. An **exclamatory sentence** shows strong feeling and ends with an exclamation point. An **imperative sentence** gives an order or makes a request. A mild command or request ends with a period, but a strong command or request ends with an exclamation point. Some imperative sentences take the form of questions but are actually mild commands or polite requests. Such sentences end with periods.

Declarative	Before reading the novel, Stephen read the preface.
Interrogative	Why did Napoleon lose the battle at Waterloo?
Exclamatory	This traffic will make us miss our airplane!
Imperative	Lock the door on your way out.
	Don't drink that sour milk!
	Donna, will you please move your car.

1.2B SUBJECTS AND PREDICATES

Simple Subjects

The **simple subject** is the noun or pronoun that names the person, place, thing, or idea that the sentence is about. The simple subject does not include modifiers. The complete subject (page 556) consists of the simple subject and its modifiers. In this book the term *subject* refers to the simple subject. In the following sentences, the simple subject is in boldface type.

> **Sigmund Freud** is considered one of the founders of modern psychiatry.

> The **last** of the artifacts that the archeologist discovered was the most interesting.

> Where will the **seminar** on computer education be held?

The simple subject of an imperative sentence is always *you*. Often, *you* is understood rather than stated.

> Be sure to study the chapter in your history book about Reconstruction. [**Think:** *You* be sure.]

Compound Subjects

A **compound subject** is a simple subject that consists of two or more nouns or pronouns of equal rank. The term *compound subject* refers to a compound *simple* subject.

> A larger **dining room,** a **den,** and a big **closet** will be added to Mr. Grabowski's house. [*Dining room, den,* and *closet* form the compound subject.]

Simple Predicates

The **simple predicate** is the verb or verb phrase that describes the action or states the condition of the subject. The simple predicate does not include modifiers and words that complete the meaning of the verb. It also does not include the adverb *not* or *never*. The complete predicate (page 556) includes all such modifiers and complements (page 558). It also includes *not* or *never*. In this book the term *predicate* refers to the simple predicate. In the following sentences, the simple predicate is in boldface type.

> subj.   pred.
> For biology class each *student* **collected** samples of forty different kinds of leaves.

> subj.   ⌐— pred. —⌐
> By this time tomorrow, our *family* **will have driven** through Sequoia National Park.

What **do** *social scientists* **view** as the major trends for cities in the next ten years?

Compound Predicates

A **compound predicate** is a simple predicate that consists of two or more verbs or verb phrases of equal rank. The term *compound predicate* refers to a compound *simple* predicate.

> Julius Caesar **led** the Roman army in one conquest after another and **expanded** the Roman Empire all the way to Britain but **was assassinated** in 44 B.C. [*Led, expanded,* and *was assassinated* form the compound predicate.]

Complete Subjects and Complete Predicates

The **complete subject** consists of the simple subject and all the words that modify it or identify it.

> ┌──────── complete subject ────────┐
> **Brown County, which is in the south-central part of Indiana,** is known for its art galleries. [*Brown County* is the simple subject.]

> ┌──────── complete subject ────────┐
> **Remembered for his courage in battle,** *Chief Crazy Horse* actually had a quiet, unassuming manner. [*Chief Crazy Horse* is the simple subject.]

> ┌──────── complete subject ────────
> *Harvard University,* **the oldest university in the United States, and** *Laval*
>
> ────────────────────────────┐
> *University,* **the oldest university in Canada,** were both founded to train people for the clergy. [Included in the complete subject is the compound simple subject, which appears in italic type.]

The **complete predicate** consists of the simple predicate and all the words that modify it or complete its meaning.

> ┌──────────────────────────
> The Vikings, who came from Scandinavia, *made* **raids on other European**
> ────────── complete predicate ──────────┐
> **countries from the eighth century through the eleventh century.** [*Made* is the simple predicate.]

> ┌──────── complete predicate ────────┐
> Film for your camera *can be bought* **at the visitors' center at the zoo.** [*Can be bought* is the simple predicate.]

Demographers *study* population trends and *predict* that the average age of

people in the United States will rise. [Included in the complete predicate is the compound simple predicate, *study* and *predict*.]

Placement of Subjects and Predicates

Subjects and predicates may be arranged in a variety of ways in sentences. The placement of the subject and the predicate often depends on the purpose of the sentence. In the examples that follow, the complete subjects are underlined once and the complete predicates twice.

Declarative Sentences

Household utensils made of pewter, an alloy consisting primarily of tin, have been used since the fourteenth century. [The subject precedes the predicate.]

Here are the periodicals that you requested from the reference librarian. [The sentence has inverted word order; that is, the subject follows the predicate.]

Into the street rolled the tennis ball. [The sentence has inverted word order.]

Because they had been studying the ancient history of Britain, Sue and Paulette, who were on a tour, were particularly interested in seeing Stonehenge. [The subject is between the two parts of the predicate.]

Interrogative Sentence

How were you able to fix the plugged drain in the kitchen? [**Think:** You were able to fix.]

Imperative Sentence

Try to finish painting the porch by this evening. [**Think:** *You* try to finish. The entire imperative sentence is the complete predicate because the subject, *you,* is understood.]

Exclamatory Sentences

The pictures that you took are beautiful!

What a fascinating exhibit that was!

EXERCISE 1   Subjects and Predicates

Underline the complete subjects once and the complete predicates twice. Write *subj.* over each simple subject and *pred.* over each simple predicate. If the subject is the understood *you,* write it in parentheses, underline it, and label it.

1. The population of the world in the year 1650 was five hundred million.
2. Between 1650 and 1850, the world's population doubled.
3. Will the rapid growth in population, now 2 percent a year, continue?
4. Because medical advances allow people to live longer, the birth rate exceeds the death rate in many countries.
5. Population experts expect continued growth and believe that the increasing population will put a strain on the world's resources, particularly food and energy.

1.2c *COMPLEMENTS*

A **complement** is a word or a group of words that completes the meaning of a verb in a sentence or a clause (page 570). Complements are always part of the complete predicate.

> The oranges sent to us from Florida were **delicious.** [The oranges were *what?* Delicious. *Delicious* is a complement.]

> This afternoon Chet is chopping **wood** for the winter. [Chet is chopping *what?* Wood. *Wood* is a complement.]

If the preceding sentences did not have complements, their meaning would be incomplete.

> The oranges sent to us from Florida were [Were what?]

> Chet is chopping [Is chopping what?]

This section covers three types of complements: objects, objective complements, and subject complements.

Objects

Objects are nouns or pronouns that follow action verbs in the active voice (see pages 595–97). There are two kinds of objects: direct objects and indirect objects.

Direct Objects. A **direct object** is a noun or a pronoun that follows an action verb in the active voice and receives the action of the verb. It answers the question *What?* or *Whom?* Verbs that take direct objects are called *transitive verbs* (page 541). Modifiers are not part of the object.

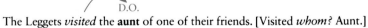

> The Leggets *visited* the **aunt** of one of their friends. [Visited *whom?* Aunt.]

> The next-door neighbors *have* a small **tractor** for clearing the snow from the driveway. [Have *what?* Tractor.]

Indirect Objects.

An **indirect object** is a noun or a pronoun that names the person or thing *to* whom or *for* whom an action is performed. An indirect object follows an action verb in the active voice. In most cases an indirect object is used with a direct object. The indirect object comes immediately after the verb and before the direct object.

The men's choir will sing **us** one more *song* to conclude the program. [**Think:** The choir will sing *(for)* us one more song.]

Will you bring **me** a *couple* of books from the library when you go there? [**Think:** Will you bring *(to)* me a couple of books?]

Compound Objects.

Like subjects and predicates, objects may be compound. A compound object consists of two or more objects that complete the same predicate.

Compound Direct Object

Jerry read several **articles** and **books** about the presidency of James Monroe.

Compound Indirect Object

We will show **Maxine** and **Paulette** as many historical sites as we have time for.

Objective Complements

An **objective complement** is a noun or an adjective that follows a direct object and explains, identifies, or describes that object. Only certain verbs take an objective complement: *make, find, think, elect, choose, appoint, name, consider, call,* and synonyms of these verbs.

Noun as Objective Complement

The votes have elected *Alexandra Smith* **state senator.** [*State senator* is the objective complement of the verb phrase *have elected*. It identifies the direct object *Alexandra Smith*.]

Adjective as Objective Complement

We considered the dancer's *performance* **brilliant.** [*Brilliant* is the objective complement of the verb *considered*. It describes the direct object, *performance*.]

A sentence may have a compound objective complement, which consists of two or more objective complements.

D.O.   O.C.

The board of trustees has appointed *Dan* the **director** of public information and

O.C.

the **coordinator** of the research department. [The nouns *director* and *coordinator* are objective complements.]

Subject Complements

A **subject complement** is a word that comes after a linking verb and identifies or describes the subject of a sentence or a clause. Subject complements often follow forms of the verb *be*. Other verbs that may take subject complements are in the following list:

appear	look	sound
become	remain	stay
feel	seem	taste
grow	smell	

There are two kinds of subject complements: predicate nominatives and predicate adjectives.

Predicate Nominatives. A **predicate nominative** is a noun or a pronoun that follows a linking verb and identifies the subject of the sentence. The root of the word *nominative* is *nominate,* which means "to name." In a sense the predicate nominative renames the subject.

P.N.

During the coming year, *Ron* will remain a **volunteer** at the local recycling center. [*Volunteer* identifies the subject *Ron.*]

P.N.

After Mrs. Sampson's expert training, *Butch* has become an obedient **dog** . [*Dog* identifies the subject *Butch.*]

P.N.   P.N.

The *broadcast* will be either a **press conference** or a **speech** by the governor. [The sentence has a compound predicate nominative, *press conference* and *speech.* Both identify *broadcast.*]

Predicate Adjectives. A **predicate adjective** is an adjective that follows a linking verb and modifies the subject of the sentence.

P.A.

The *sound* coming out of the speakers was rather **feeble**. [The predicate adjective *feeble* modifies the subject *sound.*]

The *story* that I read last night was quite **difficult** to follow. [The predicate adjective *difficult* modifies the subject *story*.]

Harrison felt **refreshed** and **relaxed** after his month-long vacation. [The sentence has a compound predicate adjective, *refreshed* and *relaxed*.]

In some sentences the predicate adjective precedes the verb or verb phrase.

Lighthearted was the *play* that we saw at the theater. [The predicate adjective *lighthearted* modifies the subject *play*.]

EXERCISE 2 ## Complements

Write the words and phrases that are in italic type in the following sentences. After each word or phrase, write the label *Direct object, Indirect object, Objective complement, Predicate nominative,* or *Predicate adjective.*

1. Winston Churchill experienced *setbacks* in his early life, but those setbacks did not prevent *him* from leading a distinguished life.
2. Churchill's childhood was *undistinguished,* for his teachers considered *him* the worst *student* in his class.
3. Churchill began to find a *direction* at the age of eighteen; at that time his father sent *him* to the Royal Military College at Sandhurst.
4. The school gave *Churchill* his first military *training,* and he became an excellent *student* of military tactics and fortifications.
5. After he had completed his education, Churchill sought *adventure,* and his experiences gave *him* the *opportunity* to become a war correspondent.

1.3 PHRASES AND CLAUSES

Phrases and clauses let you use a variety of sentence structures in your writing. This section explains the functions of both phrases and clauses.

1.3A *PHRASES*

A **phrase** is a group of related words that functions as a single part of speech but lacks a subject, a predicate, or both. This section deals with three common kinds of phrases: prepositional phrases, appositive phrases, and verbal phrases.

Prepositional Phrases

A **prepositional phrase** consists of a preposition and its object, including any modifiers of that object. In the following sentences, the prepositional phrases are in boldface type.

>   prep.   obj.
> An important challenge facing the United States **for the last two hundred years**
>
>   prep.   obj.
> has been maintaining the proper balance **between the individual's rights and**
>
>   obj.
> **society's rights.** [The second prepositional phrase has a compound object of the preposition.]
>
>   obj.   prep.
> **Which person** are you looking **for?** [**Think:** *For which person* are you looking?]

Prepositional Phrases Used as Adjectives.

A prepositional phrase that modifies a noun or a pronoun functions as an adjective. Such a phrase is sometimes called an **adjective phrase.**

Modifies Noun

The *man* **with the brown raincoat** will drive us downtown, where we will

find the *location* **of the meeting.**

Modifies Pronoun

Several **of the students** have entered the chess tournament.

Prepositional Phrases Used as Adverbs.

A prepositional phrase functions as an adverb if it modifies a verb, an adjective, or another adverb. This kind of phrase is sometimes called an **adverb phrase.**

Modifies Verb

The impressionist movement *spread* **from Europe** and influenced American artists in the early 1900s.

Modifies Adjective

The entire class was *curious* **about new energy sources.**

Modifies Adverb

The tour guide led the visitors *down* **to the lowest deck.**

A prepositional phrase can modify the object in another prepositional phrase.

A detour *took* us **around the construction site in the middle of the city.**

Appositives and Appositive Phrases

An **appositive** is a noun or a pronoun placed near another noun or pronoun to explain it or identify it.

The senior class *president,* **Amy Jones,** has brought several new ideas into student government.

Will our supervisors show *us* **trainees** the best selling techniques?

Albert Schweitzer, **doctor, missionary,** and **philosopher,** will long be remembered for his humanitarian work in Africa. [The sentence has a compound appositive: *doctor, missionary,* and *philosopher.*]

Like an appositive, an **appositive phrase** explains or identifies a noun or a pronoun. It includes all the words or phrases that modify an appositive.

Colette's *hobby,* **nature and wildlife photography,** will probably lead to an interesting job.

We **listeners with questions** can talk to the professor after the lecture.

A year of fierce snowstorms and widespread drought, *1978* will long be remembered.

An **essential appositive** or an **essential appositive phrase** is an appositive that is necessary to the meaning of the sentence. This kind of appositive should not be separated from the rest of the sentence with a comma or commas.

D. H. Lawrence's *short story* **"The Rocking-Horse Winner"** appears in numerous literature anthologies. [Lawrence wrote more than one story. The appositive is necessary to identify which story.]

A **nonessential appositive** or a **nonessential appositive phrase** is an appositive that is *not* necessary to the meaning of the sentence. Such an appositive should be separated from the rest of the sentence with a comma or commas.

Lawrence also wrote *"The Fox,"* **a story that is widely read and studied.**
— appositive phrase —
[The appositive is not necessary to identify the story being discussed.]

EXERCISE 1   ## Prepositional and Appositive Phrases

Number your paper from 1 to 15. Next to each number, write a prepositional phrase or an appositive phrase to complete the corresponding sentence. Use the kind of phrase that is indicated.

Frank, (1) ___?___ (appositive phrase), left his house (2) ___?___ (prepositional phrase) early this afternoon. As he walked (3) ___?___ (prepositional phrase), he met his friend (4) ___?___ (appositive phrase), who was waiting (5) ___?___ (prepositional phrase). They talked (6) ___?___ (prepositional phrase) and continued together (7) ___?___ (prepositional phrase). Frank and his friend passed the public library, (8) ___?___ (appositive phrase), and turned the corner (9) ___?___ (prepositional phrase). They walked (10) ___?___ (prepositional phrase) and finally arrived at the Shubert Theater, (11) ___?___ (appositive phrase). They presented their tickets (12) ___?___ (prepositional phrase) and climbed the stairs (13) ___?___ (prepositional phrase). (14) ___?___ (prepositional phrase), they were enthralled by *Hamlet*, (15) ___?___ (appositive phrase).

Verbals and Verbal Phrases

Verbals are verb forms that function as nouns, adjectives, or adverbs but retain some of the properties of verbs. For instance, they express action or being, and they may take complements. There are three kinds of verbals: participles, gerunds, and infinitives.

Participles.   A **participle** is a verb form that can function as an adjective while still keeping some of the properties of a verb. It expresses action or being, and it may take a complement.

Annoyed, *Jane* drove around the block to find a **parking** *place.* [Both *annoyed* and *parking* are participles.]

There are two kinds of participles: present participles and past participles. The present participle and the past participle are two of the four principal parts of a verb. For a complete explanation of the principal parts of verbs, see pages 586–88.

Besides functioning as adjectives, present participles and past participles can form part of a verb phrase. When a participle functions as a verb, it is not a verbal.

This section deals with present participles and past participles that function as adjectives. For an explanation of participles used as verbs, see pages 586–88.

To form a present participle, add *-ing* to the infinitive form of a verb.

Did you figure out a solution to that **puzzling** *problem*? [*Puzzling* is a present participle that consists of the verb *puzzle* and the ending *-ing*.]

To form a past participle, first determine whether the verb is regular or irregular (pages 586–87).

1. *Regular verbs.* To form the past participle of a regular verb, add either *-d* or *-ed* to the infinitive form of the verb.

Infinitive	Past Participle
exhaust	exhausted

2. *Irregular verbs.* To form the past participle of an irregular verb, use a special form of the verb. See pages 587–88 for a list of past participles of commonly used irregular verbs.

Infinitive	Past Participle
freeze	frozen
tear	torn

A participle used as an adjective may have one or more auxiliary verbs. The auxiliary verb and the participle function as a unit to modify a noun or a pronoun.

Having been lost, *Jason* vowed never to drive in the city again without a map. [*Having* and *been* are the auxiliary verbs, and *lost* is the participle.]

Participial Phrases. A **participial phrase** consists of a participle and its modifiers and complements. The participial phrase functions as an adjective to modify a noun or a pronoun. Both present participles and past participles may be used to form participial phrases.

There is *Maria* **walking briskly to city hall.**

Disappointed by the cast's mediocre performance during dress rehearsal, the *director* emphasized the importance of concentration during a performance.

Having forgotten to send a birthday card, *Ed* sent a telegram to his brother.

Notice that in the preceding sentences, the participial phrases are near the words that they modify. For an explanation of the correct placement of participial phrases, see pages 622–24.

Another kind of phrase that is formed with participles is the absolute phrase. An **absolute phrase** modifies the entire independent clause (page 570) of the sentence; it does not have a direct grammatical connection with any single word in the independent clause. An absolute phrase contains both a participle and the noun or pronoun that is modified by the participle. Consequently, the phrase is "absolute," or complete within itself.

> **The flour having fallen from the top shelf of the pantry,** I had to spend half an hour cleaning the floor. [The absolute phrase modifies the entire independent clause by telling why I had to spend half an hour cleaning.]

EXERCISE 2 ## Participial Phrases

Combine each of the following pairs of sentences by rewriting one sentence as a participial phrase. Underline the participial phrases in your rewritten sentences. You may change phrasing as necessary.

1. Cathy and Elizabeth walked down the street to the health food restaurant. The restaurant offers two dinners for the price of one before five o'clock.
2. Eugene visited his uncle during spring vacation. He took the train to St. Louis.
3. Fred was informed that he must appear as a witness in court on Monday. He told his employer that he would not be able to work that day.
4. A large crowd gathered to watch the man. He was attempting to walk a high wire. The wire was attached to the roofs of two buildings.
5. Vera had looked forward to reading the new novel. She was disappointed that it was so boring.

Gerunds. A **gerund** is a verbal that ends in *-ing* and functions only as a noun. Although it functions as a noun, a gerund has some of the properties of a verb. It expresses action or being, and it may take a complement such as a direct object or an indirect object.

Used as Subject

> According to doctors, **laughing** may be one way to treat certain kinds of illness.

Used as Direct Object

> When you study, don't forget **skimming,** which allows you to review a great amount of material quickly.

Used as Indirect Object

Sue gave **skiing** high marks after her first try yesterday.

Used as Object of Preposition

To become an artist, one must first learn the fundamentals of **drawing.**

Used as Predicate Nominative

A good way to gain exercise daily is **walking.**

Used as Appositive

Most children's favorite pastime, **playing,** actually has great educational value.

Be sure that you can distinguish between gerunds and participles. They are identical in form, but participles can function as adjectives, while gerunds always function as nouns.

Gerund Phrase.   A **gerund phrase** consists of a gerund and its modifiers and complements.

┌─── gerund phrase ───┐   ┌─── gerund phrase ───
The cheering of the crowd all but prevented us from **hearing the convention's**

┌────────────┐
main speaker.

Like gerunds, gerund phrases may perform all the functions of a noun.

Used as Subject

The marching of the band made the ground tremble.

Used as Direct Object

At this point in the hearings, the committee will avoid **debating specific policy proposals.**

Used as Indirect Object

The city has given **developing new sources of revenue** the greatest importance this year.

Used as Object of Preposition

The council has voted in favor of **setting aside additional land for public parks.**

Used as Predicate Nominative

One way to reduce grocery bills is **planting a garden of tomatoes, lettuce, beans, and cucumbers.**

Used as Appositive

Elaine's summer job, **selling sportswear in a department store,** will prove valuable in her career in merchandising.

Infinitives. An **infinitive** is a verbal that consists of the first principal part (pages 586–88) of the verb. The word *to* usually, though not always, precedes the infinitive. An infinitive may function as a noun, an adjective, or an adverb. Like a participle and a gerund, an infinitive has some of the characteristics of a verb. It expresses action or being and may take a complement.

Functions as Noun

> **To relax** is Greg's goal over spring vacation. [subject]

> Because the line for the movie was so long, we decided **to leave**. [direct object]

> The purpose of speech class is **to communicate**. [predicate nominative]

Functions as Adjective

> Phyllis has an excellent *ability* **to remember**. [What kind of ability? The ability *to remember*.]

Functions as Adverb

> At the end of the play, the people *rose* **to applaud**. [Why did the people rise? They rose *to applaud*.]

> It looks to me as if the dog is too *lazy* **to run**. [To what extent is the dog lazy? It is too lazy *to run*.]

You may form an infinitive with one or more auxiliary verbs and a past participle. Such infinitives indicate the time of the action.

> The *Super Bowl* **to have watched** was the 1969 game between the New York Jets and the Baltimore Colts.

> The *route* **to be followed** is marked in red.

Note: Do not confuse infinitives and prepositional phrases. *To* followed by a verb is an infinitive, but *to* followed by a noun or a pronoun is a prepositional phrase.

Infinitive Phrases. An **infinitive phrase** consists of an infinitive and its modifiers and complements. An infinitive phrase can function as a noun, an adjective, or an adverb.

Functions as Noun

> **To buy a birthday present** is my errand at noon.

Functions as Adjective

The best *time* **to find bargains in the stores** is the last week of December. [Which time? The time *to find bargains in the stores*.]

Functions as Adverb

A crowd *gathered* **to watch the unveiling of the new sculpture.** [Why did a crowd gather? It gathered *to watch the unveiling of the new sculpture*.]

In some sentences an infinitive phrase may be used without the word *to*.

Will you help me **put up the badminton net?** [**Think:** help me *to* put up the badminton net.]

Silently, Peg's friends watched her **practice her figure skating.** [**Think:** watched her *to* practice her figure skating.]

Sometimes the infinitive has a subject. Together, the subject of the infinitive and the infinitive make up an **infinitive clause.** If the subject of the infinitive is a pronoun, that pronoun is in the objective case (pages 612–13).

—————— infinitive clause ——————
The gym teacher told **the class to run one more mile that day.** [*Class* is the subject of the infinitive.]

—————— infinitive clause ——————
Sophie's aunt and uncle asked **her to pay them a visit when she passed through**

Cincinnati.

—————— infinitive clause ——————
Dale wants **us to start a collection of art objects from around the world.**

EXERCISE 3 ## Gerunds and Infinitives

Combine each of the following pairs of sentences by rewriting one sentence as a gerund phrase or an infinitive phrase. Use the kind of phrase indicated in parentheses. Underline the verbal phrases in your rewritten sentences.

1. Andrew sat in a quiet corner of the library all afternoon. He finished Jane Austen's *Pride and Prejudice.* (infinitive phrase)
2. Carl prepared to play a minuet for his piano recital. It took hours of practice. (gerund phrase)
3. The fisherman knit the socks that he is wearing. He used wool yarn. (infinitive phrase)

4. Truck drivers spend long hours on the road and drive through all kinds of weather. If you don't mind those things, you should look further into becoming a truck driver. (gerund phrase)
5. Last Sunday our family drove around the countryside. We looked at the beautiful fall foliage. (infinitive phrase)

1.3B   CLAUSES

A **clause** is a group of related words that contains both a subject and a predicate. There are two kinds of clauses: independent clauses and subordinate clauses.

Independent Clauses

An **independent clause** can stand by itself as a sentence. The following sentence contains two independent clauses, which are in boldface type. Notice that each clause has a subject and a predicate and that each could be a separate sentence. In the following example, the subject is underlined once, and the predicate is underlined twice.

> **Our literary club intended to read *Dune,* by Frank Herbert, but we chose Ray Bradbury's *Fahrenheit 451* instead.**

A comma and the coordinating conjunction *but* join the clauses in the preceding sentence. *But* is not part of either clause. Rather, it coordinates, or connects, the independent clauses. The other coordinating conjunctions are *and, or, nor, for, so,* and *yet.*

You can also join independent clauses with either a semicolon or a semicolon and a conjunctive adverb (pages 553–54).

> Dürer's diary, letters, and memoirs of his family survive today; scholars know more about him than about many other Renaissance artists. [semicolon]

> Dürer's diary, letters, and memoirs of his family survive today; **therefore,** scholars know more about him than about many other Renaissance artists. [semicolon and conjunctive adverb]

Subordinate Clauses

A clause that cannot stand by itself is a **subordinate clause**. This kind of clause is sometimes called a **dependent clause**. In the following examples, the subjects are underlined once, and the predicates are underlined twice. However, the clauses cannot stand by themselves because they do not express complete thoughts.

> Which is one of the vanishing species in the United States

> While we are waiting for the car to be tuned up

> Although the weather has been mild

Notice that the preceding subordinate clauses begin with the words *which, while,* and *although. Which* is a relative pronoun (page 536), and *while* and *although* are subordinating conjunctions (pages 551–52). Many subordinate clauses begin with either a relative pronoun or a subordinating conjunction. Such introductory words are part of the subordinate clause, and they join the subordinate clause to an independent clause.

> ┌──────── indep. clause ────────┐ ┌──────── sub. clause ────────┐
> Most observers admire the bald eagle, **which** is one of the vanishing species in the
>
> ┌─────────┐
> United States.

> ┌──────── indep. clause ────────┐ ┌──────── sub. clause ────────┐
> Why don't we walk around the shopping center **while** we are waiting for the car
>
> ┌─────────┐
> to be tuned up?

> ┌──────── sub. clause ────────┐ ┌──────── indep. clause ────────┐
> **Although** the weather has been mild, forecasters are predicting a harsh winter.

Clauses Used as Adjectives. A clause functions as an adjective if it modifies a noun or a pronoun. Such clauses are called **adjective clauses.** Most adjective clauses begin with a relative pronoun: *that, which, who, whom,* and *whose.*

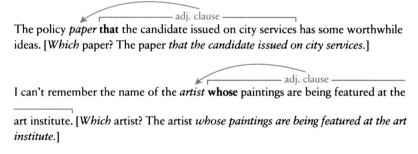

> ┌──────── adj. clause ────────┐
> The policy *paper* **that** the candidate issued on city services has some worthwhile
> ideas. [*Which* paper? The paper *that the candidate issued on city services.*]

> ┌──────── adj. clause ────────┐
> I can't remember the name of the *artist* **whose** paintings are being featured at the
>
> ┌─────────┐
> art institute. [*Which* artist? The artist *whose paintings are being featured at the art institute.*]

You may also begin adjective clauses with **relative adverbs.** Some of the relative adverbs are *after, before, since, when,* and *where.*

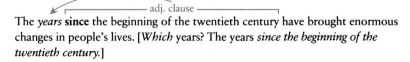

> ┌──────── adj. clause ────────┐
> The *years* **since** the beginning of the twentieth century have brought enormous
> changes in people's lives. [*Which* years? The years *since the beginning of the twentieth century.*]

Sometimes the introductory word in an adjective clause is implied rather than stated.

$$\overbrace{\qquad\qquad}^{\text{adj. clause}}$$

The *bus* the commuters usually took to work was discontinued without any announcement. [**Think:** Bus *that* the commuters usually took.]

Essential and Nonessential Clauses.
An adjective clause that is necessary to identify a noun or a pronoun is an **essential clause.** An essential clause is not separated from the rest of the sentence by commas.

Essential Clause

When our car broke down, we were lucky to find the only service

$$\overbrace{\qquad\qquad}^{\text{adj. clause}}$$

station **that** was open late at night. [The clause is essential in order to identify the station.]

A **nonessential clause** is an adjective clause that is not necessary to identify a noun or a pronoun. A nonessential clause is set off from the rest of the sentence by commas.

Nonessential Clause

The morning classes were shortened because of the

$$\overbrace{\qquad\qquad}^{\text{adj. clause}}$$

assembly, **which** featured speeches by students running for student

council. [The clause is nonessential because without it, the reader would still know which assembly is being discussed.]

EXERCISE 4 ## Adjective Clauses

Combine the following sets of sentences by writing one or more of the sentences as an adjective clause. Underline the adjective clauses in your rewritten sentences.

1. President Theodore Roosevelt was among the first people in the United States to learn judo. He was competent enough to earn a brown belt.
2. In the last one hundred years, judo has grown into an international sport. It was first included in the Olympic Games in 1964.
3. A person does not have to be big or strong to practice judo. In English the word means "the gentle way."
4. Instead of using brute strength, judo experts use timing and balance to protect themselves from their opponents. Opponents may weigh more and have more strength.
5. Judo teachers conduct their training in a gymnasium called a *dojo*. There, people take judo because it is good exercise and provides an excellent method of self-defense.

Clauses Used as Adverbs. A subordinate clause functions as an adverb when it modifies a verb, an adjective, or an adverb. Such clauses are called **adverb clauses.**

Modifies Verb

Newspapers *played* a large role in colonial America **because they supported**
——————————————— adv. clause ———————————————
and publicized the efforts of colonists protesting British rule.

Modifies Adjective

All of the neighbors were *sure* **that Mr. Wallace would recover completely**

————— adv. clause —————

from his illness.

Modifies Adverb

For her research paper, Evelyn went through the county records more

————— adv. clause —————
thoroughly **than anyone else had done before.**

An adverb clause always begins with a subordinating conjunction (pages 551–52), which is a word that shows the relationship between the subordinate clause and the independent clause. A list of frequently used subordinating conjunctions is on page 552.

Adverb clauses tell *how, when, where, to what extent,* and *why.* In the following examples, the subordinating conjunctions are in boldface type.

How

Although nervous, Sharon *greeted* the personnel director **as if** she were

——— adv. clause ———
completely at ease.

When

——— adv. clause ———
While the tide is coming in, you *should* not *stand* on those low rocks near the ocean.

Where

——— adv. clause ———
For lunch we *will meet* you **where** State and Madison streets intersect.

To What Extent

The tourists were so *eager* to see the Washington Monument

————— adv. clause —————

that they walked to it before breakfast.

Why

————————— adv. clause —————————

So that the restaurant can be sure of seating such a large party, you *should*

call ahead of time for a reservation.

Elliptical Clauses.   An elliptical clause is an adverb clause in which part of the clause is omitted. Even though the clause is incomplete, its meaning is clear; therefore, it is still classified as a clause.

┌ adv. ┐
│ clause │

You deserve more credit for the success of our fund-raising campaign **than I**. [**Think:** You deserve more credit than I *deserve*. *Than I* modifies *more*.]

————— adv. clause —————

While walking along the wharf, Larry *tripped* and *fell*. [**Think:** while *he was* walking.]

EXERCISE 5   **Adverb Clauses**

Combine each set of sentences into one sentence. Do so by rewriting one or more of the sentences as adverb clauses. You may change wording as necessary so that the resulting sentence makes sense. Underline the adverb clauses in your rewritten sentences.

1. Mrs. Sorenson has become very interested in business investing. She has signed up to take a course in investments.
2. Anne visited friends at a dairy farm in Vermont during Thanksgiving vacation. It was too expensive to fly home to Phoenix.
3. Mark crept quietly toward the deer and the fawn. He wanted to take photographs of them.
4. The officials in charge of the marathon were surprised. So many runners had qualified to run in the race!
5. The visitors lined up on the two-yard line of the home team. The crowd roared. The members of the visiting team could not hear their quarterback yell the signals.

Clauses Used as Nouns.   Clauses that function as nouns in sentences are **noun clauses.** A noun clause may function as a subject, a predicate nominative, a direct object, an indirect object, an object of a preposition, or an appositive.

Functions as Subject

```
            ┌───────── noun clause ─────────┐
```
Where the city should build a new library is the main item on the agenda at the city council meeting.

Functions as Predicate Nominative

```
                                    ┌──────── noun clause ────────┐
```
The turning point of World War II came **when the Allied forces landed successfully on the shores of Normandy.**

Functions as Direct Object

```
                              ┌──────── noun clause ────────┐
```
Research scientists are hoping **that the process of nuclear fusion will help to solve the world's energy problems in the twenty-first century.**

Functions as Indirect Object

```
                    ┌──────── noun clause ────────┐
```
Mr. Pritkin will give **whoever finds his pet poodle** a substantial reward.

Functions as Object of a Preposition

```
                                      ┌──────── noun clause ────────┐
```
The people in the train station are waiting for **whichever train arrives first.**

Functions as Appositive

```
                          ┌──── noun clause ────┐
```
It's after four-thirty, and the pranksters, **whoever they are,** are to return to my office at nine o'clock tomorrow morning.

You may introduce a noun clause with an interrogative pronoun, a subordinating conjunction, or the relative pronoun *whose.*

Interrogative Pronouns
    who, whom, whose, which, what, whoever, whomever, whatever, whichever

Subordinating Conjunctions
    how, that, when, where, whether, why

Relative Pronoun
    whose

Sometimes you may omit the introductory word in a noun clause.

```
                              ┌──────── noun clause ────────┐
```
Has anyone told the reporters **they were the winners of several awards for their documentaries this year?** [Think: informed *that* they were the winners.]

One particular kind of noun clause is the **infinitive clause.** It consists of an infinitive that has a subject. If the subject of the infinitive is a pronoun, that pronoun is in the objective case (pages 612–13) as if it were the direct object of the preceding verb. However, it is not; the entire infinitive clause serves as the direct object of the preceding verb.

┌────── infinitive clause ──────┐
They built **roads to be wider and stronger.** [*Roads* is the subject of the infinitive.]

┌─────────────── infinitive clause ───────────────┐
They designed **them to support the weight of the heavier wagons and artillery.** [*Them* is the subject of the infinitive.]

┌────── infinitive clause ──────┐
Renaissance engineers developed **pavement to serve this purpose.**

┌────── infinitive clause ──────┐
Thus gunpowder caused **Renaissance engineers to build the first paved roads.**

EXERCISE 6 ## Noun Clauses

Complete the following sentences by replacing the blank with a noun clause. The noun clause should perform the sentence function indicated in parentheses. Write the entire sentence on your paper and underline the noun clause.

1. When you walked through the tunnel, did you happen to see ___?___? (direct object)
2. ___?___ certainly left our cabin remarkably neat and clean. (subject)
3. The hope of going on the archeological dig in the spring was ___?___. (predicate nominative)
4. Although she was busy herself, Margaret always helped ___?___. (direct object)
5. Even though she receives hundreds of letters every week, the actress sends ___?___ an autographed picture. (indirect object)

1.3c ## *SENTENCES CLASSIFIED BY STRUCTURE*

Sentences are classified according to the number and kinds of clauses that they contain. The four kinds of sentences are simple, compound, complex, and compound-complex.

Simple Sentences

A sentence containing one independent clause and no subordinate clauses is a **simple sentence.** It may have any number of phrases, and it may have a compound subject, a compound predicate, or both. However, it does not have more than one clause.

Fish, underwater plants, and coral were visible in the crystal blue water.

Myra's car had a flat tire, forcing her off the road.

Compound Sentences

A sentence consisting of two or more independent clauses is a **compound sentence.** A compound sentence never has a subordinate clause. The independent clauses are usually joined with a comma and one of the coordinating conjunctions: *and, but, nor, or, for, so,* or *yet.*

```
        ————————— indep. clause ——————————          ——————————— indep. clause ——————————
```
Skydiving is an increasingly popular sport, **but** you should be in excellent physical
shape to try it.

Independent clauses may also be joined with a semicolon or with a semicolon and a conjunctive adverb such as *nonetheless, consequently,* or *still* (page 553). A comma always follows the conjunctive adverb.

```
        ————————— indep. clause ——————————          ——————————— indep. clause ——————————
```
A dirigible, a type of aircraft, is lighter than air; the first dirigible was built in
1884.

```
        ————————————————— indep. clause —————————————————
```
During the 1800s a man named John Chapman traveled throughout the Ohio
River valley and planted apple seeds; **consequently,** Chapman is known to us as
Johnny Appleseed.

Complex Sentences

A sentence consisting of one idependent clause and one or more subordinate clauses is a **complex sentence.**

```
        ————————————————— sub. clause —————————————————
```
When herders in the mountains of Switzerland want to communicate with one
another across long distances, they use a twelve-foot-long instrument that is
called an alpenhorn.

```
        ——————————————— sub. clause ———————————————
```
Paris's Arc de Triomphe, which commemorates Napoleon's victories, was not
completed until 1836 even though it was started in 1806. [The sentence contains
one independent clause: *Paris's Arc de Triomphe was not completed until 1836.*
That clause contains a subordinate clause: *which commemorates Napoleon's
victories.*]

Compound-Complex Sentences

A sentence consisting of two or more independent clauses and one or more subordinate clauses is a **compound-complex sentence.**

———— sub. clause ————
When the first synthetic fiber, rayon, was developed in 1884, the way was opened
———— indep. clause ————
for the development of modern textiles, and these textiles have revolutionized

the clothing industry.

———— sub. clause ————
Since commercial television became popular in the 1950s, the major networks
———— indep. clause ————   ——— indep. clause ———
have dominated the programming, but recent developments, which include
———— sub. clause ————
cable television and public television, may change the structure of the industry.
[The second independent clause, *recent developments may change the structure of the industry,* is interrupted by the subordinate clause *which include cable television and public television.*]

1.4 WRITING COMPLETE SENTENCES

A **complete sentence** is a group of words that has at least one subject and one predicate and that expresses a complete thought. You should use complete sentences in your writing. Two common errors in writing are the use of sentence fragments and run-on sentences. In this section you will learn how to recognize and correct both kinds of errors.

1.4A *AVOIDING SENTENCE FRAGMENTS*

A **sentence fragment** is a group of words that lacks a subject or a predicate or does not express a complete thought.

Complete Sentence
> Harriet planned to pick up the reupholstered chair on her way home.

Fragment
> Harriet planned. **To pick up the reupholstered chair on her way home.**
> [The second group of words lacks a subject and a predicate.]

Fragment
> **Harriet, planning to pick up the reupholstered chair on her way home.**
> [The group of words lacks a predicate.]

If the sentence fragment is a phrase, you can correct it by combining the fragment with a related sentence.

Fragment

> **During lunch today.** I would like to talk about the plans for the panel discussion.

Complete Sentence

> ┌── prepositional ──┐
> └─── phrase ────┘
> **During lunch today** I would like to talk about the plans for the panel discussion.

Fragment

> The zoo has acquired an anaconda. **A large snake native to South America.**

Complete Sentence

> ┌──────── appositive phrase ────────┐
> The zoo has acquired an anaconda, **a large snake native to South America.**

Fragment

> **To buy an old car and rebuild the engine.** That is what Al has decided to do.

Complete Sentence

> ┌──────── infinitive phrase ────────┐
> Al has decided **to buy an old car and rebuild the engine.**

Fragment

> I think that I saw Uncle Bill. **Waiting in line at the concession stand.**

Complete Sentence

> ┌──────── participial phrase ────────┐
> I think I saw Uncle Bill **waiting in line at the concession stand.**

Fragment

> **Paddling upstream in a canoe.** That requires a great expenditure of energy.

Complete Sentence

> ┌──── gerund phrase ────┐
> **Paddling upstream in a canoe** requires a great expenditure of energy.

If the sentence fragment is a subordinate clause used without an independent clause, you can also correct it by combining the fragment with a related sentence.

Fragment

> The entire group has decided to go to Palomar Park. **Which is featuring carnival rides at half price over the weekend.**

Complete Sentence

The entire group has decided to go to Palomar Park, **which is featuring**
————————— subordinate clause —————————
carnival rides at half price over the weekend.

Fragment

Before she leaves Florence. Harriet should be sure to see the bronze baptistry doors by Ghiberti.

Complete Sentence

┌─── subordinate clause ───┐
Before she leaves Florence, Harriet should be sure to see the bronze baptistry doors by Ghiberti.

Some sentence fragments require additions or rewording to make them complete sentences.

Fragment

The ocean, sparkling under the noonday sun.

Complete Sentence

The ocean sparkled under the noonday sun.

Fragment

The metric system, which is becoming more widely used in the United States.

Complete Sentence

The metric system is becoming more widely used in the United States.

EXERCISE 1   Eliminating Fragments

The following passage contains numerous sentence fragments. Rewrite both paragraphs, eliminating all the sentence fragments.

More than three hundred million cubic miles. That's how much water covers our planet. However, 97 percent being salty. Which leaves 3 percent fresh water. Three quarters of that fresh water is in ice caps. And in glaciers. Sixteen thousand gallons. That's how much water the average person drinks in a lifetime. Each person, using seventy gallons a day. Although the world's demand for water has more than doubled since 1960. There is still a sufficient supply to take care of humanity's needs. However, regular water shortages in certain parts of the world. Because the pattern of rainfall throughout the world is uneven. For instance, four hundred inches of rain a year in some parts of India, but no rain for several years in other parts of the world.

We can understand the effects of water shortages. When we read about the long droughts in the southwestern United States during the 1930s. When that region came to be known as the Dust Bowl. Today, many communities have devised inventive ways. To conserve water. One of the most effective being to treat sewage water and use it to water lawns and to form lakes. In spite of such efforts. There is still a great deal of waste. For instance, leaks from faucets and water pipes. Add up to 20 percent of the amount of water that a city uses. Leaks that rob the city of Chicago of one hundred fifty million gallons of water every day.

1.4B *AVOIDING RUN-ON SENTENCES*

A **run-on sentence** consists of two or more separate sentences written as one sentence. In some run-on sentences, only a comma separates the two sentences; in others, there is no punctuation at all.

Run-on

Radio and television announcers have warned people not to look at the sun during the eclipse tomorrow, doing so could result in blindness. [A comma by itself cannot connect two independent clauses.]

Run-on

Radio and television announcers have warned people not to look at the sun during the eclipse tomorrow doing so could result in blindness. [The sentences are run together without punctuation or a conjunction.]

Correct

Radio and television announcers have warned people not to look at the sun during the eclipse tomorrow, for doing so could result in blindness. [A comma and the coordinating conjunction *for* connect the two clauses.]

There are several ways to correct run-on sentences. Read the following run-on sentence. Then study the five ways in which you can correct that sentence.

Run-on Sentence

The bridge over the river is closed, a ferry will take you to the other side.

1. Separate the run-on sentence into two or more sentences.

Correct

The bridge over the river is closed. **A** ferry will take you to the other side.

2. Join the independent clauses with a comma and a coordinating conjunction (page 551).

Correct

The bridge over the river is closed, **but** a ferry will take you to the other side.

3. Join the independent clauses with a semicolon.

   Correct

   > The bridge over the river is closed; a ferry will take you to the other side.

4. Turn one of the independent clauses into a subordinate clause, and add a subordinating conjunction (pages 551–52) or a relative pronoun (page 538).

   Correct

   > **Because** the bridge over the river is closed, a ferry will take you to the other side.

5. Join the independent clauses with a semicolon and a conjunctive adverb such as *also, thus,* or *however* (page 553).

   Correct

   > The bridge over the river is closed; **however,** a ferry will take you to the other side.

EXERCISE 2   ## Eliminating Run-on Sentences

The following passage contains numerous run-on sentences. Rewrite the paragraphs, correcting all the run-ons.

The oldest map that we know about dates back about 4,300 years to ancient Babylonia, it shows an estate surrounded by mountains. As in so many other endeavors, the Greeks were ahead of their time in map making for their maps showed the world as round rather than flat, the Greeks also developed a system of longitude and latitude for identifying locations. The Romans were excellent administrators and military strategists, therefore, it is no surprise that they made worthy road maps and military maps. The most famous map maker of ancient times was Claudius Ptolemy of Alexandria, Egypt, he created a comprehensive map of the world and maps of the regions that were known to ancient travelers.

In the 1300s and the 1400s, European explorers began venturing into unknown parts of the world, consequently, they developed charts and maps to assist those who followed them. Most ships on the voyages of exploration carried chart makers and these experts made maps for coasts, islands, bays, and other geographical features that were discovered. One such map maker was the most famous explorer of all, Christopher Columbus, Martin Waldseemüller, a German who in 1507 first used the name *America* on a map was another.

USAGE AND DICTION

*H*ow is the English language used? Logic and long-continued practices have made certain ways of using words and phrases the customary ways. Knowing how to write standard, formal English is useful. In certain writing situations, such as papers and letters of application, you will want to be certain that you are taken seriously. If you use an inappropriate level of formality or nonstandard usage, you may distract, offend, or unintentionally amuse your reader.

2.1   THE SCOPE OF USAGE

The English language is dynamic. It embraces usage ranging from that found in particular occupations or professions (jargon) to that used in particular locales or by particular ethnic groups (dialect); from that used in everyday conversation (colloquial) to that used only on important occasions (ceremonial); from that used only in the past (archaic or obsolete) to that used briefly by cliques or by certain age groups (slang). Moreover, the English language is constantly changing. Words and expressions that are slang today may be accepted as part of formal usage in the future. Expressions and idioms that we commonly use today may one day be obsolete.

To communicate effectively, we must learn to recognize and to use the different levels of English usage.

2.1A   *LEVELS OF USAGE*

Formal English

Formal English is the standard English that is used for serious occasions and serious writing. It comprises the words, expressions, grammar, and standards of usage found in formal essays, research papers, scholarly writing, literary criticism, and speeches made on significant or solemn occasions. The sentences used in formal English are often long and precisely structured, sometimes employing parallelism and repetition for rhetorical effect. Formal English uses extensive vocabulary, few contractions, and almost no slang.

Informal English

Informal English is the standard English used in almost all conversation and broadcasting and in many newspapers, magazines, books, letters, and nonceremonial speeches. It is characterized by the sentence variety and length typical of conversation, by vocabulary understood and used in conversation, and by more relaxed standards of usage than those of formal English. Informal English includes contractions, colloquialisms, and slang.

Nonstandard English

Nonstandard English comprises words, expressions, and grammatical constructions that are not generally accepted as correct, although they may be accepted in certain geographic areas or by certain groups of people. Nonstandard English should not normally be used to communicate with a general audience.

2.1B *JARGON AND OCCUPATIONAL LANGUAGE*

Originally, **jargon** meant confused speech that was a mixture of several languages or dialects, or any language that sounded strange or incoherent. In some cases, it now refers to the specialized language used by persons in professions or in business.

Occupational language is the technical language used among specialists in the same profession. Although for those outside the profession it is often difficult to understand, technical language can be an efficient, precise means of communication for the specialists themselves. When the audience is more general, however, occupational language quickly becomes jargon—confused, meaningless talk characterized by vague, pretentious language. It not only obscures thought but also can confuse the reader or the listener.

Jargon

> The position afforded much interface, impacting on management objectives.

Jargon

> Our big people need to get into the paint and hit the boards if we're going to shut down their transition game.

2.1C *AVOIDING REDUNDANCY AND VERBOSITY*

Redundancy is the practice of saying or writing the same thing in several different ways to no purpose; it usually occurs because of carelessness or ignorance. **Verbosity,** or wordiness, is the practice of saying something in the most complicated way possible.

To eliminate redundancy and verbosity, use concrete words. Never avoid a short, simple word just because it is common. Use specific verbs, such as *grumbling* instead of *talking*. Repeat an idea in a phrase or a sentence only when the idea is made clearer by the repetition.

Inflated Verbosity

Having articulated his well-considered opinion to everyone gathered in the audience to listen, the author reiterated his message and fielded questions adroitly and with acuity.

Redundancy

In my opinion I think that the author expressed her theme and view of the world in what she was saying in her book.

EXERCISE

The Scope of Usage

Rewrite each of the following sentences in clear, informal English, removing jargon, redundancy, and verbosity.

1. It has been a good month saleswise, even though the net profit shows only a moderate increase over last month, which, when compared with our expectations for the new year as a whole, is disappointing.
2. It is understood that the aforementioned landowner shall lease all rights to the property, except for the rights of access outlined in the preceding paragraph, to the party of the second part, herewith referred to as Mr. Peters, for the sum of two hundred dollars per month.
3. We hope to involve ourselves in the implementation, as well as the execution, of the proposal to have installed for the well-being of those members of the community whose needs will most clearly be met by such a move, the new street light on the corner of Maple and Vine streets.
4. The gray-green color of the hospital walls, so commonplace yet so inexplicable, only served to exacerbate my already almost overwhelming sensation of nausea.
5. I am resolved, without further discussion, debate, or argument, to consider most thoroughly, if not to meditate upon, the idea, or notion, of requiring each and every member of this class, not excepting anyone, to remain following the conclusion of school if you do not immediately and forthwith cease your unnecessary, rude, impolite, and irrelevant talk.

2.2 CORRECT USE OF VERBS

Your ability to communicate increases dramatically with your ability to use verbs correctly. By changing the form of a verb, you can express its tense, the number and the person of its subject, its voice, and its mood.

PRINCIPAL PARTS OF VERBS

The four **principal parts** of a verb, the basic forms of a verb, are the infinitive, the present participle, the past, and the past participle. By using these forms alone or with auxiliary verbs, you can express the various tenses of a verb.

The infinitive and the present participle are formed in the same way for all verbs. The **infinitive** is the basic verb form that appears in the dictionary. The word *to* usually precedes the infinitive in a sentence; in some sentences, however, the word *to* is understood but not stated.

Infinitive
> Five miles is a long way *to* **walk** in the cold. Raising money for charity, however, will make us all **walk** willingly.

The **present participle** is always a combination of the infinitive and *-ing*; it is used in a sentence with a form of the verb *be* as an auxiliary verb.

Present Participle   Jenny *is* **walking** to prove to herself that she can.

Regular Verbs

Verbs are considered regular or irregular depending on how their past and past participle forms are constructed. You form the **past** and the **past participle** of any regular verb by adding *-d* or *-ed* to the infinitive. In a sentence, the past participle takes a form of the verb *have* as an auxiliary verb.

Past
> Margaret **walked** ten miles every week to get ready for the big day.

Past Participle
> We *have* **walked** several miles a week to get ready.

Here are the principal parts of two regular verbs. The auxiliary verbs in parentheses remind you that the correct form of the verb *be* is used with the present participle and the correct form of the verb *have* is used with the past participle.

Infinitive	Present Participle	Past	Past Participle
offer	(is) offering	offered	(has) offered
contribute	(is) contributing	contributed	(has) contributed

Irregular Verbs

Irregular verbs are considered irregular because they do not follow the standard rules for forming their past and past participle. Like regular verbs, however, they do use a form of the auxiliary verb *be* with the present participle and a form of the auxiliary verb *have* with the past participle. The following sentences show the correct use of the principal parts of the irregular verb *drink*.

Infinitive

You can lead a horse to water, but you can't make it **drink**.

Present Participle

The horse *is* **drinking** the water now.

Past

The horse **drank** the water when we moved away from its trough.

Past Participle

The horse *has* **drunk** all of the water.

Although no standard rules govern the formation of the past and the past participle of irregular verbs, you should have little trouble mastering their usage. You have probably already developed a good sense of what is correct by what sounds correct. Memorize the principal parts of verbs that you use frequently, and consult your dictionary for those that you do not use as often. The following list contains many common irregular verbs and should serve as a useful reference.

Infinitive	Present Participle	Past	Past Participle
be	(is) being	was	(has) been
become	(is) becoming	became	(has) become
begin	(is) beginning	began	(has) begun
bite	(is) biting	bit	(has) bitten
blow	(is) blowing	blew	(has) blown
burst	(is) bursting	burst	(has) burst
catch	(is) catching	caught	(has) caught
choose	(is) choosing	chose	(has) chosen
come	(is) coming	came	(has) come
dive	(is) diving	dived, dove	(has) dived
do	(is) doing	did	(has) done
draw	(is) drawing	drew	(has) drawn
drive	(is) driving	drove	(has) driven
eat	(is) eating	ate	(has) eaten
fall	(is) falling	fell	(has) fallen
find	(is) finding	found	(has) found
fling	(is) flinging	flung	(has) flung
fly	(is) flying	flew	(has) flown
get	(is) getting	got	(has) gotten
give	(is) giving	gave	(has) given
go	(is) going	went	(has) gone
grow	(is) growing	grew	(has) grown
have	(is) having	had	(has) had

Infinitive	Present Participle	Past	Past Participle
know	(is) knowing	knew	(has) known
lay	(is) laying	laid	(has) laid
lead	(is) leading	led	(has) led
leave	(is) leaving	left	(has) left
lie	(is) lying	lay	(has) lain
lose	(is) losing	lost	(has) lost
ride	(is) riding	rode	(has) ridden
ring	(is) ringing	rang	(has) rung
rise	(is) rising	rose	(has) risen
say	(is) saying	said	(has) said
set	(is) setting	set	(has) set
sit	(is) sitting	sat	(has) sat
speak	(is) speaking	spoke	(has) spoken
swear	(is) swearing	swore	(has) sworn
swim	(is) swimming	swam	(has) swum
tear	(is) tearing	tore	(has) torn
tell	(is) telling	told	(has) told
throw	(is) throwing	threw	(has) thrown
wear	(is) wearing	wore	(has) worn
write	(is) writing	wrote	(has) written

2.2B VERB TENSE

You use the various forms of a verb to show whether an action or a condition takes place in the present, took place in the past, or will take place in the future. The forms of a verb that express time are called **tenses.** To form tenses, you combine the principal parts with auxiliary verbs. The six English tenses are present, past, future, present perfect, past perfect, and future perfect.

To **conjugate** a verb is to list all of the forms for its six tenses. The **conjugation of a verb** also shows how the verb forms change for the first person, the second person, and the third person and for the singular and the plural.

Conjugation of the Regular Verb *Walk*

	Singular	Plural
Present Tense	I walk	we walk
	you walk	you walk
	he/she/it walks	they walk
Past Tense	I walked	we walked
	you walked	you walked
	he/she/it walked	they walked

	Singular	Plural
Future Tense	I will (shall) walk	we will (shall) walk
	you will walk	you will walk
	he/she/it will walk	they will walk
Present Perfect Tense	I have walked	we have walked
	you have walked	you have walked
	he/she/it has walked	they have walked
Past Perfect Tense	I had walked	we had walked
	you had walked	you had walked
	he/she/it had walked	they had walked
Future Perfect Tense	I will (shall) have walked	we will (shall) have walked
	you will have walked	you will have walked
	he/she/it will have walked	they will have walked

The Six Tenses of Verbs

Present Tense. To form the present tense of a verb, use its infinitive. To form the third-person singular, you usually add *-s* or *-es* to the infinitive.

◆ RULE Use the present tense to show an action that takes place now, to show an action that is repeated regularly, or to show a condition that is true at any time.

> We **walk** four miles to school.

> We **walk** every day to increase our endurance.

> We found that walking **is** good exercise. [**Think:** Walking is *always* good exercise.]

◆ RULE Use the present tense in statements about literary works or other works of art.

> *A Tale of Two Cities* **is** one of Charles Dickens's most intriguing novels. Its hero **confronts** a difficult choice.

◆ RULE Use the present tense occasionally to describe past events with special immediacy. When the present tense is used for this effect, it is called the **historical present.**

> In World War II, the English **see** London damaged severely.

In informal communication, you can use the present tense to describe future action if you include a word or a phrase that clearly indicates that the action will occur in the future.

We **walk** in the walkathon *next Monday*.

Past Tense. To form the past tense of a regular verb, add *-d* or *-ed* to the infinitive. To avoid confusion, memorize the principal parts of irregular verbs.

◆ RULE   Use the past tense to express action that occurred in the past and was completed entirely in the past.

We **walked** home from the theater last night.

Future Tense. To form the tense, combine *will* or *shall* with the infinitive form of the main verb.

◆ RULE   Use the future tense to describe action that will occur in the future.

We **will walk** in the walkathon next Monday.

Present Perfect Tense. To form the present perfect tense, use *has* or *have* with the past participle of the main verb.

◆ RULE   Use the present perfect tense to describe action that was completed either in the recent past or at an indefinite time in the past.

We **have** just **walked** farther than we have ever walked before.

Past Perfect Tense. To form the past perfect tense, use *had* with the past participle of the main verb.

◆ RULE   Use the past perfect tense to describe an action that was completed by a certain time in the past or before another action was completed.

We **had walked** the required distance before we **realized** that we could have stopped to rest.

(past perf.)   (past)

Future Perfect Tense. To form the future perfect tense, use *will have* or *shall have* with the past participle of the main verb.

◆ RULE   Use the future perfect tense to describe a future action that will be completed before another future action will be completed.

We **will have walked** ten miles before the rest of our group begins.

Tenses of Infinitives and Participles

Infinitives (page 586) and participles (page 586) have two tenses: the present and the perfect.

	Infinitive	**Participle**
Present	to walk	walking
Perfect	to have walked	having walked

◆ RULE   Use infinitives and participles in the present tense to express action that occurs at the same time as the action of the main verb.

> ┌ inf. ┐
> **Present**   I wanted **to walk** by myself.

> part.
> **Walking** alone, I saw a flock of geese.

◆ RULE   Use infinitives and participles in the perfect tense to express action that took place before the action of the main verb.

Perfect

> ┌── inf. ──┐
> **To have walked** in the walkathon makes me feel good.

> ┌── part. ──┐
> **Having walked** by myself most of the way, I gladly joined my friends for the final mile.

Progressive and Emphatic Forms and Modals

Progressive Forms.   To form the progressive, use the appropriate tense of the verb *be* with the present participle of the main verb.

◆ RULE   Use the progressive form of a verb to describe continuing action.

Present Progressive
> We **are walking** to raise money for charity.

Past Progressive
> We **were walking** near the coast.

Future Progressive
> We **will be walking** for the next two hours.

Present Perfect Progressive
> We **have been walking** for two hours.

Past Perfect Progressive
> We **had been walking** for two hours when we met the rest of our group.

Future Perfect Progressive
> We **will have been walking** for two hours by the time the main group starts.

When communicating informally, you can use the present progressive tense to express future action. Be sure to include a word or a phrase that indicates the future.

> We **are walking** in the walkathon *next Monday.*

Emphatic Forms.   To use the emphatic form, use the present or the past tense of the verb *do* with the infinitive form of the main verb.

◆ RULE   Use the emphatic form to add emphasis or force to the present and past tenses of a verb.

| **Present Emphatic** | We **do walk** every day when the weather is good. |
| **Past Emphatic** | We **did walk** before the snow began to accumulate. |

Modals.   Modals are the auxiliary verbs *can, could, do, did, may, might, must, shall, will,* and *would.* These auxiliary verbs are used with main verbs to add emphasis to a sentence or to provide shades of meaning.

◆ RULE   Use *can* (present tense) and *could* (past tense) to express ability to perform the action of the main verb.

> We **can** *call* home if we need to.

> We **could** have *taken* the car yesterday, but not today.

◆ RULE   Use *do* (present tense) and *did* (past tense) to make negative statements and to ask questions.

> We **do** not *walk* more than four miles without resting.

> **Did** you *walk* farther today than you did yesterday?

◆ RULE   Use *may* to mean "have permission to" or to express a possibility.

> His uncle said we **may** *go* now.

> We **may** *be* late if we do not hurry.

◆ **RULE** Use *might,* the past tense of *may,* to express a possibility that is somewhat less likely than one expressed by *may.*

> There is always a chance that the exam **might** *be canceled.*

◆ **RULE** Use *must* to convey the idea that the action of the main verb is required or to suggest a possible explanation.

> We **must** *return* immediately.

> We **must** *be* thoughtless to ask for such a favor.

◆ **RULE** Use *should,* the past tense of *shall,* to suggest that something ought to happen or that, although something ought to happen, it may not.

> We **should** *call* home right now. [**Think:** We ought to call.]

> We **should** *be* home right now. [**Think:** We should be, but we aren't.]

◆ **RULE** Use *would,* the past tense of *will,* to express actions that were repeated in the past or to show that you disapproved of an action in the past.

> In the winter we **would** *drive* to school every day. [repeated action]

> We were always late. Well, we **would** *leave* everything until the last minute! [disapproval]

EXERCISE 1 ## Choosing the Correct Form and Tense of Verbs

Write the following sentences, correcting all errors in the use of verbs. Underline the corrected verb forms. If a sentence has no errors, write *Correct.*

1. Having disciplined herself to read and study, Abigail Adams, the wife of President John Adams, deplored the fact that female learning was ridiculed and that girls were denied a rigorous education.
2. Fighting the New York legislature for permission to have started a school, Emma Willard went on to have made education history.
3. Public opinion about education for girls shifts back and forth until after the Civil War.
4. Some people will say that the state of women's education was a national disgrace.
5. This opinion was substantiated by European visitors who constantly commented about the uneducated women in the United States.

Sequence of Tenses

In most sentences, you use verbs that are in the same tense because the time periods described are the same. In some situations, however, you need to use verbs in different tenses to show a difference in time. You can show this difference in time effectively by changing not only the forms of the verbs but also the relationship of one verb to another.

Consistency of Tenses. When two or more actions take place at the same time, you should use verbs that are in the same tense, particularly when you write compound sentences and sentences with compound predicates. Also, remember to use the same verb tense throughout a paragraph unless the meaning of the paragraph requires that you shift tense.

◆ RULE   Use verbs in the same tense to describe actions occurring at the same time.

                       past   pres.

Incorrect   Hugh **held** the clutch in while the rest of us **push** the car.

                       past   past

Correct   Hugh **held** the clutch in while the rest of us **pushed** the car.

Shifts in Tense. If you need to show a shift from one time period to another, be sure to indicate accurately the relationships between the tenses. By changing forms and tenses, you can express precisely the time sequence that is required.

◆ RULE   If two actions occurred at different times in the past, use the past perfect tense for the earlier action and the past tense for the later one. To emphasize the closeness in time of two events, however, use the past tense for both.

        earlier   later
     past perf.   past

I **had waited** in line for hours before I **bought** my ticket. [actions that occurred at different times in the past]

        earlier   later
        past   past

We **traveled** for many miles and **reached** the coast by dark. [past actions that were close in time]

◆ RULE   If two actions occur in the present but one began in the past, use the present perfect tense for the earlier action and the present tense for the later one.

        earlier   later
     pres. perf.   pres.

Because she **has been making** calls all afternoon, Meg **feels** a sense of accomplishment.

◆ **RULE** If two actions will occur in the future, use the future perfect tense for the action that will take place earlier and the future tense for the action that will occur later.

earlier
future perf.

Because we **will have been working** on this project for several weeks before its

later
future

deadline, we **will want** to finish it correctly.

EXERCISE 2 Correct Use of Tense

Write a sentence for each set of actions indicated. Underline the verbs. If you wish, you may write your sentences about a single situation, such as a dramatic performance, an athletic contest, or a historical event.

1. Two actions occurring at the same time in the past
2. Two actions occurring in the future, one before the other
3. Two actions occurring at the same time in the present
4. Two actions occurring at the same time in the future
5. Two actions occurring in the past, one before the other
6. Two actions occurring in the present, one beginning in the past
7. An action occurring in the past and an action occurring in the present
8. An action occurring in the present and an action occurring in the future

2.2c *ACTIVE VOICE AND PASSIVE VOICE*

A verb is in the **active voice** when the subject performs the action of the verb. The active voice is generally a more direct and effective way of expressing action.

> The *audience* **applauded** the orchestra's encore.

A verb is in the **passive voice** when the subject receives the action of the verb. Use the passive voice only when you want to emphasize the receiver of the action, or when the person or thing performing the action is unknown, or occasionally when there is no other way to write the sentence. Overuse of the passive voice quickly becomes tedious and weakens your writing.

◆ **RULE** To form the passive voice, use a form of the verb *be* and the past participle of the main verb.

> The orchestra's *encore* **was applauded** by the audience.

Only transitive verbs (page 541) can be used in the passive voice. Intransitive verbs (page 541) are always in the active voice because they do not take objects.

When a verb in the active voice is changed to the passive voice, its direct object becomes the subject of the sentence, and the subject becomes the object of a preposition.

		subj.	verb		D.O.	

Active   The symphony *orchestra* **played** a Gershwin song.

Passive   A Gershwin *song* **was played** by the symphony orchestra.

When you shift a transitive verb that has both a direct object and an indirect object to the passive voice, either object can become the subject. The other object, however, remains as the complement of the verb. An object that remains as a complement in a passive construction is called a **retained object.**

Active   His friends **gave** Bill a surprise party.

Passive   Bill **was given** a suprise party by his friends.

Passive   A surprise party **was given** Bill by his friends.

◆ **RULE**   Avoid shifting from the active voice to the passive voice when describing a series of events.

Incorrect

The stable manager **fed** the horses, **was reminded** to change the straw in their stalls, and **gave** them fresh water.

Correct

The stable manager **fed** the horses, **remembered** to change the straw in their stalls, and **gave** them fresh water.

EXERCISE 3   **Active Voice and Passive Voice**

Write each verb in the following sentences and label it *Active* or *Passive*. If an active verb cannot be changed to the passive voice, write *Intransitive.*

1. Jane Austen wrote many novels about courtship and marriage, but she remained single herself.

2. Jonathan Swift's *Gulliver's Travels* satirizes humanity in a memorable way.
3. In 1926 Agatha Christie disappeared, and a cross-country search for her was conducted.
4. John Milton lost his sight but still produced poetry of great beauty.
5. Some of Maggie Tulliver's experiences in *The Mill on the Floss* were borrowed from the life of the author, George Eliot.
6. Mary Shelley wrote the classic *Frankenstein* when she was in her early twenties.
7. Charles Dickens's books were first published in serial form.
8. The popular musical *My Fair Lady* is based on George Bernard Shaw's play *Pygmalion*.

2.2D *MOOD*

In addition to tense and voice, verbs also express mood. Although you use the indicative mood more frequently, the effective use of the imperative mood and the subjunctive mood will enhance your writing.

The Indicative and the Imperative Moods

◆ RULE   Use the indicative mood to make a statement of fact or to ask a question.

Thunder often **frightens** small children.

Did you **remember** the license plate number?

◆ RULE   Use the imperative mood to make a request or to give a command.

In the imperative mood, the subject of the sentence is often understood rather than stated. Use of the imperative mood adds directness and emphasis to your writing.

Consider taking the train the next time you travel.

Take all your belongings when you leave.

The Subjunctive Mood

Of the three moods, the subjunctive mood is the most infrequently used in conversation and in informal writing. It is primarily used in formal communications, especially in diplomatic statements and in parliamentary procedure. You also use the subjunctive mood, however, to make doubtful, wishful, or conditional statements; to express something that is contrary to fact; or to ask, insist, order, request, or propose in a respectful manner.

You can use verbs in the subjunctive mood in the present tense and in the past tense.

Present Subjunctive
> If the truth **be** known, I am to be congratulated.

Past Subjunctive
> If the truth **were** known, I should have been congratulated.

The most commonly used verb in the subjunctive mood is the verb *be,* used as a linking verb or as an auxiliary verb. Study the differences between the indicative mood and the subjunctive mood in this partial conjugation of the verb *be.*

	Indicative		Subjunctive	
Present	I am	we are	(if) I be	(if) we be
	you are	you are	(if) you be	(if) you be
	he is	they are	(if) he be	(if) they be
Past	I was	we were	(if) I were	(if) we were
	you were	you were	(if) you were	(if) you were
	he was	they were	(if) he were	(if) they were

◆ RULE   Use *be* for the present subjunctive of the verb *be* regardless of its subject.

Mrs. Penwell asks that her children **be** friendly to their neighbors.

◆ RULE   Use *were* for the past subjunctive of the verb *be* regardless of its subject.

If Rudy **were** a better actor, we wouldn't have known that he forgot a line.

◆ RULE   To form the present subjunctive of verbs other than *be,* use the infinitive form of the verb regardless of its subject.

Professor Art insists that the class **listen** attentively.

◆ RULE   To form the past subjunctive of the verbs other than *be,* use *had* as an auxiliary verb with the past participle of the main verb.

If I **had seen** her, I would have invited her too.

Had I known, I would have told you sooner.

◆ RULE   To express something that is not true or that you doubt will ever be true, use a verb in the subjunctive mood in a clause that begins with *if, as if, as though,* or *that.*

Notice that something that is contrary to fact is often expressed as a wish or a condition.

Because this has been such a long day, I wish *that* I **were** home. [I am not at home.]

If I **were** you, I would ask Diane before I borrowed her book. [I cannot be you; this statement is contrary to fact.]

◆ RULE   Use the subjunctive mood in clauses that begin with *that* and that follow verbs that (1) make requests, such as *ask, prefer,* and *request;* (2) make demands, such as *demand, determine, insist, order,* and *require;* and (3) make proposals, such as *move, propose, recommend,* and *suggest.*

These clauses often appear in formal usage, particularly in standard expressions used in parliamentary procedures.

Morris recommended that the session **be postponed.**

EXERCISE 4   ## Mood

Write each verb or verb phrase in italics. Then label each one *Indicative, Imperative,* or *Subjunctive.*

1. *Hitch* your wagon to a star.
2. Edgar Allan Poe and Nathaniel Hawthorne *made* major contributions to the development of the American short story.
3. *Did* you *know* which film is an adaptation of a novel by Theodore Dreiser?
4. *Give* examples of Dickens's method of social protest in two of his novels.
5. *Would* you please *lend* me your copy of Elizabeth Barrett Browning's poems?

EXERCISE 5   ## Active Voice and Passive Voice

Write a paragraph in which you narrate a brief incident. You may invent a situation, describe a personal experience, or tell about a historical event. Use verbs in the passive voice whenever possible. Then rewrite your paragraph, changing verbs to the active voice. Finally, write a brief statement explaining which paragraph is more effective.

EXERCISE 6   ## Mood

Write a paragraph explaining to a friend how to do or make something. Use verbs in the indicative mood throughout your paragraph. Then rewrite your paragraph as a set of directions, changing verbs to the imperative mood whenever possible. Finally, write a brief statement explaining which paragraph is more effective and why.

2.3 SUBJECT-VERB AGREEMENT

2.3A *SINGULAR AND PLURAL SUBJECTS AND VERBS*

◆ RULE   A subject and its verb must agree in number.

You can change the forms of nouns, pronouns, and verbs to express number. If the subject is singular, the form of the verb should be singular. If the subject is plural, the form of the verb should be plural.

Singular
> *Grandma Moses* **was** a primitive painter who lived on farms all her life.

Plural
> Her *paintings* **are** scenes of rural life.

Verb Phrases

For a verb phrase to agree with its subject, the auxiliary verb must agree in number with the subject.

verb phrase

Singular   *Marianne* **has tried** some primitive landscapes.

verb phrase

Plural   *Marianne and I* **have taken** art lessons together.

Intervening Words and Phrases

Sometimes, words and phrases come between a subject and its verb. Such intervening words or phrases do not change the number of the subject, and, as always, the verb must agree in number with the subject. Be sure to make the verb agree in number with the subject of the sentence, not with some word in the intervening phrase.

Singular
> *Grandma Moses,* a latecomer to oils, **was** seventy-six years old when she created her first painting. [**Think:** Grandma Moses *was.*]

Plural
> The *critics* viewing her one-artist show in 1940 **were impressed** with her naive realism. [**Think:** critics *were.*]

Inverted Word Order

In some sentences, especially questions or sentences beginning with *Here* or *There*, you may have difficulty locating the subject because the verb comes before the subject. By mentally rearranging the sentence in its normal subject-verb order, you can find the subject and make the verb agree with it in number.

Singular

> In the landscape **is** a peaceful *farm*. [**Think:** farm *is*.]

Plural

> There **are** many *scenes* of farm life. [**Think:** scenes *are*.]

Singular

> **Is** Uncle George or Aunt Susan meeting us at the exhibit? [**Think:** Aunt Susan *is*.]

Plural

> Here **are** a *painting* and an *embroidery* done by Grandma Moses. [**Think:** a painting and an embroidery *are*.]

EXERCISE 1   ## Locating Subjects and Verbs

Write the verb form in each sentence that agrees in number with the subject of the sentence. Label each verb or verb phrase *Singular* or *Plural*.

1. Researchers at the University of California at Berkeley (*have constructed, has constructed*) an electric motor the width of a human hair.
2. Amazingly, the rotor in the device (*measure, measures*) only sixty microns; a human hair is seventy to one hundred microns thick.
3. Scientists here and at other research centers (*has, have*) also created gears with teeth the size of blood cells.
4. These devices, small and light enough to be inhaled, (*has been, have been*) classified as machines because of their moving parts.
5. One possible application that scientists envision for the future (*includes, include*) scissors or perhaps electric buzz saws for delicate microsurgery.

2.3B   ## DETERMINING THE NUMBER OF THE SUBJECT

In some sentences, you may find it troublesome to determine the number of the subject. To avoid confusion, pay special attention to the following types of subjects.

Compound Subjects

A **compound subject** (page 555) is composed of two or more subjects that are connected by *and, or, nor, either . . . or,* or *neither . . . nor.* A compound subject may take a singular or a plural verb, depending on (1) which conjunction is used and (2) whether the words in the compound subject are singular or plural.

◆ **RULE**   Use a plural verb with most compound subjects connected by *and*.

> **Plural**
>
> The *Prime Minister and the President* **were** to attend the meeting.

◆ **RULE**   Use a singular verb with a compound subject that refers to one person or one thing or to something that is generally considered as a unit—that is, plural in form but singular in meaning.

> **Singular**
>
> This year's most popular *author and lecturer* **is addressing** our class tomorrow. [The author and lecturer are the same person.]

◆ **RULE**   Use a singular verb with a compound subject that is composed of singular nouns or pronouns connected by *or* or *nor*.

> **Singular**   Either my *aunt or* my *uncle* **likes** to read poetry.

◆ **RULE**   Use a plural verb with a compound subject that is composed of plural nouns or pronouns connected by *or* or *nor*.

> **Plural**   Neither the farmer's *goats nor* his *sheep* **have been sold**.

◆ **RULE**   When a compound subject is composed of a singular subject and a plural subject connected by *or* or *nor,* use a verb that agrees in number with the subject that is closer to the verb in the sentence.

> **Singular**
>
>   pl.   ⌐— sing. —⌐
>
> Neither the *musicians* nor the *conductor* **is** on stage.

> **Plural**
>
>   sing.   ⌐— pl. —⌐
>
> Neither the team *manager* nor the *players* **agree** on the terms of the contract.

In following this rule, you may discover that some sentences sound awkward. In that case, rephrase the sentence.

> The *musicians* **are** not on stage, and neither **is** the *conductor*.

◆ **RULE**   When the subject is both affirmative and negative, use a verb form that agrees in number with the affirmative part of the subject.

>   pl.   sing.   pl.
>
> My *brothers, not I,* **are planning** to travel this summer.

Indefinite Pronouns as Subjects

Indefinite pronouns (pages 538–39) are pronouns that refer to people or things in general. Some indefinite pronouns are always singular and therefore always take singular verbs. The following are examples of singular indefinite pronouns:

anybody	everybody	nobody	other
anyone	everyone	no one	somebody
anything	everything	nothing	someone
each	much	one	something
either	neither		

Singular   Almost *everybody* **watches** television sometime.

Some indefinite pronouns are always plural and therefore always take plural verbs. The most common are *both, few, many,* and *several.*

Plural   *Many* **go** jogging in the park on Saturday morning.

The indefinite pronouns *all, any, enough, more, most, none, plenty,* and *some* may be singular or plural, depending on their antecedents (page 536).

Singular

All of the music presented that day **was** enjoyable. [The indefinite pronoun refers to music; it is singular and takes the singular verb *was*.]

Plural

All of the band's members **have** exceptional talent. [*All* refers to members; it is plural and takes the plural verb *have*.]

Sometimes an indefinite pronoun refers to a word that is understood rather than stated.

Even though *many* had gone, *most* **were** still at the party when we arrived. [The listener or reader would know that the pronouns refer to guests.]

Collective Nouns as Subjects

A **collective noun** (page 535) is a word that names a group of people or a collection of objects that is singular in form and may be either singular or plural in meaning. Examples include *committee, crowd, fleet, jury,* and *team.*

◆ RULE   If a collective noun refers to a group as a whole, use a singular verb.

Singular

The *crowd* **wants** action. [The crowd is thought of as a whole.]

◆ **RULE**   If a collective noun refers to individual members or parts of a group, use a plural verb.

> **Plural**
>> The *cast* **know** themselves well. [The members of the cast are acting as individuals.]

Nouns with Plural Form

Nouns such as *economics, mathematics, measles,* and *news* are plural in form but singular in meaning. Although they end in *-s,* they refer to a single thing or to a unit and therefore take a singular verb. (Notice that removing the *-s* does not make a singular noun.)

> **Singular**   *Aeronautics* **is** a subject that I have never studied.

Other nouns, such as *clothes, congratulations, pliers,* and *scissors,* end in *-s* but take a plural verb even though they refer to one thing.

> **Plural**   Your garden *shears* **are** on the workbench.

Some nouns, such as *athletics, dramatics,* and *politics,* end in *-s* but may be singular or plural, depending on their meaning in the sentence. Use your dictionary to find out whether a noun that ends in *-s* takes a singular or a plural verb.

> **Singular**   In her lecture she told us that *dramatics* **is** her avocation.

> **Plural**   His *dramatics* **are** often ignored by his friends.

Titles and Names as Subjects

Titles of individual books, stories, plays, movies, television programs, musical compositions, and magazines take the singular form of the verb even though the titles may contain plural words. The name of a country or of an organization also takes a singular verb when it refers to an entire country or group. (See pages 635 and 656 for rules regarding capitalization and underlining, or italics, for titles.)

> **Singular**
>> Hemingway's *A Farewell to Arms* **was made** into a movie.

> **Singular**
>> The *United Nations* often **sends** peacekeeping forces into troubled areas.

Words of Amount and Time

◆ **RULE**   Use singular verbs with words and phrases that refer to single units: fractions, measurements, amounts of money, weights, volumes, and intervals of time when the interval refers to a specific unit.

Singular   *One hundred yards* **is** the length of a football field.

◆ **RULE**   Use a plural verb when the amount or the time is considered to be a number of separate units.

Plural   *Five quarters* **are** all that you need to do the laundry.

When you use *the number* or *the variety* as a subject, you usually use a singular verb. When you use *a number* or *a variety* as a subject, you usually use a plural verb.

Singular   *The variety* of plants at the garden shop **is** amazing.

Plural   *A variety* of plants **are** for sale at the garden shop.

EXERCISE 2   ## Subject-Verb Agreement

Write the verb that correctly completes each sentence.

1. Neither Toronto nor Vancouver (*is, are*) as large as Montreal.
2. The entire committee (*was, were*) invited to attend the reception.
3. The bookstore and the libraries nearby (*provide, provides*) many hours of pleasure for John and his daughter.
4. Nobody (*is, are*) able to solve all the world's problems.
5. Bacon, lettuce, and tomato (*is, are*) a popular combination for a sandwich.

2.3c   ## *PROBLEMS IN AGREEMENT*

Inverted Word Order.   In some sentences, especially questions or sentences beginning with *Here* or *There,* you may have difficulty locating the subject because the verb comes before the subject. By mentally rearranging the sentence in its normal subject-verb order, you can find the subject and make the verb agree with it in number.

Singular
Near the building **was** a public park. [**Think:** park **was.**]

Plural
There **are** many ideas to be explored. [**Think:** ideas **are.**]

Singular

Is Uncle George or Aunt Susan meeting us at the restaurant? [**Think:** Aunt Susan **is.**]

Plural

Here **are** the coat and the shirt that you ordered. [**Think:** the coat and the shirt **are.**]

Sentences with Predicate Nominatives. Using a predicate nominative (page 560) can confuse subject-verb agreement when the subject and the predicate nominative differ in number.

◆ RULE   Use a verb that agrees in number with the subject, not with the predicate nominative.

Incorrect

Violets **is** one of her favorite flowers.

Correct

    subj.   P.N.

Violets **are** one of her favorite flowers. [plural subject; singular predicate nominative]

Agreement in Adjective Clauses. When a relative pronoun, such as *who, which,* or *that,* is the subject of an adjective clause (pages 571–72), decide whether the verb of the adjective clause should be singular or plural by finding the antecedent (page 536) of the relative pronoun.

◆ RULE   The verb of an adjective clause and the antecedent of the relative pronoun must agree in number.

Singular

Willie Mays, who **was** one of baseball's greatest center fielders, used to make spectacular catches. [*Who* refers to *Willie Mays,* the singular subject.]

Plural

People who **do** a job well seem to feel better about themselves. [*Who* refers to *People,* the plural subject.]

◆ RULE   When an adjective clause follows the term *one of those,* use a plural verb in the clause.

Plural

Yesterday's assignment is *one of those* that **are meant** to be a challenge.

Every *and* Many a.   As adjectives, *every* and *many a* (or *many an*) emphasize separateness when they modify subjects. *Every* teacher means "every single teacher," not "all teachers"; *many a teacher* means that each teacher is separate from all the other teachers.

◆ RULE   Use a singular verb with a single subject and with a compound subject modified by *every, many a,* or *many an.*

> *Every teacher and student* **wants** to be at the meeting.

> *Many a teacher* **corrects** papers every night.

EXERCISE 3   ## Subject-Verb Agreement

Write the verb form that correctly completes each sentence.

1. Near the congested downtown area (*stands, stand*) the Victorian houses of Carroll Avenue.
2. Their ornate architecture and their gingerbread-style trimmings are what (*makes, make*) them attractive to photographers.
3. The Bradbury Building and the Oviatt Building, both specimens of the city's nineteenth-century skyline, (*has, have*) been restored as office buildings that (*houses, house*) twentieth-century businesses.
4. Much of the architecture in Los Angeles (*seems, seem*) to reveal attempts to disguise a building's function.
5. One of the most startling sights (*is, are*) a building that (*looks, look*) like a huge ship.

2.4   CORRECT USE OF PRONOUNS

2.4A   *PRONOUN ANTECEDENTS*

All pronouns, whether they are personal, indefinite, relative, reflexive, or intensive (see pages 536–39), must agree with their antecedents in number, gender, and person (page 536).

Agreement in Number

◆ RULE   Use a singular pronoun to refer to or to replace a singular antecedent; use a plural pronoun to refer to or to replace a plural antecedent.

Singular	Plural
I, me, my, mine	we, us, our, ours
you, your, yours	you, your, yours
he, him, his	they, them, their, theirs
she, her, hers	
it, its	

Singular *Jack* said that **he** would take **his** car.

Plural Jack's *friends* said that **they** would take **their** cars.

◆ RULE   Use a plural pronoun to refer to or to replace two or more singular antecedents joined by *and;* use a singular pronoun to refer to or to replace two or more singular antecedents joined by *or* or *nor.*

Jack and Rick went to hear **their** favorite singer.

Neither Jack nor Rick wanted to drive **his** car.

Indefinite Pronouns as Antecedents.   The following indefinite pronouns are singular in meaning. Use singular pronouns to refer to or to replace them.

anybody	everybody	nobody	other
anyone	everyone	no one	somebody
anything	everything	nothing	someone
each	much	one	something
either	neither		

Singular *Each* of the women paid for **her** own ticket.

In sentences where the intended meaning of a singular indefinite pronoun is plural, use a plural pronoun to refer to or to replace the antecedent. For example, it is not sensible to use a singular pronoun in the following sentence.

Unclear

When *everybody* arrived at the theater, **he or she** bought a ticket and went inside.

Because the antecedent *everybody* really means *all* and not *each person individually,* you should use a plural pronoun or, preferably, rewrite the sentence to avoid the awkward construction.

Clear

When *everybody* arrived at the theater, **they** bought tickets and went inside.

Better

When *all* of the people arrived at the theater, **they** bought tickets and went inside.

Some indefinite pronouns, such as *several, both, few,* and *many,* are plural in meaning; use plural pronouns to refer to or to replace them.

Plural   *Several* of the students made **their** own lunches.

Some indefinite pronouns, such as *all, any, enough, more, most, none, plenty,* and *some,* can be either singular or plural. Use either singular or plural pronouns to refer to or to replace them, depending on the meaning of the sentence.

Singular

All of the color in the painting had lost **its** vibrancy. [*All* refers to *color,* which is singular; *its* refers to *all.*]

Plural

All of the books need to have **their** bindings replaced. [*All* refers to *books,* which is plural; *their* refers to *all.*]

Collective Nouns as Antecedents.   When an antecedent is a collective noun (page 535), you must first determine whether the collective noun is singular or plural in meaning. If it is singular, use a singular pronoun to refer to or to replace it; if it is plural, use a plural pronoun to refer to it.

Singular

The ad hoc *committee* voted to change **its** meeting time. [The meeting time is for the entire committee as a unit.]

Plural

The ad hoc *committee* voted to increase **their** salaries. [The committee voted for individual salaries.]

Agreement in Gender

The gender (page 536) of a noun or a pronoun is either masculine, feminine, or neuter. The masculine pronouns are *he, him,* and *his;* the feminine pronouns are *she, her,* and *hers;* and the neuter pronouns, those referring to neither masculine nor feminine antecedents, are *it* and *its.*

◆ RULE   Use a pronoun that agrees in gender with its antecedent.

Masculine	*Martin Luther King, Jr.* motivated **his** followers to take action.
Feminine	*Flannery O'Connor* based **her** stories on **her** own experience.
Neuter	A *ship* has to have **its** keel scraped annually.

Sometimes it is unclear whether the gender of a singular antecedent is masculine or feminine. If a neuter pronoun will not work, you can use the phrase *his or her* to show that the antecedent could be either masculine or feminine. This construction, however, is often awkward. If possible, rewrite the sentence so that the antecedent and all words that refer to it or replace it are plural. Sometimes you can repeat the noun that is the antecedent.

Awkward	A *lawyer* has a confidential relationship with **his or her** clients.
Better	*Lawyers* have confidential relationships with **their** clients.

Agreement in Person

Pronouns are in either the first person, the second person, or the third person (page 536).

◆ RULE   Use a pronoun that agrees in person with its antecedent.

First Person	*I will* graduate from college before **my** brother does.
Second Person	Will *you* graduate from college before **your** brother does?
Third Person	*Harriet* will graduate from college before **her** brother does.

When the indefinite pronoun *one* is an antecedent, use a third-person singular pronoun to refer to it or to replace it, or repeat the indefinite pronoun.

One often feels that **he or she** is under a microscope during exam time.

One often feels that **one** is under a microscope during exam time.

Note: In general, do not use *he* to represent both *he* and *she*. You should either repeat the noun or pronoun that is the antecedent or rewrite the sentence to make both the antecedent and the pronoun plural.

Agreement of Reflexive and Intensive Pronouns

Reflexive and intensive pronouns (pages 537–38), formed by adding either *-self* or *-selves* to personal pronouns, must also agree with their antecedents in number, gender, and person. Reflexive and intensive pronouns are always used with antecedents. Do not use them alone to replace a noun or a personal pronoun.

> **Incorrect**
>
> For the first time, Robert and I are filing income tax forms by themselves.

> **Incorrect**
>
> For the first time, Robert and myself are filing income tax forms.

> **Correct**
>
> reflexive
>
> For the first time, Robert and I are filing income tax forms by **ourselves.**

> **Correct**
>
> intensive
>
> The supervisor **herself** authorized the move.

EXERCISE 1

Pronoun Antecedents

Write the pronoun that correctly refers to the antecedent in each sentence. Make sure that each pronoun and its antecedent agree in number, gender, and person. You may have to rewrite a sentence to avoid awkwardness.

1. One of the goals of the program is for each worker to establish __?__ own production goals.
2. She is a dancer who knows when __?__ is performing well.
3. This is one of those rainstorms that last for days; I wonder when __?__ will let up.
4. Neither of the other organizations has written __?__ agenda.
5. Neither Sarah nor Jessica has __?__ umbrella with __?__.

2.4B *PRONOUN CASE*

To show the grammatical use of a pronoun in a sentence, you change its form, or **case.** The three cases are nominative, objective, and possessive.

	Singular	Plural
Nominative Case	I	we
	you	you
	he, she, it	they
Objective Case	me	us
	you	you
	him, her, it	them
Possessive Case*	my, mine	our, ours
	your, yours	your, yours
	his, her, hers, its	their, theirs

* The pronouns *my, your, his, her, its, our,* and *their* are sometimes called pronominal adjectives (page 545).

Pronouns in the Nominative Case

◆ RULE   Use the nominative case when a pronoun acts as a subject (page 555), as a predicate nominative (page 560), or as an appositive to a subject or to a predicate nominative (pages 563–564).

Subject
I would like to speak to Rosalie, please.

Predicate Nominative
This is **she.** To whom am I speaking?

Appositive to a Subject
Your *friends,* **Sandy and I,** would like you to go to the game with us.
[**Think:** Sandy and I would like.]

Appositive to a Predicate Nominative
We are the *friends,* **Sandy and I,** who helped you with your science project.
[**Think:** We are Sandy and I.]

Pronouns in the Objective Case

◆ RULE   Use the objective case when a pronoun acts as a direct object (page 558), as an indirect object (page 559), as an objective complement (page 559), as an object of a preposition (page 562), as a subject of the infinitive clause (page 569), as an appositive to a direct or an indirect object (pages 563–64), or as an appositive to an object of a preposition (pages 563–64).

Direct Object

> Mara met **her** just before school began.

Indirect Object

> She lent **her** a notebook for her first class.

Object of a Preposition

> Nancy gave it back to **her** after her class.

Subject of an Infinitive Clause

> Mr. Mitchell told **them** to see him after school.

Object of an Infinitive Clause

> Mara wanted to ask **him** why he wanted to see **them.**

Appositive to a Direct Object

> She liked her *friends,* **Mara and her.**

Appositive to an Indirect Object

> She told *them,* **Mara and her,** the whole story.

Appositive to an Object of a Preposition

> Mr. Mitchell wanted to read over their papers with both of *them,* **Mara and her.**

Pronouns in the Possessive Case

Possessive pronouns show to whom or to what something belongs. They do not include apostrophes.

◆ RULE   Use the possessive pronouns *mine, yours, his, hers, its, ours,* and *theirs* to refer to or to replace nouns.

You can use these possessive pronouns in the same way that you would use nouns: as subjects, predicate nominatives, direct or indirect objects, objects of prepositions, or appositives.

Subject

> **Hers** is the short story that won first place.

Predicate Nominative

> The second-place short story is **his.**

Direct Object

> After thinking about the plot for a long time, Kathleen wrote **hers** in two hours.

Indirect Object

> Carl gave **hers** a rave review.

Object of a Preposition

We should really find a publisher for **theirs.**

Appositive

A publisher has requested that both *stories,* **hers** and **his,** be submitted at once.

◆ RULE   Use the possessive pronouns* *my, your, his, her, its, our,* and *their* to modify nouns.

Will you visit *your* grandparents this summer?

◆ RULE   Use a possessive pronoun to modify a gerund.

Gerunds (pages 566–67) are *-ing* forms of verbs that are used as nouns. Because they function as nouns, use the possessive forms of nouns and pronouns to modify them.

Your visiting your grandparents will be a great pleasure for them. [*Your* is used instead of *you* because it is the *visiting—your visiting—*that will be a great pleasure for them.]

Compound Constructions with Pronouns

It is sometimes troublesome to choose the correct case for pronouns in compound constructions, such as compound subjects or compound objects of a preposition. To determine which case you should use, say the sentence to yourself, leaving out the conjunction and the noun or the other pronoun in the compound construction. When you have determined how the pronoun functions by itself, you can decide whether to use the nominative case or the objective case.

Thomas and **they** are responsible for the decorations. [**Think:** *They* are responsible for the decorations.]

Between you and **me,** I think David deserved to win. [Because *you* and *me* are compound objects of the preposition *between,* use a pronoun in the objective case, *me.*]

EXERCISE 2   **Pronoun Case**

Write the correct pronoun for each sentence; then indicate how the pronoun is used in the sentence.

1. (*We, Us*) guards will see that nothing is taken from the museum without permission.

---

* These possessive pronouns are sometimes called pronominal adjectives (page 545).

2. The three contestants, the twins and (*I, me*), took our places at the starting line.
3. Answering the door, we discovered that it was (*he, him*).
4. (*You, Your*) moving to another town will make it difficult for (*we, us*) to practice together.
5. Did you realize when you met them that it was (*them, they*)?

Who *and* Whom

You can use the forms of the word *who* either as interrogative pronouns (page 538) or as relative pronouns (page 538). As is true of other pronouns, the way that you use the pronoun determines which case or form of the word you should choose. *Who* and *whoever* are in the nominative case; *whom* and *whomever* are in the objective case; *whose* is in the possessive case.

Who *and* Whom *as Interrogative Pronouns.*

Who and *whom* are interrogative pronouns when they introduce questions. To determine whether to use *who* (the nominative case) or *whom* (the objective case), simply turn the question into a statement.

◆ RULE   Use *who* when an interrogative pronoun acts as a subject or as a predicate nominative. Use *whom* when an interrogative pronoun acts either as an object of a verb or as an object of a preposition.

Nominative

> **Who** is singing the lead in *Madama Butterfly*? [*Who* is the subject of the verb *is singing.*]

Objective

> To **whom** did you speak when you telephoned the White House today? [*Whom* is the object of the preposition *to.*]

If the interrogative pronoun *who* or *whom* is followed by an interrupting phrase, such as *do you feel,* you can mentally rearrange the sentence to determine the use of the pronoun in the sentence and which form of the pronoun to use.

> **Who** do you feel will best fill the position of vice president? [**Think:** Who will best fill the position? *Who* is the subject.]

In informal writing and in conversation, *who* is often used to ask a question, regardless of whether the nominative or the objective case is needed. In formal usage, however, you should follow the rules for using the nominative case, *who,* and the objective case, *whom.*

Informal	**Who** do you plan to go with to the movie?
Formal	With **whom** will you attend the plenary session next week?

Who *and* Whom *as Relative Pronouns.* When forms of the word *who* introduce subordinate clauses (pages 570–71), they are relative pronouns. Choose the form of the word to use by its use in the subordinate clause, *not* by its use in the main clause.

◆ RULE   Use *who* or *whoever* when a relative pronoun is the subject of the subordinate clause; use *whom* or *whomever* when a relative pronoun is an object within the subordinate clause.

The new teacher, **who** has been here only a week, has made many friends among the students and faculty. [*Who* is the subject of the clause *who has been here only a week*.]

My mother, **whom** many people respect, was honored at a testimonial dinner. [*Whom* is the direct object of *respect*.]

EXERCISE 3   *Who* and *Whom*

Write the pronoun that is correct in formal usage. Also, indicate how the pronoun is used in the sentence.

1. Jason's aunt, (*who, whom*) is almost ninety years old, lives with him and his family.
2. The students did not know (*who, whom*) their new mathematics teacher would be.
3. Nobody saw (*who, whom*) placed the chair on top of the flagpole.
4. Patricia, (*who, whom*) I saw just yesterday, is leaving today for a cross-country bicycle trip.
5. It was John Donne (*who, whom*) wrote, "Ask not for (*who, whom*) the bell tolls; it tolls for thee."

Pronouns in Appositive Phrases

The pronouns *we* and *us* are often used in appositive phrases, such as *we engineers* or *us pilots*. Because an appositive explains or renames the word with which it is in apposition, you must first determine how the appositive phrase is used in the sentence. If the phrase is a subject or a predicate nominative, use the nominative case of the pronoun. If the phrase is an object, use the objective case.

To determine which case to use, say the sentence to yourself without the noun in the appositive phrase.

Nominative

We engineers attended the computer conference in Los Angeles last April. [**Think:** We attended. Because *we* and *engineers* are subjects, *we* is in the nominative case.]

Objective

The refresher course for **us pilots** will be given again in the spring.
[**Think:** The refresher course for **us.** Because *us* and *pilots* are objects of the preposition *for,* *us* is in the objective case.]

Pronouns in Comparisons

In some comparisons using *than* or *as,* part of the phrase or clause is not stated but is merely implied. To choose the correct pronoun, mentally supply the missing words to determine how the pronoun is used. Because the case of the pronoun used in an incomplete comparison can alter your intended meaning, make your choice carefully. In the following examples, notice the change in meaning according to the choice of pronoun.

Nominative

I will walk as far with you as **she.** [**Think:** as far as she will walk. Use the nominative-case pronoun because *she* is the subject of the implied clause, *she will walk with you.*]

Objective

I will walk as far with you as **her.** [**Think:** as far with you as with her. Use the objective-case pronoun *her* because the intended meaning makes *her* the object of the implied preposition *with.*]

EXERCISE 4 ## Other Uses of Pronoun Case

Write the correct pronoun for each of the following sentences.

1. Will you arrive home sooner than (*I, me*)?
2. The crate was a great deal heavier than (*they, them*) thought.
3. The crate was a great deal heavier than (*they, them*).
4. Do you think my present made her as happy as (*I, me*)?
5. Mrs. Berstein asked (*we, us*) neighbors to water her lawn while she was away.

2.4c *CORRECT PRONOUN REFERENCE*

To avoid confusing your listeners or readers, be certain that the pronouns you use refer clearly to their antecedents. If you find an unclear reference, rephrase the sentence.

◆ RULE Avoid using a pronoun that could refer to more than one antecedent.

Unclear

Jerry picked Bill to be on his team because he knows the game well. [Who knows the game well? The antecedent of *he* is unclear.]

Clear

Jerry picked Bill to be on his team because Bill knows the game well.

◆ **RULE**   In formal usage, avoid using the pronoun *it, they, you,* or *your* without a clear antecedent.

The following example shows how you can usually replace the pronoun with a noun to eliminate confusion.

Unclear

I forgot my umbrella and my flashlight. When I thought about it, I laughed. [What is *it?* The pronoun has no clear antecedent.]

Clear

I forgot my umbrella and my flashlight. When I thought about my forgetfulness, I laughed.

◆ **RULE**   Do not use the pronoun *your* in place of an article (*a, an,* or *the*) if possession is not involved.

Avoid   Many of your gymnasts have been training for years.

Use   Many gymnasts have been training for years.

◆ **RULE**   Avoid using *which, it, this,* and *that* to refer to ideas that are not clearly stated.

The following example demonstrates how you can avoid making such general references.

General

We went to every game in the series, but we didn't see anyone hit a home run, which was quite disappointing. [The pronoun *which* has no clear antecedent; instead, *which* refers generally to an idea in the previous sentence.]

Clear

We went to every game in the series, but we were quite disappointed because we didn't see anyone hit a home run.

EXERCISE 5   **Pronoun Reference**

Rewrite the following sentences, making certain that all pronoun references are clear and accurate. If a sentence is correct, write *Correct.*

1. Examination of the table of contents of Shakespeare's First Folio shows that when *Timon of Athens* first appeared it replaced *Troilus and Cressida*.

2. Although there are a great many pre-Columbian metal objects in museums and private collections, we know relatively little about the techniques or implements that they employed in its manufacture.

3. Like Antwerp's, New York's rise from provincial capital to cosmopolitan center demonstrates its historical connections between the development of trade and the flowering of culture and art.

4. It is characteristic of organizations that they are not immortal; they may not seem it, but they flourish and then die just as a living organism does.

5. For all its immense intellectual vigor, the James family was one beset by personal calamities and disorders.

2.5 CORRECT USE OF MODIFIERS

2.5A *COMPARISON OF MODIFIERS*

By using different forms of adjectives and adverbs, you can compare two or more persons or things. The three degrees of comparison are positive, comparative, and superlative.

The Three Degrees of Comparison

You use a modifier in the **positive degree** to assign some quality to a person, a thing, an action, or an idea. You use a modifier in the **comparative degree** to compare a person, a thing, an action, or an idea with another one. You use a modifier in the **superlative degree** to compare a person, a thing, an action, or an idea with at least two others.

	Adjectives
Positive	That line is **long.**
Comparative	That line is **longer** than the one for the other movie.
Superlative	That line is the **longest** one that I have ever seen.

	Adverbs
Positive	Roger behaves **maturely.**
Comparative	Roger behaves **more maturely** than Eric.
Superlative	Of all the students, Roger behaves the **most maturely.**

Using Comparisons Correctly

◆ RULE Add the suffix *-er* to form the comparative and the suffix *-est* to form the superlative of modifiers with one or two syllables.

In some cases, to form the comparative modifier correctly, you must drop a final *-e,* double a final consonant, or change a final *-y* to *-i-* before adding the suffix.

> short, shorter, shortest

> funny, funnier, funniest

◆ RULE   Use *more* to show the comparative degree and *most* to show the superlative degree in three instances: with all three-syllable words, with two-syllable words that would otherwise be difficult to pronounce, and with adverbs ending in *-ly.*

> serious, more serious, most serious

> dreadful, more dreadful, most dreadful

> restfully, more restfully, most restfully

◆ RULE   Use *less* and *least* to form the comparative and superlative degrees of comparisons showing less.

> humorous, less humorous, least humorous

> hopeful, less hopeful, least hopeful

> ambitiously, less ambitiously, least ambitiously

Remember, also, that some modifiers are irregular and do not form comparisons in a standard way. You should memorize them to be able to use them correctly.

bad, worse, worst	little, less, least
far, farther, farthest	many, more, most
far, further, furthest	much, more, most
good, better, best	well, better, best
ill, worse, worst	

◆ RULE   Avoid double comparisons. Use either the word *more* or *most* or else the appropriate suffix; do not combine the two.

Incorrect   Jim is **more funnier** than anyone else in the group.

Correct   Jim is **funnier** than anyone else in the group.

◆ RULE   Avoid incomplete comparisons by clearly indicating the things being compared.

When you compare one member of a group with the rest of the group, you can avoid being unclear or misleading by using the comparative degree and the word *other* or *else*.

Unclear
> Richard plays the oboe better than anyone in the class. [This sentence says either that Richard plays the oboe better than anyone in the class, including himself, or that Richard plays the oboe better than anyone in a class of which he is not a part.]

Clear
> Richard can play the oboe better than anyone **else** in the class. [Richard is the best oboe player in **his** class.]

◆ RULE   Use the words *as . . . as* or *as . . . as . . . than* to complete a compound comparison.

A **compound comparison** really makes two statements by using both the positive and the comparative degrees of a modifier. The positive degree shows that the things being compared are at least equal or similar; the comparative degree shows that they may, in fact, be different. Because you would still have a complete sentence if you removed the second, or parenthetical, part of the comparison, use commas to set off the parenthetical part from the rest of the sentence.

> Being on time to my 8:00 A.M. class is **as** difficult **as,** if not more difficult **than,** being on time to my 7:00 A.M. class.

> Being on time to my 8:00 A.M. class is **as** difficult **as** being on time to my 7:00 A.M. class, if not more difficult.

◆ RULE   Avoid making comparisons that are illogical because of missing or faulty elements or because no comparison can be made.

To avoid having your reader or listener misunderstand your meaning, rephrase the comparison to include all of the important words.

Illogical
> Sarah writes computer programs that are as complicated as Francine. [Computer programs cannot be compared to Francine. Sarah can write programs; she cannot write Francine.]

Logical
> Sarah writes computer programs that are as complicated as Francine's. [**Think:** Sarah's programs are as complicated as Francine's programs.]

Certain adjectives, such as *perfect, unique, dead, round, full,* and *empty,* do not have a comparative or superlative degree because they express an absolute condition. Because logically nothing can be "more perfect" or "more empty," use the forms *more nearly* or *most nearly* when you use these words in comparisons.

Jim's plate was the most nearly empty at the end of the meal.

EXERCISE 1 Correct Use of Comparisons

Write the correct form of the modifier given in parentheses. Identify the degree of comparison of each correct modifier.

1. *Mutiny on the Bounty* is one of the (*more engrossing, most engrossing*) novels that I have ever read.
2. Your solution is good, but his is (*better, best*).
3. Of the four faces carved on Mount Rushmore, the one that seems (*less lifelike, least lifelike*) is Theodore Roosevelt's.
4. Does a liquid quart or a liter have the (*greater, greatest*) volume?
5. I am not certain which is the (*shorter, shortest*) book: *Ethan Frome, The Pearl,* or *Of Mice and Men.*

2.5B *PLACEMENT OF PHRASES AND CLAUSES*

◆ RULE   Place modifying phrases and clauses as close as possible to the words that they modify.

Misplacement of phrases and clauses can create unclear and unintentionally humorous sentences. To avoid misplacing modifiers, identify the word to be modified and place the modifying phrase or clause as close as possible to that word while retaining your intended meaning.

Unclear

Mrs. Santos decided to support the referendum, persuaded by the editorial. [The phrase *persuaded by the editorial* appears to be modifying *referendum,* thereby distorting the meaning of the sentence.]

Clear

Mrs. Santos, persuaded by the editorial, decided to support the referendum.

Clear

Persuaded by the editorial, Mrs. Santos decided to support the referendum.

Notice in the following example that improper placement of the modifying phrase can alter the meaning of the sentence. As you revise your sentences, check to be certain that your intended meaning is still clear.

Unclear

Strolling by the lake, a family of ducks walked in front of me. [Who was strolling by the lake?]

Clear

Strolling by the lake, I noticed a family of ducks in front of me. [Meaning: I was strolling by the lake when I noticed the ducks in front of me.]

Clear

In front of me, I noticed a family of ducks strolling by the lake. [Meaning: The ducks were strolling by the lake.]

◆ RULE   To avoid dangling modifiers, provide an antecedent for every modifying phrase or clause to modify.

A **dangling modifier** is a modifying phrase or clause that does not clearly or logically modify any word in the sentence; a dangling modifier can make a sentence unclear or unintentionally humorous.

Unclear

Before going home, the door must be locked. [Who is going home?]

Clear

Before going home, you must lock the door. [The adverb phrase *before going home* now modifies the verb phrase *must lock.*]

You can also correct a dangling phrase by changing the phrase to a subordinate clause.

Clear   Before you go home, the door must be locked.

In current usage some dangling modifiers have become accepted as part of idiomatic expressions. These are usually such present and past participles as *allowing for, based on, considering, concerning, failing, generally speaking, granting, judging,* and *owing to.*

Judging from the cover, the magazine is about computers.

Based on available information, the scholarship committee won't be meeting until July.

You can determine whether an expression is acceptable even though it may seem to be a dangling modifier by asking yourself these questions: "Does the reader expect a word for the phrase to modify, or is the phrase or clause common enough to be considered an idiom? Is the meaning of the sentence clear?"

EXERCISE 2   Placement of Modifiers

Rewrite each of the following sentences, eliminating all misplaced or dangling modifiers.

1. Being newcomers to the community, the one-way streets confused the Bryants.
2. Roasted over charcoal, we particularly like corn on the cob.
3. Having practiced the role for a month, the prospect of an audition no longer alarmed Lucille.
4. After attending college and law school for seven consecutive years, a break in the academic routine was welcome.
5. Upon receiving the defective record, it was immediately returned to the mail-order house.

EXERCISE 3   Use of Modifiers

Write sentences using each of the following phrases correctly.

1. made of a gritty substance
2. more accurately
3. in spite of repeated warnings
4. examining the beaker
5. at the age of eighteen
6. speaking in a stentorian voice
7. as miraculous
8. according to the theory of
9. most obedient
10. acting petulant
11. misinterpreting their intentions
12. feigning ignorance
13. as outspoken
14. less productive
15. if not sooner

2.6 USAGE GLOSSARY

a lot, alot   *A lot* means "a great number or amount" and is always two words; avoid using *a lot* in formal usage. *Alot* is not a word.

accept, except   *Accept* is a verb that means "to agree" or "to receive." *Except* is a preposition that means "leaving out" or "but."

> We did not want to **accept** the expensive gift.

> Beth has taken every art course offered by the school, **except** the course on silk screening.

adapt, adopt   *Adapt* means "to change or adjust" or "to make more suitable." *Adopt* means "to take or accept."

> Since he had always lived in a warm climate, it took Jeremy several months to **adapt** to our cold climate.

> The Macintosh family has decided to **adopt** a child.

advice, advise   *Advice* is a noun that means "helpful suggestion or opinion." *Advise* is a verb that means "to give or offer counsel."

> My accountant **advised** me to file my income tax forms on time. Unfortunately, I did not follow that **advice**.

affect, effect   *Affect* is a verb that means "to influence." *Effect* can be a verb that means "to bring about or achieve" or a noun that means "result."

Because our town was not directly **affected** by the flood, we could offer refuge to several families who were forced out.

The severe storm **effected** a change in our travel plans. [verb meaning "brought about"]

The **effects** of the flood were less extreme than we had thought. [noun meaning "results"]

all ready, already   *All ready* functions as a compound adjective that means "entirely ready" or "prepared." *Already* is an adverb that means "before some specified time" or "previously." Do not confuse the two.

Are you **all ready** to begin the test?

I can't believe that you've **already** finished that typing!

all right, alright   *All right* means "satisfactory," "unhurt," "correct," or "yes, very well." *Alright* is an incorrect spelling. Do not use it.

Because we were so late, we telephoned Uncle Jack to let him know that we were **all right.**

All right, who has a better suggestion?

all the farther, as far as   *All the farther* should not be used for *as far as.*

Two miles is **as far as** I will run today. [not *all the farther*]

among, between   Use *among* for comparisons involving groups of persons or things. Use *between* when only two items are being considered at a time.

Only one **among** all the race car drivers would win.

Can you tell the difference **between** a jonquil and a daffodil?

amount, number   Use *amount* with a noun that names something that can be measured or weighed. Use *number* to refer to things that can be counted.

A large **amount** of snow fell last night.

A large **number** of snowstorms are expected next winter.

anxious, eager   Both words can mean "strongly desirous," but you should use *anxious* to suggest concern or worry.

Abigail was **anxious** to get to work before the storm broke.

any more, anymore   These terms are not interchangeable. The phrase *any more* describes quantity; *any* is an adverb modifying the adjective *more*. *Anymore* is an adverb meaning "at present" or "from now on."

Is there **any more** traffic on the bridge than there is in the tunnel?

I don't drive to work **anymore.**

appraise, apprise   *Appraise* means "to evaluate"; *apprise* means "to inform."

Having **appraised** the old desk, the antique dealer **apprised** its owner that it was worth one thousand dollars.

apt, liable, likely   In informal usage, these words are often used interchangeably. In formal usage, only *apt* and *likely* are interchangeable, meaning "tending to" or "inclined to be." Use *liable* to suggest the probability of a harmful, unfortunate, or negative event or to show exposure to legal action.

Robert is **apt** to be unpleasant when he first awakens in the morning.

Mark is **liable** to strain a muscle during the game if he doesn't start practicing more regularly.

Barbara was **liable** for damages when her daughter accidentally knocked over a carton of glassware in the department store.

as, like   In formal usage, *like* is most often used as a preposition to introduce a prepositional phrase. *As* is most often used as a conjunction to introduce a subordinate clause.

Margot thinks **like** her father. [prepositional phrase]

Margot thinks **as** her father does. [subordinate clause]

In informal usage, *like* is sometimes used as a conjunction. Avoid using *like* as a conjunction in formal usage in place of *as, as if,* or *as though.*

Avoid

    The hikers felt **like** they had walked twenty miles.

Use

    The hikers felt **as if** they had walked twenty miles.

beside, besides   *Beside* means "next to." *Besides* means "in addition to."

    I parked the car **beside** our neighbor's truck.

    Besides a truck, our neighbor owns a station wagon.

between, among   See *among, between.*

between you and me   Never use the nominative case *I* as the object of a preposition. *Between* is a preposition.

    The discussion is **between you and me.** [not *between you and I*]

both, either, neither   When used to modify compound elements, place *both, either,* and *neither* just before the compound construction. The elements in the compound construction should be parallel or similar in form.

Incorrect

    Nelson intends **both** to study business and engineering.

Correct

    Nelson intends to study **both** *business* and *engineering.*

bring, take   Use *bring* when you mean "to carry to." Use *take* when you mean "to carry away."

    Bring your swimming suit with you when you come to the party.

    Remember, **take** your swimming suit with you when you go to the party.

compare to, compare with   Use *compare to* when pointing out similarities; use *compare with* when pointing out similarities and differences.

    In that metaphor the bright yellow flowers are **compared to** sunshine.

Compared with a tornado, this is a minor windstorm.

credible, creditable, credulous   *Credible* means "believable" or "worthy of belief." *Creditable* means "worthy of commendation." *Credulous* applies always to people and means "willing to believe" or "gullible."

    It was a **credible** story; we did not need to force ourselves to become involved in the plot.

    The movie director did a **creditable** job; the movie won three awards.

    Rick is a **credulous** young man; he thought that the science fiction about robots running the Pentagon was true.

data is, data are   *Data* is the plural form of the Latin *datum.* In formal English it should be followed by a plural verb. In informal English a singular verb may be used.

differ from, differ with   Thing (or persons) *differ from* each other if they are physically dissimilar. When persons *differ with* each other, they are in disagreement.

    Children **differ from** adults.

    I **differ with** Hank about the need for a new stadium.

different from, different than   Use *different from.* Do not use *different than* except to introduce a subordinate clause.

    My ideas are **different from** hers. [not *different than*]

    My ideas are **different than** hers are.

disinterested, uninterested   *Disinterested* implies a lack of self-interest; it is synonymous with *unbiased* or *impartial. Uninterested* implies a lack of any interest.

    Although I am **disinterested** in which party wins the court case, I am not **uninterested** in the principles of law that are being challenged by the case.

eager, anxious   See *anxious, eager.*

effect, affect   See *affect, effect.*

e.g., i.e. *E.g.* stands for the Latin words *exempli gratia*, meaning roughly "an example for free." *E.g.* means "for example" in English. *I.e.* stands for the Latin words *id est*, meaning "that is," and should be used to cite an equivalent. Use both sparingly.

either, both, neither See *both, either, neither.*

eminent, imminent *Eminent* means "prominent" or "outstanding in some way." *Imminent* means "about to occur."

> We were fortunate that the **eminent** historian agreed to visit our school.

> The heavy, dark clouds indicated that a storm was **imminent.**

et al. This is a Latin abbreviation for *et alii* and means "and others" (persons, not things). It is used most often in footnotes to refer to other members of a team of authors.

etc. This Latin abbreviation for *et cetera* means "and other things," "and so forth." Avoid using *etc.* in formal writing; use *and so forth* instead. Do not use *and etc.;* it is redundant.

except, accept See *accept, except.*

explicit, implicit These adjectives are antonyms. *Explicit* refers to something that is directly stated. *Implicit* refers to something that is not directly stated.

> Patty was **explicit** in her description of the swearing-in ceremonies.

> Betty's feelings about her mother were **implicit** in her willingness to help her in any way she could.

famous, noted, notorious *Famous* means "renowned or celebrated." *Noted* means "celebrated." *Notorious* means "known widely and regarded unfavorably."

> The **famous** (*or* **noted**) economist predicted that inflation would continue.

> The **notorious** prankster was finally caught and punished.

farther, further These two words are not interchangeable. *Farther* means "more distant in space." *Further* means "more distant in time or degree, additional."

> Bill swam **farther** than Tom did.

> The **further** you investigate this story, the more confused the facts seem to be.

> Conway **further** discussed his ideas about pedestrian safety.

fewer, less Use *fewer* to refer to things that you can count individually. Use *less* to refer to quantities that you cannot count and to amounts of time, money, or distance when the amount is a single quantity.

> There were **fewer** requests for help this week than last week.

> I have **less** trouble with number concepts than he does.

> I have **less** than three dollars in my pocket.

first, firstly; second, secondly Use *first* and *second*, not *firstly* and *secondly* to mean "in the first (or second) place."

> **First,** put the flowers into a vase. [not *Firstly*]

formally, formerly These two words sometimes sound alike but have distinct spellings and meanings. *Formally* means "in a formal or official manner." *Formerly* means "previously" or "at an earlier time."

> Beth spoke **formally** to the audience.

> He **formerly** was a doctor.

further, farther See *farther, further.*

good, well *Good* is an adjective. *Well* can be an adverb or a predicate adjective meaning "satisfactory" or "in good health." The opposite of feeling sick is feeling *well*.

> Fuller is a **good** writer.

> Oliver teaches **well.**

> Are you feeling **well?**

half a   Use *a half* or *half a(n)*. Do not use *a half a(n)*.

> Will drove by about **a half** hour ago. [not *a half an hour*]

have, of   *Have* and *of* sound similar in rapid speech, but they are different parts of speech. *Have* is a verb; *of* is a preposition. Be careful to say and write *have* when completing a verb phrase, especially after the helping verbs *should, would,* and *could.* *Of* is not a verb.

> We **should have** visited him earlier. [not *should of*]

hopefully   *Hopefully* means "with hope," not "I hope."

Unclear

> Hopefully, I will deliver my speech. [Do you hope to deliver your speech or will you deliver a hopeful speech?]

Improved

> I hope to deliver my speech.

i.e., e.g.   See *e.g., i.e.*

imminent, eminent   See *eminent, imminent.*

implicit, explicit   See *explicit, implicit.*

imply, infer   *Imply* means "to hint at" or "to suggest." *Infer* means "to reach a conclusion based on evidence or deduction." These words are not interchangeable.

> I **implied** in my remarks that the council should approve the plans to build a new school.

> I **inferred** from the applause that followed my remarks that the audience supported my suggestion.

in, into   Use *in* to mean "within" and *into* to suggest movement toward the inside from the outside.

> Ruth walked **into** the store to buy supplies for the camping trip.

> While she was **in** the store, she found the lantern that she wanted.

ingenious, ingenuous   *Ingenious* means "clever"; *ingenuous* means "naive."

> The **ingenious** child was always trying to invent questions that we couldn't answer.

> The newcomer was so **ingenuous** that we had to explain even the most basic things to him.

irregardless, regardless   Do not use *irregardless;* it is a double negative. Use *regardless* instead.

> We will call you when we arrive, **regardless** of the time.

its, it's   *Its* is a possessive pronoun; *it's* is the contraction for *it is.*

> The bear was standing on **its** hind legs, ready to attack.

> **It's** a nice day, so leave your heavy jacket at home.

kind of, sort of   Do not use these terms to mean "somewhat" or "rather." See also *these kinds, this kind.*

> The casserole is **rather** tasty. [not *kind of* or *sort of*]

lay, lie   *Lay* is a transitive verb that means "to put or to place something somewhere." It always takes a direct object. *Lie* is an intransitive verb that means "to be in or to assume a reclining position." It does not take a direct object. (See page 588 for the principal parts of these irregular verbs.)

> **Lay** the placemats on the table before you **lie** down to rest.

leave, let   *Leave* means "to go away" or "to abandon." *Let* means "to permit" or "to allow."

> Will you **let** me **leave** with them on the train tomorrow?

less, fewer   See *fewer, less.*

liable, apt, likely   See *apt, liable, likely.*

lie, lay   See *lay, lie.*

like, as   See *as, like.*

likely, apt, liable   See *apt, liable, likely.*

many, much   Use the adjective *many* to describe things that you can count (pencils, people). Use the adjective *much* to describe things that you cannot count (gas, truth, strength). When used as indefinite pronouns, *much* is singular and *many* is plural.

> **Many** responded to our requests for volunteers.
>
> **Much** was expected, but little was gained.

may, might   See "Modals," pages 592–93.

myself, yourself   Do not use a reflexive pronoun in place of *I, me,* or *you.*

> **Incorrect**
> My brother and **myself** enjoy sightseeing together.
>
> **Correct**
> My brother and **I** enjoy sightseeing together.

neither, both, either   See *both, either, neither.*

noted, notorious, famous   See *famous, noted, notorious.*

nothing like, nowhere near   In formal English, use *nothing like* to mean "not at all like"; use *nowhere near* to mean "not anywhere near."

> This movie is **nothing like** the one that we saw last Saturday. [formal]
>
> The studio is **nowhere near** my house. [formal]
>
> That book was **nowhere near** as suspenseful as I had thought it would be. [informal]

of, have   See *have, of.*

off, off of   *Of* is unnecessary. Do not use *off* or *off of* in place of *from.*

> We lifted the chair **off** the carpet so that we could vacuum. [not *off of*]
>
> Larry got that idea **from** his brother. [not *off*]

only   To avoid confusion, place *only* before the element that it modifies. The placement of *only* can dramatically affect the meaning of your sentence.

> **Only** Dale gave him a watch.
>
> Dale **only** gave him a watch.

> Dale gave **only** him a watch.
>
> Dale gave him **only** a watch.

persecute, prosecute   To *persecute* people is to harass or otherwise mistreat them. To *prosecute* is to bring a court action.

> The bullies **persecuted** the small children in the neighborhood.
>
> The store owners **prosecuted** the alleged shoplifter.

precede, proceed   *Precede* means "to exist or come before in time." *Proceed* means "to go forward or onward."

> Tim and Willy **proceeded** with the job, wishing that Max and Sam, who had **preceded** them in the use of the carpentry shop, had sharpened the saws.

raise, rise   *Raise* is a regular transitive verb that means "to lift"; it always takes a direct object. *Rise* is an irregular intransitive verb that means "to move upward." See page 588 for the principal parts of the irregular verb *rise.*

> Adele **raised** her feet from the table when her mother scowled at her.
>
> The moon **rises** early in the afternoon.

real, really   *Real* is an adjective; *really* is an adverb.

> It is **really** fortunate that you found your wallet. [not *real*]
>
> That is a **real** surprise!

reason is because, reason is that   *Reason is because* is redundant. Use *reason is that* or simply *because.*

> **Incorrect**
> The **reason** that I am late **is because** I missed my bus.
>
> **Correct**
> The **reason** that I am late **is that** I missed my bus.

refer back   *Refer back* is redundant. Use just *refer.*

> I **refer** to our discussion of this morning. [not *refer back*]

regardless, irregardless   See *irregardless, regardless.*

regretful, regrettable   *Regretful* means "full of sorrow or regret." *Regrettable* means "deserving regret or sorrow."

> Mark was **regretful** over the decision to close the theater.

> Closing the theater was a **regrettable** decision.

rise, raise   See *raise, rise.*

said, says, goes, went   *Said* is the past tense of the verb *say; says* is a present-tense form. Do not use *says* for *said.* Also, do not use *goes* or *went* for *said.*

> Gary called and **said,** "Do you have a tent for the camping trip, or are you going to rent one?" [not *says* or *goes*]

second, secondly; first, firstly   See *first, firstly; second, secondly.*

set, sit   *Set* is a transitive verb that means "to place something." *Sit* is an intransitive verb that means "to rest in an upright position"; *sit* does not take a direct object.

> **Sit** down next to the door, please.

> **Set** your books on the floor next to you.

slow, slowly   *Slow* is an adjective that can be used as an adverb in informal speech, especially in commands or for emphasis. *Slowly* is an adverb; it is preferred in formal usage.

> Our waiter is very **slow.** [predicate adjective]

> He is walking **slowly** from table to table. [adverb]

> Do you think that someone told him to walk **slow**? [adverb; informal]

some time, sometime, sometimes   When you use two words, *some* is an adjective modifying *time. Sometime* can be an adverb that means "at an indefinite time," or it can be an adjective that means "occasional." *Sometimes* is an adverb that means "occasionally, now and then."

> adj. noun
> He needs **some time** to be alone.

> adv.
> I would like to go to Peru **sometime.**

> adj.
> Evan is a **sometime** musician.

> adv.
> **Sometimes** I like to go away by myself.

sort of, kind of   See *kind of, sort of.*

supposed to, used to   *Supposed to* means "expected to" or "required to." *Used to* means "accustomed to, familiar with." Be sure to spell *supposed* and *used* with a final *-d.*

> You were **supposed to** take the children shopping with you. [not *suppose to*]

> They are quite **used to** you now. [not *use to*]

sure, surely   *Sure* is an adjective meaning "certain" or "dependable." *Surely* is an adverb meaning "certainly, without doubt."

> Rob was **sure** that the dog was in the house.

> The dog will **surely** return by morning.

take, bring   See *bring, take.*

than, then   Use *than* as a conjunction in a comparison. Use *then* as an adverb to show a sequence of time or events. Do not use either one as a conjunction between two independent clauses.

> The play was, in my opinion, truer to the book **than** the movie was.

> If we get home in time, **then** you may watch television.

that, which, who   Use *that* as a relative pronoun to introduce essential clauses (page 572) that refer to things or to collective nouns referring to people. Because it introduces an essential clause, do not use a comma before *that.*

> The cat **that** was crying at our door has just run away again.

Use *which* as a relative pronoun to introduce nonessential clauses (page 572) that refer to things or to groups of persons. Always use a comma before *which* when it introduces a nonessential clause.

> This book, **which** is one that I received for my birthday, is extremely interesting.

Use *who* or *whom* as a relative pronoun to introduce essential and nonessential clauses that refer to persons. Use a comma before *who* or *whom* when it introduces a nonessential clause.

> The girl **who** won that prize is Cathy's sister.

> Nadia, **who** goes to the same school as I do, is a clerk in this store.

then, than   See *than, then*.

these kinds, this kind   Use *this* or *that* to modify the singular nouns *kind, sort,* and *type*. Use *these* and *those* to modify the plural nouns *kinds, sorts,* and *types*. Use the singular form of these nouns when the object of the preposition is singular; use the plural form when the object of the preposition is plural.

> sing.
> This **kind of** *book* is easy to read.

> pl.
> These **kinds of** *books* are more difficult.

try and, try to   Use *try to* instead of *try and*.

> Please **try to** be on time. [not *try and*]

uninterested, disinterested   See *disinterested, uninterested*.

used to, supposed to   See *supposed to, used to*.

very   Use *very* only sparingly. Overuse diminishes its effect.

well, good   See *good, well*.

where . . . at   Do not use *at* after *where*.

> **Where** is that discount store located? [not *Where is it at?*]

which, that, who   See *that, which, who*.

who, whom   See pages 615–16.

-wise   Avoid using *-wise* on the end of a word to mean "with reference to" or "concerning."

> **Avoid**   **Weatherwise**, it is a pleasant week.

> **Use**   The weather has been pleasant this week.

yourself, myself   See *myself, yourself*.

SECTION

PUNCTUATION AND MECHANICS

*W*hen you speak, you use pauses and vocal inflections to help convey meaning to your listeners. When you write, you use **mechanics**—capitalization, punctuation, italics, and numbers—to convey meaning to your readers.

In the following passage from *David Copperfield* the mechanics of capitalization and punctuation have been removed.

> well ill tell you what said mr barkis praps you might be writin to her I shall certainly write to her i rejoined ah he said slowly turning his eyes towards me well if you was writin to her praps youd recollect to say that barkis was willin would you that barkis is willing i repeated innocently is that all the message yees he said considering yees barkis is willin

Here is the same passage with the mechanics correctly in place.

> "Well, I'll tell you what," said Mr. Barkis. "P'raps you might be writin' to her?"
> "I shall certainly write to her," I rejoined.
> "Ah!" he said, slowly turning his eyes towards me. "Well! If you was writin' to her, p'raps you'd recollect to say that Barkis was willin'; would you?"
> "That Barkis is willing," I repeated, innocently. "Is that all the message?"
> "Ye—es," he said, considering. "Ye—es. Barkis is willin'."

> *David Copperfield*
> —Charles Dickens

You can see that quotation marks, commas, dashes, and other mechanical devices clarify and enliven this passage. In your own writing they will allow your thoughts and opinions to come across clearly.

3.1 CAPITALIZATION

Capital letters are most frequently used to indicate the beginning of a sentence or to show that a word is a proper noun (page 534).

3.1A *CAPITALIZATION IN SENTENCES*

◆ RULE   Capitalize the first word of a sentence and the first word of a direct quotation that is a complete sentence.

Creatures that normally roam the woods at night are called nocturnal animals.

Marcie said, "**Aerial** photographs of the affected region would be extremely helpful."

Begin the second part of an interrupted quotation with a capital letter if it is a new sentence; otherwise use a lower-case letter.

"The bobsled team has just come around the final curve!" he announced excitedly. "**A** new record has been set on this course."

"That leaky pipe can be repaired," said Mr. Hobbes, "**if** I replace the worn section with a new piece."

◆ RULE   Capitalize the first word of each line of a poem.

> **Fair** daffodils, we weep to see
> **You** haste away so soon;
> **As** yet the early-rising sun
> **Has** not attained his noon.
>
> "To Daffodils"
> —Robert Herrick

Many modern poets do not capitalize the first word of each line of poetry. When you copy a poem, follow the style of the poet.

> **beauty** is a shell
> **from** the sea
> **where** she rules triumphant
>
> "Song"
> —William Carlos Williams

3.1B *PROPER NOUNS*

◆ RULE   Capitalize the names and initials of people. If a last name begins with *Mc, O',* or *St.,* capitalize the next letter as well. If a last name begins with *Mac, de, D', la, le, van,* or *von,* use capitalization according to individual family preference.

J. **O'**Shea   Hernando **de** Soto   Robert **La** Follette

Family-Relationship Words.   Capitalize a word that shows family relationship if it is part of a particular person's name or if it is used in place of a particular person's name. Usually, if a word is preceded by a possessive pronoun (page 537), or if it is used as a general term, it is not capitalized.

Grandfather Hosmer   Aunt Jeanne   Cousin Rita

Harriet told **Mother** that she would be late for dinner this evening.

Karen hoped that **Uncle Frank** would visit in September.

Her **brother** said that he wished he had a new car.

Personal and Official Titles.   Capitalize a personal or official title or its abbreviation when it is used as a name in direct address or precedes a person's name.

Capitalize the names and abbreviations of academic degrees or honors that follow a person's name. Capitalize the abbreviations *Sr.* and *Jr.*

Dean Simpson	**Superintendent** Rossi
Eleanor Brock, **M.D.**	**Governor** Ralston
David Oleson, **Jr.**	Roberta Myers, **Ph.D.**

Yes, **Senator,** the report has been delivered.

I told the **senator** that the report had been delivered.

Do not capitalize a title that follows or substitutes for a person's name unless it is the title of a head of national government.

Title Before Name	Title Following Name
Professor Fischer	Walter Fischer, **professor**
President Wilson	Woodrow Wilson, **President**

The **President** will address the nation at four o'clock this afternoon.

Gods of Mythology.   Capitalize the names of gods of mythology, but do not capitalize the word *god* when it refers to one of them.

Myths about the ancient Egyptian **god Osiris** portray the process of cyclic renewal.

◆ RULE   Capitalize the names of particular places, such as continents, countries, cities, parks, and rivers.

Bering Strait	Erie Avenue	Iceland	Ohio
Cooper River	Fairmont Park	Kalamazoo	Paraguay

Compass Points.   Capitalize compass points that refer to specific geographic regions. Do not capitalize compass points that simply indicate directions or general regions.

We spent our vacation in the **Southwest** last fall.

They traveled **west,** then **northwest** to reach their destination.

Heavenly Bodies.   Capitalize the names of planets, stars, and constellations. Do not capitalize *sun* and *moon.* Capitalize *Earth* when referring to the planet, except when it is preceded by the word *the.*

Andromeda   Neptune   Sirius   Aquarius

Photographs of **Earth** taken from satellites in space revealed many cloud formations above the planet's surface.

The path of **the earth** around the sun is called **the earth**'s orbit.

◆ RULE   Capitalize the names of nationalities, peoples, and languages.

Asian	Melanesian	Finnish
Brazilian	Hopi	Latin

◆ RULE   Capitalize the names of days, months, holidays, and special events. Do not capitalize the name of a season unless it is part of a proper noun.

Tuesday	August	spring
Winter Carnival	Memorial Day	winter

◆ RULE   Capitalize the names of historical events and periods. Capitalize the names of awards and documents.

the Middle Ages	the Treaty of Versailles
the Emancipation Proclamation	the Nobel Prize

◆ RULE   Capitalize the first, the last, and all other important words in the titles of books, newspapers, poems, television programs, musical works, paintings, and so forth. (See also pages 647 and 656–57.) Capitalize a conjunction, an article, or a preposition only when it is the first or the last word in a title or when a conjunction or a preposition has five or more letters.

"**The** Corn Grows **Up**"	*A Man **Without** a Country*
"Singing **in the** Rain"	***For** Whom the Bell Tolls*

◆ RULE   Capitalize the names of academic subjects that are languages or that are followed by a course number. Capitalize proper adjectives in the names of academic subjects.

Latin	science	French literature
Biology II	history	American history

◆ **RULE** Capitalize the names of structures and the names of organizations, such as businesses, religions, government bodies, clubs, and schools. Capitalize a word such as *school* or *club* only when it is part of a proper noun.

Abbot Hall	House of Representatives
Taoism	Gordon's Book Store
the Museum of Fine Arts	The Chess Association
the Broadcasters' **Club**	**But** a broadcasters' **club**
Essex **College**	**But** an agricultural **college**

◆ **RULE** Capitalize trade names. Do not capitalize a common noun that follows a trade name.

Tree-Ripe fruit juice   Lyle lamps

◆ **RULE** Capitalize names of trains, ships, airplanes, rockets, and spacecraft. (See also page 656.)

the *Lake Shore Limited*   *Viking II*

3.1c *OTHER USES OF CAPITALIZATION*

◆ **RULE** Capitalize most proper adjectives (page 544). Use a lower-case letter for a proper adjective that is in common usage.

Queen Anne's lace   **Persian** cat   **Gordian** knot

But oxfords [shoes]

If you are not sure whether to capitalize a proper adjective, consult your dictionary.

◆ **RULE** Capitalize both letters in the abbreviations *A.D.*, *B.C.*, *A.M.*, and *P.M.* Write *A.D.* before the date; write *B.C.* following the date.

1120 **B.C.**   **A.D.** 1970   4:30 **P.M.**

◆ **RULE** Capitalize both letters in the two-letter Postal Service abbreviations of state names.

Use Postal Service abbreviations only in addresses that include the ZIP code; do not use them in formal writing.

Minnesota **MN** 55411   Rhode Island **RI** 02915

EXERCISE

Capitalization

Rewrite each sentence, using capitalization correctly. Use your dictionary if you need help.

1. cellophane, which was first made in france, was invented by jacques edwin brandenberger, a swiss chemist.
2. "have you ever taken a train ride along the coastal route?" asked roy. "the *silver meteor* passes through the southern states."
3. for their research on the structure of crystals, sir william henry bragg and his son shared the 1915 nobel prize for physics.
4. one winter the explorers meriwether lewis and william clark camped in oregon; fort clatsop national memorial now marks the site.
5. john donne, a poet of the seventeenth century, wrote these lines in the poem "song":

> o how feeble is man's power,
> > that if good fortune fall,
> cannot add another hour,
> > nor a lost hour recall!

3.2 PUNCTUATION

Punctuation marks show when to stop, when to pause, and when to pay special attention to a particular part of a sentence. By using punctuation correctly, you help your readers understand what you have written.

3.2A *PERIODS, QUESTION MARKS, AND EXCLAMATION POINTS*
The Period

◆ RULE   Use a period at the end of a declarative sentence, a mild command, or a polite suggestion.

A rook is a bird that closely resembles a crow.

Soon the stage lights will dim, and the production will begin.

Wait here until the traffic stops.

Dorothea, would you please lower the volume of the television.

◆ RULE   Use a period after most standard abbreviations, including initials that are used as part of a person's name or title.

Do not use periods after abbreviations for most units of weight, units of measure, or chemical elements. Use the abbreviation *in.* for *inch* to show that you are not writing the preposition *in.*

Do not use periods when the abbreviation of a company or an organization is in all capital letters or when you are writing Postal Service abbreviations of state names.

Use Periods	Do Not Use Periods
Capt. Mario Venditto	**min**—minute
Julia **S.** Drake, **R.N.**	**Kr**—Krypton
Dec.—December	**gal**—gallon
Rte.—route	**AZ**—Arizona
Co.—company	**FAA**—Federal Aviation Administration
Miss.—Mississippi	

Do not confuse standard two-letter state abbreviations (which require periods) with Postal Service abbreviations (which require no periods).

Use Periods	Do Not Use Periods
Preston, **Ga.** [no ZIP code]	Rhine, **GA** 31077
Casacade, **Ky.** [no ZIP code]	Clark, **KY** 41011

◆ RULE   When a period in an abbreviation precedes a question mark or an exclamation point in a sentence, use both marks of punctuation.

When is it correct to use Dr**.**?

Note: Avoid using abbreviations in formal writing. Spell out words instead.

The Question Mark

◆ RULE   Use a question mark at the end of an interrogative sentence.

Has Del applied for the summer internship**?**

Were those old watches appraised at the jewelry store**?**

◆ RULE   Use a question mark after a question that is not a complete sentence.

The date**?** December 30.

◆ RULE   Use a question mark to express doubt about what comes before it.

Josiah Clark (1762**?**–1809) made furniture that is sturdy and usable even today.

The Exclamation Point

◆ RULE   Use an exclamation point at the end of a sentence that expresses strong feeling or a forceful command or after a strong interjection or other exclamatory expression.

He nearly escaped**!**

Don't miss the total eclipse**!**

Congratulations**!** You are the new assistant.

Wait**!** Never leave a campfire burning**!**

EXERCISE 1 **End Punctuation and Abbreviations**

Write each sentence and supply the correct punctuation.

1. Wait That flashlight needs new batteries
2. The postcard mailed from San Antonio, Texas, had a picture of La Villita, a restoration of a small city
3. The architect said, "That house is the best example of the Colonial period in this region"
4. Oh Don't forget the symbol for iron, Fe, in the equation
5. Mrs. Knudson, will you please repeat the last statistic

3.2B *COMMAS*

Commas in Series

◆ **RULE** Use commas to separate three or more words, phrases, or clauses in a series. Use a comma after each item except the last.

Donna bought **potting soil, marigold seeds,** and **fertilizer** at the plant store.

The campers **climbed the mountain, selected a campsite,** and **pitched their tents** for the night.

In preparation for the play, **Bert rehearsed his lines, Carla checked the props,** and **Florence tested the sound system.**

Do not use commas to separate items in a series if all of them are joined by conjunctions.

Did you decide to go swimming **or** fishing **or** boating last weekend?

Do not use commas to separate pairs of nouns that are thought of as a single item or as a unit.

unit

For breakfast we ordered juice, cereal, **bacon and eggs,** and milk.

Commas After Introductory Expressions

◆ RULE Use a comma to show a pause after an introductory word or phrase.

Prepositional Phrases.   Use a comma after an introductory prepositional phrase (pages 562–63) of four or more words.

After the management seminar, the participants handed in their reports.

Participial Phrases.   Use a comma after an introductory participial phrase (pages 565–66).

Wondering if she had missed her appointment, Carol raced to the elevator.

Adverb Clauses.   Use a comma after an introductory adverb clause (pages 573–74) regardless of its length.

Before she left, Sandra watered the plants.

Interjections.   Use a comma to separate *yes, no,* and other interjections, such as *oh* and *well,* from the rest of the sentence.

Yes, Sheila is eligible for the athletic scholarship.

Well, the harvest next year may be more bountiful.

Modifiers.   Use commas to separate two or more adjectives that modify the same noun. Do not use commas if the adjectives form a compound with the noun (page 545).

To determine whether to use a comma, ask yourself whether the sentence would sound right if you reversed the adjectives or if you put *and* between them. If it sounds natural, use a comma or commas. If it does not, do not use commas. Do not use a comma between the last adjective and the noun that it modifies.

Natural

Meri manages a successful, innovative business. [comma: *successful* and *innovative* each modify business.]

Natural

Meri manages an innovative, successful business.

Natural

They listened avidly to the first radio broadcast. [no comma: It is the *radio broadcast* that is first; *radio broadcast* is a compound.]

Unnatural

They listened avidly to the radio first broadcast.

Unnatural

They listened avidly to the first and radio broadcast.

Commas to Separate Sentence Parts

◆ RULE   Use a comma to separate sentence parts that might otherwise be read together in a confusing manner.

Later, former senators will gather for a formal group photograph.

Whenever **possible, alternatives** should be researched.

Repeated Words.   Use a comma to separate most words that are repeated.

What little food there **was, was** shared by all.

Rewrite sentences to avoid repeating words whenever possible.

◆ RULE   Use a comma before a coordinating conjunction (page 551) that joins the independent clauses of a compound sentence (page 577).

Josie never saw a meteor shower, **but** she viewed the Great Meteor Crater in Arizona.

Deliver this message immediately, **and** call Mr. Hutchinson before tomorrow morning.

◆ RULE   Use a comma or a pair of commas to set off words of direct address and parenthetical expressions within a sentence.

Frank, please do not forget the maps.

Her evaluations of the play have, **after all,** been positive.

◆ RULE   Use a comma or a pair of commas to set off nonessential appositives (page 564). Do not set off essential appositives (pages 563–64).

Treat an abbreviated title or a degree following a name as a nonessential appositive.

Nonessential

Karen's brother, **Steve,** will meet her at the airport tonight. [Karen has only one brother.]

Jules Verne, **the author of *Twenty Thousand Leagues Under the Sea,*** was one of the first writers of science fiction.

Wilma Sarkin, **D.D.S.,** will be the guest speaker this afternoon.

Essential

My cousin Tony moved from Boston to Los Angeles fifteen years ago. [I have more than one cousin.]

The American novelist Nathaniel Hawthorne wrote about the duality of human nature. [There is more than one American novelist.]

Julie's cat Tiny Tim purred contentedly. [Julie has more than one cat.]

◆ RULE   Use a comma or a pair of commas to set off a nonessential phrase or a nonessential clause (page 572) from the rest of the sentence. Do not set off an essential phrase or an essential clause (page 572).

Nonessential

The students, **who found the new material difficult,** met in study groups after school. [All of the students found the new material difficult.]

Every week I shop at the same store, **where I often see people whom I know.**

Essential

The students who found the new material difficult met in study groups after school. [Only the students who found the new material difficult met in study groups.]

Every week I shop at the store that is nearest to my home.

◆ RULE   Use commas before and after the year when the year is used with the month and the day. Do not use commas when only the month and the year are given.

Joanne moved into her new apartment on **July 7, 1983,** and she plans to stay there until she graduates from college.

Stuart visited Boston in **May 1979.**

◆ RULE   Use commas before and after the name of a state, province, or country when it is used with the name of a city. Do not use commas between a state and its ZIP code.

Arlene lives in **Lincoln, Wisconsin,** with her brother and sister-in-law.

Craig carefully wrote the following address on the package: John Saxon, 100 South Street, Waltham, **MA 02154.**

◆ RULE   Use a comma after the greeting, or salutation, of a social letter and after the complimentary close of any letter.

Dear Roseann,   Sincerely yours,   Yours truly,

EXERCISE 2   Commas

Rewrite the following sentences, using commas where necessary.

1. Lyndon B. Johnson was a United States representative a senator and the Vice President before he became President.
2. Sam borrowed the library book he read the first chapter and he copied some information for his research.
3. Ms. Slade a noted historian lectured about the events leading up to the Civil War the war itself and the Reconstruction.
4. We can try either Indonesian Chinese or Vietnamese cuisine in this city.
5. After his death in 1792 the naval hero John Paul Jones was buried in the chapel at the United States Naval Academy.
6. The Dobson family has purchased a new time-saving lawnmower.
7. Whatever caused it it had a disruptive effect on the whole community.
8. The outcome of their experiment unfortunately was rather disappointing.
9. Signing the contract in the presence of a witness the partners were ready to begin their business venture.
10. The architect who won the prize for the best design received the award on June 11 1975 at a small ceremony.

3.2c   *SEMICOLONS*

Semicolons are used to connect independent clauses and to clarify meaning in sentences that contain a number of commas.

◆ RULE   Use a semicolon to connect independent clauses.

Without a Coordinating Conjunction.   Use a semicolon in a compound sentence to connect closely related independent clauses that are *not* joined by a coordinating conjunction.

Many times we prepared to turn back**;** swift rapids nearly tipped the canoes.

With a Conjunctive Adverb or with an Explanatory Expression. Use a semicolon to connect independent clauses that are joined by a conjunctive adverb (page 553) or by an explanatory expression. Use a comma after the conjunctive adverb or after the explanatory expression.

The members of the diving team were excited about being in the state finals**; however,** each member seemed calm when the event began.

Hal really enjoyed his trip to Canada**; in fact,** he said that it was the best trip he had ever taken.

◆ RULE   Use a semicolon to clarify meaning in a sentence that contains several commas.

Independent Clauses.   Use a semicolon to clarify and separate independent clauses that have several commas within them, even when a coordinating conjunction is used.

> I have studied the works of Ralph Waldo Emerson, a neighbor of one of my ancestors; and I would also like to study the works of Henry David Thoreau, Louisa May Alcott, and Bronson Alcott.

Items in a Series.   Use semicolons to separate items in a series if those items have internal commas. The semicolons make clear how many items are in the series.

Unclear

> The main characters are Walter, a talented but unrecognized young artist, Pamela, a dedicated art student, Will, a famous art critic, and Harriet, a patron of the arts. [four or seven characters?]

Clear

> The main characters are Walter, a talented but unrecognized young artist; Pamela, a dedicated art student; Will, a famous art critic; and Harriet, a patron of the arts. [four characters]

EXERCISE 3   **Semicolons**

Write each sentence, adding semicolons where they are needed. You may need to replace commas with semicolons to make a sentence clearer.

1. Rhode Island is the smallest state in the country it measures forty-eight miles north to south and thirty-seven miles east to west.
2. The poinsettia grows outdoors in southern states, but, because of its vibrant red and green coloring, it is also a popular indoor plant during the winter months in cold climates.
3. Neptune was the god of the sea in Roman mythology he resembled the Greek sea god Poseidon.
4. Edgar Allan Poe published "The Raven," in 1845 as a result the poem brought him great recognition, and it is still read widely today.
5. Sara had been expecting an important call all afternoon therefore she dashed to the telephone and picked up the receiver after the first ring.

3.2D   *COLONS*

◆ RULE   Use a colon to introduce an explanatory phrase or a statement or a list of items that completes a sentence. The part of a sentence before a list may contain a demonstrative word such as *these* or *those* or an expression such as *the following* or *as follows.*

The disappointing news was reported to the waiting crowd: **the building would have to be torn down.**

New legislation will affect the following cities: **Frankfort, Louisville, and Bowling Green.**

Of the marsupials, he was able to study these: **kangaroos, koalas, and opossums.**

Do *not* use a colon to introduce a list that immediately follows a verb or a preposition.

The graphic design **includes** triangles, parallelograms, and circles. [not *includes:*]

What products are made **in** Venezuela, Bolivia, and Brazil? [not *in:*]

◆ RULE   Use a colon to separate two independent clauses when the second clause explains or completes the first sentence.

I think I know why I have read that book three times: I have the same outlook on life that the main character has.

◆ RULE   Use a colon to separate the hour and minutes in an expression of time, the chapter and verse in a biblical reference, the title and subtitle of a book, and the volume and page number of a book or magazine reference.

3:22 P.M.   *Wheels and Wagons: Early Transportation*
Genesis 12:2   *Mountaineering Monthly,* 6:72

◆ RULE   Use a colon after the salutation of a business letter.

Dear Mr. Statler: Dear Ms. Fortuna:

◆ RULE   Use a colon to introduce a direct quotation.

Dr. Doneski began her presentation with these words: "I feel honored to be speaking to such a distinguished group."

EXERCISE 4   Colons

Some of the sentences that follow need colons. Write the sentences, supplying colons where needed. If a sentence is correct as it is, write *Correct.*

1. John Paul Jones's response to the British commander's demand for surrender was "I have not yet begun to fight."
2. A golfer might use the following clubs woods, irons, and a putter.
3. For my course in traditions of Western literature, I read Genesis 2 15.
4. Before moving to her new home, Barbara read an informative book entitled *Florida Ponce de Leon to the Present.*

5. Dear Mr. Saunders

     Thank you very much for your helpful letter that suggests people to contact in the area, information to include with my application, and possible employment opportunities in the Midwest.

3.2E *QUOTATION MARKS*

◆ RULE   Use quotation marks to show that you are writing the exact words that someone said, thought, or wrote. Use quotation marks at both the beginning and the end of the quotation.

Do not use quotation marks around an **indirect quotation:** a retelling, in the writer's words, of what another person said, thought, or wrote.

Eliza asked, **"May** I borrow this tape recorder?**"**

Vic said, **"The** opera *The Magic Flute* was on the radio last night, and I really enjoyed listening to it.**"**

Vic said that he thoroughly enjoyed listening to *The Magic Flute* on the radio last night. [indirect quotation]

Dialogue.   When you are writing dialogue, begin a new paragraph and use a separate set of quotation marks each time the speaker changes.

    "Did you check the source of your information?**"** Dale asked.
    "Of course," replied Irene. "I always double-check information concerning a controversial subject.**"**

Brief Quotations.   If you are writing a brief quotation that continues for more than one paragraph, use opening quotation marks at the beginning of each paragraph, but use end quotation marks only at the end of the last paragraph.

    "No, he had never written about Paris. Not the Paris that he cared about. But what about the rest that he had never **written?** [no quotation marks]
    "What about the ranch and the silvered gray of the sage brush, the quick, clear water in the irrigation ditches, and the heavy green of the **alfalfa."**

"The Snows of Kilimanjaro"
—Ernest Hemingway

Long Quotations.   When you are copying a quotation of five or more lines, set it off from the rest of your paper by indenting it five spaces from the left and right margins. Single-space the quotation if you are typing. Do *not* use quotation marks with a quotation that is set off in this way.

◆ RULE   Use quotation marks to set off the title of a short story, an article, an essay, a short poem, or a song.

Use quotation marks to set off the title of any piece that forms part of a larger work such as the following: a single television show that is part of a series, a chapter of a book, a section of a newspaper, or a feature in a magazine. (See also page 635.)

> Miguel will recite Browning's poem **"My Last Duchess."**

> Please rehearse **"The Impossible Dream,"** the second song in the show.

> The sixth and final episode, entitled **"Today's Environment,"** was informative.

> Luke always reads the **"Hints for Hikers"** column in *Wilderness* magazine.

◆ RULE   Use quotation marks to call attention to the special nature of such words as nicknames used with a person's full name, technical terms, and odd expressions.

> Colonel Edwin E. **"Buzz"** Aldrin, Jr., participated in the historic moon-landing mission.

> The bottom of a hydroplane is designed so that the boat **"planes"** on the surface of the water.

Note: The preceding rule is for informal usage only. Avoid such usage in formal writing if possible.

◆ RULE   Use quotation marks to set off a word that defines another word.

> I use the word *calculating* to mean **"shrewd."**

Other Punctuation with Quotation Marks.   The following rules will help you to determine where and how to use single quotation marks, commas, periods, colons, semicolons, question marks, and exclamation points with quotation marks.

◆ RULE   Use single quotation marks around a quotation or a title that occurs within a longer quoted passage.

> "Watch the episode called **'The Industrial Revolution'** at eight o'clock tonight," said Mr. Creiger.

◆ RULE   Place a comma or a period inside closing quotation marks.

> "Return one day and visit**,"** suggested our guide, "for I have enjoyed showing you some of the spectacular sights this city has to offer**."**

◆ RULE   Place a semicolon or a colon outside closing quotation marks.

Grady reported, "The dam is close to overflowing"; consequently, safety measures were taken immediately.

Now I remember why I carefully read the article "How to Improve Your Memory": I didn't want to forget any of the details.

◆ RULE   Place a question mark or an exclamation point inside the closing quotation marks if it applies only to the material quoted. If the entire sentence is a question or an exclamation, place the question mark or exclamation point outside the closing quotation marks. If both the quotation and the sentence require a question mark or an exclamation point, put the end mark inside the closing quotation marks.

Loren wondered, "Did I miss the appointment?" [The quotation itself is a question.]

Did Alicia say, "I think that I will buy a digital watch"? [The entire sentence, not the quotation, is a question.]

How did you answer the question "What is your job experience?" [Both the quotation and the sentence are questions.]

EXERCISE 5   **Quotation Marks**

Write correctly the sentences that need single or double quotation marks. Be sure to use capitalization, other punctuation, and paragraphing correctly. If a sentence needs no quotation marks, write *Correct* on your paper.

1. Do you know the lyrics to the song Give My Regards to Broadway? asked Mr. Rodgers.
2. The great Charlie Bird Parker was noted for playing the alto saxophone.
3. Scholars have searched for years to find the actual urn described in John Keats's poem Ode on a Grecian Urn.
4. How does sleet differ from hail? asked Warren. Although sleet and hail are formed in nearly the same way, sleet occurs only in the winter, replied Mrs. Hartwick.
5. The artist explained that *intaglio* means engraving.

3.2F *APOSTROPHES*

Possessives

◆ RULE   Use an apostrophe to show possession.

Singular and Plural Nouns.   Use an apostrophe and an -*s* (-'*s*) to form the possessive of a singular noun or a plural noun that does not end in -*s*.

the bear's cubs	Keats's poetry	the people's choice

Plural Nouns Ending in -s. Use an apostrophe alone to form the possessive of a plural noun that ends in -s.

the settlers' land   the Elks' convention   the Davises' house

Compound Nouns. Change the last word of a compound noun to the possessive form.

the passer-**by's** comment   the bell**boys'** uniforms

Joint Ownership. Use the possessive form of only the last person's name when a thing is jointly owned. Use the possessive form of each name when two or more people each possess separate items.

Richard Rodgers and Oscar Hammerstei**n's** musicals

Wallace Stevens**'s** and T.S. Eliot**'s** poetry

Expressions Ending in -s. Use an apostrophe alone to form the possessive of most expressions that end in -s or the sound of s.

for goodness' sake   three years' work

Ancient Classical Names Ending in -s. Use an apostrophe alone to form the possessive of ancient classical names that end in -s.

Socrates' dialogues   Hippocrates' oath

Contractions

◆ RULE   Use an apostrophe to replace letters or numbers that have been left out in a contraction.

I **can't** lift these barrels by myself.

They'll be ready to leave in less than an hour.

Were the clothing styles of the **'20s** quite different?

Plural Forms

◆ RULE   Use an apostrophe and an -s (-'s) to form the plural of letters, numbers, symbols, and words that you are referring to as words or symbols.

Use italics (underlining) correctly in forming plurals with apostrophes. Do not underline the 's.

There are three *s*'s in *dissatisfied*.

The vote received twenty-five **yea's** and three **nay's**.

She told him to mind his **p's** and **q's**.

Note: The plurals of abbreviations that do not include periods are formed by adding just -*s*.

> There are several **PTAs** in our school district.

> **But** The ***PTA*'s** on the poster were faded. [referring to the letters, not to the organization]

Although names of years are written with numerals, they also usually function as words and should be treated as such.

> My grandmother told stories about growing up in New England in the early **1900s**.

Avoiding the Misuse of Apostrophes

◆ RULE   Do not use the apostrophe to form the plurals of nouns. The plural of a noun is generally formed by adding -*s* or -*es*, as in *books, families, tomatoes,* and *atlases.*

> **Incorrect**   Fortunately, we finished our **essay's** on time.

> **Correct**   Fortunately, we finished our **essays** on time.

◆ RULE   Do not add an apostrophe or -*'s* to possessive personal pronouns: *mine, yours, his, hers, its, ours, theirs.* They already show ownership.

> Are these lecture notes **yours?**

In addition, do not confuse possessive forms of personal pronouns with contractions.

> The cat washed **its** face. [not *it's*]

EXERCISE 6   ## Apostrophes

Write correctly the sentences that need apostrophes. If a sentence needs no apostrophes, write *Correct.*

1. The mens track teams at the University of Southern California held state championships throughout the 1960s.
2. How many *ss* and *is* are there in *Mississippi*?
3. Lewis and Clarks expedition to the Pacific Ocean strengthened the claims of the United States to the northwestern territory.

4. The Gianellis collie wound his chain around the chestnut tree in their back yard.

5. Saddle shoes reached their height of popularity during the 1950s.

3.2G   *HYPHENS, DASHES, AND ELLIPSIS POINTS*

The Hyphen

◆ RULE   Use a hyphen to divide a word at the end of a line.

Do not divide a word of one syllable, such as *washed* or *grieve*. Do not divide any word so that one letter stands by itself.

Always divide a word between its syllables and in such a way that the reader will not be confused about its meaning or pronunciation.

Incorrect	Marsha went to the bank Friday and **cash-ed** her paycheck. [*Cashed* is a word of one syllable.]
Correct	Marsha went to the bank Friday and **cashed** her paycheck.
Incorrect	During Jan's vacation trip, the weather was **a-greeable** and the accommodations were satisfactory. [The letter *a* stands by itself.]
Correct	During Jan's vacation trip the weather was **agree-able** and the accommodations were satisfactory.

Prefixes and Suffixes.   Divide a word with a prefix only after the prefix. Divide a word with a suffix only before the suffix.

Paula and Frank told me that they attended an important **inter-national** conference last week.

The only way to open the lock is to turn the dial in a **clock-wise** direction.

Compound Words.   For a compound word that is written as one word, divide it only between the base words. Divide a hyphenated compound word at the hyphen.

If we work quickly, we will be able to finish everything **some-time** in February.

He described his trip to the mountains during the storm as a **hair-raising** experience.

◆ RULE   Use a hyphen after the prefixes *all-*, *ex-*, and *self-*. Use a hyphen to separate any prefix from a proper noun or adjective.

all-purpose	Neo-Platonism	**But** neophyte
ex-president	pre-Alexandrian	**But** preview
self-assured	intra-Asian	**But** intrastate

Note: Do not use a hyphen between most other prefixes and their root words.

entitle   **pre**determine   **sub**standard

◆ RULE   Use a hyphen after the prefix of a word that is spelled the same as another word but has a different origin and meaning (a homograph).

| re-collect | re-count | re-form |
| recollect | recount | reform |

◆ RULE   Use a hyphen after the prefix of a word when the last letter of the prefix is a vowel and is the same as the first letter of the base word.

de-**e**scalate   pre-**e**minent   re-**e**ducate

◆ RULE   Hyphenate a compound adjective when it precedes the noun that it modifies, but not when it follows it. Do not hyphenate a compound adjective when its first word is an adverb that ends in *-ly.*

The moderator introduced **up-to-date** issues.

The issues that the moderator introduced were **up to date.**

A **barely moving** train slowed to a complete stop to avoid an obstruction.

Fractions.   Hyphenate a fraction that is used as a modifier. Do not hyphenate a fraction that is used as a noun.

Modifier   The soup was **two-thirds** water.

Noun   **One third** of the soup was vegetables.

◆ RULE   Use a hyphen to separate compound numbers from *twenty-one* through *ninety-nine.*

| | forty-nine | seventy-three |
| **But** | five hundred | ninety thousand |

The Dash

◆ RULE   Use a dash to show an interruption in a thought or in a statement. Use a second dash to end the interruption if the sentence continues.

"If we can just——"; suddenly he had another idea.

Someone——**I think it's Barbara**——will bring the table decorations.

> ***Appositives and Parenthetical Expressions.*** Use dashes when appositives or parenthetical expressions have internal commas.

We will need some equipment——**I think that a tent, sleeping bags, backpacks, and cooking utensils will do**——before we can plan an overnight camping trip.

Several colors——**orange, green, and violet, for example**——are made up of combinations of other colors.

In typing, use two hyphens to represent a dash. Do not type a single hyphen to stand for a dash.

Note: Avoid the overuse of dashes in formal writing.

Ellipsis Points

◆ RULE   Use **ellipsis points,** a set of three spaced periods (. . .), to indicate an omission or a pause in written or quoted material.

A little neglect may breed great mischief **. . .** for want of a nail the shoe was lost; for want of a shoe the horse was lost; and for want of a horse the rider was lost.

> *Poor Richard's Almanac*
> —Benjamin Franklin

> ***Other Punctuation Marks.*** If what precedes the ellipsis points is part of a complete sentence, use a period followed by three ellipsis points (. . . .). If what precedes the ellipsis points is not part of a complete sentence, use only the three ellipsis points, leaving a space before the first point (. . .). If what precedes the ellipsis points is part of a complete sentence ending with a question mark or an exclamation point, retain that mark before the three ellipsis points (? . . .).

Original passage

None of them knew the colour of the sky. Their eyes glanced level, and were fastened upon the waves that swept toward them. These waves were of the hue of slate, save for the tops, which were of foaming white, and all of the men knew the colours of the sea. The horizon narrowed and widened, and dipped and rose, and at all times its edge was jagged with waves that seemed thrust up in points like rocks.

> *"The Open Boat"*
> —Stephen Crane

Abridged Passage

> None of them knew the colour of the sky. Their eyes . . . were fastened upon the waves. . . . These waves were of the hue of slate, . . . and all of the men knew the colours of the sea. The horizon narrowed and widened, . . . and at all times its edge was jagged with waves. . . .

Sentences and Paragraphs. Use a line of periods to indicate the omission of a stanza of poetry or of an entire paragraph from written material.

EXERCISE 7

Hyphens, Dashes, Ellipsis Points

Copy the following sentences. Add hyphens, dashes, and ellipsis points where necessary.

1. Murial was obviously self conscious as she practiced her speech.
2. Please take that package if you haven't already done so to the post office this afternoon.
3. Steven wrote down the beginning of the Preamble to the Constitution: "We the People of the United States, in order to form a more perfect Union."
4. The grocery bill for one week amounted to forty three dollars.
5. I found *Robinson Crusoe* so fascinating that I read 175 pages in a single evening one third of Defoe's novel!

3.2H

PARENTHESES AND BRACKETS

Parentheses

◆ RULE   Use parentheses to enclose material that is not basic to the meaning of the sentence.

> Kathleen requested information from the FEC **(Federal Election Commission)** about the campaign funds of the congressional candidates in her district.

> The cardinal **(sometimes called the redbird)** is the state bird of Illinois.

Other Punctuation with Parentheses. Place commas, semicolons, and colons outside parentheses. Place periods outside parentheses unless the parenthetical material is a separate sentence beginning with a capital letter; then place the period inside the parentheses. Place question marks and exclamation points inside the parentheses if they are part of the parenthetical material; otherwise place them outside the parentheses.

Brackets

◆ RULE   Use brackets to enclose explanations or comments that are inserted in a quotation but that are not part of the quotation.

A guide said, "It **[the Great Salt Lake]** is four to five times as salty as the ocean."

Use brackets to enclose parenthetical information that is part of material already in parentheses.

Over a dozen oil companies are bidding for the rights to drill in the Atlantic Ocean off the New Jersey shore. (Today's newspaper also contains an article on the environmental risks of off-shore drilling **[see p. 56]**.)

Other Punctuation with Brackets. The only punctuation marks used with brackets are those within the bracketed material.

3.3 USING ITALICS AND NUMBERS IN WRITING

3.3A *ITALICS*

In printed material, certain words and symbols are set in italic type *(slanted letters like these)*. In handwriting and typing, you should underline such words and symbols according to the following rules.

◆ RULE   Italicize (underline) the names or titles of books, book-length poems, newspapers, magazines, periodicals, plays, movies, television series, paintings, trains, ships, aircraft, and so forth.

Italicize (underline) an article *(a, an, the)* that comes before a title only if it is part of the title. (See also page 635.)

The Portrait of a Lady	*Paradise Lost*
Casablanca	*Apollo 11*

◆ RULE   Italicize (underline) letters, numbers, symbols, and words when you are referring to them as words or symbols.

I marked a *21* in the last column to complete the store's inventory.

Ryan noticed that *occasionally* was misspelled in the caption.

◆ RULE   Italicize (underline) words from other languages if those words are not commonly used in English. Do not italicize foreign place names or currency.

A spontaneous shout of appreciation followed the singer's solo, the *pièce de résistance* of the evening.

But   Paula spent the day at the Musée de Louvre. This new restaurant has a standard à la carte menu. [À la carte is commonly used in English.]

Italicize (underline) a word or phrase that you wish to emphasize. Avoid overuse of this device.

"After *hours* of work," reported the excited archeologist, "we finally found evidence of a structure."

3.3B *USING NUMBERS IN WRITING*

◆ RULE Spell out numbers of one hundred or less. Spell out numbers that are rounded to hundreds and that can be written in two words or less.

> Ferdinand Magellan's expedition from Spain began with **five** ships, yet only **three** of them continued the trip to the Pacific Ocean.
>
> Were there nearly **one thousand** boxes of hats delivered yesterday?

But Nina collected **1,250** postcards from around the world.

Note: Do not mix numerals and words when writing two or more numbers in the same category.

Incorrect
> **Two hundred** general practitioners and **350** specialists attended the convention on May 29.

Correct
> **Two hundred** general practitioners and **three hundred fifty** specialists attended the convention on May 29. [Words are used to describe the numbers of people in attendance; numerals are used in the dates.]

◆ RULE Spell out any number that begins a sentence, or rewrite the sentence.

The word *and* is unnecessary in writing numbers except those numbers between *one hundred* and *one hundred and ten,* and so forth.

Incorrect 106 guardrails will be placed along that steep incline.

Correct **One hundred and six** guardrails will be placed along that steep incline.

Correct Along that steep incline, **106** guardrails will be placed.

Ordinal Numbers. Spell out ordinal numbers (*first, second, third,* and so forth) in your writing. You may write the day of the month as an ordinal number preceding the month, but the month followed by an Arabic numeral is the preferred form.

fifth day	June 8
seventh grade	eighth of June

Compound Numbers. Hyphenate compound numbers from *twenty-one* through *ninety-nine.*

thirty-two   eighty-six   ninety-three

Spell out cardinal numbers (*one, two, three,* and so forth) that occur in a compound with nouns or adjectives.

five-dollar tickets   twenty-pound turkey

◆ RULE   Spell out an expression of time unless it is a specific time using A.M. or P.M. Use numerals and A.M. or P.M. in all technical writing.

> Ruth usually leaves her apartment around **eight o'clock.**

But   My computer printout was finished at **3:51 A.M.**

◆ RULE   Use numerals to express dates, street numbers, room numbers, apartment numbers, telephone numbers, page numbers, and percentages. Spell out the word *percent.*

July 16, 1925   pages 56–101
122 San Gabriel Avenue   10 percent

Dates. When you write a date, do not add *-st, -nd, -rd,* or *-th* to the numeral.

| **Incorrect** | May 5th, 1971 | October 2nd |
| **Correct** | May 5, 1971 | October 2 |

3.4   PROOFREADING AND EDITING

3.4A   *PROOFREADING SYMBOLS*

The following symbols are commonly used to identify and correct errors in composition. Learning them will help you revise and proofread your writing.

| ⋀ | insert something | lost her ⋀ walking on stilts (*balance*) |
| # | space | bought a red # balloon |

¶	begin new paragraph	last of the heroes.¶In the next century
∿	transpose letter or words	this fabirc made has
ℯ	delete	a mountaintop top retreat
⌣	close up letters	I am happy to introduce
......	let it stand (under something crossed out)	consisted of a large percentage
≡	capitalize	the Department of agriculture
/	make lower case	Marlene gazed at the Portrait.

3.4B *EDITING SYMBOLS*

The abbreviations below are common ones that you might use when you edit a friend's draft or that your teacher might use. Page references to this text follow.

adj	adjective, 543	*gl/us*	glossary, usage, 624
adv	adverb, 547	-	hyphen, 651
agr	agreement:	*ital*	italics, 656
	pronoun-antecedent, 607	*j*	jargon, 584
	subject-verb, 600	*mod*	modifier, position of, 622
'	apostrophe, 649	( )	parentheses, 655
cap	capital letters, 632	.	period, 637
c	case, pronoun, 611	" "	quotation marks, 646
:	colon, 645	*ref*	reference, pronoun, 617
,	comma, 639	*r-o*	run-on sentence, 581
cons	consistency, 594	;	semicolon, 643
—	dash, 653	*sl*	slang, 584
dg	dangling modifier, 623	*sub*	subordination, 551
ellip	ellipsis points, 654	*vf*	verb form, 586
frag	fragment, 578	*vt*	verb tense, 588

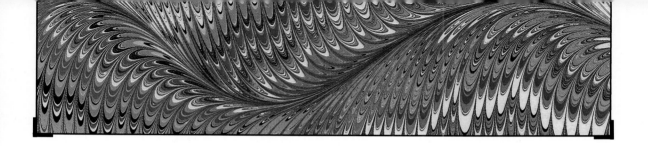

AUTHOR/TITLE INDEX

Narrative of the Life of Frederick Douglass: An American Slave, 96
National Newspaper Index, 431
Newkirk, Ingrid, 247–256
Newman, John Henry, 118, 120, 122
New York Times Index, 20, 428, 430–431

Oates, Joyce Carol, 98, 384–393
O'Brien, Eileen M., 196–200, 497–498, 499, 504
Olds, Sharon, 370–376
"Once More to the Lake" (E. B. White), 19, 29–32, 60
Origin of Species (Darwin), 437, 442
Orwell, George, 19, 98, 100–104, 119–120, 122, 123, 125, 143–147, 159–160, 275, 281, 293–300, 492, 494–495, 498, 499, 507–508, 509–510, 512, 513, 516, 522, 528–530
"Outlaws" (Carr), 80–81
Out of Africa (Dinesen), 367
Oxford, Earl of, *see* de Vere, Edward

"Paul Simon's *Graceland*" (Santoro), 338, 344–345
Perrin, Noel, 342–344
"Peter and Rosa" (Dinesen), 380
The Plug-in Drug: Television, Children, and the Family (Winn), 186
Poetry Explication, 380
Poison Penmanship (Mitford), 421–422
"The Polis" (Kitto), 527
"Politics and the English Language" (Orwell), 281, 293–300, 507–508, 510
Posner, Ellen, 349–352
"Powhitetrash" (Angelou), 110–112

The Practice of Social Research (Babbie), 424
Prudentius, Aurelius Clemens, 92–93
Psychology Abstracts, 431
Psychomachia (Prudentius), 92–93
Public Affairs Information Service Bulletin, 430
Publication Manual of the American Psychological Association, 442, 471

"Questions of Authorship" (Brown and Spencer), 174–175

Raleigh, Sir Walter, 170
Readers' Guide to Periodical Literature, 20, 428–429, 429 (fig.)
Readers' Guide to Robert Browning, 428
"Reflections on Gandhi" (Orwell), 143–147, 492, 494–495
Research Guide for Psychology, 428
"Revival Meeting" (Johnson), 87, 89
Rich, Adrienne, 7, 9
"Richard Cory" (Robinson), 379, 380, 382
"Rigid Rules, Inflexible Plans, and the Stifling of Language: A Cognitive Analysis of Writer's Block" (Rose), 57n
Robinson, Edwin Arlington, 382
Rockefeller, John D., III, 186
Rodriguez, Richard, 96
A Romantic Education (Hampl), 96
Rose, Mike, 57n
Ruskin, John, 345–348
Ryan v. New York Central Railroad, 225–228, 230–231

"Salt Lake City" (Johnson), 140–142
Santoro, Gene, 338, 344–345
The Science of Educational Research (Mouly), 424
Seeds of Chaos (Brittain), 528–529
Settle, Robert B., 424
Sex and Temperament in Three Primitive Societies (Mead), 506
Shakespeare, William, 168–184, 187, 188–189, 191, 193, 230
Shelley, Percy Bysshe, 508, 509, 512–513
"Shooting an Elephant" (Orwell), 19, 98, 100–104
"Should We Abolish the Presidency?" (Tuchman), 270–273
Simon, Paul, 344–345
Singin' and swingin' and gettin' merry like Christmas (Angelou), 123
"Singing with the Fundamentalists" (Dillard), 43–49, 490–492
"Slavery, Freedom, and Architecture" (Ruskin), 345–348
"Slouching Towards Bethlehem" (Didion), 15
Social Sciences Index, 429
The Spanish Tragedy (Kyd), 176–177
Spencer, T. J. B., 174–175, 178–179, 181, 184, 193
"Spend It All, Shoot It, Play It, Lose It" (Maitland), 19, 354–355
Spenser, Edmund, 170
Spielberg, Steven, 324, 325, 326, 327, 330, 331, 333, 334
Stanley, William, 175
"Star Food" (Canin), 98, 136, 379, 403–413
"Star-Spangled Banner," 9
Sterritt, David, 327–328, 331

662   *Author/Title Index*

"Still, Citizen Sparrow" (Wilbur), 416–417
The Story of My Life (Keller), 96
The Structure of Scientific Revolutions (Kuhn), 6n
"Such, Such Were the Joys" (Orwell), 522
"Summer Solstice, New York City" (Olds), 370–376
The Survey Research Handbook (Alreck and Settle), 424

Tarkington, Booth, 515
Taylor, Patricia, 187
Theophrastus, 127–129, 135
Thomas, Lewis, 281, 313–315
Thoreau, Henry David, 493
Timber: or, Discoveries; Made Upon Men and Matter (Jonson), 172–173
The Times [London] *Index*, 431
To Be an Invalid (Colp), 441, 447
To Know a Fly (Dethier), 266
The Trial of Dr. Spock (Mitford), 422
"The Truth About Roy McCarthy" (M. McCarthy), 195–196
Tuchman, Barbara, 16–18, 24, 37–42, 63, 129, 270–273, 276, 434, 435, 436, 438, 439, 516–518
Turabian, Kate, 442
Twain, Mark, 19, 90–91, 92, 95, 98, 104–109, 163, 165–

167, 169–171, 173, 179, 180, 181, 182–183, 183–184, 187, 188, 192, 413–415, 509, 512, 522
Twentieth-Century Short Story Explication, 380

"Unconscious Selection and Natural Selection" (Darwin), 210–215

Venus and Adonis (Shakespeare), 169
"The Vertical Negro Plan" (Golden), 523–525
The Victorian Poets: A Guide to Research, 428
"Vivisection" (Lewis), 257–259
The Voyage of the Beagle (Darwin), 121, 420, 442

Wall Street Journal Index, 431
Warren, Chief Justice Earl, 281, 285–289, 440
"Well, I Don't Love You, E. T." (Will), 19, 352–353
"What Was the Acheulean Hand Ax?" (O'Brien), 196–200, 497–498, 504
"Where Are You Going, Where Have You Been?" (Oates), 98, 136, 379, 380, 384–393

White, Justice Byron, 285–292
White, E. B., 19, 29–32, 57, 59, 60, 72–79, 139–140, 501, 514, 515, 521–522, 530
White, Theodore, 10–12, 14, 57, 60, 83–84, 85, 95, 96, 97–98, 124–125, 133, 148–150, 282, 311–313, 477–478, 479, 480, 481–482, 489, 502–503, 505, 506, 508, 518
"Whitefolks" (Angelou), 86–87, 95
"White Lies" (Bok), 201–208, 525
Whittier, John Greenleaf, 9, 177
Who's Who, 426
"Why I Write" (Didion), 18
"Why I Write" (Orwell), 513
Wilbur, Richard, 416–417
"Wilbur's 'Still, Citizen Sparrow'" (Woodard), 380, 416–417
Will, George, 19, 188, 209–210, 229, 276–279, 352–353
Winn, Marie, 186
Woodard, Charles R., 380, 416–417
"A Working Community" (Goodman), 488–489
World Book Encyclopedia, 20
Wright, Richard, 96
The Writing Life (Dillard), 70–72, 338, 354–357, 439, 493

SUBJECT INDEX

Apostrophes, 648–651
Appositive phrases, 563–564
  case of pronouns in, 616–617
  as sentence fragments, 579
Appositives, 563, 614
  to a direct object, 613
  to an indirect object, 613
  to an object of a preposition, 613
  to a predicate nominative, 612
  punctuation of, 641–642, 653
  to a subject, 612
Argument
  analysis of, 193, 216–224
  categorical, 157
  consideration of opposing viewpoints in, 158–162, 164
  definitions of, 156–158
  evaluation of, 185–187
  about facts, 156, 168–194
  guidelines for writing, 189–190, 232
  level of reader's and writer's conviction in, 172–173, 175–181
  about literary symbols, 370
  about literary themes, 366–368
  logical fallacies in, 181–187
  paragraph-length, 234–235
  peer review of, 190, 232–233
  role of probabilistic reasoning in, 171–172, 230–231, 332
  about rules, 156, 216–238
  about school policy, 235–238
  temperance in, 158, 173–175, 178–179, 191–192, 193
  tone of, 178–179
  winning, 158
  see also Proposals
Articles, citation of, 465, 467, 469, 470, 472–473
Articles [part of speech], 543
  italicization of, 655
Astrology, description of personality by, 93–94

Astronomical names, capitalization of, 635
The Atlantic (magazine), 5–6
Attention, and memorization, 51–52
Attitude, shift in writer's, 495–496
Audience, *see* Reader(s)
Author, *see* Writer
Author/framework summary, 25–26
Authorities, evaluating testimony of, 188–189
Authority
  for rules, 222, 226, 227, 228, 230, 232
  of sources, 447, 451, 455, 461
Autobiographical writing, *see* Memoir
Auxiliary verbs, 540–541, 565, 586, 588, 592–593, 598, 600

Back areas, 58, 60, 62, 67–69
Background information, in reviews, 318, 325, 326, 336, 337
Bandwagon fallacy, 182
Barnes, Wayne, 439
Begging the question, 181–182
Believing and doubting game, 160–162, 164
Benchmarks, critical, 319, 320, 328, 330, 332, 336, 337
Berry, Jean, Duc de, 516–518
Bias, in expert testimony, 189
Bibliographies
  consultation in research, 426–428
  documentation of references for, 431–432
  location of sources in, 441
  for research papers, 464–473
Bibliography card, 432, 433 (fig. 11-1)
Biographical references, use in research, 426
Black/white fallacy, 182

"Blocked by openness," 158–160
Body of essay, 476–489, 515
Boleyn, Anne, 217
Bombing, saturation, 528–529
Book Review Digest, 341
Books
  citation of, 465, 467, 469–470, 471–472
  index of articles in, 431
Box diagrams, explication of essay organization with, 485–486
Brackets, 654–655
Brainstorming, in selection of reportable events, 126
Brennan, William, 8
Bridges
  logical, 503–504, 506
  verbal, 502–503
Burden of proof, 180–181
Bush, George, 9n, 188

Cakewalk prose, 509–510, 512–513, 515
Calendar names
  capitalization of, 635
  numbers in, 657
  punctuation of, 642
Cancer, and cholesterol, 6
Capitalization, 632–637
Card catalogs
  notation of information from, 432
  use in research, 427 (fig.), 428
Carter, Jimmy, 133, 148–150, 481
Cartoons, editorial, subject and framework in, 20–23
Case [pronouns], 611–617
Catalogs, *see* Card catalogs; Online catalogs
Catalogs, bibliographical, 427–428
Categorical argument, 157
Causation
  in narratives, 364–365, 373, 377
  tenuous chain of, 184–185

Cause, relationship to effect, 269–273
Center of consciousness, narrator as, 363, 364, 372, 377
Certainty, necessary level of, in treatment of facts, 180–181
Channelization
antidotes to, 160–162, 164, 189–190
foreclosing of thought by, 158–160
Character(s)
analysis in literary criticism, 361–362, 372, 377
author as, 80–82
report on, 136
Character type
as framework, 127–128
relationship of individual personality to, 128–131
report on, 135
Cholesterol, and heart disease, 5–6, 192
Christian Science Monitor, 328
Circular argument, 181–182
Citations, 437–439
forms of, 442, 445, 447, 449, 451, 455, 464–473
in-text, 438–439, 445, 447, 449, 451, 455, 468, 471, 473
Civil disobedience, 186, 482–483
Classification, patterning essay on, 484–485
Clauses, 570–578
dependent (*see* Clauses, subordinate)
independent, 553, 570, 577, 578, 581–582, 641, 643–644, 645 (*see also* [for greater specificity] Independent clauses)
number in sentence, 518
placement of, 622–624
punctuation of, 639–640, 641, 642, 643–644, 645
subordinate, 551, 552, 570–571, 577, 578, 579–580,

582, 616, 623 (*see also* [for greater specificity] Subordinate clauses)
used as adjectives, 538, 571–572, 606–607
used as adverbs, 573–574, 640
used as nouns, 574–576
Cliché route in argument, 159–160
Clichés, 508
Cognitive psychology, insights into memory process, 51–52, 500–501, 507
Collective nouns, 535
agreement with verbs, 603–604
as antecedents, 609
Colloquialisms, 583, 584
Colons, 644–646
use with quotation marks, 647
use with parentheses, 654
Commas, 639–643, 644
connection of independent clauses with, 570
connection of compound sentences with, 577
in revision of run-on sentences, 581
separation of adjective from word modified, 544
setting off interjections with, 554
setting off nonessential clauses with, 572
use with parentheses, 654
use with quotation marks, 647
Common nouns, 534
Communication, written vs. verbal, 50
Comparative degree, 619–620, 621, 622
Comparison(s)
case of pronouns in, 617
patterning essay on, 482–484
use of modifiers in, 619–622
see also Metaphors; Similes
Compass points, capitalization of, 634

Competitive proposal, 282–283
Complements, 558–561
Complete predicates, 556–557, 557–558
Complete sentences, 578–580
Complete subjects, 556, 557–558
Complex sentences, 577
Compound adjectives, use of punctuation with, 652
Compound comparisons, 621
Compound-complex sentences, 578
Compound nouns, 535
possessive form, 649
Compound numbers, 653, 658
Compound objects, 559
Compound objects of a preposition, case of pronouns for, 614
Compound predicates, 556
Compound preposition, 549
Compound sentences, 577
punctuation of, 641, 643
Compound subjects, 555
agreement with verbs, 601–602, 607
case of pronouns in, 614
Compound words, 651
Conclusion, 515
appropriateness to context, 499
boundary of, 498
discussion of solution in, 497–498
matched pair with introduction, 499
matching with introductory scene, 491–492
restatement of author's attitude in, 496
web, 492, 494–495
Concrete nouns, 535, 536
Condell, Henry, 175
Conflict, in narratives, 365, 373, 377
Confrontation, of reader by writer, 527–530
Conjugation of a verb, 588–589, 598

Conjunctions, 550–554
  connection of series with, 639
  coordinating, 551, 570, 577,
    581, 641, 644 (*see also* [for
    greater specificity] Coor-
    dinating conjunctions)
  correlative, 551
  distinguished from preposi-
    tions, 552
  subordinating, 551–552, 571,
    573–574, 575, 582 (*see
    also* [for greater specificity]
    Subordinating conjunc-
    tions)
  use of punctuation with, 639,
    641, 644
Conjunctive adverbs, 553–554
  connection of compound sen-
    tences with, 577
  connection of independent
    clauses with, 570
  in revision of run-on sentences,
    582
  use of punctuation with, 643
Connections, between sentences,
    502–504, 506
Consensus, about facts, 230
Consumer Digest, 338
Consumer Reports, 62–63, 318–
    324, 328, 336, 338
Context, effect on literary inter-
    pretation, 380
Contractions, 583, 584, 650
Contrast, patterning essay on,
    482–484
Conviction
  of reader, 172–173, 175–177,
    178, 179, 180, 181, 190
  of writer, 177–181, 190
Coordinating conjunctions, 551
  connection of compound sen-
    tences with, 577
  connection of independent
    clauses with, 570
  in revision of run-on sentences,
    581
  use of punctuation with, 641,
    643

Cornerstone source, 441
Correlative conjunctions, 551
Counter-characterization, 131
Court, arguments before, 216–
    233, 238
Credibility
  of expert testimony, 189
  of writer, 498
Criteria, for reviews, 319–320,
    326–328, 332, 336, 337
Critical notices, 324–328, 338
Critical stance, in reviews, 321–
    322, 324, 325, 326, 336,
    337
Criticism, literary, *see* Literary
    criticism
Cromwell, Thomas, 217–219,
    223
Cults, 224–225

Dangling modifier, 623, 624
Dashes, 652–653
Declarative sentences, 554
  punctuation of, 637
  subject/predicate placement in,
    557
Deference, of writers toward
    readers, 523, 527–530
Definite articles, 543
Demonstrative pronouns, 537, 546
Dependent clauses, *see* Subordi-
    nate clauses
Description
  action as element of, 122
  use of details in (*see* Details)
  use of figurative language in,
    124
  use of verbs in, 125–126
Detail/framework summary, 24–
    25
Details
  corroboration of framework
    with, 478, 481–482
  about events, 125
  importance to memoir, 95
  and mind's formation of
    framework, 52
  from observation, 131, 133

about personalities, 127–128
about places, 119, 120, 122
recording of, 420–421
from research, 133
support of thesis with, 16–18
unexpected, 516–518
viewing through framework,
  131, 133
Dialogue, punctuation of,
  646–647
Direct address, 641
Direct objects, 558, 559, 596,
  613
  appositives to, 613
Disagreement, open statement of,
  527–530. *See also* Argument
Disorder, of thought process, 50–
  52
Distance, between writer and
  reader, 523, 525–527
Divided contrast, 484
Division, patterning essay on, 485
Documentation, of research,
  431–434, 436
Dominant idea, examination of,
  160
Double comparisons, 620
Drafting, *see* Revision
Dramatic curiosity, 490
Dramatic narrator, 363, 377
"Drift," in reporting, 119, 120,
  122
Dynamic characters, 361–362,
  377

Earnestness, abandonment of,
  523–525
Edge, replacing deference with,
  527–530
Editing symbols, 658
Editorial cartoons, subject and
  framework in, 20–23
Effect, relationship to cause,
  269–273
Either/or argument, 182, 187
Ellipsis points, 653–654
Elliptical clauses, 574

Emotion, in interpretive
works, 9–10
Emphasis, indication with italics,
656
Emphatic verb forms, 592
Encyclopedias, 20, 25
acknowledgment of ideas in, 437
authority of, 461
citation of, 465, 472
use in research, 425–426, 427
Endnotes, 445, 463
Esquire (magazine), 6
Essential appositives/appositive
phrases, 563
punctuation of, 641, 642
Essential clauses, 572
punctuation of, 642
Essential phrases, punctuation of,
642
Evaluation
of argument, 185–187
of evidence, 187–189
of film, 329
of scientific experiment, 268–269
see also Analysis; Peer review;
Reviews
Event(s)
cause of, 184–185
connection in narratives, 364–
365, 373
reports on, 123–126, 135
serial, impression of, 124–126
single, unified impression of,
123–124
Evidence, evaluation of, 187–
189. *See also* Facts
Examples
drawing inferences from, 183
filling frameworks with, 481–
482
Exclamation points, 638–639
following interjections, 554
use with ellipsis points, 653
use with parentheses, 654
use with quotation marks, 647
Exclamatory sentences, 554
subject/predicate placement in,
557

Expectations, of reader, 62–63
Experience, *see* Personal experience
Experiment, scientific, evaluation
of, 268–269
Expository essay/writing
classification pattern, 484–485
comparison and contrast pattern, 482–484
division pattern, 485
firm approach to organizing,
477–478, 479, 480, 486,
489
flexible approach to organizing, 478–479, 480, 489
formulas in writing, 476
illustration pattern, 481–482
logical connections in, 503–
504, 506
matching of introduction to
conclusion, 490–492, 494–
498, 499
outlining of, 486–488
patterns of organization, 480–
486
subject and framework in, 10–
12
thesis and details in, 14, 16–18
Eyewitnesses, testimony of, 188

Facts
acknowledgment of, 437–438
consensus concerning, 230
degree of certainty concerning,
180–181, 187–189
disputes over, 156, 168–194
drawing inferences from, 171–
173, 175–177
establishment through argument, 230–232
interpretation of, 4–7, 218–221
proposals concerning, 262
Fallacies, logical, 181–187
False analogy, 183–184
False dilemma, 182
Family
influence of television on, 186
influence on writer's life, 89–90

Family-relationship words,
capitalization of, 633–634
Field notebook
recording observations in,
419–421
use in interviews, 422
Figurative language
effectiveness of, 512
pruning of, 510
use in description, 124
Film Review Annual, 341
Films, reviews of, 324–328, 330–
335
Firm approach, to essay organization, 477–478, 479, 480,
486, 489
First Amendment, U. S. Constitution, 5, 8, 276
First draft, 64
First-person narrator, 363, 377
Flag-burning, and free speech, 5,
8–9, 216
Flat characters, 361, 362, 372, 377
Flexible approach, to essay organization, 478–479, 480,
489
Food and Drug Administration
(FDA), 180, 181
Foreign words/phrases
italicization of, 655
pruning of, 510, 513
Formal English, 583, 597, 615,
618
Formal outline, 486–488
Framework(s)
alternative, presentation by
writer, 528
analysis of, 97–98, 99
of argument, 157
character type as, 127–128
clarification in outline, 486
common ground between reader's and writer's, 63–64
corroboration with details,
478, 481–482
definition of, 7–9
distortion of understanding by,
126–127

Literary criticism
  analysis of character in, 361–362, 372, 377
  analysis of plot in, 364–365, 373, 377
  analysis of point of view in, 362–364, 372, 374, 377
  analysis of setting in, 360–361, 371–372, 374–377
  analysis of symbolism in, 368–370, 373–374, 377
  analysis of theme in, 365–368, 373, 374–376, 377
  guidelines for writing, 376–378
  identification of problem in, 358, 365, 366, 374–376, 378, 379–380
  organization of, 485
  peer review of, 378
  proposing solution in, 358, 374, 376, 378, 379
  sample essay, 374–376
  understanding as object of, 358–359
Literature, report on characters from, 136
Logic
  concept of argument in, 157
  defects in, 181–187
  in interpretive frameworks, 9–10
  method of argument in, 168
Logical bridges, 503–504, 506
Long-term memory, 51, 52
Looping, and creation of back areas, 67
Loose division, 485
Los Angeles Times, 327, 519, 520
Lynching, 274

McCarthy, Roy, 195–196
Magazines
  acknowledgment of ideas in, 437
  citation of, 465, 467, 470, 473
  indexes to, 428–430, 431
  reviews in (*see* Reviews)

Main verb, 540
Major premise, 157, 220
Meaning
  attachment to objects, 368–369
  communication with images, 507–508
Mechanics, 632. *See also* Capitalization; Italics; Numbers, use in writing; Punctuation
Memoir
  analysis of, 97–98
  dual role of author in, 80–82
  examples of, 88, 96
  exercise in writing, 99
  guidelines for writing, 94–95
  historical framework for, 82–85
  importance of framework for, 82
  peer review of, 95
  psychological framework for, 90–94
  research for, 418
  social framework for, 85–90
Memory
  long-term, 51, 52
  of observations, 420
  of reader, 500–501, 507–508
  searching for details, 95
  short-term, 51–52
  stabilization through writing, 52–53
  stimulation with imagery, 507–509
  transitory nature of, 51–52
  working, 52, 53, 501
Metaphors
  effectiveness of, 512
  pruning of, 510
  relation of setting to theme with, 374, 375
  stimulation of memory with, 507
  use in description, 124
Miller, George, 51–52, 54
Mindset, of reader, 63–64

Minor premise, 157
Modals, 592–593
Modern Language Association (MLA), citation style, 442, 468–471
Modifiers
  correct use of, 619–624
  use in comparisons, 619–622
  use of punctuation with, 640–641
  see also Adjectives; Adverbs
Mood [verbs], 597–599
Moon landing, 191
More, Sir Thomas, 216, 217–219, 220, 222, 223
Ms. magazine, 499

NAACP, 274
Names, agreement with verbs, 604. *See also* Calendar names; Place names; Proper adjectives; Proper nouns; Titles [of works]
Narratives
  interpretation of (*see* Literary criticism)
  self-contained, 80
  subject and framework in, 12–14
Narrator
  dramatic, 363, 377
  limited, 363, 377
  limited omniscient, 364, 372
  omniscient, 362–363, 377
Nationalities, capitalizing names of, 635
Natural History (magazine), 499
Negligence, liability for, 225–228
Nelson, Craig, 6
The New Leader, 325
Newman, John Henry, 7
Newsday, 327, 439
Newspapers
  citation of, 470
  indexes to, 428, 430–431
  letters to, 269–273
  and politics, 520
  reviews in (*see* Reviews)

Periodicals, *see* Journals, scholarly; Magazines; Newspapers
Periods, 637–638
  effect on reader's scanning of passage, 501
  use with ellipsis points, 653
  use with parentheses, 654
  use with quotation marks, 647
Person, agreement of pronouns and antecedents in, 610–611
Personal experience
  building frameworks from, 10–11
  presentation as shared experience, 82
Personalit(y)(ies)
  astrological descriptions of, 93–94
  author's discovery of, 90–94
  moralistic conception of, 92–93
  relationship to character type, 128–131
  reports on, 126–131, 135–136
  simplification of, 133
Personal pronouns, 536, 537, 651
Persuasion, *see* Argument; Proposals
Photocopies, of research sources, 436
Photography, interpretation of subject by, 6, 7
Phrases, 561–570
  placement of, 622–624
  punctuation of, 639–640, 642
  as sentence fragments, 579
Physical evidence, evaluation of, 188, 189
Place(s)
  characterization by inhabitants, 121–122
  idea of, 119–120
  identification in literary criticism, 360, 371–372, 376
  literal, 119–120
  reports on, 119–122, 135

Place names
  capitalization of, 634
  punctuation of, 643
Plagiarism, 436, 438
Plot, analysis in literary criticism, 364–365, 373, 377
Plural-form nouns, agreement with verbs, 604
Plural forms, and the apostrophe, 650–651
Poems
  analysis as narrative, 370–376
  capitalization in, 633
  elision of, 654
  subject and framework in, 23–24
Point-by-point contrast, 483, 484
Point of view, analysis in literary criticism, 362–364, 372, 374, 377
Poisoning the well, 182–183
Positive degree, 619, 621
Possession, indication with apostrophe, 649–650
Possessive case, 612, 613–614
Possessive nouns, 545
Possessive pronouns, 537, 545, 651
Postal codes, 636, 638, 643
Post hoc fallacy, 184
Precedent, in interpretation of rules, 222, 226, 227, 228, 230, 232
Predicate adjectives, 560–561
Predicate nominatives, 560, 612, 613
  appositives to, 612
  case of, 615, 616
  and subject-verb agreement, 606
Predicates, 555–558
  complete, 556–557, 557–558
  compound, 556
  placement of, 557
  simple, 555–556, 557–558
Prefixes, 652
Prepositional phrases, 549–550, 562–563, 564

punctuation of, 640
  as sentence fragments, 579
  used as adjectives, 562
  used as adverbs, 562
Prepositions, 548–550
  distinguished from adverbs, 550
  distinguished from conjunctions, 552
Present emphatic tense, 592
Present participles, 564–565, 586–588, 623
Present perfect progressive tense, 591
Present perfect tense, 589, 590, 594
Present progressive tense, 591, 592
Present subjunctive tense, 598
Present tense, 588, 589–590, 591, 594
Presidential power, 270–273
Prewriting outline, 486
Primary sources, 441, 445, 447
Principal parts of verbs, 542, 564, 568, 586–588
Probabilistic reasoning, role in argument, 171–173, 230–231, 332
Problem
  development in introduction, 496–497
  identification in literary criticism, 358, 365, 366, 374–376, 378, 379–380
  match between solution and, 268–273
  selection for research paper, 440–441
  statement in proposal, 262, 263, 264–265, 266, 267, 268, 272
  validity of, 274, 279
Problem-centered writing, *see* Proposals
Problem/solution essay, 266–269
Product labeling, 187
Product reviews, *see* Reviews

Progressive verb forms, 591–592
Pronouns, 535–539
  agreement with antecedents,
    607–611
  alluding to key nouns with,
    502
  case of, 611–617
  correct use of, 607–619
  creation of informal tone with,
    526
  demonstrative, 537, 546
  indefinite, 538–539, 546, 603,
    608–609, 610–611
  indication of writer's perspec-
    tive through, 492
  intensive, 537–538, 611
  interrogative, 538, 546, 575,
    615
  personal, 536, 537, 651
  possessive, 537, 545, 651
  reference to antecedents, 617–
    619
  reflexive, 537, 611
  relative, 538, 546, 571, 575,
    582, 606, 616 (*see also* [for
    greater specificity] Relative
    pronouns)
  used as adjectives, 545–546
Proof
  burden of, 180–181
  scientific, 268–269
Proofreading, 657–658
Proper adjectives, 544
  capitalization of, 635, 636
  separation from prefix, 652
Proper nouns, 534
  capitalization of, 633–636
  separation from prefix, 652
Proposals
  advice column, 262–266
  analysis of, 281
  competitive, 282–283
  failure of, 273–274, 276
  guidelines for writing, 279
  letters to the editor, 269–273
  match between problem and
    solution in, 268–273
  organization of, 485

parts of, 262, 263, 264–265
peer review of, 280
problem/solution essay, 266–
  269
for publication, 282
refutation of, 276–279, 280,
  282
research for, 422–423
summary of, 281
see also Argument
Protagonist, 365, 373, 377
Psychological framework, for
  memoir, 90–94
Psychology, insights into memory
  process, 51–52, 500–501,
  507
Publication, preparing proposal
  for, 282
Public figure, interview-based report on, 136
Public opinion polls, 182
Punctuation, 637–655. *See also*
  under names of punctua-
  tion marks

Quarrels, 156
Question marks, 638
  use with ellipsis points, 653
  use with parentheses, 654
  use with quotation marks, 647
Questionnaires, 422–424
Questions, interview, 421–422
Quotation marks, 646–648
Quotations
  acknowledgment of, 438
  bracketed material in, 655
  elision of, 654
  indirect, 447
  from interviews, 422
  of research sources, 445, 447,
    449, 451, 453, 455, 457,
    459, 461
  of secondary sources, 436
  use in literary criticism, 375

Reader(s)
  acceptability of proposals to,
    273–274, 276

communicating with, through
  imagery, 507–509
conviction of, 172–173, 175–
  177, 178, 179, 180, 181,
  190
of critical notices, 324, 325
deference of writers toward,
  523, 527–530
distance between writer and,
  523, 525–527
effect of proposals on, 279–
  280
engagement of, 490, 514–530
establishing connections for,
  502–504, 506
expectations of, 62–63
explication of framework for,
  20
"general educated," 61
intermediate, 60–61, 65
of interpretive reviews, 328,
  330, 336
knowledge of, 63
matching tone of introductions
  and conclusions to, 499
memory of, 500–501, 507–
  508
opinions of, 63–64
persuasion of, 158, 162, 164
of research, 439
simplicity of style in communicating with, 509–513
of technical reviews, 336
ultimate, 60, 61, 64, 65
visualization of, 61–62
writer's concern with, 58–65
Reader/framework summary, 26
Reading, for research, 434, 436
Reagan, Ronald, 63, 276–279,
  282
Reasoning, probabilistic, 171–
  173, 230–231, 332
Recursiveness, of writing process,
  56
Redundancy, 584–585
Reference [pronouns], 617–619
Reflexive pronouns, 537
  agreement with antecedents, 611

Savage, Albert R., 224–225
Savvy Woman (magazine), 131
Scenes, parallel, building introduction and conclusion on, 490–492
Scenic narration, 363
School policy, arguments about, 235–238
School prayer, 276–279
Scientific American (magazine), 176, 189
Scientific writing
  citation style for, 471–473
  evaluation of, 268–269
  problem/solution arrangement in, 266–268, 496–498
Seat belts, 514–515
Segregation, racial, 12–14, 22–23, 63–64, 186, 523–525
Semicolons, 643–644
  connection of compound sentences with, 577
  connection of independent clauses with, 570
  in revision of run-on sentences, 582
  use with parentheses, 654
  use with quotation marks, 647
Sentence fragments, 578–581
Sentences
  capitalization in, 632–633
  classified by structure, 576–578
  complements in, 558–561
  completeness of, 578–582
  connections between, 502–504, 506
  elision of, 654
  phrases and clauses in, 561–578
  punctuation of, 637, 638, 639, 641–644
  purposes of, 554
  readers' processing of, 500–501, 502
  structure of, 554–578
  subjects/predicate division, 555–558

varying structure of, 518–520
  see also Topic sentence
Serials, citation of, 465, 472
Series, punctuation of, 639–640, 644
Setting, analysis in literary criticism, 360–361, 371–372, 374–377
Sex roles, influence on writer's life, 90
Sexual stereotypes, in popular films, 330–334
Shaftesbury, Lord, 16–18, 24, 63, 129
Shakespeare, John, 180, 183
Shawn, William, 59
Short-term memory, 51–52
Similes
  effectiveness of, 512
  pruning of, 510
  relation of setting to theme with, 374, 375–376
  stimulation of memory with, 507
  use in description, 124
Simple predicates, 555–556, 557–558
Simple sentences, 576
Simple subjects, 555, 557–558
Simplicity, as ideal for style, 509–513, 515
Single quotation marks, 648
Slang, 583, 584
Social framework, for memoir, 85–90
Social lessons, influence on writer's life, 90
Solution
  discussion in conclusion, 497–498
  infeasible, 274, 278–279
  in literary criticism, 358, 374, 376, 378, 379
  match between problem and, 268–273
  statement in proposal, 262, 263, 265, 266, 267–268, 272–273
  undesirable consequences of, 276, 278

Sources
  acknowledgment of, 437–439
  authority of, 447, 451, 455, 461
  availability of, 424–425
  citation form, 442, 445, 447, 449, 451, 455, 464–473
  cornerstone, 441
  currency of, 459
  documentation of, 431–434, 436
  for literary criticism, 379–380
  location of, 441, 447
  primary, 441, 445, 447
  for research, 424–434, 436–439
  summarization of, 445, 449
Sow's ears, 19
Static characters, 361, 377
Stereotypes
  negative, influence on writer's life, 89
  in reports on personalities, 127
  sexual, in popular films, 330–334
Story
  analysis of, 359–370
  as basis for memoir, 94–95
  see also Narratives
Straw man, 183
Strict division, 485
Strong verbs, 520–522
Structures, capitalizing names of, 636
Style
  making choices about, 530
  reader's expectations concerning, 62
  separation from substance, 515
  simplicity of, 509–513, 515
  submergence of subject in, 509–510
  texture, 516–522
  tone, 178–179, 268, 499, 523–530
  underdeveloped, 514–515
Subject
  of argument, 157

Topic sentence, 14, 477, 478, 479, 480, 486, 489, 507, 508
Trade names, capitalization of, 636
Transitional markers, 504, 506
Transitive verbs, 541
    voice of, 596
Trial, as forum for arguments, 216–233, 238
Truth
    and framing of subject, 9
    about literary works, 358
    use of interpretation in reaching, 5, 7, 12
    writer's concern with, 528, 530

Ultimate audience, 60, 61, 64, 65
Uncertainty
    as condition of argument, 157, 158, 168
    permissible, in treatment of facts, 180–181
Understanding, as object of literary criticism, 358–359
Understood "you," 555, 557
Unpublished sources, citation of, 471
Usage
    glossary, 624–631
    levels of, 583–584
    modifiers, 619–624
    pronouns, 607–619
    scope of, 583–585
    verbs, 585–607

Values, see Framework(s)
Vazquez, Amado, 151–153
Vehicles, capitalizing names of, 636
Verbal bridges, 502–503
Verbals, 564–570

Verbosity, 584–585
Verb phrases, 540, 542
    number of, 600
Verbs, 539–543
    action, 539, 540
    active and passive voice, 510, 511, 595–597, 599
    agreement with subjects, 600–607
    auxiliary, 540–541, 565, 586, 588, 592–593, 598, 600
    changes in form, 542
    conjugation of, 588–589, 598
    contribution to texture, 520–522
    correct use of, 585–607
    creation of informal tone with, 526
    irregular, 565, 586–588
    linking, 540, 598
    modification by adverbs, 548
    mood of, 597–599
    principle parts of, 542, 564, 568, 586–588
    regular, 565, 586
    specific, 585
    strong, 520–522
    tense of, 588–595
    transitive and intransitive, 541, 596
    use in description, 125–126
    weak, 520, 521, 522
Vices, battle with virtues, 92–93
Victorian era, religion and politics in, 16–18
Vietnam War, interpretation of facts concerning, 4–5, 7
Virtues, battle with vices, 92–93
Voice [verbs], 510, 511, 595–597, 599
Voter registration, 22–23

War, endangerment of civilians in, 528–529

Watergate scandal, 270–273, 519–520
Weak verbs, 520, 521, 522
Web conclusion, 492, 494–495
Wheeler, John, 4, 7
Whittaker, Florence, 224–225, 230, 231, 232
"Who" and "whom," correct use of, 615–616
Windowpane style, 510, 513
Word families, 502
Words
    foreign, 510, 513, 656–657
    readers' processing of, 500, 501
    selection and editing of, 510, 513
    usage notes, 624–631
Working memory, 52, 53, 501
Works Cited section, research paper, 464–473
Writer
    as character, 80–82
    concern with reader, 58–65
    conviction of, 177–181, 190
    credibility of, 498
    deference toward readers, 523, 527–530
    distance between reader and, 523, 525–527
    historical influences on, 85
    as interpreter, 80–82
    overview of processes of, 64–65
    shift in attitude of, 495–496
    social influences on, 89–90
    solitary processes of, 50–56
Writer's block, 56–58, 499

Yearbooks, 20
You, understood, 555, 557

Mount Vernon, NY 10553. Excerpted by permission from CONSUMER RE-
PORTS, August 1989.

DETHIER, VINCENT: From Vincent Dethier, *To Know a Fly*, copyright 1962. Reproduced with permission of McGraw-Hill, Inc.

DEUTSCH, PHYLLIS: From review of "E.T." by Phyllis Deutsch from *Jump Cut* No.
28, April 1983, pp. 12–13. Reprinted by permission.

DIDION, JOAN: "Marrying Absurd" from *Slouching Towards Bethlehem* by Joan
Didion. Copyright © 1967 by Joan Didion. Reprinted by permission of Farrar,
Straus & Giroux, Inc.; Excerpt from "Quiet Days in Malibu" from *The White
Album* by Joan Didion. Copyright © 1976, 1979, 1989 by Joan Didion. Re-
printed by permission of Farrar, Straus & Giroux, Inc.

DILLARD, ANNIE: Copyright © 1984 by Annie Dillard. Reprinted from *Encounters
with Chinese Writers* by permission of University Press of New England;
"Singing with the Fundamentalists" reprinted by permission of the author and
her agent Blanche C. Gregory, Inc. Copyright © 1985 by Annie Dillard; Excerpt
from *The Writing Life* by Annie Dillard. Copyright © 1989 by Annie Dillard.
Reprinted by permission of Harper & Row, Publishers, Inc.

DINESEN, ISAK: From *Winter's Tales by Isak Dinesen*. Copyright 1942 by Random
House, Inc. and renewed 1970 by Johan Philip Thomas Ingerslev c/o The Rung-
stedlund Foundation. Reprinted by permission of Random House, Inc., and The
Rungstedlund Foundation.

EDENS, MICHAEL: Michael Edens, "Mothballed," *The Nation* magazine/The Nation Company, copyright 1989. Reprinted by permission.

GELMIS, JOSEPH: © 1982 *Newsday*/Joseph Gelmis.

GOLDEN, HARRY: Excerpt from *The Best of Harry Golden* by Harry Golden. Copyright © 1967 by Harry Golden. Reprinted by permission of Harper & Row,
Publishers, Inc.

GOODMAN, ELLEN: "C. Everett Koop" reprinted by permission of the author; "A
Working Community" from *Keeping in Touch* by Ellen Goodman. Copyright ©
1985 by The Washington Post Company. Reprinted by permission of Summit
Books, a division of Simon & Schuster, Inc.

HITT, JACK, et al.: Copyright © 1988 by *Harper's Magazine*. All rights reserved.
Reprinted from the August issue by special permission.

HUNT, GEORGE W.: Reprinted with the permission of America Press, Inc., 106 West
56th Street, New York, NY 10019. © 1989 All Rights Reserved.

JOHNSON, JAMES WELDON: From *Along This Way—The Autobiography of James
Weldon Johnson*. Copyright 1933 by James Weldon Johnson, renewed copyright
© 1961 by Grace Nail Johnson. Reprinted by permission of the publisher, Viking
Penguin, a division of Penguin Books USA Inc.

KING, JR., MARTIN LUTHER: "Letter From Birmingham Jail" from *Why We Can't
Wait* by Martin Luther King, Jr. Copyright © 1963, 1964 by Martin Luther King,
Jr. Reprinted by permission of Harper & Row, Publishers, Inc.

LEWIS, C. S.: From *God in the Dock* by C. S. Lewis. Copyright 1970 C. S. Lewis Pte
Ltd., reproduced by permission of Curtis Brown, London, and Collins Publishers.

MAITLAND, SARA: Copyright © 1989 by The New York Times Company. Reprinted by
permission.

MARTIN, JUDITH: Reprinted with permission of Atheneum Publishers, an imprint of
Macmillan Publishing Company from *Miss Manners' Guide to Excruciatingly Cor-*

rect Behavior by Judith Martin. Copyright © 1979, 1980, 1981, 1982 by United Feature Syndicate, Inc.

MCCARTHY, MARY: Excerpts from *Memories of a Catholic Girlhood,* copyright © 1957 and renewed 1985 by Mary McCarthy, reprinted by permission of Harcourt Brace Jovanovich, Inc.; Excerpts from "The Athlete of Evasion and the Prodigal Son" in *The Mask of State: Watergate Portraits,* copyright © 1974, 1973 by Mary McCarthy, reprinted by permission of Harcourt Brace Jovanovich, Inc.

MILLER, ROBERT KEITH: From Robert Keith Miller, *Mark Twain,* copyright 1983. Reprinted by permission of Frederick Ungar Publishing Co.

MITFORD, JESSICA: From Jessica Mitford, *Poison Penmanship,* copyright 1979. Reprinted by permission of the author and the author's agents, Scott Meredith Literary Agency, Inc., 845 Third Avenue, New York, NY 10022.

MUNRO, ALICE: "Day of the Butterfly" from *Dance of the Happy Shades* by Alice Munro. Copyright © 1968 by Alice Munro. Published by McGraw-Hill Ryerson Limited. Reprinted by arrangement with Virginia Barber Literary Agency, and McGraw-Hill Ryerson Limited. All rights reserved.

O'BRIEN, EILEEN M.: With permission from *Natural History,* Vol. 93, No. 7; Copyright the American Museum of Natural History, 1984.

OATES, JOYCE CAROL: Copyright © 1965 by Joyce Carol Oates. Reprinted by permission of John Hawkins & Associates, Inc.

OLDS, SHARON: From *The Gold Cell* by Sharon Olds. Copyright © 1987 by Sharon Olds. Reprinted by permission of Alfred A. Knopf Inc.

ORWELL, GEORGE: "Marrakech" and "Why I Write" from *Such, Such Were the Joys* by George Orwell, copyright 1953 by Sonia Brownell Orwell and renewed 1981 by Mrs. George K. Perutz, Mrs. Miriam Gross, Dr. Michael Dickson, executors of the Estate of Sonia Brownell Orwell, reprinted by permission of Harcourt Brace Jovanovich, Inc., and Martin Secker & Warburg Ltd.; Excerpt from "Killing Civilians" in *The Collected Essays, Journalism and Letters of George Orwell: As I Please, 1943–1945,* Volume III, copyright © 1968 by Sonia Brownell Orwell, reprinted by permission of Harcourt Brace Jovanovich, Inc., and Martin Secker & Warburg Ltd.; "Reflections on Gandhi" by George Orwell, copyright 1949 by Partisan Review and renewed 1977 by Sonia Orwell, reprinted from his volume *Shooting an Elephant and Other Essays* by permission of Harcourt Brace Jovanovich, Inc., and Martin Secker & Warburg Ltd.; "Shooting an Elephant" from *Shooting an Elephant and Other Essays* by George Orwell, copyright 1950 by Sonia Brownell Orwell and renewed 1978 by Sonia Pitt-Rivers, reprinted by permission of Harcourt Brace Jovanovich, Inc., and Martin Secker & Warburg Ltd.; "Politics and the English Language" by George Orwell, copyright 1946 by Sonia Brownell Orwell and renewed 1974 by Sonia Orwell, reprinted from his volume *Shooting an Elephant and Other Essays* by permission of Harcourt Brace Jovanovich, Inc., and Martin Secker & Warburg Ltd.

PERRIN, NOEL: From *First Person Rural* by Noel Perrin. Copyright © 1978 by Noel Perrin. Reprinted by permission of David R. Godine, Publisher.

POSNER, ELLEN S.: Ellen Posner, "Learning to Love Ma Bell's New Building," *The Wall Street Journal,* Arts & Leisure Page, October 12, 1983, p. 26. Reprinted by permission of the author.

SANTORO, GENE: "Paul Simon's *Graceland,*" *Down Beat,* December 1986, pages 32–33. Reprinted by permission of *Down Beat.*

THOMAS, LEWIS: From *The Medusa and the Snail: More Notes of a Biology Watcher* by Lewis Thomas. Copyright © 1978 by Lewis Thomas. Reprinted by permission of the publisher, Viking Penguin, a division of Penguin Books USA Inc.

TUCHMAN, BARBARA: From Barbara Tuchman, *Bible and Sword*, copyright 1956, pp. 177–178. Reprinted by permission of New York University Press; "Should We Abolish the Presidency?" from *A Distant Mirror: The Calamitous 14th Century* by Barbara W. Tuchman. Copyright © 1978 by Barbara W. Tuchman. Reprinted by permission of Alfred A. Knopf Inc.; From *Practicing History* by Barbara Tuchman. Copyright © 1981 by Alma Tuchman, Lucy T. Eisenberg & Jessica Tuchman Matthews. Reprinted by permission of Alfred A. Knopf, Inc.

TWAIN, MARK: From *The Autobiography of Mark Twain*, edited by Charles Neider. Copyright 1917, 1940, © 1958, 1959 by The Mark Twain Company. Copyright 1924, 1945, 1952 by Clara Clemens Samossoud. Copyright © 1959 by Charles Neider. Reprinted by permission of Harper & Row, Publishers, Inc.; "Corn-Pone Opinions" from *Europe and Elsewhere* by Mark Twain. Copyright 1923 by Mark Twain Company, renewed 1951 by Mark Twain Company. Reprinted by permission of Harper & Row, Publishers, Inc.

WHITE, E. B.: "Once More to the Lake" from *Essays of E. B. White*. Copyright 1941 by E. B. White. Reprinted by permission of Harper & Row, Publishers, Inc.; From "Education" from *One Man's Meat* by E. B. White. Copyright 1939 by E. B. White. Reprinted by permission of Harper & Row, Publishers, Inc.; Excerpt from "Foreword" from *Essays of E. B. White*. Copyright © 1977 by E. B. White. Reprinted by permission of Harper & Row, Publishers, Inc.

WHITE, THEODORE H.: Excerpts from *In Search of History* by Theodore H. White. Copyright © 1978 by Theodore H. White. Reprinted by permission of Harper & Row, Publishers, Inc.; Reprinted with permission of Atheneum Publishing Company from *The Making of the President 1960* by Theodore H. White. Copyright © 1961 Atheneum House, Inc.; Excerpts from *America in Search of Itself* by Theodore H. White. Copyright © 1982 by Theodore H. White. Reprinted by permission of Harper & Row, Publishers, Inc.; "Direct Elections: Invitation to National Chaos" reprinted by permission of the Estate of Theodore H. White.

WILBUR, RICHARD: "Still, Citizen Sparrow" from *Ceremony and Other Poems,* copyright 1950 and renewed 1978 by Richard Wilbur, reprinted by permission of Harcourt Brace Jovanovich, Inc.

WILL, GEORGE: "Against Prefabricated Prayer" and "Well, I Don't Love You, E.T." reprinted with permission of The Free Press, a Division of Macmillan, Inc. from *The Morning After: American Successes and Excesses, 1981–1986* by George Will. Copyright © 1986 by The Washington Post Company; "Lotteries Cheat, Corrupt the People" © 1984, Washington Post Writers Group. Reprinted with permission.

WOODARD, CHARLES R.: *Explicator*, Volume 36.6, February 1976. Reprinted with permission of the Helen Dwight Reid Educational Foundation. Published by Heldref Publications, 4000 Albermarle St., N.W., Washington, D.C. 20016. Copyright © 1976.